New Austrian Film

LIVERPOOL JMU LIBRARY

3 1111 01448 4644

New Austrian Film

Edited by

Robert von Dassanowsky and Oliver C. Speck

berghahn
NEW YORK · OXFORD
www.berghahnbooks.com

First published in 2011 by

Berghahn Books
www.berghahnbooks.com

©2011, 2014 Robert von Dassanowsky and Oliver C. Speck
First paperback edition published in 2014

All rights reserved. Except for the quotation of short passages
for the purposes of criticism and review, no part of this book
may be reproduced in any form or by any means, electronic or
mechanical, including photocopying, recording, or any information
storage and retrieval system now known or to be invented,
without written permission of the publisher.

Library of Congress Cataloging-in-Publication Data

New Austrian film / edited by Robert von Dassanowsky and Oliver C. Speck.
  p. cm.
  Includes bibliographical references and index.
  ISBN 978-1-84545-700-6 (hardback) -- ISBN 978-1-78238-510-3 (paperback) --
ISBN 978-0-85745-232-0 (ebook)
  1. Motion pictures--Austria--History. 2. Motion picture industry--Austria--History.
  I. Dassanowsky, Robert. II. Speck, Oliver C.
  PN1993.5.A83N49 2011
  791.43'09436--dc22

                                                                2011000954

British Library Cataloguing in Publication Data

A catalogue record for this book is available from the British Library

Printed in the United States on acid-free paper.

ISBN: 978-1-84545-700-6 hardback
ISBN: 978-1-78238-510-3 paperback
ISBN: 978-0-85745-232-0 ebook

Contents

Introduction

New Austrian Film:
The Non-exceptional Exception

Robert von Dassanowsky and Oliver C. Speck

In an article in 2006, the *New York Times* introduced a series of screenings of Austrian productions with the following statement: "In recent years this tiny country with a population the size of New York City's has become something like the world capital of feel-bad cinema" (Lim 2006). As the critic portrays the major directors, a picture emerges that probably sums up a common sentiment regarding New Austrian Film: not unlike other cinematic new waves, Austria's artists are engaged in a bitter fight against the prevailing petit-bourgeois mindset of their fellow citizens. From this perspective, however, it must appear that New Austrian Film is caught in a deadlock, a fight against its nation's very image, be it the postwar self-stylization as neutral Austria, Nazi Germany's first victim, or even the ironic self-perception as a leftover of *Kakania*, Robert Musil's famous satirical moniker for the *k.und k.* (imperial and royal) Austro-Hungarian dual monarchy. In an effort to break the illusions of the "official" Austria and its long avoidance of dealing with its fascist past, New Austrian Film is not only highly critical and counter-traditionalist (albeit using traditional genres) but it takes on the very mechanisms of spectatorial trust in cinema. And with a strong female participation that is significantly prominent, we can see how gender affects cinematic style and mood in dealing with contemporary dystopias. Despite the challenges to the audience, the reductionist "feel-bad cinema" label is itself only another totalizing concept that current Austrian filmmakers would smash.

The problem with seeing the struggle against the petit bourgeoisie as the common denominator of New Austrian Film, even as its main creative force, is that any work debunking the former image as counter-factual and the latter as a disguise for xenophobia and parochialism would already and inevitably be a reaction against those powerful, prior discourses. Indeed, a director's wildest imagination seems to be trumped by the sordid details of what appears to be a uniquely Austrian trauma that is constantly emerging before the eyes of the fascinated spectator. Nothing that is done to the mentally challenged hitchhiker in *Hundstage/Dog Days* (2001) by Ulrich Seidl, a film we would credit with an uncanny foresight, can match the ordeal of Natascha Kampusch, who escaped in the summer of 2006 after more than eight years in captivity. Any portrayal of the bourgeois as a pervert with a double life, clichéd or not, must fail in the light of the monstrous Josef Fritzl who held his daughter, Elisabeth, for twenty-four years as a sex slave in an underground prison. The case of Fritzl is especially telling, not because of the apathy on the part of his neighbors and the authorities (a point that has been stated ad nauseam), and not because it prompted Austria's then Chancellor Alfred Gusenbauer to announce on television that he would launch an image campaign to counter the "international slander" of Austria that ensued,[1] but because the sadistic jailer himself was more than willing to produce images, thereby psychologizing and thus excusing himself, portraying himself as unloved and abused by his mother, as controlled by forces beyond his control—in short, as a victim himself.

It is exactly here, in this discourse of victimhood, that we have to locate what was described above as a deadlock: images on television, in the newspaper, and on the web are clearly already on the side of power, insofar as they allow the perpetrator to redefine himself as a victim. Any attempt to counter these images could not rise above the level of former Chancellor Gusenbauer's campaign, a reactionary mode that inevitably leads to *ressentiment*. The problem for New Austrian Film could thus be summed up as finding a way to save the perspective of the victim, this impossible position that is always already occupied by power. At this point, we can also see a first indication that this problem is directly linked to fascism, not for historical reasons but for what could be called structural reasons. As Walter Benjamin argued in 1935, in his lucid essay "The Work of Art in the Age of Mechanical Reproduction," fascism aestheticizes political life. Indeed, Benjamin pinpoints the novelty of German fascism in this fusion: politics and art are no longer different realms. The danger in this development, however, does not concern the loss of a somehow "auratic" status of the work of art, which could now be used for any form of propaganda, but a conflation of momentous consequences—it is now the experience of art that constitutes the community: "The violation of the masses, whom Fascism, with its *Führer* cult, forces to their knees, has its counterpart in the violation of an apparatus which is pressed into the production of ritual values" (Benjamin 1969: 241). This apparatus, of course, does not stop working just because Nazi Germany surrendered and Austria was allowed to reposition itself in the political landscape of the Cold War. As Benjamin points out, "the mode of human sense perception changes with humanity's entire mode of existence" (ibid.: 222). In other words, this mode of perception prevails and, if we can trust the diagnostic power of New Austrian Film, finds its expression above all in television. We can thus state that the attacks of New Austrian Film are not aimed at a specific Austrian petit-bourgeois milieu, but at the general mode of existence that carries this ideological apparatus and that lingers on not only in Austria.

At this point, an affinity with another conflation becomes clearer, which Michel Foucault calls "biopolitics," and which, again, is not specific to Austria or even Germany, but whose emergence is linked to modernity: "For the first time in history … biological existence was reflected in political existence; the fact of living was no longer an inaccessible substrate that only emerged from time to time, amid the randomness of death and its fatality; part of it passed into knowledge's field of control and power's sphere of intervention" (Foucault 1978: 142). The fascist state, to stay with the most obvious example, regulates not just everyday life, but the biological life of its citizens.

In postwar Austria, as in the rest of the Western world, biopolitics already transformed society into what Gilles Deleuze, in an extrapolation of Foucault's thesis, calls a "society of control": "We are in a generalized crisis in relation to all the environments of enclosure—prison, hospital, factory, school, family. The family is an 'interior,' in crisis like all other interiors—scholarly, professional, etc. where there is no longer an outside to the system" (Deleuze 1986: n.p.). As Michael Hardt (1993: 141) explains in his reading of Deleuze, the dialectics between inside and outside still regulate the system of the modern nation-state. Here, the public space of politics has only an indirect influence on the clearly separated, private space of the family. With the gradual erosion of this distinction, the difference between "us" and "them," nature and culture, public and private collapses into a system where the outside is basically abolished, where everything is interiorized. The consequences are far reaching: the others now "only" have a different culture, nature needs our protection, and what used to be public space is privately owned and operated, thus the frequent appearance in New Austrian Film of shopping-malls, fast-food chains and video stores as kinds of cultural wasteland, a perfect illustration of the concept of a society of control.

Again, we have to come to the conclusion that there is neither a mourning for nor a destruction of the Austrian *Heimat* or "homeland" in New Austrian Film, but an astute analysis of these postmodern spaces which clearly appear as "non-places," to borrow a famous concept of Marc Augé. A non-place, as Augé defines it, is "a space which cannot be defined as relational, or historical, or concerned with identity" (Augé 1995: 78–79). The people we see drifting through Austria in these films could also be traveling through any other landscape. As we can clearly see, just to give some examples, in Barbara Albert's *Nordrand/Northern Skirts* (1999) and in Michael Haneke's *71 Fragmente einer Chronologie des Zufalls/71 Fragments of a Chronology of Chance* (1994), no relations, historic roots or regional identities can help the protagonists with positioning themselves, and any references to Austria appear as secondary, as they also do in Ruth Beckermann's filmic travelogues.

As was pointed out above, defining the impossible position of the victim as a point in the societal *dispositif*, to stay in the Foucauldian framework, is important for an understanding of New Austrian Film. The films under discussion in the present volume do not deal with fascism because of Austria's arguably problematic relationship to its fascist past, but because they recognize that unfortunately nothing about this *dispositif* is truly exceptional: the filmmakers from "this tiny [sic] country" are fully aware that Austria is not an exception but the rule.

In his book *Homo Sacer*, Giorgio Agamben (1998) expands Foucault's notion of biopower, concentrating on the fact that the modern state not only controls the life of its own citizens but also excludes certain people from the body of its citizenry, and in turn regulates their biological life. According to Agamben, biopolitics is always inscribed in the founding act of sovereignty. Here, he follows the often-quoted statement by Carl Schmitt that the sovereign is the one who can declare a state of exception. This founding act, initially a performative utterance—"We declare ourselves sovereign!"—paradoxically creates two related "zones of indistinction," as the one who utters the declaration is at the same time part of the group and equally above the law, because the sovereign can always suspend the law and declare martial law. Implicit in the declaration is also a primary exclusion from the group, the automatic ban on all who do not belong. These *personae non gratae* are not protected by any law and can be incarcerated or killed with impunity; indeed, stripped of all political rights, inmates have nothing but their "bare life," as Agamben explains.[2] Hence his provocative notion that the site of biopolitics is the camp and not the prison—a prisoner, though separated from society, is at least protected by the penal code. Agamben clearly sees the same mechanism at work in modern politics as well as in fascist Germany: the dangerous precedent set by the Nazis, one still perpetrated today, is the creation of in-between spaces where de facto people can be kept in legal limbo.

Looking at New Austrian Film, we can quickly see that the common denominator here is the temporary creation of a zone of exception. The most obvious example is, of course, Stefan Ruzowitzky's Academy Award-winning film, *Die Fälscher/The Counterfeiters* (2007),[3] where, inside the concentration camp, another forbidden zone is erected that, in turn, simulates normalcy—people do their job, eat, party, and so on. Inside this bubble, however, the law is an absolute dictate of usefulness, as the life of the inmates depends entirely on one specific skill; indeed, as the film strongly suggests, this secret zone inside the camp is the repressed truth of capitalism, because the simulation of value is reality and absolutely no surplus hinders efficiency. Here, *The Counterfeiters* offers a far more critical insight into the workings of a camp and the questions of morality than Steven Spielberg's epic *Schindler's List* (1993).

From this perspective, zones of exception appear everywhere in New Austrian Film. Michael Haneke constantly reminds us in his films that the central institutions of modernity—family, school, and the military—are in crisis and are themselves subject to a state of exception. His first three feature films, the so-called "glaciation of feelings" trilogy, address the failure of these institutions directly: the husband and wife in *Der siebente Kontinent/The Seventh Continent* (1989) destroy all their belongings, including the "bare life" of their daughter and the fish. The two white-gloved killers in the two versions of *Funny Games* (1997, 2007) turn the gated community into a camp with astonishing ease and their rigged bets and wagers represent the law of the moment for the unfortunate victims; while *Le Temps du loup/Time of the Wolf* (2003) takes place in a post-apocalyptic, lawless landscape, where the zone of exception is omnipresent.

We can state that the Austrian exception is best understood as a paradoxical exception; what makes these films exceptional is the astuteness with which they analyze and represent an unexceptional and generalized postmodern condition. Yet it is the history, the very development of New Austrian Film—the *nouvelle vague viennoise*, the Austrian New Cinema, Vienna's Po-mo Neo-realism, what ever it may be called—that is truly exceptional in the development of contemporary Western and specifically European cinema. Despite the slow lifting of popular amnesia (in and outside the country) regarding Vienna's film tradition and that of its old cinematic relationships—with Budapest, Prague, Berlin, Paris, London, and most of all Hollywood—Austria's recent international filmic presence since the 1990s is neither the proverbial "overnight success" nor is it a national film emergence in the truest sense of the phrase. Austria has been at this point before, but the deep fractures in the nation's identity since the trauma of its (re)birth in 1918, with five political incarnations in the twentieth century alone (sharing some of that with its neighbor and historical partner Germany) has taken a toll on continuity in its cinema. Each new cinema generation has had difficulty in reconnecting with the one before it, until all that seemed to remain were counterproductive clichés and a frustrated desire to reinvent. But without a strong auteurial tradition, and the need to export, even beyond the German-speaking world, such retrenchments tended to move with market demands rather than with risk. Each time creative risk became a factor in Austrian filmmaking, it had something to do with the disruption of the very concept of the nation. Perhaps this makes its cinema all the more demonstrative of what Austria is: as a multicultural melting-pot that attempted cultural homogeneity, and not without lingering debate, it is embracing its difference from the linguistically based nation-states and collected regions that surround it, a difference it already represented as a polyglot dynastic empire that colonized itself, ever eastward and southeastward, much like the United States in its move westward to expand a nation based around an ideal, rather than an ethnicity. Austrian film, when it arrived, was naturally multicultural, as was its post-1918 national industry—even at times transnational—and as were its larger mirrors, Canadian film and, most importantly, Hollywood.

The desire to develop a new wave in Austrian cinema has been active since the postwar era. In the midst of the great commercial boom of the late 1940s and 1950s, attempts were made to cultivate an Austrian neo-realism that would be analogous to that of Italy, and thus reflect on Austria's sociocultural problems. The ten year Allied occupation of Austria ultimately scarred Austrian self-esteem. The myth of sovereignty, the search for a future role in Cold War Europe, and the de-Germanization of its immediate past in favor of the "good" history of the imperial era and Vienna's artistic heyday, merely shut down the audience's desire for critical approaches in favor of escapism, unproblematized national allegory, and visual pleasure. The Second Republic, which officially began in 1955, and the wearisome move towards it since 1945, marked a return to traditional film genres in comedy and drama, in the *Heimatfilm*, and the historical biopic. Many important filmmakers, performers, and crews that had made Austrian film internationally popular in the era of silent and early sound film, and those that had remained or survived the Nazi annexation, were still at work. Although tarnished by the immediate past, the old star system (Paul and Attila Hörbiger, Paula Wessely, Hans Moser, Hans Holt, Hans Thimig, Theo Lingen, Curd Jürgens, the Marischka family) mixed well with the new discoveries (Oskar Werner, Romy Schneider, Josef Meinrad, Maria Schell, Nadja Tiller, Peter Alexander, Senta Berger, Gunther Philipp, Johanna Matz) and held the nation's loyalty, even when many of the newer generation soon left for Munich, London, Paris, or Hollywood in search of more adventurous material, only to be regarded there as an even more limited "type." The public and the critics also continued to trust in the traditional creativity of veteran directors such as Willi Forst, Hubert and Ernst Marischka, Eduard von Borsody, Karl Hartl, and Géza von Cziffra; these recalled Austria's silent era, its socially critical melodramas, its female film pioneer, Louise Kolm-Fleck, and the monumental epics of producer Sascha Kolowrat and Austro-Hungarian directors Michael Kertesz (Michael Curtiz) and Sandor Korda (Alexander Korda), which rivaled D.W. Griffith and C.B. DeMille for world popularity. These veterans were active in the creation of Austria's most recognizable genre in early sound, the Viennese film. Created by writer Walter Reisch and star performer/director Willi Forst, it was not only exported internationally but remade in Berlin and then Hollywood studios, where Austrian film talent that sought wider possibilities, rejected the clerico-authoritarian regime (1934–1938) known as Austrofascism, or fearing Nazi revolution or annexation, joined many of their German counterparts from Berlin. Austria essentially hosted two film industries after 1933: that of mainstream production approved for German import (Nazis in and outside of the country had infiltrated Austrian production to the point of forcing "Aryanization" in the sovereign state), and that of the *Emigrantenfilm*, which consisted of German immigrant and anti-Nazi or Jewish Austrian talent coproducing in an internationalist style with studios in Hungary and Czechoslovakia, even the Netherlands and Sweden. While these latter attempts found critical and popular favor at home and, indeed, around the globe, annexation by Nazi Germany in 1938 (the *Anschluss*) halted this Central European film experiment and shifted much of its talent to Hollywood.[4] The "entertainment" role of Vienna in the Reich consisted of more of what it always had done best, the Forst-led Viennese film, operetta, and comedies, along with a few overtly propagandist narratives. Nevertheless, many of these lavish period films suggested the forbidden fantasy of a lost imperial Austria and its unique culture, rather than the country's integration into a multifaceted concept of a greater Germany.

The imperial film epics of the 1950s which emerged from the Viennese film genre and lost themselves in the opulent melodrama of Habsburg royalty and the music-laden fantasies of old Vienna in the nineteenth century, along with biopics on composers such as Mozart, Beethoven, and Schubert (from veterans and new purveyors of the style, such as Hubert Marischka and Franz Antel), were the exact opposite of their antecedents during the Reich—nation building rather than national deconstruction. Given the long Allied occupation, the imperial fantasy and *Heimatfilm* context seemed to define Austria with a false sense of continuity and a world popularity that at once distanced Austria from its Nazi past and its definition as a German province, while it brought it ever closer to West Germany in film production needs. These Agfacolor films, like the postwar Hollywood Technicolor celebration of American cultural superiority, conveyed through opulent studio back-lot musicals, wide-screen trivial comedies, and Biblical epics, were reassuring. They battled the onset of television and brought Austria to the world entertainment market again, if not to the critical world of cinema, which found its important impulses in Italy, France, Sweden, Britain, and even in the Eastern Bloc (East Germany, Czechoslovakia, Poland, Hungary, Yugoslavia).

Ironically, as significant as cinema had been in defining and redefining postimperial and republican Austria, and in sending its creative messages abroad, it was never seen as a national art with the pride and support given to literature, theater, opera, or the concert hall. The lack of national film funding in Austria, which was only sparsely begun in 1980, the exhaustion of the mainstream film genres, and the retirement or demise of many of Austria's veteran film talents by the 1960s, brought no government support for the growth or even teaching of film. Instead of the national pride that greeted French, British, or Italian New Wave cinema and cultivated global attention, Austrian commercial film was co-opted by West German, then ever wider, international multi-productions (generic spy films, broad comedies aimed at dubbing distribution, period extravaganzas that flopped) and television, and ceased to exist by 1968. The avant-garde turned against narrative structure rather than trying to change it with new techniques and subject matter, and Viennese Actionism—a mix of shock and protest performance art about and utilizing film—attacked the complacency and traditionalism of Austrian art, society, and politics, alienating audiences (if not critcs).[5] This supported the growing impression abroad and eventually at home that Austria was not a "film nation."[6]

The exception that is the current new wave in Austria is that it grew uniquely from a slow return to narrative and documentary film forms, and attempted to please no one except its makers and communicate with a local audience. From its scattered beginnings in the late 1970s, its artists rejected commercial filmmaking not only because this was a dead concept following the collapse of the industry and its Austrian-German remnant in the sex comedy, and with the impact of the Actionists, but because it was poverty cinema that made the auteur a necessity rather than an artistic conceit. The very modest means and the need to experience a different Austrian reality (even "history") engendered a new film generation that looked at styles abroad but found their vision and voice in critical topics set in recognizable circumstances. Austrian film history was distant, unloved, and served only as a measure of what was being made differently.

By the time the 'new wave' label began to identify the second decade of this youthful cinema, limited international coproduction (usually Austrian-German) was common again, and several narrative films had garnered noteworthy attention in and outside Austria. Among these was the groundbreaking television film, *Der Fall Jägerstätter/The Jaegerstaetter Case* (1972) from Axel Corti, a rare attempt at exploring dissident life in Austria during the Third Reich; the psychological study of contemporary urban-underclass xenophobia, Peter Patzak's *Kassbach* (1979); the starkly neo-realist *Schwitzkasten/Clinch* (1978) by Canadian-turned-Austrian filmmaker, John Cook; actor/director Maximilian Schell's *Geschichten aus dem Wiener Wald/Tales From the Vienna Woods* (1979), a critical look at impoverished life under Austrofascism from the play by Ödön von Horváth; and Wolfgang Glück's *Der Schüler Gerber/The Student Gerber* (1980), a period allegory about fascism and self-destruction. Axel Corti's television trilogy, *Wohin und Zurück/Somewhere and Back* (1986), which followed Gabriel Barylli's Jewish refugee character Freddy Wolf though the war, made Barylli a near star in the US for a brief time when the wrenching final segment, *Welcome in Vienna*, about Wolf's return to Austria as part of the American occupation force in 1945, aired on public television networks. *Die Praxis der Liebe/The Practice of Love* (1985), written and directed by one of Austria's leading avant-garde experimentalists of the 1960s, VALIE EXPORT (who insists her name be written in capital letters as a brand), was a successful foray into traditional narrative form and helped her find wider reception for her feminism and political criticism. Finally, Niki List's national box-office smash, the neo-noir comedy *Müllers Büro/Mueller's Office* (1986), and Josef Hader and Alfred Dorfer in Paul Harather's now classic adaptation of their tragicomic odd-couple play *Indien/India* (1993), proved that popular entertainment could be critical and did not have to return to outmoded production forms and themes. Even the social comedies of television director Reinhard Schwabenitzky, the most mainstream Austrian filmmaker at the present time, have grown within this cinematic new thought and look.

The Vienna Film Fund and a nascent national film subsidy helped solidify the new growth to some extent, but it was and still remains among the weakest financial support structures in Europe. With few traditional venues for distribution available, new companies and concepts such as the artist-run Sixpack Film (or sixpackfilm), which promotes short and experimental work, brought together a very disparate creative scene. The term New Austrian Film is thus one of convenience. This new wave did not replace or integrate itself into entertainment film as elsewhere in Europe. It did not have to battle dominant entertainment film (and lose) as in the US. Although politically critical it was not brought about by sweeping national political change, nor does it emerge from cinematic colonialism. It is not based on a manifesto as was the early Oberhausen-led New German Film of the 1960s and the second generation New German Cinema in the 1970s and 1980s, or like the followers of the Danish Dogme 95 approach (although there are a few Austrian Dogme-inspired films). It is the exception, one that grew organically from the uniqueness of the destruction of its cinematic parent, from its resistance to official history and national image, and from the multicultural shadow that has always been a natural part of the internationality of this national cinema. Its categorization can only be found in its self-starting and casual collaboration, rather than in some overriding doctrine, in its ability to exist against all economic and market-driven odds, and in emerging critical sympathy to a multi-segmented and detached national film history/culture that has only recently been represented as significant by archives, retrospectives, and research.[7] The exception is also the fact that New Austrian Film can be defined by what it is not—as Austria itself has always been.

We have endeavored to give this collected volume the type of methodologically and stylistically variant quality found in the films examined. From close readings to psychological study; from sociopolitical to semiotic analysis; from formalistic examination to impressionistic reportage and interview—the volume as a whole reflects the aspects that unite and separate these films and their makers. Balancing the general and the exceptional might be the only way to do justice to these recent films from Austria. Margarete Lamb-Faffelberger explores the very roots of the new film era in her discussion of VALIE EXPORT, as she looks at the artist's questioning of cinema as theory and practice in the 1960s and 1970s, her feminism, and her current stance on the relationship between performance and the screen. New Austrian Film's origins in the dominant film style and unlikely camera of the versatile entertainment showman of the Second Republic, Franz Antel, is the subject of Joseph Moser's examination of Antel's series of commercial films (1981–2003) dealing with a curmudgeonly Vienna butcher by the name of Bockerer that move towards an early attempt to "come to terms" with the previously cinematically taboo subject of the *Anschluss*, Nazism, Allied occupation, and Cold War consequences. Similarly, Wolfgang Glück's film *38* (1987), about a Jewish journalist and a gentile actress caught between the final days of Austrofascism and the approaching Nazi *Anschluss* is dissected by Felix Tweraser as a mixed attempt to reinvent the historical drama for a generation that rejects the totalizing force of that genre and to open the topic of historical fascism in Austrian cinema. Glück gave Austria its first international success in decades and garnered an Oscar nomination for Best Foreign Language film but lack of critical enthusiasm at home articulated the new generation's desire for new cinematic structures informed by the deep caesura of the 1960s and 1970s and a concentration on the fascistic residue in contemporary Austria. Christina Guenther provides a close-up from this landscape and considers Ruth Beckermann's representation of Jewishness and women in the construction of Austrian historical memory and contemporary cultural identity through her experimental documentaries and transgenre works as one of the very few Jewish filmmakers at work in Austria today.

Barbara Albert's *Nordrand/Northern Skirts* (1999) provided the international breakthrough for the more established phase of New Austrian Film in the late 1990s. It approaches the marginalization of the new multicultural population in Vienna played against the transitory nature of the postmodern urban environment and the xenophobia encouraged by Jörg Haider and the so-called Freedom Party. The dominance of female characters and her specifically female approach make it the exception in New Austrian Film. As film critic Ed Halter writes, these "quiet, cool, and subjective [films] achieve a detached, contemplative air so rarely attempted by overcompensating American cinema, communicating a bittersweet beauty through the simple evocation of interior life" (Halter 2003). Dagmar Lorenz approaches this postfeminism inside and outside of Albert's landmark film, and finds the lingering sexism and gender-related abuse that makes female independence difficult.

Meanwhile, Imke Meyer looks behind the scrim of a post-9/11 globalist, consumerist society at the leveling mechanisms that at once antagonize individualism and cause isolation in a nation still at odds with its national identity in Albert's follow-up film, *Böse Zellen/Free Radicals* (2003). The dystopian mosaics of Albert's oeuvre are mapped out according to her use of space and spatial distinctiveness by Mary Wauchope, who finds the filmmaker's subversion of the mythical Vienna and tourist Austria to be illusory points of identity and non-security, particularly for women. Yet, Albert's desire and need for a "new community of women," as Lorenz calls it, shaped by these dystopian aspects is most perceptible in the working interrelationship of women filmmakers in Austria today. The collaborative quality of New Austrian Film has manifested itself as a creative network that has replaced the historical male dominance of Austrian cinema with a female direction that is unique among the "new" cinemas in Europe. Seemingly at the center of this shared creativity, and also representative of its auteurism, is Kathrin Resetarits, in whose work and near iconic (self-)representation Verena Mund finds complex messages of perception regarding "image"—be it gender, socioculturally, or culturally defined—and its ambiguous reflection in popular media. Catherine Wheatley asks if there is a postfeminist, feminine, or female aesthetic arising from this cinematic imprint, using Valeska Grisebach's *Sehnsucht/Longing* (2006) as her case study along with films by Jessica Hausner and Ruth Mader. Her analysis of a specific reflexivity defined by time, space, and spectatorial gaze which opposes the "meta-texutal ruptures" in continuity by male New Austrian filmmakers does not lead to a conscious male-subversive counter-cinema (Mulvey, et al.) for her, but ultimately forms a cinematic *écriture féminine* constructively coexisting with male presence in these films.

One can look to Michael Haneke, who has risen to the kind of critical international attention not given to an Austrian director since Willi Forst, as heading up the "other half" of New Austrian Film—that of a possible male aesthetic, but one that does not oppose or position itself against female filmmaking, instead sharing equally in the talents available and the networking that has brought this new wave to the fore. If Haneke is a pan-European filmmaker—German born, Austrian citizen, Austrian, French, and German creative loci, and multicultural ethnic concerns—whose internationalism contributes to his universality, then Ulrich Seidl provides the opposite approach to locating similar universally identifiable dystopias: a sharply localized camera aimed at the anomie and brutality of everyday life in faceless suburbs and among "average" working and middle-class Austrians—the heart of the non-exceptional exception. Eva Kuttenberg approaches Haneke's earliest filmic success, *Der siebente Kontinent/The Seventh Continent* (1989), which influenced the breakthrough films of Albert and Hausner, by examining the "glaciation" that concerns the filmmaker in the contemporary industrialized world, and specifically in the Austrian vernacular. The implosion of the consumerist dream, its deception and dehumanization, results in an allegorical reduction of the Second Republic and its value system to rubble. Haneke's baiting of the audience's desire for (Hollywood and Hollywood-style) horror and human torture refashions this film into the notorious *Funny Games* (1997), in which the middle-class family unit and its safety in possessions and privacy is brutally deconstructed by sociopathic visitors—from the outside in (and off camera), suggesting that even if they did not do it themselves as in *The Seventh Continent*, it can be done for them. The security, class, even civilized behavior, identified with Austria's high-art culture are myths, which Gabi Wurmitzer delineates. In *La Pianiste/The Piano Teacher* (2001), based on Nobel Prize-winning author Elfriede Jelinek's allegorical novel of self-destructive sadomasochistic impulses in an Austria repressing its fascist past, as played out behind the elegant facades of Vienna's traditional music world, Haneke becomes more specific. As Catherine Wheatley argues, this film represents the sexual redux of Haneke's *Funny Games*, in which the sex acts are de-eroticized, out of frame, and contextualized by power and control. Wheatley also positions the film vis-à-vis the sexually explicit French body-genre films of Breillat and Noé. Given Haneke's penchant for allegorical tales of sociopolitical repression and its contemporary destructive legacies, he moves interestingly into that rare form for a contemporary Austrian filmmaker, the historical film, with a pre-First World War story of ritual punishment at a German school, *Das weiße Band/The White Ribbon* (2009). It revisits and re-envisions the few period explorations of early twentieth-century youth, including *Der junge Törless/Young Toerless* (1966), a new-wave German film by Volker Schlöndorff based on the novel by the Austrian author Robert Musil, Glück's aforementioned *Der Schüler Gerber*, but also rare historical dramas about war and identity, such as Axel Corti's *Radetzkymarsch/Radetzky March* (1995) and Stefan Ruzowitzky's *Die Fälscher/The Counterfeiters* (2007). Perhaps the continued astringency of narratives on contemporary dystopias has made the critical historical feature a renewed possibility in the next phase of New Austrian Film.

With a more direct attack on the structures of contemporary work-a-day society, Matthias Frey details Ulrich Seidl's transference of a sensibility reminiscent of Diane Arbus from his controversial documentaries to equally distancing narrative visions of deception without satisfaction, and survival without redemption. These are heightened by Seidl's "staged reality"—using non-actors to give his narrative films the aesthetic of his unyielding documentaries. And it is this painterly quality that Justin Vicari finds so compelling in the difficult tableaux of Seidl's work, which capture attempts at individualism that often breaks through the crust of social conformity with cruelty and self-debasement. He gives Seidl's films a pedigree in the Austrian art of the *fin de siècle*, particularly in connection with Gustav Klimt and his visions of "sexual angst and malevolence, where sensual arousal goes hand in hand with terror, torture, and pain." Like Haneke, Seidl refuses to offer straightforward political solutions. Martin Brady and Helen Hughes read his social criticism by examining three films spanning the filmmaker's career which have the theme of migration as their subject: *Good News* (1990), a study of migrant newspaper vendors in Vienna; *Mit Verlust ist zu rechnen/Loss is to be Expected* (1992), a postsocialist documentary written with Michael Glawogger, on a failed courtship across the Austrian-Czech border; and the feature film which created controversy regarding the exploitation of the exploited for the purpose of bringing their plight to the screen at the 2007 Cannes Film Festival, *Import Export* (2007), which tells the story of bilateral migration between Austria and the Ukraine. Seidl's "anthropology of migration" is examined in the context of Jean Rouch's *cinéma-vérité*, and his hyperstylization is demonstrated to offer a unique way of looking both at contemporary migration and at migrants themselves. The filmmaker's unflinching camera is shown not only to "voyeurize the voyeurs" but also to gaze severely yet democratically on transnational movements in the "new Europe."

Continuing in this vein, Nikhil Sathe inspects films by Barbara Albert, Houchang Allahyari, Ruth Mader, Jörg Kalt, Ulrich Seidl, and Andreas Gruber, which confront the very concept of space, division, and identity slippage in the national and the post-Soviet Central European imaginary. Austria as border and borderland; Austria as mythic center and actual periphery.... The *huis clos* situations that Andreas Böhn analyses in his contribution on films by Christian Frosch, Florian Flicker, and on Haneke's *Caché/Hidden* (2005), are all zones of indistinction, lawless zones, where the law is suspended, albeit momentarily, and where, in turn, a temporary totalitarian law allows the role reversal of perpetrator and victim. The directors transfer this to the relationship between spectator and image, breaking down a traditional cinema of audience trust to one that forces the spectator to question convention, expectation, and the very manipulation of entertainment. Reflecting this and focusing on Florian Flicker, Gundolf Graml looks at Flicker's reimagined postmodern road movie, *Suzie Washington* (1998), in which true identity and destination is only a surface concern. Instead, the protagonist's saga exposes the stations of her journey for their imagined sociopolitical representations and their cultural frictions within the ever-expanding EU. Erika Balsom takes on the subversion of such dominant cinema structures by exploring the work of Martin Arnold, Gustav Deutsch, and Peter Tscherkassky, three of the influential post-Actionist experimentalists of "found film" who tap hidden subtexts, turn narratives against their ideologies, and realign spectator–image relationships.

Stefan Ruzowitzky is a distant second to Michael Haneke in terms of international recognition, but unlike Haneke, who disintegrates the dominant film aspects of his work, Ruzowitzky recontextualizes traditional genres and utilizes their associated "entertainment value" to break apart their totalizing nature and create narratives that also reflect on the nature of cinematic storytelling. The horror film has been almost non-existent in Austrian and German cinema since early sound, and Ruzowitzky's approach to the internationalist concept of this box-office attraction, the German-produced *Anatomie/Anatomy* (2000) and its sequel *Anatomie 2/ Anatomy 2* (2003), shows why it was generally avoided after 1945. Alexandra Ludewig analyses how the director plays with general audience expectations and the inescapable shadow of a true historical horror subtext, Nazi dehumanization and scientific experimentation. Likewise, Rachel Palfreyman surveys the rebirth of the most durable genre in Austrian and German cinema, the *Heimatfilm*. While still set in provincial surroundings and displaying the natural beauty that made the genre such a visual and escapist pleasure, it has shed clichéd characterizations, banal folk wisdom, and contrived happy endings for a more realistic (and historically suggestive) depiction of social oppression and of class and gender abuse in

Ruzowitzky's *Die Siebtelbauern/The Inheritors* (1998). It would, of course, be a film set during the Nazi period that gained New Austrian Film its greatest Hollywood attention and the country's first Oscar for Best Foreign Language Film despite the fact that Austrian filmmakers had already been a presence and an influence on the international festival circuit for more than a decade. Critics suggested the following year that "studios are guilty of mining the Holocaust for awards season gold"[8] when Stephen Daldry's cinematic adaptation of the Bernhard Schlink novel on Nazism, guilt, and objective reception, *Der Vorleser/The Reader* (2008), was deemed a favorite along with six other Nazi-period films. Götz Spielmann's equally sexual meditation on crime, revenge, and redemption, *Revanche* (2008), gave Austria its second foreign-language Oscar nomination in a row, but it was Ruzowitzky's unique way with genre film and its vocabulary that not only gave Hollywood what it had obviously wanted all along: a fess-up; an Austrian film on Nazism.[9] It was of course a breakthrough in Austria as well, a popular film that dealt with the painful and obscured Nazi past and the Holocaust. A pendent perhaps to the sixty-plus years it took Germany to present its own nuanced version of Hitler and his last days, Oliver Hirschbiegel's *Untergang/Downfall* (2004), as its cinema had already begun to face a new aspect of its history, East Germany. Raymond Burt shows how Ruzowitzky intentionally uses the relative safety and order of traditional narrative structure and documentary camera movement to approach the heretofore unapproachable topic of an Austrian concentration camp, where the exchange of power provides the spectator with a far more nuanced look at "unrepresentable" territory than otherwise seen in recent cinema. A far different genre revision is the Austrian comedy, which has usually been tied to Vienna's cabaret tradition with performers ranging from Jewish monologists of the 1930s, to theater actors turned golden-age comedy film stars, to the biting satire of performer Helmut Qualtinger in the 1960s and 1970s. As Regina Standún argues, the resurgence of the local Austro-comedy, which already iconizes its new-classic talents, is less pratfall and more a gritty neo-realist look at the foibles of an unremarkable life reflected in the darkest shades of humor. The least internationally marketed or exported films of the new wave, they have achieved significant box-office success at home and in the German-speaking region, occasionally achieving greater popularity than the ubiquitous and seemingly unassailable Hollywood or internationally coproduced blockbuster import.

The hypocrisy of the elite, the purveyors of high culture, and of the Catholic Church, is Wolfgang Murnberger's target, and he deflates these icons deftly in the guise of mainstream entertainment as one of the most commercial filmmakers in critical Austrian film (along with Reinhard Schwabenitzky and Harald Sicheritz). His cinematic take on the detective story, *Komm, Süßer Tod/Come Sweet Death* (2000), based on the novel by Wolf Haas, resulted in a bona fide national and regional box-office smash. Despite his more mainstream entertainment style, Murnberger, no less than Haneke, forces the viewer to question cinematic convention and spectatorial expectations in a moral context. Also subverting mainstream form and style is Michael Glawogger, whose slightly surreal features and documentaries on the often shocking absurdities of contemporary society are discussed by Christoph Huber in an impressionistic manner that mirrors the tone of the director's form and demonstrates the style of reportage greeting film in Austria today. From his first feature film—*Die Ameisenstraße/Ant Street* (1995), in which the introverted inhabitants of an old apartment building are all but ignored during the vast renovation work undertaken by its new owner—Glawogger has concentrated on the marginal, the forgotten, and the exceptionally unexceptional. That this film has been understood as an allegory of everything from the official repression of "untidy" aspects of Austrian history to the construction of the European Union, suggests the odd universality Glawogger achieves while at the same time being arguably the most Austrian-focused filmmaker of the new wave. Even his documentaries, such as the voyages across overcrowded urban slum landscapes in *Megacities* (1998) and the look at intensive hard labor in *Workingman's Death* (2005), have something of the hallucinatory about them. The films seem conscious that image cannot be reality, and reality is but perception—an equation that exposes the constructs of Jörg Haider's absurd exclusionary politics in a country where multiculturalism is fundamental to the nation, as in the Glawogger/Barbara Albert/Ulrich Seidl/Michael Sturminger documentary, *Zur Lage – Österreich in sechs Kapiteln/State of the Nation – Austria in Six Chapters* (2003). Glawogger takes on the exploitation cinema of the 1960s and 1970s but replaces its hedonism with a tragicomic futility that speaks of the limits of self-realization, as in the anti-sex-comedy sex comedy, *Nacktschnecken/ Slugs* (2004), in the episodic look at three contemporary families related by Holocaust history, *Das Vaterspiel/Kill Daddy Good Night* (2009), or in the Tarantinoesque, druggy road-movie grunge of *Contact High* (2009).

"The image is all and also nothing" might be a motto for the Austrian new-wave documentary which in its meditative manner forces the spectator to become the narrator, as in such hypnotic eco-films as Nikolaus Geyrhalter's *Unser täglich Brot/ Our Daily Bread* (2005), which stares at the horrible beauty of food production; Erwin Wagenhofer's *We Feed the World* (2006), or Udo Maurer's *Über Wasser – Menschen und gelben Kanister/About Water – People and Yellow Cans* (2007). And while the image is always questioned, this approach manages to capture the elusive, and move the spectator without the overtly objective manipulation found in most post-9/11 documentaries on the condition of our social and natural world. Arno Russegger looks not only at filmmaker Hubert Sauper (like Haneke, an Austrian living and working in France) and his previous documentaries on the fight for human dignity, be it in Africa or among abused women in contemporary Paris, but also at the documentary's place in the new wave and its mistrust of the "official." His theoretical dissection of Sauper's multi award-winning and Oscar-nominated *Darwin's Nightmare* (2004), on the widespread corruption surrounding the fishing industry in Lake Victoria, Tanzania, which has resulted in unmitigated ecological and human disaster, approaches the filmmaker as helpless witness rather than polemicist, and its resulting spectatorial effect.

Sara F. Hall's analysis of Götz Spielmann's *Antares* (2004) shows the formalistic aspect of the New Austrian Film in its early turn-of-the-century manifestation:

cyclical, episodic, and medially reflexive. In this way Spielmann's sexually attentive observation of a controlled set of people who simultaneously interact with and without the social mask is no different from the structures of Albert and Seidl. In fact, they reach back to the Viennese literary impressionist work of Arthur Schnitzler and his 1897 play *Reigen* (published first in 1903 due to censorship difficulties), which has spawned so many adaptations and modernizations, and is often known by its French title, *La Ronde*. Hall finds Spielmann's film to be one of body politics, image propaganda, and ultimately a troubled humanism that positions itself against the Hollywood constructs of sexuality and the sexual female, as well as against the romantic notions of touristy Austrian images. Perhaps it is this clinical distance that makes New Austrian Film seem difficult and a "feel-bad cinema" to some. Overtaken by the aesthetic of the ugly it searches for and captures human discord that cannot easily or ever be resolved.

More than just an unusual choice by Austria to represent the country at the 2010 Oscars, *Ein Augenblick Freiheit/For a Moment, Freedom* (2009), a film about exile and immigration shot in Farsi, Turkish, English, and German by the Austro-Iranian director Arash T. Riahi, was a volley against xenophobia and a validation that New Austrian Film is as multifaceted and polyglot as Austria's cinema history has been. The concept of national cinema has always been an elastic one here, even as Austrian filmmakers of the past have struggled to survive in a limited market and between "seeing" the nation and selling the country. In an interview with Catherine Wheatley, Götz Spielmann discusses the changing qualities, reception, and markets of New Austrian Film from a primary perspective and voices his views regarding his *Antares* follow-up, the Oscar-nominated *Revanche* (2008). Along with other recent work, it seems to mark the return of the genre film and suggests the shifting aesthetics of Austrian feature film to come.

Notes

This collaborative effort generated enough discourse on the subject for several books. The industry and patience of our contributors is clear in their work and we hope in the overall concept of the collection. We are most grateful to Berghahn Books, especially to Mark Stanton, who understood the excitement and possibility of such a project, and to our anonymous readers, who encouraged us by pointing out not only what worked but also what did not—and let us grow beyond both. For their support, suggestions, critique, and assistance regarding various aspects of this collection and the life that went on around it we thank: Josef Aichholzer, Ernst Aichinger, Peter Bondanella, Marie Cadell, Rolando Caputo (*Senses of Cinema*), Craig Decker (*Modern Austrian Literature*), VALIE EXPORT, Fernando Feliu-Moggi, Chris Fujiwara (FIPRESCI-*Undercurrents*), Matthias Greuling (*Celluloid*), Sabine Hein, Johannes Hofinger, Florian Kröppel, Daniel Lindvall (*Film International*), Gary Morris (*Bright Lights Film Journal*), Scott Murray (*Senses of Cinema*), Margaret Ozierski, Martin Rauchbauer, Clemens Ruthner, Stefan Ruzowitzky, Wendelin Schmidt-Dengler, Hubert Sauper, Götz Spielmann, Christoph Thun-Hohenstein, Jacqueline Vansant, and Martin Weiss. We are also grateful to the Austrian Cultural Forum (New York and Washington, DC), the Modern Austrian Literature and Culture Association (MALCA), the German Studies Association (GSA), the Goethe Institute, Los Angeles, and the Austrian Film Commission.

1. ORF [Österreichischer Rundfunk]. 2008. "Gusenbauer Plans Image Campaign to Counter Abuse Criticism," 30 April. Retrieved 11 October 2008 from: http://www.aparchive.com/Search.aspx?kw=gusenbauer&st=k#1U563145.

2. Agamben summarizes his arguments as follows: "1. The original political relation is the ban (the state of exception as zone of indistinction between outside and inside, exclusion and inclusion). 2. The fundamental activity of sovereign power is the production of bare life as originary political element, and as threshold of articulation between nature and culture, zoë and bios. 3. Today it is not the city but rather the camp that is the fundamental biopolitical paradigm of the West" (Agamben 1998: 181).

3. Prior to this Stefan Ruzowitzky had made *Anatomie/Anatomy*, a horror film that features doctors who define their patients entirely as "bare life", using them for experiments. *Das Experiment/The Experiment* (2001), by Austrian resident Oliver Hirschbiegel, could also be called a meditation on the establishment of a zone of exception. Inspired by the Stanford prison experiment, the guards in this film quickly establish a totalitarian regime, stripping the inmates of all political rights.

4. Ulrich (2004) is a hefty compendium of Austrian and Austro-Hungarian expatriate and exiled talent in the Hollywood film industry. Many of these actors, directors, and film artists were also active in Berlin, Budapest, Prague, London, and Paris prior to or following their Hollywood years.

5. Hermann Nitsch presented the first Actionist art in his showing at the Galerie Dvorak in Vienna in March 1963. The bloody carcass of a lamb was hung from the ceiling and then moved through the room in a shaking motion in order to splatter blood on the viewers. Blood was poured from buckets onto the floor, and an actor flung raw eggs against a wall. The shock value of the Actionists is to be found not only in their provocation of traditional art venues and art audiences, but also in the radicalism of their materials and the use of the human body. Blood, animal entrails, and carcasses figure strongly in their early performances in what is intended as a ritualistic or Dionysian "rapture". Later, the naked human body was directly involved in the action. A selection of Austrian actionist film (1967–1970) can be seen online at: www.ubu.com/film/vienna_actionists.html. The interview with Actionist Otto Mühl by Andrew Grossman explores this subversive and alienating creativity from the artist's perspective.

6. For a detailed examination of the decline of the Austrian film industry after the 1950s and non-narrative avant-garde experimentalism, see Dassanowsky (2006).

7. Historical studies of Walter Fritz provided the only substantial volumes on Austrian film history from the 1960s into the 1990s. With the re-emergence of Austrian film there has been a significant increase in published studies. The Filmarchiv Austria issues restored film classics and rarities on DVD and well-produced director, era, and genre book-length studies, while the Austrian Film Museum and Vienna's Synema Society for Film and Media concentrates on more recent cinema. Contemporary film is examined in Horwath, Ponger, and Schlemmer (1995), and Schlemmer (1996). Elisabeth Büttner and Christian Dewald (1997, 2002) have attempted to examine Austrian film history in a thematic/theoretical frame. In English, there is Riemer (2000), Lamb-Faffelberger (2002), Lamb-Faffelberger and Saur (2004), and Dassanowsky (2005). The Austrian Film Commission publishes annual catalogues and its online site includes summaries of current and forthcoming productions in all genres, interviews with filmmakers, and current news: http://www.afc.at.

8. AFP. 2009. "Filmmakers 'using Holocaust as Oscars bait'". *ABC News*, 19 February. Retrieved 14 May 2009 from: http://www.abc.net.au/news/stories/2009/02/19/2495396.htm.

9. The first nomination of an Austrian film in this category was Glück's *Anschluss* love story, *38* (1987).

References

Agamben, G. 1998. *Homo Sacer: Sovereign Power and Bare Life.* Stanford, CA: Stanford University Press.

Augé, M. 1995. *Non-Places: Introduction to an Anthropology of Supermodernity.* London: Verso.

Benjamin, W. 1969. "The Work of Art in the Age of Mechanical Reproduction," in *Illuminations*, ed. H. Arendt. New York: Schocken, 217–51.

Büttner, E., and C. Dewald. 1997. *Anschluss an Morgen: Eine Geschichte des österreichischen Films von 1945 bis zur Gegenwart.* Salzburg: Residenz.

———. 2002. *Das tägliche Brennen: Eine Geschichte des österreichischen Films von den Anfängen bis 1945.* Salzburg: Residenz.

Dassanowsky, R. von. 2005. *Austrian Cinema: A History.* Jefferson, NC: McFarland.

———. 2006. "Austria's 1960s Film Trauma: Notes on a Cinematic Phoenix," *Undercurrent* 3. Retrieved 11 October 2008 from: http://www.fipresci.org/undercurrent/issue_0306/dassanowsky_austria.htm.

Deleuze, G. 1986. "Post-scriptum sur les sociétés de contrôle," in *Pourparlers.* Paris: Minuit.

Foucault, M. 1978. *The History of Sexuality, Vol. 1*, trans. R. Hurley. New York: Vintage.

Halter, E. 2003. "Das Experiment," *Village Voice*, 12–18 November. Retrieved 14 May 2009 from: http://www.villagevoice.com/2003-11–11/film/das-experiment.

Hardt, M. 1993. *Gilles Deleuze: An Apprenticeship in Philosophy.* Minneapolis: University of Minnesota Press.

Horwath, A., L. Ponger, and G. Schlemmer (eds). 1995. *Avantgardefilm Österreich: 1950 bis heute.* Vienna: Wespennest.

Lamb-Faffelberger, M. (ed.) 2002. *Literature, Film and the Culture Industry in Contemporary Austria.* New York: Lang.

Lamb-Faffelberger, M., and P.S. Saur (eds). 2004. *Visions and Visionaries in Contemporary Austrian Literature and Film.* New York: Lang.

Lim, D. 2006. "Greetings From the Land of Feel-bad Cinema," *New York Times*, 26 November. Retrieved 11 October 2008 from: http://www.nytimes.com/2006/11/26/movies/26lim.html.

Riemer, W. (ed.) 2000. *After Postmodernism: Austrian Literature and Film in Transition.* Riverside, NJ: Ariadne.

Schlemmer, G. (ed.) 1996. *Der neue Österreichische Film.* Vienna: Wespennest.

Ulrich, R. 2004. *Österreicher in Hollywood*, 2nd edn. Vienna: Filmarchiv Austria.

Part I

Early Visions/Influential Sites

Chapter 1

"The Experiment Is Not Yet Finished": VALIE EXPORT's Avant-garde Film and Multimedia Art

Margarete Lamb-Faffelberger

Introduction

> I have screamed with the voice that belongs to me.
> I have bitten with the teeth that belong to me.
> I have scratched with the nails that belong to me.
> I have cried with the tears that belong to me.
> I have seen with the eyes that belong to me.
> I have thought with the thoughts that belong to me.
> I have laughed with the laugh that belongs to me.
> I have kissed with the mouth that belongs to me.
> I have slept with the dreams that belong to me.
> That is the life that belongs to me.
> —"Images of Contact" (1998)

VALIE EXPORT is a well-known and internationally renowned Austrian experimental filmmaker and avant-garde artist.[1] During a career spanning forty years, she has produced a powerful oeuvre—provocative, uncompromising, and aesthetically refined. It is comprised of expanded cinema productions, body performances, body–material interactions, conceptual and digital photography, video environments and installations, laser installations, experimental and feature-length films and documentaries, as well as drawings, sculptures, and texts on contemporary art, art history, and feminism. When she entered the scene in the late 1960s, a radical shift in consciousness sparked by guilt feelings about the horrors of the Second World War had taken hold of the younger generation in both Western

Europe and the United States. In the world of the arts, the revolutionary new concept of intermediality—crossing the boundaries between art and technology—as well as the body as "extended" medium had been embraced by the avant-garde.

EXPORT's oeuvre reflects the sociopolitical challenges of her generation as well as the innovative aesthetic theories of her time. She employs her own body as a medium of gendered critique to provoke social change, particularly with regard to the prevailing conservative mind-set towards women. This marks her work as distinctly feminist. Until the 1980s, her work was largely misunderstood and misinterpreted by both the public and Austria's art critics. For the most part, the Austrian media displayed a typically snobbish and downright hostile attitude. But even within Austria's art scene, her work was eyed with suspicion.[2] In 1989, she lost in a bid for a professorship at Vienna's esteemed University of Applied Arts. Between 1990 and 1994, she taught at the University of Wisconsin, Milwaukee and at the Academy of Arts in Berlin. From 1995 until 2005, she held the position of Professor of Multimedia and Performance at the Academy of Media Arts in Cologne, Germany. For her groundbreaking art, she has earned much appreciation and deep respect from far beyond Austria's borders. At last, however, her international success has spawned recognition from within. In 2000, EXPORT became the tenth recipient of the prestigious Oskar Kokoschka Prize.[3]

Numerous studies and analyses have been made of EXPORT's work, including a recent book by Szely (2007). Her work is discussed and presented not only in the context of multimedia art, into which it has been pigeonholed over the past decade, but in the context of film. In September 2007, EXPORT validated Szely's argument that she has always been a filmmaker.[4] In this chapter I look at EXPORT's explorations of the body, the image, language and the photographic apparatus, and of their interface and boundaries as well as their relation to space and time in our postmodern world. The emphasis—consonant with Szely's analysis—lies on reading her oeuvre as a body of moving images.

In 1967, Waltraud Höllinger reinvented herself by adopting the pseudonym VALIE EXPORT, coupling femaleness with the concept of marketing. She got the idea from Smart EXPORT, a popular Austrian cigarette brand, and produced two photographs entitled "VALIE EXPORT – Smart EXPORT" as self-portraits. The word "VALIE" (sharing its sound with her nickname Wali, but implying "value") is placed over the brand logo and her face is superimposed on the small circle in the center of the pack around which the text *semper at ubique, immer und überall* ("always and everywhere") is printed. On the second image, EXPORT takes up a macho pose, chin up, disheveled hair, eyelids drawn, the cigarette lit between her lips. The stretched-out hand cockily offers a close-up look at the pack VALIE EXPORT. Since cigarettes impart market value and, of course, connote virility, her message reads: "I am a woman performing as a man; I proffer myself/my work as a commodity."

EXPORT's aesthetic and theoretical principles were informed by several avant-garde movements, such as the work that emerged from Black Mountain College in North Carolina, and Fluxus, which is known for its political engagement and antiauthoritarian stance in the wake of the conservative politics that culminated in America's involvement in the Vietnam War.[5] The idea of "intermedia" (coined by Fluxus member Dick Higgins in 1965) spurred EXPORT's imagination. The pioneering radical feminist work of American women artists—for example, Carolee Schneemann's studies of visual traditions, taboos, and the body in relation to society—were equally important to EXPORT. She was also familiar with the avant-garde scene in postwar Austria, knew the writings by the Wiener Gruppe and was acquainted with the Viennese Actionists, whose happenings and performances she frequently attended. Yet, she never worked directly with them. Even though she shared their aim of breaking social, sexual, and cultural taboos and their preference for the human body as the principal material for their work, she radically repudiated the violation and destruction of the woman's body that was an essential part of the artistic expression of the Actionists. In contrast, EXPORT took a decisive stand against the status quo of the sexual politics of the time, which tolerated the objectification of women and hindered women from becoming active in their own right. Her feminist stance is rooted in American and European second-wave feminism, and in the political rebellion that culminated in the anti-Vietnam War movement and in the student movement in West Germany. Furthermore, what set her work decidedly apart from that of the Viennese Actionists was her revolutionary application of media technology—film, photography, video, and, since the 1990s, digital technology. Already in her earliest work, EXPORT utilized a range of media (action/performance, photography, film, and video).

To gain a fuller understanding of her radical work and its significant impact on the younger generation of artists and filmmakers, it is crucial to take these international currents in the arts and their theoretical underpinnings into consideration. The following components can be identified in her work: "Attention to materials and objects, random selection, spontaneous actions, the elimination of binding categories and formal boundaries between various media, as well as between art and life, and an antiauthoritarian stance on sociopolitical and cultural questions that includes a critical view of the cultural apparatus" (Mueller 1994: xvi).

Expanded Reality: Expanded Cinema and Feminist Actionism

> When we say expanded cinema we actually mean expanded consciousness.
> —Gene Youngblood, *Expanded Cinema* (1970)

After the Second World War, artists in Austria were largely isolated from the avant-garde art scene that evolved in the United States and Western Europe. Therefore the idea of film as a means of personal expression and sociopolitical critique was not rooted in the tradition of auteur cinema but was instead related to the avant-garde movement of the late nineteenth and early twentieth century and its radicalism in painting, literature, music, architecture, and philosophy. In the 1960s, film "happenings" combining projection with performance were in vogue.[6] These were often spontaneous and relatively inexpensive to stage. Moreover, Gene Youngblood proclaimed that expanding cinema was necessary for the formation of a new social and artistic consciousness: "Expanded cinema ... like life is a process of becoming, man's ongoing historical drive to manifest his consciousness outside of his mind, in front of his eyes" (Youngblood 1970: 54). Accordingly, EXPORT explains, "expanded cinema" was understood to mean not only "the expansion of the optic phenomenon but also the deconstruction of the dominant reality and the language that it construes" (EXPORT 1997: 61). The expansive art concept led experimental filmmakers to explore and investigate the effects of media communication on individual cognitive processes, on human language, perception and thought, and on the social environment. Her photo essay "Zur Mythologie der zivilisatorischen Prozesse/On the Mythology of Civilizing Processes" (EXPORT 1972) investigates the communicative function of symbols (signifiers) and signs (signification), and the interpretative and consumer behavior of society. Throughout her career, these concerns have remained central to her intellectual explorations as demonstrated in her artistic production (see EXPORT 2003b).

EXPORT launched her first expanded cinema projects in 1967, several of them in collaboration with Peter Weibel.[7] *Abstract Film No.1* was her first expanded cinema art piece. It demonstrates the model of producing a film without using celluloid. *Auf+Ab+An+Zu/Up+down+on+off* from 1968 is a film-action piece in which the spectator turns into an emancipated actor who supplements the movie since the projection and the montage take place simultaneously. Expanded cinema expressions include the street as stage where space and time are contiguous with everyday life and consumerism. In the late 1960s, it was assumed that "real life" was happening in the urban public space where anti-war protests, student revolts, and demonstrations for equal rights for women took place. The inner-city space, or "underground," evoked opportunities for a new kind of reception of EXPORT's provocative and aggressive street performances such as *Tapp- und Tastkino/Touch Cinema*. Here, EXPORT wears a styrofoam box like a megasized T-shirt over her torso. The box constitutes the cinema; the two slits in the front simulate the entrance doors to the auditorium; and her bare breasts simulate the screen. The spectator's hands are invited to enter and "view" (touch) the "film" (breasts) for exactly twelve seconds. The performance is photographed. These images are legendary. The hands of the man are stuck inside the box, seemingly cut off at the elbows. He looks at the face above the box, perhaps hoping to discern her pleasure but her face is flat, mask-like. She is surrounded by a crowd of spectators, yet there is nothing to see. The "screen" is invisible. The action happens inside, out of sight: camera obscura.

For EXPORT, the expanded cinema concept also means the deconstruction of the voyeuristic scope of film. Her strategies of expansion are aimed at the desexualization of both object and subject and, therefore, exclude pleasure in the meaning of the Lacanian concept of *jouissance*. In 1969, she shows her sex head-on. In Munich's Stadtkino, she walked up and down the aisles sporting a rifle and wearing pants with a triangular opening in the crotch that exposed her genitalia.[8] The viewers, experiencing no pleasure in seeing the erotic in such a way, are shocked and turn their gaze away. This occurs, as the art historian Régis Michel explains, because the performance forces the spectator into a situation in which they do not watch the spectacle as "voyeur", and the sex (of the artist) itself gazes at the spectator and thus annuls their power to observe (Chukhrov 2007). EXPORT also conceived the poster *Aktionshose – Genitalpanik/Action Pants – Genital Panic* as a reproducible piece of art, which bridges the gap between high art and popular culture, when the public space was already satiated with images fueling the consumerist boom of the economic miracle and the capitalist marketing of the perfect or ideal female body.[9] Moreover, discussions about theories of high culture versus mass culture, the increasing power of the culture industry, and the growing influence of technology on society and culture—by Michel Foucault, Claude Lévi-Strauss, Marshall McLuhan, and the Frankfurt School, for example—were well under way.

The human body as the site for inscriptions of social codes is central to all of EXPORT's work: "The center of my artistic work is comprised of the human body as medium for information, as bearer of signs, of meaning and communication. I deal with the depiction of mental conditions, with the sensation of the body when it loses its identity" (EXPORT, in Burnham 1982: 34). A persuasive case in point is the 1968 street performance *Von der Mappe der Hündigkeit/From the Portfolio of Doggedness* when EXPORT—walking her leashed "dog" (Peter Weibel) that follows her meekly on all fours through the inner city of Vienna—explores the question: "What changes when man behaves like an animal even though man is not animal?" (Lebovici 2003: 146). Despite the fact that gender is not central to the concept of the performance, it nevertheless demonstrates a strong opposition to the misogynist worldview of the Viennese Actionists. "VALIE EXPORT owes a lot to the Actionists. But the patriarchal status of the passive feminine is everything that she challenges. Not in words. In deeds. She is the artist, and it is her body, which she displays. The body of the woman: counter-power of the patriarchate," asserts Régis Michel (2003: 27). Indeed, for EXPORT the body is "the screen on which society arranges its daily slapstick and forces wo/man to be its actor" (EXPORT, in Hofmann and Hollein 1980: 88). The female body is the scene of the action. It is motor and repository. It is dispatcher, conductor, and receiver of feelings and forces, sensations and energies. It is the battleground of life, illness, and death. It is the place where the self realizes its boundaries and defines where and how it will encounter the world outside. "The body of a woman is in reality selfless, [it is] not her own ... [She is permitted] to function through her body only in relationship to the man, in relation to society," explains EXPORT (ibid.: 95).

Body Sign Action from 1970 demonstrates the meaning of her assertion. The woman's skin functions as a screen (*Hautleinwand*) (EXPORT 1997: 54). The photograph lens zooms in on the left upper thigh that displays a garter. Yet the garter is not real; it is a tattoo, an indelible mark on the artist's own body. Tattoos manifest the linkage between society and ritual. Therefore, the tattoo of the garter (sexual fetish and concurrently, a genuine piece of woman's clothing at a time when women had few personal rights and no public voice) carries the meaning of reconstructed female history. In 1971, EXPORT uses her body in *Eros/ion* as a transmitter and screen of traces of socially inscribed conditions and realities in her investigations of the relationship between the social signs of culture and the body, and between material and the body: First, the naked female body rolls over broken glass that cuts her skin. Bloodstains become visible as the body continues across a smooth glass surface and paper. As the glass splinters are transformed into signs through the aesthetic process, the artist changes and overcomes the socially prescribed significance of the meaning and image as material. In her performance *Homometer II* from 1976, EXPORT's abdomen—or more accurately, the loaf of bread that hangs from her neck—functions as the projection screen. When the spectator/actor is asked to cut into the loaf of bread, the seemingly benign act of obtaining nourishment becomes a reprehensible act of violence against the body. Literally carving into the skin is the focus of her short film *Remote-Remote* (1973). In a close-up shot, the tip of a sharp knife cuts with relentless persistence into cuticles. The incessant scratching noise is unsettling; the sight of the skin being torn up and blood—that is, menstruation—oozing from the wound into a bowl of milk—motherhood—on her lap is unnerving. "The drama of wo/man's self-depiction transpires in the lacerations of the skin" (EXPORT 1996: 339). The transformation of internal pain to the outside of the female body is symbolic of both suffering and survival.

These expanded cinema pieces and much of EXPORT's subsequent work reveal her fixation on externalizing inner feelings and emotions. Her visualization of subjectivity and the unconscious counteract our cultural code of rationality and objectivity—the cogito—as the highest form of human mental life, which is indubitably male.

Making Visible the Invisible: Conceptual Photography

> The illiterate of the future will be the person ignorant
> of the use of the camera as well as the pen.
> —Laszlo Moholy-Nagy (1946)

Throughout her career, EXPORT has been primarily concerned with the crisis in perception of our fragmented world, where signs are deprived of their ability to represent, images are no longer anchored in reality, and words have lost their referent. Conceptual photography thus affords EXPORT the opportunity to investigate the dimensions of time and space and their effect on the photographic process while utilizing the aesthetic as well as the visual, material potential of the apparatus. To make visible the constructs of reality—the virtual realities that shape our perception (cognitive maps) of the world today—EXPORT dismantles the media's representations.

The photomontage *Train* (1972) serves as an early example of her conceptual work. Her starting point is the dissection of the space–time structure in perceived reality: "We know that reality is never present in its totality. The experience of reality is composed of various multifarious identities and is actually only a selection from the perspective of the viewer" (Faber 2003: 71–72). Conceptual photographic experiments about the relationship between image and word are depicted in *Schriftzug/Handwriting-writing Train* (1972) and *Be-Weg-ung/Movement-Trace* (1973). In 1968, EXPORT created her first serial conceptual photographic exploration entitled *Finger Poem*. The stills are arranged side by side, each showing the frontal view of the artist's upper body as she creates letter after letter with her hand and fingers. She writes a poem without a pen and delivers a message without uttering a word. Its subtitle "I say the showing with the signs by signing the legend" (*Ich sage die zeige mit zeichen im zeigen der sage*) alludes to the Heideggerian notion of language as a representation by image and by concept and also refers to Derrida's (1978 [1967]) examination of writing and the associated phenomenon of iterability.

During the 1970s, EXPORT worked on two major photographic cycles entitled *Body Configurations in Nature* and *Body Configurations in Architecture*. Once again, her work centers on the visualization of the loss of communication when the female body rejects social norms. "Insertion," "Elongation," "Conformance," "Application," "Adaptation," "Addition," and "Elevation" are stills that depict the female body blending into the topography of the urban and natural landscape. In various poses— bent out of shape—it is applied to the worn surface of the urban and natural environment. The stills of the twisted female body as decor in spatial arrangements, therefore, not only frame a certain space but also time. EXPORT explains:

> The parallel between landscape and the mind and between architecture and the mind is mediated by the body ... because the parallel has its origin in the external opposition between mind and body, and also because the body bears the stamp of other factors, just as the landscape does. The landscape shows the marks made by space and time ... the disposition of its parts, such as trees, rocks and hills, shows the effects. [The] parts of the body ... also show the stamp of inner states and express them. This analogy of scenic and bodily arrangements, these common forms of revealing mood, have served since the beginning of pictorial art as projection surfaces for expression: external configurations, whether they are in the landscape or in the picture (which thus turns into the landscape) serve as the expression of internal states. (EXPORT 1979: 61)

The two *Body Configurations* are brilliant in their magnification of a woman's situatedness and forceful inscription into the official, the rational, the elevated public space. The series of photographs can be interpreted as female resistance to the public, hegemonic space, the "transparent space" that denies difference.[10] Transparent space is oppressive space and the female body in it is the "intelligible body" (see here Bordo 1993) or "docile body" (see here Foucault 1977) that bears the wounds of the dominant cultural inscriptions of "normalcy." In *Body Configurations*, the female body remains in the public space, although this comes at a price. It is reduced to the status of a trivial element and fades into the surface structure of the public urban landscape (in Lacanian parlance, aphanisis).

EXPORT's systematic structural studies of the female body continue in her interrogation of well-known European paintings and sculptures. By exploring the historical archive of body postures, she reveals the double structure of the body as both instrument and cultural record. Taking Leonardo da Vinci's famous studies of proportion and the "secret" link between geometry, the body, and the mind—the "human measure" (*das menschliche Maß*)—as her point of departure, she delineates her theory in the essay "Corpus More Geometrico" (EXPORT 2003a). This begins with a quote from Maurice Merleau-Ponty, "The body is to be compared, not to a physical object, but rather to a work of art, which places the body squarely in the realm of signification" (Merleau-Ponty 2002: 174). Indeed, the traditional, dominant function of the female (nude) body in Western art is to be present for the gaze of man.

EXPORT investigates the depiction of women in Renaissance art works, in which the real and the ideal are blended together, signified by idealized features and stylized attributes, in the presentation of the female self as defined by society:

> I use body parts or segments of body expression which have largely been used when portraying women ... [However, they] are not the norm for the traditional representation of woman ... I give these body parts a new and different medial expression and bring them ... into a new and different context. By overlapping the first image with a second image, the first one is destroyed, by overlapping the second with a third the second is destroyed, and so on. Nevertheless, it remains the same body with which I am dealing. (EXPORT, in Rötzer and Rogenhofer 1988: 155)

For instance, in *Madonna with Vacuum Cleaner* (1976), we see a woman sitting in the pose of Mary against the backdrop of Sandro Botticelli's famous *Madonna of the Pomegranate* fresco. Instead of holding the child, she cradles a vacuum cleaner in her arms. The substitution of the soft for the firm, of the living (the child) for a machine, reduces and demolishes the intactness of the maternal posture. Two photomontages— *Birth Madonna* and *Knitting Madonna*—are further variations on this theme. The exaggerated depiction of suffering and the idealized portrayal of woman as mother— in this case Michelangelo's famous *Pieta*—is confronted with the crude realism of a housewife's everyday life symbolized by the washing machine and the knitting machine. Hence, the spectator who has been conditioned to identify with the idealized figure in art, instantly and abruptly calls the static portrayal of the female body through the ages into question.

EXPORT subscribes to a particular visual philosophy of decoding role-prescribed embodiments by countering all fixations with multimedial ruptures, which she terms—with reference to the anagrammatic writings of the German poet Unica Zürn and the visual art of Hans Bellmer—"medial anagrams." In the framework of the anagrammatic play, both versions of the word/image, both combinations, are equal. The reference of word and image to reality, their signifying function, is momentarily—though not irremediably—suspended. In *The Real and Its Double: The Body* (1987), EXPORT takes Bellmer's action of disassembling and reassembling the body and Zürn's deconstruction and reconstruction of language as the same artistic process of anagrammatization. She asserts that "objectual or verbal anagrammatizing results from the inadequacy of the body as social construction of woman. The interchangeability of body parts and parts of sentences stands for the interchangeability of the self of woman as body" (EXPORT 1987: 15; see Lamb-Faffelberger 1996: 231–45). Consequently, EXPORT's intermedial (and intertextual) feminist discourse can be called an anagrammatization of gender.

An Anagrammatization of Gender: Experimental Films

> Movies are a world of fragments.
> —Jean-Luc Godard

VALIE EXPORT's focus on the divided female body in its object status and subject awareness anticipated the musings of feminist deconstructionist film theory that renounced the aesthetic principles of the dominant Hollywood cinema and exposed its realist texts as purveyors of bourgeois ideology. Laura Mulvey, in her groundbreaking essay "Visual Pleasure and Narrative Cinema" (Mulvey 1975), argues that the eye of the camera constructs the spectator as a male who identifies with the protagonist that drives the narrative, while woman is put on view as an object for the voyeuristic gaze. She is the muted object, the blind spot; she is the wound. EXPORT rejects "Hollywood and its pleasures" and attempts to write a film language that speaks outside the canon (Penley 1988: 6). "Feminism both as methodology and personal experiential stance, which had left an indelible mark on EXPORT's art during the 1970s, continued to be the single most important impulse and thematic source in her work in the 1980s" (Mueller 1994: 183).

EXPORT's experimental film *Syntagma* (1983) is conceived as "an index ... a sort of notebook ... re-assembled into moving images" (Lebovici 2003: 154). This eighteen-minute short, informed by theoretical reflections, combines avant-garde filmmaking and editing techniques with EXPORT's extensive work with the female body. *Syntagma* is an amalgamation of materials from her expanded-cinema pieces, performances, video, and conceptual photography saturated with non-diegetic synthetic sound and the occasional voiceover, all of which propel forward EXPORT's prevailing concern with the reappropriation of woman from her perception of alienation. For instance, we recognize elements of EXPORT's interactive video installation *Split Reality* and her 1974 performance piece *Seeing and Hearing Space*.[11] Another dominating element in *Syntagma* is the incessant movement that forces the viewer to continually alter their perception of space.[12] *Syntagma* is all about the indivisibility of space, time, the female body, and the gaze and paradox of perception. Its clever opening sequence illustrates the medial constructedness of these entities. The short begins with a sequence of two well-manicured (cultured) hands of a woman pushing apart two strips of film leader that travel from the top to the bottom of the screen which, as if they were heavy gates, seem to resist somewhat their forced separation. The electronic sound level rises with the widening of the space. Once the opening is broad enough for the fingers to fully emerge from the dark space (we are thinking of a birthing event) the finger/bodies begin to communicate by spelling s-y-n-t-a-g-m-a (compare the work *Finger Poem*, discussed above). After the credits, a woman split-in-two walks through an open space. Actually, the split screen shows one woman-segment walking towards the camera and the other walking away from it, each at a different distance to the camera. Then they both walk toward it, one in front and the other behind in the depth of the screen. While the movement of the fragmented body goes on and on—stepping high-heeled (cultured) across the black-and-white image of bare feet (natural)—a female voiceover (in German and English) recites a text based on R.D. Laing's *The Divided Self* (1960): "The body clearly takes a position between me and the world. On the one hand, this body is the center of my world, and, on the other, it is the object of the world of the others." Subsequent shots again evoke the metaphor of birth: the woman walking down an escalator into the womb of the city, and into and out of an underground train, this captured by a security camera and viewed on a monitor. The woman returns to the surface. There she is invisible (absent) while the camera picks up her pace and moves through the streets. The viewer only sees the image of her face in the side mirrors of cars as she walks past them. The cityscape becomes visible. It is a montage of superimposed stills telescoped and mirrored, expanding and contracting upward, downward, and sideways. The spectator also, though barely, notices the female body fading into the urban landscape as it is wrapped around the bottom of a staircase: she fills the gap (compare the *Body Configurations* works discussed earlier). The woman is visible indoors where she sits at a table; here, clever editing makes her appear successively on all sides of the table, and again she is doubled up: the woman in the foreground, her black-and-white version in the background, and vice versa. She leafs through the pages of a book while the sound-montage announces time in constant repetition, and she walks through rooms at an increasingly frantic pace until the "eye" of the camera looks through the window onto the building vis-à-vis her. In another shot, the woman tenderly touches a mirror image of herself that alternates between a photograph and its negative, while simultaneously we see the woman alternate with her filmic negative. In bed, her partly covered body, seen from directly above, is superimposed with body fragments in black and white, and each change of shot is accompanied by the disquieting thud of a staple gun. Some of the most complex images are the shots of body parts in nature. One shot is of a lakeside beach, but a brush paints the word *welle* ("wave") in blue into what is first erroneously perceived as real sand. Another image shows footprints in the sand in which a pair of bare feet stand. Then the camera moves back, and into view comes the studio where the scene is staged—a smart *trompe l'oeil*, tricking the viewer's perception!

Syntagma's anagrammatic language seeks an answer to the relationship between the carnal sensual body and the public body, or, more precisely, between the female body and the "doubly gendered" city based on the assumption "that the language of the body as present is merged with the language of the body as absent, in the triumph of culturation *as* body, which is also a triumph *over* the body" (EXPORT 1987: 15; see also Bronfen 1992). Fragmentation means, once more, "a place of construction, an open-ended process of reshaping women's lives" (Mueller 1994: 190). While the film tells much about woman's loneliness, pain, and dissolution, it also hypothesizes the expansive body, which sets foot into the exterior world that it desires to communicate with and to coinhabit. Margret Eifler contends that "woman's social manifestation ... does in fact situate her within a schizophrenic soliloquy [which] actually marks the beginning of a self-willed healing process" (Eifler 1996: 119). Kaja Silverman's interpretation goes further. She reads *Syntagma*'s "necessary repetition of the body's imaging and sensory mapping as,

> a corporeal text in two languages or forms. Neither of these languages has priority over the other. Each must constantly be respoken, or—like Latin—risk death. Each is the potential site for the introduction of disruptions and innovations into that text. Finally, what happens to one body inevitably reverberates within the other, although always in a different form. As the image of a flesh-colored foot superimposed over its black and white counterpart tells us, the body is neither one nor two; it is two in one. (Silverman 2000: 22–23)

Indeed. It is the "two-in-one" woman who is taking part in the everyday practices of our postmodern world with its hyperproduction of culture, its preoccupation with instantaneity, and its mad drive for profitability and increased market share, which have transformed our perception of space and time to such a degree that we have practically lost the experience of real space through the perceived acceleration of time (see Harvey 1989: 290–94). Already in the 1970s, Henri Lefebvre foresaw that "any revolutionary project today, whether utopian or realistic, must, if it is to avoid hopeless banality, make the reappropriation of the body, in association with the reappropriation of space, into a non-negotiable part of its agenda" (Lefebvre 1991: 405).

Despite the advances that women have made in becoming-being, besides their notable gains in selfhood in the past two decades, we cannot yet declare victory for women (not even for the female urbanite professional and her househusband) over the city/streets because the shared human burden of postmodernity—the impossible, yet inescapable task of regrounding meanings and values in the absence of grounds—remains to be addressed (see Parsons 2000).

Narrative Films: *Invisible Adversaries, Human Women,* and *The Practice of Love*

> I always see film as a sculpture that, for me, has varying levels of ways of observing it.
> —VALIE EXPORT, 2003

EXPORT's interrogations of the female body are dialectically bound to her explorations of the technological apparatus of cinema, and the structures and functions of video imagery and film. Between 1976 and 1984, she released three feature-length films, *Invisible Adversaries, Human Women,* and *The Practice of Love,* which are in line with much of women's filmic practice of the time in that they are narrative-driven, political, and oppositional.[13] It was "an essential and symbolic field of action in the art of women of the seventies to explore alternatives to commercial productions and to test the tenuous relation between intimacy and [the] public sphere and between reality and the imagination" (EXPORT, in Mueller 1994: 150). EXPORT's films, like other experimental films by women made in the 1970s and 1980s, transgressed closely guarded taboos by documenting the private sphere. At the time, these films were marginalized and did not receive serious critical attention due in no small part to the fact that they did not fit neatly into the categories of the first or second avant-garde as defined by the influential film theorist Peter Wollen (1975).[14]

Unsichtbare Gegner/Invisible Adversaries (1976) is a 112-minute, 16mm color film which EXPORT cowrote with Peter Weibel.[15] Part of the film is preconceived, but large segments of text and several scenes were improvised during shooting. EXPORT inscribes herself into the film at several levels—for example, through examples of her art that are incorporated into the film. Also, Anna (Susanne Widl) shares the art of photography with the filmmaker. Anna's relationship to Peter is paralleled by EXPORT's personal relationship to Weibel. However, the final version of the film comes together at the cutting table where EXPORT creates a visually fascinating essay on gender and experience, culture and environment. As Alison Butler explains, EXPORT's "multiple self-inscription constitutes a simultaneous insistence on and dispersal of her subjectivity which erodes the qualitative distinction between extradiegetic and intradiegetic authorship" (Butler 2002: 76).

The film's narrative takes the viewer on a haunting excursion into psychic disintegration and eroded identity but refuses the viewer the opportunity of arriving at a definite conclusion about the protagonist's sanity. In the tradition of the "fantastic film" it pivots between a psychoanalytic case study and science fiction (Sobchack 1996). The loose storyline—which lacks a plot in the traditional sense—concerns the effects of mysterious beings from outer space (Hyksos) who penetrate people's minds to take over the world. Anna becomes obsessed with her fear of the aliens who she perceives as responsible for the rot and rising aggression around her. She also notices with dismay that she is slipping from one crisis into another while seeking increasingly morose subject matter for her camera. Because she is desperately trying to understand the mechanisms of her marginalization, she finds it necessary to take photographs of what she interprets as the destructive work of the Hyksos and claims, "My visual work is like a monologue ... I cannot believe the reality of my environment ... my paranoia surrounds me." The disjointed, uncanny outer world reflects her inner state of mind (see Widmann 2007). Anna's gradual becoming-woman, her subjectification process, occurs within three constellations: Anna alone, Anna in public, and Anna with Peter. Anna alone in her private sphere notices her doppelgänger in the mirror, and everyday household items are made strange. They surrealistically come alive. Parallel shots create a visual link between the handling of food and women's customary everyday practices: washing food becomes equal to bathing, scaling fish corresponds to shaving the body, breading and broiling is like putting on make-up. Anna's photographs of public places and events show distorted objects and an ever-increasing violence. Her relationship to Peter turns sour with constant arguing. Finally, Anna's psychiatrist diagnoses her as a paranoid schizophrenic, and her delusions of the doppelgänger effect in people are reflected in her photographic art. For instance, the picture she takes of her doctor shows his two likenesses side by side.

EXPORT's brilliant film-cutting techniques—such as superimposition, unusual camera angles, negative imaging, quick cutting, juxtapositions, and complex patterns of montage—reflect her love affair with the aesthetics of the classical avant-garde. While there is some narration in the film, she makes use of what Robert Stam calls "reflexivity." The film points to its "own mask and invites the public to examine its design and texture" (Stam 1985: 1). By skillfully exploiting these practices, she creates an anagrammatic mode of captivating visual vocabulary in a fascinating stream of imagery and sound. She conceives the interpolation of her video, performance, and installation art, the "ready-mades," in terms of "self-contained signifying units" that provide commentary (Mueller 1994: 126). For instance, near the beginning of the film, Anna develops photographs in her darkroom. As she dips her picture of a vagina into the chemical liquid, a man's coarse grunting sound is heard that has a risibly pitiful effect on the viewer. In the next sequence, EXPORT fuses segments of her video piece *Stille Sprache/Silent Language* (1974) into the storyline. She also brings into the film perhaps her most significant conceptual photographic work of the 1970s. Situated in a film studio, the filmmaker projects a photograph of a Tintoretto painting onto the screen. Anna stands in front of the canvas and tries to recreate the posture of the woman in the artwork. She absurdly distorts her body to cover the projected image. Using video technology, EXPORT overlaps the female image of the famous painting with that of Anna by fading the pictures in and out of the monitor's screen. This anagrammatic technique shows clearly that the woman's pose in the painting is merely the art world's canonized projection of the ideal female body. Equally jolting are scenes based on the concept of a performance piece from 1972, in which Anna walks unsteadily through the streets and parks of the city on her ice skates, and her ensuing dream sequence, in which she sleeps with her skates on. The interpolation of stills from her conceptual photography cycle *Body Configurations in Architecture* accentuates further Anna's precarious and labile position in the public environment. Image after image in rapid montage is slapped onto the screen with a loud bang to illustrate how little public space is available to Anna as her body squeezes itself between buildings and wraps itself around the sidewalk. More than a decade before Judith Butler's (1990) influential study, EXPORT effectively visualizes the "performativity of gender."

Invisible Adversaries confronts several of Freud's theories, such as so-called castration anxiety, his investigation of the phenomenon of paranoia, and the "uncanny." What is more, the film exposes Freud's description of the pathological state of "ego-doubling, ego-splitting and ego-exchange" as the established role expectation for women since it posits "doubling and splitting ... as the manifestation of an alienation from physicality induced by representation (Benjamin's 'mechanical reproduction')" (Butler 2002: 74). Even though, the film does not offer a resolution it ends in optimism for Anna, and so for the future of women. We see Anna stepping into bed, the place of rejuvenation. She wears a hiking outfit and seems ready to climb the next mountain that comes between her and her goals. Duplicating the first shot of the film, the camera's eye moves from the inside of Anna's room, through the window, panning across Vienna's rooftops before returning to the room. There is a future for Anna, and indeed we meet her again in EXPORT's second feature film.

In *Menschenfrauen/Human Women* (1980), Anna (played again by Susanne Widl) works in an architectural firm and is happily married to the journalist Franz (Klaus Wildpolz). However, her husband is romantically involved with three other women: Gertrud (Maria Martina), Petra (Christiane von Aster), and Elisabeth (Renée Felden). In this film, the women's storylines create a narrative mosaic. Once again, EXPORT collaborated with Weibel on writing the script and directing the film. As in the first feature, they incorporate autobiographical components and materials that they acquire during shooting. In addition, they insert into the script a number of elements (visuals, texts, information from newspapers) based on actual events. *Human Women* is considered a consciousness-raising film that deals with issues critical to the second-wave feminist movement in Western Europe and the U.S.A. and its debates about patriarchal structures, emancipation, and equal rights.

The female characters represent four types of women whose life experiences and expectations have a profound influence on their personal development. The process of subjectification for each of them takes a dramatically different course. Gertrud is a divorcee who lost the custody battle for her son to her ex-husband and teaches at a high school. Her political engagement and keen sense of justice for human (women's) rights gets her into trouble with her boss. When she loses her job and also realizes that Franz's interest in her has diminished, she suffers from agonizing feelings of loneliness and isolation. Gertrud increasingly exhibits self-destructive behavior—such as bulimia—that ultimately leads to her suicide by electrocution. The second woman, Elisabeth, also has a son, and she suffers from a painful longing for her absent father, who did not return from the war. Though absent, he continues to keep a strong hold on the family through his widow, who continues the disciplinary regime of Elisabeth's father. Elisabeth now works as a barmaid and desperately desires the love of a man—including affection and respect from her adolescent son—but she repeatedly falls for deceitful niceties from men and all the lovers she takes in mistreat her emotionally and physically. In the final scene, she sits in the train anxiously awaiting Franz. However, she is again left behind when he, arriving late, tries to jump onto the departing train but trips and slides under its wheels. Petra, the third woman (and the least-developed character), is a kindergarten teacher and a playful, happy-go-lucky person. Anna and Petra become friends as soon as they realize they are both expecting a child fathered by Franz. They rejoice in their decision to leave Franz and to raise their children together.

Despite the fact that the emphasis is on the storyline, aesthetic experiments again are cleverly woven into the fabric of the narrative. In particular, video interpolations serve to signal and support the views and mind-set of the four women but also are employed to create effects of foreshadowing and estrangement. In the introductory sequence, Elisabeth is seen in a flashback as a young girl barricading herself in a small room while there is loud banging on the door. She cries and screams that she "needs a room of her own" while her mother, incensed by her daughter's apparently obnoxious behavior, informs her that only boys have a right to such a place. In another sequence, Elisabeth piously kneels in church during Holy Communion and whispers, "God is a man." EXPORT's body performance *I (Beat (It))* from 1978, in which she wades through water with heavy lead bandages strapped around her thighs to render her almost completely immobile, is recreated to visualize Gertrud's exhausting feelings of weariness and exasperation. As Gertrud sits at the typewriter, she sees alternating images of herself wading through water and flashbacks of once-happy moments with her lover Franz. The soundtrack alternates accordingly and switches back and forth between a poetic text by the filmmaker and an actual TV interview of a female student who had received a prison sentence for attempted bank robbery. The final scene of the film, where the two pregnant women, Petra and Anna, walk in the sand on the beach, is reminiscent of EXPORT's conceptual art *From the Humanoid Sketchbook of Nature* (1973).

This final scene signals a victory of sorts: Petra, the kindergarten teacher, and Anna, the business woman, fully embrace motherhood after dismissing Franz, the father of their children, and turning to each other for friendship, affection, and support. In an earlier scene, the two women celebrate their newly gained sisterhood in a neighborhood restaurant. Their cheerful laughter draws attention from guests at surrounding tables. Several elderly women shake their heads disapprovingly. When Petra and Anna kiss each other across the table, the patrons' voices grow louder and demand that the pregnant women, who are perceived to be "wives" acting immorally as "lesbians," leave the establishment immediately. Despite its comic effect, the message of the scene is somber.

Central to feminist investigations at the time was the critical analysis of the separation of public and private spheres. In addition, feminists showed that within the private realm, woman cannot claim "a room of one's own" (to use Virginia Woolf's well-known phrase) for regeneration and creativity, nor is she protected from abuse within the private sphere. In *Human Women*, EXPORT "pulled away the lace curtains and sharpened the soft focus on the idyllic hearth to reveal it as one of the more powerful mechanisms in divesting woman of her 'self'" (Mueller 1994: 161). Despite its significant contribution to feminist discourse and its success at the box office, the film did not garner much critical acclaim. Rather, critics disapproved of EXPORT's supposed return to the nature-versus-nurture model by celebrating motherhood as a viable lifestyle. Even more troubling for many was the film's inadvertent center-staging of the male ego by surrounding Franz's machismo with four women. However, EXPORT's hope that, as it is put in the film, "we must create a human society in which motherhood does not restrict woman in her creativity and determination," remains valid, at least for (upper) middle-class women in our postmodern Western world.

EXPORT's art is always political. Cinematic experimental art—which is generally considered apolitical—turns highly political as she explores the limitations of film in drastic ways and ruptures the usual passive reception characteristic of the medium.

In addition, she remains interested in the shifting relations and the linkage between the public and the private. In 1985, EXPORT released her third and (so far) last feature-length narrative film, *Die Praxis der Liebe/The Practice of Love*. The main character is a professional woman by the name of Judith Wiener (Adelheid Arndt). She is an ambitious investigative journalist who lives in Vienna and enjoys the attention bestowed upon her by her two lovers, the physician Dr Josef Frischkoff (Hagnot Elischka) and psychiatrist Dr Alphons Schlögel (Rüdiger Vogler). When she comes upon a murder victim in the subway, she is drawn into the case of a gun-smuggling operation and upon further investigation discovers that one of her boyfriends is involved in these illegal machinations.

The film is narrative driven, and the plot's background is based on an actual scandal that rocked the Austrian political landscape at the time. The strong-willed, spirited Judith Wiener is part of the new postfeminist generation who fully embraces its gain in subjecthood. Women like Judith stay single (longer), are highly educated, and enjoy successful careers. The public and the private are no longer two wholly separate entities. In fact, the interconnectedness of the two in Judith's world shapes the story. Judith easily moves within the public sphere, and explores and examines its space above and beneath the surface. Her inquiries are only partly due to her profession. As a member of the new generation of women, she is used to questioning and challenging the status quo. While Judith walks with self-confidence and poise, the two men in her life seem to be slipping on shifting ground. Unlike Franz in *Human Women*, whose oversized male ego desires the love of four women, Josef and Alfons do not expect the same kind of devotion from Judith. Rather, their relationship is cast as a supporting role. On the one hand, it underscores Judith's standing within the social order; and on the other hand, their medical profession hints at an ailing society in need of healers and shrinks. In fact, violence—spilling out from the private into the public and swelling to a horrifying torrent of war—flows as a theme through much of EXPORT's work.[16] Looking for answers to the basic sociological question: "What kind of world do we live in?" she searches for human signs of love. The guarded optimism emanating from her films seem to indicate that EXPORT believes in love's existence.

The question of the structure of looking—always central to EXPORT's cinematographic work—evolves in her first and third narrative films into the problematic of surveillance/counter-surveillance and its resulting paranoia and linkage to female experience. Already crucial to the making and understanding of *Invisible Adversaries*, it reappears in *The Practice of Love*, where the notion of the "private eye" comes into play. Peering into private space and inspecting public space is reminiscent of the film noir genre, but the fact that the investigator is a woman reverses the convention. She is not the femme fatale but rather "the mirror opposite of the film noir antihero, or perhaps just a positive view of the much feared femme fatale" (Mueller 1994: 166). Judith's acts as a private eye, her investigations through pictures and questions, controls the story. At the same time, Judith becomes aware that she, too, is being watched. As she faces a situation that seems more than she can handle, she begins to understand that women continue to have limited options when trying to reverse the structure of looking. EXPORT "enacts a radical instability of subject and object, and a partial dissolution of subjectivity which continually undercuts its own impulse to attain power. This instability places EXPORT's mode of counter-surveillance under the sign of paranoia" (Sicinski 2000: 76). Near the end of the film, Judith returns to her apartment and finds it totally trashed. The villains have destroyed everything while hunting for incriminating photos and recordings. In the final scene, Judith stands next to her packed suitcase near the window of her apartment, and the voiceover announces the departure of a flight from Vienna to Chicago. Fearing for her life, she is ready to go into exile. This film, like the others, ends with guarded optimism: Judith can start a new life in America.

Expanded cinema techniques—various processes of the way of looking and seeing; the extension of artistic expression into space and time; the expansion and diversion, rupture and fusion of conventional forms of film—are once again present in *The Practice of Love*, such as the framing of Judith's gaze. As the metal frame of the gate in the underground slowly descends in front of her, the camera's eye on the inside sees the shadow of the gate's mesh moving across Judith's face, and each small opening becomes a frame of her eyes. Another interpolation presents fragmentary elements in black and white and superimpositions of Judith's and Josef's bodies, while the pendulum swinging back and forth induces the notion of time. Then the male gaze is literally printed onto Judith's breasts, and the faces of Josef and Judith are canvasses for the face of the other. Lacan's mirror stage is evoked when Alfons's reflections in the left and right segments of the dresser's tri-part mirror are "gazing" at Judith's image visible in its middle section. Furthermore, EXPORT most effectively exploits the technique of applying material to the celluloid itself, a common practice in art films. Alfons and Judith are embroiled in a verbal confrontation. While the sound swells to a deafening intensity, Judith, crouching on the floor, swings her hand to the right and knocks everything off the coffee table. With her hand swinging back, she draws a line across the face of her lover. Her ostentatious gesture, underscored by a maddening scratching noise, informs Alfons—and the viewer—of the end of their relationship. Another insertion into the narrative is the video installation used for the final conversation between Judith and Josef. Three monitors are visible, two on the bottom; the bottom two each show the mouth of one of the actors, and a larger one above displays both mouths on its split screen. Judith is standing next to the TV rack with her back to the monitors. She speaks into the open space in front of her while her lip movements are seen on one of the lower monitors and on the split screen above. Josef is physically absent. His voice can be heard, but only his lip movements are visible. This scene—using language without the physical presence of its origin—is a restaging of *Split Reality* (discussed above). Here, it serves to demonstrate EXPORT's ubiquitous concern about the (technological) mechanisms of aggression and devastation that she perceives as the cause for the dangerous volatility of today's society. As Mueller explains, "The powerful image of Judith surrounded by her video equipment and confronting the absent Josef brings the film's many references to the technology of communication to a surprising conclusion" (Mueller 1994: 181).

During the 1980s, in addition to *Syntagma* and her three feature-length narrative films, EXPORT produced four films for Austrian television: *Das Bewaffnete Auge/ The Armed Eye* (1984), *Tafelbemerkungen/Table Quotes* (1985), *The Yukon Quest* (1986), and *Actionism International* (1989).[17] Her 16mm short, *Wollust – Ein perfektes Paar oder Die Unzucht wechselt ihre Haut/Lust – A Perfect Pair or Indecency Sheds its Skin* was EXPORT's contribution to *Sieben Frauen – Sieben Sünden/Seven Women – Seven Sins*, a 1986 production by the German television channel ZDF.[18] EXPORT's short offers an allegory of lust, power, and morality. It displays the human (male and female) body as a walking billboard for the products it uses and as a disposable entity in today's "shallow" society where the facility to analyze critically and evaluate the dimensions of commercialization have been lost.

Conclusion

In 1967, Guy Debord asserted that only through the creative process with its mode of diversion can humankind in postmodern society regain its authority and control over the "spectacle" of commercialism, of the constant dumbing and numbing of the pacification and depoliticization of the masses (Debord 1992: 22). EXPORT clearly appreciates Debord's premise. Her oeuvre is a lucid examination of the fundamental conventions and contradictions of the society we live in. Subversion, diversion, and reversion are the major principles of her feminist art. For nearly four decades, she has employed these strategies of inner resistance and has prominently inserted and asserted herself in the (male) world of the "spectacle."

Notes

1. I am greatly indebted to VALIE EXPORT for her gracious support and for making materials and information available to me. I also thank my colleagues and friends, especially Paul Schlueter, for providing valuable advice. The title is from EXPORT's retrospective at the Greek Film Archive's Fifth Avantgarde Film Festival, Athens, 2008. The artist insists her name be spelled in capitals in print. Unless otherwise noted, translations are my own.

2. "I couldn't gain real recognition, neither in the male world of artists nor in that of filmmakers. I was always treated as a co-pilot. For instance, [after] I was on stage, the audience asked other filmmakers about what I did, I wasn't asked at all, as if I wasn't there. Nowadays, one cannot imagine how ignorant the art world was of female artists" (EXPORT, in Lebovici 2003: 147).

3. Every other year, the Austrian art academy bestows an acclaimed artist of international reputation with this highest honor. The award—underwritten by the Austrian government—is normally delivered by a government representative. At the time of the award ceremony in May 2001, Austria was ruled by the coalition government of the conservative ÖVP and the right-wing FPÖ, or Freedom Party, under the leadership of the notorious Jörg Haider. By refusing to accept the award, EXPORT demonstrated her political astuteness and conviction. What is more, she dedicated the award to a collaborative art project entitled "Media analysis of fascist politics, political manipulation, and manipulative construction of deceit and truth in image and information technologies" (*Mediale Analyse faschistoider Politik. Politische Manipulation und manipulative Konstruktion von Lüge und Wahrheit in Bild- und Informationstechnologien*).

Other prizes bestowed on EXPORT are the Gustav Klimt Prize in 1998, the Decoration of Honor in Gold of the City of Vienna in 2003, the International Prize for Art and Culture of the City of Salzburg in 2004, and the Republic of Austria's Decoration of Honor for Science and the Arts in 2005. Currently, EXPORT serves as the commissary for Austria at the Venice Biennale of Art.

4. "I have always used film and photography simultaneously, starting with 8mm films, then 16mm, slides, and expanded cinema where I used my own body and myself as person and selected the medium according to the idea or mission or topic that I wanted to express," EXPORT told my students via videoconferencing in September 2007. The conversation is archived at Lafayette College and the Elfriede Jelinek Forschungszentrum at the University of Vienna.

5. The term "happening" was coined at Black Mountain College in 1952 when John Cage performed his *Theater Piece No.1* as the first multimedia happening. Cage's experimental compositions are recognized as an American source of Fluxus, which was founded by George Maciunas in 1962 as an interdisciplinary production of art, a commitment "to move the frame beyond the screen". See Dwoskin (1975: 235–44).

6. *Mosaik im Vertrauen* (1955) by Peter Kubelka is recognized as the first avant-garde film made in Austria. During the 1960s, Kurt Kren shot many happenings of the Viennese Actionists: *Ana: Action Brus* (1964) and *Self-mutilation* (1965). In 1967, Kren created *Sinus b, TV* and the legendary *20. September*.

7. At the same time, together with Peter Weibel, Kurt Kren, Hans Scheugl, Gottfried Schlemmer, and Ernst Schmidt Jr., EXPORT co-founded the Austrian Filmmakers Cooperative as a protest against Peter Kubelka's film museum.

8. "I told the audience that they had come to this particular theater to see sexual films. Now, actual genitals were available, and they could do anything they wanted to it [sic]. I moved down each row slowly, facing people. I did not move in an erotic way. As I walked down each row, the gun I carried pointed at the head of the people in the row behind. I was afraid and had no idea what the people would do. As I moved from row to row, each row of people silently got up and left the theater. Out of film context, it was a totally different way for them to connect with the particular erotic symbol" (EXPORT, in Askey 1981: 80).

9. EXPORT also conceived a photo series by the same title. The art critic Bojana Pejic suggests that EXPORT's "artist poster" symbolizes the beginning of the evolution of art and feminism in the late 1960s when mass culture and mass consumerism became part of our everyday practices (Pejiç 2007: 55).

10. The term "transparent space" was coined by feminist geographers, such as Gillian Rose and Linda McDowell, in the 1990s (see Gwin 2002: 20).

11. *Split Reality*, conceived in 1967, was produced as video action in 1970 and as an interactive video installation in 1973. It "splits" reality into a sound level and a visual level through the application of a record player, a video recorder, and a TV set. The split images that occur in *Syntagma* are an extension of EXPORT's 1974 performance *Seeing and Hearing Space*, in which she used two video cameras and a mixer to create a closed-circuit action. The performer stands in front of a screen, and simultaneously her captured face appears on the monitor's screen, where it is constantly altered. The spectator sees the full body of the performer in the room, and at the same time the performer's likeness in a state of permanent alteration on the screen. As in *Split Reality*, the personality conveyed by the medium appears to be schizophrenic.

12. Already in 1973, EXPORT investigated this phenomenon in the expanded cinema piece *Adjugated Dislocations I+II*. The perception of spatial continuity is conveyed by two 8mm film cameras, one of which is strapped to the artist's torso, the other to her back. By "wearing" the apparatus, the artist is the camera. A third 16mm film camera documents the various spatial situations, moving from room to room over corridors, into the street, across the square and out into the open countryside. When all three perspectives are projected in parallel, the recording process becomes visible alongside the filmic representation.

13. In addition, a film entitled *Unica* was planned for 1987/88. EXPORT also wrote a script for a film adaptation of Elfriede Jelinek's 1983 novel *Die Klavierspielerin*. Unfortunately, the last two film projects could not be realized due to a lack of funding.

14. Koch (1988) demonstrates that EXPORT's feature films successfully bridge both avant-gardes as defined by Wollen. Wollen identified films of the first avant-garde by their absence of verbal language and narrative, whereas films of the second avant-garde remained within the bounds of narrative cinema.

15. For detailed information on the process of film production and the collaboration between EXPORT and Weibel, see Mueller (1994: 126–29).

16. See, e.g., *Hyperbulia* (1973), *The Practice of Life* (1983), *Tattooed Tears* (2001), as well as the installations *Scream* (1994), *Head-Apharäse: Dead Bodies Don't Cry* (2002), and *Kalaschnikow* (2007).

17. On these films, see Benzer and Schwärzler (2007: 51–59).

18. The other six contributions were by Chantal Akerman (*Portrait d'une paresseuse*), Maxi Cohen (*Anger*), Laurence Gavron (*Il Maestro*), Bette Gordon (*Greed: Pay to Play*), Ulrike Ottinger (*Superbia – Der Stolz*), and Helke Sander (*Völlerei*).

References

Askey, R. 1981. "An Interview with VALIE EXPORT," *High Performance* 4(1): 80–99.

Benzer, C., and D. Schwärzler. 2007. "Kuratieren und Kollaborieren: VALIE EXPORT im Dialog mit dem Fernsehen," in S. Szely (ed.), *EXPORT: LEXIKON*. Vienna: REMAprint, 51–59.

Bordo, S. (1993). *Unbearable Weight: Feminism, Western culture, and the body*. Berkeley: University of California Press.

Bronfen, E. 1992. *Over Her Dead Body: Death, Femininity and the Aesthetic*. New York: Routledge.

Burnham, L.F. 1982. *High Performance*. Los Angeles: Astro Artz.

Butler, A. 1990. *Gender Trouble: Feminism and the Subversion of Identity. Thinking Gender*. New York: Routledge.

———. 2002. *Women's Cinema: The Contested Screen*. London: Wallflower Press.

Chukhrov, K. 2007. "Body as the Political Excess," in H. Saxenhuber (ed.), *Special Exhibition of the 2nd Moscow Biennale in the National Centre for Contemporary Art Moscow (NCCA) and Ekaterina Foundation from 4th March until 3rd April, 2007*. Vienna: Folio-Verlag, 176.

Debord, G. 1992. *Society of the Spectacle*, trans. K. Knapp. London: Rebel Press.

Derrida, J. 1978. *Writing and Difference*. Chicago: University of Chicago Press.

Dwoskin, S. 1975. *Film Is: The International Free Cinema*. Woodstock, NY: Overlook Press.

Eifler, M. 1996. "VALIE EXPORT's Iconography: Visual Quest for Subject Discourse," *Modern Austrian Literature* 29(1): 119.

EXPORT, VALIE. 1972. "Fotomappe ZYKLUS ZUR ZIVILISATION. Zur Mythologie der zivilisatorischen Prozesse, mit einem Begleittext von Günter Brus." Wien: Ed. Kurt Kalb.

———. 1979. *Photography as Art, Art as Photography*. Cologne: DuMont.

———. 1987. *Das Reale und sein Double: Der Körper*. Bern: Benteli.

———. 1996. *White Cube/Black Box*. Vienna: EA Generali Foundation.

------. 1997. "Body Sign Action," in *Split-Reality, VALIE EXPORT.* Vienna: Museum Moderner Kunst, Stiftung Ludwig/Springer.

------. 2003a. "Corpus More Geometrico," in Neue Gesellschaft für Bildende Kunst (ed.), *VALIE EXPORT: Mediale Anagramme.* Berlin: NGBK, 105.

------. 2003b. "Expanded Cinema as Expanded Reality," *Senses of Cinema* 28: n.p.. Retrieved 1 July 2008 from: www.sensesofcinema.com.

------. 2007. "Auf+Ab+An+Zu," in H. Saxenhuber (ed.), *Special Exhibition of the 2nd Moscow Biennale in the National Centre for Contemporary Art Moscow (NCCA) and Ekaterina Foundation from 4th March until 3rd April, 2007.* Vienna: Folio-Verlag, 88–89.

Faber, M. 2003. "Die Beobachterperspektive: Zu VALIE EXPORTs konzeptueller Fotografie," in Neue Gesellschaft für Bildende Kunst (ed.), *VALIE EXPORT: Mediale Anagramme.* Berlin: NGBK, 71–72.

Foucault, M. (1977). *Discipline and Punish: The Birth of the Prison.* New York: Pantheon Books.

Gwin, M. 2002. *The Woman in the Red Dress: Gender, Space, and Reading.* Urbana: Illinois University Press.

Harvey, D. 1989. *The Condition of Postmodernity.* Oxford: Basil Blackwell.

Hofmann, W., and H. Hollein (eds). 1980. *VALIE EXPORT: Biennale di Venezia.* Vienna: Bundesministerium für Unterricht und Kunst.

Koch, G. 1988. "A Pain in the Body, a Pleasure in the Eye," *Kunstforum International* 97: 123–26.

Lamb-Faffelberger, M. 1996. "L'avant-garde feministe autrichienne: Innovations esthetique. VALIE EXPORT et Elfriede Jelinek," in Dieter Hornig, Georg Jankovic and Klaus Zeyringer, eds. *Continuités et ruptures dans la littérature autrichienne.* Paris: Editions Jacqueline Chambon, 231–45.

Lebovici, E. 2003. "Entretien avec VALIE EXPORT," in Michel Régis, ed. *VALIE EXPORT.* Paris: Editions de l'Oeil, 143–56.

Lefebvre, H. 1991. *The Production of Space.* Oxford: Basil Blackwell.

Merleau-Ponty, M. 2002. *Phenomenology of Perception,* trans. C. Smith. New York: Routledge.

Michel, R. 2003. "I Am a Woman: Three Essays on the Parody of Sexuality," in Michel Régis, ed. *VALIE EXPORT.* Paris: Éditions de l'Oeil, 27.

Mueller, R. 1994. *Fragments of Imagination.* Bloomington: Indiana University Press.

Mulvey, L. 1975. "Visual Pleasure and Narrative Cinema," *Screen* 16(3): 6–18.

Parsons, D.L. 2000. *Streetwalking the Metropolis: Women, the City, and Modernity.* Oxford: Oxford University Press.

Pejiç, B. 2007. "On Pants, Panics and Origins," in H. Saxenhuber (ed.), *VALIE EXPORT. Special Exhibition of the 2nd Moscow Biennale in the National Centre for Contemporary Art Moscow (NCCA) and Ekaterina Foundation from 4th March until 3rd April, 2007.* Vienna: Folio-Verlag, 54–63.

Penley, C. (ed.) 1988. *Feminism and Film Theory.* London: Routledge.

Rötzer, F., and S. Rogenhofer. 1988. "Mediale Anagramme: Ein Gespräch mit VALIE EXPORT," *Kunstforum International* 97: 150–59.

Sicinski, M. 2000. "VALIE EXPORT and Paranoid Counter Surveillance," *Discourse* 22(2): 71–91.

Silverman, K. 2000. "Speak, Body," *Discourse* 22(2): 8–24.

Sobchack, V. 1996. "The Fantastic," in G. Nowell-Smith (ed.), *The Oxford History of World Cinema*. Oxford: Oxford University Press, 312–21.

Stam, R. 1985. *Reflexivity in Film and Literature*. Ann Arbor, MI: UMI Research Press.

S. Szely (ed.) 2007. *EXPORT: LEXIKON*. Vienna: REMAprint.

Widmann, T. 2007. "Unvorhergesehen, nicht-vorgegeben," in S. Szely (ed.), *EXPORT: LEXIKON*. Vienna: Sonderzahl, 21–30.

Wollen, P. 1975. "The Two Avant-gardes," *Studio International* 190 (978): 171–75.

Youngblood, G. 1970. *Expanded Cinema*. New York: Dutton.

Chapter 2

Franz Antel's *Bockerer* Series: Constructing the Historical Myths of Second Republic Austria

Joseph Moser

The debate over Austria's founding myths has played a central role in the study of Austrian literature, film, history, and culture since 1986. Kurt Waldheim's election as federal president and Jörg Haider's election as head of the FPÖ (Freedom Party) in that year triggered a large discussion of the country's past.[1] The founding myth of Austria as Hitler's first victim and the resulting picture of Austria's collective innocence in the Second World War and the Holocaust were the most prominent misconceptions, ones which have been rejected largely by most Austrians. The country's neutrality in the Cold War; the economic miracle and ensuing prosperity of the postwar period, which was weaker than in West Germany; and the reluctance to confront the Nazi past, which was stronger than in Germany, were other important factors in shaping the Second Republic. Franz Antel's four-part *Bockerer* series supports and partially deconstructs several myths that are vital to the historical and national identity of contemporary Austria, and they are more a reflection of historical interpretation in the 1980s and 1990s than an accurate depiction of the historical periods in which the films are set.

While Franz Antel is an old-guard filmmaker and most of his work—having slipped into the realm of kitschy films ranging from *Heimat* comedies to soft-sex films in the 1960s and 1970s—precedes New Austrian Film, the *Bockerer* series represents a much more complex part of his oeuvre. As Robert von Dassanowsky argues, the first part of the series—*Der Bockerer* (1981)—can be seen as inaugurating New Austrian Film (Dassanowsky 2005: 212). Released well before the events of 1986 raised Austria's public awareness about the country's past, this film breaks an overriding taboo in Austrian film by covering: the *Anschluss* (the annexation of Austria by Nazi Germany), so-called *Arisierungen* ("Aryanization") of Jewish property as well as Austrians' active involvement in Nazi Germany. It both supports the founding myth of Austria as the first victim of Hitler's aggression, apologizing for the past as was common practice in Austria in the early 1980s, and at the same time gives a critical account of Austrians' participation in the Third Reich. The first part of the *Bockerer* series is based on Ulrich Becher and Peter Preses's 1946 play with additional scenes written for the film by H.C. Artmann. While some differences between the play and the film will be identified, this chapter concentrates on Antel's adaptation because the film was much more successful in the public sphere than the play; in addition, the film is also a product of the 1980s whereas the play was written in exile and then premiered in Austria a few years after the war. While the play confronted an audience in the immediate postwar era that was unsure of Austria's future, the film met an Austrian audience that no longer questioned the legitimacy of the sovereign republic of Austria, yet simultaneously lacked a conscious awareness of the country's recent past. In one of the few scholarly interpretations of the play and the film, Jacqueline Vansant compared the two and argued that Becher and Preses's Bockerer was a self-reflecting and critical observer of his times, which Antel's Bockerer is clearly not (Vansant 1991: 277). Antel decided to adapt the play after seeing it in 1980 (ibid.: 272). The fact that Antel's Bockerer is a more naive person is indicative of the public's ignorance of history in the 1980s. There are also three sequels to the first film—released in 1996, 2000, and 2003—all of which were written by Antel himself. These films deal with the Allied occupation of Austria, the 1956 uprising in Hungary, and the Prague Spring of 1968 respectively. The addition of these three sequels shifted the historical emphasis of *Bockerer* from the period of the Nazi regime to the postwar era, a time that was significantly less troubled and controversial for Austria. This is a rather unfortunate shift of emphasis from a difficult part of Austrian history to the cold war, in which Austria had a relatively easy position as a neutral country. In fact, in each of the three sequels, Austrians help either Russians, Hungarians or Czechs with coping with the Soviet military occupation. Austria is depicted as a lucky and prosperous nation that managed to escape the turmoil of the Cold War.

The first part of the series is as much a reflection of the final years of the Kreisky era as of Antel's personal preferences for certain groups.[2] The film stylizes the Austrian working class as a major anti-Nazi group rather than showing how support and rejection of the Nazis in Austria did not fall along class lines. Nonetheless, five years before the Waldheim scandal, this film addressed difficult historical topics that only few in Austria at the time wanted to see discussed. *Der Bockerer* is the story of a Viennese butcher and his family and friends during the time of the *Anschluss* and immediately after the war. Bockerer's good-hearted stubbornness and naivety, which come as no surprise given his name—*Bock* is German for billygoat—help him live through the period of the *Anschluss* without siding with the Nazis. When the first part of the series premiered in 1981, many Austrians recognized some of the country's favorite actors: Karl Merkatz, in the role of Bockerer, had only a few years earlier completed his work as the boisterous working-class archetype Mundl Sackbauer on the popular TV series *Ein echter Wiener geht nicht unter/A True*

Viennese Does Not go Under (1975–1977), a friendlier and more outgoing adaptation of the character of Archie Bunker, the bigoted paterfamilias from the American television series of the 1970s, *All in the Family*. In *Der Bockerer*, Merkatz plays a similarly gregarious and naive character, which the audience feels sympathetic towards, which is clearly different from the reaction Archie Bunker inspires. Much like Mundl, Bockerer always starts screaming when he encounters an injustice or feels betrayed. His honest working-class demeanor makes him likeable to some, while other viewers find his coarse and loud language and impulsive reactions irritating. In *Der Bockerer*, Klaus-Jürgen Wussow plays a Gestapo officer; Teddy Podgorski is one of his underlings. Dolores Schmidinger, who was also in *Ein echter Wiener geht nicht unter*, was cast as the jovial prostitute Mitzi. Franz Stoß and Heinz Marecek, who were in the Austrian TV series *Die liebe Familie/ The Dear Family*, played a *Hofrat* (Austrian honorific title) and the Jewish doctor Rosenblatt respectively, representing the Viennese upper class as they had already done in their previous work. Other popular TV actors included Alfred Böhm, Senta Wengraf and Ida Krottendorf. There was also a small cast of older actors, who had had successful careers during the Nazi period, such as Hans Holt and Marte Harell. With the exception of Klaus-Jürgen Wussow, all of the major actors are Austrians. This is significant as the film concentrates on Austria and Austrians, and the Germans are noticeably perceived as foreigners and invaders. Antel's focus on portraying Austrians in this film strengthens the film's role in building Austria's national identity.

Bockerer represents the quintessentially good Austrian, a construct developed around the idea of Austria's innocence during the Second World War. Despite the conception of the main character as an anti-Nazi Austrian, the film also shows Austrian collaborators, including the notorious Schebesta, a window maker, who "Aryanizes" an apartment and who has the Jewish owners deported. Other Austrian Nazi collaborators include Bockerer's wife, who prefers to celebrate Hitler's birthday over her husband's, both of which incidentally fall on the same day. Bockerer's son, Hansi, joined the SA well before the Germans arrived, however, and over the course of the film Hansi turns out to be a misguided youth and a victim of his errors. The number of Austrians supporting the Nazis in this film is actually remarkably high, but all the Austrian Nazi supporters have flawed characters and do not live up to the standards of the honest working-class male embodied in Bockerer and his friends. According to Oliver Rathkolb (2005: 105), this conception of the honest, hard-working male is crucial to the myth of reconstruction after the Second World War.

Apart from Bockerer, there are only two other characters whose views of the *Anschluss* are beyond reproach. The first is his friend, railroad worker, and socialist resistance fighter, Hermann, who is killed by the Nazis in the concentration camp at Dachau. Hermann and Bockerer end up in a brawl with some Germans outside a *Heurigen* (Viennese vineyard), which later leads to Hermann's arrest and deportation. Bockerer pays for his friend's ashes to be transferred from Dachau back to his widow in Vienna. Hatzinger, another friend, who joins him to play tarot cards, is also very unhappy with the regime, but he tries to stay out of any conflict with the Nazis and survives unscathed.

Schebesta, a small businessman and thus a member of the petit-bourgeois class, is the vilest Nazi supporter in the film. Right after the *Anschluss*, he cold heartedly "Aryanizes" an apartment and robs the Jewish owners, Herr and Frau Blau, of all their possessions before deporting them, presumably to their deaths. In the first scene, Schebesta is introduced as he joyously eats sausage in Bockerer's butcher shop and offers to buy liver cheese for one of the German soldiers who he claims have arrived to liberate them. Both Bockerer and the soldier do not understand from what Austrians have been liberated. Schebesta's character, as well as the first scene with the soldier, are not in the play and were invented by Artmann for his film. From the very beginning Schebesta is depicted as an overzealous Nazi who proudly wears the party badge on his jacket. The second time Schebesta appears in the film he is chatting with Herr Blau in the doorway of his window store, assuring Blau that he will help him and his wife get away. He advises Blau to put all his money in an envelope and his jewelry in a box. The third time Schebesta appears on the screen, he is guiding two Germans in black trench coats up to Blau's apartment, where he forces Blau to sign away all his possessions. Then he asks for the money, but as Frau Blau pretends that she does not know what he is talking about one of the Germans throws her against a commode, breaking it. This prompts Schebesta to alert the German: "Comrade, watch out for my furniture." Finally, Schebesta helps to drag the Blaus to a truck, assuring Blau, "You will get to leave" and "Where do you think, Davos?" Schebesta's strong Viennese accent emphasizes that this legalized looting is not a German but an Austrian action. The topic of *Wohnungsarisierungen* (the "Aryanization" of apartments) in Vienna has been of great interest to historians over the last ten years, but in 1981 it was still an underdiscussed topic, even though it was a mass phenomenon in Vienna in the spring of 1938.[3] This scene in the film would be very strong if it were not for the fact that Schebesta goes insane and his insanity is soon uncovered as he starts impersonating Hitler. This first becomes apparent when he serves as an overzealous *Luftschutzhelfer* (air-raid warden). Throughout the film, Schebesta slowly starts acting and looking like Hitler. He screams orders, imitating Hitler's upper Austrian high German, and wears a Hitler moustache and combs his hair like his beloved Führer. In the next scene, Schebesta stands in front of his store screaming "A hundred thousand pieces of broken glass, and no glass, no glass" (*Hunderttausend Scherben und es gibt kein Glas, kein Glas*), and he then runs past Bockerer's store. Bockerer simply says that Schebesta should be sent to Steinhof, Vienna's large and famous mental hospital, which is exactly what happens. The war, which Schebesta supported passionately, has ruined him. After the war, he breaks out of Steinhof and visits Bockerer, who is in bed at home with a fever. Schebesta enters the bedroom and declares that he is the Führer and that he needs to hide in Bockerer's apartment. Thinking that Hitler has invaded his bedroom, Bockerer jumps out of bed and calls Schebesta a mass murderer and vegetarian. This in itself should be an insult to an honest butcher. As Schebesta flees from Bockerer's apartment, he is met by the Herr Inspector, who is now dressed in an Austrian uniform, and two wardens from Steinhof who wrap him in a straightjacket. Schebesta's insanity undermines the strong scenes of the "Aryanization" in the Blaus' apartment. Some of the final scenes are comic and tragic. Both his insanity and support for Hitler are thus portrayed as an exception rather than the rule, and this makes his acts against the Jewish couple seems less common a historical event than these so-called "Aryanizations" actually were.

There are several more comical moments in the film. There is a silly historian, who moves into the Blau's apartment, referred to in the play as Dr Galleitner. He is studying the supposedly great times that the people are living in and writing a book on how Jewish freemasons killed Mozart, a humorous mockery of Nazi scholarship. He pretends to be a vegetarian, partially imitating Hitler. While this historian is not clinically insane, he represents the intellectual elite, who are aloof from the struggles of everyday life during the war. He stands in stark contrast to the average honest working-class ladies who stand in line for meat in front of Bockerer's butcher's shop. Fräulein Mitzi, who works at the Café Tosca, a seedy nightclub, asks the professor if there would be any meat on this day to celebrate the victory in Paris. The academic's answer is "Your inclinations are particularly carnal" (*Sie sind aber besonders fleischlich eingestellt*); this is clearly a humorous insert that is not in the play. The professor claims he is buying meat for his dog, though Mitzi and a superintendent standing next to him know that he does not have one. Finally, the professor announces: "If the Führer orders that meat should be bought, then meat has to be bought." Bockerer steps out of his store, telling the waiting crowd that there will be no meat today, explaining that they have already eaten all the meat from Belgium and Norway, and the sneaky French probably hid their own meat. He tells the shoppers to run over to the North Sea Hall and look for fish. The historian uses pompous terms, such as *Weltgeschichte* (world history). At the same time, he is a fraud, since he is not willing to admit that he does eat meat. The hard-working superintendent behind the historian sees through his disingenuous comments and again represents the good, naive Austrian who does not blindly support Nazism. Even Mitzi, also a member of the working class, is more skeptical of the times than the academic. The historian's views are the exception, not the rule.

The position that Bockerer's family takes to the *Anschluss* is complicated as both his son and wife initially support the Nazis and then soon come to regret their actions. His wife, Binerl (short for Sabine), naively follows the new regime without understanding it. Antel portrays here a negative interpretation of a mother and wife, who as a woman is too ignorant to ask the questions that Bockerer raises about the Nazi regime. The loss of her son is her punishment for her support of the Nazi regime. As a woman, she also does not fit into the perfect ideal of the honest mature working-class male, and consequently she does not understand the world as well as Bockerer. This sexist depiction of Binerl is a major flaw of both the play and the film, but it is not uncommon for Antel's, and Becher and Preses's, generation.

Hansi, Bockerer's son, begins the film as an ambitious young SA man, but becomes weary of the organization when his superior, Gstettner, reveals that he is gay and in love with Hansi. Initially, the SA draws Hansi away from helping his father in the store and away from his girlfriend. Antel's portrait of Hansi reveals a naive and impulsive youth, who is easily manipulated by an older man and goes as far as to torture Jews on the streets of Vienna. However, when he is faced with detaining his father after the vineyard brawl, he lets his father go. Hansi gives in to Gstettner's advances to help his father, but finally breaks up with him. This turns out to be a fatal decision for Hansi, as after leaving Gstettner for his girlfriend his former gay lover has Hansi drafted into the regular Wehrmacht and deployed to the eastern front where he is killed. This is the son's punishment for having left his paternal house and for having gone along with the crimes of the SA after the *Anschluss*, as well as for his ambiguous sexual orientation.

The SA officer Gstettner is an important character in his own right. In one scene, he is wearing a yellow velvet bathrobe over his uniform, drinking champagne while trying to seduce Hansi. He hugs the young man's neck and caresses his ear. Hansi tries to resist, but gives in as he realizes that his father is in danger of being arrested. Gstettner calls the Gestapo agent, von Lamm, to have Bockerer released after being arrested for having been seen talking to a resistance fighter. Apart from the fact that this scene depicts Franz Antel's homophobia and the cliché of the gay man seducing innocent young men—an idea which is unfortunately common among Antel's generation—it is interesting how Gstettner refers to von Lamm as "one of us" (*einer von uns*), implying that von Lamm is gay and/or a Nazi. The Austrian SS man Gstettner, through Antel's lens, becomes strange and unusual by being gay. The portrayal of Gstettner implies that both homosexuals and Nazis are not the norm in Austria. After the war, Gstettner shows up in Bockerer's shop asking for their famous liver cheese, which he would like to serve to a French general for whom he is now working. Bockerer's wife wonders where she has seen Gstettner before, but cannot remember. Thus, Gstettner gets away without being punished until the second part of the series. He slips under the radar, which conforms to Antel's and his generation's view of gay people. Gstettner, much like Schebesta, marks a radical departure from the play in showing Austrians participating in the Nazi regime. Hansi, on the other hand, is portrayed more sympathetically in the film, while in the play he is ideologically convinced of National Socialism to the extent of even repeatedly insulting his father for not tagging along politically. Antel does not seem to have been comfortable in portraying Hansi in this light, perhaps because the majority of older viewers in 1981 would have been around Hansi's age at the time of the *Anschluss*.

Another group that does not fit into Antel's conception of the honest working-class Austrian male is the haute bourgeoisie. Throughout the film, we see short scenes of Frau Hofrat and her guests playing bridge, scenes which are absent from the play. Like many Austrians at the time, the members of this small bridge club are simultaneously opposed to, but also in support of, Nazism. One of Frau Hofrat's friends—played by Franz Stoß, whom most Austrians recognized as Herr Kommerzialrat on *Die liebe Familie*, and who was famous for playing sophisticated upper-class characters—argues that both the Nazi's organizational skills and military conscription are praiseworthy. Another member of the bridge club, played by Hans Holt, praises the *Arbeitsdienst* ("labor service") because he feels that it did away with unemployment.[4] In *Der Bockerer*, Senta Wengraf's character, who is dressed elegantly, befitting a *Hofrat*'s wife, and who uses a disproportionate number of

French words in her nasal upper-class Viennese accent, is ambivalent about the Nazis. She is for the most part not interested in politics until her daughter returns home with her grandson, whose father (Hansi) had died at the Eastern front. There is some historical truth in the idea that the haute bourgeoisie tacitly supported Nazism; however, they are portrayed much more negatively than Bockerer. There is an implication in the film that this group of people should have taken a firmer stand against Nazism, instead of just standing by, even though, for the most part, this is what Bockerer does. However, since there are significantly fewer *Hofräte* than working-class people in Austria, their views are again the exception rather than the rule. The fact that these people play bridge, instead of tarot, further symbolizes their arrogance and pretensions when compared to Bockerer's circle of friends.

The depiction of the Jewish Dr Rosenblatt in both the play and the film is problematic. Right after the *Anschluss*, he manages to obtain an American visa. While the film makes clear that only a few people were able to get such visas, there is later a scene at the Westbahnhof where a large group of people are seen boarding the *Emigrantenexpress* ("emigrants' express train"). Dr Rosenblatt runs around Vienna with a mop and bucket to avoid being bullied by SA men into washing the sidewalks. He manages to escape and returns as a smart American lieutenant. One cannot help but think that Dr Rosenblatt benefited from his persecution; after all it made him emigrate to a more prosperous country. Bockerer is saddened by Rosenblatt's departure and calls his name as the train leaves the station. The Gestapo agent Pfalzner interrogates Bockerer on the spot for having Jewish friends. The final scene of the film shows Rosenblatt returning to Bockerer's store in an American army jeep and dressed in military uniform. Bockerer's wife and Hatzinger are all overjoyed to see him, which represents a change of heart for both, as they had previously felt uncomfortable playing tarot with a Jew after the *Anschluss*. They send him in to see Bockerer, who is playing cards with his grandson. As he looks up to see Rosenblatt, he smiles and announces jovially, "Your turn, Mr Rosenblatt" (*Ihr Blatt, Herr Rosenblatt*).

At this point Strauss's *Blue Danube Waltz* begins to play in the background and it seems as if the Second Republic can now start happily. The Rosenblatt character shows Austrian Jews having benefited from emigrating to the US, and it is implied that Austria welcomed returning emigrants with open arms. This, of course, undermines the tragic fate of the Blaus in the film. It goes without saying that the kitschy ending—with the waltz playing in the background and Bockerer's remark, *Ihr Blatt, Herr Rosenblatt*—marks a simple happy ending that undoes some of Antel's criticism of Austria and projects the idea of a new harmonious Austria. While the final line is directly taken from the play, Vansant (1991: 280) rightly argues that Antel should have changed this to a more appropriate ending for the early 1980s.

Historic newsreel footage is used in the film at the beginning, when German troops invade Austria, as well as towards the end, when footage of the destruction of Vienna is shown. The narrator comments on the images of destruction: "And then we received the bill for the fight of Mr. Hitler. *Mein Kampf,* he said, but we had to risk our necks. Vienna is a pearl, he said, the Herr Führer, and he was going to give it the right setting. One can see that now."[5] This announcement towards the end of the film undoes most of the criticism of Austrians' involvement in the Nazi regime, as it clearly implies that Austrians were victims of Hitler's insane megalomania. There is no doubt that the audience in 1981 appreciated this point of view, as it helps to overcome the critical depiction of Austrians in the first half of the film.

The second Bockerer film, *Der Bockerer II – Österreich ist frei* (1996), picks up on the theme of Austrian suffering during the Allied occupation. Set roughly in 1947, this film is reminiscent of the adaptation of Graham Greene's *The Third Man* (1949). The international police patrol the first district of Vienna and the Soviets and Americans are struggling to get along as the cold war begins to unfold. Bockerer works for the Soviet administration as a butcher, and most foods are rationed and the black market is rampant. Somewhat reminiscent of the character Alida Valli in *The Third Man*, a young Russian woman, Elena, who works for the Soviet military as a translator, tries to escape to the American zone. While the plot of the film is significantly less intense than the first, Antel seeks to portray the rebirth of a new Austria. Similar to the character Hedwig Bleibtreu in *The Third Man*— who laments about the Allied forces: "I envisioned the liberation much differently" (*Die Befreiung habe ich mir ganz anders vorgestellt*)—Bockerer complains about the Soviets being "worse than Hitler" (*schlimmer als wie beim Hitler*). This exaggerated and inappropriate remark, however, is balanced by the fact that despite all the hardship of the times Bockerer gets along splendidly with both the Americans and the Soviets. Austrians like Bockerer appear destined to serve as politically neutral Europeans. In addition to his old Austrian and neo-American friend Rosenblatt, in this film he meets Major Nowotny from the Soviet army. Nowotny is an old friend of Bockerer's from his days in the *Schutzbund* (the Social Democratic paramilitary organization during the interwar period), when the two men fought side by side in the Karl-Marx-Hof in 1934. During an argument with Nowotny, he tells him: "An Austrian stays an Austrian" (*ein Österreicher bleibt ein Österreicher*). Nowotny, who is still infuriated by the fact that Bockerer helped Elena cross over to the American sector, finally gives in to this sentiment as Bockerer invites him to play tarot cards, and Strauss's *Blue Danube* plays in the background. The scene is followed by newsreel footage of the signing of the State Treaty in 1955 and Chancellor Figl declaring "Austria is free!" (*Österreich ist frei!*)—all of this accompanied by Beethoven's ninth symphony in the background. After having survived the Nazi years in the first film, the second neatly shows how Bockerer lives through the days of the Allied occupation, but Antel unfortunately equates the two. Further, he uses Bockerer's "clean" history in the Nazi period to suggest that most Austrians did not deserve the postwar occupation.

Despite the fact that this film supports the myth that Austria suffered from the Allied occupation, and that the State Treaty and neutrality for the country did not arrive soon enough, Antel does point to the fact that denazification was not a success and that continuity with the Nazi era was also a factor of the new Austria. The Gestapo agent Pfalzner from the first film is shown in the second working in the passport office, and he asks Bockerer for a letter of reference for the denazification board. Bockerer refuses to help Pfalzner, however, and at his hearing he gets away despite Bockerer's refusal by simply using his Viennese *Schmäh* (wit) in order not to reply to some of the questions. Pfalzner also denounces one of the members of the denazification board, saying he knew him from the *Gauleitung* (district government under Nazi rule). This scene clearly illustrates how former Nazis continued to hold high-ranking positions in Austria. When Bockerer needs a passport with a false identity for Gustl Pühringer, a recently returned POW whom Bockerer slowly adopts as his son, Pfalzner is more than happy to oblige. The threatening Gestapo man has become a friendly passport agent, hoping to secure Bockerer's good will in case he should need someone to vouch for his past. Although very few Nazis were actually punished by the Austrian government, Gstettner, the gay SA officer who, in the first film, sent Hansi Bockerer to Stalingrad, is arrested by Nowotny for black marketeering and sent to Siberia. Obviously, Antel wanted to close the chapter on Gstettner and not let him get away like Pfalzner; however, it would have been historically incorrect to have the Austrian justice system punish Gstettner for his Nazi activities. The difference between the depiction of Gstettner and Pfalzner, however, opens up the unfortunate distinction between "good" and "bad" Nazis in the postwar era.

The third film, *Der Bockerer III – Die Brücke von Andau* (2000), continues the portrayal of Austria as a sovereign and neutral country in the midst of the cold war after the signing of the State Treaty. Set in 1956 in a now free Austria and at the time of the Budapest uprising, the film follows a plot similar to Anatole Litvak's *The Journey* (1959), which starred Deborah Kerr, Yul Brynner, and Jason Robards. Following the mythical final departure of Soviet soldiers from Vienna, Bockerer's grandson Karli and his adopted son Gustl set out on a business trip to Budapest to collect some meat. Bockerer once more uses his connections with the former Gestapo agent Pfalzner to obtain a new passport for Gustl, again highlighting the fact that denazification was far from perfect, and then Gustl, Karli and Bockerer's assistant travel to Hungary. However, the van is confiscated by Hungarian rebels, and Bockerer has to travel to Budapest, where he finally gets his friend Major Nowotny from the Soviet army to help him retrieve it. Nowotny tries to warn the rebels that the Soviets are sending tanks to Hungary and finds himself at an impasse, neither being able to return to his troops nor knowing where to turn. Karli saves the daughter of a Hungarian freedom fighter and ends up being killed in the fighting. Bockerer, Nowotny, and Gustl meanwhile flee for the border, heading for the bridge near Andau, at which point the film follows a plot similar to *The Journey*. The three find themselves at an inn on the Hungarian side of the border. Bockerer and Gustl help to take down a wooden watch tower to rebuild the bridge and then they help people flee over the bridge to Austria. In the process of getting his van across, Bockerer is shot, yet he kindly donates the meat he has brought with him to feed the refugees on the Austrian side of the border.

At the end of the film, Bockerer promises to make a real Austrian out of the deserter Nowotny. The communist Nowotny is redeemed as an Austrian, who has come to his senses, affirming Antel's anti-communist views. Rosenblatt, now an Austrian civilian, comes over to play a game of tarot. However, instead of the happy ending that marked the two previous films, the young Hungarian woman arrives to report that Karli has been killed. The film ends with a newsreel announcer bombastically declaring: "Karli was only one among 100,000" (*Karli war nur einer von 100.000*). Much like his father Hansi, Karli died because he did not steer clear from conflict, unlike Bockerer, who embodies the neutral Austrian.

The fourth film of the series, *Der Bockerer IV – Der Prager Frühling* (2003), echoes much of the sentiment of the third film, and is probably more significant for tying up loose ends of the soap-opera aspects of the series rather than introducing any new ideas about Austria's postwar history. The first third of the film is devoted to Fräulein Annerl, the widow of Hermann (the resistance fighter who died at Dachau) in the first film, who has been Bockerer's live-in maid since Binerl's death. After offering the informal *du* to Hatzinger, Rosenblatt, and Nowotny at one of their tarot games, Bockerer finally proposes to her. They are married by the former Gestapo agent Pfalzner, who has advanced in life to become a district mayor (*Bezirksvorsteher*) and is now trying to democratically secure the goodwill of his constituency by performing weddings. Bockerer does not want to be married by this former Nazi, but gives in to Annerl. In the shape of Pfalzner, the *Bockerer* series does not hide the fact that former Nazis continued their careers in public service in Austria after the war, very often peaking in their professions in the late 1960s. The newlywed couple decides to spend their honeymoon in Czechoslovakia, where Gustl has started a butcher's shop with his sister Milena, a Czech citizen. Putting the wagon before the horse, Gustl is hoping for the political liberalism of the Prague Spring to lead to the legalization of privately run businesses. While this plotline is not necessarily the most believable, the film is less about Czechoslovakia and more about Austria and its relative prosperity and political stability in the late 1960s. Milena Czerny not only happens to be the co-owner of a butcher's shop but also an aspiring journalist. Bockerer, Annerl, Hatzinger, and Elena (the escaped translator from the second film) end up being caught up in the collapse of free broadcasting in Czechoslovakia. Bockerer frees Gustl from jail by asking the minister on live television to pardon him and finally helps Milena relocate the television studio to an alternative location. Bockerer saves Milena from being arrested by the Soviets, while again he loses his van just before reaching the border and smuggles her out in a circus caravan. Bockerer gets out of the circus vehicle overjoyed to be back in Austria and encounters an Austrian border guard who is not interested in what is happening in Czechoslovakia and just wants to see his papers, insistent on following *Vorschriften* (regulations). The film series comes to an end with Bockerer screaming at the official, "Where are we now, with the Nazis again or with the Russians? Over there, people are being shot and that is in the middle of Europe. And you are only worried about laws and regulations."[6] Austria has become a free and democratic country, where the ORF (Austrian television channel) is in a much more fortunate situation than broadcasters in Czechoslovakia. Nonetheless, Pfalzner and the authoritarian border guard show that a free society cannot be built overnight, but rather that it is a gradual process that leads to democratization. In contrast to Austria's eastern neighbors and the successor states of the former Habsburg territories, the Second Republic is portrayed as being very lucky and successful.

The entire *Bockerer* series is complex in the sense that it critically points out Austrians' involvement on the one hand, while simultaneously being flawed for stylizing the anti-Nazi Bockerer as one of many anti-Nazi Austrians. Bockerer, who is actually exceptional, becomes the norm for Austrians during the Nazi regime. The focus of the final three parts of the series overemphasizes the Cold War in the series and this also distracts from Austria's history in the Holocaust and the Second World War.

Notes

1. For the first four decades after 1945, Austria unquestioningly regarded itself as the "first victim" of Hitler's aggression. The election of the former UN Secretary General, Kurt Waldheim, as president in 1986, however, divided the country politically. Waldheim's service in the German Army during the Second Word War fell under the scrutiny of a historical commission that cleared him of any involvement in war crimes. Nonetheless, the country was split between those who supported Waldheim and those who rejected the idea of public office for any former officials of the Nazi regime. In the same year, Jörg Haider was elected the leader of the extreme right-wing populist FPÖ, and over the following years, up until 2000, the party received growing support from mostly younger voters, who favored a German nationalist ideology that included an uncritical approach to Austria's past. The divisions in Austrian society that were caused by Waldheim and Haider, however, contributed to an increased interest in inquiry into Austria's Nazi past.
2. Bruno Kreisky was Chancellor of Austria from 1970 to 1983. As head of the SPÖ he ruled Austria with a majority government from 1971 to 1979. For further information, see Bischof and Pelinka (1994).
3. The Austrian Historical Commission has made the topic of *Wohnungsarisierungen* one of its priorities in researching Austria's past in the Nazi period. Results from the Commission's findings are available at: http://www.historikerkommission.gv.at.
4. Hans Holt and Marthe Harrell were both young stars in Wien Films produced during the Nazi time. The legendary Wien Film, which produced films with a Viennese and Austrian focus even during the Nazi period, was also the place where most of Antel's films were produced. This is why he even wrote an illustrated book about the studio's history (see Antel and Winkler 1991).
5. *Und dann haben wir die Rechnung präsentiert bekommen für den Kampf vom Herrn Hitler. Mein Kampf hat er gesagt, aber hinhalten haben wir unseren Schädel müssen. Wien ist eine Perle, hat er gesagt, der Herr Führer, und er wird ihr die richtige Fassung geben. Man sieht es.*
6. *Wo san mir denn, wieder bei die Nazi oder bei die Russen? Da drüben werden die Menschen erschossen und das ist mitten in Europa. Und Sie haben keine anderen Sorgen als Gesetze und Vorschriften.*

References

Antel, F. and C.F. Winkler. 1991. *Hollywood an der Donau: Geschichte der Wien-Film in Sievering.* Vienna: Edition S.

Bischof, G. and A. Pelinka. 1994. *The Kreisky Era in Austria.* New Brunswick, NJ: Transaction Publishers.

Dassanowsky, R. von. 2005. *Austrian Cinema: A History.* Jefferson, NC: McFarland.

Rathkolb, O. 2005. *Die paradoxe Republik.* Vienna: Paul Zsolnay Verlag.

Vansant, J. 1991. "Ways of Remembering: *Der Bockerer* as Play and Film," in D.G. Daviau (ed.), *Austrian Writers and the Anschluss.* Riverside, CA: Ariadne Press.

Chapter 3

Historical Drama of a Well-intentioned Kind: Wolfgang Glück's *38 – Auch das war Wien*

Felix W. Tweraser

The New Austrian Film of the 1980s began to produce popular historical dramas portraying Austria during the *Anschluss* and the ensuing period of Nazi rule. Peter Turrini's *Alpensaga* (1976–1980), Franz Antel's *Der Bockerer/The Bockerer* (1981), Axel Corti's *Eine blaßblaue Frauenschrift/A Woman's Pale Blue Handwriting* (1984) and *Wohin und zurück/Somewhere and Back* (1985/86), and Wolfgang Glück's *38 – Auch das war Wien/38 – Vienna Before the Fall* (1986) found large audiences domestically, and in the case of Glück's film, which was nominated for the Academy Award for best foreign-language film in 1987, was successful on the international market. Such films stand out because of a relative lack of interest among New Austrian filmmakers in depicting the time of Nazi rule in Austria (1938–1945), with many focusing their attention instead on the residue of Naziism still evident in Second Republic Austria. Antel's and Glück's films were both adaptations of texts that were honest, unsparing, and differentiated in their descriptions of the *Anschluss* period of Austrian history and Austrians' complicity in the Nazi takeover: Ulrich Becher and Peter Presses' play *Der Bockerer* (1946) and Friedrich Torberg's *Auch das war Wien* (published posthumously in 1984, but written during Torberg's exile in Prague and Zurich in 1938/39). While Antel's film, in particular—through its melodramatic effects—renders the more threatening or troubling aspects of its literary source harmless, Glück's film also sacrifices a more historically nuanced and difficult narrative in favor of easily identifiable characters and situations and relatively facile conceptions of individual responsibility and guilt. The film is wedded to a good/evil and before/after binary that elides historical complexity and gradations of guilt, responsibility, and victimization. Additionally, the way the audience is encouraged to identify with the Jew Martin Hoffmann, and the way he is characterized as a naive victim, perpetuates the myth of collective Austrian victim status with respect to National Socialism that saturated postwar Austrian society.

In the following, I analyze the artistic choices that inform Wolfgang Glück's film adaptation of Torberg's work, looking specifically at Glück's deployment of the camera, the use of Viennese locations, other aspects of the film's *mise-en-scène*—including the set design, casting choices, and type of acting and movement favored—and the relationship between diegetic and nondiegetic sound, in order to draw more general conclusions about its power to catalyze audience interest and challenge common historical assumptions about the *Anschluss*.[1] In general, Glück errs on the side of maximum audience accessibility and identification—knowing that his audience is composed primarily of citizens socialized in a country loath to dig too deeply into its Nazi past—for instance, in his assertion that the central character, Martin Hoffmann, must seem inherently likable (Kahl 1988). I put the film's release in the historical context of 1986, the year in which the first major broad-based inquiry into Austria's past took place during Kurt Waldheim's campaign for the presidency, and when Jörg Haider assumed power in the FPÖ. In the analysis of certain key scenes I compare the original source material of Torberg's novel (Torberg 1984)—at its best a probing indictment of Austrian attitudes, artistically constructed as a series of dances and narrated in the present tense for maximum immediacy, suspense, and surprise—with Glück's rendition. The film garnered generally favorable early notices, but has not received much attention in film studies, probably because it hews very closely to the conventions of linear, ponderous storytelling characteristic of historical realist film.[2] The one scholarly study to date itself comes to a mixed conclusion, praising Glück's intentions and effort to awaken Austrians' historical consciousness, but faulting the film's lack of artistic innovation and its flattering of the audience's taste (Wauchope 2004: 220–21).

The appearance of *38 – Auch das war Wien* in 1986 coincided with seismic social and political developments in Austria and a gradual unmooring of the self-serving mythology of collective victim status crucial to the founding and, indeed, success of the Second Republic.[3] The broad consensus that prevailed in Austrian political culture bound various constituencies across party lines. What bound this consensus together, in addition to Austria's assertion of victim status during the period 1938–1945—incidentally a policy promoted by the Allied powers and articulated in the Moscow declaration of 1943—was a less-than-forthright official and private confrontation with shared responsibility for the Nazi period, but also the country's rapid reintegration into the Western sphere of influence during the cold war. Over time, these foundational myths have lost their force because of changing geopolitical circumstances. The increased general interest in Austrians' complicity with National Socialism was an unintended consequence of Kurt Waldheim's presidential campaign in 1986 and the end of the Cold War has allowed more attention to be paid to continuities in Austrian history. The political and social realignments that have taken place in Austria since 1986, while amply described and reflected in print media, also have symbolic and visual analogs in public space: in the ephemeral interventions attached to demonstrations, temporary art exhibitions, and performances that have characterized the last two decades; and in the more permanent changes in the physical commemorative landscape, which provide more opportunities for introspection, reflection, and expiation, all activities encouraged by an artistic endeavor such as *38 – Auch das war Wien*. Glück has pointed out the particular resonance of the film's year of release: "Another film about National Socialism? In times in which matters arise that we thought had been overcome, a past with which even fifty years later we have not come to terms is supposed to be ignored: in such times as the year 1986 such a film cannot be too much."[4] As an early and earnest effort to reawaken historical consciousness and reflection about the *Anschluss* and its consequences, something that was less than self-evident in 1986, *38 – Auch das war Wien* deserves considerable credit.

The film depicts the romance between the Jewish writer Martin Hoffmann (Tobias Engel) and the non-Jewish actress Carola Hell (Sunnyi Melles), set against the backdrop of Vienna in the months preceding Austria's annexation by Nazi Germany on 12 March 1938. Martin and Carola rent an apartment together and pursue their professions, Martin contracting with the publisher Sovary (Romuald Pekny) to produce a new play (one that is supposed to be apolitical), and Carola acting, on the stage at Vienna's Theater in der Josefstadt and in Berlin, in a production of Lessing's *Emilia Galotti*, but also on screen in escapist fare produced by a Vienna-based but already Nazi-controlled company, Wien-Film. The demands of their professional obligations and the intensity of their romance conspire to blind them to the nature and immediacy of the Nazi threat in Vienna, though warning signs abound: Carola's interrogation by the Gestapo in Berlin (prompted by her unintentional but politically charged comments and her association with a Jew); the repeated admonitions of Martin by his best friend Toni Drexler (Heinz Trixner), an anti-Nazi journalist at the *Neues Wiener Tagblatt*, to leave Austria while he can; and the subtle and ominous turn in anti-Semitic behavior in Vienna's public places, where Martin is now accosted openly. In spite of such warning signs, and carried away by the euphoria of their coming child, and by Austrian national pride prompted by Chancellor Schuschnigg's defiance of Hitler and call for a national plebiscite on 9 March, Martin and Carola drop their plans to organize visas for the US and so are unable to flee Austria in time; Carola is able to get to Prague, but Martin, in the film's final scene, is arrested on the street—Blutgasse—by the Gestapo. The publisher Sovary commits suicide, Toni Drexler is arrested, and the *Diktatur der Hausmeister* ("dictatorship of the custodians," Torberg's term in the novel) commences.

Glück is at pains to render the public and private scenes in a historically realistic fashion, filling the frame with Viennese landmarks and baroque exteriors that visually recall the glory of the multinational, multilingual, and religiously tolerant Empire. An important subplot involves Martin and Carola's landlady Frau Schostal (Ingrid Burkhard), whose socialist husband has been imprisoned since the Civil War of February 1934 but whose son joins the SA, the *Sturmabteilung*, or Storm Troopers; her empathetic attitude towards Martin, and her family's various political allegiances, all occurring under the umbrella of the *Ständestaat*, the corporatist state under which both Nazis and socialists were illegal, provide important historical background.

While analysis of the film is my focus, it may be interesting to note which plot and characterization elements Glück downplays or changes completely in his adaptation of the novel. The specific nature of Martin Hoffmann's Jewish identity, and the multifaceted history and character of political anti-Semitism in Austria, things described at some length in the novel, are rather cryptically addressed in the film.[5] Other interesting departures from the source material include the location of Martin and Carola's apartment: in the novel it is in the leafy district of Döbling, on the Eroicagasse not far from the vineyards that ring Vienna, while in the film the apartment is in the city's center (First District), on the Webergasse. Whereas the novel emphasizes the apartment as an idyll and escape, physically removed from the more obvious social and political changes taking place in Vienna, the film locates it in the city's center, reinforcing the central characters' apparent blindness to what is going on right in front of them. Glück also inserts a scene on New Year's Eve 1937/38, one full of gaiety and harmony, to underscore the naive optimism of the central characters. More problematically, while the novel endeavors a nuanced description of how and why Austrians were drawn to National Socialism and its anti-Semitic ideology in the first place, the film's openly anti-Semitic characters—the *Hausmeister*, the Nazi functionaries, Frau Schostal's son, and Karl Brandt, an actor—are all conceived and acted with such a cartoon-like evil quality that it blocks any audience identification or introspection about the many gradations of involvement and support that the majority of Austrians provided at the time. This happens to the extent that, when compared to the more naturalistic and underplayed acting styles of everyone else in the cast, it supports the retrospectively comfortable notion that Austrians were victims of an alien invasion of nerdy evildoers. In addition, Glück abandons many of the novel's more interesting formal aspects—its musical structure, or its use of a narrative present tense to heighten immediacy, danger, and surprise, yielding a relatively fast pace—in favor of a much more ponderous and straightforward narrative strategy. In some ways the last quarter of the film, in which Glück uses more quick cuts and disorienting changes of scene, is the most effective; it is also the part of the film that, from a strictly formal standpoint and in terms of pacing, comes closest to the original.

Glück introduces his Viennese locations with wide-angle shots of such familiar landmarks as the Riesenrad in the Prater and the Stephansdom, shooting with a filtered lens for a hazy, dreamlike effect. Such establishing shots suggest a mood of nostalgic, at times sentimental, identification to the viewer, who is encouraged to conjure notions of Vienna's golden age prior to the fall of the Austro-Hungarian monarchy. As the angle of the shot narrows, often initially including the characters in the middle distance, Glück maintains specific references to totems of Vienna's imperial glory. A good example of this is an extended early scene, shot on location in the Volksgarten: Glück's camera tracks left and right to encompass the surrounding buildings on the Ringstraße, the reflecting pools and rose plantings in the garden, and records the ease with which Martin and Carola move through this landscape.

The overall mood created by the languid camera movement, bathing the scene in the warm, natural light of a late September afternoon, and the correspondingly relaxed manner of the actors, is one of absolute comfort and safety in one's surroundings. The topic of conversation is also relatively frivolous: Martin and Carola discuss the propriety of his sending flowers to her at the theater while she is rehearsing a role and they talk about moving into an apartment together. And yet, Glück effectively underscores Martin and Carola's false sense of security when Carola says, "I don't bother with politics" (*Ich kümmere mich nicht um Politik*), or when Martin, in response to Carola's account of her mother's misgivings about their relationship, says: "Tell your mother that I'm not Jewish!" (*Sag' deiner Mutter, dass ich kein Jud' bin!*) Over the course of the film, Carola (as befits her given name, Hell, which in German connotes not just light but also clear-sightedness) begins to see the danger of her naive position, particularly in scenes where she views herself on screen in a typically escapist Nazi production, while Martin, as he witnesses and experiences scenes of anti-Semitic agitation, becomes less inclined to disavow his heritage. Nevertheless, in this early scene at least, Glück leaves little to chance: it concludes with the camera, which has been tracking the actors the whole time, coming to rest on the statue of Empress Elisabeth, while the actors exit the frame.

The interior scenes shot at landmark sites emphasize the security that they provide from the increasingly labile public sphere. Martin is a regular, a *Stammgast*, at the legendary Café Herrenhof. His close relationship with the headwaiter Alois reinforces his sense of belonging, and our introduction to the cafe includes an incident in which Martin receives special treatment (a nice contrast to the final scene in the Herrenhof, in which Martin must vacate the premises because of the Gestapo). There are numerous scenes of rehearsals in the theater in der Josefstadt, where Carola is a member of the company. Though there are references to the outside world, the director of the production is at pains to emphasize that the theater is an apolitical sanctuary. The busy offices of the *Neues Wiener Tagblatt*, with posters of Chancellor Schuschnigg on the wall, suggest connections to the rich tradition of independent journalism inherited from the monarchy and the First Republic, but it also functions as a bastion of Austrian national pride in the face of the threat coming from Germany. In a final scene, the lobby of the Grand Hotel provides an oasis of safety in a world that is collapsing. All these familiar locations evoke a (lost) sense of security in a past that is increasingly threatened by the new masters in Austria. The interior of Carola and Martin's apartment is also shot to emphasize its comfort and convenience, but also its quality of sanctuary and retreat with respect to the world outside.

The world of arts and letters in which Martin, Carola, and their circle of friends move did not always respond quickly to the political developments occurring around it. Glück's film is accordingly set in the theaters, publishing houses, coffeehouses, and editorial rooms that make up that world. These institutions' response to the Nazi threat becomes a key register in the film, working in dialogue with what occurs on the political stage, but often effectively and affectively hindering the characters' realization that their environment is changing, even within the confines of their presumed sanctuaries. In response to the Nazis' efforts to instrumentalize works of human creativity to support their political goals, the products of Germany's literary tradition and cultural heritage accordingly become contested markers of identity. Over the course of the film, Carola plays the title role in Lessing's *Emilia Galotti* and Luise in Schiller's *Kabale und Liebe*, classical roles, laden with socially and politically critical potential, in the genre of bourgeois tragedy. The rehearsals for *Kabale und Liebe* become an important symbolic grid for the political changes occurring outside the theater. In spite of the theater director's assertion that "Politics doesn't interest me," Carola and her Jewish leading man advocate a more politically engaged interpretation of the drama. The Nazi Karl Brandt is an understudy in the theater company, and is accordingly treated initially with ridicule by the others, but by the end of the film he has taken over the male lead and is in many ways running the whole show, and Carola loses her role to a more politically acceptable understudy as well. The theater director's final words on screen, though, in the latter instance directed at Carola's understudy, are exactly the same as they had been to Carola before the *Anschluss*. Here Glück subtly underscores the continuity of personnel and the compromises made by some of Austria's leading artistic figures—Hörbiger and Wessely, among many others—who stayed during 1938–1945 and allowed their own celebrity to be exploited by the Nazis. The publisher Sovary represents the most specific link to the cosmopolitan, multilingual, and multiethnic Habsburg tradition, a position he articulates when describing his relationship to his secretary: "We two— Pekarek and I—she from Prague and I from Budapest, thrown together in Vienna with Jewish roots. For me, that constitutes what it means to be Austrian."[6] Both novel and film emphasize that this tradition has come to an end: Sovary commits suicide. Glück composes the sequence preceding Sovary's suicide by contrasting the seeming safety of the hotel lobby and the resigned aplomb with which he concludes his life—a cognac with Martin, an exaggerated tip for the waiter, lifting his hat (twice) as he climbs the stairs, all the time with the camera tracking left and right to follow him—with the horror of his final act.

Some of the casting choices are interesting and suggestive, though they may undermine Glück's stated intention of audience identification with the central character. The cabaret singer who performs "The Song of the Little Austrian" ("Das Lied vom kleinen Österreicher"), Gerhard Bronner, had been forced to emigrate in 1938 because he was Jewish, returning to Vienna after the war and performing for many years at the Kabarett Simpl. Lukas Resetarits, also a mainstay of the postwar cabaret scene in Vienna, plays with welcome panache the anti-Nazi cab driver who is willing to take Martin to the border so he can escape. The casting of Tobias Engel and Sunnyi Melles in the roles of Martin and Carola walks a fine line between individuation and stereotype. Engel's Semitic features mark him as Jewish, and some shots seem to go out of their way to emphasize these features; one scene depicting an anxious phone conversation between Martin and Carola, for instance, shoots Martin in a phone booth inside the Café Herrenhof, and the low angle and intense backlighting have the effect of exaggerating his features in a disturbing manner. Martin is also shot at times in extreme close-up; the only other characters to be similarly shot are other Jews at the train station, who, like Martin, are unable to flee

Vienna because of the border closures, but these secondary figures are not developed as three-dimensional characters. Nevertheless, the use of extreme close-up links the figures visually in the mind of the viewer. The relatively discreet romantic scenes shot in the interior of the apartment often depict Martin coming up to Carola from behind, a predatory move that is somewhat troubling, in that it recalls the use of the sexually predatory Jew in the visual propaganda favored by the Nazis.

Glück combines diegetic and nondiegetic elements in the film's soundtrack in order to suggest connections that are not immediately apparent. The diegetic music employed—Strauss on the radio on New Year's Eve, the song in the cabaret when celebrating Schuschnigg's fleeting defiance of the Nazis—occurs in scenes where the principle characters are comfortable in their surroundings and expressing Austrian national pride (on another occasion one hears the "Horst Wessel Song" off-screen after the Nazi takeover.) The cabaret song's lyrics are decidedly double-edged, lampooning the Austrian's tendency to go along with whoever is in power at the moment, while at the same time expressing pride in Schuschnigg's defiance of Hitler:

> I, the little Austrian,
> Want nothing but my peace,
> And, as a little Austrian, just watch,
> The big ones, if you please.
> ...
> Still when it's gotten too mad,
> It's gotten too mad indeed,
> Then we hold speeches,
> But no longer our mouths,
> Then even Schuschnigg shows,
> What he's made of.[7]

The use of diegetic music from traditionally Viennese waltzes and cabaret connotes lightness and gaiety, and Glück is careful to employ such music to reinforce the moments when the principle characters are carried away by optimism about their future.

The relatively infrequent use of nondiegetic sound immediately prompts the question of why it is employed when it is. Two musical compositions for the film accompany several scenes: one is a dissonant orchestral wall of sound that features over the opening credits and in a scene of maximum anxiety for Martin, when he is forced to hide from the Gestapo even in his regular coffee house. The other film music is a heavily produced sentimental melody that accompanies some of the romantic scenes between Martin and Carola, for instance the scene in the Volksgarten; it additionally accompanies the final scene when they are separated at the train station, and plays over the final credits. This "love theme," aside from being somewhat annoying as music, undermines some of the visuals, particularly in Martin and Carola's final scene together, a moment of high anxiety, set to a slow, cloying melody.

More effective is the use of sound to underscore the visuals of ominous changes in public space: a transitional exterior scene on New Year's Eve 1937, in which

Martin encounters children playing happily in a tree, is accompanied by a familiar musical theme, but this is gradually drowned out by the sound of boots of "illegal" Nazis marching by in the background; exterior scenes of Jews forced by mobs to label Jewish-owned businesses and erase campaign slogans from the cancelled plebiscite, respectively, are accompanied by anti-Semitic insults and general abuse by the mob, though to leave these insults free-floating—by not synchronizing them to a particular figure visually—arguably lets the viewer off the hook.

Martin's final wanderings through Vienna's streets are accompanied by typical slogans uttered in organized fashion by a group of SA brown shirts, and corresponds to the visual changes in the streets' appearance that have taken place, seemingly overnight: propaganda banners and posters are everywhere, *Hausmeisters* fanatically clean their house fronts, children carry Nazi flags, and so on. A particularly suggestive blending of diegetic and nondiegetic sound accompanies the exterior sequence accompanying Martin and Carola's sudden departure. (This sequence follows a scene shot in the apartment, in which their joy at sharing the news of Carola's pregnancy is suddenly interrupted by a phone call from Toni, who informs them that Schuschnigg has resigned and that they need to leave Vienna immediately.) The audio track supporting this taxi ride into an unknown future is appropriately eclectic, using the ambient diegetic sound of a group of Nazis marching by and singing, while at the same time strains of Strauss's *Radetzkymarsch*—diegetic or not remains unclear—compete for attention. The cacophony of colliding sounds resolves itself in a return to the dissonant wall of sound that plays over the opening credits. Thus the sudden visual turn from euphoria to a completely uncertain future is aptly echoed in a disharmonious audio track.

Glück's film hits its stride in the final quarter, a series of briskly paced scenes that simultaneously show Martina and Carola's growing awareness of their threatened status and a more distanced objective look at how the streets of Vienna are changing. A key scene in this development is set in the interior of the Wien-Film studios, where members of the production company are gathered after work to view the rushes. The viewer does not know this yet, though, since the scene is introduced by Carola in full screen—grainy, black and white—performing a musical tap-dance number with her partner. The viewer sees various takes of the same number, and the director finally asks for one to be played without the audio track. As this version plays, Glück cuts to a shot of the viewing area (now shot in color), and narrows in on Carola's reaction to the footage. Sunnyi Melles plays the scene subtly and effectively, as the viewer watches her express a gamut of emotions, culminating in realization and disillusionment. The dialogue with the director that ensues after the lights go up is perhaps superfluous, but serves to underscore her realization: "One should always see prints without the sound … you see everything more clearly. Everything that's missing. Nothing uttered about the character, relationships, or atmosphere. They all miss the mark of what is true and important." Carola, who had accepted the film offer thinking that she could remain politically detached from the terms of her compromise, realizes that the whole endeavor is artistically and morally bankrupt, unchallenging for the participants and providing only escape for the audience. From this point on, Carola's political consciousness is awake: she confronts the director of *Kabale und Liebe* to draw out more of the political content of the play, and she encourages Martin to go ahead and get their visas before it is too late.

A series of exterior scenes, shot mainly from a high angle, show Martin walking through a Vienna that no longer provides any security at all. This sequence, set to a suggestive mixture of ambient street noise, sloganeering, and the ominous film music, effectively emphasizes Martin's existential loneliness: he is no longer part of any community. The places that had provided security no longer are open to him, but he is not part of the Jewish community either, as he stands aside observing the organized persecution of Vienna's Jews from a distance. By shooting the street scenes from above, Glück adopts the camera position of a silent witness to the barbarity that is unfolding. From the time that Martin and Carola receive the news from Toni that they must leave Vienna immediately, Glück adopts faster pacing: the scenes do not last as long; the locations change in a jarring way, requiring some orientation on the part of the viewer; and the narrative point of view (established through the positioning of the camera) alternates between Martin's perspective and that of an Olympian witness looking on from above. Glück's cutting strategy effectively suggests that events are spinning out of control and that the principle characters no longer have an overview of what is unfolding. The pacing of these scenes mirrors Torberg's narrative strategy, which establishes maximum surprise and immediacy through adoption of the present tense.

In sum, Wolfgang Glück's *38 – Auch das war Wien* depicts the time before the *Anschluss* in a realistic, historicizing manner. Glück's careful attention to the details of the *mise-en-scène* yields a product of seemingly reliable verisimilitude, placing the viewer in the volatile atmosphere of 1938 Vienna, while the romantic story provides the viewer with many emotional points of identification with the victims of Nazism in Austria. The film's earnest depiction of the exteriors is also part of its main weakness: in unfolding a tableau of general victimization to an invading horde, and having those Austrian Nazis who appear on screen act in an overheated, cartoonish manner, the film ends up reinforcing the myths it seeks to deconstruct, allowing the viewer the comfort of thinking that such things are impossible and that no truly patriotic Austrian would collaborate with the Nazis. The high percentage of the population that enthusiastically supported Hitler—and the disproportionate number of Austrians directly involved in the institutional structure of the Holocaust— necessarily fade into the background of such a presentation.

Notes

1. The film, originally released in fall 1986, is now available on DVD as part of the collection "Der österreichische Film: Edition der Standard", a compilation of 100 important Austrian films re-released by Hoanzl of Vienna in 2006.
2. See, for instance, Seidel: "[Glück's] film about the days of Austria's Anschluss to Nazi Germany has the ambition to be authentic. In fact this has been accomplished, although at the price of an incontrovertible didacticism." Seidel's remarks, taken from a review in the *Frankfurter*

Allgemeine Zeitung, 8 September 1986, appear on the DVD sleeve of *38 – Auch das war Wien* (Vienna: Hoanzl, 2006).

3. Gertraud Steiner Daviau writes that the film "served as a prelude to the widespread media coverage and the many books, articles, and international conferences that appeared in 1988, on the occasion of the fiftieth anniversary of the Anschluss". Retrieved 15 December 2007 from: http://www.filmreference.com/Films-Thr-Tur/38-Auch-das-War-Wien.html.

4. Glück's remarks are taken from "Das Ziel: Die Widersprüche aufzeigen," which appears on the DVD sleeve for *38 – Auch das war Wien* (Vienna: Hoanzl, 2006).

5. As Rice remarks: "Throughout the novel, Martin is portrayed as a talented dramatist, a good friend, and a sympathetic mate to Carola, but what makes Martin Hoffmann a subtly and richly developed character is his Jewishness. He is a Jew who has never allowed his Jewishness to control his life, thus isolating himself from the collective, as he discovers in the final pages. He views the world through Semitic eyes, comprehending the difficulties and complexities of being a Jew in a non-Jewish world, while at the same time the world itself views Martin Hoffmann according to his ethnic heritage. In true Torbergian fashion, the reader is presented with a protagonist who must make his way through a hostile environment only to discover that he remains an outsider" (Rice 2001: 108).

6. *Wir zwei—die Pekarek und ich—sie aus Prag und ich aus Budapest—hier in Wien zusammengewirkt—mit jüdischem Firmament. Das ergibt für mich den kompletten Begriff des Österreichischen.*

7. *[I]ch will als kleiner Österreicher / nichts wie mei Ruh' / und schau als kleiner Österreicher / immer nur den Großen zu / ... / Doch wenn's uns zu bunt wird / dann wird's uns zu bunt / dann halten wir Reden / und nicht mehr den Mund / dann zeigt selbst der Schuschnigg / das, was in ihm steckt* (Kramer and Prucha 1994: 85).

References

Kahl, K. 1988. "Unruhe vor dem Sturm," *Kurier*, 4 March, 37.

Kramer, T. and M. Prucha. 1994. *Film im Lauf der Zeit: 100 Jahre Kino in Deutschland, Österreich und der Schweiz*. Vienna: Ueberreuter.

Rice, M.H. 2001. "Nazis and Jews: A Thematic Approach to Three Exile Works by Friedrich Torberg," Ph.D. dissertation. Cincinnati, OH: University of Cincinnati.

Torberg, F. 1984. *Auch das war Wien*. Munich: Langen-Müller.

Wauchope, M. 2004. "Identity and Perception in the Film *38 – Vienna before the Fall*," in M. Lamb-Faffelberger and P.S. Saur (eds), *Visions and Visionaries in Contemporary Austrian Literature and Film*. New York: Peter Lang, 211–22.

Chapter 4

Cartographies of Identity: Memory and History in Ruth Beckermann's Documentary Films

Christina Guenther

It is at the margins of documentary film[1] that Jewish-Austrian filmmaker Ruth Beckermann has explored the central sociopolitical questions that launched and still inform much of her work: "Who are we, children of the second generation? What characterizes us?"[2]

Born to Holocaust survivors in 1952, Beckermann writes that only as an adult in the 1980s was she able to speak about the feelings caused by the overt marginalization of Jewish life in postwar Austria. In a 1989 collection of essays *Unzugehörig*, she writes that her Jewish compatriots perceived their Viennese childhood and youth in spatial terms as a "no-man's land," "a ghetto-existence" marked by *Unzugehörigkeit* or "not belonging" (Beckermann 1989: 117). For Beckermann, public erasure of Jewish existence in the Second Republic was particularly disconcerting in a land that had aided in the destruction of European Jewry. Indeed, during her youth any aspect of Jewish identity was only expressed or performed within the safe confines of family and the significantly reduced Jewish community. Beckermann likens the post-Holocaust Jewish community in Austria to a fragile structure. In her words: "Jewish presence in Austria after 1945 is bound up with a host of identity problems. It is a precarious house of cards built on painful experiences and hope-filled ideals" (ibid.: 107).[3] The image suggests that Jews intent on rebuilding communities in the Second Republic repressed painful memories of persecution and loss in favor of an idealized Habsburgian tradition characterized by an enlightened multicultural tolerance. It is, therefore, not surprising that this struggle undermined any affirmative sense of Jewish Austrian identity on the part of her parents' as well as her own generation.

Since the early 1980s, having completed a doctorate in journalism and art history at the University of Vienna in 1977, Ruth Beckermann has been making documentary films that explore and represent Jewish identity in the Second Republic, a process that has involved working through both transgenerational trauma and survivor guilt on the one hand, and working against invisibility in postwar Austria on the other. Her films reveal that, as a Jew in Austria today, claiming a geographical place and sociopolitical space is an ongoing project that involves a steadfast engagement with historiography.

The margins, thus, represent a familiar territory to Beckermann, and she uses this metaphoric and aesthetic site as a point of departure for her exploration of post-Holocaust Jewish-Austrian identity. Often working as an ethnographer to draw attention to the elision of personal and collective memories, she succeeds in her films in constructing a counter-memory. Her visual and aural texts challenge the dominant narrative of Austrian history and national identity, one very much attached to the idea of a homogeneous ethnicity and religion and grounded in a particular Alpine landscape. Interestingly, the political and social margins that Beckermann inhabits with her films are not represented as a static or fixed position or an inert backdrop; travel is instead often the organizing principle. In fact, in a 1996 interview about her first three films she emphasizes that all her films represent "journeys in a way, [even if] very different ... in form and structure" (Beckermann, in Reiter 1997: 22),[4] during which she refigures post-Holocaust Jewish-Austrian identity in terms of routes rather than roots.[5]

A cultural observer self-consciously filming from within her own localized subculture, a "participant observer," travel also remains a central trope in most of Ruth Beckermann's "film essays" since 1996. Her particular genre of ethnography takes the form of filmic travelogues in which she probes the interconnections between identity, memory, history, and documentary. In this chapter, I would like to reflect on how, with her "filmic maps," Beckermann creates her own variant of experimental ethnography. I shall focus on two of her ethnographic travelogues—*Die papierene Brücke/Paper Bridge* (1987) and *Zorros Bar Mizwa/Zorro's Bar Mitzvah* (2006)—films made almost twenty years apart.

As a preface to my analysis of Beckermann's ethnographic travelogues, a brief discussion of what I mean by "experimental ethnography" may be useful. I borrow the term from Catherine Russell (1999), who attempts to highlight the potential of melding two seemingly autonomous practices on the margins of mainstream filmmaking: experimental film and ethnographic film. She defines this interplay of filmmaking in terms of a "collision of social theory and formal experimentation" (ibid.: xi). In this process of dissolving disciplinary boundaries, "'culture' is performed in various fragmented and mediated ways, always challenging various structures of racism, sexism, and imperialism that are inscribed implicitly and explicitly in so many forms of cultural representations" (ibid.: xii). Experimental ethnography, then, is less about representing "other" cultures than about reflecting on the discourse of culture in representation.

Beckermann questions in her films how identity and culture in Austria have been imagined in connection with mystified autochthony, in terms of groundedness in particular "Austrian" landscapes and cityscapes. A central question for her, too, is how Jewish identity in particular continues to be constructed as "other," as not belonging within the dominant homogenizing national culture of the Second Republic. Her use of the trope of movement or travel is particularly effective here as an integral component in the construction of identity. Movement and metaphors of mobility in the films subvert the notion of *Bodenständigkeit* (a concept that connects authenticity and indigeneity, rootedness in the land) as a basis for legitimizing "true" Austrian national identity.[6] Movement in Beckermann's films, especially train travel, also evokes a landscape of loss, invoking the absence of the decimated Jewish-Austrian community in Vienna.

As a filmmaker clearly sensitive to the rhetoric of conventional documentary— with its claims to truth and the "real" and its commitment to 'empirical evidence' and objectivity—Beckermann explores in a consciously subjective manner through interviews and voiceovers, and via a montage of photographs and archival footage, as well as through her frequent use of *mise en abyme*, how Jewish identities are continually reinscribed in and performed through family and community narratives and ritual. In most of her films, Beckermann herself also occasionally appears—even if on the periphery, posing questions in an understated way, trying to understand the people, places and events that she is filming. Visible yet unwilling to provide explanations in her films, Beckermann documents her struggle to make meaning of what she sees, thereby breaking through the binary opposition of "us" in terms of filmmaker and spectators and "them," the subjects being filmed and interrogated.

To return to Catherine Russell, for a moment: citing James Clifford, she problematizes the traditional conventions of ethnographic film with its "assumption that something essential is lost when a culture becomes 'ethnographic'" (Russell 1999: 5). This so-called "salvage paradigm" with its attendant mastering or controlling gaze can be resisted in ethnographic documentaries by first recognizing allegory as a structure of representation in ethnography where "individual subjects become representative of cultural practices and even 'human' principles" and, second, "by opening ourselves to different histories" (ibid.: 5).

Russell's two-fold interpretation of Clifford's strategy for resisting the "salvage paradigm" and its ideology in ethnographic film is useful as a framework for understanding how Beckermann adapts her genre of travel documentary to construct alternative histories and identities. For Russell, the idea of "different histories" refers to the voices and histories of the colonized, and to the new forms of subjectivity articulated through texts that might be described as autoethnographies or indigenous ethnographies" (ibid.: 5). Indigeneity in Beckermann's documentaries is never represented in uniform or "authentic" terms. Moreover, it is always also "generationally inflected,"[7] continually reinterpreted and practiced by each generation. Time, thus, serves as a particularly relevant coordinate. By juxtaposing herself, her personalized questions and select commentary with diverse visual images and political perspectives in her films, Beckermann foregrounds the fact that her representations of Jewish life are neither representative nor monolithic; in effect, she thereby refutes the notion of an authentic identity—as Jewish, as Austrian, as a member of the second generation—particularly qualified to represent *the* Jewish experience.

Furthermore, as Beckermann consciously makes public the marginalized private sphere of Jewish life and memory, she calls into question the teleological historiography that is implied by the "salvage paradigm" in ethnographic documentaries. There is no origin, no final goal or arrival at a destination; central to her films is the process of investigation and experimentation with forms of representation. Taken together, then, Beckermann's film essays offer a form of memory in which we may simultaneously look backward and forward, return and recuperate what has been yet also depart on a journey of discovery. Beckermann retrieves marginalized cultural histories of Jews in the Austrian context even as she represents dynamic Jewish identities, neither mute nor vanishing, self-conscious constructions of the "other" in present-day Austria and for the future.

Paper Bridge: A Vienna Film

As ambivalent and cynical as she is about her hometown, Vienna—a city that, as she observes, "profits as ever from the architectural, scientific and artistic legacy of its murdered and expelled Jews" (Beckermann 2001: 3)[8]—remains, in both her writing and her films, the center of her artistic engagement.[9] In *Wien retour – Franz West/ Vienna Revisited* (1983), *Die papierene Brücke/Paper Bridge* (1987), and *homemad(e)* (2001), as well as in her writing (Beckermann 1984, 1989), Beckermann's project is to survey and memorialize public and private spaces in Vienna and in eastern regions belonging to the former Habsburg Empire where Jewish life existed before 1938 and where it once again exists today. I therefore refer to these films as Beckermann's Vienna films.[10]

In contrast to the two later Vienna film essays, the first, *Vienna Revisited*, utilizes the genre of the documentary in a more conventional mode of "social truth-telling" (Warren 1996: 7). She documents Jewish life and tradition in Vienna's Leopoldstadt of the 1920s and 1930s, the Zweite Bezirk, or Second District, that was home and a culturally significant shared space for some 60,000 Viennese Jews. To do this, she uses a doubled perspective: Franz West/Weintraub's personal recollections contrast with archival footage from the 1920s. West/Weintraub's narrative of his political development as a communist activist reveals the affinity between and solidarity among the dispossessed. The narrative constructs a bridge between Leopoldstadt and the workers' districts, and Red Vienna, which was devastated during the early 1930s with the rise of the Austrofascist movement. Interestingly, for a young man like West/Weintraub, *Heimat* ("home") had as much to do with the strong ties to Leopoldstadt's Jewish communities as it did to Vienna's working-class movements.

As the title *Vienna Revisited* indicates, the film represents a return to the city, although Beckermann chooses to capture an alternative Vienna. The places central to the film are not the familiar ones of the multicultural imperial capital with their mystified, glorious traditions—the Ringstraße, St Stephan's Square, Hofburg, Burgtheater, the State Opera, and the posh shopping areas of the First District, so cherished by even Beckermann's parents' generation. Instead, Beckermann places Leopoldstadt, the so-called Mazzesinsel, in the limelight, moving it from the margins to the center of her Vienna film. By equating Vienna with the Isle of Mazzo's Leopoldstadt, she valorizes a specifically Jewish perspective on the city during the 1920s. In a subsequently published collection of photographs and documents, she cites a Jewish joke of the times that further illustrates the centrality and significance of the district to Habsburg Jews. The joke goes as follows: "When a Habsburg Jew returns from a trip to Vienna, he is asked about everything he saw. He answers, 'I saw the North station, and the Prater Star and the Schiffgasse and the Carl Theater'— 'And the Hofburg palace and the Burgtheater?'—'No, I didn't make it to the outer districts'" (Beckermann and Teifer 1984: 12)[11]

If *Vienna Revisited* represents Beckermann's project of historical restoration, an artistic reconstruction of Leopoldstadt's cultural and political geography that young Jewish intellectuals like Franz West/Weintraub considered home, her second film, *Paper Bridge*, represents a far more subjective or personal quest, namely an exploration of Viennese space as the dialectic between separation and the desire to be close.[12] In *Paper Bridge*—unlike in her first Vienna film—Beckermann uses the less restrictive film essay, a genre which allows the filmmaker to work through a central question of urgent personal importance without being constrained finally to assert any definitive answers.[13]

The personal, autobiographical nature of Beckermann's quest is clearly underscored by her own explicit presence in the film in the role of both narrator and interviewer. Once again her search for identity is cast as a journey. She reverses the trajectory of her forebears who, traveling westward, arrived as hopeful immigrants in Vienna from the eastern margins of the Habsburg Empire. Surveying—indeed probing—the actual geographical sites from which her father, together with thousands of Eastern European Jews of his and earlier generations, migrated to Vienna is the center of her venture. In the course of this filmic journey, Beckermann attempts to capture images of those physical places and inhabitants made mythical through familial and cultural narratives. Some forty years after the defeat of the Third Reich, these places are consciously and artistically refracted by her own experiences, emotions, and imagination as she visits them. In her words, "I not only wanted to trace the vestiges of my family history, but also wanted to find out how the proven histories and transmitted stories blend with my own experiences and feelings."[14]

The first and final frames of the film essay are, then, set in Vienna, the site from which Beckermann embarks on her search for identity and belonging, even as she interrogates the relationship between geographical origin and identity.[15] The opening scene, a view from her private apartment through the gauze of a curtain and down onto a bustling street corner, evokes the sense of extraterritoriality, the disconcerting limbo that she describes in an essay about her youth in Vienna. The view through a diaphanous fabric suggesting invisibility, separation, and diffusion is a recurring motif in the film. At times the filter is glass, at other times a curtain, at still other times fog or steam. Thus, the experience of space in the film—whether perceived in the present or in a mythical past—is associated with opacity and removed.

Positioned in the first frame of *Paper Bridge* behind a transparent screen, separated from the city, we the observers metaphorically experience the same sense of distance from urban life. In addition, we are encouraged to imagine the process of evoking stored memories, spatialized in the film by emptied-out space, an attic, an abandoned storage room. Memory work is as much a solitary imaginative process as it is an archeological dig or the uncovering of old, worn, lost, and forgotten objects from specific sites.

Beckermann discovers that she cannot really locate the sites of her family's past; she can only approach the central geographical locations of her Jewish heritage and identity, tangentially conveyed to her via paper bridges—stories and photographs—for, as she herself observes, "Can one even arrive in the childhood of one's parents?" "Are there pictures and places that correspond to the stories with which I was raised?"[16]

At another moment she observes of those spaces of her heritage, "the closer they are, the less attainable" (*je näher, desto unerreichbarer*). Here the existential paradox has a very real cause: we know that although her destination is Czernowitz, her father's hometown, she was not granted permission to film there by the Soviet authorities.

Beckermann illustrates her ambivalence toward Vienna in a second scene early in the film, prior to her departure for the Bukovina, the birthplace of her father. In transit through the city, casually peering through the window of a Viennese streetcar from an aisle seat, she contrasts the imposing *Gründerzeit* architecture of the Ringstraße with the Vienna of the Nazi era, in which her grandmother, Rosa, went underground in order to survive. The starkness of the juxtaposition between present and past is accentuated by Beckermann's treatment of sound in the sequence. The anonymous, urban, voice-recorded announcements of streetcar stops, cast in the *heimisch* Viennese accent contrasts with the voice-over commentary through which we learn that Rosa was able to survive in Vienna by silencing her own voice, her own accented German. Her self-imposed muteness was the condition of her survival, although, as Beckermann herself hastens to add, Rosa also depended on the support of a few kind Viennese.[17]

Eastern Europe is a somewhat nebulous and desolate rural space in contrast to the vibrant urban scenes of contemporary Vienna, even if Beckermann chooses to emphasize her separation from the latter. A shot approaching an isolated frontier crossing marks her departure from the city, and as she passes this insubstantial, decontextualized, geographical boundary that seemingly delineates separate sovereign states, she also enters a space of different, foreign, even exotic sounds. Approaching, finally, her father's birthplace, the Bukovina, a region that today straddles the boundary between Ukraine and Romania, Beckermann reveals a wintery landscape, small towns with muddy streets and run-down structures, even Jewish cemeteries. The remaining Jewish community in the region is elderly and minuscule; most of the Jewish men and women, inhabiting a gendered space in the synagogue where Beckermann films them, are on the verge of emigrating to Israel, as we learn from the narrator. Yet they look like displaced extras in a film. The foreignness of Romanian space is most clearly perceived through the archaic existence of the community who live in a preindustrial world defined by an outdated, codified hierarchy of gender.

One of the final scenes of the east in *Paper Bridge* is set in Osijek, Yugoslavia, where an American film company has hired Viennese Jews, incidentally including fellow writer Robert Schindel, to serve as extras in *War and Remembrance*, a television miniseries with segments set in the concentration camp Theresienstadt. The heated debates that the actors engage in during scene-breaks revolve around means and possibilities of Jewish collaboration and resistance during the Third Reich and reflect the difficulty of recuperating memories and, with it, an affirmative identification for Jews in the Second Republic.

Beckermann ends her "Jewish quest" (*Heimatsuche auf jüdisch*) with a return to modern Vienna. The parts of Eastern Europe and the former Soviet Union she has visited represent a wasteland in relation to which Beckermann can develop neither a sense of identification nor one of belonging (Lorenz 1997: 237). In this last sequence she places herself squarely within two aspects of the cityscape: the "center" figured by the central public square, and the Jewish textile quarter with its historical buildings. No longer sequestered behind the curtains of the private space of her apartment, she ventures into public spaces. Nonetheless, her claim to belong to the city is problematized by the montage of a documentary-style sequence of images in which Waldheim supporters who have gathered in front of St Stephan's Cathedral to demonstrate against protesters (who are forcibly removed by police) make no secret of their anti-Semitic feelings, even belligerently taking on Beckermann and her father. Beckermann shows the angry exchange only briefly. The choice at the end of the film, to reappropriate the Jewish textile district, is not unproblematic either. The camera focuses on the windowpanes as they reflect the textile district, reminding us of the unstable and transparent quality of space evoked at the beginning of the film.

What does Vienna signify for Beckermann's generation at the end of the 1980s? Vienna in Beckermann's film is the ambivalent space where familiarity and comfort coexist in tension with the sense of not belonging, a tension that leads to continuous intellectual engagement. *Paper Bridge* impresses upon us that members of Beckermann's generation must construct their own places of belonging via the memories of their parents and grandparents. And, they must rely on their own imaginations to demystify by defamiliarizing the notion of territorial identification or belonging, an identification always bound by time. Beckermann's visual and aural trek in search of her paternal roots ends with the realization that locating Jewish identity in terms of rootedness within a fixed, geographically definable space such as Vienna is impossible: charting identity signifies a never-ending nomadic enterprise, a continuous routing or path-finding without a specific destination. Through narration juxtaposed with images of actual geographical sites, cinema itself provides passages to re-experience the past, even if in mediated forms.

Staging the Bar/Bat Mitzvah in Twenty-first Century Vienna

Ruth Beckermann's most recent documentary film, *Zorro's Bar Mitzvah* (2006), seems to corroborate the very positive sentiment expressed on the cover story of a contemporary issue of *Profil*, Austria's equivalent to *Time Magazine*: "Shalom Vienna: Spirit of Optimism in Vienna's Jewish Community."[18] Beckermann's film showcases four lavish yet culturally diverse Bar/Bat Mitzvahs in contemporary Vienna. In fact, this film represents the first of Beckermann's documentaries to specifically feature the celebration of Jewish life in Austria today. If most of her documentaries (from 1980 through 2001) are testimonials or witness films, elegiac enactments of the mourning process, invested in constructing a counter-memory, Beckermann's latest documentary, in which she "performs ethnography" (Schechner and Appel 1990: xv), represents Jewish cultural ritual in a type of experimental reflexive film.

The subject of *Zorro's Bar Mitzvah* is, of course, again a political one as it bears witness to the renewed existence of Jewish life in the Vienna of the twenty-first century. With this film, Beckermann goes public with a private, familial, cultural, and religious event, the bar/bat mitzvah, or Jewish rite of passage, a foundational practice that is invisible and even exotic in the context of the Catholic Austrian majority culture.[19] The film thus stands in stark contrast to her own experience of growing up Jewish in postwar Vienna, exterritorialized and in the gaping divide between the private Jewish sphere and the dominant non-Jewish Austrian public arena of the 1950s through 1980s.

Beckermann's documentary, set in the Vienna of the new millennium, seems thus to confirm that the second and third generations of Jews in Austria are actually initiating a transformation that includes developing a robust sense of identity that is founded not exclusively on a history of deadly Nazi persecution or even nostalgia for an idealized Habsburgian past. In Beckermann's documentary about a celebration that marks the point when children become "sons or daughters of the commandment" and, thereby, assume both the privileges and obligations of fully fledged membership in the adult Jewish community, four youngsters' initiation rites underscore how this modern identification process is both confidently and creatively enacted in present-day Austria. Indeed, Beckermann's bar/bat mitzvah film attests to the existence of a colorful, sophisticated, and affluent, intercultural Jewish-Austrian community living in Vienna today.

Moreover, Beckermann's coming-of-age film not only illustrates and publicly acknowledges this aforementioned "spirit of optimism" among Vienna's next generations of Jews; it fulfills a concrete pedagogical objective. It initiates—especially young German-speaking—gentiles into the vocabulary and grammar of the bar mitzvah. Beckermann's official website[20] includes a ten-page .pdf file of pedagogical materials for *Zorro's Bar Mitvah* developed by two educators (Sonja Haberbusch in conjunction with Maria Wildam) for a primarily non-Jewish Austrian school audience unfamiliar with both the tradition, meaning and structure of the bar/bat mitzvah. In addition, under the rubric "facts" we find a description of this family celebration, its three components or stages, its symbolic, religious and social meaning as well as diagrams of the way in which *T'ffilin*, or prayer bands, are properly applied.[21] This same concern for educating her audience is clearly evident in her film. With her camera, Beckermann accompanies four very different 12- and 13-year-olds through aspects of their bar/bat mitzvah preparation, ceremony and celebration, and the attendant excitement and anxiety unique to each. Moreover, in her opening credits, the four youngsters are identified as costars by their first names, Tom, Moishy, Sharon, Sophie; indeed, each is given equal billing in the film one after the other through the three phases. The use of first names further personalizes the experience for young gentile children and emphasizes the role that the youngster plays as the central figure in this Jewish initiation rite.

Mixing observational passages (watching with her camera) with interviews with the four teenagers and their families about what this coming-of-age ritual means, Beckermann creates a frank intimacy of perspective that undermines the process of "othering" so typical of traditional ethnographic film. Furthermore, Beckermann's film constructs "otherness" in terms of a diversity of the Jewish community in Vienna that cannot be associated with a single ethnicity and where multilinguality is the norm. Vienna is clearly identified as the backdrop of each ceremony. But each of the youngsters has a multicultural background and is at the very least bilingual. While each speaks a Viennese-inflected German, German is not the mother tongue. In fact, the exact multiethnic background of each child is not necessarily explicitly revealed in each case in the film. Moreover, the cameraman, André Wanne—the self-styled "Bar Mitzvah Filmmaker"—who is hired by the individual families to film the three stages of the celebration, and whom Beckermann, in turn, follows with her camera throughout the film, emphasizes that there is no "typical" celebration or event within this intercultural Jewish community whose location happens to be Vienna.

Through her mix of aesthetic devices such as interviews, camera angles, and above all *mise-en-scène*, Beckermann's ethnographic performance film is as much about making visible an otherwise invisible yet significant initiation rite in the Austrian context as about how conscious Jews are about remembering the ritual even as it is being performed or invented. Documentary theorist Bill Nichols reminds us that "documentaries always were forms of representation, never clear windows onto 'reality'; the filmmaker [is] always a participant-witness and an active fabricator of meaning, a producer of cinematic discourse rather than a neutral or all-knowing reporter of the way things truly are" (Nichols 2005: 18). Thus, the film reflects on the role of memory-making within the diverse Jewish communities of Vienna.

Beckermann highlights how a particular feature of this Jewish ritual includes the impetus to stage, document, and remember the performance even in the process of experiencing it. It is a consciously staged event, carefully choreographed for the camera, so that it can be viewed again later, even as a form of entertainment, by friends and family. Beckermann thereby foregrounds the tension on the one hand of bearing witness to the "reality" of the event, and memorializing it and of actually experiencing it as an entry into adulthood on the other. Beckermann reminds us in this self-conscious filming process that her view is not a comprehensive one, one that can capture the event in its totality. Beckermann draws attention to a third metatextual layer: to the artifice of the mechanics of memory-making. She undermines the illusion of a complete view by having her camera observe the cameraman, André Wanne, filming the event and then editing the film clips. Occasionally, Wanne's camera blocks Beckermann's gaze, so that we can only hear but not actually see the events—sometimes we are confronted with someone's back, for instance. In any case, the boundary between personal experience and public performance of becoming a Jewish adult throughout the film remains fuzzy and the film problematizes the possibility of freezing experience into memory as it occurs.

The performative nature is further emphasized by the fact that three of the youngsters are encouraged to "star" in video clips created specifically to invite family and friends to their bar/bat mitzvah or to be viewed later as entertainment. Each child and witnessing family members and friends are also encouraged to pay attention to the camera that is recording the performance—even if they are not supposed to look directly into it, as Sophie tells her friends. Thus, the actual coming of age as a religious, social, and ethnic ritual becomes "official" when it has not only been witnessed by the immediate community in the present but can be transmitted to absent members and/or viewed again in the future. There is, by the way, also an entertainment dimension. The cameraman who is also a videographer tells us in the film that these video clips become a popular form of entertainment for friends and relatives. The title of this documentary, in fact, refers to the role that Sharon chooses for himself and that he enacts almost professionally in the Vienna woods with a whole film crew, props, and stuntmen.

Beckermann does not present a single interpretation of the bar/bat mitzvah that might be representative. She contrasts generational perspectives, thereby keeping her film open-ended. The Zorro film clip, whose production Beckermann includes in her documentary, is a case in point. Sharon has chosen to play Antonio Banderas, a Hollywood icon representing sexy masculinity, opposite Catherine Zeta-Jones. Beckermann wonders on camera about the choice of Zorro as a "motto" for Sharon's bar mitzvah, but Sharon's mother tells her that Zorro is quite appropriately associated with Spain and the family's Sephardic roots. Zorro's ethnicity as an outsider outlaw is indirectly evoked. Interestingly, in an interview with Anja Salomonowitz about the film, Beckermann reveals that in her correspondence with the owner of the Zorro trademark, she has found out that Zorro may well have been a recusant Jew, a *morrana* dedicated to *tikkun olam*, the salvation of the world (Beckermann n.d.).

It is the grandparental generation in Beckermann's film that broaches the topic of gender difference within Judaism. The gendered gaze of the camera, too, reveals fractures within the community along gendered lines. Beckermann includes one bat mitzvah, and we are hard pressed not to notice that it differs from the other ceremonies because Sophie does not wear the prayer bands. But it is the grandmother who rolls her eyes when her husband applauds the practice of separating men and women in the bar mitzvah or in the synagogue in general. Furthermore, Beckermann captures the gendered nature of the ceremony with her camera by documenting the physical division between men and women at the Wailing Wall in Israel, at the Orthodox Jewish ceremony and celebration, and during the Sephardic celebration. Beckermann's camera at times challenges gendered boundaries by looking from the male space at the women behind barriers and at other times peering with the women through the barriers at the men celebrating in the central space of celebration.

The open-endedness of the film is enhanced by Beckermann's brief but intimate conversations with each of the teenagers and with their parents and grandparents. She asks the youngsters and their families to reflect on the meaning and experience of the bar and bat mitzvah, challenging any notion of objectivity in her ethnographic study in the process. The answers vary: For the grandparents it symbolizes coming of age, and against the backdrop of deadly discrimination it is a reminder of survival. For Sophie's mother, it is what her daughter wants, a ceremony prescribed by religion (*unsere Religion sagt, wir müssen*), as well as an opportunity to see many dear friends and reaffirm a sense of community. Sophie recites the line from the speech that she presents at the synagogue, that the bat mitzvah initiates her into the generation of Jewish women. For Moishy and his father, Orthodox Jews, and for Tom, it means a shift of spiritual responsibility; Moishy now carries his own sins; Tom's mother remarks that as she is married to a gentile, there is now through Tom a true Jewish man in the house who can perform the rituals and say the prayers. For all four youngsters, the ceremony is constitutive of Jewishness. But all four of the youngsters expose an uncertainty about the ceremony through their self-conscious laughter and gestures.

In conclusion, then, *Zorro's Bar Mitzvah* reflects on the Jewish initiation rite and its performative significance in both affirming and recreating a communal identity that extends across various generations, nationalities and ethnicities. The film represents an ethnographic practice in which filmmaker Beckermann steps away from the "salvage paradigm" particular to ethnographic documentaries with their ontologies of loss or their mission of preservation. She documents in a self-conscious and even self-critical manner how from within her minority culture as a Jew in Vienna she constructs this "other" culture, one that hearkens back to a historical textual foundation (the Torah) that while influenced by a vibrant interculturality redefines itself through generational interpretation for the future.

Significantly, Beckermann's film goes beyond representing a celebration of renewed Jewish culture in Austria today. It highlights a diasporic consciousness that is not simply equivalent to multiculturalism, which—as Boyarin and Boyarin remind us—is invariably tied to a single, impermeable national or ethnic identity, or to a pluralism which "reduces incommensurate differences to equivalent shades upon a single palette" (Boyarin and Boyarin 2002: 9–10). The Jewish diasporic community as showcased in this film through four ethnically mixed and unique performances of the bar mitzvah is "founded on generational connection and attendant anamnestic responsibilities and pleasures," on family connections and practices that aid memory (Boyarin and Boyarin 1995: 313). The members of this ethnically mixed community that Beckermann has chosen to represent in her film are "rediasporized"—that is, situated only temporarily in Vienna and maintaining a commemorative relationship to the notion of homeland, or rather an imagined series of homelands which sit on top of one another, a palimpsest.[22] Sephardic Spain, symbolized through the American popular film *Zorro*; Jerusalem and the Wailing Wall; the United States primarily through Sophie's language of preference and her father's speech; Eastern Europe through the Yiddish spoken by Moishy at his celebration—all are evoked and commemorated as variants of homeland. In other words, as these young people and their extended families enact the Jewish ritual of coming of age they convey a heterogeneous sociopolitical community, one that is not predicated on an identification with a territorial nation-state. This diasporic community thus challenges the notion of an ethnically fixed homogeneous nation situated within permanent geographical boundaries. I am reminded of what Daniel and Jonathan Boyarin have suggested about the potential of diasporic Jewish culture in our interconnected contemporary world: "diasporic identity is a disaggregated identity. Jewishness disrupts the very categories of identity because it is not national, not genealogical, not religious, but all of these in dialectical tension with one another" (ibid.: 333). Indeed, with her films, Beckermann seems to point to the potential of a diasporic model that contests discourses of autochthony, indigeneity and territorial self-determination in favor of an alternative and imaginative way of theorizing identification in a world that has grown increasingly interdependent.

Notes

I am grateful to the Institute of the Study of Culture and Society at Bowling Green State University for the research fellowship in Spring Semester 2008 that facilitated the completion of this article. Special thanks to Dr Vivian Patraka, director of ICS, and to my fellow ICS scholars for their lively conversation and encouragement.

1. "I'm interested in the fringes or periphery of documentary films" (*Mich interessieren beim Film die Randbereiche des Dokumentarfilms*) (Beckermann, in Reiter 1997: 22).
2. In her voiceover in *Die papierene Brücke/Paper Bridge* (1987), Beckermann poses the question: *Wer sind wir, die Kinder der 2. Generation? Was macht uns aus?* All further translations of Beckermann citations in this article are the author's.
3. *Jüdische Existenz in Österreich nach 1945 ist mit einer Fülle von Identitätsproblemen verbunden. Sie ist ein wackeliges Kartenhaus, gezimmert aus schmerzlichen Erfahrungen und hoffnungsvollen Phantasiebildern.*
4. *Es sind eigentlich alle drei Reisen, in gewisser Weise, aber von der Form und vom Aufbau sind alle drei verschieden.*
5. See also Pile and Thrift 's observation that "[n]owadays, identity is often hedged about with spatial metaphors, with what Gilroy ... calls the 'spatial focus' ... The ethnic absolutism of 'root' metaphors, fixed in place, is replaced by mobile 'route' metaphors which can lay down a challenge to the fixed identities of 'cultural insiderism', metaphors like diaspora" (Pile and Thrift 1995: 10).
6. In *Nach Jerusalem/Toward Jerusalem* (1990) and *Ein flüchtiger Zug nach dem Orient/A Fleeting Passage to the Orient* (1999), Beckermann again problematizes metaphors of groundedness or rootedness as the basis for identity, albeit in very different ways. Beckermann continues to develop her poetics of geography with *Toward Jerusalem*, a film in which the road from Tel Aviv to Jerusalem becomes a chronotope, a site of encounters where identities, histories, languages,

and religious and political practices occasionally intersect but also coexist in parallel worlds. Beckermann thereby multiplies and interrogates the spatial metaphors that are often used to validate communal or national identity. In effect, she re-evaluates the notion of geographical origin or locatedness that often serves as an integral category of identity. In *A Fleeting Passage to the Orient*, Beckermann constitutes her subject, the Empress Elisabeth ("Sissi"), in spatial terms within the first frames that show us an Austrian snowscape viewed from a fast-moving train. Swiftly follows a view from an ocean liner traveling through a vast, somewhat amorphous seascape with a final panning shot of a Middle Eastern cityscape. Beckermann's voiceover observes that the Egyptian orient is the proper context for her "Elisabeth film", a counterview of Sissi, the outsider. A seascape, not a snowscape, is where Beckermann chooses to relocate this romanticized woman, icon of a glorious Habsburg past, on the occidental periphery (*am entferntesten Ort*). Here, Beckermann feels she can invoke her version of Elisabeth, the ex-centric European, who claimed "I belong nowhere, not in concepts nor in a tradition" (*ich passe nirgends hinein, nicht in Begriffen oder Tradition*), and whose favorite retreat was to lose herself as a cosmopolitan flâneur in the metropolitan centers around the world.

7.   Irene Kacandes suggested this term as an alternative to Marianne Hirsch's "postmemory" at the "Trajectories of Memory Conference: Intergenerational Representations of the Holocaust in History and the Arts", Bowling Green State University, Ohio, March 2006.

8.   [P]*rofitiert nach wie vor von dem architektonischen, wissenschaftlichen und künstlerischen Erbe der ermordeten und vertriebenen Juden.*

9.   As Lorenz notes, "Although Beckermann has lived in Paris for several years, Vienna remains the site of her intellectual involvement" (Lorenz 1997: 242).

10. Portions of this section first appeared in Guenther (2004).

11. *Als einer von einer Reise nach Wien zurückkommt, wird er gefragt, was er alles gesehen hat: 'Ich hab' den Nordbahnhof gesehen und den Praterstern und die Schiffgasse und das Carltheater.'— "Und die Hofburg hast du nicht gesehen und das Burgtheater?'—Nein, in die äußeren Bezirke bin ich nicht gekommen.'"*

12. Compare Renate Posthofen's reading of the film: a "quest for a virtual and spiritual home, and the recovery of her cultural and historical roots. It leads the filmmaker to explore the reality of her life in Vienna and how it relates to her Jewish heritage" (Posthofen 1997: 266).

13. In an interview with the *Linke*, Beckermann explains: "Ever since *Vienna Revisited* I have been preoccupied with challenging the narrow confines of the form of the documentary film. I wanted to find forms where language was not simply used as commentary, ancillary to the images that served as evidential material. Because with such stories facts are less significant than feelings and legends ... *Vienna Revisited* adheres to a very strict documentary form" (*Schon seit* Wien retour *habe ich mich damit beschäftigt, wie ich diese engen Formen des Dokumentarfilmes überschreiten kann. Ich wollte Formen finden, in denen die Sprache nicht nur als Kommentar verwendet wird und die Bilder nicht nur als Beweisstücke behandelt werden. Weil es gerade bei einer solchen Geschichte weniger um die Fakten geht als um Gefühle und Legenden ...* Wien retour *ist nach einer sehr strengen dokumentarischen Form aufgebaut*) (Hirt 1987: 30). For a helpful discussion of the film essay, see Lopate (1996): For Lopate, both essay and film essay center on "a continual asking of questions—not necessarily finding 'solutions,' but enacting the struggle for truth in full view" (ibid.: 245). Lopate includes five characteristics of the film essay, all of which apply to Beckermann's films: 1) a connection between words and images; 2) a unified voice; 3) a central tension or argument; 4) a personal point of view; 5) eloquence or articulateness (ibid.: 246–47).

14. *Ich wollte nicht nur den wenigen Spuren meiner Familiengeschichte nachgehen, sondern herausfinden, wie sich die erwiesenen und erzählten Geschichten mit meinen eigenen Erlebnissen und Gefühlen vermischen* (Beckerman n.d.).

15. In a more recent interview, Beckermann states that for her, "[b]elonging has nothing to do with a plot of land or a country" (*Zugehörigkeit hat für mich nichts mit einem Boden oder mit einem Land zu tun*) (in Reiter 1997: 19).

16. *Wie kann man auch in der Kindheit der Eltern ankommen? Gibt es Bilder zu den Geschichten, mit denen ich aufgewachsen bin?*

17. Compare this with Beckermann's statement: "There were people in this city of Vienna who saved my grandmother. Yes, my Eastern-Jewish, Yiddish-speaking Oma Rosa was able to survive here ... Because there were people who helped her. (*Weil es Menschen gab, die ihr halfen ... Ihre Stimme ist leise, man hört sie kaum im Gebrüll der anderen*) (Beckermann 2001: 6).

18. *Profil*, 20 February 2006.

19. Bar mitvah is the initiation rite for boys, while the bat mitvah is the girls' equivalent.

20. See: http://www.ruthbeckermann.com. A filmography and description of her films and press releases can be found on the website as well.

21. See: http://www.ruthbeckermann.com/zorroderfilm/fakten.php.

22. Jonathan and Danial Boyarin posit that a "distinctive feature of Jewish diaspora is the repeated experience of *rediasporization*. This results in a situation where, to borrow from Homi Bhabha, the imaginary Jewish homeland is 'less than one and double': Zion longed for and imagined through Cordoba, Cairo, or Vilna, and these frequently palimpsested one on the other such that Cairo becomes a remembered Cordoba and the new Jerusalem a remembered Vilna" (Boyarin and Boyarin 2002: 11). Prior to this, they reflect on reasons why the Jewish diaspora might still be considered as a precise model of the diasporic experience. "One of these is the persistence of Jewish communities, not only outside the homeland, and not only in the absence of political hegemony enjoyed by fellows in the homeland, but, for centuries, in the absence even of a substantial community of fellows actually living in the homeland, such that the Jewish diasporic relation *to the homeland* ... is primarily commemorative, rather than kin-based or economic" (ibid.: 11).

References

Beckermann, R. 1984. "Historischer Essay," in R. Beckermann and H. Teifer (eds), *Mazzesinsel: Juden in der Wiener Leopoldstadt 1918–1938*. Vienna: Löcker Verlag, 1–29.

———. 1989. *Unzugehörig: Österreicher und Juden nach 1945*. Vienna: Löcker Verlag.

———. 2001. "Auf der Brücke: Rede zur Verleihung des Manes Sperber-Preises, Wien, 16/10/2000," *German Quarterly* 4(1): 1–7.

———. 2002. "Illusionen und Kompromisse: Zur Identität der Wiener Juden nach der Schoah," in G. Botz, I. Oxaal, M. Pollak, and N. Scholz (eds), *Eine zerstörte Kultur: Jüdisches Leben und Antisemitismus in Wien seit dem 19. Jahrhundert*. Vienna: Czernin Verlag, 382–92.

———. 2006. "Dokumentarfilm in Österreich: Das Geheimnis des Familienfilms, Ruth Beckermann und Arash im Dialog," *Ray: Filmmagazin*, October, 92–96.

———. n.d. "Zur Produktion," an introduction to her text on *Die papierene Brücke*.

Boyarin, D. and J. Boyarin. 1995. "Diaspora: Generation and the Ground of Jewish Identity," in K.A. Appiah and H.L. Gates (eds), *Identities*. Chicago: University of Chicago Press, 305–37.

———. 2002. *Powers of Diaspora: Two Essays on the Relevance of Jewish Culture*. Minneapolis: University of Minnesota Press.

Guenther, C. 2004. "The Politics of Location in Ruth Beckermann's 'Vienna Films'," *Modern Austrian Literature* 37(3/4): 33–46.

Hirt, E. 1987. "Immer wieder Illusionen haben..." *Linke*, 2 April, 29–32.

Lopate, P. 1996. "In Search of the Centaur: The Essay-film," in C. Warren (ed.), *Beyond Document: Essays on Nonfiction Film*. Hanover, CT: Wesleyan University Press, 243–70.

Lorenz, D. 1997. *Keepers of the Motherland: German Texts by Jewish Women Writers*. Lincoln: University of Nebraska Press.

Nichols, B. 2005. "The Voice of Documentary," in A. Rosenthal and J. Corner (eds), *New Challenges for Documentary*, 2nd edn. Manchester: Manchester University Press, 17–33.

Pile, S. and N. Thrift. 1995. "Introduction," in S. Pile and N. Thrift (eds), *Mapping the Subject: Geographies of Cultural Transformation*. London: Routledge, xx–xx.

Posthofen, R. 1997. "Ruth Beckermann: Re-activating Memory – In Search of Time Lost," in M. Lamb-Faffelberger (ed.), *Out of the Shadows: Essays on Contemporary Austrian Women Writers and Filmmakers*. Riverside, CA: Ariadne, 264–76.

Reiter, A. 1997. "Ruth Beckermann und die jüdische Nachkriegsgeneration in Österreich" and "Wovon man geträumt? Auszug aus einem Interview mit Ruth Beckermann," *Mit der Ziehharmonika: Literatur/Widerstand/Exil* 14(4): 19–24.

Russell, C. 1999. *Experimental Ethnography: The Work of Film in the Age of Video*. Durham, NC: Duke University Press.

Schechner, R., and W. Appel (eds). 1990. *By Means of Performance*. Cambridge: Cambridge University Press.

Warren, C. 1996. "Introduction, with a Brief History of Nonfiction Film," in C. Warren (ed.), *Beyond Document: Essays on Nonfiction Film*. Hanover, CT: Wesleyan University Press, 1–22.

Part II

Barbara Albert
and the Female Re-focus

Chapter 5

A New Community of Women: Barbara Albert's *Nordrand*

Dagmar Lorenz

The work of the Austrian filmmaker Barbara Albert is informed by feminist theory and an awareness of the ideas feminist intellectuals and artists advocated in the 1970s and 1980s.[1] Her film *Nordrand/Northern Skirts* (1999) suggests that there are new options available to women coming of age at the turn of the new millennium. Yet it takes exceptional circumstances for her protagonists to recognize and avail themselves of their opportunities and forge a life of their choosing against the pressures of their misogynist environment.

Nordrand was Albert's first major feature film and an immediate success, receiving the Thomas-Pluch Film Script Prize, the Vienna Film Prize, and the Fipresci Prize at the 1999 Biennale in Venice. Nina Proll, in the role of Jasmin, was awarded the Marcello Mastroianni Prize. *Nordrand* integrates feminist concerns with issues at the forefront of Austrian turn-of-the-millennium debates: the rise of the rightwing FPÖ, the so-called Freedom Party, and increasing hostilities against "foreigners" (*Ausländer*) encouraged by this party. In the intricate network of Albert's film, problems of gender and ethnicity are interlinked. *Nordrand* examines the lives of two women associated with the milieu of Vienna's traditionally proletarian northern suburbs. The scenes in this environment reveal that whatever working-class consciousness may once have existed here has been replaced by an underclass lifestyle revolving around television, beer, and sex.

One of Albert's protagonists, Jasmin, is an Austrian working-class woman; the other, Tamara, a young health professional, comes from a Serbian middle-class background. Her superior class status is offset by her outsider position as a non-Austrian. As these women find themselves faced with difficulties that threaten their chances of self-realization, they join forces and embark on an unconventional path

LIVERPOOL JOHN MOORES UNIVERSITY
LEARNING SERVICES

together to ensure the independence that they did not find within their families and in their relationships with men. The film ends when the two heterosexual women establish a household together, one of them expecting a child, the other one focusing on her career. This arrangement provides them with much-needed stability and security. *Nordrand* ends on a vision of an individualistic solution to the complex problems faced by Viennese women.

A report on Viennese young women published in 1999, the year Albert's film was released, provides a stark account of the plight of young women.[2] The information provided in this report helps to situate *Nordrand* within its proper context. The overwhelming problems revealed in the report and in Albert's film suggest that the feminist movement as well as the changes in legislation it effected have made little difference in the everyday lives of women. In 1999, women still lag behind in terms of education, job chances, social status, and quality of life. Rather than institutional changes and collective action, Albert emphasizes the potential of individual women making a difference to their lives through solidarity and commitment. The postfeminist dilemma identified in *Nordrand* calls for women to muster the determination to help themselves. There is no one else helping the protagonists to turn their lives around and overcome the trauma of abuse and neglect. The pessimistic aspect of Albert's film is the message that there is no social network to sustain women; the positive aspect is the assumption that women have the strength and resourcefulness to take care of themselves and each other.

Nordrand is set in what Horwath calls the "wintry and very unglamorous Vienna north side," partly at the women's places of work, a pastry shop and a hospital, and in different locations throughout the city (Horwath 2007). The images characterizing the diverse urban population show that Vienna has become increasingly complex. As Alexander Horwath observes, "The film recognizes that Vienna has become a melting pot again for the first time since the 1930s" (ibid.). Motivated by her opposition to the xenophobia of the Freedom Party, Albert emphasizes the potential for cross-cultural empathy and cooperation within a small group of differently marginalized individuals: an Austrian working-class woman, a Serbian refugee, a Romanian, and a Bosnian man. Underscoring the exceptional disposition of the protagonists, the film provides as a backdrop scenes of war and population displacement in border areas, police raids against immigrants and refugees in the city, and mob activity by young men, all of which define the mentality prevalent around 1999. Jasmin's home environment, the suburban working-class housing projects, is of particular interest because the plight of women in this social stratum is readily apparent. Albert's film lacks the leftist fervor of the 1960s and 1970s but rather registers ubiquitous social problems: the disintegration of the proletarian family, alcoholism, addiction to television, brutality against women, and economic problems. The film also suggests positive potential within this group, notably women's capacity for mutual support and affection, expressed in the bonding between mother, daughters, and sisters in Jasmin's family.

In contrast to the leftist and feminist critical literature of the 1960s, 1970s, and 1980s, Albert's analysis of Viennese society does not instill activism. The spectrum of the problems in 1999 is too diffuse, involving issues of ethnicity, religion, class, and nationality, personal as well as social problems. Gender-related challenges are explored within this larger framework in a culture and class-specific context. For instance, the Bosnian Senad, Jasmin's rescuer, displays an entirely different attitude towards sex and intimacy than Jasmin's loutish Austrian boyfriends. Senad recognizes Jasmin's feminine side immediately despite her unflattering clothes and expresses his appreciation for her with a gift he buys with his last few schillings: a blond-haired angel doll. The fact that he also returns Jasmin's lost wallet with its contents untouched lends further credence to this chivalrous gesture as an expression of a kind of old-fashioned respect for women that seems absent among the Austrian males. The latter treat Jasmin rudely and, instead of making her gifts, supply her with alcohol and take advantage of her when she gets drunk. Shockingly, they do not seem to care whether she lives or dies and leave her in freezing temperatures on the bank of the Danube canal after a night of partying.

Jasmin appears to be conditioned to expect no better. She understands her buddy's ruthlessness in light of her own family situation and has even come to enjoy rough, indiscriminate sex to which she responds with wild laughter. Her defiance represents an appropriate albeit self-destructive reaction to her situation, which is emblematic of the international political scene as well. Images and sounds of war— explosions and destruction—repeatedly remind the viewer of the ongoing war in the Balkans. Impressions of gang crimes in Vienna's streets are set parallel to the military scenery. Both types of images pertaining to the public sphere point to a spreading machismo, which is amplified by Albert's soundtrack, featuring harsh rock and hip-hop, an acoustic signal of the progressive marginalization of the feminine sphere. At a New Year's Eve celebration, however, the four lovers—Jasmin, Senad, Tamara, and Valentin—dance to the sounds of a Viennese waltz reminiscent of the romance and glamour of a past era.

For the women protagonists in *Nordrand* it takes near-catastrophes to reassess and readjust their lives. Jasmin has a narrow escape from death and Tamara learns about her brother's death while her Austrian boyfriend is deployed in the Balkans. The women face an unwanted pregnancy, have an abortion, and break up with their Austrian lovers, who only add conflict to their lives. Soon thereafter they enter into more gratifying relationships with Eastern European men, but those entanglements do not last either since the men leave Vienna. However, it is not relationship problems but pregnancy that constitutes the turning point in the women's lives. At a moment of existential need, Jasmin and Tamara recognize the true character of their boyfriends. Jasmin is beaten and thrown out of her lover's apartment when he learns that she is pregnant. He has no intention of helping her with the abortion, let alone taking care of a child. Tamara becomes aware that marrying her Austrian boyfriend would create intolerable dependency for her. Facing up to their own desires, Jasmin and Tamara understand that the traditional way of life—marriage and the nuclear family—is not an option for them at this point.

Until their pregnancies, Jasmin and Tamara lived without self-scrutiny with regard to social norms and the example of their parents. Tamara's ambition was professional achievement, Jasmin's being popular with men. Tamara ends her pregnancy because her career is more important to her than motherhood and marriage; but she becomes pregnant again soon after the abortion. Jasmin realizes that she wants a child, but not a husband. Juxtaposing two women of different background, interest and talent, who make different reproductive choices, Albert, steering clear of biological essentialism, treats motherhood as a matter of individual preference. Nonetheless, the emotional closeness that arises between Jasmin and Tamara as a result of their common background as classmates and their ordeal at the abortion clinic suggests that shared social and biological experiences can become the basis for a deep friendship. Finally, Albert's theme is the creation of a new sisterhood, a new community of women in the midst of, and yet apart from, the male dominated public sphere.

In her next film, *Böse Zellen/Free Radicals* (2003), Albert explores difficulties women of different age groups encounter in their private lives and their work environment, their lack of preparedness for disaster, and the failure of science to calculate risk. In this film, extreme events—a plane crash and a car accident—place women in borderline situations that call for a reassessment of their expectations and options. The women who succeed do so by embracing life in the moment (Holden 2007). Important topics in Albert's films are the disadvantages women have traditionally suffered and the fact that these problems persist in the postfeminist era, counter to the widely held notion that women have "got it made." Regressive trends, her films show, jeopardize the gains made in the struggle for equality.[3] But Albert also explores new lifestyle options open to average women, including reproductive choices, better employment chances, and single life as a result of better career opportunities. She also reveals the way that these new possibilities can be used against women. Jasmin, for example, is pressured by her lover to have an abortion. Thus a woman's right to choose becomes the obligation to choose what the man prefers. Other male characters take advantage of a woman's earning capacity or exploit crisis situations to assert control, as is the case with Tamara's boyfriend.

The gender-related problems examined in *Nordrand* also include the excessive stress to which women like Jasmin's mother are exposed in their dual role as homemakers and workers, and the oppression they suffer within the domestic sphere. Women are relegated to second-class jobs, have limited access to education, and encounter assaults on their dignity by men who treat them as commodities when they are young and lose interest in them when they grow older. More generally, *Nordrand* explores the interconnectedness of gender-related problems and age discrimination and substance abuse. The close-up portraits of Jasmin and Tamara show and implicitly criticize the subservient roles these women adopt at their work place and their submissive behavior towards men. The flashbacks to their childhood suggest that these problems are the product of negative formative experiences.

The findings of the 1999 Wiener Report on Viennese young women mentioned above correspond to the women's condition depicted in *Nordrand*. For example, the report documents that it is common for girls and young women to experience neglect, violence, and sexual abuse (Lechner et al. 1999: 63). All of these conditions are present in the family of Jasmin, whose father is a tyrant and an alcoholic who beats his wife and molests his daughters, turning from the older girl to the next younger one. When he can no longer maintain his dominant role with Jasmin he avails himself of her younger sister, still a little girl. Since Jasmin has ceased to be the object of his desire she is now the target of his scorn. He ends up evicting her from the family home because the presence of an unruly grown-up daughter obviously aware of his conduct undermines his authority.

The relationship between Jasmin and her mother is one of affection and tenderness, but also of neglect. In one scene the two women fall asleep in each other's arms in front of the television. In another scene the females of the household watch an escapist television program about a fairy-tale princess that appeals to their unfulfilled yearnings for love and status. In both instances the women seem relaxed, even joyful, in the absence of the short-tempered, unkempt father. The mother's submissive demeanor in his presence indicates that she is intimidated and unable to oppose him. Even though she fails to protect her daughters, her maternal love represents a positive element in Jasmin's chaotic home life. Later, it is again the mother who shows concern by stopping at the pastry shop where Jasmin works, bringing her some necessities and reporting family events.

The information provided in the Wiener Report underscores the frequency of domestic sexual abuse, a prominent theme in Albert's films. It is estimated that in 1999 there were 10,000 to 25,000 sexually abused children in Vienna, and that every third girl between the ages of one and sixteen had been a victim of sexual violence, most likely between the ages of six and eleven. Of the thirty-four children aged between one and six listed in the report as victims of sexual abuse, nineteen are boys and twenty-five girls. These figures imply that the more helpless a child appears, the more attractive she or he is to potential abusers, almost all of whom are male (ibid.: 63, 66). *Nordrand* posits as a possible remedy against male violence an exclusively female environment for Jasmin's future child. From the role males play in *Nordrand* this seems to be the logical conclusion. Male characters are shown to occupy a marginal and even destructive position vis-à-vis their families. This applies particularly to Jasmin's father, who lives with his wife and children. Yet, even more congenial characters like Senad and Roman are difficult to imagine in the role of caregivers and homemakers. Cast as rescuers and lovers—note for example the significance of the romantic name Valentin—they are passing strangers, troubadours, but not family men. The inability of many men to contribute to a nurturing family environment is also indicated by the Wiener Report. It claims that in most cases sex offenders are familiar to their child victims, often relatives or family friends (ibid.: xx). Only 6 to 15 per cent percent of the perpetrators are strangers. According to the report there is a greater likelihood for offenses to be detected in the working-class milieu, which makes Albert's chosen setting the appropriate one for the film. In more affluent groups the likelihood of sex crimes being covered up is assumed to be greater. Yet, *Nordrand* shows that a law of silence also prevails among proletarians, who protect abusers.

Jasmin's mother does not warn or defend her daughters but pampers them. Thus she inadvertently teaches them that abuse is a woman's destiny. Even though the attempts at female bonding in Jasmin's family provide a respite from abuse, they occur on the home territory of the drunken and violent father—there is never a question of leaving him or notifying the authorities, and the existing condition is not remedied. *Nordrand* focuses on the plight of the female child, which is also the case in the Wiener Report. The latter also reveals that violence in the wider sense—including neglect, undernourishment, homelessness, and a lack of educational and emotional support—affects children of both genders in shocking numbers. Boys are approximately three times more likely than girls to suffer physical violence leading to injuries and even death. Girls, on the other hand, are more frequently the victims of sexual and psychological abuse (ibid.: 64, 65). With these findings in mind the viewer of *Nordrand* can conclude that the young Austrian ruffians in Albert's film, Jasmin's friends, are shaped by a background of abuse.

More specifically, however, Albert brings to light a wide spectrum of brutality against women and provides insights into the conditioning of female children for their role as recipients of violence, while boys are socialized to become its perpetrators. *Nordrand* provides glimpses into the role of the military and its glamorization through hero worship and military parades. The film also points to the function of the media and political culture in the construction of gender. Male children are encouraged to identify with soldiers and embrace the ideal of the fighter. At the parade sequences little boys are shown emulating the smug behavior of young men; girls and women look on and cheer. Included in *Nordrand* is television footage showing tanks and soldiers in fighting gear, images that are juxtaposed to others that reveal the plight of refugees hunted by border patrols, thereby documenting the terror wrought by the military. Fast frame changes suggest that the aggression created by the war is ubiquitous and extends into the civilian sphere, including the women's working environment. Tamara, an aspiring nurse, is faced with misogyny and xenophobia in her hierarchically structured hospital environment. She is humiliated by one of her superiors, a nurse who dresses her down because of a trifling matter. The contrast between the women in this scene stands out: Tamara is dark-complexioned, and the nurse blond with a demeanor and tone of voice that call to mind the culture of the Nazi BDM (Association of German Girls).

Nordrand traces violence within the urban environment from the perspective of the two women protagonists, who are accustomed to verbal and at times physical abuse—slapping, pushing, hitting. Growing up under those conditions, Jasmin and Tamara have become desensitized to the gender bias of their society. Albert's depiction of the harassment the young women encountered in school and their gender-specific professional choices are confirmed by the Wiener Report. It documents that in the school system traditional gender stereotypes are reinforced (ibid.: 18) so that girls feel more limited in their career options.[4] In *Nordrand*, the most important factor in the two women's development is the nuclear family, which in Jasmin's case resembles a battleground. Tamara, who is physically but not emotionally separated from her family, lives alone. Neither situation seems beneficial to the women's psychological development: Jasmin lives with the traumata inflicted at home, Tamara with those resulting from the trauma of war and her displacement.

Jasmin, her sisters, and their mother live like prisoners in their own home, while Tamara is at liberty to choose and furnish her own living quarters. Compared to the constant emotional insults sustained by Jasmin, Tamara's lot seems preferable. However, Tamara lacks even the questionable kind of companionship Jasmin enjoys. Early on in the film Tamara's plight as a loner becomes obvious. She has developed a spectacular ability at manipulating a Rubik's cube, an achievement that provides her with a modicum of respect among her classmates, who otherwise treat her as an outsider. To the viewers it is clear that the toy also serves as a substitute for human interaction.

The Wiener Report sheds further light on the situation of refugee girls like Tamara. It states that in 1999, 22,000 girls born outside Austria, many of them from the former Yugoslavia, lived in Vienna under varying circumstances (ibid.: 55). Tamara belongs to the fortunate group of foreign-born girls who, having grown up and attended school in Austria, lack language problems and are entitled to residence and work. The report also mentions other, less-fortunate girls who face deportation and have severe communication problems (ibid.: 55–60). Tamara enjoys a freedom unknown to Jasmin and possesses the social skills expected from a woman professional. She has an eye for fashion and a mind of her own. Yet she is miserable, homesick; she misses her parents and lives in constant worry about her brother. Her anguish shows on her face during her telephone calls to Serbia, which are often interrupted and thus become symbols of her fragmented world. Torn between her memories of home and her daily concerns in Vienna, she is caught up between two spheres.

Jasmin and Tamara are exceptional in that they muster the strength to solve their most pressing problems on their own. Bonding with one another gives them a distinct advantage. Jasmin lacks the wherewithal to provide for herself and her child, but Tamara is in a position to help her. Jasmin, on the other hand, is the better homemaker and able to provide a nurturing home environment. Thus the film ends on a carefully optimistic note even though Albert's outlook is anything but upbeat. Her film registers the deterioration of social and professional chances for women in the postfeminist era as well as the backlash against earlier progressive trends. Horwath aptly characterizes Albert's ambivalence towards the situation at the end of the 1990s as "a complex web of emotions, of quiet desperation and utopian outbursts. It's the aesthetic opposite of the 'strong' and hierarchical imagery promoted by Haider and his lackeys" (Horwath 2007).

Prominent Austrian feminist authors, including Elfriede Jelinek and Marlene Streeruwitz, articulated in their turn-of-the-millennium publications the view that the feminist movement had failed. They also observed that feminism and women's rights initiatives were even dismissed by women who adopted the patriarchal model in an attempt to reap some of the benefits of capitalism. Austrian women writers who continued to pursue a feminist agenda were relentless in pointing toward the widening gender gap in the increasingly oppressive global society. *Nordrand* participates in this critical feminist discourse by addressing the legacy as well as the failures of feminism through Jasmin and Tamara, characters of the filmmaker's own generation. *Nordrand* is less polemical than Jelinek's and Streeruwitz's dramas, but Albert's film, too, conveys the view that the struggle for women's equality has been lost, at least in the public arena, and it focuses on the private realm as the final frontier in the fight for women's rights.

Albert's outlook may seem more optimistic than Jelinek's or Streeruwitz's, whose recent works imply that patriarchal structures and commercialization leave no room for alternatives—every possible form of expression seems to be subsumed by the capitalist paradigm (see Jelinek 2000; Streeruwitz 2006). In contrast, *Nordrand* ends on a positive note, suggesting that solidarity among women is still possible on the basis of shared gender-specific needs and experiences. Rather than interpreting the concept of sisterhood in political terms, as was the case during the women's movement, Albert represents mutual support among women as an individualistic choice. At the same time, the household Jasmin and Tamara make can be viewed as a model transforming not only two women's lives, but also the lives of those around them.

Postmodern Viennese film and literature often thematizes the diversity of Austrian society to debunk the myth of national homogeneity promulgated in the national narrative of the postwar era. *Nordrand* exposes the breaking apart of traditional structures such as national identity, the nuclear family, patriarchal society, and it questions established notions of gender.[5] Reviewers of the film have, however, ignored its central themes: pregnancy, abortion, and motherhood, and the gender-specificity of life choices. An examination of these issues provides further insight into the basic assumptions in the film. *Nordrand* swiftly moves from its original topic, the plight of foreigners in Vienna's increasingly multicultural society, to its primary concern, alterity in the most basic sense, the physical, emotional, and social difference betweens men and women. It turns out that all forms of otherness, of which Albert presents many, are derivative of gender patterns. Ethnic diversity among the characters is used by the filmmaker as a tool to identify gender characteristics that emerge regardless of cultural setting.

In all likelihood the father of Jasmin's child is the Bosnian Senad, who ends up returning to Sarajevo, thus placing his national identity ahead of other concerns. Tamara, a Serbian and likewise from Sarajevo, stays in Vienna to become a surrogate parent to Jasmin's child. The two-woman household will, in other words, be made up of members of traditionally opposed groups. The tolerance that arises between Jasmin and Tamara, who have distinctly different lifestyles and aspirations, is based on their resolve to support a new life, and their household represents a cross-cultural matriarchal model opposing the national model of the male-dominated society. Jasmin in her role as homemaker and future mother diffuses cultural, religious, and national tensions between the four persons at Tamara's Christmas party.

Nordrand is not primarily about heterosexual relationships either, although sexuality is an important theme as the frequency of its representation suggests. Jasmin, who resolutely defends her right to be promiscuous, has sex with different men, including the sensitive Senad, who seems unable to fulfill her sexual appetites. Tamara and her Austrian lover Roman are also seen in intimate poses, but the romance is disrupted when she announces her pregnancy. In a later scene she is shown in a tender embrace with Valentin. Other male–female relationships include the abusive marriage of Jasmin's parents, Jasmin's father's incestuous relationship with Jasmin's younger sister, Jasmin's entanglements with brutal working-class males, and her tryst with a fellow employee, who ends up paying for her abortion. There are also hints at a frustrating involvement between Tamara and a Serbian man prior to her relationship with Roman. These affairs, none of which lead to a lasting commitment and ultimately seem not to matter, serve to debunk myths of female monogamy and exclusive romantic love. Albert breaks the nexus of heterosexual love, marriage and family. Love as experienced by Tamara and Valentin is characterized as exceptional, but it is an end in itself, as are Jasmin's casual encounters. The form sexual relationships in *Nordrand* take, some being more passionate and romantic than others, but all of them equally valid, undermines the symbolic code of passion and romantic love discussed by Niklas Luhmann: Albert's film questions and rejects the bourgeois ideology of love, which once again gained cachet in the postfeminist era under the guise of subjectivism (Luhmann 1982: 9).

Contrary to the often surrealistic and satirical representation of gender constructs and relationships in the works of Austrian avant-garde women writers, such as Jelinek and Streeruwitz, gender-related abuse and violence in *Nordrand* are portrayed in realistic, class- and culture-specific terms. The violence against women and female children in a milieu whose members have little interest in education has taken its toll on Jasmin who cannot extrapolate herself from this milieu entirely. Tamara, with her middle-class expectations, has developed more refined tastes and ambitions. Yet, both women make traditional career choices by entering service-oriented jobs, although it is suggested that Jasmin has artistic and Tamara scientific talents which remain untapped. *Nordrand* also shows that it is impossible for men and women to establish egalitarian relationships. Rather, they communicate through service, sex, and violence enacted by males and endured by females. Only in the absence of males as authority figures is Jasmin able establish an alternative lifestyle. Within her nuclear family she is used to compensating for the brutality in her daily life by cuddling, eating junk food, and escaping into the illusionary worlds of television. In contrast, Tamara's fashionable but sterile apartment, and her rigidity and controlling attitude, suggest the kind of self-discipline and perfectionism that result from isolation.

For their friendship to last, the women have to come to terms with conflicts dating back to their schooldays when Tamara was jealous of the gregarious and popular Jasmin. Meeting at the abortion clinic, they realize that their views of each other were superficial and mistaken, and because of their shared dilemma they find common ground. In her differentiated approach Albert steers clear of stereotyping. Tamara's boyfriend wants to keep the child, but she rejects him to remain true to herself, whereas Jasmin is jilted by her lover.

Jasmin and Tamara differ in every respect, in their attitudes towards their careers, relationships, sexuality, motherhood, and love, yet their ability to negotiate and adjust their expectations makes for a basic understanding. The male protagonists, on the other hand, are without exception shaped by experiences involving violence inaccessible to the women characters. The male realm is visually and acoustically associated with aggression, war, and the military. Even in the civilian sphere male bonding occurs by way of aggression, as a sequence towards the end of the film reveals: Jasmin crosses a bridge on foot and is faced by a phalanx of young men taunting and threatening her. She walks on, quickly and resolutely, an individual apart from the pack. Tamara's Austrian lover is associated with guns and tanks. In one scene he crawls through a field, armed and surveying the terrain with his binoculars like a hunter. The fleeting impressions of Tamara's native former Yugoslavia reinforce the image of male aggression. The landscapes and cityscapes are in a state of devastation, populated by uniformed male hunters and their human prey—civilians, women, and children. The opposing parties are represented by the Austrian Roman in military gear and the refugee Senad in civilian clothes. Trying to escape, Senad crouches on the ground, unarmed. Such images link gender with political and social categories. Soldiers with their tanks and guns—the phallic significance is obvious—are inscribed as masculine; vulnerable civilians as feminine.

This iconography extends into the Viennese context. Dark-complexioned male "foreigners" are often shown standing in groups that quickly disband when lighter colored Austrian policemen appear. The outsiders, in other words, adopt a behavior traditionally marked as feminine. Undermining this stereotypical model, the color markings are applied in reverse to the female characters: Austrian women are typecast as blond, especially Jasmin with her flowing blond curls. Their lack of education, submissiveness, and lowly service functions epitomize the traditional image of femininity, but Jasmin's mannish clothes—tight jeans and a bomber jacket—suggest the opposite. At the pastry shop, Jasmin has to wear a pink uniform that lends her an exaggerated, sugary kind of femininity. Tamara, on the other hand, prefers flattering dresses, but at the hospital she has to wear a nurse's uniform. These contradictory images show the constructedness of gender. Garments are part of social role play.

Beneath the costumes Tamara is an energetic, unsentimental woman. Because of her earning capacity she assumes the masculine role in her relationship with Jasmin, a mother and homemaker at heart. Albert's gender patterns suggest homosocial structures, but homosexuality is not the topic of *Nordrand*. The Austrian males, configured as aggressive, possessive, and patriarchal are clearly not compatible with Tamara and Jasmin, and the women become involved with Eastern European men. Tamara's Valentin has androgynous qualities amplified by his soft features, curly pony tale, and his black cape-like coat. Nimbly climbing a tall fence in search of a man who cheated him out of his money, he evokes the bisexual figure of Dracula. In keeping with his feminization, Valentin displays strong emotions, rage, grief, pain— he cries on camera—but also love and tenderness. Senad, less flamboyant than Valentin, is portrayed as a compassionate and creative individual. He saves Jasmin from freezing to death and pursues her in a somewhat timid, respectful fashion. Both Valentin and Senad lack the aggressive sexuality associated with the Austrian males. For example, Senad does not respond when Jasmin tries to satisfy him manually as she lies fully dressed next to him in a men's homeless shelter. Neither the environment nor the fact that Jasmin feels obliged to repay him for saving her life seem to appeal to him. For Senad, as for Valentin, as the sequence of the latter's love making with Tamara suggests, intimacy is an integral aspect of the sexual act.

Desensitizing substances, notably alcohol, are a part of the Austrian males' lifestyle. They seem to require mood altering chemicals to cope and are seen either in a state of stupor or overstimulation. In contrast, the two Eastern European men and the two women protagonists do not get drunk even at the joyful New Year's Eve celebration in St Stephan's Square. In the company of her Austrian buddies, whose behavior is reminiscent of her father's, Jasmin does not hold back. The respective scenes suggest that for Jasmin to interact with these men requires that she, too, needs to be drunk.

Albert's gender scale calls to mind the model of masculinity and femininity of Otto Weininger (1906). Rather than the extremes of masculinity and femininity, individuals with similar physical and emotional characteristics attract each other. The androgynous Valentin appeals to the energetic character of Tamara more than Roman, the military male. The sensitive Senad, who is incapable of talking about his traumatic war experiences, appeals to the more feminine Jasmin on a deeper level than her macho Austrian lovers. According to Weininger's gender scale, Jasmin and Tamara also complement one another.

But not even the gentler Eastern European males end up meeting Tamara's and Jasmin's needs. As the men move on, the women settle down in preparation for the child. This ending suggests that for Tamara and Jasmin to achieve a life of their own choosing they have to rely on their own strength. This rather modest solution by no means implies that Albert is not a feminist. On the contrary, *Nordrand* is a radical film in that it calls for gender segregation for the good of the human race. The examination of gender differences leads to the conclusion that even the most compatible men and women are still incompatible. Thus *Nordrand* restates a fundamental message of the earlier feminist movement for the new global situation shaped by war, radicalized nationalism, and misogyny.

The hope that personal solutions may still be an option to meet the crisis of Western civilization, that measures may still be taken by women for the sake of their children, is a far cry from the grander revolutionary dream of the feminist movement of the 1970s and 1980s, which aimed at reshaping the status of women and the social order worldwide. Albert's film concludes with the same simple image with which it opened: children at play, and a little girl pulling a butterfly kite. Yet this image implies more trust in the future and the legacy of feminism than can be found in the works of some of Albert's feminist contemporaries.

"All of us have a great longing for the father. The women's movement has not progressed beyond that. Now we can see ourselves in our misery. I think, we are worth less than ever before," Streeruwitz (1999: 450) has her character Tini asserts in the drama *Boccaleone*, published the year *Nordrand* was released.[6] Streeruwitz, like Albert, addresses the plight of asylum seekers, but she places the topic within the context of the international trade in human body parts. In Streeruwitz's work every nook and cranny of the public sphere seems co-opted by patriarchal structures.

Likewise, the works of Jelinek show no alternative sphere to commercialism and male dominance. *Nordrand* portrays the nuclear family as destroyed from the outside and from within. Heterosexual relationships provide no lasting love and protection for women and children—the only place they do so is in the illusionary realm of television. Yet, Albert validates a model of personal solidarity among women. It offers mutual support and motherly love, compassion, and tolerance, qualities that she inscribes as feminine. Thus Jasmin's and Tamara's household represents a paradigm for a subtle power shift and potential social transformation.

Notes

1. Born in Vienna in 1970, Albert studied journalism, German literature, and theater at the University of Vienna, and continued her studies at the Vienna Filmakademie. Aili Zheng (2001) provides a brief discussion of Albert's work preceding *Nordrand*. Zheng notes that the poetic images characteristic of *Nordrand* were already present in Albert's earlier work, notably in the episodic film *Slidn'—Alles bunt und wunderbar* (1998), of which Albert directed the first part entitled "Tagada". In this piece, metropolitan Vienna and its multifaceted population at the turn of the millennium constitute the setting and shape the protagonists of *Nordrand*. The characters interact with the city as much as they do with one another. Sites and situations specific to Vienna play a major role in the characters' inner journey towards coming to terms with their feelings and defining their individual identities, which according the Zheng are "uncertain" at the outset. Albert probes into the "fragmented lives in the transitional spaces on the margins of urbanism" (Zheng 2001: 64).
2. See Lechner, Pimminger, Reiter, and Willsberger (1999). Hereafter this source is referred to simply as the Wiener Report.
3. Hempel (2001: 17) explains that "feminist backlash" may signify a counter-movement against the achievements of the women's movement, but might also refer to an alleged postfeminist epoch in which all goals of the feminist movement have been accomplished and have become obsolete as points of discussion.
4. The Wiener Report notes that the gendered socialization of boys and girls, as well as the attitudes of teachers, prevent girls interested in the sciences and technical fields from making choices (Lechner et al. 1999: 18, 22).
5. Since the 1980s, films by Jewish filmmakers of the postwar generation address Jewish topics: e.g., Nadja Seelich and Lukas Stepanik's *Kieselsteine* (1983), Ruth Beckermann's *Die papierene Brücke* (1987), and *Gebürtig* (2001), codirected by Robert Schindel and Lukas Stepanik, all explore Vienna's hidden Jewish past and a reemerging Jewish culture in post-Shoah Austria. They document an unacknowledged Austrian diversity, thus countering the discourse of Austrian continuity based on the "Habsburg myth" set forth in Ernst Marischka's 1950s *Sissi* films and perpetuated in Rodgers and Hammerstein's legendary musical, and Robert Wise's 1965 film, *The Sound of Music.*
6. Wir haben alle eine große Sehnsucht nach dem Vater. Mehr hat die Frauenbewegung nicht fertiggebracht. Wir dürfen uns jetzt in unserer ganzen Armseligkeit sehen. Ich denke, wir sind weniger wert denn je.

References

Hempel, N. 2001. *Marlene Streeruwitz: Gewalt und Humor im dramatischen Werk.* Tübingen: Stauffenburg.

Holden, S. 2007. "Drowning in a Wake of Loss," *New York Times,* Retrieved 29 May 2008 from: http://query.nytimes.com/gst/fullpage.html?res=9807E5DC153FF932A2 5753C1A9659C8B63.

Horwath, A. 2007. "'Northern Skirts' Raises Austrian Politics and Artists' Concerns in the Age of Haider." Retrieved 27 June 2007 from: http://www.indiewire.com/ots/ fes_00NDNF_000329_Nordrand.html.

Jelinek, E. 2000. *Gier.* Hamburg: Rowohlt.

Lechner, F., I. Pimminger, A. Reiter and B. Willsberger. 1999. *Wiener Mädchenbericht: Zahlen und Fakten.* Vienna: Frauenbüro der Stadt Wien.

Luhmann, N. 1982. *Liebe als Passion.* Frankfurt: Suhrkamp.

Streeruwitz, M. 1999. "Boccaleone," in *Die Theaterstücke.* Frankfurt: Fischer, 431–82.

———. 2006. *Morire in levitate.* Frankfurt: Fischer.

Weininger, O. 1906. *Geschlecht und Charakter.* Vienna: Braumüller.

Zheng, A. 2001. "Regie, Produktion, Drehbuch: Ein Interview mit der Filmemacherin Barbara Albert," *Modern Austrian Literature* 34(1/2): 69–78.

Chapter 6

Metonymic Visions: Globalization, Consumer Culture, and Mediated Affect in Barbara Albert's *Böse Zellen*

Imke Meyer

Introduction

In 1999, Barbara Albert's feature film *Nordrand/Northern Skirts* was nominated for a Golden Lion at the Venice Film Festival.[1] As Robert von Dassanowsky observes, the showing of Albert's film at the festival spoke to the fact that a "new era" had really begun in Austrian cinema, as "no Austrian film had competed in decades" in Venice (Dassanowsky 2005: 259). Dassanowsky ranks Albert along with Michael Haneke and Peter Tscherkassy as one of "the three most internationally significant Austrian filmmakers recognized for their stylistic impact" in the last decade of the twentieth century (ibid.: 253).[2] Albert followed up *Nordrand*, the first feature-length film she wrote and directed on her own, with *Böse Zellen/Free Radicals* (2003) and *Fallen/ Falling* (2006), and these subsequent works indeed bear out Dassanowsky's assessment of her promise at the end of the last decade. Albert's emerging body of work shows the imprimatur of a style that strikes the viewer as at once deeply personal, Austrian, and global, while Albert's films are bound together by a cinematic language that is becoming legible as that of an auteur. On the following pages, I want to read Albert's *Böse Zellen* as a film whose language and use of metonymic techniques allow for a unique cinematic engagement with consumer culture and globalization in general, and with Austria's position within these larger force fields in particular.

Böse Zellen introduces the viewer to a globalized post-9/11 Austria that is dominated on the one hand by chaos and arbitrariness, and on the other by rigidity and control. The film depicts a country that is struggling to react to the forces of globalization at a point in its history when it has still not yet fully grappled with the burdens of its fascist past. *Böse Zellen* opens with a sequence that invokes thoughts both of fascism and of globalization: it highlights supervision of the individual by various authorities and tightened travel restrictions all over the globe after 9/11. At the same time, the film's opening passage alludes to chaos theory in a repeated shot of a butterfly flapping its wings—an activity that, according to the popularized version of chaos theory, can cause unforeseen events such as hurricanes in areas far removed from the original location of the butterfly (a phenomenon widely known as the "butterfly effect").

The non-descript cityscape through which Albert's characters move is dotted with signifiers of both cultural imperialism and globalization (McDonald's restaurants and the Coca-Cola logo are frequently visible, for instance). An Afro-Austrian character repeatedly encounters prejudice in an Austrian environment that the film depicts as wanting to cling to homogeneity in the face of globalization. The promise of happiness—"We will make you happy!" (*Wir machen Sie glücklich!*) an advertisement for standardized suburban housing repeatedly announces—can be realized only within the tightly circumscribed framework of choices consumer culture offers. Product choice, though, remains, in the end, a solely arbitrary decision. The paradoxical intertwining of control and arbitrariness is most strikingly illustrated towards the end of the film: one of the characters wins a raffle and is handed the keys to one of the suburban houses that has been coveted by all the characters in the film. The raffle carefully controls the distribution of the desired icon of bourgeois domesticity. The winner is made to feel special. At the same time, the recipient of the prize is chosen at random—he or she really could have been anybody, and are therefore not really special at all. The promise of individuality and "specialness" is broken at the very moment at which it is realized.[3] Andreas, the winner, has a vague sense of the betrayal consumer culture perpetrates as he walks through the sterile rooms of the standardized house he now owns.

The characters' emotions, attached to complex personal and national histories, are mediated and harnessed by a globalized consumer culture. Yet the expression of genuine affect is not completely disabled within this setting, but curiously becomes possible again at precisely those points where the inauthenticity of a commercialized world dominated by mass media seems to reach its apex. Andreas' disappointment upon winning the house is palpable. Kai, a teenager plagued by guilt feelings over a car accident he caused, finally finds release on the trashy TV show *Verzeih mir/Forgive Me*. What Adorno and Horkheimer termed "the trace of the better" (*die Spur des Besseren*) seems to survive in the globalized post-9/11 culturescape depicted in Albert's film (Horkheimer and Adorno 1971: 128). I will attempt to highlight here some of these "traces of the better," as well as what I would like to call the metonymic techniques Albert's film uses to make them visible. *Böse Zellen* manages to reframe the seemingly (and paradoxically) familiar images of alienation in global consumer culture, allowing us to see in them the unexpected: elements of individualism and cultural particularities that stubbornly refuse to blend into the faceless façade of consumer capitalism. At the same time that it insists on its national identity, though,

Albert's film transcends a purely Austrian perspective by entering into a kind of cultural, political, and aesthetic dialogue with the nation's global context that does not erase all dimensions of cultural particularity.

Metonymy and Surveillance

Nostalgic and politically regressive notions of Austria as a postimperial, postfascist, newly harmless and cozy alpine homeland have been banished from Albert's film. There are no visuals of majestic mountains, green meadows, or cute farmhouses populated by *Lederhosen*-clad down-to-earth country folk. Instead, the built environment consists of the faceless architecture of chain stores, shopping malls, and standardized suburban housing. Industrial areas in Austria look no different from those in Rio de Janeiro, where the film's opening is set. Here, it seems as though Austria's attempts to distance itself from its fascist national past and to gain a foothold in a globalized world has caused the erasure of spatial and cultural architectures that can be read in nationally specific terms. Rio de Janeiro is identified in the film by the famous Sugar Loaf Mountain. But the city sights we are shown are hardly different from the ones we see in Austria. They could, in fact, be anywhere— cranes in a harbor, suburbs, and urban traffic chaos. The city in which the bulk of the film is set, finally, can only be identified as Austrian via language, and not via any culturally specific visual markers. Sterile apartment complexes, shopping centers, a multiplex cinema, car parks, and domestic spaces either filled with bland middle-class furnishings or cluttered by the cheap products a capitalist economy uses to turn individuals into consumers make up the environment through which the characters move.

The film first introduces us to Manu, one of the female protagonists. At the end of a vacation in Brazil, she flies home to Austria, but her flight crashes. Miraculously, Manu survives the crash, and the film then jumps forward six years to a supermarket where Manu stocks shelves. She has a daughter, Yvonne, and is married to Andreas, who works at the local mall's cineplex. Yvonne attends a kindergarten where she is taught by Manu's best friend Andrea (who, like Manu's husband, goes by the nickname Andi). One night, Manu and her girlfriend Andi go dancing. On the way home, Manu is killed by Kai, a teenage driver whose car swerves across the road. Kai's girlfriend Gabi is injured in the car crash and becomes a quadriplegic. Other connections between the characters abound: Manu's brother Lukas teaches physics to a high-school class attended by Kai, Gabi, and Patrizia. Patrizia, whose parents were killed in a murder-suicide, lives with a one-legged man—possibly her grandfather—who has a sexual relationship with Manu's mentally unstable sister Gerlinde. Yvonne's kindergarten is located in the same building as a choir practice room. One member of the choir is Belinda, an overweight petite-bourgeoise white woman, who is the mother of the Afro-Austrian character Sandra. Sandra befriends Manu's brother Lukas. Belinda buys a vacuum cleaner from Reini, a German man who picks up women at the local disco, among them Andrea and Gerlinde. In the end, the paths of all characters cross at the opening ceremony of a new wing of the local shopping mall.

As the film opens, we see a tightly framed shot of Manu dancing in a room to the tune of the "Macarena," a pop song.[4] As the camera pans around, we look out of a window that frames a view of Sugar Loaf Mountain and the surrounding bay. The spectator finally locates Manu in Rio de Janeiro, and identifies her as a tourist packing her bags in a hotel room. Manu takes a photograph of the view from her hotel room and then takes a bus to the airport. The shots out of the bus window could be shots of a city virtually anywhere in the world: we are shown houses crowded on a hillside, streets teeming with traffic, anonymous warehouses, container terminals, and shipping facilities in a harbor. When Manu is at the airport, she asks a passerby to take her picture against an anonymous airport background that could be located anywhere. When we see Manu writing a postcard to her boyfriend Andreas ("Andi"), she describes her environment as a "paradise" that offers "sea" and "beach"—things that the camera does not show us.

The camera likewise denies us a view of the famous *Christ the Redeemer* statue that overlooks Rio de Janeiro. Once we know that we are in Rio, we are waiting for a camera shot of this well-known sight. Instead, Manu's departure from Rio is intercut with scenes from a choir practice in Austria. These scenes are introduced by a shot of Jesus' body on a white crucifix. Before Manu even arrives back in Austria, then, Brazil and Austria have become metonymically linked through the image of the white Jesus figure that is absent from the place where we expect to see it—Rio—and that then moves into view as the first element that visually introduces an Austria that, for the most part, looks and (thanks to the pop songs in the film's soundtrack) sounds as though it could be practically anywhere—even, for that matter, Brazil.

The metonymic link between Brazil and Austria sets the tone for the entire film. Throughout the movie, characters become connected to each other in unexpected and surprising ways, and linkages between seemingly disparate contexts are opened up with the help of metonymic shifts. At the same time, though, the specificity of Austria is not completely erased. Rather than completely eliminate that which is Austrian in the film, the metonymic links to other contexts often broaden the notion of what Austria might be. On the one hand, the film argues that the culture industry infects everything with sameness (Horkheimer and Adorno 1971: 108). On the other hand, it also shows that in the very end, the forces of consumer culture encounter resistance: small measures of cultural specificity and individuality survive.

After a metonymic link has been established between Brazil and Austria, a concrete one emerges: Manu boards a flight to take her back to Europe. The character's movement provides the direct link between two continents. The film introduces a measure of irony already at this point, as it turns out that a concrete link is more difficult to establish than a metonymic one, in spite of the fact that travel movements are under tight control. For instance, a disembodied voice from the flight deck explains to the passengers seated on the plane that a delay has occurred because a fellow passenger, whose ticket was not in order, had to leave the plane along with his luggage. A lone suitcase is visible on a baggage cart outside the plane, and a single passenger is shown boarding a bus to take him back to the terminal. Before the plane takes off, Manu, who is squeezed into a middle seat, asks a flight attendant: "Can I still go to the toilet?" Manu is told that she has to wait until after take-off. In other words, strict passenger and luggage screening procedures are in place, and travelers are expected to control their bodily functions and adapt them to the needs of the safety procedures.

Screening and controls are meant to eliminate errors and unforeseen events from the travel process. It turns out, however, that total control is not possible (see Dassanowsky 2005: 283): Manu's plane crashes. We are shown a butterfly flapping its wings in an unknown location.[5] We then see a piece of white sky outside the flying plane. The sky morphs into white curtains that adorn the choir practice room in Austria. The camera pans over the choir and then focuses on a kitschy painting in which an angelic child kneels in front of a lake; the dark clouds above are parted by a beam of light that shines down upon the child. The camera zooms in on the painted clouds, which in turn transform into dark storm clouds that engulf the plane that is carrying Manu and the other passengers. The plane shakes violently. After a cut, we are shown a bird's-eye view of dark waters; soon, debris from a plane crash floats into view. We also see a rescue boat that carries Manu—she appears to be the plane crash's only survivor. Whereas at this point the film has managed to establish numerous metonymic links between Brazil and Austria, the establishment of a concrete link—a passenger flight from Brazil to Austria—fails due to a plane crash, a crash that occurs in spite of tight control mechanisms and travel safety regulations.

While the film shows that control is not possible, it is not saying that effects have no causes. Rather, it seems to suggest that while these causes are present, it would be virtually impossible to trace our way back to them from a given occurrence. Did the butterfly we were shown in a separate shot cause the plane crash with the flapping of its wings? The film's editing suggests there might be a link, but a clear and concrete one can hardly be established. Later in the film, Manu's brother Lukas is seen teaching a high school class about chaos theory and fractals, and he states, "Chaos and order exist contiguously and simultaneously in complex, non-linear systems."

Similarly, meaning seems definitely to reside in the images presented in the film's opening sequences; it cannot be arrested and expressed in a linear fashion, however. For instance, the kitschy painting of the angelic child seems to suggest that the beam of light shining down upon it is sent by a protective higher power. On the other hand, because the image of the painted clouds changes into the storm clouds that down the plane, it would appear that the source of the light can also be the source of less benevolent forces. When we are shown the painting again later in the film, therefore, we wonder whether the beam of light can really only signify benevolence and grace, or whether it is not akin to a search light, a surveillance device trained upon a helpless child. And do we envision these higher powers—whether benevolent or not—the film seems to ask, merely because it would be too difficult for us to extract meaning from reality if we had to do so using chaos theory equations and fractals?

By engaging with the topics of surveillance, control, and metonymic connections, Albert's film does not merely inscribe the contemporary Austria it depicts in a global context, for it likewise inscribes itself into the context of the history of Austrian postwar cinema. For instance, to give two examples, Valie Export's *Die Praxis der Liebe/The Practice of Love* (1984) thematized voyeurism and electronic surveillance in a context that linked the issues of nation, history, and gender. Michael Haneke's *71 Fragmente einer Chronologie des Zufalls/71 Fragments of a Chronology of Chance* (1994) likewise establishes a chain of metonymic links in the context of a critique both of voyeurism and of the mass media. Thus, Albert's film very consciously seeks to engage not just with the sociocultural context of contemporary Austria, but it reflexively engages with the medium's national history.

In keeping with the themes of surveillance and control, the film signals early on that outside of the framed cinematic image entities are present that nevertheless have an impact on what happens inside the frame. For instance, as Manu has her picture taken by a passerby at the airport, she first looks in the direction of the camera held by the passerby and then tilts her head slightly to the right to gaze in the direction of somebody located outside the frame. Improbably, it is this image of Manu gazing at the viewer of the film that appears in a photo album later on in the film, rather than the image of her that would have appeared in the view finder of the camera the passerby used to take her picture. In addition, it is not clear how Manu's camera survived the plane crash along with her, so that her vacation photos could be later placed in an album. Thus, the flip side of control emerges here, too: imponderability and chaos always seem to accompany efforts of control and surveillance.

The theme of surveillance inscribes itself into both the film's content and its form. Throughout the film, we see numerous high-angle and bird's-eye shots, of characters as well as of spaces; the high school student Patrizia and Manu's daughter Yvonne, for instance, are shown from above in their beds. The high-school locker room as well as the cemetery are at various points represented through high-angle shots. Often, the camera eye seems to follow right behind a character, looking over his or her shoulder. When the camera pans it often stops ominously in the middle of nowhere. For instance, we meet the high-school student Kai as he fast-forwards through a video recording of an episode of the TV show *Aktenzeichen XY...ungelöst*, a program similar to *America's Most Wanted*. It tries to help catch criminals by presenting reenactments of crimes on TV and by encouraging its viewers to be vigilant—to engage in acts of observation and surveillance, as it were. The episode we see in the film focuses on Kai's older brother Patrick, who, prior to Kai's birth, was abducted in a small forest and later found dead. Following this scene, we are shown a woman with her dog who jogs through a wooded area that looks similar to the one represented in the TV show.[6] The dog runs away and does not come back, even though its owner calls for it repeatedly. The camera pans in the direction in which the dog ran. Since we make a connection between the TV show and the forest shown now, we almost expect to see the dog standing next to a dead child's body. But the camera movement stops before anything in particular moves into view. In all of these instances, the camera seems to narrate from a perspective that is that of an entity more powerful than the characters. As spectators, we partake of the camera's power to the extent that we get to share its perspective, but on the other hand we are also made to feel uneasy by its movements because the source of its powers remains hidden from us. The odd mix of feelings of recognition, familiarity, and indeterminacy that the camera's view invokes in the spectator is nothing short of uncanny. It is never revealed from whose perspective the camera narrates. We are watching the unfolding of stories whose author remains concealed, and by cutting pan shots short or not moving into view characters whose voices we hear, the author seems to tell the spectators that parts of the narrative may also remained concealed. Not knowing who the author is, not knowing who is looking, as it were, creates anxiety and uneasiness. The manner in which the theme of surveillance is represented in the film, then, makes the realms of chaos theory, religion, and psychoanalysis appear uncannily contiguous.

Substitution, Re-enactment, and Mediated Affect

The *Aktenzeichen XY...ungelöst* episode is one of the many instances in the film in which reality is replaced by a re-enactment, substitutes are inserted into emotionally highly charged spaces, or affect is accessed by mediation. For instance, Kai, who is perceived by his classmates as cool and good looking, often talks to Patrizia, who is a loner who is bullied at school and teased about her looks. Kai himself, though, often stands apart from his classmates and is drawn to Patrizia. This might be explained by the fact that Kai often feels as though he were not simply his own person, but rather an inadequate substitute for his dead brother. In the hallway of his parents' house, two large framed photos are mounted on the wall, illuminated by spotlights that seem both to echo and retroactively to question the source of the beam of light that shines upon the angelic child in the painting that adorns the choir practice room. One of the framed photographs shows Kai, the other his dead brother Patrick. In the pictures, both boys appear to be of roughly the same age. Placing the photos of the two boys—one dead, the other alive—next to each other in this manner produces an uncanny effect of oscillation between simultaneity and presence on the one hand and a reminder of loss and absence on the other. It is as though Kai's aging vis-à-vis the state of development arrested in the photos were an indication not of his growth, but rather a measure of the time that has elapsed since his older brother's death.

While Kai may feel like a substitute for his murdered brother, in effect he becomes an involuntary murderer himself when the car accident he causes kills Manu and cripples Gabi. The vague guilt he feels over being alive when his brother is dead can now be concretized in his emotional torture over the accident. Kai's decision to present the story of the car accident and Gabi's paralysis on the TV show *Verzeih mir* allows him to enact in front of a national audience his feelings of guilt and shame—some of which are linked to the car accident, but some of which, as explained earlier, have a much longer history. The public confession of guilt over the car accident can substitute in the economy of Kai's emotions for confessions of guilt over other issues, such as the fact that he is alive whereas his brother is dead. The release and relief Kai experiences are visceral, in spite of the highly artificial structure of the show and the staged nature of the confession.

Patrizia, whose name already signals a relation to the dead brother Patrick, enters the emotional realm Patrick occupies for Kai, and Kai feels an impulse to protect her from the abuse of her classmates. At some point, Kai asks Patrizia how her parents died. She puts the fingers of her right hand into the shape of a pistol, puts them to Kai's head, imitates the sound of a gun shot, turns her hand to her own head, and imitates a second gun shot sound. Earlier in the film, when Patrizia had experimented with a Ouija board in her room, a book fell from its shelf. The book's title is *Erstkommunion: Festtag meines Lebens* ("First communion: celebration of my life") and contains some generic photos of church scenes. In addition, personal photos of Patrizia have been pasted in as supplements to the generic story told in the book. This arrangement already makes it seem as though the claim that a particular individual life was celebrated here is false, and that the communion is rather a generic event with minor individualized elements. Patrizia then opens the book to a page that shows a picture of her flanked by what seem to be her parents. The faces of the parents have been removed from the photo, though. Thus, it seems as though the parental bodies depicted in the book might also be merely generic—substitutes for a real thing that has long since left the scene of life. When Patrizia visits the cemetery, we see that the faces of Patrizia's parents instead smile down from oval-shaped portraits on their tombstone. The "celebration of my life" thus becomes linked to death. When Patrizia uses gestures to re-enact her parents' murder-suicide for Kai, her actions are overdetermined, as she implicitly also gestures towards the violence that has marked both her and Kai's lives.

Another context in which substitution and reenactment are highlighted in the film are the group therapy sessions that Belinda's daughter Sandra attends. Viewed in the larger context of Austrian cultural history, these therapy sessions seem both to gesture towards Freud and the indelible imprint psychoanalysis has left on the country, and to signal a radical departure from the therapy techniques of the traditional talking cure. Sandra's group therapy sessions take place in a largely empty room with white walls and light-colored floors—surfaces well suited for projection, it would seem. During the sessions, the patients are asked to use other patients as stand-ins for people important in their lives. These stand-ins are then to be arranged in constellations that are meant to convey the affective proximity or distance or emotional history a given patient has with other people in his or her life. We observe Sandra during a number of these exercises. In other scenes in the film, we see her interact with some of the people for whom she then finds substitutes during the therapy sessions, namely her mother Belinda and Manu's brother Lukas. After Sandra arranges the substitutes in the therapy room, she is repeatedly asked by the therapist: "Does this feel right to you?" After Sandra confirms that it does, the therapist moves on to query the substitutes about how they themselves feel—as though they were really able to channel those for whom they are substituting, based simply on the position they are taking in a given constellation in the room.

Here, then, as in the various substitution constellations between Kai and Patrizia, the substitute and the real, the artificial and the actual, the fake and the authentic bump up against each other and curiously merge. It is as though at rare points a dialectical image were produced when chains of substitutions are arrested, and a constellation emerges that is able to capture the actual emotional states of the characters. Thus, in an especially striking therapy scene, Sandra adds to the Lukas substitute two other substitutes who are to stand in for his sisters, Manu and Gerlinde, even though Sandra has never met them. The real Manu is dead at this point of the film. The substitute standing in for Gerlinde, the mentally unstable sister, happens to be wearing a tank top decorated with a film strip design, and she keeps saying that she is afraid and uncomfortable, feeling as though somebody were standing behind her and observing her. Thus, this substitute, whose clothing makes a playful comment on representation and projection, who has never met Gerlinde, and who presumably knows nothing about her state of mind, curiously intuits something that might just be true about Gerlinde and many other characters in the film; namely, that they feel exposed to surveillance and observation, and that they are subject to a vague and indefinable threat.

Fear of the Other and Globalization

On a number of levels, Albert's film engages with the presence or suspected presence of something foreign in a seemingly familiar context. Many of the characters apparently feel that, if it were possible to locate these foreign elements, the sense of being exposed to a vague and indefinable threat could be conquered: it could be translated into an engagement with a known enemy. For instance, though it is not clear to the spectator that Yvonne really suffers from any physical discomfort after her mother's death, her father Andreas has her repeatedly hospitalized so she can undergo tests. Andreas tells Yvonne that she might have *böse Zellen* (literally "evil cells") inside her and that the doctors need to locate and eliminate them. It is easier to deal with the concrete presence of "evil cells" than to treat the invisible emotional wounds Yvonne's mother's death has caused.

No "evil cells" are ever found in Yvonne's body, though. When her aunt Gerlinde visits her in the hospital, she tells Yvonne that "they" look for evil cells in everybody, "but we have none, no matter how badly they want us to have them." Gerlinde, the mentally unstable character, may thus be the one that gains some actual insight into the working mechanisms of fear. The film repeatedly examines a fear of foreignness—both figuratively via the suspected "evil cells" in the human body, and literally via the presence of "others" in a formerly homogeneous society.

As an Afro-Austrian, Sandra stands out as "other" in her environment. The spectators may wonder why Sandra has a white mother. Was Sandra adopted? Is Belinda her biological mother, and was Sandra's father a man of color? The film does not satisfy whatever curiosity the audience may feel, and in this manner, *Böse Zellen* manages to make us think about the ways in which familial bonds come about. The film does not allow us to take these ties for granted by assuming direct biological lineage and/or racial homogeneity of families. While on the one hand the film establishes surprising links between seemingly disparate contexts, on the other hand it questions links normally taken for granted, such as family bonds. The film is thus able to emphasize that, ultimately, a constructedness and arbitrariness inheres in such relations, too.

Albert's film does not fetishize race. The attention Sandra's physical attributes are paid by the camera is no different from the attention the bodies of Caucasian characters receive. By simply presenting Sandra's skin color as a given, the camera distinguishes its gaze from orientalist and exoticizing tendencies that otherwise permeate the still largely homogeneous white suburban environment through which the characters move.[7] Here, Sandra is confronted with racism. For instance, she works in a cosmetics store, and while demonstrating the use of a skin care product to a white customer, the customer complains that it is impossible for Sandra to test the product's efficacy because her skin is too dark. Sandra is likewise subject to orientalist prejudices in, for example, the marketing campaigns of big corporations: the film makes this glaringly obvious by placing Manu's brother Lukas and Sandra in a McDonald's restaurant that is decorated with posters and placemats advertising an African safari trip. These advertising materials translate the colonial gaze and its object, the "dark continent," into the only seemingly more benign gaze of Western tourism.

The global is expanded to the cosmic in another scene. In the hospital, Yvonne has a conversation with Gerlinde about their relative position in the universe. Yvonne asks: "And behind the universe, what is there?" Gerlinde replies: "It goes on endlessly there, there is nothing behind it." Yvonne, mildly shocked, says "But that is ... " and Gerlinde, nodding with widened eyes, responds: "Yes!" It is as though Gerlinde were explaining to Yvonne, who understands immediately, that they have been subject to a giant hoax, and that in actuality, their position and the reality that surrounds them are utterly irrelevant, engulfed as they are by an infinite nothingness that cannot accommodate transcendence, either.

This disorientation and "transcendental homelessness" (*transzendentale Obdachlosigkeit*, Lukács 1994: 32) the characters experience is mirrored in the political realm. At no point does the film explicitly tell us that we are in Austria. National particularity has been drained from the built environment—it appears faceless and non-descript. The characters are identified as Austrian only by their dialect. Ironically, the one character who states that she is "from Austria" is the Afro-Austrian Sandra—yet she has to contend with the prejudice that she cannot be from Austria because she looks like an "other." The political disorientation is captured brilliantly in a scene in which Gerlinde picks flowers from a bed that adorns the middle of a busy traffic island. The camera moves around the flower bed, and at some point a round blue placard, decorated with stars of the EU logo, moves into view. A large golden euro sign occupies the middle of the placard. The constant traffic flow around the flower bed signals commerce, interchange, and intercourse. The circular nature of the traffic flow simultaneously points to the seeming beauty of an orderly closed system and to its futility: if everything moves in a circular pattern, nothing will ever truly get anywhere. The EU nations—the golden stars—are governed by capitalism: the euro symbol dominates the stars and robs them of any individuality. Nature has been displaced by commerce, and only small fenced-in patches of it survive.

Capitalism, consumer culture, globalization, and European political integration have robbed Austria of many of its national particularities. However, Austria's social, political, and cultural history are inscribed into the film as traces that are faint but nevertheless legible: as already mentioned, Sandra's therapy sessions conjure up memories of Freud; the alienated sexual encounters that take place in the film and that link the characters in various ways invoke thoughts of Arthur Schnitzler's *Reigen/La Ronde* (1900);[8] and the fur coat Gerlinde wears throughout the film make her and her radically alienated sexuality appear like a distorted afterimage of Leopold von Sacher-Masoch's *Venus im Pelz* ("Venus in Furs," 1870).[9] One of the national particularities that remain much more easily legible in the film, though, is the burden of Austria's fascist past and the accompanying guilt. Much of the vague guilt that the characters feel may not be attributable to concrete events, but rather to Austria's dark past.[10] When Gerlinde compulsively drinks milk to cleanse herself of an imaginary poison, one cannot help but contrast this white milk with the "black milk of daybreak" of Paul Celan's post-Holocaust poem "Todesfuge" ("Deathfugue").[11] Thus, Sandra's therapist is probably both right and wrong when she states: "Regardless of what happened in the past, it will only resolve itself once we stop looking for guilt." On the one hand, Austria may only become truly the same as other nations once it stops focusing on historical guilt. On the other hand, if it no longer focused on its guilt, it would lose one of its last national particularities, and, by abandoning its moral responsibility to engage with the past, it would create more guilt. Engaging with the past and living up to its historical responsibilities simultaneously admits Austria to the global community of nations and keeps it from ever truly being the same as these other nations.

Conclusion

Albert's film presents an incisive critique of capitalism, consumer culture, and the more problematic leveling effects of globalization. At the same time, though, it shows us characters that are not completely squashed under the weight of racism, exoticism, or commercialism. Rather, meaning continues to emerge in unexpected moments, and "traces of the better" survive. The universal "web of deception" (Adorno 1973: 342) that surrounds the characters may be seamless, but they choose to assemble meaning right in front of its seemingly impenetrable surface by making use of its detritus. Lukas, for instance, explains the meaning of fractals to Sandra while she moves french fries around on a McDonald's "livecam" placemat that shows safari images of Africa.

A character in Wim Wenders's *Im Lauf der Zeit/Kings of the Road* (1976) complains that "the Yankees have colonized our unconscious." In Albert's film, US pop culture is ever present, but in contrast to the effect ascribed to it in Wenders's film, it does not seem to overwhelm completely or colonize the collective unconscious. Rather, the characters often adopt it joyfully, constructing new meaning out of imported pop-cultural forms. For instance, Manu and her girlfriend Andi happily sing along to the band a-ha's song "Take on Me"—the band itself is Norwegian and adapted American pop patterns to European tastes. Similarly, as Patrizia walks through a depressing underpass[12] in what could be the Wiener Neustadt, she encounters a street musician who plays John Phillips and Scott McKenzie's 1967 song "If You're Going to San Francisco (Be Sure to Wear Some Flowers in Your Hair)." While the hippy anthem, due to its use in too many contexts, may have lost some of its original counter-cultural potential, it acquires new meaning here and seems to provide the soundtrack to a liberated feeling that emerges in Patrizia. Here, the Wiener Neustadt and San Francisco become linked, but in such a way that neither overtakes, nor completely assimilates, nor colonizes the other. Meaning is constituted horizontally, rather than in a metaphorical or vertical manner that would establish hierarchies and privilege one context of signification over another.

It seems as though meaning is often formed in precisely the contexts where it is least expected. The trashy TV show *Verzeih mir* is the mechanism that finally allows Kai to find affective release for his guilt feelings and to open himself up towards a relationship with Patrizia. The joy Manu and Andi feel dancing to commercial pop songs in a generic disco is palpable, as is the consolation that Belinda gets from her collection of kitschy stuffed animals.[13] In the course of his study of fractals, Lukas discovers structures that repeat themselves and that exhibit a beauty that gives him real pleasure. The beautiful and potentially infinite repetition of these structures contrasts starkly with the sometimes limiting repetition compulsion that is enacted in much post-Holocaust Austrian culture as authors and filmmakers struggle to create narratives that address the historical burdens of Austria's fascist past.[14]

Meaning, in all of these instances of unexpected creation, is established metonymically—that is, horizontally. It is only fitting, then, that the vertical logic of religion and higher authorities is also transposed by the film onto a horizontal plane. Towards the end of the film, Manu's friend Andi drives up a mountain and lays herself down in the snow, spreading her arms as a crucified figure would.[15] The white of the snow and Andi's white sweater evoke the white *Christ the Redeemer* statue in Rio that we never see and that was replaced by the white crucifix adorning the choir rehearsal room in Austria. Religion has thus been brought down to earth, and meaning has been made non-hierarchical. It has joined a horizontal human plane. It remains one of the film's final paradoxes and ironies that, in order to become visible and reveal its meaning, this horizontal plane has to be shown from a vertical high-angle camera perspective.[16] Via its form, the film here manages to gesture towards the imponderable and the inexplicable—that which will not yield to surveillance or to our attempts to understand it, but which itself possesses the power to reveal new angles. It is appropriate, then, that the film ends with a shot of Manu's daughter looking at a puddle in whose reflecting surface oil traces form fractal-like shapes that just may yield beauty and meaning, but whose origins remain imponderable. Through the eyes of Albert's camera, we are not presented with an easy feel-good movie. But Austria may here not quite appear to be the "land of feel-bad cinema" that it has recently been proclaimed to be (Lim 2006: 14).

Notes

1. I would like to thank the participants of my University of Pennsylvania spring 2007 seminar on travel in German and Austrian cinema, as well as the students in my fall 2006 and fall 2009 Bryn Mawr seminars on postwar Austria, for their spirited discussions of Albert's film. I would also like to thank the University of Washington's Department of Germanics for the opportunity to introduce an earlier version of this essay at the department's Annual Alumni Lecture Series. I also would like to thank Bryn Mawr's Center for Visual Culture for giving me a forum to present my work on Albert. I am grateful for the valuable feedback I received.

2. Dassanowsky's assessment is shared by others. For instance, Derek Elley ranks Albert "among the forefront of younger European talent" (Elley 2003).

3. Very similar betrayals of the consumer through the mechanisms of capitalism and the culture industry have, of course, been analyzed by Max Horkheimer and Theodor Adorno (1971: esp. 108–50).

4. Interestingly, "Macarena," a popular Andalusian name, also refers to the Virgin of Macarena, an incarnation of the Virgin Mary. The song thus establishes a metonymic link to the famous *Christ the Redeemer* statue in Rio which we expect to see, but are in fact never shown.

5. This butterfly is also reminiscent of a butterfly-patterned kite that is shown twice in Albert's *Nordrand*. This link to the earlier film is strengthened by shared concerns of both works: globalization, human isolation, a critique of capitalism, and a search for possibilities of expressing affect.

6. As the woman jogs, we also see a one-legged character walking in the background, who may or may not be Manu's sister's lover. The one-legged character establishes a link both to Manu's sister's lover and to Belinda, who later on badly injures her leg when she throws herself in front of a train in a suicide attempt. The image also provides an association with the paralysis Kai's girlfriend Gabi will suffer later.

7. The movie was filmed in the Wiener Neustadt, in Vienna, and in Bratislava (Slovakia).

8. The traffic island—signifying, as it does, commerce and intercourse—likewise seems to allude to *Reigen*-like structures.

9. I owe thanks to my colleague Christiane Hertel for this observation.

10. In an interview included on the 2005 US KinoVideo DVD edition of *Böse Zellen*, Albert states that she feels there is "something dark" in Europe, "but especially in Austria."

11. For the original of Celan's poem, see Celan (1986: 41–42). The phrase "black milk of daybreak" is taken from John Felstiner's translation (Felstiner 1995: 31).

12. I owe thanks to Andrea Gogröf-Voorhees for sharing the observation that this underpass may also be an ironic comment on how quite literally shallow the 1960s "underground" has become in the context of a globalized consumer culture.

13. Albert's earlier feature *Nordrand* also engages the idea that real affect is released in response to some of the culture industry's worst manifestations. For instance, in *Nordrand*, some of the characters—members of a highly dysfunctional working-class family that lives in an apartment

in a depressing housing complex on Vienna's northern edge—watch on TV portions of a well-known fairy tale film, *Drei Nüsse für Aschenbrödel/Three Hazelnuts for Aschenbrödel*, a GDR-Czech coproduction from the 1970s. This highly romanticized and often sentimental film produces tangible affective responses in the characters in Albert's film—the film allows them to express empathy and hope. In this and other contexts, Albert's take on her characters manages to be utterly non-patronizing.

14. On this repetition compulsion, see Heidi Schlipphacke (2010).
15. This scene prefigures one in Albert's later feature *Fallen*, in which the same actress, along with four other characters, stands on a hill and spreads her arms like a crucified figure.
16. My thanks go to Diana Behler for her insightful comments on this aspect of the film.

References

Adorno, T.W. 1973. *Ästhetische Theorie*. Frankfurt am Main: Suhrkamp.

Celan, P. 1986. "Todesfuge," in *Gesammelte Werke, Vol. 1*. Frankfurt am Main: Suhrkamp, 41–42.

Dassanowsky, R. von. 2005. *Austrian Cinema: A History*. Jefferson, NC: McFarland.

Elley, D. 2003. "*Free Radicals,*" *Variety*, 18–24 August, 24.

Felstiner, J. 1995. *Paul Celan: Poet, Survivor, Jew*. New Haven, CT: Yale University Press.

Horkheimer, M. and T.W. Adorno. 1971. *Dialektik der Aufklärung*. Frankfurt am Main: Fischer.

Lim, D. 2006. "Greetings from the Land of Feel-Bad Cinema," *New York Times*, 26 November 2006, Retrieved 11 October 2008 from: http://www.nytimes.com/2006/11/26/movies/26lim.html.

Lukács, G. 1994. *Die Theorie des Romans. Ein Geschichtsphilosophischer Versuch über die Formen der großen Epik*. Munich: Deutscher Taschenbuch Verlag.

Schlipphacke, H. 2010. *Nostalgia after Nazism: History, Home, and Affect in German and Austrian Literature and Film*. Lewisburg, PA: Bucknell University Press.

Chapter 7

Place and Space of Contemporary Austria in Barbara Albert's Feature Films

Mary Wauchope

Each of the three feature films of the Austrian filmmaker Barbara Albert— *Nordrand/ Northern Skirts* (1999), *Böse Zellen/Free Radicals* (2003), and *Fallen/Falling* (2006)— focuses on a group of characters who repeatedly cross paths within a limited geographic area of Austria: the city of Vienna in *Northern Skirts*, and small Austrian towns in *Free Radicals* and *Falling*. Typical of such "ensemble films" is that the community which develops among the main characters functions in many ways as a microcosm of the larger community in which they live. Through her characters, then, Albert paints a picture of modern Austria (and by extension of the Western industrial world in general) as members of a community impacted by globalization, commercialism, and world politics; a community which faces isolation and a lack of direction and is disappointed by unfulfilled dreams. But the world Albert portrays is not without hope. Her characters do at times have moments of meaningful connection with others, however fleeting, and find brief moments of happiness and peace with themselves when they are able to break free of the constrictions which confine them.

Place and space play a key role in each of these films in treating issues of life in the modern world. Over recent decades a reassessment of theories of space and place has been undertaken in various disciplines from architecture to cultural studies, and film theorists have looked to such sources as Bakhtin, Benjamin, Certeau, Bachelard, Lefebvre, Deleuze, and Gardies to enrich discussions of the functions of space in film. In addition, recent work by geographers and the development of organizing systems like chaos theory and fractal science can be particularly fruitful in providing a framework for discussion of the functions of space and place in Barbara Albert's feature films.

The imaginary Austria of film—whether those films have been made at home or abroad—has played an essential role in characterizing such typical Austrian film genres as the "Viennese film" with its baroque buildings and grand boulevards, and the *Heimatfilm* with its picturesque rural settings. Such stereotypical national landscapes were an equally essential component of the film which has surely done more than any other to construct an image of Austria worldwide, the American-made *The Sound of Music* (1965), set in the beautiful scenery of Salzburg and its surroundings. A characteristic feature of the films of many current Austrian filmmakers, however, is that they challenge the identification of Austria with these iconic images and attempt instead to reimagine the Austria of film to reflect the changing experience of place in today's world. Consistent with such trends, the feature films of Barbara Albert problematize concepts of geographic space and belonging, of home and nation, and of insider versus outsider status.

Albert's first feature film, *Northern Skirts*, emphasizes Austria's location in relation to Eastern Europe and is set against a backdrop of the upheaval of the early 1990s in that region. During this time Austria (and in particular its capital, Vienna, which is the location of the film's story) was directly affected by migration resulting from the opening of Eastern European borders and by the dissolution of Yugoslavia. *Northern Skirts* focuses on four young characters who reflect an Austrian community affected by these migrations: Jasmin is a native-born Austrian; Tamara is born to Bosnian Serbs but grew up in Austria; Valentin comes from Romania; and Senad is a Bosnian Muslim. The title of the film, *Northern Skirts*, refers to a specific geographic location, the neighborhood on the outskirts of northern Vienna where the main characters live. But the title points as well to Austria's geographic location to the north of the Balkans and the civil war in former Yugoslavia. More broadly, the term *Northern Skirts* also points to a long-held image of Austria as a borderland, outpost, and bridge. As the dominant power in Central Europe, the Austrian Empire was long seen to function as the boundary between Eastern and Western Europe. And as far back as the siege of Vienna in the sixteenth century, Austria was seen as the final outpost of Europe and Western civilization, protecting it against the Ottoman Empire and invaders from the Orient beyond. Postwar Austria has also been characterized by its location, this time seen as a mediating bridge between Western Europe and outlying regions, whether due to its role as mediator between East and West in the Cold War, as a transit location for Eastern European Jews moving to Israel, or as a central location for offices of international organizations like the UN and OPEC.

Recent work in cultural geography, however, suggests that a view of place as static and discretely set off from other places by its boundaries does not reflect the reality of space as it functions for real communities, particularly in the world of today with its unprecedented global interactions. James Clifford, for example, argues : "The new paradigms begin with historical contact, with entanglement at intersecting regional, national and transnational levels. Contact approaches suppose not sociocultural wholes subsequently brought into relationship, but rather systems already socially constituted relationally, entering new relations through historical processes of displacement" (Clifford 1997: 7). If the contemporary Austria of *Northern Skirts* can be seen as a bridge, then, it is a bridge like the places which cultural theorist Homi Bhabha (1994: 5) describes as a liminal space of borders, thresholds, and in-betweenness where negotiations of various cultures take place and where the bridge itself functions as the space for a developing community.

The Austria of *Northern Skirts* is not shown to be shut off from the outside by its borders. Rather, its borders are riddled with connections to places beyond and its community extends beyond borders as well; for example, Tamara is originally from Sarajevo and Valentin an illegal migrant from Romania. The border itself is shown to be porous. The southern Austrian border is seen when Tamara's boyfriend performs his military service as a guard there. But the border is not well fortified and moments later Senad from Bosnia manages to come across it undetected. The movement across Austria's borders goes in the other direction as well: Tamara's parents have returned to Sarajevo; Valentin longs to go to the US; and a Russian waitress plans to move to Australia.

Communications technology also provides for connections to the outside: reports of the war in Bosnia and the end of the socialist regime in Romania on radio and television are interspersed throughout the film as background noise and imagery, and frequent phone calls connect people from different countries. A liberal use of inserts, a common stylistic device in all Barbara Albert's feature films, also links Vienna to the outside, showing: family members in Romania and Bosnia; traveling shots of streets in those countries; a girl in Russia receiving a doll which was sold by Valentin in Vienna; and a still shot of the Russian waitress in her travel goal, Australia. The film's structure reflects the fact that in Albert's Vienna the local and the global are not exclusive. The integrity of an Austria which is defined by its geographical borders and which can keep out what lies beyond those borders is thereby challenged through the film's narrative and editing. This is consistent with the open view of place expressed by many contemporary geographers. For example, Doreen Massey writes, "the particularity of any place is ... constructed not by placing boundaries around it and defining its identity through counterposition to the other which lies beyond, but precisely (in part) through the specificity of the mix of links and interconnections *to* that 'beyond'" (Massey 1994: 5).

In the 1990s, a more traditional view of nations and borders was alluded to when the concept of Austria as a final outpost was taken up again in a new context: some now saw Austria as an outlying state of the European Union securing the borders against an influx of unwanted immigration from the south and east. This image of Austria was popularized by Richard Lugner, a supporter of the Austrian Freedom Party (FPÖ) and later a leader of the Austrian Independent Party, both of which had gained support in part by playing on Austrians' fears of being overrun by immigration from the south and east. Lugner called for a "Fortress Austria" (Karacs 1999: 1), using a term which mirrored the phrase "Fortress Europe," which critics of the European Union had used to decry a perceived tendency of the EU to define itself as much by its exclusion of outlying economically disadvantaged regions as by membership of the states within. It is precisely this image of Austria which Barbara Albert rejects in *Northern Skirts*. In commenting on her choice of the mid 1990s as the time period for her film, Albert talks of her disappointment in the political trends in Austria at that time, with "the rise of right-wingers everywhere, which resulted in the other parties also moving a bit further to the right" (Flos 2007). In *Northern Skirts* she deconstructs this image of Austria as an outpost excluding outsiders and as a place for Austrians only. Rather, the image of Austria she presents is consistent with a more open view of geographic place as articulated by Massey:

> the particular mix of social relations which are thus part of what defines the uniqueness of any place is by no means all included within that place itself. Importantly, it includes all relations which stretch beyond—the global as part of what constitutes the local, the outside as part of the inside. Such a view of place challenges any possibility of claims to internal histories or to timeless identities. (Massey 1994: 5)

Eschewing images which might suggest the mythic Austria of many earlier films (or ones made use of recently in the political arena), *Northern Skirts* avoids the iconic landmarks of Vienna. Rather than the typical tourist image of the city, we see generic locations typical of urban settings in Western industrialized nations, such as high-rise apartment buildings and colorless city streets. Mobility and transition characterize the inhabitants' lives, as reflected by numerous traveling shots from moving forms of transportation and by the many scenes set in locations of transience: bridges, buses, metro and train stations, a dormitory for refugees, a club which is a gathering place for Serbian immigrants, the van from which Senad does business and in which he lives. When characters do approach landmark settings in the film, the specificity of those places is obscured. For example, shots filmed in the Danube Park do not highlight the famous river and a New Year's celebration on St. Stephen's Square does not show the whole St. Stephen's cathedral. Likewise, sequences shot in an Aida patisserie do not highlight the cultural appeal of the traditional Viennese coffee shop, but rather concentrate on images of the business processes that take place behind the scenes of this large restaurant chain. There are no orienting establishing shots or identifying street signs, and changes in scene are not connected by transition shots that contribute to an intact overview of the city. The cinematography contributes, then, to a deconstruction of a mythical image of Austria as characterized by its famous landmarks. These disjointed images of place reflect the lack of connection among members of the community of contemporary Vienna as portrayed in the film.

Any coherence to the Austrian community in *Northern Skirts* comes not from common geographic origins, but from interactions which occur within the geographical space. As Massey writes: "If ... the spatial is thought of ... as formed out of social interrelations at all scales, then one view of a place is as a particular articulation of those relations, a particular moment in those networks of social relations and understandings" (Massey 1994: 5). The structure of the ensemble film is particularly well adapted to reflect a spatial interconnectedness which develops through the social interaction of a community. In *Northern Skirts* it is in the spaces of Vienna that the paths of the four main characters cross and that a community of sorts develops among them. Jasmin, the "native" Austrian, moves among a diverse community whose members are of various ethnicities and immigration status in which concepts of insider and outsider no longer have much significance. And, in fact, where common nationalities do exist, they do not necessarily lead to a sense of belonging among individuals: Both Senad and Tamara come from Sarajevo in a Yugoslavia which is undergoing partition, but they are divided by ethnic differences which have been compounded by war. In one scene Jasmin suggests that Tamara and Senad speak Serbo-Croat together. But Bosnian-Serb Tamara clearly wants nothing to do with Bosnian-Muslim Senad. Likewise he claims to speak the language "Bosnian" rather than a dialect of their common language, Serbo-Croat.

None of the four main characters of *Northern Skirts* is at home or settled in a traditional manner in Vienna. Tamara lives in her family's apartment alone, since her family has returned to Sarajevo, and at the end of the film she decides to return as well. Valentin fled Romania after Ceaucescu was deposed in order to enter Austria illegally, but he sees Vienna only as a stopover on his way to the United States. Senad is a refugee fleeing war in Bosnia who lives temporarily in a dormitory for asylum seekers. All of the characters are outsiders in some way in Vienna and have only meager access to the opportunities of more privileged Austrian society. We learn that Serbian-born Tamara envied Jasmin when they were children for her privileged status as a native-born Austrian, but in the Vienna of *Northern Skirts*, Jasmin has become as marginal an inhabitant of the city as Tamara. As Linda McDowell writes, "As soon as it is recognized that cultures are fluid and temporary social constructions, made and remade over time—Clifford's translocal culture—it is apparent that movement involves the remapping of cultural identities and practices for all those involved" (McDowell 1999: 210). The film's title, then, is also a metaphor for the characters' marginal status at the outskirts of society.

In spite of the lack of connection between place and identity among those in *Northern Skirts*, they, like characters in all of Albert's films, long for a sense of belonging. The old paradigms for concepts like home and family have become problematic, however. Tamara is torn between the home she has grown up in and the home in Sarajevo to which her family has returned. Jasmin lives in a home with a sexually abusive father and an ineffectual mother. When she finally moves out, the boyfriend she had expected to move in with rejects her. She looks for solace in ways she can: she and her sister watch, entranced, a romantic fairy tale on television which contrasts sharply with life in the household around them; she moves from sexual encounter to sexual encounter seeking human contact; and she drinks too much. At one point Jasmin spends the night unconscious on the street out in the cold and at another she shares a bed with her latest sexual partner in a home for refugees. She becomes, then, homeless in her home town much like the illegal immigrants and refugees who have sought a safe haven there.

All three of Albert's films have women as primary characters and these women face particular struggles in dealing with traditional gendered patterns for life which conflict with other desires for seeking fulfillment. When Tamara and Jasmin attempt to set up house together, Jasmin clings to the superficial symbols of home (afternoon coffee and cake, a Christmas wreath) but when she begins to stay out all night, their homelife falls apart. And neither Jasmin nor Tamara is prepared to start a family of their own. Tamara leaves her boyfriend, Roman, after she gets pregnant, and the two women reconnect as adults when they meet again after many years in the waiting room of an abortion clinic.

Albert's characters comprise a community which is emblematic of such understandings of a globalized world in which place is not a static and bounded spatial dimension, but rather a dynamic and open-ended dimension characterized by the interactions which take place there.

Although the depiction of their Vienna may be much harsher than that of earlier genre films set in Austria, there is a hopeful note that the dynamism and diversity of its community will allow the characters to prevail in the end. Despite the fact that issues of home and community are not resolved in *Northern Skirts*, the film ends with a rather uplifting shot of Tamara standing at the window of the train which will take her back to Sarajevo. She has a smile on her face and clearly enjoys the feel of the wind against her face and the speed with which she moves past the objects outside. This open-ended final scene leaves room for the possibility of a better future for the characters of *Northern Skirts*.

Albert's second feature film, *Free Radicals*, is the story of a large ensemble of diverse characters, all living in the same town, each of whom shares a home, a workplace, a classroom, or a place of worship with other characters. It has in common with *Northern Skirts* themes of isolation in a globalized, modern society. As in *Northern Skirts*, the places in *Free Radicals* are populated by a diverse population whose network as a community is determined more by the location where they cross paths than by any significant human relationships among them. While *Free Radicals* also does not include images of a stereotypical Austria, Albert does find her characters' inability to achieve their goals particularly characteristic of contemporary Austrian society: "What I find fascinating is that the figures are often so passive, even in my films, how determined by others, driven by conditions and necessity. That is, in my experience, very Austrian" (Albert, in Hermes 2004).

In *Free Radicals* place and space again play a key role in conveying the film's themes as characters turn to what Yi-Fu Tuan has termed mythical spaces, "an intellectual construct" which is "a response of feeling and imagination to fundamental human needs" (Tuan 2001: 99). While in *Northern Skirts* characters idealized geographic places into mythical spaces—the US for Valentin, who drives around in a van painted with the American flag, and Australia for his Russian coworker—in *Free Radicals* it is made clear that these places will not ultimately fulfill characters' dreams. For example, Manu, a young wife and mother, takes a vacation in Brazil and writes home a postcard in which she describes the place as "paradise." But the Brazil which Manu describes is seen instead through images which contradict this view: an impersonal room in a high-rise hotel, a sterile airport, and the stereotypical scenes of a Third World country as seen from a bus on the way to the airport.

The ideal space of home and the idealized family are as elusive for the characters of *Free Radicals* as they are for those in *Northern Skirts*. Manu dies in a car crash, leaving a husband and young daughter behind. Her sister, Gerlinde, who is described by Albert as one with a borderline personality disorder, has sex with an older physically challenged man so that she will have a place to live. A middle-aged single mother, Belinda, is so disappointed by having her romantic advances rebuffed that she throws herself onto the tracks of an oncoming train. Both the father and mother of high-school student Patricia killed themselves, leaving her an orphan (we see a family photograph from which she has cut out the faces of her parents). Manu's widower, Andreas, begins a relationship with Manu's best friend, Andrea, but their attempts to become a family fail in the end. A running theme in *Free Radicals* is that of a dream house being raffled off. This dream space for many of the town's inhabitants is depicted on a banner next to the slogan: "We make you happy." But the happiness this mythical place promises does not become a reality. Andreas wins the house where he and Andrea could create a home and family right at the time when Andrea has realized their relationship is not what she wants. While Andreas looks at the house, Andrea drives up into the mountains and lies down in the snow.

Commercialism is pervasive in the lives of the characters in *Free Radicals*, and some of them compensate for their lack of human interaction by amassing material goods. Middle-aged single mother Belinda, who admits to being lonely, is particularly vulnerable. When her daughter Sandra visits, all she can talk about are the lottery games she is playing and her most recent purchases. Their only outings together are to the mall, where she delights in the free gifts and prizes. And through the course of the film we see characters play a game involving scratch cards for which the main prize is the new dream house. It is appropriate, then, that the two main public gathering places where the characters of *Free Radicals* cross paths are two shopping centers (and that the winner of the dream house is announced at the grand opening of a new wing of a mall).

But the space of *Free Radicals* also extends to include other levels or dimensions of (potential) reality. Some characters turn to virtual experiences of human connection when other forms fail. A young man named Kai watches a videotaped news report of his brother's kidnapping; because his brother disappeared before Kai was born, Kai only knows his brother through this virtual representation. Another of Kai's significant relationships is mediated through the world of television as well. A talk show, *Verzeih mir*, on which guests ask someone for forgiveness, is playing in the background when Kai and his girlfriend, Gabi, kiss. Later, when Kai asks Gabi to forgive him for the car crash which paralyzed her, she answers with a line she has just heard on the talk show, which she is watching in her hospital room: "I've made up my mind that I never want to see you again." Eventually Kai decides to go on the talk show himself to ask Gabi for forgiveness on television, but his relationship, mediated through the world of television, cannot be repaired.

Characters in *Free Radicals* also look to various systems for understanding the world, including psychotherapy, organized religion, and the occult, to provide them with answers and direction. Sandra, an Afro-Austrian who never knew her father, turns to psychotherapy by trying to work through her family and identity issues at counseling sessions. Her counselor's treatment method involves having patients act out with other patients the encounters they would like to have with their own family members—offering another form of virtual relationship rather than real human contact. Other characters turn to religion or contact with the spirit world to satisfy their needs: Belinda seeks community at church, where she sings in the choir until after her suicide attempt, and Patricia tries to communicate with the spirit world via her Ouija board. When Manu's widower begins an affair with her best friend, he says he cannot continue because he feels as if Manu is watching them. References to a possible afterlife appear frequently in inserts—of the sky, of clouds, of religious symbols—which point to the importance of these dimensions for the themes of isolation and community in *Free Radicals*.

Free Radicals points to other systems as well for making sense of the world, "secondary realities" as Albert refers to them (in Prenner 2003). While in *Northern Skirts* we see connections between Austria and the places beyond its borders, in *Free Radicals* we see a web of interconnections throughout the world and between various realms within the world. The connections between the inhabitants of a small Austrian town and events, however minor, in other parts of the world are potentially explained in *Free Radicals* through references to chaos theory. When Manu leaves Brazil at the beginning of the film, we are shown a shot of a butterfly in a forest. The proverbial flap of the butterfly's wing is seen, followed by the supposedly resulting storm which brings down Manu's plane. Although Manu survives the plane crash (as sole survivor) she dies six years later in a car crash. There seems to be no reason for survival in the one case but not in the other. Chaos theory promises to explain the seeming inexplicable, as Manu's brother Lukas explains in a fast food restaurant, using french fries to illustrate his points.

Lukas seeks a sense of order in the world in another realm as well. A physics teacher, he is intrigued by fractal science, because, as he says, fractals show a "transition from chaos to order." Throughout the film Lukas explains the system of fractals: "Even in seemingly utter chaos, there are always structures and patterns." Wendy Everett goes so far as to include *Free Radicals* in a group of films which she terms "fractal films." She looks to the science of networks as a model for the complex narrative structures of such films, which

> are structured by various interwoven narratives that trace the fragmented experiences of an undefined number of characters. In most cases the relationships between the characters develop apparently randomly, in unpredictable and dynamic ways that demand a creative reading on the part of the spectator. Because of the multiple 'realities' implied by their parallel or intersecting stories, the films offer neither stasis nor closure, but merely ongoing change and process. (Everett 2005: 163)

The very structure of *Free Radicals*, then, can be seen to reflect its themes of changing concepts of community in contemporary society.

This view of a multilayered reality is also mirrored by the spatial dimensions in the film. At moments of significant events for which one might be expected to look to a larger plan or system (whether religion or fractal science) for answers—for example, scenes of the aftermath of the crash of Manu's plane or of the car cash which killed Manu; a shot of Manu's grave followed by Manu's daughter crying out in bed; high schoolers trying to conjure up spirits with a Ouija board; Andrea lying in the snow—the camera shoots from overhead, providing a vantage point for a clear overview of the world and a viewpoint for a potential protective observer. In addition, the frequent juxtaposition of dissimilar shots without transition reflects the possibility of the world existing on more than one level. For example, before Manu's plane crashes, we see a shot of billowing clouds in the sky which she sees out of the window. The film then cuts to a church choir singing "From heaven above I came to earth," then to a crucifix, and then to a picture of a praying child with a zoom in on the sky in the picture, before cutting to an overhead shot of debris on the ocean from the plane crash. The editing suggests that the crash is connected to the cosmic or spiritual realms highlighted in *Free Radicals*.

Chaos theory, fractals, network systems—all attempt to show an order, a logic, a pattern of cause and effect, in a world where little order of this type is apparent, but which religion and the spirit world provide for some characters. But in *Free Radicals* these secondary realities are only potential. They, like the film, do not provide conclusive answers or a direction for life. But although the film raises questions about the meaning of life without answering them, it does provide its viewers with some solace. Andrea, who has gone off to lie down in the snow, eventually opens her eyes, looks into the camera, then pulls herself up and moves off-screen. The film also ends on a somewhat upbeat note. In the final sequence of *Free Radicals* we see a shot of an overcast sky, then a pan down to an empty lot. Shot from above, Yvonne, the daughter of Manu, and Gerlinde, the woman with the borderline personality disorder, run around playfully in the rain. This sequence provides no closure for the characters or answers to the questions the film poses, yet it does show these two lonely people finding a moment of pleasure in the rain. Albert explains: "you're looking for these understandings and these fittings together. And then in the end you can just say 'Okay, you live and die and that's it.' Maybe it doesn't matter that you don't understand, because you will never understand."[1]

Albert's third feature film, *Falling*, tells the story of a group of former high-school friends who are reunited after fourteen years at the funeral of one of their teachers. In this film, all of the main characters are women. Their reunion causes them to remember the hopes and dreams of their youth, which were greatly influenced by Michael, the teacher who has just died. Reminiscing about their past together also leads them to reassess their present lives, which brings to this film the familiar themes of longing for community, family, and home. A space which plays a particularly important role in *Falling* is that of an idealized place or utopia. Albert sums up the themes of the film thus: "I would call *Falling* a personal sketch of figures who are questioning their lives. It is about utopias, about dreams, but also about the question of how resigned one has become: Does your own life match the one you wanted?" (in Steininger 2007).

As in *Northern Skirts* and *Free Radicals*, the characters of *Falling* are dissatisfied with their lives. The traditional patterns for attaining idealized relationships, family and home prove to be ineffective for these women as well. Carmen has become an actress in Germany and her romantic flings are now the topic of articles in celebrity magazines. Nina is expecting a child (with a man who was deported two weeks after she became pregnant) simply because, she says, she didn't want another abortion. She and a new bride fight with each other because Nina and the groom were kissing on his wedding day. Another of the women, Alex, has a steady boyfriend at home, but has sex with the groom in a bathroom. She later symbolically throws the bride's veil into a bonfire. Nicole's daughter, Daphne, must live with her grandfather because her mother is in jail.

Place plays a particularly important role in this film, since it is set in the small town where the women grew up and to which they have now returned in order to attend their teacher's funeral. The film begins with a shot of a particular place, a long take in black and white of a meadow. We discover in the course of the film that this place has special importance for the film's characters and that it is representative of their youthful hopes and dreams. When the women reminisce about their school days we discover that they had had a special place in their younger years, a clearing, where they had dreamed about building a house. When the women later come upon just such a clearing by chance, they determine that this is indeed the meadow of their youth. An insert of a tree in black and white makes it clear that this is the place from the film's opening shot, a place which has functioned as a mythical utopia for the women.

The town itself does not provide the women with a sense of home or communal belonging in any traditional way. We never see their families or the places they lived. During the reunion, they become reacquainted with each other, but they also gravitate back to negative relationships and self-destructive behaviors. The very structures of the town at times shut them out. For example, when we are first introduced to Nina, she stands hemmed in by a large, blank white wall in the background and by two big rectangular signs made out of stone in the foreground. The words on the signs are only partially visible and letters have fallen off, adding to the confusion of this opening scene of the film's narrative. This first scene contrasts sharply with the open, peaceful scene of the meadow which precedes it—the landscape of the film's first shot—which is further separated from the sequence introducing Nina by several seconds of blank screen. The narrative then begins with Nina speaking to someone off-screen, then walking behind one of the stone signs to have a conversation. We begin our characters' stories, then, in a place which places barriers around them, a place very unlike the meadow which opens the film. We soon discover that, as Nina is boxed in by the architecture of the town in this early sequence, the women in *Falling* are boxed in by the routines of their daily lives and by their own lack of initiative to move beyond them.

The women in *Falling* are, like the characters of Albert's previous films, looking for meaning and direction in their lives. Indicative of this is a scene where the women drive together in a car. Alex, who is in the back seat sleeping off too much alcohol, suddenly wakes up and asks: "Are we there yet?" Her companions can only answer: "Where?" But by the end of the film, Albert offers her viewers more optimism in *Falling* than she does in her previous films. At Michael's grave, jaded Carmen sarcastically thanks him for destroying her illusions, but then she also thanks him sincerely "for the dreams." When the women express resignation about the lives they now lead—"we keep busy, shop, go on vacation, check out the sales, shop some more." "That's life."—Brigitte encourages them to fight again for their ideals and assures them: "An alternative world already exists." Albert again uses the device of inserts frequently in this film. Here they function as flashbacks from the past or as characters' memories. The story of these women is also linked to the future through inserts which present stills from sequences that are yet to come in the narrative's chronology—highlighting the changes which are to come and which provide some sense of hope for a better world in the future.

As in Albert's other films, we once again see characters seek in organized religion a place for solace. We first meet the characters in *Falling* in the funeral chapel, where they join the church choir in singing "Heaven is a Wonderful Place." But the main characters find little comfort in religion's rituals: they disrupt the funeral service with a ringing cell phone and laughter, and Carmen later spits on the grave of their former teacher. But confrontation with Michael's death leads them nonetheless to seek some understanding of death which will help them understand life. The women's lack of a satisfactory and consistent framework for understanding death is indicated by the appearance of one of Albert's unusual inserts which is taken from a future sequence in the film—and appears twice. When one of the women mentions seeing an old classmate earlier, a shot of a young man walking in a train station is shown; another of the women explains that he is dead from a drug overdose. Yet the audience later discovers that the shot of this young man was an outtake from a later sequence in which Carmen waits at the train station to leave town. We again see the shot of the young man who then walks up to Carmen and speaks to her; Carmen remarks that she had heard he was dead. Death, like life, proves to be unpredictable and the unpredictable sequencing of shots in *Fallen* contributes to this.

In all three of Albert's films, key scenes make reference to the space up above, whether through shots of kites flying during Tamara and Jasmin's childhood in *Northern Skirts* or the many overhead shots in *Free Radicals*. In *Falling* there are numerous inserts of the sky. Whether their reference is to heaven or the heavens, black-and-white inserts of rolling clouds in the sky clearly allude to the meadow seen in the opening black-and-white shots of the film. When the women happen upon this meadow of their youthful dreams again, a particularly powerful event takes place. They walk to the edge of a cliff and lean into the wind which comes across it. In a moment of euphoria, they are supported by the wind, kept from falling (a reference to the film's title), floating in the sky; they are in communion with each other. This mythical place of youthful ideals and hopes, then, provides them for a moment with the sense of community and support that they seek.

We see other scenes of such joyful energy in the film, in which characters break out of their daily routine by jumping on a trampoline, playing a game, or riding a mechanical bull. Such scenes occur in *Northern Skirts* as well, for example, when Tamara stands at the train window traveling home to Sarajevo or during a New Year's Eve gathering when Jasmin, Tamara, Senad, and Valentin enjoy a moment of joy as they celebrate with beer and song amidst the crowd in St. Stephen's Square. Popular music and dancing frequently provide the impetus for such moments of release for Albert's characters, especially in *Free Radicals* and *Falling*. Albert has said in an interview, "Dancing is the longing to feel alive" (in Hermes 2004). In *Falling*, Carmen and Daphne connect while listening to CDs in the car, and when a vehicle later pulls up into a Burger King parking lot with its radio playing, all of the women move to the beat and some even get up to dance. At the core of Albert's depiction of modern life, then, where people randomly come into contact but rarely truly connect, is this contradictory hope for a life of fulfillment kept alive by brief moments of connection and happiness.

One of the hopes which the women of *Falling* had had when they were young was to remain free—as they believed their teacher Michael was. When the women return to their old school, they remember the social and political engagement they exhibited in their school days and recall a favorite phrase from that time, "We are free," and begin writing it over and over on the chalkboard. When Carmen later asks Nina, "Do you still want to be free?" Nina answers, "More and more." Relating this freedom to their youthful political engagement and that of their teacher in the student movement of the 1960s, the women sing together lines of "We shall overcome," the gospel song which became an anthem of the U.S. Civil Rights Movement and plays in various versions throughout the film: "We shall overcome. We shall all be free someday." While the film leaves open whether the women will make the same choices they did when they were younger, it is clear that through their reunion they have at least rediscovered the freedom to make their own choices again. Albert has said in an interview, "It was important for me to show that my women can get active and say: 'I'm organizing my life myself'" (in Steininger 2007).

In their striving to survive day to day, the women have allowed themselves to become resigned to their situations, giving up the freedom to live their lives according to their own ideals. Albert sees this as a contradiction in humans: "we are so happy when we have moments when something is logical ... things fit together. We need this order and structure ... We always build this logical system, this structure and this order, because without it we are lost. But on the other hand, we also want to feel free."[2] This contradiction of wanting home and a sense of belonging on the one hand but freedom on the other is apparent in Albert's earlier films as well: in *Northern Skirts* when Jasmin wants to create a household with Tamara, she nevertheless stays out all night against Tamara's wishes. And in *Free Radicals* Andrea wants to create a home with Andreas, but just at the moment when he is looking at the dream house he has won, she drives up into the mountains and lies down in the snow. But the moments of release the characters in all three films engage in provide them with an opportunity, even if only momentarily, to break free of the situations in which they find themselves and of the contradictions with which life presents them.

This option of breaking loose—whether induced by sex, alcohol, popular music, or being reunited with old friends—is portrayed at the level of the film frame in both *Free Radicals* and *Falling* through the cinematography of dancing scenes where women allow themselves to lose control. For example, in *Free Radicals* Andrea goes out dancing after Andreas has told her they should see less of each other. She begins to dance so wildly that the handheld camera does not keep her within the frame. In *Falling*, Alex (played by the same actress), who has admitted that she self-medicates to relieve her pain, is also no longer contained by the frame when she finds release by dancing wildly with the bride (they even remove their tops) to a song with the words "You make me want to lose control." Albert has said of such sequences, "I want to let the actors, the characters, try to, like … as if they want to get out of the frame."[3]

The most obvious example of a character in *Falling* who lacks freedom is Nicole, whom we see enclosed in a prison cell after being brought back into custody. She was to return to prison after the teacher's funeral, but she missed the deadline and was taken in forcibly. When the police tackle Nicole as she walks through a mall, Carmen, who has until that point been mostly preoccupied with phone calls to her agent back in Germany and has expressed the most disappointment in their former teacher, finally becomes engaged in the events around her. She tries in vain to free Nicole from the grasp of the police and cries out in solidarity "Long live freedom." An insert follows of a still photo—in the future or just a possibility?—of all of the women running with Nicole outside the prison walls, providing a hopeful image of freedom even for Nicole.

Brigitte has remained most steadfast in her commitment to her youthful ideals (and those of her teacher Michael). We find out that she not only continued to be close to their teacher throughout his life, even his lover off and on, but that of all the women she has come closest to carrying on his life's work by becoming a teacher. The film concludes with Brigitte discussing change and social engagement with her students, encouraging them to fight for their own hopes and ideals. At home on her bulletin board, next to a flyer for a demonstration against the war in Iraq, is a picture apparently drawn by one of her students. It is labeled with the word "Family," that ideal community which characters in all of Albert's films seek, and the word "Utopia," a place which represents youthful hopes and idealism, including that mythical place of the meadow where the women of *Falling* reconnect with their own youthful ideals.

In each of Barbara Albert's features we are confronted with characters in contemporary Austria who are trapped in difficult social or political situations and in unfulfilling everyday routines. Although the images can be harsh, Albert's films are not without glimmers of hope. Her films contrast, through narrative and cinematography, places in which her characters are hemmed in and dissatisfied to spaces—whether a global world where boundaries and borders are broken down, multiple realms of potential reality, or the places of dreams and hopes which provoke people to reassess their lives and create an alternative world—where they can break free from limitations, whether imposed from outside or coming from their own lack of initiative. There are spaces in Albert's worlds where characters are able, even if only for a moment, to find joy and freedom in a world of change and a community in transition.

Notes

1. Albert's remarks are taken from "Interview with Barbara Albert, Austrian Filmmuseum, Vienna (October 7)," which comes with the DVD of *Free Radicals* (Kino Video, 2005).
2. Source: see n.1.
3. Source: see n.1.

References

Bhabha, H. 1994. *The Location of Culture*, New York: Routledge.

Clifford, J. 1997. *Routes: Travel and Translation in the Late Twentieth Century.* Cambridge, MA: Harvard University Press.

Everett, W. 2005. "*Fractal* films and the architecture of complexity," *Studies in European Cinema*, 2 (3) Winter, 159–171.

Flos, B. 2007. "'Ich habe meine Bilder der letzten Jahre gesammelt': Auszüge aus einem Gespräch zwischen Barbara Albert und Birgit Flos," *ZDF.de*, 19 March. Retrieved 25 March 2007 from: http://www.zdf.de/ZDFde/drucken/0,6753, 2007.2003545,00.html.

Hermes, M. 2004. "Das Bedürfnis nach dem Hier und Jetzt: Interview mit Barbara Albert." *Die Tageszeitung*, 4 April. Retrieved 5 April 2004 from: http://www.taz. de/pt/2004/04/01/a0258.1/textdruck.

Karacs, I. 1999. "'Fortress Austria' Takes a Sharp Turn to the Right," *The Independent*, 3 October, p.1.

Massey, D. 1994. *Space, Place, and Gender*. Minnesota: University of Minnesota Press.

McDowell, L. 1999. *Gender, Identity, and Place: Understanding Feminist Geographies.* Minneapolis: University of Minnesota Press.

Prenner, C. 2003. "Gewollte Hilflosigkeit," *Evolver*, 16 December. Retrieved 25 March 2007 from: http://www.evolver.at/stories/Interview_Barbara_Albert.

Steininger, T. 2007. "Barbara Albert über 'Fallen'," *Österreich*. Retrieved 25 March 2007 from: http://www.oe24.at/zeitung/kino/article 25224.ece.

Tuan, Y.-F. 2001. *Space and Place: The Perspective of Experience*. Minneapolis: University of Minnesota Press.

Chapter 8

Connecting with Others, Mirroring Difference: The Films of Kathrin Resetarits

Verena Mund

Kathrin Resetarits is known for working in more than one field. In early 2006 she was named "Shooting Star" at the Berlin Film Festival. In fall 2007 she published *Vögel sind zu Besuch*, her first book of prose, by which time her short film *Ägypten/Egypt* (1996) had made it into the classics of experimental filmmaking shown in museums and other art venues.[1] While in general her manifold interests (and successes) seem rather unusual, within the recent generation of Austrian filmmakers this is a more common occurrence.

Two things have been striking about New Austrian Film in recent years. First, the core of the Viennese new wave appears to be female: Barbara Albert, Jessica Hausner, Kathrin Resetarits, and Mirjam Unger are the names most commonly mentioned in this respect.[2] Often Ruth Mader or the German Valeska Grisebach are also listed; both, too, were students at Vienna Film Academy in the mid 1990s, as was Jasmila Žbanić of Sarajevo.[3] Second, while the prevalence of women in this group is acknowledged fairly widely, the fact that a remarkable amount of networking takes place among these filmmakers is rarely mentioned. Not surprisingly, during their time as students at the Academy, teamwork was a factor in their short films or feature debuts, but, even afterward, they went on relying on the network established during those years, not least because many of them were able to fulfill several functions and work in different positions. Žbanić, for example, made short appearances in Jessica Hausner's short *Flora* (1995) and in Barbara Albert's *Sonnenflecken/Sunspots* (1998), as well as in her short documentary *Somewhere Else* (1996/97). Nina Kusturica, best known for her feature *Auswege/Sign of Escape* (2003), also worked as an editor and producer on Mirjam Unger's *Wiens verlorene Töchter/*

Vienna's Lost Daughters (2007). In 2003 she founded the production company Mobilefilm together with Eva Testor, who besides directing films is a cinematographer and shot Jörg Kalt's *Richtung Zukunft durch die Nacht/Direction Future Through the Night* (2002) and *Crash Test Dummies* (2005). Cinematographer Christine A. Maier shot Jasmila Žbanić's *Grbavica* (2006) and all of Albert's short films as well as her famous *Nordrand/Northern Skirts* (1999), and also shares the credit for cinematography in Resetarits's *Egypt*. Albert herself wrote the script of Kusturica's *Sign of Escape* and produced Žbanić's *Grbavica* as well as Hausner's debut feature, *Lovely Rita* (2002). Hausner, in turn, together with Albert, Martin Gschlacht, and Antonin Svoboda, cofounded the production company Coop99, produced films by Svoboda and Hans Weingartner, and operated as assistant director on Resetarits's *Egypt* and *fremde/Strangers* (1999), as did Valeska Grisebach on Resetarits's *Ich bin Ich/I am Me* (2006). And Resetarits herself had prominent acting roles in Albert's *Sunspots*, *Böse Zellen/Free Radicals* (2003) and *Fallen/Falling* (2006), as well as in Kalt's *Direction Future Through the Night* and *Crash Test Dummies*.

Although the prevalence of women in the Viennese new wave is not based on an agenda, the women of this group predominantly pursue an interest in women characters and women friendships in their films, and Resetarits is no exception in this regard. In *Strangers* she focuses on her female protagonist and the women around her, and as a result men have limited visibility. Not that there are no men in this film; they even have an important impact on the events. Yet, the film positions them as peripheral. The men are extras, first-class customers at the protagonist's workplace, or we see them as film stars on TV. The protagonist's ex-husband is "present" only in a phone call with the protagonist while we neither see nor hear him, or, when he is actually in a scene with his daughter at IKEA, we see the daughter but he is visible only by virtue of his hand pushing a shopping cart.

Whereas the female prevalence in recent Austrian filmmaking has value in terms of marketing, the group's networking appears almost to be an obstacle in this regard. Since, as Bert Rebhandl puts it, "Austrian cinema has abandoned its former 'great men policy' and has re-shaped itself as a field" (Rebhandl 2005: 64), it has become more difficult to describe or present this cinema in those terms of film reception most common today; namely, the perspective of auteur cinema.[4] So, for the programmers of the 2006 film series "Austria: State of a Nation" at the Lincoln Center, New York, "it is tempting to call it a movement," but instead of paying any further attention to this idea, the programme notes go on to emphasize that "this is a collection of individuals, each pursuing his or her own idiosyncratic vision".[5] The series included works from the era of the so called 'great men policy', such as films by Ruth Beckerman, Nikolaus Geyrhalter, Michael Glawogger, Michael Haneke, and Ulrich Seidl. The recent generation of New Austrian Film was also represented, not as a network, or a "field," but again as two auteurs: Barbara Albert and Ruth Mader. Although Albert's cowriting of Mader's *Struggle* is mentioned in the film descriptions—the only exception of a listed screenwriting credit—it does not serve as a characterization of the network in recent Austrian cinema. Instead it emphasizes Albert as "prime mover,"[6] a more important auteur than others. Yet, more revealing is that Mader had collaborated with Albert and Martin Leidenfrost on a screenplay before, and that Albert also worked with Mader's cinematographer Bernhard Keller on *Fallen*; or, for that matter, that Keller was also cinematographer on Grisebach's *Be my Star* and *Longing*. What is obscured through this reduced focus on the auteur is the work relations that exist across films, such as *Struggle* and *Northern Skirts*, as well as other films of the Viennese new wave that the film series was supposed to represent. On the other hand, a focus on networking has the advantage of highlighting various connections between the "great men" and the "reshaped field" of filmmakers, to use Rebhandl's distinction again. For example, Monika Willi edited *Northern Skirts* and, together with Nadine Muse, Haneke's *La Pianiste/Die Klavierspielerin/ The Piano Teacher* (2001); she also worked on Kalt's *Direction Future Through the Night* and Glawogger's *Workingman's Death* (2005). Resetarits played in Albert's *Sunspots*, which also included in the film series, and has been an assistant director fairly regularly in Haneke's productions as well. The list of examples could be extended.[7] Thus, with a focus on networking, relations come into view that are different and more complex than a (too) simply structured genealogical concept allows. This is even more true if, as in the case of the Viennese new wave, multifunctional collaboration takes place to a great extent. Resetarits alludes to the advantages of her multifunctional experiences when she remarks, "[w]hile acting one cedes oneself and hands oneself over to someone else [the director]. That is why the trust an actor has to build up is so important. As a director I used to underestimate this too much" (in Schiefer 2006).[8]

Moreover, an auteur view may mislead in discussing the work of the new wave filmmakers only in reference to the "great men," as, for example, when Bert Rebhandl writes about the work "of a group of younger male and female filmmakers" as a "reaction" to Seidl and Haneke (Rebhandl 2004: 6). Ruth Mader, in contrast, rigorously rejects such contextualizing (Dassanowsky 2006), and, significantly, she does so in an interview when her comments about the collaboration on *Struggle* have just been ignored: "'I again collaborated on the script with Martin Leidenfrost and Barbara Albert. This team was already successful with my short film *Gfrasta*. We have developed a fine system of writing together.' 'Some critics at Cannes see a mixture of Michael Haneke and Ulrich Seidl in your style ... ' 'I totally disagree'" (Greuling 2003). Emphasizing the structure of work relations has little chance against the story of "great men," a genealogy of auteurs. The ideal of this concept is the autonomous individual standing out because of creativity, intellect, or power. A focus on networking, on the other hand, does not neglect the special role of a director within a film production, but instead provides a different context, where the filmmaker is described within a set of work relations—something the auteur approach misses. Here such a background of work relations mostly remains unseen. In her film *Strangers*, Resetarits also seems to make this point, where she casts a Hollywood star as the "autonomous individual."

In *Strangers* there is a juxtaposition of two worlds, the world of the singular star and the world of the collaborative group. The film can be described as typical of the working-girl genre, where a usually insignificant female employee meets the man she adores from the world of the rich and famous (Volkening 2007). At the beginning of the film, Matt Damon is introduced to us in a TV interview as he is about to fly to Vienna. We watch this interview together with the protagonist at her home. She works as a receptionist in the VIP lounge of Vienna International Airport and, importantly, is a fan of Damon's. So, on the one hand we have the singular star in the spotlight, a man who simply seems to be beautiful, and on the other we have the protagonist who puts a lot of work into dressing up for her encounter with the star. In order to make this encounter possible, the protagonist is helped by her colleagues, a group who also support her after her big disappointment. "This guy can't even say thank you," she reports when sitting together with them. But it is not his impoliteness alone that causes her frustration. From the very beginning something is wrong: Damon is not alone. This is not as she has experienced him on TV, not as she envisioned him when she planned to address him personally. Damon came with three bodyguards around him, she tells her colleagues, "all of them at least one foot taller than himself." Just by being there, the bodyguards demonstrate that every effort to address Damon would be in vain. Moreover, they make clear that Matt Damon is not simply Matt Damon. He might be a person, but he is also definitely a (star) image—Resetarits shows him only once: during the TV interview. The camera zooms slowly out, making the TV set visible as it frames Damon, and thus emphasizing the fact of the image. Further, if one tries to meet the star beyond the image, one is confronted with bodyguards, assistants, managers, and press agents: a whole company that keeps the image of Matt Damon "alive." A network, though, that usually remains unseen.

Not only do networks depend on communication, communication is also the main benefit of a network. But the positive impact of a network on one's work is not limited to the transmission of isolated bits of information. When Emily Artmann told Resetarits that Geyrhalter Films, which had produced a film Artmann had edited before, would be interested in unusual documentaries and might agree to produce Resetarits's *I Am Me*, her first project after leaving the Vienna Film Academy, this was more than "simple" information.[9] It came from someone whom Resetarits knew from her time at the Academy and who had edited her film *Strangers* before, someone who shared a history of networking with Resetarits and was supposed to communicate with her as the editor of the new project. Communication between people who developed relationships through sharing projects and discussions is able to transmit much more detailed and specific information, as Resetarits explains when she compares working with Albert and Kalt to working with other directors: "With Bärbel and Jörg ... it is the way that we share the same understanding of film, share the same goals; that provides me with reliability. And we speak the same kind of language as well" (in Schiefer 2006). What Resetarits is talking about is sharing a code: a set of communication modes and conventions developed in everyday life through shared experiences and background discussion and which facilitates the transmission of complex messages. The reliability or comfort of group communication advances with the code's potential to condense complexity. A very compact communication mode, for instance, is inherent in humor that may be vague or ambiguous regarding the message, but also funny to those who are in on the joke; that is, those who may share a particular sense of humor and have prior knowledge and thus are able to work with the vagueness and ambiguity. Erhard Schüttpelz takes humor as a model to describe communication within a young art scene and points to the potential for the creativity it opens up. As a mode of communication that, besides the concrete message, transmits the awareness of being part of a group, it makes the group comfortable with experimenting or neglecting conventions of established production (Schüttpelz 1995: 55–57). This aspect becomes apparent when Resetarits compares her acting in TV productions to her working with Albert and Kalt. "First of all, I am interested in [working with Albert and Kalt], because they are doing something that I dare to do" (in Schiefer 2006). In this environment it is not just that she feels comfortable; with Albert and Kalt she also is confident in taking risks.

Group communication is also an issue in films of the Viennese new wave. Women's networks and friendships, for example, are an important aspect of Albert's *Sunspots*, *Free Radicals*, and *Fallen*, as well as of Unger's *Ternitz, Tennessee* (2000) and her short *Speak Easy* (1997).[10] Resetarits, however, stands out in her analysis of conditions of communication, as well as in her reflections on film as a medium and on film reception as a communicative act.

In *Strangers* we often see the protagonist on the phone at her own workplace. She is talking to different people: to a colleague, to her mother, to her ex-husband. Sometimes she is joking, but only in certain conversations. Resetarits watches the receptionist setting everything in motion to make the encounter with Matt Damon possible: she calls her colleague in order to change shifts, her mother about baby-sitting her daughter, and, as this does not work out, her ex-husband regarding the same issue. The sound of her voice changes from phone call to phone call. Her efforts to overcome her feelings of guilt dominate the call with her mother, whereas the talk to her ex-husband sounds more like a battle about resources. These calls are quite different from the calls to her colleagues: only then does it seem she discusses the pros and cons of Damon on the one hand and a shift change on the other. Only then is she not afraid of disclosing her crush on Damon. Overall, her voice sounds more relaxed, but also a self-parodying of her embarrassment and barely-contained excitement. "I promise you'll be my maid of honor," she jokes when her colleague agrees to swap shifts. And after Damon is gone, her colleagues help her through the disappointment again by joking and by sharing in the mockery of men.

As Resetarits uses the phone calls to introduce her protagonist, we hear about her desire as well as learn about her social environment. Resetarits does not show this context though: she just shows the protagonist on the phone, which "presupposes the existence of another telephone, somewhere," one at least (Ronell 1989: 3). We do not see the others communicating with her, nor do we hear them. We hear only her part, rather than the complete conversation, so attention is drawn to the fact that there is communication going on, as well as to the various modes of communication in play: for example, the sound of her voice, or what she is doing with her hands while speaking. To calm down, she lights a cigarette, a signifier of sensual pleasure, of even an endlessly increasing desire for pleasure (Klein 1993: 43–46). While doing so she keeps the phone between her head and shoulder, her ear unremittingly adhering to this "technical materialization of desire" (Genth and Hoppe 1986: 6). The receptionist is excited about the prospect of a possible encounter with the Hollywood star, and the last thing she wants now is to work. And the phone, as a machine of simultaneous presence and absence (Ronell 1989: 84–85), allows her to make necessary arrangements to let it happen, as well as to extend her joy and excitement through sharing it with her colleagues. The intensity of the protagonist's desire is even more clearly pointed out at the moment of interruption: the receptionist is forced to put down both, phone and cigarette, when disturbed by an arriving customer.

Resetarits's protagonist is not only a receptionist by profession, receiving requests and giving out information, as several monitors at her desk showing flight schedules or images from surveillance cameras underscore. Even as an individual, she lives through communication and is described as a receiver and a sender of information. The phone emphasizes this. When she is shown a couple of minutes later, grabbing a walkie-talkie, the wall behind her covered with a huge world map, her profession has already become a metaphor for the conditions of her being.

The object of the receptionist's desire is also mediated through TV. At some point, when the protagonist is watching the interview, her view of Damon is disturbed by her daughter's head moving in front of the TV. From the beginning, there are conflicting interests, and communication means negotiating them. It does not have to be done through words though. Accordingly, while the daughter tries to push herself in front of the TV to gain her mother's attention, the mother cranes her neck to look around her daughter without letting her attention be pulled from the interview.

Just as the desires and dreams of the mother are challenged by the moral imperatives to be a good parent and pay attention to her daughter, the daughter has to prove that she is capable of following orthographic rules and fulfilling standards of being a reasonable person for her age, a person capable of participating in and following the communication norms of society. The daughter has problems at school; she is assumed to be dyslexic and must also take a test to check her intelligence. Can she talk reasonably, even though she has trouble spelling? Does she know what she is talking about? Can she understand what people say to her? At the end of the film, Resetarits poses the more crucial question as being whether we understand the girl.

If communication is understood as sending and understanding or recognizing messages between people, there is always the problem not only of understanding what a message means but also whether the receiver has understood or will understand one's own message. As the basic situation of communication is characterized by this double contingency, the success of communication, according to Niklas Luhmann, is rather unlikely (Luhmann 1984: 217–19). Yet the probability of success is enhanced when there is a history of inter-individual communication in addition to general standards of communication. In *Strangers* we learn about the importance of this inter-individual background and how it is able to provide successful communication despite the fact, or maybe even because, standards of communication are neglected.

As they are driving home after the intelligence test, the receptionist turns on some music in the car, and immediately the girl says, "Mama, the one with the flute!" It takes the receptionist some time to find the right tape, but obviously there is no question about which song her daughter means: soon Bob Seger's "Down on Main Street" starts with its peculiar electric guitar tune. Both mother and daughter seem to relax and continue driving. Obviously, in this situation to insist that there is no flute in this song would seem beside the point and even confusing. Communication works here through a replacement of meaning, which has apparently been processed through past mutual experiences. Mother and daughter are communicating on the basis of their shared knowledge, according to which "Down on Main Street" is the "song with the flute." If the girl had asked for "the song with the electric guitar," her mother probably would have chosen another song, or she would have had to ask for clarification.

We watch this scene through the car's windshield. It gives a view of the scene, but, at the same time, it limits this view by reflecting buildings, trees, and other signs of the city. The windshield underscores the exclusion of this environment as well as ourselves from communication between the receptionist and the girl, which is guided by an inter-individual experience not accessible to us.

The daughter's intelligence test is used by Resetarits to analyze modes of communication rather than to show how the girl is coping with the tasks. She follows the reaction in the faces of the girl and the tester, and it is from this and from the sound of the tester's voice that the audience gets an idea about how successfully the girl completes the tasks. Sometimes the camera takes a bird's-eye-view of the table where both the girl and the tester are sitting. The framing cuts their bodies out of the picture, so that we only see their hands interacting with each other in a laboratory-like setting. Although functioning as tools to hold or move objects, the hands almost become agents in themselves, playing like hand puppets in the test situation. The girl's hands seem to be insecure, moving slowly and hesitantly, while the hands of the tester resolutely lay out cards, which are to be set in the correct order by the girl. "Can you do this, too?" the tester asks. Even before the girl's hands start moving, the tester's hand enters the picture again, this time holding a clock and setting it up. The pressure of standardization and measurement determines this situation, which might have a big impact on the girl's future life. Only a very few limited patterns of response will be accepted, leaving no place for unusual reactions, creative as they may be.

Not surprisingly, hands also play a big role in Resetarits's best known film, *Egypt*, a ten-minute-long documentary on sign language. Hands—as well as faces and even whole bodies as we learn throughout the film—are moving in a way that we don't understand and that often make us feel estranged. At the end of the film this will have changed. *Egypt* could be described as a series of experimental sets that constitute a multilevel syllabus to introduce hearing persons to sign language as well as to their own communication handicaps. In this performative and downright playful film, the didactic dimension evolves out of the fact that we, the audience, do not learn by simply being told but by being part of the performance. The playfulness is based on and structured by the conditions of film as a medium. Resetarits makes us aware of these conditions by cutting off one dimension of the medium. The sound is turned off through (almost) the whole film. In the beginning, though, we are not quite aware of this fact: we see a girl, who presumably watches TV. With the next cut we now see what kind of film she is watching. However, we do not understand what is going on in the scene, because, as we now become aware, we, unlike the obviously amused girl, cannot hear the film scene. The film places us in the position of a deaf person. But Resetarits also gives us time to realize something more: the women we see on TV have a very accentuated and slow lip movement. We have seen such a strange lip movement before: their manner of talking seems similar to singing. If we were to hear the women singing, their lip movement would not appear strange to us at all. But because the sound is turned off it does seem odd, at least as long as we have not figured out that it is just singing that we see—something quite usual to us, if we see and hear it simultaneously. Without sound, as we learn, the world also looks different to us.

In the next sequence, we again see strange lip movements. This time it is a woman translating intertitles into sign language for us. Unlike the scene with the silently singing lips, this time we do understand the lip movement, because we have seen the written words before. We can rely on them when we go on watching—a further step toward overcoming the feeling of awkwardness. Our attention is drawn by the turned-off sound, and we watch with mouths agape. And we see: the lips are not alone in this translation; they are joined by hands gesturing, making signs. For example, the woman's upright hand turned at a slight angle and moving forward obviously says "shark," as it mimics what we see of a shark above the waterline, namely its dorsal fin. This makes sense to us. Other intertitles follow, each of which seems more complex and more impossible to translate into a few hand signs or gestures than the preceding one: "widow," "revolution," "Marilyn Monroe." And each time we are surprised anew by the creativity and the effectiveness of sign language in expressing complex concepts. Our attitude begins to change, and more and more the cliché of sign language as a substitute communication fades.

After having enhanced the regard for sign language, *Egypt* shows us that, even if we are not well-versed in sign language, we do understand more of it than we might assume. We might not get the differences between "stone fish," "parrot fish," and "snow fish" in sign language at once, when the teacher introduces these signs to the class. But when a student raises her hand, we do understand that she has questions about them, too. Of course this is due to the obvious context, but in part, it is also due to the fact that what is at first sight an "exotic" way of communicating includes deictic, emblematic, or pantomimic gestures, which hearing persons also make use of in order to communicate (Löffler 2003). We might point with our hand or finger to ourselves, or to the person we are talking to, just like the woman in *Egypt* recounting an old Viennese song in sign language. We might also tap our forefingers against our foreheads, like the student who has questions about the different fish signs, or we might cover our ears with our hands, not in order to protect them but to signify noise, just like the man in *Egypt* who does so at the social gathering for coffee and cake of a group of older people talking sign language. Immediately we understand what he means. At the same time, watching the "noise" of the group he is referring to makes clear to us that perpetual communication does not work on the basis of single signs alone, even if they have a conventional character. The ease of chatting (in sign language) needs grammar and something like idioms and metaphors, a syntactical as well as a paradigmatic structure, in other words the evolved structure of a language (Linz and Grote 2003: 318–19). Otherwise the chatter would not flow.

At the center of *Egypt* is a story narrated in sign language, which provides the film with its title as well as refering to the theoretical background for its perspective on sign language and the perception of it in Western culture.[11] The story is told by a student in a classroom about two Austrians who, after having read about Egypt, decide to take a look at it themselves and end up finding a big treasure in the tomb of a pyramid—we have heard this kind of story a thousand times before; we know it from films, novels, and also archaeologists' reports. It is always about people who, having studied ancient history or having found old maps, make use of their knowledge about a foreign culture in order to find a buried treasure for themselves or their home country. *Egypt* places us in the position of these colonial protagonists. They mirror certain aspects of our own attitude to the world of sign language, which at the beginning of Resetarits's film remains as exotic to us as Egypt and its pyramids do to the two Austrians in the story. We are also confronted with an unapproachable but appealing phenomenon: "hieroglyphics," strange, pictorial signs which tell stories we understand very little if at all and which we keep trying to decipher. Similar to hieroglyphics in colonial thinking, sign language is usually perceived as a culture which is technologically underdeveloped. We are used to looking at sign language as a handicapped substitute, a troublesome way of communication. And this is exactly the way the boy in the classroom starts to tell the story. As if he intended to present the cliché, he begins with the title: e-g-y-p-t. One after another, each single letter is mimicked by his fingers— troublesome indeed. He even has to make a second start with the proper name that has no separate sign of its own but needs to be spelled out by hand. But this tedious start is left behind when the boy gets into the flow and his fascinating body language lets the story mutate into a vehicle for the way he narrates it. Compared to the boy's eloquence, our own body language is atrophied. But on top of that, the boy's narration even raises doubts about the eloquence of our spoken language.

As in sign language, besides hand and lip movements, facial expressions, arms, and even the whole body also function as mediums of communication, the talking body not only representing the sender of the message but its medium as well. In the image of the talking body, concepts of the individual as well as of language and society overlap—which is not limited to the context of sign language, but is also true for communication in general: "If one starts examining communication, one encounters nothing like a precisely distinguishable fact, but two endless horizons, the psyches of the individuals involved on the one hand and the society of the two individuals on the other" (Baecker 2005: 10). Building on this idea, one could say *Egypt* deals with the language horizon of communication and develops visual descriptions of it. For instance, in a classroom the teacher sits facing the camera, speaking in sign language. Although we do not hear anything, we know she is not talking to herself, that there are other people talking too, though we hardly see them. There are just their hands reaching into the picture from left and right, talking hands that represent people less as individuals than as participants of communication. The hands show that communication is taking place: the teacher is not only making signs separately, she is surrounded by language being practiced.

Unlike *Egypt*, Resetarits' most recent film *I Am Me* focuses on the other "endless horizon" of communication. What interests her here, she says, is the topic "'I and the other' or, the question, how do I connect with the other? Is this possible at all, or not? I examine this by means of two twins, who are eight and eleven years old" (in Schiefer 2006). A double question of who's who is the starting point of the film, which is mainly structured by a concept of mirroring. Not only are we watching twins, two people looking like a person and their mirror image, but the film even presents a reflection of this mirror image as well: a second pair of twins.

"That's me." "No, that's me." Two fingers are pointing at the same girl in a photo. In a way these "finger puppets" reprise those from the test scene of *Strangers*. This time they are fighting about who may point at the girl in the photo, about who may be the girl—who is standing right next to a girl looking exactly the same. And, watching this play-like scene in *I Am Me*, we are the last to be able to decide who indeed is "me." As in *Egypt*, we are part of the play. "I intend to put the spectator into a situation where he is confronted with two human beings he is unable to distinguish," says Resetarits, "maybe sometimes he does, but then again he does not" (in Flos 2006).

The disturbing aspect of *I Am Me* is not so much the fact that we are unable to distinguish the individuals in the film, but that we cannot be sure of our own judgment. The film again and again performatively emphasizes to us the assessment we made a moment ago; namely, that the insight we thought we had reached about who's who, does not help us understand what happens all through the film between these girls who look exactly alike. The film makes clear to us that our judgment about the girls, about their relationship, was a judgment of and for that moment—and we can't even be sure of that, can we? Is Anasthasia the one who rather curiously follows the TV show while her sister—Olga?—hiding behind her, almost does not dare to look at the screen? So is Anasthasia also the one taking the lead while singing together with her sister? Or was this rather the one who was better in gymnastics and dancing? But we were already certain this is Olga, weren't we? The film—whose German title, *Ich bin Ich*, is symmetrically shaped in an even stricter way than the English one—does not only show us mirror-like structured images or analog scenes of both pairs of twin eating, watching TV, or making music. Simultaneously it also makes us reflect on our own judgments; it, too, holds a mirror up to us. Are we able at all to gain an impression and to assess the situation without understanding who is who?

I am Me shows us that we are indeed unable to adopt a point of view and communicate it until we have an understanding of the individuals involved (cf. Goffman 1959: 49). And mostly this understanding is nothing but guessing anyway. In order to reach an understanding we have to rely on the impression we get from each twin through her appearance and conduct. Do the twins wear the same clothes; or if not, in what way are they different? What kind of interests does each of them have? Or, what are their favorite colors and animals, as Resetarits asks each of the older twins. Strikingly, both girls draft or correct their answers in reaction to their sister's. After the first girl has listed a handful of animals as her favorite ones, the other twin tops her, responding that all animals are her favorites, whereupon her sister immediately corrects herself: "Actually, it's the same with me, too." Thus, while we base our sense about the self of each girl on the impressions we get from their answers, their selves are not the causes of these impressions (cf. ibid.: 252). We are confronted rather with representations of their selves, a message from each girl about herself. The "real self," as such, is not accessible. "A person is neither what other people say about him or her nor his or her own description of him- or herself".[12]

In order to communicate one has not only to read the impressions of the other individual, but at the same time one has to give impressions about oneself. Everyone has to play a role, too. "To *be* a given kind of person ... is not merely to possess the required attributes, but also to sustain the standards of conduct and appearance that one's social grouping attaches thereto" (ibid.: 75). We all have to learn those standards, to learn how to play roles, roles which people expect us to perform: to learn to be a convincing adult, to look like a woman, to behave like a twin. What kind of behavior might the twin girls think we expect them to perform for us? And how do we think they should behave? Whereas the younger twins, at least Anasthasia, present themselves as being very close, to such an extent that it is as if, for the two, it is not possible to imagine existing without the other, the older twins seem to aim at giving the opposite impression. Beverly and Jill, the older ones, almost seem to deny that they are twins. Rather, they try to distinguish themselves from one another, and sometimes it looks like they are eager to take every situation as a contest. Who's better in playing the memory game? Who is faster at finishing their yogurt? In the beginning Resetarits presents a shot of them that serves as a portrait of their relationship, but at the same time it could be taken as an allegory of the film's thesis as well. We see the two girls standing next to each other in front of a mirror, which is the only actual mirror in the film. They are wearing the exact same shirt; it is a glamorous one, as if they want to go out to a party. The girls are brushing their hair to bind it into a perfect ponytail. Competition seems to be in the air, each girl focused on herself while looking at her mirror image. Who is the best, who is the most beautiful one? We see two girls looking exactly the same while also trying to stand out—the latter ironically also making them the same. It is like a kind of *tableau vivant* of what Resetarits outlines when contemplating her film: "[W]hat constitutes the difference between one individual and another, is interchangeable. It doesn't really differentiate us from others; on the contrary it's something we have in common: the consciousness of being an individual".[13] Turning their heads, and with the help of the mirror, Jill and Beverly check how they look when seen from the side. They try to control how they look when seen by other people: do they make the kind of impression they are aiming at? It is this act of aiming at, as such, that lets us understand each of them as an individual, and not so much what they are aiming at. But the eagerness of the girls is also just an impression we get through an image. Resetarits underscores this by filming the whole scene while the camera is turned onto the mirror. The film does not actually show the girls but only an image of them as reflected in the mirror.

Whereas this image might not be able to transmit the impression each of the girls has in mind—namely, to look more distinguished than her twin sister—we can sense something in the image which the twins were probably not aiming for: when the girls check their mirror images, they do it to check their hair, not because they want to appear to be competitive. Funnily enough, that is how communication often works, which Resetarits understands from her experience as an actress—control over the impression people have of you is not a given:

> The exciting thing about acting is that the body is your tool and at the same time it is a black hole. One only knows so little about oneself, and in the mirror one always looks completely different…. It might happen that while acting one is trapped with one's foot somewhere and goes on acting nevertheless, because one doesn't want to break off, and just feel terrible about it. But then exactly this scene might be interesting, and people say, "here this woman looks so mysterious." (Resetarits, in Schiefer 2006)

"Communication is a problem … a multitude of problems" (Stanitzek 1995: 24–25). That is what makes it difficult but also attractive. And precisely because communication is more than one problem it develops momentum, a momentum, which is not controllable and can achieve unexpected results. But Resetarits is aware of the fact that these results might be very creative. In order to make use of this momentum, confidence in the work situation is needed as well as the capability to adopt different perspectives on this complex setting. Her working environment in Vienna has provided Resetarits with both.

Notes

1. See, e.g., "Ecstatic Bodies," the exhibition curated by Florian Wüst, which showed at E-M Arts/Fondazione Morra, Naples (http://www.em-arts.org/independent/edition-2003/index_ eng.html), and at the Piet Zwart Institute, Rotterdam (http://pzwart.wdka.hro.nl/fama/ programme2/archive/2003-2004/experiencememory).
2. See Leipziger Cinemathek (2000), Marsilius (2001), Hermes (2004), and Perthold (2004). In a text on the sleeve of *Speak Easy* (Vienna: Hoanzl, 2006), Isabella Reicher also refers to a "'nouvelle vague Viennoise' shaped by female filmmakers".
3. Notably, documentary filmmaker Anja Salomonowitz is almost never listed in the context of Viennese new wave; meanwhile, Nina Kusturica and Marie Kreutzer are rarely mentioned.
4. Similar to Rebhandl, Manfred Hermes distinguishes "auteur directors like Haneke and Seidl" from "a generation appearing since the late 1990s and represented by names like Barbara

Albert, Kathrin Resetarits, Jessica Hausner or Nina Kusturica" (Hermes 2004: 36). He later adds Ruth Mader.

5. Walter Reade Theater. 2006. "Austria: State of a Nation," film programme. Retrieved 14 October 2007 from: http://www.filmlinc.com/wrt/onsale06/austrian06.html.
6. Walter Reade Theater. 2006. Calendar. Retrieved 14 October 2007 from: https://tickets.filmlinc.com/php/calendar.php?month=12&day=3&year=2006&sid=&cmode=0&org=.
7. Albert wrote the script for Glawogger's *Slumming* (2006), which was also part of the film series.
8. Moreover, Resetarits is a writer: see, e.g., Resetarits (2007). She also co-writes the comedy routines of her father Lukas Resetarits.
9. Author's interview with Kathrin Resetarits, 25 November 2007.
10. Seibl (2004: 15) points to the lack of female bonding in Ulrich Seidl's *Hundstage* (2001) compared with Albert's *Free Radicals*.
11. The story also refers to the connection between silent film and Orientalism, a reference which cannot be developed further here. See, e.g., Lant (1997).
12. Resetarits; quote taken from a 2006 film description of *I Am Me* (my translation; V.M.).Retrieved 2 Novmeber 2008 from: http://www.sixpackfilm.com/catalogue.php?lang=de&page=&pid=&oid=1493&s=&searchstring=.
13. Source: see n.12.

References

Baecker, D. 2005. *Kommunikation*. Leipzig: Reclam.
Dassanowsky, R. von. 2006. "Austria Hungry: The Return of a Film Nation," *Bright Lights Film Journal* 51. Retrieved 28 September 2007 from: www.brightlightsfilm.com/51/austria.htm#ref25.
Flos, B. 2007. "Ich-Spiegelungen," *Diagonale*. Retrieved 12 October 2007 from: http://2006.diagonale.at/main.jart@rel=de&content-id=1095956399245.htm (my translation; V.M.).
Genth, R. and J. Hoppe. 1986. *Telephon! Der Draht, an dem wir hängen*. Berlin: Transit.
Goffman, E. 1959. *The Presentation of Self in Everyday Life*. Garden City, NY: Doubleday.
Greuling, M. 2003. "'Viele Schauspieler sind vom Fernsehen zerstört.' Interview mit Ruth Mader," *Celluloid 2*, 10–13.
Hermes, M. 2004. "Filme aus Österreich: Utopische Löcher im Elend," *Spex* 4: 36–38.
Klein, R. 1993. *Cigarettes Are Sublime*. Durham, NC: Duke University Press.
Lant, A. 1997. "The Curse of the Pharaoh, or How Cinema Contracted Egyptomania," in M. Bernstein and G. Studlar (eds), *Visions of the East: Orientalism in Film*. New Brunswick, NJ: Rutgers University Press, 69–98.
Leipziger Cinemathek. 2000. "Vier Frauen – vier Filme. Österreich 1996–99: B. Albert, J. Hausner, K. Resetarits, M. Unger," film programme. Retrieved 23 September 2007 from: http://www.cinematheque-leipzig.de/archiv.php?Filmid=868.
Linz, E. and K. Grote. 2003. "Sprechende Hände. Ikonizität in der Gebärdensprache und ihre Auswirkungen auf semantische Strukturen," in M. Bickenbach, A. Klappert, and H. Pompe (eds), *Manus Loquens: Medium der Geste – Gesten der Medien*. Cologne: Dumont, 318–37.
Löffler, P. 2003. "Was Hände sagen: Von der 'Sprechenden' zur 'Ausdruckshand'," in M. Bickenbach, A. Klappert, and H. Pompe (eds), *Manus Loquens: Medium der Geste – Gesten der Medien*. Cologne: Dumont, 210–42.

Luhmann, N. 1984. *Soziale Systeme*. Frankfurt am Main: Suhrkamp.

Marsilius, J. 2001. "Die 'Nouvelle Vague Viennoise'." Retrieved 23 September 2007 from: http://www.3sat.de/3sat.php?http://www.3sat.de/film/reihen/16243/index.html.

Perthold, S. 2004. "'Die Zukunft des Österreichischen Films ist weiblich...' Eine Präsentation von 10 Kino-Filmregisseurinnen und Drehbuchautorinnen," in City of Vienna (ed.), *Frauenkulturbericht 2003*. Retrieved 23 September 2007 from: http://www.wien.gv.at/kultur/abteilung/pdf/frauenkunst2003c.pdf.

Rebhandl, B. 2004. "Nicht anders möglich: Der neuere österreichische Spielfilm und sein Mangel an Realitätssinn," *Kolik Film* 1: 6–10.

———. 2005. "Insel-Entertainment," *Kolik Film* 3: 64–66.

Resetarits, K. 2007. *Vögel sind zu Besuch*. Vienna: Czernin.

Ronell, A. 1989. *The Telephone Book: Technology, Schizophrenia, Electric Speech*. Lincoln: University of Nebraska Press.

Schiefer, K. 2006. "Shooting Stars 2006: Gespräch mit Kathrin Resetarits," *Austrian Film Commision*. Retrieved 3 October 2007 from: http://www.afc.at/jart/prj3/afc/main.jart?rel=de&reserve-mode=active&content-id=1164272180506&tid=1155914583936&artikel_id=14049.

Schüttpelz, E. 1995. "Die Akademie der Dilettanten (Back to D.)," in S. Dillemuth (ed.), *Akademie*. Munich: Press Verlag, 13–57.

Seibl, A. 2004. "Frauen im Anderswo: Weiblichkeitsbilder im jüngeren Österreichischen Spielfilm," *Kolik Film* 1: 11–17.

Stanitzek, G. 1995. "Kommunikation (communicatio & Apostrophe einbegriffen)," in J. Fohrman and H. Müller (eds), *Literaturwissenschaft*. Munich: Fink, 13–30.

Volkening, H. 2008. "Working Girl – Eine Einleitung," in S. Biebl, V. Mund, and H. Volkening (eds), *Working Girls: Zur Ökonomie von Liebe und Arbeit*. Berlin: Kadmos, 7–22.

Chapter 9

Not Politics but People:
The "Feminine Aesthetic" of Valeska
Grisebach and Jessica Hausner

Catherine Wheatley

In November 2003, the Brooklyn Academy of Music (BAM) in New York ran a program of films entitled "Breaking the Rules: New Austrian Cinema," showcasing what Ed Halter, in his preview of the series, referred to as "some of the finest films of recent years" (Halter 2003). Ten months later, London's National Film Theatre (NFT) ran a similar program, which included seven of the fourteen works screened at BAM. Given that the NFT season was devoted solely to Austrian women filmmakers, the figures bear out quite literally a comment made by programmer Geoff Andrew: "One of the truly extraordinary aspects of the upturn in Austrian cinema's fortunes is the role played by women ... [O]f the directors who have come to the fore in the last few years, at least half are female" (Andrew 2004: 19).

Headlining the program were films by Barbara Albert—whose *Böse Zellen/Free Radicals* (2003) was the gala screening—as well as those by Jessica Hausner, Ruth Mader, and Valeska Grisebach.[1] These names are perhaps the most frequently referenced of a group of Austrian women filmmakers who have continually gained in profile and achievement over the course of the 2000s. Many of them have collaborated on each other's films: Albert and Hausner formed the production company Coop99 in 2000, together with fellow director Antonin Svoboda and photographer Martin Gschlacht; Albert has written scripts for several of her compatriots' films, including Nina Kusturica's *Auswege/Signs of Escape* (2003) and Mader's *Struggle* (2003); and Hausner advised on Grisebach's *Sehnsucht/Longing* (2006). Andrew points out that these collaborations do not preclude diversity in terms of content, form, or tone: "[t]he women here may very often focus (albeit far from narrowly) on female experience, but their films boast a real variety of approaches and attitudes" (Andrew 2004: 19). Nonetheless, he concedes, there are constants. Aesthetically, there is a tendency towards realism and an almost documentary approach. Thematically, the films often turn around personal dramas and the evocation of nuanced relationships and interior lives (ibid.: 19).

What is most remarkable about a number of the films made by women directors in Austria since the turn of this century is, however, the absence of a social agenda: although political concerns fall within the films' purview, they are rarely the central focus.[2] At stake here is not politics but people. This eschewal of explicit sociopolitical critique marks a distinct break with recent Austrian cinema history, cleaving away from both the satires of male New Austrian filmmakers such as Wolfram Paulus, Peter Patzak, and Wolfgang Glück and the feminist tracts of VALIE EXPORT or Friederike Petzold, for example (or even Kitty Kino's attenuated efforts). While clear echoes of their cinematic antecedents can be found in the works of Albert, Hausner, and Grisebach, the films are notable for their deployment of what might be termed a "feminine aesthetic," which draws on modernist devices not to produce a Brechtian *Verfremdungseffekt* ("Alienation effect") in service of an ideological agenda, but rather to encourage spectatorial engagement with a plurality of meanings.

Using Grisebach's *Sehnsucht* as a case study, this chapter seeks to examine this feminine aesthetic within the context of German and Austrian cinematic history and to investigate some of the ways in which *Sehnsucht* typifies a new cinematic form that is ringing the changes for a new direction in Austria filmmaking. Before beginning, however, a caveat of sorts is needed, which has to do with claiming Grisebach as a specifically "Austrian" filmmaker. Born in Bremen in 1968, Grisebach grew up in Berlin, studying there and in Munich and Vienna, and subsequently attended the Vienna Film Academy, where she was taught by Patzak, Glück, and Michael Haneke. She returned to Berlin to make her graduation film, *Mein Stern/Be My Star*, in 2001 (produced with Austrian and German funds) and subsequently *Sehnsucht* (German funded). This dual heritage has led to Grisebach having a rather hybrid status in discourses of national cinema: on the one hand she has been spoken of alongside directors such as Ulrich Köhler, Henner Winckler, and Maria Speth as part of a new "Berlin School" (see, e.g., Knörer 2006); on the other she has close links to Coop99 and her films, as we I will discuss below, demonstrate clear hallmarks of her education in Vienna. One might say that she is typical in this respect of a generation of German-speaking directors working in a "transnational" or at least pan-European context, of which Fatih Akin and Michael Haneke stand out as two obvious examples. It is sadly beyond the scope of this article to engage with such issues, but some acknowledgement of them is nonetheless necessary when discussing "Austrian" filmmakers.

Heimat and its Aftermath: Cinematic Contexts

Given Grisebach's problematic national status, positioned as she is between the twin posts of Austria and Germany, it is perhaps appropriate to begin an analysis of her major work to date with reference to the *Heimatfilm*, a genre which similarly traverses borders between the two countries. Despite Thomas Elsaesser's claim that the *Heimat* film is unique to Germany (Elsaesser 2005: 134), Austria itself has a long tradition of such films (see, esp., Steiner 1987), both in their "straight" incarnations (depictions of rural idylls in which traditional values prevail) and in the shape of the "New *Heimat* film" (critiques of Austrian society, primarily focusing on its Nazi past, which satirize the genre).

Sehnsucht tells the story of metalworker and volunteer fireman Markus Koplin, who lives a quiet existence in rural Zuehlen with his wife and childhood sweetheart Ella. The affectionate portrait which Grisebach paints of *Sehnsucht*'s bucolic backdrop demonstrates evident affinities with traditional incarnations of the *Heimat* film. Postcard landscapes are matched by intimate domestic scenes of villagers eating, drinking, and celebrating in traditional style: the men swigging schnapps, the women cutting *Kuchen*. The villagers' work and social routines are observed in detail, with emphasis placed on the menial nature of the former and the communal tone of the latter. Numerous close-up of Markus in his workshop are contrasted with depth shots of him at work on a water tower and a fence, contributing to the creation of a stable community, while the scenes in which the various characters socialize show them in groups, both collegial (Markus's dinner with his fellow firemen) and familial (two family dinners with wife Ella and mistress Rose situates Markus's relationship with each woman as part of a wider dynamic, in which the promise of future offspring is implicit). The film's totem, the maypole, may be absent from the *mise-en-scène*, but in its place has been substituted a bonfire, around which Ella and Markus dance and swig beer. Aurally, the film makes use of both traditional music, such as the *Lieder* that Ella performs with her ladies' choir, and contemporary techno tracks: O-Zone's "Dragostea Din Tea"[3] and a 2002 remix of Alcazar's "Crying at the Discotheque" provide the soundtrack to the film's two scenes of celebration. Grisebach's deployment of the pop soundtrack serves not so much to ground the film in the present (or the recent past, both songs having been released in the early years of this decade) but to ironically underscore the anachronistic way of life in Zuelen, juxtaposed as they are with scenes of elderly couples in Bierkellers and boot-shod villagers swaying by the bonfire.

That *Sehnsucht* not only draws on the formal iconography of the *Heimat* film but moreover enters into a dialogue with its bourgeois romanticism is also clear. Tassilo Schneider relates the genre to the "Hollywood domestic melodrama," and describes films that "typically center around domestic crises caused by generational conflicts, sharing with their American counterparts both a preoccupation with the crisis of patriarchal authority and a privileging of female agency and of the point of view of women protagonists" (Schneider 1995: 60).[4] Schneider goes on to argue that after the end of the Second World War, "the sustainment of traditional patriarchal structures proved problematic," and that the "social space where this ideological crisis manifested itself most immediately and most urgently was the family." He then identifies three main character types that are typical of the *Heimat* film: "weak, morally ambiguous father figures ... strong and prominent women, and ... troubled sons and daughters (ibid.: 61). Anton Kaes presents a slightly different reading of the genre when he stresses the conservative and nostalgic nature of these films. He writes that "in the first years after the war, *Heimat* signified above all an experience of loss, a vacuum that Germans filled with nostalgic memories" and that the films made during the 1950s "portrayed Germany as a rural, provincial homeland" and "concentrated on untainted, politically naïve and innocent Germans" (Kaes 1989: 166).

These critical accounts of the genre centre around two perceived attributes common to most *Heimat* films. First is the emphasis that these films place on gender and the domestic. *Sehnsucht* dispenses for the most part with the generational conflicts that Schneider sees as central to the genre—indeed family is given as a nurturing, supportive institution, most prominently through the characters of Ella and her grandmother—but it is undeniably rooted in a crisis of the masculine and a privileging of female agency (if not always perspective). Markus may be the film's protagonist—it is his viewpoint that dominates our understanding of narrative events—but his identity is opaque and uncertain by comparison with the two women he shares his life with. We are given no explanation as to why he embarks upon an affair with waitress Rose: his small-town life is given to us as neither joyless nor confining. In fact in the film's establishing sequences, the simple moments of pleasure that Markus finds with Ella are tenderly evoked, as we see the two sharing a quiet conversation at their kitchen table, or coiled round each other in sleep. "I would do anything for you," Markus tells her as he departs for the fateful weekend away where he will meet Rose. Yet the scenes he shares with his mistress show us another Markus, who dresses in a pristine white cricket sweater rather than a fleece and hiking boots, who sips *Sekt* (Austrian sparkling wine) on the lawn rather than swigging beers round a bonfire.

Markus appears as a passive figure, unable to detach himself from either of the female forces between which he prevaricates. Both Ella and Rose, on the other hand, know quite clearly what they want and are able to articulate their desires both orally and physically. Ella initiates the first sexual encounter we see take place within the film, between herself and Markus with the words "Sleep with me" (*Schlaf mit mir*), and although she is portrayed as the more romantically and physically insecure half of the couple, the imperative tone of her words belies a determination borne out by the ensuing sequence, which resembles less a love scene and more a wrestling match. Ella clings onto Markus despite his lacklustre efforts to keep her at bay: pushing her chest away from his rather than embracing her breasts, pinning her arms above her head when she tries to wrap them around his neck during their "love-making." A proliferation of close-ups emphasizes the subtle nuances of this sexual battle, lingering on Markus' clenched fists and Ella's clawing fingers in order to reinforce the sense of claustrophobia inherent to the relationship. By contrast, Rose and Markus's first night together is elided from the narrative altogether, replaced instead by a cut from Markus dancing alone to him waking up in a strange bed. The next cut takes us to the kitchen, where Markus encounters a beatific Rose, smiling tenderly at him. He must later inquire as to what took place between them, a question which

Rose meets with an enigmatic gaze. Whether or not she was the sexual initiator, then, Rose is placed in a position of superior knowledge and power in comparison to Markus. It might be a stretch of the critical imagination to posit that Markus is effectively twice raped: taken once by force and once as a result of his own schnapps-induced oblivion. Nonetheless, he is clearly at the mercy of two stronger personalities than his own, and it is his inability to choose between them or to free himself of them that constitutes the "crisis of masculinity" at the centre of the narrative.

The second quality inherent to the genre which has a particular pertinence for Grisebach's film is the association of the *Heimat* film with nostalgia. Linda Hutcheon has suggested that nostalgia is an idealization of the past, which in itself effaces history:

> Nostalgia, in fact, may depend precisely on the irrecoverable nature of the past for its emotional impact and appeal. It is the very pastness of the past, its inaccessibility that likely accounts for a large part of nostalgia's power.... This is rarely the past as actually experienced, of course; it is the past as imagined, as idealized through memory and desire. (Hutcheon 2000: 195)

Hutcheon concludes that "nostalgia is less about the past than about the present" because "the ideal that is not being lived now is projected into the past" (ibid.:195). She is thus led to condemn nostalgia itself as essentially regressive and naive, as a failure to engage with the actual, experience of the present. Her argument reiterates Frederic Jameson's critique of what he calls "nostalgia films," which represent the past of a chain of empty stereotypes. According to Jameson, these films "can be read as dual symptoms: they show a collective unconscious in the process of trying to identify its own present at the same time that they illuminate the failure of this attempt, which seems to reduce itself to the recombination of various stereotypes of the past" (Jameson 1991: 296).

It is precisely this unease about the idealization of the past and concomitant effacement of present political realities that provided the impetus for later rethinkings of the genre by (mainly Austrian) directors such as Wolfram Paulus, Peter Patzak, and Wolfgang Glück.[5] The New *Heimat* films of the late 1970s and early 1980s subvert generic convention in order to expose the ideological whitewashing it enacts, dealing directly with Austria's Nazi past, its rigid morality based on Catholicism, and what Thomas Elsaesser refers to as the "intellectual aridity of village life" (2005: 134). Here, the Alpine idylls of summer tourists and skiing instructors peel away to reveal still lives of brutalizing everyday existence in the provinces. For some, traditional peasant structures make way for mafia-like agribusiness and political wheeler-dealing—for example, Christian Berger's *Raffl* (1984). Others combine the Nazi past with the traditional Austrian provincial theme, such as Paulus's *Heidenlöcher* (1985).

The latent violence which pervades *Sehnsucht* seems to serve as a mitigated version of that which explodes into many of these films. Indeed, a climate of frustration and silent rage serves as a backdrop to many of the films being produced by women directors in Austria today. Ruth Mader's *Struggle*, which charts the progress of a young polish woman who (illegally) emigrates to Austria and becomes involved in a violent sexual scene, stands out as the most confrontational of these works. However, it is Jessica Hausner's *Lovely Rita* (2002) and *Hotel* (2004) that alongside Grisebach's film seem to forge the strongest links with the *Heimat* film as incarnated within New Austrian Film. Like Grisebach, Hausner draws on the iconography of the *Heimat* film. *Hotel's* action takes place in a remote mountain setting, evoking the snow-capped spectacle of the 1930s and 1940s *Bergfilme*, predecessors of the *Heimat* film, although its tone has more in common with Stanley Kubrick's *The Shining* (1980) and Michael Haneke's 1997 *Funny Games* (on which Hausner worked as script girl), its elliptical structure evoking an atmosphere of mysterious tension which the film never fully resolves. Hausner's previous work, her debut feature *Lovely Rita*, is set in a suburb of Vienna, and as such its links to the *Heimat* film and its variants might be less self-evident. But the suburban setting bears at times an uncanny resemblance to the pastoral backdrop of *Sehnsucht*: small towns, it seems, are small towns. The parochial attitudes of Rita's family and school friends, the sparse scenery and surrounding woodland, the overtones of Catholic zeal and fascist patriarchy (epitomized by Rita's father) conspire to position *Lovely Rita* as the modern variant on the New *Heimat* film. It is little surprise then when *Lovely Rita* concludes with an act of cathartic violence, the inevitable climax to the film's simmering tensions. Disaffected schoolgirl Rita's eventual murder of her parents has garnered the film comparisons with Haneke's *Benny's Video*, in which a young man kills a friend "to see how it feels." Haneke's film is at pains to show the myriad ways in which Benny is a product of the society in which he lives, a society in which affect has been replaced by televisual effect, sentiment numbed, perception reduced to living life through a lens. His action is therefore a logical response to a society in which one can no longer distinguish between a "real' death and one staged with "ketchup and plastic." By contrast in *Lovely Rita*, critic Leslie Felperin claims, the focus "is strictly on the family, rather than society at large" (Felperin 2002: 52). In Felperin's reading, Hausner condenses sociopolitical critique into a study of the "casual cruelty" of family dynamics (ibid.: 52), although she adds that Rita's final gaze directly into the camera implies that "Austria should take some of the blame."

Felperin's concise but cogent reading offers one way of understanding Rita's behavior, implicitly aligning it with the melodramatic tradition which Schneider sees as characterizing the *Heimat* film. Certainly, the film conforms to the key premises of the genre as delineated by Schneider: generational conflict, female agency, and the point of view of women protagonists. But close attention to detail offers another perspective on the film's narrative, in which Rita's actions can be seen to be the result of intensely personal desires and frustrations. Rita's family, although certainly strict, are far from draconian; indeed, Rita seems to share—or at least have shared—a close relationship with her father, whose anger is only prompted by Rita's ongoing refusal to lift the toilet seat after use. Upon learning of her repeated truancy, their reaction is to confine Rita to her room. When her abortive sexual liaison with younger teen Fexi is revealed, it is his parents who impose a ban on their relationship. Throughout, Rita's parents reveal themselves as tolerant, but not indulgent, mostly loving, if somewhat selfish, parents. Likewise, Rita's staunchly Catholic, bullying schoolmates are not painted as wholly villainous representatives of the petite bourgeoisie: indeed, the film's final scene sees the ringleader (whom Rita has previously locked in a dressing room in order to steal her part in the school play) invite Rita to her home—a gesture of conciliation which Rita ultimately refuses.

With society, school, and family thus absolved of blame for Rita's behaviour, we might look to the character herself for clues as to how we might understand her actions. Rita is on the cusp of womanhood; as such, her rift with her father seems the natural consequence of "Daddy's little girl" growing up. Treated as a child by the institutions and adults who surround her, yet expected to take responsibility for her actions, she is deeply resentful of authority and yearns for a connection with someone else. The liminality of her identity is explored in her relationship with Fexi as the two alternate between acting as playful children (chasing one another, throwing snowballs) and sexually mature adults. Her "playtime" with Fexi is Rita's only relief from what the starkly abrupt editing makes clear is the unspeakable monotony of her existence. Reading the film thus, it is tempting to view Rita's murder of her parents as an outburst of frustration in the wake of her attempt to run away with Fexi: her parents dispatched, she is able to live life on her own terms. However, it is not Rita's parents but Fexi who sabotages the attempt to run away, and Rita's new found freedom is revealed as something of an anticlimax. Taking flight after the murder (carrying out the stalled train journey she had hoped to take with Fexi), Rita checks into a hotel and makes herself a prisoner in her room, adopting the method of punishment favoured by her parents. The boredom of daily existence is only redoubled when it is of our own making: Rita's sole action is to right an unevenly hung painting on the wall, and eventually she returns home to the corpses of her parents. Rather than the final glance to camera, it is the penultimate image that perhaps best encapsulates Rita's tragedy: as flies buzz around her mother's corpse, the lamp automatically switches off—set on a timer which will continue to perform the same action day in, day out.

The Feminine Aesthetic

Rita's actions can be seen, then, as a form of *abreagieren* (giving vent to frustration), a term frequently associated with the New *Heimat* film, and used, in Thomas Elsaesser's words, "to encompass violence within the family, silent rages and sexual humiliations, a culture of resentment that leads to racism, xenophobia and anti-Semitic aggression: all phenomena which have marred Austria's liberal self-image" (Elsaesser 2005: 29–30). But they can also be seen as the result of a profound desire for change, for something more than the quotidian teenage life in which Rita feels trapped. It is a sentiment perhaps best expressed by the title of Grisebach's film, described by the director as "a very personal feeling" (Grisebach 2006).

In the press notes to *Sehnsucht*, issued with the BFI release of the film, Grisebach comments that, "love affairs often become a stage for longing … wishes are to come true, exciting things are supposed to happen to you … you become a dramatic figure" (ibid.). It is arguably this desire for excitement and for self-validation that motivates Rita's seduction of a middle-aged bus driver as well as her midnight flight with the critically ill Fexi. Indeed, *Sehnsucht* serves as an apposite epithet to sum up the themes of many of these new films, all of which focus on the minutiae of human relationships, the desires and disappointments which face us as human beings. Here, "longing" implies a bittersweet yearning for the life not lived. In Rita's case, this is a life not yet lived—her rush towards adulthood is an attempt to discover alternatives to small-town life; in Markus's case it is a life not chosen, a road not taken. His is a feeling that seems to underlie so many extra-marital affairs—driven not by unhappiness, but curiosity.

Where Patzak, Berger, and Glück employ the individual as a cipher, a condensation of societal mores, Hausner and Grisebach instead see society as a mere backdrop to the individual experience. Critic Ed Halter describes their films (along with those of Barbara Albert) as "[q]uiet, cool, and subjective," stating that they "achieve a detached, contemplative air ... communicating a bittersweet beauty through the simple evocation of an interior life" (Halter 2003). The aggressive polemics of the New *Heimat* film are therefore replaced with an observational tone, which may in Grisebach's case find its roots in her background as a documentary filmmaker.[6] *Lovely Rita* can be seen as granting each of its characters some sympathy; in *Sehnsucht*, the camera refrains from judging any of its characters. Rather, opacity gives way to a kind of transparency. The opening suicide and subsequent discussions of it, for example, hint at a death foretold: it is combined with a considered use of lingering close-ups which emphasize key objects, such as a soldering iron and a knife, in order to lend a sense of fatality to proceedings, but in a manner that is un-resolved. That is, the spectator suspects the narrative will take a tragic turn, that these characters perhaps love too much and too openly to be healthy, but what precisely will occur is undetermined, so that when (after the red herring of Rose's fall from a balcony, which she survives) Markus's climactic suicide takes place, there is a sense of inevitability, but not determination. Infused as the film is with an atmosphere of dread, the viewer's initial inclination is to attempt to establish whether it is Ella or Rose, each of whom expresses their passion so openly, who will be the shadow cast upon Markus' life. Greeting Markus the morning after their first liaison, Rose's unwavering smile seems to have something of the stalker about it, while Ella's desperation to cling to her husband both physically and emotionally takes on the manner of a disturbed child. However, as the film unfolds, neither emerges as either demon or angel—and, remarkably, Markus' affection for each woman seems genuine. Life with neither woman is given as better or worse—simply different.

As such, *Sehnsucht* offers a welcome antidote to the binarism between the wife and the lover, the good woman and the whore, which according to Molly Haskell (1974) is so often a feature of the melodrama: both relationships have a validity which renders the notion of choosing between them as resolutely difficult for the spectator as it is for Markus himself. Of greater note is the fact that the film never vilifies Markus, despite his cowardice—or greed—and its increasingly horrific consequences, offering instead an extraordinarily sensitive portrait of marital infidelity. Grisebach's background in documentary film is perhaps most evident in an admirable neutrality towards her characters, which seemingly maintains a respectful distance while at the same time capturing the tiniest nuances in their body language: the preponderance of close-ups and low lighting convey a sense of intimacy, rather than claustrophobia, and focus our attention on the minutiae of physical reaction. When Markus finally leaves Ella, the heart-wrenching decision is elided into four shots: a profile of him in the doorway of their shared home, putting on his coat; the back of Ella's hung head; a bag on a table; Ella's tear-stained face. In such a manner, Grisebach combines stylistic tropes from the Dardennes brothers and Bruno Dumont: keeping the dialogue to a bare minimum, she allows the camera to linger over her characters bodies and faces, asking us to read them for signs of an inner life.

The spectator is thus forced to work at piecing together the external indications of character in order to create meaning. That is, while the film takes a loosely melodramatic structure, psychology is attenuated in such a way that the "meaning" of each character's behavior emerges only through the individual spectator's reconstruction of the film's events via a process of critical and emotional engagement with the onscreen representation. To this end, Grisebach draws on a number of reflexive devices. Like Hausner and Mader, she makes effective use of non-professional and inexperienced actors in order to reinforce the film's naturalism but also its Bressonian opacity. She also devotes a substantial portion of the film's running time to chronicling the everyday, forcing the film viewer to acknowledge the minutiae of the characters' existence. It is a device which owes a debt to Chantal Akerman, whose *Jeanne Dielman, 23 Quai du Commerce, 1080 Bruxelles* (1976) seems to have served as an influence for many of the women directors making up the group under discussion. Mader's *Struggle*, for example, features a twenty-five-minute, near wordless montage of immigrant workers in Austria picking strawberries, gutting turkeys in a slaughterhouse, polishing glasses and placing them in a case, and scrubbing down someone's pool. The accumulated evidence of repetitious labor, for minimal wages, all perfectly framed by the camera, shot after shot, day after day, prompts a critical engagement with the social implications of what is effectively indentured servitude, just as Akerman's chronicling of one woman's domestic routine provokes engagement with feminist causes. For both films, the overall effect or impression arises through a combination of real-time filming and cumulative imagery. Slow intercutting and tightly framed close-ups force the viewer to consider the features of banal activities. Both follow a directive of obsessive compulsion, in which balance is construed through the guise of an overly ritualized presentation of quotidian routines shot in real time. They are structured by a combination of display (of tasks) and elision (of "events"). In each film, a sense of stasis is built up by the repetition of key anecdotal moments and episodes.

As I have already noted, Mader's work is by far the most politically engaged of the group of films under consideration here, and has perhaps more in common with the overt social critiques of Ulrich Seidl than films such as *Lovely Rita* and *Sehnsucht*— although as Robert von Dassanowsky points out her films leave much more to the imagination than Seidl's do (Dassanowsky 2005: 280). But we can see the mode of reflexivity that *Struggle* draws upon as an exaggerated version of that operating within Grisebach's and Hausner's films: in all three cases the spectator is prompted to read meaning into the film as a result of the film's observational strategies. These films do not tell, they show. Like Akerman's *Jeanne Dielman* they are aimed at restoring realism to the cinematic experience, maintaining continuity editing but doing so in such a way that the spectator is forced to engage rationally with the minutiae of the filmic image. As such, they rely on what I have elsewhere termed a "feminine" or "benign' form of reflexivity, which allows the spectator an extended period of time to reflect upon the image and thus distances them from the action on screen (Wheatley 2008). This is directly opposed to the "masculine," "aggressive" reflexivity of Haneke or Seidl, which is frequently explicitly metatextual and can be seen as building on Eisensteinian montage techniques, rupturing continuity to jar the spectator into critical awareness. Such "aggressively" reflexive films are not concerned with distancing the spectator from the cinematic action, but with emphasizing their proximity to it. That is, where benign reflexivity calls the spectator's attention to the film, aggressive reflexivity calls their attention to their self, with the object of bringing about a change in the spectator's film-watching practice. It is probably because the impact of aggressive reflexivity upon the spectator is much stronger and the experience of it much more determined, that it is so often brought to bear in the service of polemics—one might think, for example, of the now infamous "rewind scene" in Michael Haneke's *Funny Games*, which calls the spectator's attention to their willing consumption of the violent spectacle.

In referring to the critical aesthetic of Grisebach's film as "feminine," I do not wish to connect it to the director's gender nor to any explicit attempt at addressing gender concerns within the film's narrative or form. Although I have cited Akerman as a stylistic influence, I do not believe that Grisebach, Hausner, or even Mader, see themselves as being specifically part of a woman's "counter-cinema"—as practiced by Laura Mulvey, Sally Potter and others—which sets out to subvert the patriarchal norms of Hollywood cinema by engagement in experimental practice (see Smelik 1998).[7] What I have in mind rather is a form of cinematic *écriture feminine*, which seeks to disrupt traditional oppositions, such as those of masculine/feminine, documentary/fiction, political cinema/engagement. *Sehnsucht* combines the traditions of classical entertainment (in the form of the *Heimat* film), with its critique (in the form of the New *Heimat* film); it privileges feminine agency but offers us a male protagonist; and it uses documentary techniques to tell a fictional narrative—itself based on a true story.[8] Further troubling any facile division we may make is the film's coda, which effects a radical reframing of all that has gone before. A cut from Markus being airlifted to hospital takes us to a group of five adolescents, apparently aged in their early teens, discussing his story, which they have been given as hearsay. The discussion not only troubles the "factual" status of all that has gone before, some details of which are altered in the rendition (for example Rose is transformed from waitress to fellow fire officer) but the teller of the story is a young girl—so the masculine point of view is suddenly rescinded as events are suddenly reframed by their female narrator.

Like the closing image of *Lovely Rita*, the final scene of *Sehnsucht* offers a moment of "aggressive" reflexivity, which ruptures the hermetic seal separating the spectator from the filmic image. As such, another set of divisions is broken down: if the eternal paradox facing feminism is one of opposing, and therefore validating, patriarchal norms, then the incorporation of the masculine into the feminine is perhaps one way of circumventing this double bind. Moreover, in both cases, the "meaning" of this moment of reflexivity is left open: there is no final message given, rather the film is further opened out for interpretation. The two films thus function as what Hélène Cixous might term "gift economies" (Cixous 1987), in which nothing is expected in return for the experience of film viewing. That is to say that we, as spectators, are not expected to reach a set of fixed conclusions as to the film's "meaning," nor are we expected to alter our own behaviour (in the form of our viewing practices) as a result of watching. Instead, the works offer themselves up as pluralities of meaning, from which the spectator can derive their own sense, with no interpretations prescribed or proscribed. As such, they are generous films. But they are also, potentially, hopeful films, in which a bleak melodrama can become, as the young teens at the film's end put it, "courageous," "romantic." If the salient quality of New Austrian Film has been "its willingness to confront the abject and emphasize the negative," making it "the world capital of feel-bad cinema" (Lim 2006), the possibility that the feminine aesthetic opens up for more positive visions—if not of society as a whole then at least of personal relations within it—maybe its most valuable contribution to Austrian cinema.

Notes

1. The other works included were Sabine Derflinger's *Vollgas/Step On It* (2001), Ulrike Schweiger's *Twinni* (2003), Nina Kustirica's *Auswege/Signs of Escape* (2003), written by Barbara Albert, Martina Kudlacek's *Im Spiegel Maya Deren/In The Mirror of Maya Deren* (2001), and a series of short films by Anja Salomonowitz and Kathrin Resetarits.
2. There are of course the usual exceptions to such a sweeping generalization: Mader's *Struggle*, concerned with the progress of a young Polish woman to Austria, stands out as an obvious example; Albert's contribution to the documentary *Zur Lage/State of the Nation* (2002), co-directed with Ulrich Seidl, Michael Glawögger, and Michael Sturminger, is another.
3. This song is "Dragostea din tei," informally known as "The Numa Numa Song" – and is the most successful single by the Moldovan pop group O-Zone, sung in Romanian, originally released in June 2004.
4. David Sorfa points out that the *Heimat* film and Hollywood domestic melodrama perhaps merge in the form of Douglas Sirk (Sorfa 2007: 96).
5. It is worth noting that Grisebach studied below the latter two at the Vienna Film Academy, along with another oft-cited name in Austrian cinema, Michael Haneke, and it is perhaps no coincidence that *Sehnsucht* opens with the image of a suicidal couple smashing their car into a tree: a pivotal narrative trope in Haneke's two-part TV film *Lemminge/Lemmings* (1979).
6. Grisebach produced three short documentary features—*Sprechen und Nichtsprechen* (1995), *In der Wueste Gobi* (1997), and *Berlino* (1999)—before moving into fiction with her short film *Mein Stern/Be My Star* (2001), although these were not given cinematic releases.
7. Indeed, although this chapter is concerned primarily with women filmmakers, one could make a case for the inclusion of male-gendered filmmakers amongst those working with a "feminine aesthetic": German Stefan Krohmer's *Sommer '04* (2006) stands out as one such example.

8. Grisebach describes the origins of the project thus: "Some years ago, I was in a small village in France, in Burgundy. I was staying with friends who lived on the village main street, and opposite us was a smart house where a builder lived. And then one day someone told me that this married man had met another woman when he was on a business trip and had fallen in love. By chance, his wife found out and nothing was as it had been after that: his wife left him, and the man shot himself in the heart with a shotgun, although he survived. Unfortunately, I could never find out any more" (in Glombitza 2006: 19).

References

Andrew, G. 2004. "Now About These (Austrian) Women..." *National Film Theatre Programme*, September, 18–21.

Cixous, H. 1987. *The Newly Born Woman*. Manchester: Manchester University Press.

Dassanowsky, R. von. 2005. *Austrian Cinema: A History*. Jefferson, NC: McFarland.

Elsaesser, T., with M. Wedel (eds). 2005. *The BFI Companion to German Cinema*. London: BFI.

Felperin, L. 2002. "Lovely Rita" [review], *Sight and Sound*, 12(2): 52.

Glombitza, B. 2006. "Beneath the Magnifying Glass," *German Films* 1(2): 18–19.

Grisebach, V. 2006. "Directors Statement," BFI Pressnotes to *Sehnsucht / Longing.*

Halter, E. 2003. "Das Experiment," *Village Voice*, 12–18 November. Retrieved 20 May 2008 from: http://www.villagevoice.com/film/0346,halter,48566,20.html.

Haskell, M. 1974. *From Reverence to Rape: The Treatment of Women in Movies.* Harmondsworth: Penguin.

Hutcheon, L. 2000. "Irony, Nostalgia and the Postmodern," in R. Vervliet and A. Estor (eds), *Methods for the Study of Literature as Cultural Memory.* Amsterdam: Rodolpi, 189–287.

Jameson, F. 1991. *Postmodernism, or, the Cultural Logic of Late Capitalism*, Durham, NC: Duke University Press.

Kaes, A. 1989. *From Hitler to Heimat: The Return of History as Film.* Cambridge, MA: Harvard University Press.

Knörer, E. 2006. "Luminous Days: Notes on the New German Cinema," *Vertigo* 3(5): 3–5.

Lim, D. 2006. "Austrian Filmmakers with a Heart for Darkness," *International Herald Tribune*, 27 November. Retrieved 28 December 2007 from: www.iht.com/bin/print.php?id=3682336.

Schneider, T. 1995. "Finding a New *Heimat* in the Wild West: Karl May and the German Western of the 1960s," *Journal of Film and Video* 47(1–3): 50–60.

Smelik, A. 1998. *And the Mirror Cracked: Feminist Cinema and Film Theory.* London: MacMillan.

Sorfa, D. 2007. "Uneasy Domesticity in the Films of Michael Haneke," *Studies in European Cinema* 3(2): 93–104.

Steiner, G. 1987. *Die Heimat-Macher: Kino in Österreich 1946–1966*.Vienna: Verlag für Gesellschaftskritik.

Wheatley, C. 2008. *Michael Haneke's Cinema: The Ethic of the Image*. Oxford: Berghahn.

Part III

Michael Haneke and Ulrich Seidl:
A Question of Spectatorial Destination

Chapter 10

Allegory in Michael Haneke's
The Seventh Continent

Eva Kuttenberg

Michael Haneke's directorial debut, *Der siebente Kontinent/The Seventh Continent* (1989), premiered in the US in 1990 at New York's Museum of Modern Art in the New Directors/New Films series after garnering attention at Cannes in 1989, remains little known outside the circle of international film scholars and festivals.[1] In Austria, this cinematographic milestone established Haneke as a provocative innovator who set the stage for a new generation of filmmakers, from Barbara Albert to Jessica Hausner,[2] but US interest was shortlived in spite of positive reviews in major newspapers.[3] To date, discussions in the Anglophone world have been limited to peripheral references in the context of Haneke's "glaciation trilogy," which also includes *Benny's Video* (1992) and *71 Fragmente einer Chronologie des Zufalls/71 Fragments of a Chronology of Chance* (1994).[4] The lack of attention to *The Seventh Continent* as an independent work is even more surprising for two simple reasons: First, Haneke himself highly rates the film and counts it among his favorites.[5] Second, *The Seventh Continent* draws on a popular genre, the family melodrama, and its cultural context is less driven by a national agenda than by an overall concern about the nuclear family in a state of crisis in the late 1980s.

After enduring the visually intense experience of watching nearly two hours of an unassuming middle-class family drift toward collective suicide, the viewer of *The Seventh Continent* might wonder "what the picture wants," an expression borrowed from W.J.T. Mitchell (2005: 37). Mitchell's kinship with Haneke rests in the power of images effectively communicating lack and absences and in Haneke's case, causing profound discomfort and signaling a social order in a state of disarray. He attains this visual effect via complex double structures. First, he creates a rather familiar setting with intimate glimpses of daily family routine while distancing the viewer by focusing on objects and mechanical devices. Playing intimacy against detachment, he overtly signals failing communication and disintegration in the postindustrial world. Haneke then precisely amasses shots of minute details to map large-scale social change rooted in and exemplified by the nuclear family: patriarchy declining in spite of professional success; feminism failing in spite of gracefully combining motherhood and work; innocent childhood ending with participation in a collective suicide.[6] To depict how the family's orderly world closes in and traps them in a dead-end position, forcing them to make the most radical irreversible decision, Haneke shies away from a didactic model of problem presentation and strategies of resolution and instead employs allegory as "a genuine structural element" to map contingencies (Frye, in Owens 1980: 69), invite multiple readings, and help "preserve a certain ambiguity".[7] Thematically the film is an allegory of life in our oversaturated consumer society; of laws, the purpose of life, and rigid structures; and ultimately of the steadfast rise of the middle class, working hard to attain material comfort and convenience decades after the war. Social progress is then turned on its head when a well-to-do family descends into self-destruction. As such the film allegorizes social and cultural paradigms, including popular culture.

Haneke's highly theoretical and artistic agenda, his repeatedly stated aversion to symbolism (the antidote to allegory),[8] and his use of the aesthetics of transgression to challenge the standards of postmodern Western consumer society make him a conceptual artist drawing on allegory as technique and content. In an insightful, now canonical, essay, Craig Owens considers allegory both as a practice and a criticism of visual arts and broadly defines it as a doubling of texts (Owens 1980: 68). In *The Seventh Continent* doubling occurs on structural, thematic, and rhetorical levels. Select scenes depicting everyday routines are repeated in their entirety with only minor modifications. The film is designed as a family drama and inspired by an actual event heavily publicized in the media. The daily hype, in turn, plays a pivotal role in the family's life by keeping the dialogue among the characters to an absolute minimum and substituting interpersonal communication with an impressive repertoire of mass media excerpts, from newspapers to radio and television broadcasts to music. Language is limited to citation, when for instance mother and daughter engage in the ritual of the evening prayer. Referencing Walter Benjamin's work, Owens identifies allegorical strategies typical of modern literature and postmodern art. A preeminent allegorical practice is the palimpsest, in which "one text is *read through* another, however fragmentary, intermittent, or chaotic their relationship may be" (ibid.: 69). It is important precisely because of the fleeting references and other texts, drastically reduced fragments incorporated not to assure intertextuality and interconnectedness or restore meaning and a historic framework, but in a manner that underscores ever-increasing isolation and fragmentation. *The Seventh Continent* begins like a Chuck Close painting, with individual dots for which only the large screen affords a unifying frame. Unlike one of Close's paintings, where the dots add up to an image, the film maps disintegration into pixels and culminates in characters literally pulling the plug on their existence.

Owens lists appropriation and the cult of the ruin as additional characteristics of allegory. Haneke's strategies of appropriation include the poignant use of images, genre, and media to add new meaning to the story and maintain a sense of ambiguity. The act of systematically demolishing one's home signals more than a radical break with the typical lifestyle in a Western postindustrial consumer society. This destructive reaction to stifling monotony defies the allegorical cult of the ruin because it is a step toward self-annihilation. The omnipresence of the media mirrors the complexity of our world and underscores the importance of home and family as a protective shield, however faulty, against the outside world. The film also reminds us of how we deal with the constant barrage of news by shutting it out. Such an attitude inevitably builds tension, since the mind wards off the flood of information seeping into our perception, numbing our senses, and demanding constant repression. To make his point, Haneke dots superficial private bliss and professional success with remarks about loss, illness, and intrigue. Authenticity, individuality, and spontaneity are gone in a lifestyle that privileges materialistic over emotional well-being and a setting where family life is coterminous with social life.

Moreover, Owens attributes to allegory a fundamental double role of "technique and attitude" (ibid.: 68). In *The Seventh Continent,* form meets content and structure meets effect in a visual "poetics of enunciation" highlighting the banal quotidian as a quintessential aspect of our lives, if not the sole purpose (Mitchell 2005: 29 n.2). Routine certainly provides structure; at the same time, it covers up an enormous void that Haneke reveals through his clinically precise optics, employed with such rigor that realism borders on hyperrealism.[9] In other words, through brilliant visual allegories, he astutely maps both a "purely physical" material world and "an aggregation of signs" beneath it (Cowan 1981: 110).

In his discussion of Walter Benjamin's theory of allegory, Bainard Cowan reminds us that "in Benjamin's analysis, allegory is preeminently a kind of experience … an outward form of expression and an inner experience" of a world no longer perceived as permanent and thus coupled with "a sense of transitoriness, an intimation of mortality" (ibid.: 110). The film's prevailing mood is literally and figuratively overcast. For turning theory into cinema, Haneke seeks inspiration from "the complete cinema stylist," Robert Bresson, whose films are "tightly constructed to the exclusion of all but the bare essence of the material he intends to explore … presented with rigorous, almost fanatic, attention to detail" (Katz 1998: 173). For *The Seventh Continent* Haneke adds dramatic cuts and extensive use of black film. The stringent structure is punctuated with witty analogies between technological devices and internalized, automatic behavior and close-ups of mundane tasks.

The film's evocative scenes illustrate how "transforming things into signs is both what allegory does—its technique—and what it is about—its content" (Cowan 1981: 110). Repeated shots of a beautiful fish tank allegorize a largely mute family devoid of personality but quite pleasant to look at. By appropriating the genre of the family drama, Haneke can center the film on domestic scenes and the satisfaction of basic needs, from sleep to personal hygiene. Sadly, this family "has everything—and nothing," and although "there is no joy, no humanity … everything is up-to-date"

(Vogel 1996: 73, 74). Similarly, in his landmark study of Austrian film, Robert von Dassanowsky reads *The Seventh Continent* as "firmly couched in … the social drama genre tradition, which he [Haneke] then deconstructs and subverts" (Dassanowsky 2005: 253). In an interview with Thomas Assheuer, Haneke elaborates on the comment that catastrophes in his films often originate in the family and explains the importance of this fundamental dramaturgic strategy: it ensures a high level of identification and serves as an ideal model to address problems that pertain to society at large (in Assheuer 2008: 87). In *The Seventh Continent* the family constitutes a deceptive mental safe haven. Since the outside world rarely penetrates, and then only through carefully issued dinner invitations or a rare intrusive phone call, the family's home resembles an eerie sanctuary, the imaginary, sought-after seventh continent—a paradoxical state of mind in which determination and the desire for oblivion coexist. In the film's third part, libidinal energy is unleashed in massive vandalism and violence when the family destroys their belongings and commits suicide.

Haneke's Cinema of Precision as Subversion

Calling himself an "optimist [who] tries to shake people out of their apathy" (Haneke, in Horton 1998) is a mild understatement of what Haneke does to viewers of *The Seventh Continent* while chronicling a life lived by numbers and schedules systematically spinning out of control. Haneke offers no explanation but lots of detail about family life in the late 1980s in a media-saturated setting typical for an industrialized nation driven by money and conformity. The lives of the engineer Georg Schober (Dieter Berner), his wife Anna (Birgit Doll), and their daughter, Eva (Leni Tanzer), revolve around home, school, and work. Particularly revealing is the mother's profession: she is an optician, trained to treat the eye as a potentially malfunctioning organ that can be fixed with corrective lenses. Her diagnostic clinical gaze is inevitably reductive, disregarding emotional and psychological investments in an individual's gaze. These creatures of comfort evoke utmost discomfort as we closely watch them over the course of three years, from 1987 to 1989, in this tightly structured film. The first part and year introduces the family and the wife's emotionally troubled brother; the second reinforces the idea of no life outside their rigid routine, opening with perfectly timed sex and culminating in psychic breakdown when Anna bursts into tears and cannot stop crying after the family drives by an accident with several fatalities. In the third and final part, all three prepare for and commit suicide. Their (self-)destructive lifestyle is characterized by severely limited interpersonal communication bordering on narrative surrender, numbing popular music, an onslaught of news reports, and mechanically performed tasks, from setting the radio alarm for 6 A.M. every morning to the ritual of getting up, waking up the daughter, having breakfast, and going to work and school. The eternal recurrence manifests itself in repeated shots of tying shoelaces and parking the car in the same spot day after day. Such deadening repetition conveys paralysis, stagnation, and isolation of and within a family on the verge of collapse, despite professional promotion and affluence. Trapped in a lifestyle no longer desirable or tolerable, they epitomize Benjamin's "dialectics at a standstill" (Benjamin, in Day 1999: 108). The pronounced focus on routine goes beyond meticulously documenting everyday trivia and in a variety of ways articulates the disintegration of social structure, interaction, and subsequently individuality. Once family structure, the nuclear family, the link between the individual and the collective, is no longer sustainable, society as a whole is at risk of collapsing into a homogeneous mass and losing its balance. The Schobers are trapped by a desire to escape the present yet unable to envision a future or bring about change, and each of them fails in their own way to reconfigure "family" as a source of strength and site of rejuvenation. Instead it turns into "a site of social upheaval" and "a site of representation of such upheaval" (Sobchack 1987: 178).

Emotional glaciation is inscribed in faces, where expressions of shock and profound anxiety alternate with frozen masks of polite indifference when they sit "petrified" in front of the television or in their car while having it cleaned (Ivanceanu, in Metelmann 2003: 252). Close-ups of objects, actions, or body parts further destabilize the viewing experience and are cues for emotionally tense moments. For instance, a client undergoing an eye examination with her head positioned in an optical diagnostic machine readily shares an anecdote about a nearsighted classmate who had to wear extremely ugly glasses that made her fellow students laugh. In a desperate act of revenge, the girl put a curse on the entire class, wishing on them failing eyesight and ugly glasses. And as a prank in their senior year students indeed all wore ugly glasses. Anna and her brother cannot conceal their surprise when they learn that the girl did not respond with liberating laughter but instead wet herself and thus intensified her humiliation. Also noteworthy is the fact that this laconic family feels compelled to share the episode during dinner, freely adding witty remarks to help them overcome their initial speechlessness about blatant teenage cruelty. In the course of the same dinner, the camera zooms in on exaggerated chewing motions to alert viewers of yet another emotionally charged moment to come. The pleasure of enjoying a good meal is cut short by the guest's sudden emotional breakdown. Deviating from his assigned role, the patriarchal, jolly uncle who was believed to have fully recovered from mourning the loss of his mother violates social protocol. In the family's world, emotions, from sharing a good laugh to comforting each other in sadness, are kept to a minimum. Should someone's indifferent mask unexpectedly crack, it causes embarrassment and impatient inquiries. At the sight of the sobbing uncle, Eva is shocked, her father embarrassed, and her mother clueless about how to help him. Watching television is the ultimate remedy to re-establish the routine and avoid any further discussion.

Linguistically, Haneke begins with the smallest unit, the sign. Oddly redundant in the strict sense of plot comprehension are numeric and letter signs. The film opens with a condensed allegory: a close-up of a license plate getting covered with foam at a car wash is rather emblematic of a family's existence reduced to numbers and about to vanish, neither quietly nor without leaving a trace. The bilingual warning sign at the car wash—*Nicht bremsen*, Do not break—allegorizes their staying the course and inability to leave a well-trodden path or envisioning alternatives. The sign on Eva's school, missing several letters, hints at failing educational institutions. Among the print media are a newspaper article about a girl gone blind, a prescription pad, and reams of computer-generated data. Two-way communication is limited to hollow, feel-good formulas exemplified in Eva's evening prayer and platitudes highlighting speech as schematic and conventional rather than individual. Entertaining guests is not done for the pleasure of company but as a calculated move to reciprocate an invitation and celebrate a promotion with the boss. Time and again Haneke depicts the family members intensely searching for proper words, a clear indicator of fading interpersonal communication: Georg is ill at ease when his now-retired former boss unexpectedly shows up at work to retrieve his personal belongings. An exchange between doctor and patient is shockingly brief, while a phone conversation between Eva's mother and the teacher is somewhat more natural; as is to be expected, Anna declines a one-on-one meeting and settles the matter over the phone. The teacher stands out as a more successful communicator, trying to unveil the mystery of Eva's sudden blindness at school. She gets Eva to talk, albeit only after threatening to leave her alone. When the mother, in turn, carefully chooses her questions to inquire about her daughter's loneliness, Eva responds with mere guttural utterances and gestures. By far the most comprehensive narratives are Anna's letters and Georg's suicide note about a life not lived. The letters again illustrate disconnection: text and image are at odds with each other when Anna reads her first letter out loud, Georg walks through the maze of industrial halls to his desk, and Eva is mentioned but we actually see Georg's boss instead. Most importantly, Haneke employs the letter as a monologue, a report to the audience about the state of affairs in the family.

Collective Suicide as a Family Affair, and a Home in Ruins

"Allegory concerns itself, then, with the projection—either spatial or temporal or both—of structure as sequence; the result, however, is not dynamic, but static, ritualistic, repetitive," Owens (1980: 72) contends. By capturing the static, ritualistic, and repetitive elements in the family's life, Haneke gets viewers' attention, only to catapult them out of their comfort zones. The setting of a family drama is particularly convenient for such an endeavor. Rather than portraying a life span from childhood through adulthood to old age or closely knit generations, the film zooms in on the nuclear family about to finish dutifully playing by the rules of consumer society and surrounding themselves with electronic gadgets, from the automatic garage door to the stereo equipment. They consolidate their efforts for one last ritual, the destruction of their material possessions and themselves. Their lifestyle "is a terrible indictment of consumer capitalism itself—or at the very least, an alarming and pathological symptom of a society that has become incapable of dealing with time and history," a conclusion Fredric Jameson (1983: 117) draws about the postmodern practice of pastiche as it surfaces in nostalgia films and increasingly also in movies with contemporary settings. Here, Jameson broadly defines postmodernism and points to the correlation between "the emergence of new formal features in culture with the emergence of a new type of social life and new economic order ... postindustrial or consumer society, the society of the media or the spectacle" (ibid.: 113).

During the Second World War in Austria, the family stood for Nazi power and ideology. In the postwar years, families plunged into consumerism and adapted to a budding democracy largely driven by economic growth. The generation depicted in Haneke's film has internalized repression without ever articulating hopes or dreams. Family ties neither originate in nor are sustained by emotional bonds, only by rituals, from meals to running errands. The family is held together by their communal living space, along with a rigor and discipline vividly displayed in their carefully orchestrated and rehearsed routine; this serves as a perhaps bewildering, perhaps uncannily familiar reminder of how a large portion of our lives deals with the everyday.[10] Their home, with its select mass-produced items, lacks character; it looks ascetic and functional rather than cozy. A nightstand with a lamp, glass of water, newspaper, and watch perfectly resembles that of an anonymous hotel room. Most personal items only enter the picture when they are about to be destroyed; for instance, the daughter's drawings. Similarly, emotions only erupt when pain is overwhelming.

In the film's third and longest part, the homage to the trivia of daily existence turns into horror when, in the same systematic manner in which they approached life, the Schobers prepare for death. Although a family vacation is well within their financial means, they do not escape the everyday but instead spend their last holiday with Georg's parents to bid them farewell. There they finalize their plan for action. About three years earlier they had already established a viable method of killing themselves with an overdose of prescription drugs they have been hoarding. Clearly, their premeditated act is a logical consequence of their lifestyle and not a sudden impulse. Finally taking charge of their lives re-energizes them and gives them a clear goal and purpose. Under the pretense of preparing for a long trip, they sell their car, withdraw all their money from their savings accounts, quit their jobs, and excuse their daughter from school. With newly purchased tools, they silently work side by side and demolish their home, which is fully equipped with all conveniences of modern life, pausing only for lavish meals during which they happily smile at one another. This tense pairing of destruction and consumption as hedonistic pleasure and indulgence deserves a closer look. The bizarre family banquet in the partly destroyed home suggests a historic shift from modern consumerism to the austerity and rubble of the postwar years and allegorizes postwar Austrian attitudes of turning one's back against the past. The family enacts the famous Paul Klee painting *Angelus Novus,* turned into a cultural icon by Walter Benjamin, for whom this figure was the angel of history pushed into the future by a fierce storm called progress. Trashing one's possessions means radically rejecting postwar values and society's ideology of preserving and accumulating wealth to ensure steady growth. The family bluntly dismisses the most cherished capitalist possession by flushing a grand total of 478,000 Austrian schillings, bundles of hard-earned money, down the toilet. Some filmgoers perceive this gesture, captured in a three-and-a half-minute long shot, as more appalling than the parents making their child an accomplice in suicide.[11]

By breaking up each and every piece of furniture and tearing up neatly folded shirts, drawings, and family photographs, they fill the tabula rasa of their lives with debris, obliterate their common memory frame, and leave nothing intact to aid others in reconstructing their memory. The wrecked home and their decomposing bodies are the most brutal reminders of materialism and materiality turned into their exact opposites—destruction and debris. Ironically, for Benjamin, ruins are "the allegorical emblem par excellence ... for history as an irreversible process of dissolution and decay" (Benjamin, in Owens 1980: 70). Typically, however, ruins are not the product of action but wither away because of a lack of interest and shifted priorities. Watching these individuals painstakingly taking apart their home makes one wonder why they go through all this trouble. Why not vanish without a trace or simulate a fatal car crash? Obviously they want to be found along with the remnants of their lives. But why? Perhaps to deny allegory its ultimate triumph of adding meaning and instead to bring out its other extreme: "The obscurity, fragmentariness, and arbitrariness of allegory all signify the absence of a fulfilling event; this absence, in turn, serves to invoke that event with greater urgency" (Cowan 1981: 119). Engaging in massive destruction is liberating not in the sense of getting rid of a life they no longer value but as an exit strategy. Creating a scenario of no return helps them stay their course and follow through with their plan that also includes their daughter, who took them by surprise when she emphatically responded "Me too" to the chilling lines in a cantata that claimed, "I look forward to death." Once the father smashes the fish tank, the daughter suffers a panic attack at the sight of life forcefully ended and the mother fully realizes what is yet to come. They do not allow outsiders to derail them, such as when the maintenance crew of the phone company inquires about their telephone connection, the husband explains he did not want to be reached, but the crew does not become suspicious enough to intervene.

With the escalating violence, irony reaches its peak when the father reminds Eva to put on good shoes so that she does not get hurt. This sudden kindness and concern for her well-being contrast with her mother's earlier sentiments. When Eva initially signaled her loneliness, it actually provoked violence and brought her more pain. Inspired by an article about a blind child showered with love, she simulated sudden blindness at school in an effort to live out her fantasy of a warm, caring environment, and succeeded in getting her teacher's attention. Reinventing herself as a victim backfired, however, when her mother's fury caused her further victimization as this simulation was curtailed with a slap in the face.

An even bigger slap in viewers' faces is the unabashed depiction of every single step of their group suicide arranged in a strict, inverted hierarchical order: child, wife, husband. After drinking a fatal overdose, Eva recites her usual prayer. Georg records Eva's and Anna's times of death on the wall. After Georg is dead, a series of flashbacks from his life, including close-ups of his daughter and wife and even his boss, are blended in. There is nothing aesthetically seductive in the depiction of suicide; the grim reality of life coming to an end speaks for itself through a body struggling for its last breaths. The gripping final scene has the television still on but no longer showing a picture.

Several disquieting explanatory texts are added onto the film and ought to be read in concert with Owens's assertion of allegory as "the model of all commentary" (Owens 1980: 69). The first appended passage puts the reality of the suicides in question because— notwithstanding Georg's suicide note, which reassures his parents of their unanimous decision to terminate their existence—the parents initiate a police investigation for murder. Another title reveals that the film is based on an actual suicide. In an interview with Serge Toubiana, Haneke explains his cinematic response to a news report and how he was troubled by a journalist acting like an armchair psychologist, trying to make the incomprehensible plausible.[12] Interestingly, only his second draft of the script no longer sought to explain the inexplicable and refrained from patronizing the viewer.

Consumption and Deception

Consumption is intimately linked to the fragmentation of the body when close-ups of hands and feet in motion minimize emotional investment and imitate and mock clinical optics. For instance, a lengthy sequence depicts the trivia of filling up with gas, paying the bill, turning the key in the ignition, putting the stick shift in gear, stepping on the gas, and eventually putting the vehicle in motion; this chain of events, or rather non-events, concludes with a shot of the vacant space where the car left a trace of liquid. Again, the ordinary act invites an allegorical reading of transience and eternal recurrence, the hopelessly repetitive nature of the transaction.

Haneke's allegorical criticism is most effective when he disguises chores as leisure activities. Shopping in a supermarket is disguised as a pleasure trip, involving a casual stroll through the well-stocked aisles of a supermarket, gracefully reaching for items here and there and letting them slide into the shopping cart.[13] In the dramatic finale of this dance of consumption, the cashier types in number codes at a maddening pace, and the only faces shown are those of the butcher and the cashier. This sets them apart as people who work while the others just shop and succumb to the lullaby of background music and intermittent advertisements.

Similarly, three trips to the car wash disguise a chore as a family outing, doubling as a bizarre endurance test to acquire indifference toward their surroundings. Moreover, the family allegorizes their sense of a world gradually closing in on them by being trapped in an "iron cage" (Larcher 1996: 32; 2005: 28). During the first trip, all three family members sit in silence in their car, engulfed by deafening noise as the brushes go over the metal that protects them against the outside. The second trip alerts viewers of a looming catastrophe when the mother suddenly bursts into tears after they drive by a fatal car crash where body bags make death an absolute reality. Had they watched the accident on the local news, it would have resulted in yet another incident of "mediated invisibility" (Naqvi 2007: 47). The third and final trip, oddly enough, occurs shortly before they get rid of the vehicle and thus affirms their conformity, since a clean car sells better at the junkyard and the more cash they obtain, the more they have to flush down the toilet.

The final father–daughter outing is to the secondhand car dealership, which looks more like a junkyard. This emblem of decay, turns into a peculiar performance space for a requiem, Alban Berg's violin concerto "To the Memory of an Angel", written to commemorate the untimely death of Manon Gropius, the daughter of Mahler's widow Alma and her second husband, architect Walter Gropius. This scene is unusual in its sharp contrast to Haneke's style of stripping images to their bare essentials. If music adds "a veneer of humanity," this short musical segment almost takes on a life of its own (Peucker 2000: 183). It invites a poignant allegorical reading of humanity reduced to rubbish framed by its specific setting or "metaphor for transcendence" (Haneke, in Assheuer 2008: 118).

Allegorical Optics

Disquieting camera shots of electronics—TV screens, appliances, and the clock radio—sectioning life into measurable units and imposing a rigid time frame onto their lives evoke detachment and abstraction. At the same time, the camera is a twenty-four-hour surveillance device in the life of the family, exposing the everyday in its totality. Visual intensity is achieved by forcing a temporal structure onto the viewer: in some scenes, images do not vanish after they have been consumed because the camera stays on the respective object or person in a prolonged final shot (Seeßlen 2005: 52). In other scenes, a black screen suddenly interrupts the picture and literally blocks out the image. Haneke composes a visual score and uses the camera to create a unique rhythm, not unlike that of John Cage's music, as Jameson would argue, in which "the hearing of a single chord or note [is] followed by a silence so long that memory cannot hold on to what went before, a silence then banished into oblivion by a new strange sonorous present which itself disappears" (Jameson 1983: 121). Jameson reminds us that postmodernism extends to the visual as well as the performing arts, an argument deliberately pursued by Haneke, who emphasizes the film's affinity to music rather than words in his interview with Toubiana.[14] A captivating symphony of hands too busy to caress a loved one efficiently performs routine tasks: reaching for door handles, turning switches on or off, opening or closing bedroom curtains, pouring coffee and juice. The body has mutated into a robot mechanically performing a series of tasks largely connected to "the duty to consume" (Stallabrass 1996a: 151). Dramatically reduced to a biological entity, deprived of sensuality and *joi de vivre*, the body only needs to be fed, cleaned, and rested.[15] In a physical education class, the teacher's monotonous drill—"hop, hop, hop"—mutes the faintest idea of pleasure.[16] Rather than dancing or swaying to the rhythm, the family sits motionless in front of the television while watching a music contest, just as they sit in the final hours of their lives.

For Owens, "allegory does not restore meaning but adds meaning" and "generates images through reproduction of other images—a film still, a photograph, a drawing"

(Owens 1980: 69). By far the most complex visual allegory is borrowed from the world of advertisement: a poster of an Australian beach, reappearing throughout the film with minor modifications. This desolate, barren beach with huge rocks, brown sand, murky water, and a view obstructed by a mountain clearly is an antidote to romantic beach fantasies of crystal-clear azure water, white sand, palm trees, lush vegetation, happy, relaxed people, and an open view of the horizon. In his interview with Toubiana, Haneke explains that the initial still image is a montage of three different units—a beach, the ocean, and a mountain—with a peculiar sound collage and animated waves washing ashore.[17] Owens alerts us to a potential "allegorical motive" in photomontage, for it is the "common practice of allegory to pile up fragments ceaselessly, without any strict idea of a goal" (ibid.: 72). Rather than constituting a counterpoint to the family's daily monotony or an escape fantasy, the poster replicates the atmosphere of their gloomy home and dismantles their family life as a montage of bits and pieces that are valuable in their own right, such as a successful career, a comfortable home, and a pretty daughter. Yet they are no more than page fillers in the family scrapbook, soon to be torn up page by page and image by image.

The travel advertisement brackets the film's first part. It initially appears when the family is leaving the car wash and looks slightly out of place when taken at face value, but seems decidedly less so when read as a symbol of an exit strategy. It reappears after Anna has put her daughter to bed, wishing her sweet dreams. At this point it becomes clear that the poster reflects an escape/suicide fantasy shared by the family. Most evocatively, it resurfaces in the third part, after Georg takes a last look around the family's home, goes inside, and pulls down the shades. This sequence allegorizes their escape fantasy as one of radical withdrawal. Haneke employs the poster as a visual code for a pre-suicidal state of mind and a suicide committed, because after Eva swallows the fatal overdose, the beach scene is blended in. Similarly, the image of the Australian beach confirms Georg's suicide. Ironically, the closer the family drifts to death, the more the poster comes to life by depicting the motion of waves actually washing ashore.

The poster renders the mindset of the family visually, and its strategic use throughout the film captures the essence of Haneke's filmmaking: he creates a cinematographic text based on a newspaper article about a family suicide and thereby documents minute details to attain an enhanced version of realism—a hyperrealism that on the surface is more blurred than the original, "a little like Photorealism, which looked like a return to representation after the anti-representational abstractions of Abstract Expressionism, until people began to realize that these paintings are not exactly realistic either, since what they represent is not the outside world or, in other words, the latter's image" (Jameson 1983: 123). And as Jameson poignantly reminds us, "false realisms ... are images of other images" (ibid.: 123), an apt statement about filmmaking capturing the fate of a family that no longer emerges as a group of individuals but as a deindividualized persona. In terms of geography, false realism is rather obvious because Australia is not the seventh continent. What else does the picture mean, aside from providing an overt clue about a looming catastrophe and complete withdrawal? In the third part, it clearly points to nonexistence, signifies erasure, and stands for the family's lack of affection, their "emotional glaciation."

The television set and its broadcasts emerge as the optical master allegory; it reliably fills the void, provides companionship throughout life and death, and remains the only object "surviving" its owners. Julian Stallabrass has said that television involves "one-way communication" contributing to the "homogenization of identity" (Stallabrass 1996b: 189, 198). Haneke uses it to reinforce the everyday by incorporating two television commercials about basic consumer products, detergent and cotton pantyhose. Both commercials are significant more for what they lack than for what they reveal. We hear them without seeing them, and they do not exploit consumer anxieties. Moreover, Stallabrass reminds us how "the television, this 'piece of talking furniture' … becomes a constant accompaniment to existence; switched on forever like a light, the most mobile element in the living-room, kitchen or bedroom, from which it is hard to drag the eyes away to attend to a person or a book" (ibid.: 207). Television broadcasts create a presence to be ignored and an excuse to ignore each other; they banish the "fear of silence" and limit conversation to occasional comments without generating dialogue; and they help viewers avoid eye contact. They do not encourage interaction or constitute a source of information. For that Haneke uses radio broadcasts, to induce "a scattered, disconnected, interchangeable and ephemeral state of 'informedness' which one can see will be erased by the very next moment to be replaced by new information" (ibid.: 199). In its double function, the clock radio coincidentally also delivers a steady stream of devastating news about everything from war to hostage takings, which is neither discussed nor processed but is merely white noise against which to perform the morning routine, perfectly blended into the everyday without requiring engagement.

And it is precisely such a double bind that characterizes Haneke's *The Seventh Continent*—on the one hand reduction, precision, fragmentation; allegory and proliferation of meaning on the other. Extreme close-ups both enhance realism and blur images by ripping parts out of context, fragmenting and thereby transcending images, and evoking figurative meanings. These paradoxical stances are at the core of the film, and Haneke's allegorical cinematic practices challenge mainstream film technique and viewers. For Grundmann, Haneke "debunks[s] the desirably normal as the oppressively normative that gives rise to violence and dysfunction in the first place" (Grundmann 2007: 6). He does so most successfully by not smoothing over rifts but continuously reviving tension between text and image, film and black screen, visibility and invisibility, ignorance and recognition, disappearance and sudden emergence, mediated reality, obscured fantasy, and void. The only potential pitfall of Haneke's highly intellectual agenda is his own ambition. Allegory can reach another extreme and make suicide seem as surreal and inadvertently as logical as did the news report that prompted him to make the film. Turning the family into the black sheep of the flock of humanity overshadows the conceptual challenge to depict life (and death) in the postindustrial world without patronizing viewers and offering one too many explanations.

Notes

1. Part of this chapter was presented at the 2008 annual convention of the German Studies Association. I wish to thank Michael D. Richardson for thoughtful comments, and Paul Reitter for mentioning Vivian Sobchack's work.

2. Haneke's *71 Fragmente einer Chronologie des Zufalls/71 Fragments of a Chronology of Chance* (1994) in particular became a manifesto for future filmmaking (Hermes 2004: 10–11). In 2007 and 2008, when this article was written, three collections in German had extensively dealt with *The Seventh Continent*: Horwarth (1991), Grabner, Larcher, and Wessely (1996), and Wessely, Larcher, and Grabner (2005). The first of these, Horwath's pioneering study, also includes the film script. While Metelmann (2003) still offers the most sophisticated close reading of *The Seventh Continent*, Catherine Wheatley (2009) sees the film as a stepping-stone in Haneke's career.

3. Reviewing it for the *New York Times*, critic Vincent Canby deemed the film's "visual style its state of mind" (Canby 1990). In the *Chicago Tribune*, Michael Wilmington described the film as "a calm chronicle of hell" (Wilmington 1994). Meanwhile, for the *Chicago Reader*, Jonathan Rosenbaum wrote that this "powerful, provocative and highly disturbing Austrian film [is] a shocking and potent statement about our times and superior to the two other films in Haneke's trilogy" (Rosenbaum 2004). See also Thomas (2001).

4. See, e.g., Peucker's work on Haneke's family trilogy (Peucker 2000); Riemer's interview with producer Veit Heiduschka (coincidentally also the founder of Wega Film), mentioning his advice on the making of a trilogy to ensure better marketing (Riemer 2000: 63); and more recently, Grundmann's overview of Haneke's oeuvre (Grundmann 2007).

5. In Nina Kusturica and Eva Testor's film *24 Realities per Second – A Documentary on Michael Haneke* (2004), Haneke also includes *71 Fragments of a Chronology of Chance* and *Code Inconnu* (2000) among his favorite films.

6. Metelmann asserts: "Through images Haneke shows the absence of words, the loss of meaning generating social communication, reflected in a visual medium that attains an 'auratic quality' through similar trends as the written medium" (Metelmann 2003: 212).

7. Haneke, in Kusturica and Testor's film *24 Realities per Second – A Documentary on Michael Haneke* (2004).

8. Meindl extensively comments on Haneke's aversion to symbolism: see, e.g., Meindl (1996: 73).

9. See Larcher's discussion of Haneke's *überrealistisch* (Larcher 1996: 31; 2005: 26).

10. References to ritual surface repeatedly in Haneke criticism: see, e.g., Larcher (1996, 2005) and Naqvi (2007).

11. See Serge Toubiana's interview with Michael Haneke on the DVD of *The Seventh Continent* (Kino International Corp., 2006). Here, Haneke explains how he anticipated that reaction in Cannes, where people indeed walked out of the theater during this scene. Moreover, he points out that the gesture of destroying money is not his idea but was a real act committed by the family whose collective suicide inspired the film.

12. See note 11.

13. Stallabrass notes that "the chore aspect [of shopping] is increasingly concealed" (Stallabrass 1996a: 151).

14. See note 11.

15. Metelmann deems the disappearance of the body a quintessential Haneke theme (Metelmann 2003: 9, 225).

16. Metelmann reads the physical exercise as an analogy for a professional career where some get stuck, others need a little push, and others do just fine (Metelmann 2003: 72).

17. See note 11.

References

Assheuer, T. 2008. *Nahaufname, Michael Haneke: Gespräche mit Thomas Assheuer.* Berlin: Alexander Verlag.

Canby, V. 1990. "Film View: With Movies Like These, One Never Knows," *New York Times*, 1 April, p. 15.

Cowan, B. 1981. "Walter Benjamin's Theory of Allegory," *New German Critique* 22: 109–22.

Dassanowsky, R. von. 2005. *Austrian Cinema: A History.* Jefferson, NC: McFarland.

Day, G. 1999. "Allegory: Between Deconstruction and Dialectics," *Oxford Art Journal* 22(1): 105–18.

Grabner, F., G. Larcher and C. Wessely (eds). 1996. *Utopie und Fragment: Michael Hanekes Filmwerk.* Thaur: Kulturverlag.

Grundmann, R. 2007. "Auteur de Force: Michael Haneke's 'Cinema of Glaciation'," *Cineaste* 32(2): 6–14.

Hermes, M. 2004. "Die Neue Wiener Schule: Der aktuelle österreichische Film und sein sozialer Realismus," *Das Kino-Magazin* 4: 10–11.

Horton, A.J. 1998. "De-icing Emotions: Michael Haneke's Retrospective in London," *Kinoeye.* Retrieved 03/29/2003 from: http://www.ce-review.org/kinoeye/kinoeye5old.html.

Horwath, A. (ed.) 1991. *Der Siebente Kontinent: Michael Haneke und seine Filme.* Vienna: Europaverlag.

Jameson, F. 1983. "Postmodernism and Consumer Society," in H. Foster (ed.), *The Anti-aesthetic: Essays on Postmodern Culture.* Port Townsend, WA: Bay Press, 111–25.

Katz, E. 1998. *The Film Encyclopedia*, 3rd edn. New York: Harper Perennial.

Larcher, G.. 1996. "Michael Hanekes Filmtrilogie: Negative Dialektik zwischen Ethik und Ästhetik," in F. Grabner, G. Larcher and C. Wessely (eds), *Utopie und Fragment: Michael Hanekes Filmwerk.* Thaur: Kulturverlag, 30–36.

———. 2005. "Theologie und Ästhetik: Fundamentaltheologische Prolegomena und filmische Konkretionen zum Werk Hanekes," in C. Wessely, G. Larcher and F. Grabner (eds), *Michael Haneke und seine Filme: Eine Pathologie der Konsumgesellschaft.* Marburg: Schüren, 13–31.

Meindl, H. 1996. "Zum Erhabenen in der Kinotrilogie Michael Hanekes," in C. Wessely, G. Larcher, and F. Grabner (eds), *Utopie und Fragment. Michael Hanekes Filmwerk.* Thaur: Kulturverlag, 55–79.

Metelmann, J. 2003. *Zur Kritik der Kino-Gewalt: Die Filme von Michael Haneke.* Munich: Wilhelm Fink.

Mitchell, W.J.T. 2005. "What do Pictures Want?" in *The Lives and Loves of Images.* Chicago: University of Chicago Press, 28–56.

Naqvi, F. 2007. "Mediated Invisibility: Michael Haneke," in *The Literary and Cultural Rhetoric of Victimhood: Western Europe, 1970–2005.* New York: Palgrave MacMillan, 47–72.

Owens, C. 1980. "The Allegorical Impulse: Toward a Theory of Postmodernism," *October* 12: 67–86.

Peucker, B. 2000. "Fragmentation and the Real: Michael Haneke's Family Trilogy," in W. Riemer (ed.), *After Postmodernism: Austrian Literature and Film in Transition.* Riverside, CA: Ariadne Press, 176–88.

Riemer, W. 2000. "Producer's Challenge: Art and Commerce. Interview with Veit Heiduschka," in W. Riemer (ed.), *After Postmodernism: Austrian Literature and Film in Transition.* Riverside, CA: Ariadne Press, 62–67.

Rosenbaum, J. 2004. "The Seventh Continent," *Chicago Reader*, 2 April, pages not available.

Seeßlen, G. 2005. "Strukturen der Vereisung: Blick, Perspektive und Gestus in den Filmen Michael Hanekes," in C. Wessely, G. Larcher and F. Grabner (eds), *Michael Haneke und seine Filme: Eine Pathologie der Konsumgesellschaft.* Marburg: Schüren, 47–65.

Sobchack, V. 1987. "Bringing It All Back Home: Family Economy and Generic Exchange," in G.A. Waller (ed.), *American Horrors: Essays on the Modern American Horror Film.* Chicago: University of Chicago Press, 175–94.

Stallabrass, J. 1996a. "The Duty to Consume," in *Gargantua: Manufactured Mass Culture.* London: Verso, 151–70.

———. 1996b. "Looking-glass TV," in *Gargantua: Manufactured Mass Culture.* London: Verso, 189–213.

Thomas, K. 2001. "Screening Room: A Cool-Eyed Perspective: 'Violent World' Spotlights Michael Haneke, a Frank Observer of the Modern Human Condition," *Los Angeles Times*, 22 November, p. 38.

Vogel, A. 1996. "Of Nonexisting Continents: The Cinema of Michael Haneke," *Film Comment* 32(4): 73–75.

Wessely, C., G. Larcher and F. Grabner (eds). 2005. *Michael Haneke und seine Filme: Eine Pathologie der Konsumgesellschaft.* Marburg: Schüren.

Wheatley, C. 2009. *Michael Haneke's Cinema: The Ethic of Image.* New York and Oxford: Berghahn Books.

Wilmington, M. 1994. "Take 2. Friday's Guide to Movies & Music," *Chicago Tribune*, 4 November, p. K.

Chapter 11

"What Goes without Saying": Michael Haneke's Confrontation with Myths in *Funny Games*

Gabriele Wurmitzer

Anna, Georg, and Schorschi Schober (and their dog), are the protagonist family in both versions of Michael Haneke's *Funny Games* (1997 and 2008). They arrive at their remote vacation home on a lake in the countryside, and within an hour of reaching the place their lives are turned upside down by two well-spoken and courteous strangers dressed completely in white, Peter and Paul. Slowly and politely the family members are verbally disarmed, tortured, and killed, one after the other, by the young men. Twelve hours later, having just drowned his last victim, Anna Schober, Paul knocks on the door of a house across the lake. Planning to repeat the actions of the past night, the verbal and physical torture "game" is about to begin again. The suggested repetition of previous events at the end of the film denies the viewer closure as well as an understanding of a motive for the strangers' acts of violence, and evokes viewer responses that range from confusion to anger.

When the original version of *Funny Games* premiered at the Cannes Film Festival, it appalled spectators to such an extent that many, including the German director Wim Wenders, walked out of the screening (Frey 2003). The most common responses were "torture" (Heinzelmann 1997), "shocking suspense thriller" (Pilipp 1999: 358), and "unmotivated torture" (Falcon 1998: 11). The reactions to the main characters' victimization were unusually strong, considering that throughout Haneke's filmic oeuvre unjustified aggression plays an important role. The director had already stunned his audiences with the meaningless suicide of a family in *Der siebente Kontinent/The Seventh Continent* (1989), the cruel as well as senseless murder of a teenage girl in *Benny's Video* (1992), and an irrational killing spree in *71 Fragmente einer Chronologie des Todes/71 Fragments of a Chronology of Chance* (1994).

Underlying the inescapable physical and psychological violence in *Funny Games* is an obvious attack on filmic representations of cruelty presented as a harmless form of entertainment.[1] Bloodshed and carnage have become integral parts of our lives through the press, the news, literature, and the entertainment industry. Michel de Certeau (1984) claims that the media has increased its immense influence on our perception of the world. Indeed, Western society is inundated with factual and artificial imagery, and accepts what the news and entertainment industries offer to the point where fiction merges with reality. Over time, depictions of actual and fictitious brutality meld to become no more than amusement for its own sake. Haneke openly criticized Austrian (and US) society's carefree acceptance of violence as offered by the visual media: "[T]his permanent presence of violence—in television series, films, documentaries—means that a Coca-Cola advertisement takes on the same level of reality as news footage. That is the danger: everything becomes drained of reality, so violence appears easy to exercise and with few consequences" (Falcon 1998: 12). Making the audience members aware of "their role as consumers in relation to screen violence" (ibid.: 12) was one reason why the director unapologetically confronted Austrian moviegoers with it when *Funny Games* was released in 1997.

For its tenth anniversary, Haneke decided to painstakingly replicate the successful original and aim it at the American public. Badly received, the 2007 (released in 2008) US shot-by-shot remake of *Funny Games* has been denounced for its unconcealed critique of the media's influence on society, which seemed outdated and overly didactic to reviewers in the twenty-first century (Buß 2008; Lane 2008: 92–93). The North American audience perceived the filmmaker's intentions as too transparently displayed and a distraction from the plot.

Both films, the original and the remake, establish direct contact between the viewers and the action on screen during the scenes where Paul addresses the camera directly, and each member of the audience is called upon to participate in the game which the young men play with the family.[2] Paul addresses the camera and spectators several times. Every time his tone and attitude are jovial. Playfully he directs questions at the viewers, ponders the fate of the family, and makes jokes about the suffering victims involving all who watch the film. In one such scene Peter and Paul bet with Anna and Georg that the family will be kaput in twelve hours, and Paul looking directly into the camera asks: "What do you think? Do you think they have a chance to win? You are on their side, aren't you? So, where do you place your bets?" The suffering Anna wants her misery to end immediately. But Paul denies them quick deaths because he has resolved to entertain his audience: "We do want to offer something to the audience" (*Wir wollen doch dem Publikum etwas bieten*), he explains looking at the parents.

Paul's congenial tête-à-tête with the camera conveys clearly "that we, too, are partaking of his murderous game—indeed, that it's all laid on for our entertainment" (Romney 1998: 36). However, the practice of making spectators aware that they are persistent observers of grotesque on-screen events was no longer new and surprising in 2008, which accounted for the absence of enthusiasm for the new version of the film. In addition, American viewers were already conscious of the fact that mass media has the power to normalize violence and render it invisible through its ever-present portrayals on TV and on the cinema screen.

This chapter will step away from the discussion of Haneke's critical use of violence. Instead it will engage with his subtle but profound attack in the film on everyday speech and society's trust in social myths. Because German is the director's native tongue, the film adaptation discussed here will be the 1997 German-language release. Although he oversaw every aspect of the film during the remake, including an accurate translation of the dialogue, the verbal exchanges in the English-language remake did not affect the audience as much as those of the original. Additionally, and importantly in the context of this essay, the linguistic finesse with which Haneke's protagonists express themselves is much more pronounced in the original German, and also alludes to important perceptions of class differences in Austria. The characters in *Funny Games* have a bourgeois background. Circumstances, such as the large vacation home on the lake, the expensive Range Rover, the sail boat, and the Callaway golfing equipment characterize their social milieu.

The visual cues are supported by the polite language, predominantly used by upper-middle-class society. Representing attitudes and ideas of Austrians from a certain class through the lifestyle and conversations of the protagonists allows Haneke to zoom in on a fundamental element of social interaction: myth. He asks: How can ideas that have been absorbed into public discourse and normalized be subverted through language and used to cause harm? So far, Haneke scholars have overlooked the fact that the family, as representatives of Western society, succumbs to the intruders because their blind reliance on several social myths is abused and ultimately destroyed.

Myth: "Which Story Would You Like? Which Would Satisfy You?"

"Myth is a type of speech … [E]verything can be a myth provided it is conveyed by a discourse," writes Roland Barthes (1972: 109). Applying Barthes's concept of myth to support the claim that Haneke launched an attack on society's faith in social myths is particularly valuable, because the protagonists in *Funny Games* lose control over their lives precisely at the moment when Peter and Paul upturn their "profoundly naturalized" discursive belief system (Hall 1980: 132). Barthes's concept of myth and its role in articulated language brings to light the implications and dangers of residing within the confines of a fabricated yet naturalized framework of meaning.

With the help of myths, social rules—made up of signs, codes, and conventions within a group—construct reality (Jakobson 1971: 570–79). Individuals in any society are bound to its social rules in "specific socio-cultural contexts within which [they] are socialized" (Chandler 2006: 156). Semiotician Daniel Chandler emphasizes that learnt social codes, in addition to language, convey meaning and information beyond the immediately visible connotations (ibid.: 154). In any given group, comprehension of implied meaning is based on the understanding of codes. When the codes are misused, communication breaks down and renders some members helpless. In *Funny Games* this effect can be observed in three instances. The family's reliance on unwritten codes and implicit language conventions opens the door for Peter and Paul to destroy the myth of polite society, the myth of safety, and the myth of the underprivileged as criminal.

Engaging with established beliefs, Haneke exposes an additional, important component of the essential linguistic framework sustaining society: the principle of "what-goes-without-saying" (Barthes 1972: 11). For Barthes, what goes without saying are particular myths which are considered common sense and accepted as truths (ibid.: 155). Common sense is also defined as an artificial value system that makes it possible for individual stories (mythologies) to become general myths that are deemed truths—such as, for example, that light means safety. Common sense behaves as if it was a fact, that being on a well-lit path at night is an assurance of safety, and going along a dark street means danger. But such common-sense beliefs may turn back onto themselves and be shown to be misleading or wrong.

The Myth of Polite Society

The myth of polite society refers to the complex social codifications of the Western bourgeoisie, which regulate human interactions within language groups of the same class. Although considered natural, the codes of conduct are socially constructed and not universal, and have to be learnt by all members. Because every individual within the same environment grows up immersed in social codifications, his or her existence has become invisible and they are applied subconsciously: they "are experienced as the evident laws of a natural order—the further the bourgeois class propagates its representations, the more naturalized they become" (Barthes 1972: 140). As innate behavior patterns of individuals, they are not questioned, even when their performance becomes a hazard.

Within the social context of the Haneke's film, this system means that all participants consider it natural to honor each other with respect and adhere to common language codes and principles which are based on politeness and respect. Social relations may be reduced to a few superficial niceties, such as greeting someone in passing, or can involve generous displays of friendship; perhaps, giving someone the last batch of eggs, after they have dropped the first two sets. Anne and Georg rely on implied social rules to regulate the world around them. The intruders, Peter and Paul, however, reverse the codes and conventions guiding their behavior and bring the artificiality of the myth of polite society to the surface.

The first meeting between the Schober family and the young men seems innocent enough. Fred and Eva Berlinger, their neighbors on the lake, are seen chatting with two young men dressed in white, Peter and Paul, in their backyard, as the family drives by. Anna asks Georg: "Who are the boys?" (*Wer sind denn die Bubis?*) Georg answers unconcerned: "I do not know, I believe Fred has a nephew that age." Assuming positive relations instead of being alarmed by the unusual occurrence, Georg establishes an, albeit fictional, connection between their friends and the strangers and decides that they cannot be dangerous; otherwise the four would not appear so amicable. For the protagonists it seems natural that both men belong to the same social sphere as the Schobers and Berlingers. Despite Fred's peculiar aloofness, which Anna points out to Georg, they have no further suspicions. Trusting in social convention, the couple remains blind to the dangerous situation their neighbors are in. Initially, Peter and Paul, although strangers to the Schobers, are awarded their trust because they are presumed to be part of the Berlinger family. Adhering to the rules of proper social behavior, and an unspoken belief in the myth of polite society, means that strangers should be treated with the same courtesy that is afforded to friends. When it finally becomes obvious that the Berlingers are not friends with the men but victims of the same cruelties that Peter and Paul inflict on the Schober family, the neighbors are dead, and Anna, Georg, and Schorschi have already become hostages.

At the beginning of the interactions between the Schober family and the two men, conversations are pleasant and conducted with the proper etiquette. Fred Berlinger and Paul come to Georg's dock to help him with the boat. Fred introduces the stranger: "Paul is the son of a business friend." Although not a nephew, as Georg suspected, the trustworthiness of Paul is not in question. Fred intentionally refers to Paul as the son of a business friend, rather than a business partner. Friends are valued more than business partners. It would be considered rude to pry for details. Paul behaves exemplarily, bowing his head as he addresses Anna with the words: "Good day, madam!" (*Guten Tag, gnädige Frau!*) The formal speech used in this scene signifies that Paul belongs to the same social class as the two families.

Language in isolation does not signify anything, unless it is used within a system of signification which all members of a group have learned and internalized (Barthes 1973: 14). Paul is trustworthy because he speaks the same language as the group of friends. Only a short while later, Anna will do what Fred did, introduce Paul to her friend Gerda. This interaction opens the door to Gerda's house at the end of the film. Their modus operandi, abusing the myth of polite society by adopting bourgeois language and behavior, is always the same; and it works every time in the film.

The Myth of Safety

For bourgeois society, being safe and feeling so have become important features of a comfortable life. One place, above all others, which has been mythologized as a protection from danger is undoubtedly the home. A multitude of saccharine idioms, such as "Home sweet home" and "There's no place like home," refer to society's ostensibly fundamental need for safety and comfort within four walls. It is a place of security precisely because it is owned, and ownership entitles one to decide who may enter and who should leave. There is an almost stalwart belief that the home is the ultimate safe haven. This seems especially true when it is located in a scenic area, away from the potentially dangerous unknown, protected by fences and gates.

Anna and Georg Schober's property is situated in just this kind of area. "A fence surrounds the property, the electronic entrance door in the front and the lake in the back secure the place from intruders. The bourgeois (*Bürgersleut*) believe, *My home is my castle.*"[3] Their vacation home appears to be a restored farmhouse. With its thick walls and heavy doors, window shutters and strong locks, it seems to be a fortress. When the dog Rolfi wanders into the residence to investigate the living room and the kitchen, where most of the action will take place, the material comforts of the house— expensive furnishings, big TV, remodeled kitchen—can be seen in the background. The strong walls, a high fence around the house, carefully selected furniture, and a fridge and pantry full of groceries visualize the belief in the myth of safety. A fortified bastion such as this will make it possible for the family to hide inside for some time, should there be a threat from the outside.

Of course, all this is useful only if the threat from the outside is recognized as such and prevented from entering. Peter comes to the house first, and Anna hesitates to let him into her safe zone. But then he reminds her: "We have seen each other already, when you stopped your car at the gate." The key point has been made: Anna has already seen Peter and Paul with the neighbors, which implies again that he is a friend of their friends, therefore safe to enter her house. She invites him in.

Peter introduces himself as a family friend of Fred and Eva Berlinger, and Anna has no further reservations about letting the stranger into her home. On his way out he drops the four eggs she has just given him and asks her for more. This time, he drops the cell phone into the sink as well as the second batch of eggs on the floor. Although Anna's irritation with the apparent clumsiness of Peter increases, she remains polite, as the social code prescribes it. When she finally asks him to leave, she gives a reason: "Before you destroy the rest of the kitchen, you should take your eggs and leave!" Asking someone to depart without reason is considered rude in her social circles. Her reason for wanting him to go away is valid: he is causing damage to her property and has to be prevented from doing more harm. Anna still feels safe enough inside her residence to tell Peter politely but firmly to go away. But before he has time to step out, his friend Paul suddenly walks through the door into the hallway.

Both Peter and Paul are now in Anna's private sphere, Paul already behaving as if he belonged there. When she insists that they leave the house immediately, Paul does not even notice her request and does not respond to her. Right away he focuses on the golf clubs standing in the corner and asks to try them out. Anna is barely given time to respond: "If it makes you happy" (*Wenn es Sie glücklich macht*). Paul leaves, while Peter remains in the house and shows no sign of intending to go away any time soon. When Paul marches back into the foyer again, Anna is more than simply annoyed, she slowly begins to show signs of panic: "Now, please leave!" (*Also, gehen Sie jetzt, bitte!*) By herself, Anna is physically not able to throw the two men out, and they behave as if they do not understand why she is getting irate and wants them to leave her property. The "bourgeois castle" (*bürgerliche Burg*), as Metelmann (2003:

136) puts it, has been taken over by the two men within a very short time of the family's arrival there.

Finally Georg returns from working on the boat, but he does not understand the seriousness of the situation. Again, the myth of politeness demands respectful treatment of guests. And because this is his house, and he also is convinced that he is safe inside, he does not support his wife's demand to immediately get rid of the men. But within minutes he is overpowered by brutal force. Paul hits his leg with the golf club. Not only have two strangers just raided a vacation home on a quiet country lake, the owners are helplessly watching. Georg is unable to run away, and Anna cannot call for help, because the cell phone is wet from being dropped into the dish water. The entire family is now held hostage in their own "castle" by two strangers, who have nothing better to do than to torture a helpless family. Their "funny games" are about to begin.

Anna drags the injured Georg into the living room and onto the couch. Peter and Paul, trying to be "helpful," follow her and sit down on the opposite couch. The *mise-en-scène* for the rest of the film is the living room. Within minutes it is transformed into a site of terror. All the misery that the solid walls and strong locks are there to keep out has been let in by the owners themselves. Peter and Paul sit on the couch and make themselves comfortable, behaving as if nothing has happened.

At this moment the parents realize that they are captives in their own house. Subverting the myth of one's own house being a safe haven, Haneke turns the secluded place into a prison, with two efficient wardens, for the family. Now securely inside, how will the family be able to get rid of their tormentors? Georg can neither defend the family nor escape, he cannot even walk. Anna is in an intractable situation. She could run, but she does not want to leave her helpless husband and her son behind.

In addition to locks and gates, light gives an illusion of safety. Society has come to rely on the myth that nothing bad can really happen during daylight or in well-lit areas at night. Schorschi's escape attempt proves that myth wrong. When he darts to the front door during a scuffle between the adults, it is shut and locked, which perversely prevents him from escaping. The door keeps evil in rather than out, as intended, and the boy has to climb out of a window on the second floor to get away. Another skillful turning of the tables: rather than breaking in, he has to break out of his house, a purported site of safety.

The next hurdle in the escape attempt is the insurmountable electronic gate and the tall fence, both again designed to keep danger out. Earlier in the film Peter had mentioned that he was able to access the property via a hole in the fence, "a gap through which violence enters" (Ossenagg: 2005: 140). Schorschi cannot find the hole in the dark. This opening may or may not exist, but the idea illustrates further a macabre constellation that lets violence into the safe zone but prevents escape from it. Eventually Schorschi wades through the lake to get around the fence and runs to the Berlinger house for help. The darkness of the night makes him feel safe. However, nearing the house, the motion sensor activates the outside lights which illuminate Schorschi, exposing him to his pursuer. The camera swings around and we see Paul approaching through the dark like a white ghost. The boy reaches the door, runs into the brightly lit house, not into the safety of the light but to be caught and brought back to his parents.

Myth of the Underprivileged Criminal

Two young men destabilize the system of bourgeois conventions that differentiate each social class from the next, abusing Anna and Georg's reliance on social codes. Peter and Paul's pleasant appearance and polite behavior suggest an upper-middle-class background, yet at the same time belie their cruel intentions. Cleanly dressed, educated, respectful, and well-mannered, they wear this particular social identity with natural ease. Hall writes: "Certain social codes may ... be so widely distributed in a specific language community ... and learned at so early an age, that they appear not to be constructed ... but 'naturally' given. Simple visual signs appear to have achieved a 'near-universality' in this sense" (Hall 1980: 132).

In the bourgeois mind, the portrayal of criminals follows a particular mythological pattern. A criminal is imagined as exhibiting one or more of the following characteristics: drug-addiction, alcoholism, profanity, aggression, poverty, dirtiness, unkemptness, and mental illness. A decent person, on the other hand, is recognized through good looks, intelligence, cleanliness, and polite conduct. The myth flattens a complex idea and fashions it into a simple formula which can explain who is a criminal and who is not. Barthes formulates this effect as myth's tendency to abolish complexity and to organize a world which is without contradictions, because it is "wallowing in the evident, it establishes a blissful clarity: things appear to mean something by themselves" (Barthes 1972: 143). Through myth the world is seen as a display of essences. The idea of the criminal is essentialized and naturalized at the same time. With the help of myth, it goes without saying that a criminal is necessarily a dirty, profane, poor man. Because the two young people do not fit that image, they must not be criminals in the bourgeois mindset. Myth makes ideas seem natural and innocent.

Paul, during a dialogue with Peter, illustrates this and makes visible how illusory the myth of the criminal is. Horrified and pain-stricken, Georg asks: "Why are you doing this?" and Paul presents a satisfying story about a baseless criminal:

> PAUL: Listen, his father got a divorce when he was so tiny, and took a younger woman ...
> PETER: He is lying! My mother got a divorce, because ... because ...
> PAUL: Because, she wanted to keep the little cuddle bear all to herself, and ever since, he is gay and a crook.
> PETER: You are an asshole!
> PAUL: In reality, he is from a filthy, deprived family, has five siblings, they all are addicted to drugs. The father is a drunkard, and you can imagine what his mother does. That means, he is screwing her. Tough, but true.

This story is of course incongruous with the appearance and manners of the young men, and Georg replies: "You are disgusting. Could you at least cut out the obscenities in front of the child?" Instead, Paul offers another answer to Georg's initial query: "But of course. Which answer would you like? Which one would satisfy you? In fact, you know as well as I that what I told you is not true." If none of what Paul says is true, then why say it at all? The film exposes the fiction of myths and learned social codes. The myth of the criminal, which had been accepted as natural and true by the family, is debunked because the killers neither fit the profile, nor do they have a motive for their deeds.

Haneke has explained why he chose to give his tormentors a bourgeois identity: "this form of senseless violence is a very bourgeois affair. When the film came out I collected seven different newspaper articles from seven different countries describing very similar cases. They were always boys from bourgeois homes, not deprived or drug-addicted" (Falcon 1998: 12). The director dismantles this myth not only in his fiction. He finds proof for it in real life as well. Newspaper articles confirm that the myth of the criminal impedes our judgment and makes us overlook signs that would otherwise have alerted us to danger.

Subverting myth after myth, Haneke takes certainties away from the protagonists and the viewers. He forces the peaceful family into a violent situation from which they are unable to escape. For the spectator, there is nothing that can be relied on in the film. Too many invisible structures have been laid bare, such that interactions between the Schober family and the two men have become unpredictable. Language and behavior codes have been overturned, and it is never clear whether politeness, empathy, or feelings of safety are real or feigned. Peter and Paul are effusively courteous, obsequious, and sycophantic. At the same time they are cold-blooded murderers. The trust in being safe with others of one's own social class prevents the family from recognizing danger from within, because of their unconditional belief in the myth of polite society. Peter and Paul use the same behavior patterns and the same language as the family but turn them inside out and thus silence them.

Myths are expressed in language. Language is "essentially a collective contract one must accept in its entirety if one wishes to communicate … it can be handled only after a period of learning" (Barthes 1973: 14). In this sense, myths are like language, they have to be learned, accepted, and shared by a community. The murderers are very well acquainted with bourgeois language conventions and mythologized ideas. They enter the lives of the Schobers and Berlingers intent on overturning them and exposing their belief system, which is an unstable social framework held together by common sense and things that go without saying.

Many who have seen the original film admit they would not want to watch it at home in their comfort zone. Precisely because the idea of a comfort zone is exposed as a myth in the film, it becomes a trap. *Funny Games* is a loop, without beginning or end and thus devoid of the closure that we have become accustomed to. The action in *Funny Games* is akin to a Möbius strip, neverending and lacking a beginning, and only ever showing us one side, the side of violence, the side of the victim. The victims are never given a chance to become perpetrators. There is no outside force sweeping in to save them. Haneke works with extremes in this film. He does not make any concessions to the viewer, emotionally or intellectually. He engages the audience on several levels in this film. One evident aspect is violence; Haneke "shows how we are all obliged to co-exist with violence" (Joos 2006: 92). The other, more subtle attack is aimed at everyday speech and society's trust in social myths. Social codes and myths have become part of bourgeois life to such an extent that many ideas go without saying, appearing to be natural constituents of the world as we know it.

Notes

1. Haneke has spoken about the media's influence on perceptions of violence (see Sharrett 2003), an issue also discussed by Riemer (2004) and extensively elaborated on in Metelmann (2003). The amount of academic discourse on *Gewalt* ("violence") in Haneke's films is considerable: see, e.g., Metelmann (2003) and Wessely (2005).
2. For discussions of this moment in the film, see Pilipp (1999), Riemer (2004), and Metelmann (2003).
3. Italics in the original. Metelmann implicitly criticizes Haneke's propensity to dwell on the isolated lives of ignorant *Bürgersleut* (see Metelmann 2003: 133).

References

Barthes, R. 1972. *Mythologies*, trans. A. Lavers. New York: Hill and Wang.
———. 1973. *Elements of Semiology*, trans. A. Lavers and C. Smith. New York: Hill and Wang.
Buß, C. 2007. "Gewaltstudie *Funny Games U.S.* Sadismus für Nostalgiker," *Spiegel Online*, 29 May. Retrieved 15 March 2009 from: http://www.spiegel.de/kultur/kino/0,1518,556248,00.html.
Certeau, M. de. 1984. *The Practice of Everyday Life*, trans. S. Rendall. Berkeley: University of California.
Chandler, D. 2006. *Semiotics: The Basics*. New York: Routledge.
Falcon, R. 1998. "The Discreet Harm of the Bourgeoisie," *Sight and Sound* 8(5): 10–13.
Frey, M. 2003. "Michael Haneke," *Senses of Cinema*, August. Retrieved 15 March 2009 from: http://www.sensesofcinema.com/contents/directors/03/haneke.html.
Hall, S. 1980. "Encoding/Decoding," in Centre for Contemporary Cultural Studies (eds), *Culture, Media, Language: Working Papers in Cultural Studies 1972–1979*. London: Hutchinson, 128–38.
Heinzelmann, H. 1997. "Funny Games," *Kinofenster*, November. Retrieved 15 March 2009 from: http://www.kinofenster.de/filmeundthemen/ausgaben/kf9711/funny_games_film/.
Jakobson, R. 1971. *Selected Writings, Vol. 2*. The Hague: Mouton.
Joos, J.-E. 2006. "Une Violence sans sujet: David Cronenberg et Michael Haneke," *Parachute* 123: 80–119.
Lane, A. 2007. "Recurring Nightmare: *Funny Games*," *New Yorker*, 17 March, 92–93.
Metelmann, J. 2003. *Zur Kritik der Kino-Gewalt: Die Filme von Michael Haneke*. Munich: Wilhelm Fink.

LIVERPOOL JOHN MOORES UNIVERSITY
LEARNING SERVICES

Ossenagg, K. 2005. "Der wahre Horror liegt im Blick," in C. Wessely, G. Larcher, and F. Grabner (eds), *Michael Haneke und seine Filme: Eine Pathologie der Konsumgesellschaft.* Marburg: Schüren, 115–44.

Pilipp, F. 1999. "Michael Haneke's Film *Funny Games* and the Hollywood Tradition of Self-referentiality," *Modern Austrian Literature* 32(4): 353–63.

Riemer, W. 2004. "Michael Haneke, *Funny Games*: Violence and the Media," in M. Lamb-Faffelberger and P. Saur (eds), *Vision and Visionaries in Contemporary Austrian Literature and Film.* New York: Peter Lang, 93–102.

Romney, J. 1998. "Fatal Impact," *New Statesman*, 30 October: 36–37.

Sharrett, C. 2003. "The World That Is Known: An Interview," *Cineaste* 28(3): 28–31.

Chapter 12

Unseen/Obscene:
The (Non-)Framing of the Sexual Act
in Michael Haneke's *La Pianiste*

Catherine Wheatley

> I would like to be recognized for making in *La Pianiste*
> an obscenity, but not a pornographic film.
> —Michael Haneke

In his introduction to a series of articles on the depiction of sex and the sexual act in contemporary cinema, *Sight and Sound* editor Nick James touches upon a subject which is gaining increasing attention in academic articles and critical reviews: the appearance of sexually explicit acts and images in aesthetically ambitious films (James 2001: 21). Amongst the films that he lists as examples of this cinematic trend are Breillat's *Romance* (1999) and *À ma soeur!/For my sister* (2001), Noé's *Seul Contre Tous/I Stand Alone* (1998) and *Irréversible/Irreversible* (2002), Despentes and Trinh Thi's *Baise Moi/Fuck Me* (2001), Chéreau's *Intimacy* (2001), Von Trier's *Idioterne/The Idiots* (1998), and Haneke's *La Pianiste/Die Klavierspielerin/The Piano Teacher* (2001).

The inclusion of Michael Haneke's *The Piano Teacher* amongst these films is not, at first glance, particularly surprising. Based on a novel by Elfriede Jelinek, the film's narrative follows the emotional and sexual trajectory of Erika Kohut (Isabelle Huppert), a middle-aged piano teacher who, over the course of the film, gives outlet to her repressed sexuality by watching pornographic films, spying on copulating couples, mutilating her own genitalia, and eventually attempting to embark upon a sado-masochistic relationship with a young student, Walter (Benoît Magimel). But while the film's content ostensibly aligns it with the other works that he discusses, visually, *La Pianiste* relentlessly confines the sexual act to the off-screen space. As James admits, "there is no real sex in this film" (James 2001: 21). Its place within the canon of sexually explicit works seems then somewhat problematic, for unlike the vast majority of the films listed above Haneke's film contains no graphic depictions of sex (whether penetrative or oral), and therefore cannot be said to contain any elements of "hardcore" cinema—the characteristic which John Phillips sees as being definitive of this category of films (Phillips 2001:133). Although, as Kimberley Cooper rightly points out, Haneke's film, like many of those listed by James, creates 'a visceral reaction in [its] audience' and has 'aroused a fervent moral polemic' as a result of its provocative and confrontational approach to the spectator (Cooper 1999: 45), in withholding the sexual act from the image frame, the film repositions the spectator in a manner that is radically different to the films with which it is grouped by James, Phillips, Cooper, and numerous other critics. Through a comparison with two of the key films that are consistently referenced alongside Haneke's—Breillat's *Romance* and Noé's *Irréversible*—this chapter will examine precisely how this repositioning takes place, and what its implications are for the spectator of *La Pianiste*.

The "Sexually Explicit Art Film"

In order to see how Haneke's film diverges from the other films that James mentions, we must begin with a brief examination of some general characteristics of what can be seen as an emerging sub-genre. While there is a degree of critical awareness of a trend in cinema that incorporates formal properties of pornography into what are, for the lack of a more precise term, known as "art films," engagement with its key features is at present somewhat undeveloped, and so far no coherent approach has been established. Fragmented attempts at providing some sort of label include, for example, Ginette Vincendeau's description of *Baise Moi* as an example of the "auteur's sex movie" (Vincendeau 2002: 38), and Barbara Creed's categorization of *Romance* as part of a "post-porn" movement comprised of films which "take pornography out of its traditional context and rework its stock images and scenarios" (Creed 2003: 74). But both Vincendeau and Creed tend towards formal analysis, overlooking to some extent questions of intention. If we take the *Oxford English Dictionary* definition of "pornography" as a guide, we can consider it to be "the explicit description or exhibition of sexual activity in literature, films, etc., intended to stimulate erotic rather than aesthetic or emotional feelings." So while the explicit portrayal of sexual activity is what links the films in Vincendeau's and Creed's analyses to the pornographic genre, then some account also needs to be taken of whether these portrayals are intended to stimulate erotic feelings, or a more intellectualized response—or indeed both.

One of the few extended analyses which approaches this question of intention comes from Lisa Downing (2004), who, in a study of French cinema's new "sexual revolution," proposes and examines a selection of interpretative strategies for viewing what she terms the "sexually explicit art film." She describes this as, "an experimental cinema that blurs the boundaries between art film and porno flick … a genre of film which seeks to dismantle the prohibition regarding the exposure of the body and of 'real' sexual activity in narrative film" (ibid.: 265–66), concluding that the majority of the films discussed under the moniker of the "sexually explicit art film" can be characterized as postmodern micro-narratives, hypothesizing that the generic marker of the group may be their refusal of totalization.

Downing's article includes textual analyses of both Catherine Breillat's *Romance* and Gasper Noé's *Irréversible*, two films which repeatedly emerge as better-known examples of the sexually explicit art film. The two films could not, in many ways, appear more different both visually and ideologically—indicative of the vast number of visual styles and ideological positions which the sub-genre seems to subsume. However, they each demonstrate a postmodernist bent not only in their concern with framing the sexual act, but also through an underlying quality of excess which permeates the films' form and content. What links *Romance* and *Irréversible*, along with many of the other films that make up the subset, is perhaps their alignment with what Carol Clover, speaking primarily of horror films and pornography, has termed "body genres" (Clover 1987: 189): films which privilege the sensational, most prominently in pornography's portrayal of orgasm and in horror's portrayal of violence and terror. Extending Clover's definition to include the sensation of pathos in the melodrama, Linda Williams states that visually, each of these excesses could be said to share a quality of uncontrollable convulsion or spasm—of the body "beside itself" with sexual pleasure, fear and terror, or overpowering sadness. Aurally, excess is marked by recourse not to the coded articulations of language but to inarticulate cries of pleasure in pornography, screams of fear in horror, sobs of anguish in melodrama (Williams 1987: 209).

It is easy to see how films such as *Irréversible* and *Baise Moi* conform to this genre of body films. Both films caused a critical uproar with their explicit and graphic depictions of rape and murder, and *Irréversible*'s physical effects on its audiences are by now well documented.[1] It strikes me, however, as somewhat peculiar that *Irréversible* is posited as "post-porn," for response to the film has focused primarily on the graphic depictions of violence which, as Nick James and Mark Kermode have underlined, align *Irréversible* more closely with cinematic horror than pornography (James and Kermode 2003). In fact, the film contains two depictions of the sexual act. The first (or rather the second, since the film plays in reverse order) is a love scene between a heterosexual couple, Alex and Marcus. It is perhaps erotic, but certainly bears little relation to pornography, resembling the softly-lit love scene between Julie Christie and Donald Sutherland in Nicolas Roeg's *Don't Look Now* (1973) in form and content rather more than a scene from any hardcore porn flick. There is no graphic depiction of genitalia, or penetration, and what is foregrounded is the tenderness between the couple rather than the act of intercourse itself. The second scene featuring the sexual act (in terms of biology if not motivation), has garnered rather more critical attention—possibly as a result of its violent overtones—the act it shows being the film's now infamous nine-minute rape scene. As Downing notes, one element shared by a vast number of these "sexually explicit art films" is the inclusion of scenes of rape (Downing 2004: 277). It is difficult to know how to approach these scenes, as rape is more often construed as an act of violence than a "sexual" act, having to do with the desire to exert power rather than the desire for sexual satisfaction. However, in the context of these films, the act of rape is usually depicted in a graphic manner which places genitalia and penetration firmly within the frame. It is for this reason that I have opted to discuss the scene within the context of the sexual act—the emphasis being placed on the sexed body, rather than sexual urges.

The first hour of *Irréversible* is characterized by aesthetic excess. As David Sterritt puts it, "the camera never stops shaking, bobbing, turning upside down, moving in and out of focus—showing us nothing and everything. Its movement mirrors the chaos and violence of the situation and the characters' wildly out of control state of mind" (Sterritt 2005: 205). The rape scene, by contrast, is shot with a static camera positioned at ground level. The excesses that operate in this scene are not those of movement but of time, image and sound. The sheer length of the sequence accounts for much of its effect, along with the brutality of the rapist's actions and speech and, perhaps more importantly, the gut-wrenching screeching of the victim. While it does not draw on the soft lighting or close-up editing of pornographic scenes to sexualize the rape—as, arguably, Kaplan's *The Accused* (1988) and Peckinpah's *Straw Dogs* (1971) do—*Irréversible* thus extends some of the excesses of body genres— horror, pornography—in order to confront the spectator with the violence of rape.

Romance might initially appear more problematic with regards to its categorization as a "body genre." The film offers a frank depiction of genitalia, penetration, and oral sex, shot mainly from the point of view of the protagonist, Marie, a young woman who, having been sexually spurned by her lover, sets out on an extended quest for sexual satisfaction with other men. Her visually explicit exploits are, however, accompanied by a voiceover in which she tries to make philosophical, political, and emotional sense of her own behavior, providing precisely those coded articulations of language that Williams sees as definitive of pornography by their absence. By giving voice to Marie's thoughts, Breillat thus goes some way to attenuating the excessive effects of the genre. Nonetheless, *Romance* incorporates a number of scenes that depict the body "beside itself," images presenting explicit sexual acts and sexual responses, and it is noteworthy that Marie's voiceover is frequently silenced during these scenes. This is most remarkably the case in an episode where Marie is "raped" by a stranger. An anonymous man offers Marie money to perform cunnilingus on her, to which she assents without saying a word. Having performed the act, the man then turns Marie over and enters her from behind. As he continues, Marie seems to sob, and when he leaves, she shouts that she is not ashamed. This scene is perhaps the least visually explicit of the film's depictions of the sexual act (there are no close-ups, no exposed genitalia here), yet it reverts to the aural conventions of the body genre: the only indication of Marie's emotional response—rather than her physical one—comes with her post-event assertion. Otherwise the soundtrack is dominated by moans and whimpers.[2]

Marie's initiation into bondage by her employer Robert likewise refuses voiceover, replacing it with the cathartic weeping that is her reaction to being tied up. Although the heroine eventually vocalizes her response in a dialogue with Robert, her sobs dominate the visual and audio tracks for some forty seconds before she speaks. Her shudders and gasps can be seen both as a substitute for the catharsis of sexual climax, and as the overwhelming spectacle of the body in anguish that Williams associates with melodrama. It is no coincidence that the title of Breillat's film is that of the genre that Ann Douglas once referred to as "soft-core emotional porn for women," for the film incorporates and to some extent exploits the excesses inherent to both genres (Douglas 1980: 26).

By privileging a feminine perspective, Breillat at once reframes the sensational effect of the pornographic genre and redoubles it. In *Romance*, philosophy, sexual politics, and contradictory emotions "co-exist," as Linda Williams writes, with "hard-core, arousing sex" (Williams 2000: 23). This juxtaposition of the act and its critique is typical of the somewhat paradoxical approach to genre which appears within the majority of the films that make up this sub-set of sexually explicit "post-porn." If Breillat and Noé's films are postmodernist on a level of content—in their refusal of grand narratives—they equally demonstrate a visual postmodernism, which lies not only in their deployment of an aesthetics of excess, but also in their use of generic pastiche, parody, and intertext. In Downing's interpretation of the films as postmodernist micro-narratives, she states that the films incorporate generic elements in order "to challenge and mobilize their meanings, using them not as ends in themselves but as a lens imported into the cinematic collage in order to show the narrative events from a different perspective, for a few moments, a few frames" (Downing 2004: 278). However, the result of this proximity between critique and conformity is, as Downing acknowledges, a sense of ideological confusion: "we, the viewers, find ourselves with a moral and ideological collage that is as difficult to navigate as it is thought-provoking" (ibid.: 278). *Irréversible* and *Romance* can be read—and indeed have been read by various critics and academics—as troubling the conventions of horror and pornography.[3] Unfortunately, this collage also leaves the spectator free to read the film in any number of other ways, including as erotic spectacles in themselves.

In his response to John Ellis's essay "On Pornography" (Ellis 1992), Paul Willemen states that fantasy images, framed image-objects, and what we see around us are three different things existing in different spaces (Willemen 1992). Each involves different relations between subject and look. The actualization of fantasy scenarios into framed image-objects necessarily passes through the "defiles of the signifier," in Lacanian terms, as well as through the distortion processes unconscious signifiers are subjected to when passing into consciousness (ibid.: 179). As Lacan has it, "[desire] is an effect in the subject of that condition which is imposed upon him by the existence of the discourse to cause his need to pass through the defiles of the signifier (Lacan 1977: 264). Concrete images, which are what pornography images—in any context—needs must be, require a social setting and an individuation which "pure" fantasy can do without: as Willemen puts it: "A sexual fantasy can proceed very satisfactorily without having to specify the pattern on the wallpaper. A filmic fantasy cannot" (Willemen 1992: 179). This leads to a double-bind situation, where on the one hand, Willemen states, the surfeit of specific details due to the need for a frame to be filled produces an excess of signification. But on the other hand, this excess is also a loss: the lack of fit between the represented scenario and the fantasy transmuted into concrete images. In pornography, this inevitable mismatch plays a particularly important role because it is more acutely experienced. Pornographic imagery directly addresses the viewer with the fantasy itself so the fantasy no longer needs to be reconstructed: the actors' bodies, the lighting, the sets, the noises on the soundtrack, everything is excessively concrete and never quite coincides with the selective vagueness of a fantasy image. Willemen's conclusion then is that in pornography it is the loss generated by the friction between the fantasy looked for and the fantasy displayed which sustains the desire for ever-promised and never-found gratification (ibid.: 179).

It is this very mismatch upon which Breillat and Noé play, filling the gaps in the fantasy with images and noises which do not simply fail to correspond with the spectator's pornographic fantasy, but which do so deliberately in order to actively reframe and so expose it in its philosophical, political, or moral implications. However, the use of excess to trouble pornographic convention is problematic in two ways. Firstly, it depends on incorporating these very conventions into the film, and indeed foregrounding them through devices which expand and elaborate on them: we might say that the base materials of the films are the excesses of pornography, which are then blurred but not banished by the films' postmodernist strategies. Secondly, the films underestimate the extent to which the spectator may be willing to sift through the excesses of concrete imagery in order to expose the basic fantasy image that lies beneath the layers of excess, and take pleasure in it despite the filmmakers' attempts to foreclose this possibility. Hence those critics and reviewers who have found *Romance* and *Irréversible* titillating, despite the moral repugnance the films might inspire.[4]

A Cinema of Restraint

One alternative to the aesthetic of excess that characterizes the "sexually explicit art film" is a cinema of restraint, provided by Haneke's film. If *Romance, Irréversible* and the other films that comprise the sub-genre of the "sexually explicit art film" can be seen as postmodernist works, *La Pianiste* is grounded firmly in modernist convention. The film operates on the principles of minimalism, precision, and distanciation seen in the works of Robert Bresson and Michelangelo Antonioni, amongst others. Its formal structure depends heavily on ellipsis and litotes, devices that suppress, rather than extend, information and sensation. Scenes are separated from one another with black spacers that fragment the narrative and distance the viewer, and Godardian sound edits intermittently divorce the visual from the sonic. Shots are filmed, for the main part, from a fixed position, the camera's only movement a restricted and restrictive pan. These reflexive devices have the opposite effect of Noé's rumbling soundtrack and whirling camerawork, placing the spectator at a distance from the filmic event. As J. Hoberman explains, this immediately attenuates the presentation of the film's sexual content, such that "[w]here Jelinek's novel maps a forcefield of sexual repression, Haneke rationalizes its flow" (Hoberman 2002: 107).

Within this context of formal restraint, the sexual act occurs "on screen" but outside of the cinematic frame, thus depicting the act but not the body. One way in which Haneke achieves this is by constraining sexual imagery to the spoken. In the flat that Erika shares with her mother, she and her suitor Walter barricade themselves in a bedroom and start to kiss, first standing, then sitting together on the bed. Calling a halt to proceedings, Erika tells Walter that before they can continue he must read the letter that she had given him earlier. Shifting positions, Walter and Erika are framed as physically separate from one another as, in a deadpan voice, Walter proceeds to enunciate Erika's written request to be tied up, beaten, and abused. When Walter pauses, she pulls out a box of whips, ropes, and other bondage toys and spreads them out for him to see. The couple remain out of physical contact and the objects remain immobile, displayed almost as *objets d'art* on the floor: they are not incorporated into a sado-masochistic work of art with Erika as its centerpiece as happens to Marie in *Romance*. Haneke sets out the script and the props but refuses to play out the scene. The explicit acts that Erika describes are divorced from their physical representation: voiceover is not an adjunct and nor is it even a substitute, for Walter's monotone reading refuses any eroticism, and excess is denied at either the visual or aural level.

Elsewhere the sexual act occurs within the film as part of the visual track. The spectator witnesses three narrative instances of "intercourse," but in each case the sexual act either occurs in the off-screen space or is obscured within the frame. Erika and Walter's first sexual encounter occurs in the women's toilets of the Conservatory where she teaches: a white-tiled septic space bleached in pale light. Erika enters, shortly followed by Walter. He peers over the top of the stall she is using to watch her urinate, although we are not given access to what he sees. When she exits the stall, he kisses her, and they slide to the restroom floor in an embrace, initiating what resembles a classic love scene. The camera, however, remains at a distance throughout, situated at the farthest point from the two lovers in the room. Erika abruptly tells Walter to stop and stands up again. She unbuttons his trousers, at which point Walter shifts so that he has his back to the spectator, his body blocking Erika's body from view. Walter's black clothing and large frame both resemble and effectively act as the black rectangles that censors often place over genitalia in film, blocking out the act so that we cannot either see her arms or his penis. The camera next cuts to a reverse-shot taken over Erika's shoulder so that we are facing Walter, but now the framing has been tightened, so that Walter's penis and Erika's hands are outside the lower border of the image frame. Erika then herself slides into this filmic space beyond the bottom edge of the frame, as she kneels to perform fellatio on Walter. At this point, the circumscribed frame is practically drained of content. Walter's torso is framed against a white background: there is very little movement, and no sound other than his laboured breathing. Indeed, when Walter tries to articulate the aural excesses of pornography—"That's it, I'm coming"—Erika silences him, threatening to stop if he does not keep quiet. The white doors of the toilets form a background of vertical lines with Walter's body a black stripe across the centre of the screen, drawing our attention to the upper and lower limits of the frame, and the space that lies beyond them. Walter's gaze towards this space reinforces the implied presence of the sexual organ and the sexual act, prompting us to follow his eyeline down to the natural conclusion which we cannot see, but easily imagine. The characters' gazes in fact serve as a constant reminder of the sexual act's presence in the off-screen space. When Erika watches Walter masturbate, a series of shot/reverse-shots between the two allow us to ascertain their spatial relationship to one another, so that when we are shown a close-up of Erika's face, it is clear exactly where she is looking and what she is looking at. It is an effective device: as reviewer Alexander Walker put it, "absolutely nothing genital is visible in this sequence, yet 'its' presence is painfully tumescent" (Walker 2001: 29).[5]

On the other two occasions that Erika and Walter (attempt to) engage in a sexual act, the explicit is similarly transformed into the implicit through its non-framing. When Walter rapes Erika, the static camera focuses on the characters' faces: Walter's turned away from the camera for at least half the scene, Erika's impassive as she stares into space. The only noise is Walter's breathing, the shot is void of any excess. His orgasm is marked as much by silence as by noise, as he holds his breath before releasing it in a grunt. Indeed throughout the film, the image of a body "beside itself" through orgasm is delayed or disposed of, the only exception coming late in the film and functioning as a remarkable reorientation of cathartic climax. In an earlier scene at the ice rink where Walter plays hockey, Walter's body once more acts as a screen, obscuring Erika's attempts to perform fellatio on him. The camera is placed at a distance, so both the arrangement of bodies within the frame, their relative lack of motion and relative proportion to the frame make it difficult for the spectator to discern what is taking place. But the frame is suddenly filled with movement as Erika pushes Walter off her and bursts into the foreground of the frame, vomiting heavily. The "money shot" here becomes something disgusting and obscene; not a moment of satisfaction, but a moment of repulsion and rejection.

La Pianiste does however feature one series of "classically" explicit sexual images within the frame. Early in the film, we see Erika aggressively enter the space of a porn arcade. She goes into a video booth, whereupon there follows a seven-second shot of a split-screen monitor showing four separate image tracks: each a clip from a generic hardcore porn film. The film cuts back to Erika as she selects an image (and interestingly, while all the other image tracks show the men's faces but not the women's, Erika selects a scene of a woman lying on her back on a table while fellating a man, so that her face is visible while he is reduced to the status of disembodied member), then back to the selected porn film on the monitor. The pornographic image track recurs on the cinematic screen twice more, as the film continues to intercut between it and Erika watching it. The camera then lingers on Erika as she reaches into a wastepaper basket and pulls from it the tissues used by a previous occupant to wipe up his ejaculate. She inhales the tissue deeply while watching the film, her face impassive: her reaction a visual inversion of the excesses of masturbation.

Shame, Guilt, and the Obscene

The use of films-within-films is a recurring feature of Haneke's films. Here, it serves a number of purposes in addition to foregrounding Erika's pursuit of passive pleasure. Firstly, it functions as a generic reference as well as a point of contrast: this is pornography in its most raw and basic form—both pornography as a "norm," and pornography separated from any artistic pretension. Its inclusion thus serves to underline the deviations that Haneke makes from these norms. Secondly, it also serves to remind us what is implicit in Haneke's film. These images act almost as visual aids, to be recalled whenever the spectator is prompted to imagine what it is that lies outside the cinematic frame (that is, the erect penis).

Equally significant, however, the scene creates a *mise en abyme* of the spectator's situation, directly foregrounding the act of voyeurism. The intradiegetic images on the monitor employ the process of enunciation characteristic of pornographic imagery, what Paul Willemen refers to as direct address. Direct address imagery is offered explicitly, in Mulvey's terms, "to be looked at," stressing the addressee's look as opposed to the addresser's intervention, and so is particularly liable to bring the "fourth look" into play in full force (Willemen 1992: 174). This "fourth look" is not of the same order as the other three (intradiegetic looks, the camera's look at the profilmic event, and the viewer's look at the image), but, in Lacanian terms, a look imagined by me in the field of the "other" which surprises me in the act of voyeurism and causes a feeling of shame (Miller 2003: 6–7).

Any articulation of images and looks which brings into play the position and activity of the viewer as a distinctly separate factor—as the body genre of pornography does—also destabilizes that position and puts it at risk, for when the scopic drive is brought into focus, the viewer also runs the risk of becoming the object of the look. But the fourth look emerges particularly strongly when the viewer's scopic drive is being gratified in relation to an object or scene that heightens the sense of censorship inherent in any form of gratification. Its direct implication in both the social and the psychic aspects of censorship, of the law, introduces the social into the very act of looking while remaining an integral part of textual relations. In simpler terms: the fourth look gains in force when the viewer is looking at something they are not supposed to look at according to an external system of censorship (as in clandestine viewings), or according to an internal system of censorship (the superego) or, as in most cases, according to both censorships combined. In this way, that fourth look problematizes the social dimension, the field of the "other", in the cinematic institution as well as in the photographic and televisual ones. And this social dimension manifests itself as shame (Willemen 1992: 174).

Of course, it is possible for a film to intentionally invoke the fourth look in order to confront the spectator with their own voyeurism through the use of reflexive devices, and this is the case to a greater or lesser extent for each of the films that make up the category of "sexually explicit art films." Through reflexive devices, they foreground the director's artistic control and induce a feeling of shame at having been "caught" looking. But what happens when we are not looking at something we should not be looking at, but wanting to see something we know we should not want to see? This is when guilt comes into play.

Shame and guilt are part of the same series of emotions, having to do with blame, responsibility, regret, remorse, and so on. If we seek to distinguish the two, an important reference is Jacques-Alain Miller's suggestion that shame is a primary affect and guilt is a secondary one (Miller 2003). This primary/secondary difference between shame and guilt is an interesting distinction: in his analysis, Miller suggests that while both are related to an awareness of ourselves as a result of a relationship with the Lacanian "other's" gaze, guilt, unlike shame, is not only the recognition of having done wrong but, more significantly, it can be the consequence of mere thought. It can even be the result of thoughts, particularly unconscious thoughts, which would never be acted on. In this case, we are not judged by another, but by ourselves. Thus, Miller points out, in Freudian terms the superego censures and punishes us for the sins we commit; but it also punishes us for the sins that we do not commit (ibid.: 11). The relevance to the cinematic spectacle is self-evident, since the spectator's relationship to the cinema is not one concerned with action but with urges: it is our desires that define our relationship to the cinematic image. And in Haneke's film the emphasis on interiority is redoubled since we do not look at the explicit image, but imagine its presence outside the image frame. The non-framing and the aesthetics of restraint that operate within *La Pianiste* can thus be seen to transmute the Lacanian feeling of shame into a Freudian sense of guilt through their engagement of the spectator's imaginative faculty.

Discussing *Romance*, Breillat claims that the meaning of an image is wholly dependent on whether it is looked at with a vision that is "hideous and obscene" or "with love" (Sklar 1999: 26). But what are we to understand by the term "obscene"? The word comes from the Latin *caenum*, "filth," but this seems to leave us little to go on. It is perhaps useful at this juncture to turn to legal definitions of the term, relating to obscenity law. Martha Nussbaum's illuminating discussion of obscenity and the law (Nussbaum 2004) underlines the point that legal accounts of the obscene typically refer to the disgusting properties of the work in question as they relate to the sensibilities of a hypothetical "average man." The legal standard in the US set by *Miller v. California* in 1973 holds that "a work may be subject to state regulation where that work, taken as a whole, appeals to the prurient interest in sex; portrays, in a patently offensive way, sexual conduct specifically defined by the applicable state law" (ibid.: 134). This determination is made from the point of view of "the average person, applying contemporary community standards" (ibid.: 135). Likewise, the *Oxford English Dictionary*'s definition of the term is "[o]ffensively or repulsively indecent, esp. by offending accepted sexual morality."

What both definitions of the obscene foreground is not the intentions of the creator but the response of the viewer. Breillat seems to intend by the above statement that the meaning of an image is dependent upon the way in which the director views it and imbues it with that vision. Downing interprets the formula as follows: the meaning of an image is wholly dependent upon the ideological positions that it appears to uphold. Or, in other words, meaning depends on the ideological position that the film implies (Downing 2004: 278). Haneke, however, turns this formula on its head: the meanings of the images in *La Pianiste* are dependent upon the ideological positions that a spectator infers. *La Pianiste*'s mobilization of the spectator's imagination shifts the responsibility for a film's "meaning" from the director to the spectator, and if the spectator is responsible for the production of meaning, then they are responsible for that meaning's moral implications. *La Pianiste* uses non-framing to restore to the sexual act the potential for obscenity by foregrounding the viewer's response to the image, thereby functioning as a provocation to the spectator to reconsider their own relationship to the consumption of the sexual image in moral terms.

Haneke's film occupies an ambiguous position vis-à-vis to the sub-genre of "postmodern porn" that Downing distinguishes. It constitutes a critique of pornography and the alienation of sex from emotion, and in this sense supports a film such as Breillat's. It also critiques the society that represses and censors sexual images such as those we see in *Romance*, which can perhaps educate their spectators about human relationships in the way that commodified pornography cannot. But at the same time *La Pianiste* offers no alternative, no "better way" of making films or of adjusting society's attitude to sex and sexuality. Haneke flatly refuses the representation of the sexual act in any form other than the abject and alienated. In this sense, it is an extremely pessimistic—perhaps even nihilistic—piece of cinema. But Haneke does make the film pertinent to the spectator in a way that neither Breillat nor Noé achieves. What is truly obscene about *La Pianiste* is not that it offends accepted sexual morality, but that by foregrounding the ob-scene—by way of its linguistic derivation, that which cannot, or should not, be seen—the film leads the spectator to ask whether "accepted" sexual morality itself is offensive.

Notes

1. For an extended account of *Irréversible*'s physical effects on film audiences and the controversy surrounding the film, see Sterrit (2005: 205).
2. The word "rape" occurs in inverted commas here since the scene has been variously construed as a straightforward rape, a near-rape, and a consensual act, indicating a confusion about what happens on screen which serves as evidence in itself of the scene's opacity. For an extended discussion of this ambiguity, see Martin (2000).
3. For examples pertaining to both, see Wilson (2001), and James and Kermode (2003).
4. For examples pertaining to each film, see Wilson (2001) on *Romance*, and Felperin (2003). Incidentally, when I went to hire *Romance* from my local video rental shop, I was intrigued to find it in the "Erotica" section, rather than "French film."
5. In an interview with Claire Mellini, Haneke reveals that he originally shot the scene with Benoît Magimel's penis visible within the frame but then decided against using the shot in the final edit in order that the spectator, as he puts it, "becomes shocked by the act itself, and not by its place within a narrative" (Mellini 2001: 99).

References

Clover, C. 1987. "Her Body, Himself: Gender in the Slasher Film," *Representations* 20: 187–228.

Cooper, K. 1999. "Beyond the Clean and Proper,' *Vertigo* 1(9): 45–46.

Creed, B. 2003. *Media Matrix: Sexing the New Reality*. Crow's Nest, Australia: Allen and Unwin.

Douglas, A. 1980. "Soft-Porn Culture," *New Republic*, 30 August, 25–29.

Downing, L. 2004. "French Cinema's New 'Sexual Revolution': Postmodern Porn and Troubled Genre," *French Cultural Studies* 15(3): 265–80.

Ellis, J. 1992. "On Pornography," in Screen Editorial Collective (eds), *The Sexual Subject: A Screen Reader in Sexuality*. London: Routledge, 146–70.

Felperin, L. 2003. "Irreversible," *Sight and Sound* 13(3): 47–48.

Hoberman, J. 2002. "Prisoners' Song," *Village Voice*, 2 April, p. 107.

James, N. 2001. "The Limits of Sex," *Sight and Sound* 11(6): 21.

James, N. and M. Kermode. 2003. "Horror Movie," *Sight and Sound* 13(2): 20–22.

Lacan, J. 1977. *Ecrits: A Selection*. Trans Alan Sheridan. London: Tavistock.

Martin, A. 2000. "X Marks the Spot: Classifying Romance," *Senses of Cinema Online Film Journal*, i.4. Retrieved 24 March 2006 from: http://www.sensesofcinema.com/ contents/directors/02/www.sensesofcinema.com/contents/00/4/romance. html.

Mellini, C. 2001. «Désaccords mineurs pour piano forte: Entretien avec Michael Haneke et Elfriede Jelinek,» *L'Avant-Scène du Cinéma* 504 : 95–102.

Miller, J.-A. 2003. 'Note sur la honte et la culpabilité," *La Cause freudienne* 54: 6–19.

Nussbaum, M. 2004. *Hiding from Humanity: Disgust, Shame, and the Law*. Princeton, NJ: Princeton University Press.

Phillips, J. 2001. "Catherine Breillat's *Romance*: Hard Core and the Female Gaze," *Studies in French Cinema* 1(3): 133–40.

Sklar, R. 1999. "A Woman's View of Shame and Desire: An Interview with Catherine Breillat," *Cineaste* 25(1): 24–26.

Sterrit, D. 2005. *Guiltless Pleasures*. Mississippi: Mississippi University Press.

Vincendeau, G. 2002. "Baise Moi," *Sight and Sound* 12(5): 38.

Walker, A. 2001. "The Piano Teacher," *Evening Standard*, 8 November, p. 29.

Willemen, P. 1992. "Letter to John," in Screen Editorial Collective (eds), *The Sexual Subject: A Screen Reader in Sexuality*. London: Routledge, 171–83.

Williams, L. 1987. "Film Bodies: Gender, Genre, and Excess," in R. Stam and T. Miller (eds), *Film and Theory: An Anthology*. Oxford: Blackwell, 207–22.

———. 2000. "Cinema and the Sex Act," *Cinéaste* 27(1): 20–25.

Wilson, E. 2001. "Deforming Femininity: Catherine Breillat's *Romance*," in L. Mazdon (ed.), *France on Film: Reflections on Popular French Cinema*. London: Wallflower, 145–57.

Chapter 13

The Possibility of Desire in a Conformist World: The Cinema of Ulrich Seidl

Mattias Frey

At the Berlin premiere of *Hundstage/Dog Days* (2001), Ulrich Seidl prefaced the screening by wishing the audience "a disturbing evening."[1] Like the films of his compatriot Michael Haneke, with whom he shared the stage that evening, Seidl's work constitutes a cinema of disturbance and contains a damning critique of Austrian society. Unlike Haneke, however, Seidl finds the disturbing not in extraordinary outbursts of violence or helplessness, but rather in the everyday strangeness all around us, a world he represents formally in blurring and ultimately deconstructing the boundaries between fact and fiction, documentary and feature film. He is seen by many, alongside Egon Humer, as the most important Austrian documentary filmmaker of the 1990s and has only strengthened this position in the last few years.

Seidl has repeatedly emphasized in interviews and public appearances that he never intended to be a documentary filmmaker. Like others working in Austria's subsidy-dependent industry, Seidl stumbled upon the documentary as a means to realize his cinematic aspirations without having to resort to delivering commercial fare. Even before shooting *Dog Days*, his first official "fiction film," he refused to consider himself a documentarist, maintaining that his entire oeuvre "transcends the boundaries between fiction and documentary" (Rothe 2002). The filmmaker's stylized, laconic regard of quotidian quirks transcends social reportage and the discourses of authenticity and reality which inform other domestic documentaries. Seidl is uninterested in life's few happy moments, a stance he justifies by asserting the contrast between his project and a wedding photographer's job ("No Wedding Photographer" became the title of a touring Seidl retrospective). He captures characters who play the roles of their own lives. His stylized *mise-en-scène* reaffirms the constructedness of European social space, investigating the possibility of desire in a world intolerant of deviation from normality.

That Seidl is no wedding photographer of the traditional kind is evident in *Der Ball/The Ball* (1982), his graduation project at the Vienna Film Academy. Chronicling a graduation dance in a small Austrian village, the fifty-minute piece unveils the hypocrisy and gluttony of an inhibited, ritualistic society. The first shots of Seidl's films are always emblematic or programmatic. *The Ball* begins with a pastoral prospect of a fog-draped village, a church protruding from its center, before cutting to the second image, a pan over a much less idyllic traffic intersection. This opening betrays the film's narrative rhythm: "official" portraits immediately undermined by a raw revelation. Two types of sequences fuel this logic over the course of the film. The first are "interviews," shot in static, unbroken takes with village officials: the mayor, the school principle, an attorney, the deputy mayor, the school doctor, and other authorities in the town. These are not exactly traditional interviews, however, but rather monologues which the subjects have memorized or even read from a script. The subjects appear in a less than flattering manner; their attempts at self-presentation are plainly laid bare. The second type of sequence shows the preparations for the ball or scenes from the ball itself. As the village attorney explains, "the ball is a social event," one which assumes a deadly earnestness, particularly for the village youth. Via shot scale and editing, the rehearsal assumes an almost militaristic formality. The camera focuses on detail shots of dresses and accessories, revealing the very plain faces and bodies of the people that wear them only later. A montage sequence telegraphs makeup preparations. In a tableau anticipating Seidl's later *Models* (1998), a mirror blocks the viewer's access to a girl's face. The young woman is a test object: she is experimented upon with substances (makeup) and (beautician's) machines. One man "sunbathes" in a solarium. The procedures appear alien; they resemble torture. The soundtrack hones in on the industrial, terrible noises which the machines produce. The sound of the girl's laughter at the end of this sequence, however, is withheld.

The debutante attempts a reply to the crucial question, "Why do you go to the ball?" But whereas any other filmmaker would have used a close-up "talking head" to document this intensely climactic moment, Seidl delivers the scene in a long shot. Through this distance Seidl seeks to show that the question "why?" is moot. His graduation film chronicles the perversion of desire in a homogeneous society. Directly after one of the village elders lauds the boys' "possibility to have different suits," the film cuts to a series of men in identical attire. The ballroom resembles a prison, or the empty paper factory of Humer's *Postadresse: 2046 Schlöglmühl* (1990). Music rattles irritatingly through the ominous hall: the black voices and jovial refrains of "Sentimental Journey" and "All of Me" jar with the village's severity and homogeneity.

The play of contrasts culminates in the exposed hypocrisy of the townspeople during the ball itself. Sober monologues precede licentious behavior at the dance, increasingly captured in hellish red tones. Synchronized line dances yield to drunken "chicken dances." As an interviewee reports in a voiceover that future couples "meet" at the dance, a man and a girl sloppily canoodle on the edge of the dance floor. After the ball ends, the concluding shots dwell, once again, on the sleepy village. In this second viewing, however, the "innocent" hamlet appears manifestly superficial and repressed.

Still Lives

After having finished at the Academy, Seidl suffered rejection letters and undertook documentary assignments for ORF (the Austrian Broadcasting Corporation) and 3Sat, a German/Austrian/Swiss channel. His breakthrough came in 1990 with the theatrical release of a controversial feature-length documentary. *Good News oder: Von Kolporteuren, toten Hunden und anderen Wienern/Good News or: Of Paperboys, Dead Dogs, and Other Viennese* (1990) is a dialectic essay which juxtaposes the squalid conditions of South Asian immigrants who sell newspapers in Vienna's outer districts with observations of Viennese tabloid readers. Structurally, *Good News* makes ironic the symbiotic relation between the distribution and consumption of news in Vienna: that is, between the immigrant sellers and the partially xenophobic buyers. Two distinct spaces emerge: first, "native" Austrian living rooms, captured in tripod shots resembling photographs; and, second, the cold corners and shanty towns where the sellers dwell, frequently filmed with a restlessly mobile camera. The often solitary whites' stillness contrasts sharply with the South Asians' group behavior: they chant, clap, and dance in long, hand-held sequences. Seidl, in form and in content, recreates the meaning of "still lives." As distinct as these worlds appear, both are subsumed under the heading "Vienna" and connect in the circulation of a specific medium. The film suggests that both groups ultimately exist on the edge of society.

Seidl's camera captures the pathetic subjects in stylized tableaux, lingering within static frames for uncomfortable lengths of time, a mannerism which has led reviewers to link his work to the photography of Diane Arbus. This technique, although still evolving in this film, marks Seidl's later documentaries with ever greater effectiveness. Its roots are essentially twofold: first, in Brecht's *Verfremdungseffekt*, a theatrical device in which an irritating distance between actors and audience creates a critical space; and, second, a tradition of painterly cinema. Seidl's appropriation of this painterly cinema amounts to its deconstruction, however. Whereas André Bazin praised Rossellini's *Paisà* (1946) for its depiction of a staged event in a "realistic" cinematographic language, using long takes and deep focus (Bazin 1967), Seidl uses these techniques in his documentary films, using primarily non-professional "actors," to achieve the exact opposite effect: a stylized, plastic world. In this sense Seidl is also working against the contemporary equation—in documentary reportage as well as in the Dogme 95 cinema—of a shaky camera with the "real."

One exemplary use of the painterly in *Good News* is an extreme long shot of a seller near the beginning of the film. The man, clad in his clown-like, yellow and red uniform, stands in a tram shelter backed by a black-and-white advertisement for a rival tabloid. The billboard features a businessman reclining in a chair reading the *Abendzeitung*, his tie blown back presumably by the airplane in the background of the image. The slogan reads: "A New Wind Will Be Blowing, Starting 12/12." Surrounding the shelter is the foreground of the gray cobblestone street and the white of snow-covered trees. In this composition, several issues are at stake. First, the newspaper seller enters into a dialogical relationship with the advertisement, in a way that recalls—but is certainly more earnest than—Jean-Luc Godard's *Made in USA* (1966). Second, by virtue of shot scale and staging, this seeming idyllic Viennese winter landscape dwarfs the seller's body and foregrounds his blackness. Greater forces circumscribe his existence.

Although *Good News* engages with the subject matter of TV reportage, it explicitly rejects that form. Distinctly missing are the reporter's voiceover and subjective physical presence—their intrusive personality, problem-solver image, and comforting, surrogate subject position for the spectator. As is often the case in Seidl films, the subjects look to the filmmaker in the off-screen space during static shots or after speaking. The unspoken questions, "Was that good? Was that what you wanted?" are plainly legible in their faces. Gazes from passersby into the camera, furthermore, are consistently left in, establishing yet another level of voyeurism.

Indeed, *Good News* was very much an object of curiosity in Vienna during its initial run and stimulated public discussion throughout German-speaking Europe. After a few weeks the film had been seen by an audience larger than most domestic genre films and remained a presence in Austrian cinemas for several months. The exceptional performance of *Good News* at the box office allowed Seidl the financial freedom to pursue his next project. *Mit Verlust ist zu rechnen/Loss Is to Be Expected* (1992) moves from the outer districts of Vienna to the border zone between Austria and the Czech Republic. It begins with an arresting image: a weary, perhaps drunk or handicapped man undresses in a dark, non-descript room and performs a strip-tease to radio static and an audience of one: the camera. Seidl maintains that this behavior and the tolerant attitude with which the Czech villagers regard it are meant to serve as a contrast to Austria (Wulff 1995: 253–54). There, just a few kilometers over the border, such a man would be locked away on the basis that he is disturbing the "image" of the community. This is an example of a tactic central to Seidl's works: each maps social spaces which are geographically close and yet totally different.

The film proceeds to chronicle the affair between Josef Paur, an Austrian widower, and Paula Hutterová, a widowed senior of German descent who lives in the Czech village just over the border. In some ways the story follows a familiar pattern to *Good News*. Josef is the bored Western pensioner and Paula the overworked victim of socialism's legacy. He desires a companion and maid to spice his routine; she longs for a more comfortable existence. Ultimately, their lives are too incompatible to sustain the romance. Containing much more narrative than previous efforts, *Loss Is to Be Expected* anticipates Seidl's later dramatic work.

Seidl's next project, *Tierische Liebe/Animal Love* (1995), would, however, be his most economically narrated and most controversial. It explores a motif introduced in *Good News*, namely, the obsessive attention Austrians pay to cats, ferrets, and dogs. The film returns to the middle-class Viennese milieu portrayed in *Good News* and once again records its sterile homes with an icy distance. To these people, pets represent conversation partners, therapists, playmates, bedfellows, and fashion objects to be groomed meticulously. The film's argument proves to be metacinematic. The animals function as projection screens for human desires. *Animal Love* reveals a pathetic loneliness and desperation behind all the care and attention. According to Seidl this is the subtext of his entire oeuvre: "hell is us" (Rothe 2002).

Animal Love is Seidl's most difficult work. One critic ascribes it a "hitherto unknown nihilism" (Grissemann 2007: 132). While graphic depictions of masturbation, pornography, sex, and bestiality are not uncommon in Seidl, here they assume a hostile, destructive tone. The filmmaker's attitude toward his subjects becomes much more exhibitionistic than, as the director has claimed, "intimate" (ibid.:140).

The Insanity of Normality

Models (1998) sketches the fantasies and realities of young models. Although supermodels figure as the vaunted objects of desire in our society, Seidl fixes on the everyday tics and banal insecurities from which these women suffer: persistent cellulite, bosom dilemmas, catty competition, and the inability to be alone. A world of glamour whose shine and luster Seidl rubs away, *Models* aims at an unmasking, harking back to *The Ball*.

Indeed, the film opens with a shot familiar from *The Ball*: a woman seated, her face hidden behind a hand mirror whose design matches the pattern of the bathroom tiles. Vivian's blond hair peeks out over the mirror, which structurally displaces and semiotically replaces her face. She repeats the mantra, "I love you," to herself. Her décolleté—the only part of her body accessible to the spectator—functions as a revealing synecdoche for her entire being. The image certainly introduces the theme of vanity, but also the concept of constant self-assurance in pursuit of the elusive perfect body. In addition, the composition anticipates moments in which the camera is placed behind a mirror. The camera in *Models* functions, literally and figuratively, as a mirror. It is a point of vanity and and—often illusory—reflection.

Seidl's gaze is unrelenting. The "glamorous" retch over a toilet or awkwardly sleep with a photographer. Nevertheless, the subjects' often seemingly misguided feelings remain primary and the spectator must engage with them with both disbelief and affection. Midway through a one-night stand, Vivian asks her newly befriended partner, "what do you feel for me?" as if she truly expects him to tell her he loves her. After another cocaine binge, Lisa drinks alone and telephones a friend. The spectator can only be suspicious as to whether her "I'm losing the connection to reality" is not merely another plea for sympathy and attention. The women worry that their boyfriends might be philandering at the very same time that they wish to be—or in fact are—unfaithful themselves.

Models documents subjects who are constantly on display. Its originality is its examination of precisely those situations in which the models are not supposed to be "acting"; it probes the moments beyond the poses. In several scenes Vivian interrogates her boyfriend Werner while she sits on the toilet urinating or changing her maxi pad. Later, the pair discusses their faltering sex life in a *mise-en-scène* that recalls Rainer Werner Fassbinder's *Die bitteren Tränen der Petra von Kant/The Bitter Tears of Petra von Kant* (1972). Werner reclines on the bed in the background, while his girlfriend crouches on the bed's edge in the foreground. Both look forward, towards the camera; when Vivian demands that Werner look at her, one wonders how he could.

The process of modeling itself is telegraphed in a series of stylized sequences. One *tableau vivant* has a row of silent models sitting on the casting couch, looking into the camera, for which each then rehearses her interview monologue. "Blond is always good," a fashion photographer reassures a young woman nervous about missing the trend in hair color. The body as commodity, an equation present throughout Seidl's work, including *Import Export* (2007), is central to *Models*. Each girl treats her body as a vehicle which should be preserved and altered—for example, Lisa's prominent nips, tucks, and enlargements. As ever, the whirls and giggles of the tools which abet this process command prominent attention: waxing strips, the Stepper, the bathroom scale, neon tanning beds. In one montage sequence, the circular motions of anti-cellulite machines resemble the primitive psychiatric contraptions of Friedkin's *The Exorcist* (1973).

Dog Days (2001), Seidl's fiction film debut, represents much less a departure than a continuation of his narrative strategies. The film unfolds in a Viennese suburb over two hot, sticky days. The characters and their isolated, lonely lives are introduced much in the vein of Seidl's documentaries. The focus remains the daily, mundane activities which lay bare the "insanity of normality" (Wulff 1995: 245). There is the jealous boyfriend and his meek lover juxtaposed with the retiree who spends his time tending his immaculate lawn and weighing packages of sugar to ensure he has not been swindled. There is the woman who walks from a session of rough sex at a swinger club directly into the main halls of the mall where children play. She lives together with her estranged husband. The pair mourn the death of their child, yet the film never gives details of this story.

Even in form and style, it is difficult to separate *Dog Days* from Seidl's documentaries. Indeed, it is impossible to differentiate between the amateurs and the few professional actors that Seidl hired for the film. In this feature, just as in Seidl's documentaries, the characters are "playing the role of their own lives" (Wulff 1995: 249), which the production history certainly bears out. The pimp and the alarm salesman in the film, for example, have the same professions in real life (Nord 2002). As Seidl reveals in an interview: "I don't make any difference between feature films and documentaries. That's why the term 'staged reality' was coined. That means the people in my film are non-actors, but sometimes don't act that way. And that irritates some people. They want to think and see in tidy categories" (in Elstermann 1996).

Dog Days is a disturbing suburban story told with irony, but with neither restraint nor a final redemption. Since all characters are both victims and perpetrators in some sense, the basic question of justice—what does one deserve?—is blurred. Seidl borrows from Werner Herzog's visual circle metaphors. Driving "donuts" in a parking lot recalls the ending of Herzog's *Stroszek* (1977). Furthermore, motifs recur. For example, Miss Lower Austria dances at a nightclub before her jealous boyfriend; later an old woman jiggles for her husband in their living room. These circles and recurrences suggest a cyclical history of vulnerability and (self-)destruction.

In *Jesus, Du weißt/Jesus, You Know* (2003), Seidl again mines the "insanity of normality." The film opens with a woman praying before the camera: "I thank you, Father, for this film, I thank you, Father, for the days of shooting, that they went so well." The concept is simple. God-fearing Viennese pray alone in a church. The pious Austrians say out loud that which they usually direct towards God in silent meditation. One woman wishes her husband would stop watching so many talk shows. A young man is unsure whether he wants to become a monk or marry his girlfriend. A university student is concerned that he is obsessed with erotic TV-films. The last woman, finally, asks Jesus for money to hire a private investigator to pursue her unfaithful husband.

Occasionally, the spectator gains access to the subjects' predicaments away from the space of the church. The film cuts, for example, to the woman at home sewing or ironing, while her husband presumably watches talk shows and ignores her. In a larger sense, the film pursues a thesis about communication. Why do these people voice their problems alone at church rather than engaging in dialogue with their beloved? *Jesus, You Know*, like Seidl's previous films, places the spectator in a bind. On the one hand, the "characters" in the documentary are genuinely ridiculous. On the other, one feels guilty for laughing at such vulnerable creatures. This is another boundary Seidl attempts to blur, "the border between something being funny and the moment at which laughing completely escapes us" (Köhler 2002).

Away From Here

Import Export (2007), Seidl's second fiction film, reprises key elements of *Loss Is to Be Expected*: both films examine the ambiguous boundaries between "Eastern" and "Western" Europe. Seidl's later film opens with a man repeatedly trying but failing to start his motorcycle. A menacing, anonymous highrise looms in the background. We are in an unforgiving Ukrainian suburb resembling the Yugoslavian locations of Welles's adaptation of Kafka, *Le Procès/The Trial* (1962). It is an industrial wasteland of transit zones: makeshift pathways between cranes and bulldozers and the corridors of the hospital where Olga, the female protagonist, works. The affectless setting is more terrible than the similar but expressedly stylized locations in Butterworth's *Birthday Girl* (2001), Dusl's *Blue Moon* (2002), or even Moodysson's *Lilja 4-ever* (2002). Edward Lachman's handheld camera follows Olga walking through the halls of her shoddy flat. The promising poster of a waterfall in the bathroom functions like the utopian prints in Michael Haneke's *Der siebente Kontinent/The Seventh Continent* (1989): an imaginary window to a better world. Olga is dissatisfied with her lot and when the paychecks stop arriving, the trained nurse begins moonlighting at a bordello for internet porn. Still unable to make ends meet, she emigrates to Vienna.

The Austrian capital, where the jobless Paul trains to be a security guard, is just as cold and barren as the Ukraine. In a desolate former quarry, men run in a circle and fire imaginary bullets, while the noise of the autobahn drones in the background. Paul is unlucky in love, too. He brings an attack dog to his girlfriend's apartment in the mistaken belief that it might kindle their romance. Increasingly hounded by acquaintances seeking to collect debts, Paul drives with his stepfather to the East in order to set up some gumball machines. Meanwhile, Olga has started working as a nanny and maid in a wealthy Viennese household. When it becomes apparent that the kids like Olga more than their fussy mother, the jealous boss fires the beautiful Ukrainian immediately and without any explanation. Olga next gets a job as a cleaning lady in a nursing home; bureaucratic rules prevent the former nurse from caring for the patients. That the residents nonetheless appreciate her more than their bored, native Austrian caretakers leads to grumbling and, in the end, a vicious attack by a vengeful nurse.

Import Export treads between the comic and the tragic. The spectator wants to laugh and cry at the same time; the intense situations foreclose an "appropriate" response. In one grotesque scene, Paul's stepfather instructs his stepson on the "power of money" by forcing a prostitute to bark like a dog. In another sequence, Olga receives an impromptu language lesson in German for her clients: "I would like to suck your cock." When an online customer demands of Olga that she "stick [her] finger up [her] ass," the set design makes the scene ironic: a poster behind the woman reads, "love is like a red, red rose." Later, Paul attends a workshop for the unemployed in which the teacher (played by the German comic Dirk Stermann) advises the motley crew to follow the rule LMAA—*Lächel mehr als Andere* ("smile more than the others"). This acronym parodies the letters' usual meaning: *Leck mich am Arsch* ("kiss my ass"). Such moments recall the promotional instructional video in *Good News*. In that film the immigrant sellers receive lectures in pictograms and slogans: "keep smiling, keep selling."

Import Export is two films told in parallel montage, two films which subtend, but—unlike in Robert Altman or Krzysztof Kieślowski—never neatly meet. The two stories rhyme, beginning with the reverse motion of going West, or East, in a utopian dream of self-improvement with mixed results. The scenes interact dynamically. Dancing sequences follow each other consecutively: Paul alone in an Eastern European club, Olga with an elderly patient in the basement of the old people's home. The motion of the youths who strut around Paul after his humiliation echoes Paul's circular movements in his guard training. These graphic "echoes" correspond to the film's sound design. As ever, Seidl attends to the white noise around us, which *Import Export* reproduces as a refined soundscape. In one tracking shot, we see a series of wax machines. The various models glide over empty cubicles; each buzzes and hums uniquely. In the nursing home scenes, the senile outbursts of the patients or the laughter of the cleaning ladies over lunch form a hypnotic rhythm, an a cappella music of the quotidian. These strangely aesthetic tones yield an uncanny, yet sweet cacophony.

Import Export scrutinizes monetary and bodily circulation. The circuits, however, do not necessarily close; the connection between the protagonists is the telos "away from here." The story ultimately investigates a deeply rooted pattern of behavior: the will to demoralize and humiliate as the expression of one's own powerlessness. In terms of its subject, the film is close to Barbara Albert's *Nordrand/Northern Skirts* (1999), Ruth Mader's *Struggle* (2003), or Michael Klier's *Überall ist es besser, wo wir nicht sind/The Grass is Always Greener* (1989); meanwhile, the nursing home documentary/fiction method of observation and interaction recalls Elliot Greenebaum's *Assisted Living* (2003). The work as a whole is nonetheless unmistakably Seidl.

For critics, Seidl ridicules his subjects, cynically exhibits them, and ignores their sense of worth. Indeed, Seidl transports us to places which have been declared private: sex clubs, living rooms, as well as fenced-off swimming pools and gardens. He shows us individuals at their most vulnerable: unemployed, in prayer, naked, or senile. Seidl's important intervention, however, is to interrogate whether these areas have been declared taboo out of respect for the individuals in these places or states, or rather because we, as spectators, fear identifying with these people.

Seidl renders the social rituals which we take for granted—whether they be the village ball, buying a newspaper, or seeing a model in an advertisement—strange and uncanny. Although the director is currently working on his first picture explicitly about mass tourism (Philipp 2007), in a sense his entire oeuvre treats this issue. His gaze is anthropological. It places us in the awkward position of being a tourist in our own society.[2] Seidl poses less the basic social question: Is this normal? Instead, he challenges us to re-examine whether that which we have long since tacitly accepted as normal or abnormal can be absolutely classified in those categories. He asks: Is anything normal?

Other directors have surely treated the "problems" present in Seidl's work—globalization, the relations between Eastern and Western Europe, the Catholic Church, and the role of outsiders in society. No other filmmaker, however, employs such radically different strategies to address them. Other contemporaries, such as Fatih Akin, use melodrama and evoke visceral emotions in their spectators. Seidl—channeling influences such as the films of Werner Herzog and Rainer Werner Fassbinder, Diane Arbus's photography, Francis Bacon's grotesque portraits, and the "still life" tradition in painting—challenges the spectator not only to feel but also to think about the constructedness of our society. He probes relations. These are the personal relations individuals forge with their partners, pets, or God, but also the relations at work when we watch films. His films ask whether we are to be passive members of the cinematic flock—letting images flicker by at twenty-four frames per second—or whether we should engage with the screen in a critical way.

Notes

This chapter is a significantly revised version of "Border Zones: The Films of Ulrich Seidl," *Senses of Cinema* (July–September 2004).

1. Seidl's remark was made before the screening of *Dog Days* at the Freiluftkino Museumsinsel in Berlin, 27 June 2002.
2. Walter Wippersberg's *Das Fest des Huhnes* (1992) takes this principle to the satirical extreme. It spoofs ethnological documentaries, presenting an African who supposedly reports on the strangeness of the "natives" from the Upper Austria.

References

Bazin, A. 1967. "The Evolution of the Language of Cinema," in *What Is Cinema? Vol. 1*, ed. and trans. H. Gray. Berkeley: University of California Press, 23–40.

Elstermann, K. 1996. "Dafür genieren sich die Leute," *Taz*, 2 September, p. 17.

Grissemann, S. 2007. *Sündenfall: Die Grenzüberschreitungen des Filmemachers Ulrich Seidl*. Vienna: Sonderzahl.

Köhler, M. 2002. "Es ist die Wirklichkeit, die provoziert," *Berliner Morgenpost*, 1 August, http://www.morgenpost.de/printarchiv/film/article505928/Es_ist_die_ Wirklichkeit_die_provoziert.html.

Nord, C. 2002. "Ich lebe mit meinen Figuren," *Taz*, 1 August, p. 13.

Philipp, C. 2007. "Der Bildhauer der Wirklichkeit," *Der Standard*, 10–11 November, p. 33.

Rothe, M. 2002. "Die Hölle sind wir selbst," *Berliner Zeitung*, 1 August, http:// www.berlinonline.de/berliner-zeitung/archiv/.bin/dump.fcgi/2002/0801/ berlinberlin/0029/index.html.

Wulff, C. 1995. "Eine Welt ohne Mitleid: Ulrich Seidl und seine Filme," in P. Illetschko (ed.), *Gegenschuss:16 Regisseure aus Österreich*. Vienna: Wespennest, 240–54.

Chapter 14

Dog Days:
Ulrich Seidl's *Fin-de-siècle* Vision

Justin Vicari

"We're about to enter the twenty-first century," says one of the passing characters in Ulrich Seidl's *Hundstage/Dog Days* (2001). In Seidl's vision, we can build up the urban landscape to our heart's content, expand our superhighways and strip malls as far as the eye can see—but we're still working with the same primitive bodies, hearts, brains, and sex organs that we've always had. Underpinning all progress is the chronic latent threat of a return to savagery, not in the form of some sweeping apocalypse but in all those small daily moments when the limitations of the human stand starkly revealed: a lonely old widower taking out his dentures at bedtime and dropping them into a glass; a wrinkled, cellulite-riddled woman in an abusive relationship, pulling up her flab to snip her pubic hair with scissors.

Seidl has an accomplished and compelling eye for such grotesque moments and he frames them not only with a filmmaker's sense of the lushness of movement in space and time, but with a modern photographer's awareness of the flatness and confinement of the frame. Seidl begins and ends *Dog Days* with a series of static shots of people posed in familiar surroundings—sunbathers lounging on porch decks; a naked couple embracing against red curtains at a sex club—that have the disarming frontality of portrait photographs. In one memorably tight, medium close-up, Seidl shows a woman riding in an elevator, trying to ignore an old man who is aggressively looking her body up and down: this oppressive juxtaposition of watcher and watched within a single shot inscribes the divided nature of Seidl's own voyeurism, always willing to push situations to extremes and bring out the worst in his characters, but at the same time bearing a seemingly troubled heart that sometimes goes out to the fragile lives whose pain he records.

If Seidl's earlier documentaries have garnered comparisons with Diane Arbus's calmly composed observations of human oddities, then *Dog Days*, his first film that is not a documentary, bursts convincingly into lurid Nan Goldin terrain, with its seedy nightclubs, its flashes of neon, and especially its battered women. In fact, *Dog Days* has two of these: a young beauty-pageant winner, Miss Lower Austria (Franziska Weiss), whose boyfriend (René Wanko) is constantly accusing her of cheating on him (which she is not); and a middle-aged teacher (Christine Jirku), whose paramour, Wickerl (Viktor Hennemann), brings home a clueless young stud named Lucky (Georg Friedrich) and tries to impose a *ménage à trois* on her. There are other stories, all taking place during the same summer heatwave and crosscut by Seidl into a downward-spiraling tapestry of human misery: a salesman (Alfred Mrva) of home alarm systems is threatened by his clients at a housing co-op if he doesn't find out who's been keying their cars; a retarded or mentally-ill girl (Maria Hofstatter) hitchhikes with various strangers, whom she regales with manic Top Ten lists and advertising jingles; an old man (Eric Finsches) seduces his housekeeper (Gerti Lehner) on the fiftieth anniversary of his marriage to his late wife; and a young married couple live in tense, angry silence after the mysterious death of their child, the husband (Victor Rathbone) pushing the wife away and the wife (Claudia Martini) carrying on affairs under the husband's nose.

So Seidl's title, we see, has two meanings: the sweltering humidity of summertime, and a kind of evolutionary (or counter-evolutionary) cycle in which people begin to act more and more like their canine counterparts. Seidl's subject is the limits of the human—the human becoming all-body, becoming animal. "Heat always produces an exceptional kind of situation in people," the director has remarked. "When it's extremely hot out, people either become aggressive or apathetic".[1] Dismissing all the typical movie-making ways of simulating heavy sweating (by spraying the actors down with water) as "tricks," Seidl chose to film *Dog Days* only when the air temperature topped 100 degrees, and, going one better, turned on the heat in the apartments he used as sets. The effect is palpable: the cast (made up of non-professional actors) drifts slowly in a haze, bleary-eyed.

Is it the rigorous documentarian in Seidl who imposed this condition of verisimilitude—or is it the philosopher, who seems to want to show that most of our human energies are misdirected, misguided; in a word, wasted? Many of those static shots of sunbathers show them lying next to big unused swimming pools, whose shimmering blue water promises easy relief from the heat. But the sunbathers never get into the pools. Suggesting that there is an innate futility to all human endeavors, Seidl demonstrates the ways in which people displace their true emotions into furious, compulsive, even self-defeating activity. The feuding husband and wife also have a swimming pool: a sunken, drained one that the husband uses as a handball court, pounding out his rage with tennis ball and racquet. Brilliantly, Seidl establishes a feeling of hours spent at this pastime in a sequence of a few shots that move rapidly from late afternoon light to early-sunset dimness, and finally to darkness.

Watching *Dog Days* we discover truth not as a result of the emoting of actors, but simply by observing the characters' actions, which always seem to hover at extremes of banality or barbarism. When the film is not simmering up to the boiling point or exploding outright into violence, it is deliberately and overwhelmingly mundane: we see the old man mowing his lawn, the teacher picking at a cold chicken carcass in her kitchen. Like the conversational style of the hitchhiker, who rattles off her nutty Top Ten lists ("Do you know the ten sexiest TV news anchors?") and the ingredients in mass-produced foodstuffs, all the day-to-day activity in Seidl's film is little more than "factoid" behavior, performed by rote and lacking in genuine meaning.

Factoid behavior—shopping, driving, housework—cements the social order together in its comforting routines but has a depressingly numb and deadened quality. Ultimately, it has little to do with the characters' true humanity. Almost by contrast, the hitchhiker's nervous, out-of-context spouting of advertising jingles has the bizarre feel of Dadaist poetry or nonsense rhymes for children; but she is wrong in her fundamental assumption that these quoted slogans and sound bites are a way to genuinely connect with other people. Adverts are a widespread part of culture, but almost a "dirty little secret" of culture, a zone apart from "polite" social intercourse, designed to work subliminally and never enter the conscious mind. To remind people of the ways in which they are conditioned by advertising on a daily basis becomes an affront, virtually taboo. "You watch a lot of TV, don't you?" the salesman asks the hitchhiker, disparagingly. When she first makes her appearance, hurtling toward the old man in a supermarket parking lot, her bubbling-over energy and blue streak of dialogue seem completely antic by contrast with the dull, quotidian pace Seidl has been establishing in previous scenes. By hurling her own storehouse of factoids at the hapless Samaritans who agree to give her rides, the hitchhiker both affirms the universal discourse that holds society together and at the same time seems to mock it, revealing it to be a parade of hopeless banalities.

On the other side of the banal factoid life lies barbarism. In *Dog Days* violence is not so much something transcendently evil, or even particularly a source of power— many of the scenes of violence feel half-hearted, awkward, almost impotent; and in fact none of the characters achieves what they really want by resorting to violence— but rather a way for the characters' true "humanity" to return and express itself. Violence is the only element in life that is not a factoid, memorized, pre-packaged and dished up for easy consumption. To an extent, this is also true of the film's occasionally graphic sex scenes, fumbling and largely unconvincing attempts to regain a human nature that has been somehow denatured. These sex scenes are also tinged with irony in their very matter-of-factness. When we first see the adulterous wife, for instance, she is engaged in a three-way at an underground sex club, stark naked, bobbing up and down like a would-be porn star, but still wearing her clunky tortoise-shell glasses, a funny indication that some part of her has not been completely abandoned to this act.

Seidl gives some of the most appalling nudity in *Dog Days* to the "ugliest" of his couples, the old man and his housekeeper. She bears a vague resemblance to Linda Hunt, and toward the end of the film she performs an arthritic striptease for the old man, grotesquely wiping her baggy white-cotton panties all over her sagging body while he smirks with approval.[2] Although hysterically incongruous, the relationship between the old man and the housekeeper is handled by Seidl with a certain tenderness. In their most touching moment together, he asks her to put on his late wife's favorite dress and then plays a game with her where she has to search for the bouquet of flowers and box of chocolates he has hidden in the garden.

Such tenderness, however, cannot compete with the brutality of the world. Ironically, it is the hitchhiker, the most child-like and least sexual character in *Dog Days*, who is ultimately violated. Fearing reprisals from the co-op residents whose cars have been keyed, the alarm-systems salesmen turns her over to the angry mob, who take turns torturing her for hours in an empty apartment. Finally, one of the men rapes her. This showdown between the hitchhiker (a composite of consumerism and advertising jingles) and the salesman becomes a metaphor for the destructive energies of capitalism. She lives by the slogans and catchphrases used to sell products and hype celebrities, even though it is clear she has "dropped out" of the culture itself; she has no car of her own, after all, but is reduced to bumming rides from other people. In the end, a salesman, a key player in the economic system, turns on her and brings about her destruction. Is Seidl suggesting that a market economy always rises up against its own adherents and hangers-on, the "little dogs" who get eaten by the bigger ones? We see that the hitchhiker's life is expendable, no more important than the old man's Rottweiler, poisoned in the last scene, possibly also by the salesman, in revenge for the old man telling him earlier that a guard dog is the most reliable alarm system of all.

Seidl's critique is further strengthened visually by the fact that capitalism has totally effaced the physical landscape of *Dog Days* into an ersatz Westernized festival of kitsch. This is an anonymous Vienna; Seidl avoids showing any of the antique architecture that once defined this capital of the old world. Instead, we see the crass end results of the "Disneyfication" of Europe. Real estate developments, highrises, superhighways, and strip malls all serve as backdrops for scenes of real or threatened violence (many of these scenes look as though they could be taking place in America). Like worshipped totems losing their influence and becoming vestigial, the dehumanized (and dehumanizing) architectural forms of advanced capitalism elicit a tendency to destruction, graffiti, and vandalism; but this destruction ends up being visited mainly on the nondescript people who shuffle across the vacant parking lots, haunt the shopping plazas, and drive the endless highways.

The fact that the hitchhiker becomes a scapegoat for the pent-up tensions of a community is dramatized by Seidl in the sudden thunder shower that breaks the heat wave immediately in the wake of her violation. Although she has been talking nonstop for almost the entire film, she loses her voice during and after her ordeal: the hitchhiker's function as Greek chorus is silenced, and with it the sense of guilt and meaning which the classical chorus was meant to invoke in ancient cathartic drama. The other bedraggled characters, staring out at the rain, remain isolated and, for the most part, seem to find little real relief. And rather than blame this anonymous ex-urban wasteland—or indeed the system itself—for their increasing dehumanization, there is evidence that the characters come to support it more and more: on his scales at home, the old man weighs pre-packaged sacks of coffee from the supermarket and is angered to find that one of them is a little lighter than the others; he takes it back to the store, demanding his money back from the dubious manager. If human variability happens to slip into the gear-work of mass production, it ends up being viewed as a cheat, an unfairness, a lie.

What makes the hitchhiker's rape so ironic (and sad) is how painstakingly Seidl has shown us that all of her love and human feeling were invested in mass culture and consumerism. She tries to teach one of her rides the advertising jingle, "Haka Finishes Your Kitchen," set to the tune of the Parisian cancan, now purged of any sexual innuendo and transformed into a nursery-school singsong. Her favorite pop song is a romantic, 1960s-sounding ballad, "Monja," drenched in reverb—but over it Seidl lays tracking shots of a shopping mall, the true object of the hitchhiker's longing. Later, Seidl uses similar tracking shots of a neon-lit strip mall, replete with McDonald's, while we hear the hitchhiker singing an old German hymnal ("Everlasting is Thy Reign"). If consumerism is shown to be a kind of modern belief system, the focus of fanatical devotion, we see that religion itself has degenerated into another form of consumerism. "I like the Virgin Mary and the baby Jesus," the hitchhiker says. "I've got a statuette at home and 'Lordes' water. The bottle looks like the Virgin Mary, and you can unscrew her head. And the 'Lordes' water is inside." "You mean Lourdes," her driver corrects her, but the distinction hardly seems to matter to the hitchhiker's enjoyment of this "holy object" as a trinket, or the absurdity of a society's attempt to mass-produce "miracles."

Real transports of the spirit never get very far, bogged down in tawdriness and animosity. There is a flurry of scenes in the middle of *Dog Days* where many of the characters begin to sing to each other, as a way of attempting to connect or, more often, to spar, to take back personal identity against the threat of hostile encroachment. The adulterous wife and her lover (Christian Bakonyi) begin to seduce each other by duetting a Greek drinking song; the manic husband drowns them out by shouting a nonsense ditty: "The little horse goes hop, hop, hop!" Likewise, as part of their escalating violence against the middle-aged teacher, Wickerl and Lucky demand that she sing "La Cucaracha"; instead, she sings the love aria from *Carmen*, in a surprisingly strong soprano. The men drown her out, bellowing and gyrating in an obscene dance. It is no coincidence that Seidl has so many of his characters singing; his use of frail amateur voices, easily drowned out, offers a harsher vision of loneliness and isolation than the celebrated group-song montage in Paul Thomas Anderson's *Magnolia* (1999), but the idea is similar: we all yearn to connect on a pure, spiritual level, but ultimately we cannot achieve this. If it is true that people can become more fragile and child-like when they sing, more emotionally open, then Seidl demonstrates that this child-like fragility (in the hitchhiker, especially) becomes an immediate target. The fractured, wandering a cappella voices of the characters in *Dog Days* are the discordant music of subjectivity that has lost itself and gone astray, trying to sound its way home in the dark like a bat.

Fearful of being too vulnerable in a heartless world, love always turns cruel in *Dog Days*, even sado-masochistic, and can only express itself as tenderness under extreme duress. At one point the husband, at the end of his rope, holds a gun to his wife's lover, but not to harm him; he orders the astonished lover to drink a beer with him, as if the two men were buddies. Later, Lucky, ashamed of having helped Wickerl beat and violate the teacher, holds a gun on this couple and forces her to berate him, slap him, and finally burn his hand with a cigarette; but instead of enjoying this act of turning the tables on her abuser, she breaks down sobbing and comforts Wickerl, telling him she loves him. In fact, this questionable moment where a woman affirms the right of her boyfriend to abuse her is one of the few moments in *Dog Days* that could conceivably be described as "romantic."

But even this love, as Seidl has already shown, is really just a substitute for a deeper, more primal bond, that between the teacher and her elderly mother. When we first see her arriving at her apartment, the middle-aged woman plays back her answering-machine messages, the first of which is from her mother, a rambling litany of aches, complaints, recriminations—"Why don't you call me?" While this message plays, we see the teacher impassively going to the bathroom with the door open, and changing her clothes. Then, with a harsh electronic bleep, the mother's voice gives way to the second message, Wickerl proclaiming the teacher as "my favorite tush!"—a crudity that erases the cringe-inducing guilt of the mother's voice while at the same time reifying it in a further lowering of the woman's self-esteem. It is a compact mini-essay on Freud (perhaps the most famous of Austria's native sons, after all): the painful emotions that surround the relationship with the mother get deferred into the "easier" romantic attachment with the man, but because of the psychical remainder left over from the mother, we see that this romantic attachment soon becomes difficult and painful as well.

Freud is not the only historic Austrian evoked in the teacher's apartment: her walls are decorated with Gustav Klimt prints. The most famous of the Viennese Secessionists, Klimt painted pictures full of sexual angst and malevolence, where sensual arousal goes hand in hand with terror, torture, and pain. Klimt is the painter par excellence of the sado-masochistic imagination. When Lucky first returns to the teacher's apartment after her violation, he tells her that at first he enjoyed abusing her, fascinated "to see how some people can act toward other people." This is almost a description of Seidl's own philosophy, and the mixture of pain and pleasure that attends upon watching *Dog Days*. But what has grown out of this morbid fascination is a feeling of love for his victim: to her astonishment, Lucky attempts to kiss her. She pushes him away and he tells her that, for him, love is pain: "it hurts" when you fall in love and then when you fall out of it again.

This theme of the past's baggage, weighing the individual down in the present, comes up again and again in *Dog Days*. Both Lucky and the young man who is dating Miss Lower Austria announce to their respective love objects that every girl they've ever loved has cheated on them, let them down, hurt them. It is their broken, disillusioned hearts that make them violent toward women—not a convincing excuse for their behavior perhaps, but one that acknowledges the problem of surviving any kind of heartbreak. For these young men, love has become irredeemably painful, so their girlfriends must accept a certain amount of pain in order to love them. For Seidl, sado-masochism isn't so much a specific and identified taste or fetish as an inevitable part of what it means to try to love anyone in the first place: sadism is a compensation for masculine fears of vulnerability; masochism is the coin of devotion paid by the female who loves. One might balk at this implication that sado-masochism could be considered an inevitable, practically a universal condition, but in terms of the couples in *Dog Days*, the director makes a fairly convincing case.

It is also baggage from the past—the death of their child, symbolized by a makeshift crucifix on the side of a highway—that plagues the husband and his adulterous wife. Seidl films them visiting this crucifix in separate cars; she watches from the other side of the road and waits while he lays flowers; in this sequence the sightlines are similar to "normal" angle–reverse-angle shots in conversation scenes, suggesting that the now-severed couple "speak" to each other only through their dead child. It is only after new devastation in the present—her affair—that they can begin a rapprochement about the past: during the rainstorm she goes outside and sits on the empty swing and after a few moments he joins her; they still do not speak, but this shared activity, so redolent of childhood innocence, suggests that perhaps they will start again. Similarly, Wickerl and the teacher are brought back together by Lucky threatening them with the gun. He breaks them down to the point where they are helpless and cling to each other, needing each other again. This is not Lucky's intention; he hoped to break them apart. When we gamble against our own pasts, we run the risk of reliving them, making them occur again in the present; but there's also the possibility of healing. So the old man—on what would have been his fiftieth wedding anniversary to his late wife—seduces his housekeeper, recreating with her the love that has died.

Seidl has stuck to some of the grounding tenets of documentary filmmaking in *Dog Days*: he uses non-professional actors, and though the script was plotted out by Seidl and Veronika Franz, the dialogue is largely improvised. Seidl seeks to capture his protagonists in their representative milieux, surrounded by the everyday objects that define them; he has a knack for the "prop" that perfectly exemplifies a character, that creates an instant, bull's-eye feeling of naturalism: the overstuffed armchairs and oil paintings of dogs in the old man's house, or, in the husband and wife's house, the huge garish fish tank that dominates the scene where she attacks him, trying to get him to open up and talk to her again.

This is also why Seidl has filled the teacher's apartment with Klimt prints: *Hygeia, the Stoclet Frieze*, and others. Her abuse at the hands of Wickerl and Lucky takes place under a "sofa-sized" reproduction of Klimt's strange early painting, *Idyll*, where a cameo of the Madonna and child is flanked by languorous nude Adonises. The hard-to-read symbolism of this frieze turns on the question of whether the male figures are there to protect or to threaten the nurturing female element that stands between them. Klimt insisted on a return of everything that had been repressed out of the smooth workings of social progress: his subjects are primal myths of the libido rising up to tear asunder the fabric of everyday life. In particular, female bodies in Klimt become pliable and plastic, twisted and elongated in ways that are physically impossible; or they are swallowed up in background patterns that reduce the female subject to the status of a decorative object.

Klimt's *Idyll* also presides over the scene where the crazed Lucky takes Wickerl and the teacher hostage, trying to make things right between them by an act of desperate violence. Lucky sticks a lit candle in Wickerl's buttocks and makes him sing the Austrian national anthem. "Land of hammers, with a bright future," Wickerl bellows tunelessly, "people with a gift for beauty." It is Seidl's most outrageous, bitterly sardonic tableau, provoking both cringing and a kind of disturbed laughter, and it suggests that Seidl's *fin-de-siècle* vision, like Klimt's a hundred years ago, is filled with a deep disgust for propriety, for the gentility of social rituals.

The most pessimistic of the current European directors—Michael Haneke, Bruno Dumont, Catherine Breillat, and Gaspar Noé among others—proceed from the belief that the breakdown of modern society has rendered individual lives all but definitively meaningless. These directors depict a human condition that has lapsed back into a state of savagery, but it almost does not matter if the people in their films suffer pain or feel happy, live or die. For these directors, all of Western culture—even its vaunted freedoms, its sexuality, and its art—is viewed as being utterly played-out, at the end of its tether, and wholly given over to assuming the death drive. Seidl, on the other hand, has a streak of subverted romanticism. He seems to want us to care about his cracked-crystal characters: the hitchhiker's destruction, the husband and wife's tentative reunion, Wickerl's humiliation—all of these climaxes resonate with an appropriate thrum of sorrow, relief, terror. And yet these apotheoses are also strongly tinged with the outrageous extremity of black comedy, Seidl's personal form of stylization. It is not as if the characters' lives were utterly meaningless, but rather exist in quotation marks. "People can be so cruel"—the old man's remark after finding his poisoned dog—is not so much a convincing emotional epiphany as perhaps a final tossed-off factoid, what we expect him to say at this decisive moment, and almost a thesis (under-)statement for *Dog Days* itself.

In true black comedy—the kind that operates in Luis Buñuel's *The Exterminating Angel* (1962), Jean-Luc Godard's *Les Carabiniers* (1963), Werner Herzog's *Even Dwarves Started Small* (1970), or Rainer Werner Fassbinder's *Satan's Brew* (1976)— disgust takes precedence over sorrow, disturbing situations are handled lightly, people are depicted as slightly ridiculous in their agony, and the actors or characters are so blatantly grotesque that it is often hard to sympathize with them, even when we recognize their fates as harsh. "Reality is always so much harsher than what you can show in a film," Seidl has said,[3] sounding slightly defensive about the amount of violence in *Dog Days* while at the same time tipping his hand about how he views reality itself. The sardonic laughter that is occasionally provoked by his film is, finally, the triumphant response of the misanthrope who can sit back and revel in revealing people to be exactly as bad as he suspected in the first place.

Notes

The original version of this article appeared in *Film Quarterly*, Vol. 60, Number 1, Autumn 2006.

1. *Dog Days*, DVD special features (Kino International, 2004).
2. Set to a woozy, 1930s-style tango, these scenes of loopy, repellent eros resemble the perverse fantasies solemnly enacted by the hustlers in Gus Van Sant's *My Own Private Idaho* (1991).
3. *Dog Days*, DVD special features (Kino International, 2004).

Chapter 15

Import and Export: Ulrich Seidl's Indiscreet Anthropology of Migration

Martin Brady and Helen Hughes

Good News, Bad News: "Poet of the Wretched"

Ulrich Seidl has been described, quite accurately, as a "poet of the wretched" (*Poet des Trostlosen*; Grissemann 2007: 112). His films constitute an inimitable and instantly recognizable anthology of loneliness, deprivation, voyeurism, and cruelty. Renowned and often reviled for their extreme subject matter—pet fondling (*Tierische Liebe/Animal Love*, 1995), infantilism (*Spaß ohne Grenzen/Fun Without Limits*, 1998), rape (*Hundstage/Dog Days*, 2001), xenophobia (*Zur Lage/State of the Nation*, 2002), religious fanaticism (*Jesus, Du weisst/Jesus, You Know*, 2003), internet sex (*Import Export*, 2007)—and their inscrutable hyper-stylization—obsessive symmetry and static full-frontal tableaux—his documentaries and fiction films have been the object of impassioned debate in Austria and abroad since his first film for cinema, the ironically titled *Good News* (1990), was released in Austria in March 1991. As an "oppositional artist by profession" (*Berufs-Oppositionskünstler*), Seidl has been compared to German directors Rainer Werner Fassbinder and Christoph Schlingensief (Grissemann 2007: 203). A list of his twenty-five favorite films, drawn up in 2004, included works by such provocateurs as Pasolini, Buñuel, Herzog, and von Trier (see ibid.: 289).

A methodical, self-critical, and measured director, Seidl has made only two feature films and five documentaries for the cinema in twenty years (together with a handful of television films and shorts). Of these seven films, three have the theme of migration, or projected migration, as their subject: *Good News* (1990), a study of Bangladeshi, Egyptian, and Pakistani newspaper vendors in Vienna; *Mit Verlust ist zu rechnen/Losses to be Expected* (1992), the story of the attempt by an aged Austrian widower to court a Czech woman across the Austrian–Czech border; and *Import Export*, a fictional tale of a young Ukrainian woman who moves west to Vienna as a migrant worker and a young Austrian man who, together with his stepfather, travels east to seek his fortune in Slovakia and the Ukraine.

Despite the astonishing stylistic consistency across Seidl's work, these three films also demonstrate a series of historically and geographically determined shifts in their study of migration, from a distanced (and distancing) inquisitiveness in *Good News*, through incursions into the intimate, emotional sphere of isolated lives on either side of a visible border in *Mit Verlust ist zu rechnen*, to an exploration of shared impoverishment and cultural difference in *Import Export*. Significant in themselves as works of one of the most striking voices in contemporary European auteurist cinema, these three films also chart shifts in perspective (literal and metaphorical) on post-Cold War Europe, East and West. In particular they chronicle a shift from borders marked by political and historical (physical) boundaries to internalized, social separation determined by such factors as economic inequality and cultural mistrust.

These shifts will be examined in what follows, both in terms of the representation of migration from East to West and from West to East and in the way these movements are encrypted cinematically. Seidl's eccentric framing and unconventional cinematography emphasize the physical and metaphysical spaces of migration and shed light on the unfamiliar whilst simultaneously estranging the familiar.

Seidl's gaze is unflinchingly "indiscreet" (Grissemann 2007: 88), but it is not voyeuristic. In its premeditated use of the camera as a tool for provocation, Seidl's method is in fact close to that of the early pioneers of *cinéma-vérité* in France around 1960. The ethnographic filmmaker Jean Rouch, in particular, believed that the value of cinema as an anthropological tool lay in the ability of the cinematic apparatus to provoke extreme reactions. To cite one of the most famous examples: in his landmark study of life in Paris during the Algerian war, *Chronique d'un été/Chronicle of a Summer* (1961), Rouch and codirector Edgar Morin provoked one of the participants in their anthropological study of the Parisian "tribe" (Rouch 2003: 167) to recount her experience of returning to France after losing her father in a concentration camp. The result, according to Rouch, was "the creation of something that goes beyond the tragic: an intolerable mis-en-scène [*sic*], like some spontaneous sacrilege that pushed us to do what we had never done before" (ibid.: 153). This "sacrilege," which Rouch later termed "the staging of 'real life'" (ibid.: 33), also occurs in a scene in which the same young Jewish woman, Marceline, shows the number tattooed on her arm to a group of young Africans who initially don't understand its significance:

> That was a provocation.... They had thought the tattoo was an adornment of some kind. All of us were deeply affected. The cameraman, one of the best documentary people around, was so disturbed that the end of the sequence is out of focus. I stopped filming to give everyone a chance to recover. Now, is this a 'truthful' moment or a 'staged' moment? Does it matter? (ibid.: 211–12.)

According to Steven Feld, Rouch's films demonstrate "that film and anthropology share the same essential concerns with the nature of intersubjectivity" (Feld 2003: 14). This is also the case with the three films of Seidl discussed in this essay. What is more, Rouch's famous contention that for the visual ethnographer "fiction is the only way to penetrate reality" (ibid.: 6) is also shared by Seidl, who has repeatedly claimed that his documentaries always contain fictional elements, whilst his fiction films have their roots in documentary practice. As Rouch put it:

> For me, as an ethnographer and filmmaker, there is almost no boundary between documentary film and films of fiction. The cinema, the art of the double, is already the transition from the real world to the imaginary world, and ethnography, the science of the thought systems of others, is a permanent crossing point from one conceptual universe to another; acrobatic gymnastics, where losing one's footing is the least of the risks. (Rouch 2003: 185)

Seidl's films are "difficult" films: the two documentaries are drawn out, at times enigmatic, and eschew commentary and exegesis; the feature film is violent, harrowing, and sexually explicit. In their exploration of contemporary issues— migration, the aging population, unemployment—these three films offer material for the exploration of social and economic integration in the "New Europe" and the representation of migration in the media that is engaging, distinctive in style, and humorous.

Gazing at Others

Stefan Grissemann's recent and comprehensive monograph on Seidl, which covers his work up to and including *Import Export*, attempts to define "the Seidl system" (Grissemann 2007: 19). This expression in itself is an indication that Seidl's cinema appears to involve a severe and unyielding approach to its own cinematic language. A key part of the Seidl system is the choice of subject matter, placing his films in a tradition of Austrian writers, filmmakers, and artists—including such dissenting voices as Thomas Bernhard, a favorite of Seidl,[1] and Michael Haneke—who have responded with ferocity to the culture of this relatively small, predominantly Catholic country with its remnants of an imperial past. Grissemann opens with the assertion that the director has a special affinity with outsiders and minorities that is rooted in his own cultural make-up:

> Seidl flouts conventions of decency and taste in order to portray life as he sees it—as a fascinating farce.... But in fact through his uncompromising visual language Seidl restores to the people and events he shows their rightful place in life; it is as though he wants to rescue all that is suppressed and repressed in society, as well as the rage and irritation of his protagonists, and restore it to reality... Seidl admits that he has always had an 'emotional kinship with minorities who subsist beyond the bounds of bourgeois normality' because he has himself 'always felt like an outsider'. He identifies the roots of his interest in social failures and eccentrics in his own Catholic upbringing,

with which he never felt at ease. For his own part he categorically rejects work that is straightforwardly 'political'. Instead he believes that he is 'holding up a mirror' to the audience. The discomfort that inevitably results from recognizing oneself in it explains, he believes, why people simply accuse him of 'distorting' reality. (ibid.: 8–10)[2]

The accusation, which has accompanied all of his films to date, is that his gaze on others—be they dog-owners kissing their pets (*Tierische Liebe*), Viennese racists calling for the annihilation of Islam (*Zur Lage*), nude men masturbating to Mozart (*Brüder, lasst uns lustig sein/Brothers, Let Us Be Merry*, 2006), or demented geriatrics (*Import Export*)—is intrusive, voyeuristic, exploitative, and cynical. Seidl's considered response is that his aim is "to trigger consternation" (*Betroffenheit auszulösen*; Grissemann 2007: 33). Although his protagonists habitually perform humiliating, ostensibly ludicrous acts for the camera—unsurprisingly, the striptease is a Seidlerian leitmotif—their exhibitionism is often framed by long-held, photograph-like tableaux in which the "performers" stare back at the camera and thus, in the cinema, return the gaze of the audience. At times the extreme nature of this exchange reminds one not only of the participatory tradition in Austrian performance art—of the Viennese Actionists in general and Hermann Nitsch in particular—but also of that cerebral, reflexive genre of European, essayistic filmmaking which has its roots in the French new wave.

Voyeurizing the Voyeurs

Staring Back is the title of a book by the veteran French documentary filmmaker Chris Marker, in which he collects images from more than half a century of his films that demonstrate a reciprocity, a democracy even, of gazes (Marker 2007). Perhaps the most famous of these is the transnational encounter at a market place in Praia, Cape Verde, in *Sans Soleil/Sunless* (1984).[3] A film ostensibly about a Westerner's encounter with Japan, *Sans Soleil* tackles themes as diverse as the legacy of Portuguese colonialism and the functioning of memory. The camera's gaze is that of a fictional male narrator, Sandor Krasna (a pseudonym for Marker himself), whose epistolary musings are narrated by an off-screen female voice.[4] One of his preoccupations is catching the eyes of local women:

> It was in the market places of Bissau and Cape Verde that I could stare at them again with equality: I see her, she saw me, she knows that I see her, she drops me her glance, but just at an angle where it is still possible to act as though it was not addressed to me, and at the end, the real glance, straightforward, that lasted a twenty-fourth of a second, the length of a film frame. All women have a built in grain of indestructibility, and men's task has always been to make them realize it as late as possible. African men are just as good at this task as others, but after a close look at African women, I wouldn't necessarily bet on the men.[5]

It is this twenty-fourth of a second that is reproduced in *Staring Back* (Marker 2007: 67), alongside images from across the globe, many of them capturing frozen moments of revolt, revolution, and protest (including demonstrations against the Vietnam War, against the French state in 1968, and, more recently, against Jean-Marie Le Pen). In this volume of photographs and brief epigrams, moving images become photographs; in Seidl's case, conversely but analogously, movement is frozen quasi-photographically. As Marker writes, introducing a sequence of images that includes the African woman in Praia: "In this malignant, undefinable world, the speed of the shutter stopped the rarest moment, a moment of certainty" (ibid.: 64).

"Staring back," as opposed to the unidirectional, unequal and potentially violent act of "staring," acquires, in Marker's films and his book of stills from them, a quasi-metaphysical dimension, a transcendence which has also been identified, by a number of commentators, in *Import Export* (Grissemann 2007: 225; Huber 2008: 26). Not only is the voyeur's invasive gaze reflected back, but it is also translated, potentially at least, into communication. Moreover, as unambiguous signals of cinematic reflexivity, these reciprocal gazes, mediated by the camera apparatus and editing hand, reflect obsessively on "remembering and forgetting ... and on the relation that the filmic image bears to these processes" thereby charting "the limits of access to other people and other cultures through images" (Cooper 2006: 49).[6]

As we shall see, it is an anthropology of indiscreet, yet often also discrete, gazes—of eye contact—that also connects Seidl's films, and their view of foreigners in particular, with Rouch.

How to Look at Foreigners

The encounters, and gazes, in *Good News* are noticeably more tentative, fleeting, unresolved, and distant than in the other films of Seidl discussed here. Indeed it can be asserted, perhaps rather sweepingly, that the camera adopts a point of view more recognizably inquisitive and subjective than in either *Mit Verlust ist zu rechnen* or *Import Export*. In its scope, the film is ambitious, perhaps overly so, as its somewhat arch subtitle suggests: *Von Kolporteuren, toten Hunden und anderen Wienern/On Newspaper Vendors, Dead Dogs and Other Viennese*.[7] Alongside the newspaper vendors, we are shown—by way of contrast—petty bourgeois white Austrians at home, in their allotments, at the vet—a "place of care perverted" (*Ort der pervertierten Fürsorge*; Schmid 2003: 47)—and in various states of inebriation in Viennese bars.

The migrant workers themselves are shown primarily on the streets selling the (*Neue*) *Kronen Zeitung* and *Kurier*. The training sessions designed to teach them the basic German expressions and body language required to sell the newspapers ("Keep Smiling, Keep Selling") are conducted bilingually, as are the tense encounters with the management on payday. The migrants are also shown at home with their families (often in cramped, dingy, rundown accommodation), praying in the mosque, and celebrating at a wedding. Just as the migrants and indigenous population are shown to inhabit mutually exclusive spaces, so the camera captures their activities differently. This is particularly apparent in the recording of interior spaces. The indigenous Viennese families are framed, in typical Seidl fashion, symmetrically and full-frontally, usually with a static camera, occasionally with a mechanically precise pan. These rigid, highly constructed, tableau compositions remind one, as Seidl himself has hinted, of Catholic altarpieces:

> It is a moment of suspension, of interruption in a film without it actually coming to a halt. People pose as if for a photographer and their gaze into the camera meets that of the spectator. For me this is a magic moment which either moves or disturbs me. Space is important in this context. I give people a lot of space, which is why they often come across as being very small. Here my pictures become altars. (Seidl, in Schmid 2003: 55)[8]

The rigidity of these tableaux is, superficially at least, reminiscent of the poses struck by the migrant street vendors in their surreal red and orange uniforms on the wintery streets of Vienna. However, it soon becomes apparent that their immobility is neither photographic nor quasi-ecclesiastical, but obligatory: they are expected, as a condition of their employment, to stay at their designated vending locations for the best part of thirteen hours a day. Their immobility is economically determined, rather than socially or culturally inherited—as appears to be implied, in the case of the indigenous population, by Seidl's tableaux of *Heimat* pictures and religious iconography. To underscore this distinction, Seidl follows a supervisor driving at night through the streets of Vienna to record even the most minor deviation on the part of the vendors from the company guidelines: not occupying precisely the allocated pitch, failing to smile or present the papers correctly. Whilst Seidl has induced his fellow countrymen to take up their rigid poses for the camera, the migrants have been obliged to pose by their employers.[9] Seidl also appears to be showing how the migrant body requires forcing into a space, in this instance a cityscape, already inhabited by a schooled population (one which may itself appear alien to the outsider and which Seidl's cinematography certainly estranges).

It has been pointed out in criticism of *Good News* that Seidl does not confer on the migrant workers the right to speak, or at least to be understood, whilst the white Austrians are nothing short of garrulous. On the few occasions the audience does hear the vendors speak in their own languages there are no subtitles. According to Lars Henrik Gass, this voicelessness, coupled with the straightjacket of Seidl's trademark static framing, imprisons the vendors within the diegesis:

> [I]t becomes apparent that nothing can take place in the image which Seidl has not planned. That is exactly what I would call him to task for; it becomes utterly boring and one begins to hope that at least one person will break out of Seidl's filmic concept and say he is fed up. In this film, for example, the Pakistanis who are being depicted never have a chance to speak. (in Danquart et al. 1996: 35)

What Gass appears not to have registered is the subtle disparity between the way the film captures the home-life of the indigenous Austrians and the way it chronicles the milieu in which the migrants move. And it is precisely movement, freedom of movement even, which is the issue here.

The "I Love Austria!" Sticker

Perhaps the most striking sequences in *Good News* cinematographically are those in which the camera enters the spaces in which the migrants' communal activities of worship and celebration take place. These spaces—part public, part private—are shown to be vibrant, colorful, but "hidden" spaces behind the facades of Vienna, both literally and metaphorically. The sequences repeatedly begin and close with a tilting pan up to sky, revealing that the meeting halls are located in courtyards set back from the main thoroughfares (indeed the camera never locates them in relation to any recognizable Viennese landmarks); these are places that are explicitly marginal and concealed.[10] Grissemann, on the other hand, suggests that the camera's unblinking eye, the absence of cuts within these sequences, serves to embed these enclaves into the structure of the city:

> The migrant culture, which at times appears quite mysterious, lies just behind the facades of Vienna's houses. A direct path leads into these foreign places without a cut. The camera's gaze travels from the grey streets through staircases and antechambers into the hidden centers of Islamic culture in Vienna. (Grissemann 2007: 88)[11]

These episodes are, however, visually more ambiguous than Grissemann suggests—the camera never actually quite makes it back to the street; instead the sequences either end before the connection with communal space is fully established, or the gaze shifts upwards to the heavens (which is only shared space in a conceptual or metaphysical sense).

In an extended sequence of bravura hand-held camerawork, the film explores the Anadolu Camii mosque, entering and leaving the space through a series of corridors, stairs, and doors. The labyrinthine invasion of the "foreign" space is cinematographically reminiscent of the work of Carl Theodor Dreyer (especially in *Vampyr*, 1932), another filmmaker on Seidl's list of favorites. The camera passes a grocery shop and hairdresser before entering the mosque itself and observing the praying Muslims from behind. It does not linger on any of these "exotic" sights and ignores the inquisitive gazes of those it passes—it moves through the space, registering its contours but without engaging with it or those who inhabit it. As if to highlight the "otherness" of the mosque, the sequence is unexpectedly—and arguably rather crassly—interrupted by an elderly white Austrian woman, framed statically and full-frontally, reading from a newspaper article on the dangers of an increasing global population. The woman's immobility (despite the underground train she is seated in) is in stark contrast to the vibrant life seen in the mosque. Seven times during the film the focus is shifted in this way from the newspaper sellers to the newspaper consumers. The articles are read by symmetrically posed readers in various environments, both public and private: by a railway line, in the underground, in hospital, at home on a sofa, on a dark street, in the pub. These readings open the film to contemporary political debates in a quasi-Brechtian way. However, the articles of the *Kronen Zeitung* do not provide statistics à la *Kuhle Wampe* (in that instance to support the arguments of the workers' movement), but rather point to the alien and contradictory environment in which the migrants are attempting to build a life: there is a request for nominations of model Austrians, articles on the need to have pride in old age, on a film written by an animal psychologist, on a young man who shakes his baby to death, a lonely hearts advert, and—at the end of the film—an explanatory note accompanying a free "I love Austria!" sticker.

It is in the more straightforward juxtapositions that Seidl's partisanship perhaps breaks through his rigid geometry, although here too understanding is expressed in terms of movement in space: "In *Good News* for example I don't simply look at the newspaper vendors, but rather I try to feel what they feel and enter into their world emotionally" (Grissemann 2007: 94).[12] Seidl describes his empathy in structural terms: rather than rigidly staring (*zuschauen*, "looking at"), he makes a move towards the vendors emotionally (*hineinfühlen*, "enter into their world emotionally"); in Seidl's "system," empathy and solidarity are expressed geometrically.

Whilst the film's gaze on the migrant workers, certainly in their own social environment, tends to be characterized by distanced (and distancing) inquisitiveness, there are a handful of encounters that suggest tentative stabs at cross-cultural communication. These advances tend to involve older Austrian women—pre-figuring the liaisons of *Mit Verlust ist zu rechnen*—and are themselves not devoid of the condescension that Fassbinder caricatured in his portrayal of Emmi in *Angst essen Seele auf/Fear Eats the Soul* (1974). One woman, for example, appears to believe that her local newspaper vendor will only understand her if she speaks to him in clipped, ungrammatical German; she also takes it upon herself to explain to the vendor that Austrian citizens receive less government support when ill and out of work than foreign workers. These encounters—which include a scene with a vendor who has married an Austrian (and in which we learn her name, Renate, but not his)—and the rapid-fire sequence of white Austrians describing an average day remind one forcefully of the transnational encounters in Rouch and Morin's *Chronique d'un été*. The stilted artificiality of certain scenes in the latter, including the discussion between a white Renault worker (Angelo) and a black student (Landry), pre-figure the "staging of reality" in Seidl's film.

Film historian Erik Barnouw has commented on Rouch's notion of the filmmaker-as-provocateur in the following terms: "The direct cinema documentarist took his camera to a situation of tension and waited hopefully for a crisis; the Rouch version of *cinéma vérité* tried to precipitate one.... *Cinéma vérité* was committed to a paradox: that artificial circumstances could bring hidden truth to the surface" (Barnouw 1993: 254–55). As Rouch himself put it:

> We contract time, we extend it, we choose an angle for the shot, we deform the people we're shooting, we speed things up and follow one movement to the detriment of

another movement. So there is a whole work of lies. But, for me and Edgar Morin at the time we made that film this lie was more real than the truth.... It's a sort of catalyst which allows us to reveal, with doubts, a fictional part of all of us, but which for me is the most real part of an individual. (Rouch, in Eaton 1979: 51)

These remarks are strikingly similar to Seidl's comments regarding his staging of reality to generate greater authenticity:

I think my films are very artificial because they are heavily influenced by my visual language. I record things that happen, i.e., reality, and place it in a frame. As a director I also try at the same time to keep things moving.... I'm not interested in portraying reality, although I do attach great importance to realism and authenticity. (Grissemann 2007: 23)[13]

In one of the final scenes of *Good News*, Seidl introduces, somewhat unexpectedly, a precise contemporary political context for his film, as a man reads a passage from the *Kurier* informing its readers that the aforementioned complimentary "I love Austria!" sticker is intended to signal support for "the democratic values in Austria" in the face of current upheavals in East and West. It is these upheavals which form the context for the proposed, but ultimately unrealized, migration from East to West in Seidl's next film, *Mit Verlust ist zu rechnen*.

Shared Anthropology

Rouch coined the term "shared anthropology" (Eaton 1979: 45) to describe his collaborative, participatory staging of reality through fiction, an attempt to synthesize the methods of two of the pioneers of documentary film, Robert Flaherty and Dziga Vertov: "It is [the] permanent 'ciné-dialogue' that seems to me one of the interesting angles of current ethnographic progress: knowledge is no longer a stolen secret, later to be consumed in the Western temples of knowledge. It is the result of an endless quest where ethnographers and ethnographees meet on a path that some of us are already calling 'shared anthropology'" (Rouch 2003: 185).[14] Of Seidl's films, *Mit Verlust ist zu rechnen* is the one with which this notion sits most comfortably, not least given that the idea for the film came from the central character. There is also an attendant shift from the distanced, inquisitive gaze of *Good News* to what might be termed a "participant camera" (Eaton 1979: 45). Although this may be explained, in part at least, by Seidl's employment of a different cameraman, Peter Zeitlinger (who also works with Werner Herzog), it is also inseparable from the genesis of the film: whilst Seidl was scouting locations along the Austrian–Czech border for a long-cherished historical costume drama on the life of the nineteenth-century bandit Johann Georg Grasel, he was approached in Safov by a local Czech woman of German descent, Paula Hutterová, who wanted to know what he and his colleagues were up to; it was talking to her that gave Seidl the idea of shooting a documentary about "life between East and West" (Grissemann 2007: 108).

At the outset, it appears that *Mit Verlust ist zu rechnen* will indeed be a film about migration. Paula is a widow, and she has met a recently widowed Austrian pensioner, Sepp Paur, who lives across the border in the Austrian village of Langau (with a population of 700, making it little more than three times the size of Safov) and is searching for a new partner to keep his life (and house) in order. In a classic Seidl composition, we see Sepp literally on the lookout for a new companion, standing by an unmanned border crossing with a pair of binoculars trained on the tiny hamlet in the distance.

Seidl's film is unmistakably partisan. Whilst both protagonists are warmhearted and endearing characters, it is the Czech way of life, for all its shabbiness and deprivation, and its postcommunist weirdness, that Zeitlinger's roving camera captures with palpable empathy. This is something that will emerge again, more than a decade later, in *Import Export*. As Seidl admitted: "The East has always fascinated me. I find a lot there that is interesting, good, fantastic. I feel comfortable there and can't join in the chorus of voices condemning the 'backwardness' of the East.... In questioning Western prosperity on the other side, with its fitted kitchens and freezers, I am taking sides with the East" (Seidl, in Grissemann 2007: 115, 116).[15] Unsurprisingly, this empathy manifests itself formally in the cinematography. Whilst the camera that follows Paula about her everyday chores (collecting her meals on wheels, washing, clumsily killing a chicken with an axe) is fluid and, at least by Seidl's standards, even relaxed, the petty-bourgeois Austrians across the border are exposed to the full force of Seidlerian stylization, most strikingly in a droll, rapid-fire sequence of Austrian housewives demonstrating their kitchen appliances (just as their male counterparts had shown off their electric lawnmowers in *Good News*). This is not to say that the film generally resorts to drawing crass distinctions between East and West. Indeed, one of the most striking features of *Mit Verlust ist zu rechnen* is the fact that, despite the supercilious pronouncements of some of the Austrians on their Czech neighbors, it is actually quite difficult to distinguish between life on either side of the border:

> It is symptomatic that Seidl investigates the relationship between the postcommunist East and the capitalist West—a theme he will pick up again years later in *Import Export*—based on two villages which in many ways are virtually indistinguishable from one another, which represent two sides of the same coin and are close to one another both literally and metaphorically. (Grissemann 2007: 115)[16]

Borderlands

It is in this unexpected twist to Seidl's portrait of provincial life across the newly-porous East–West border that his film differs from those East German documentaries of the same period with which it appears, initially, to have so much in common. *Mit Verlust ist zu rechnen* is, for example, in many of its details strikingly similar to Andreas Voigt's *Grenzland: Eine Reise/Borderlands: A Journey*, also of 1992. Voigt's film charts a journey north along the German–Polish border, interviewing locals on both sides of the Cold War demarcation line. In its programmatic gaze eastwards—turning its back, so to speak, on the advancing *Wessis* (post-reunification West Germans)—Voigt's film is also a partisan expression of solidarity with Eastern neighbors. Here too we see predatory Westerners looking over the border, binoculars in hand; here too we see the consumer durables of an affluent capitalist society juxtaposed with privation just across the border. The languorous, relaxed tone of Voigt's film, verging at times on the comical, is, however, very different from Seidl's "dark poeticization of landscape and ways of life" (Grissemann 2007: 107). Seidl's film may indeed articulate a certain fondness for the candor of the East, but it is entirely free from the optimistic generosity which allows *Grenzland* to prize the quietly inebriated and philosophical mindset of the Poles as an antidote to the rampant consumerism of post-unification Germany (Hughes 1999). In Seidl's own words, his film is an essay on loss which transcends the vagaries of shifting political boundaries: "From the loss of homeland via the loss of youth, the loss of love, the loss of a spouse, the loss of sexuality, the loss of money to the loss of life" (Seidl, in Grissemann 2007: 118–19).[17]

Voigt concludes his film with an emotive symbolic image—the camera passes out from the mouth of the Oder into the open waters of the Baltic to new horizons, accompanied by a catchy, if moody jazz soundtrack. Seidl's story of the potential migration of Paula to the West, prefigured by a series of more or less surreal forays across the border (to Sepp's house, the Prater, a sex shop, and a department store), ends with a terse intertitle informing us simply that: "Paula did not move over to join Sepp. She prefers to continue receiving her meals from the co-operative kitchen. Sepp on the other hand is still on the lookout for a suitable wife."[18]

This is, one could argue, a piece of "good news" within the diegesis. Migrating from Safov to Langau has been shown to be a small move geographically, but a very large one culturally. Paula resists the lure of well-stocked supermarket shelves, Austrian toiletries, and modern kitchen appliances not only because of her age but also because the economic benefits are outweighed by an anticipated loss of personal freedom. The ironic twist is, of course, that this very freedom is secured, in part at least, by the remnants of a despotic system (the state which provides the meals on wheels is portrayed in the film as a faceless source of Kafkaesque edicts and eerie piped music which fills the winter streets of Safov). The landscapes are also important here: in no other Seidl film do they play such a prominent role, with the result that *Mit Verlust ist zu rechnen* has the feel of a post-reunification *Heimatfilm*. Many austerely beautiful shots of the landscape do not feature human beings at all, and when they do—in a series of extraordinary static tableaux of farmers and villagers silently facing the camera like figures in some nineteenth-century genre painting or Richard Oelze's surrealist *Erwartung/Expectation* (1935/36)—the locals both east and west of the border seem (literally) rooted in the ground.

In these "stagings" of life—which Birgit Schmid (2003: 48) terms "staged realities" (*inszenierte Wirklichkeiten*)—Seidl transgresses the boundary between fact and fiction, between documentary and *Spielfilm* (feature or, literally, "acted" film), more consistently (and hermetically) than in *Good News*: "I didn't realize how far I would end up crossing the boundary between documentary film and feature film" (Seidl, in Grissemann 2007: 109).[19] Although the film had no predictable outcome, at least insofar as the migration story was concerned, there is a uniformity to the imagery which is unsettling. As Schmid puts it, Seidl is "an obsessive stylist, almost a geometrician of the visual who measures out his images" (ibid.: 46).[20]

In this film, however, the rigidity is inextricable from the diegesis—the story of a migration that never materializes—and it is this that prevents the film becoming simply formalist or excessively mannered. Moreover, there is subtlety to the film's choreography—which includes the more informal tracking shots following Paula around Safov referred to above—which gives it a range and rhythm that prefigure *Import Export*, the film which, in Grissemann's view, introduces into Seidl's oeuvre "more open, 'humanistic' traits" (*offenere, "humanistische" Züge*; Grissemann 2007: 222).

Moralist or Social Pornographer?

Seidl has pointed out in numerous interviews that in *Import Export*: "there are no external borders. External borders fall, of course, but internal ones remain. It is these that I show" (Seidl, in Grissemann 2007: 217).[21] This alone makes the film highly contemporary as a film about migration. Although it shifts from East to West and back again some twenty-one times—in a complex rhythm that gains momentum towards the end—the three protagonists are never shown crossing borders (although Seidl had originally envisaged this in his treatment). On four occasions intertitles provide geographical information: in the second and fourth episodes we are informed that we are in the Ukrainian town of Snizhne and Vienna respectively, and as Paul and his stepfather Michael head east we are told that they stop off in Košice in Slovakia on their way to Uzhhorod (formerly Uzhgorod) in the Ukraine. Of the unidentified locations, not all are immediately recognizable geographically—the opening shot of a man attempting thirteen times to start a motorcycle is one such, another is the extraordinary scene shot, as Seidl explained in an interview, against the backdrop of the run-down Roma housing estate Luník IX outside Košice.[22] As Christoph Huber has noted: "Tellingly, national borders play no role in the film (the belatedly identified Ukrainian opening shot might just as well show Austria). Rather, social and existential boundaries take on weight" (Huber 2007: 47).[23]

Import Export charts two journeys which intersect once (in a Viennese railway station), but without the main characters ever meeting. Olga (Ekateryna Rak), a young nurse from Snizhne, leaves her mother and child behind in the Ukraine to search for work in Vienna, where she arrives a third of the way into the film. Paul (Paul Hofmann) and Michael (Michael Thomas) set off from Vienna at the mid point of the film to deliver chewing gum dispensers to Slovakia and a fruit machine to the Ukraine. Following a sordid and degrading encounter between his stepfather and a local prostitute, Paul walks out of the Uzhhorod Intourist hotel they have been staying in and, failing to find work in the city, is last seen attempting to flag a lift, although it is not clear in which direction he is intending to travel. His stepfather is left behind in the Ukrainian hotel and, in the film's final episode, Olga is shown laughing with her fellow migrant workers in the Viennese geriatric hospital where she works as a cleaner. Her future remains uncertain as without a husband she has no prospect of a permanent right of abode. The film's trajectory is thus very different to that of *Mit Verlust ist zu rechnen*, in which the protagonists are shown moving energetically across borders, only to stay on where they have lived all their lives. By the end of *Import Export* none of the three central characters has any immediate prospect of staying put.

As schematic as the film sounds from this skeletal synopsis, it in fact confounds expectations on a number of levels, not least as a film of migration. For example, despite encountering demeaning treatment at the hand of her employers and superiors—she is suddenly fired as an *au pair* ("that's how it is over here" her employer claims), and bullied by a hospital nurse (who informs her that she may have been a nurse in the Ukraine, but "over here you're a cleaner")—Olga is in fact able to rely on support from a Ukrainian friend in Vienna and is neither isolated nor systematically abused. In the case of Paul, Seidl is equally determined to avoid stereotypes: "In his portrait of the male protagonist Seidl plays from the outset with signals pointing to far-right culture. But they lead us down the wrong track; Paul is not on the far right and neither a xenophobe nor a neo-Nazi" (Grissemann 2007: 214).[24]

According to Grissemann, it is not the maltreatment of migrant workers themselves that is the issue here but rather the "toughness of the world of work in Europe" (*Härte europäischer Arbeitswelten*; ibid.: 222), a theme it thus shares with Christian Petzold's *Yella* (2007) another feature film that combines a fictional narrative with documentary authenticity.[25] The most recognizably Seidlerian set pieces are reserved for the training sessions that both Paul and Olga have to endure in their search for work—in self-defense and interview techniques in Paul's case, and in the correct procedure for cleaning the teeth of taxidermic specimens and hospital toilets in Olga's. All of these sequences are tempered with considerable humor, however. It is in his portrayal of groups at the mercy of invisible social and economic forces that Seidl is at his most uncompromising and shocking. The appalling living conditions in Luník IX and the degrading institutionalization of the dementia patients in the geriatric hospital where Olga works provide, along with Seidl's trademark scenes of sexual degradation, some of the most shocking scenes in the film; they are also the scenes in which the documentary mode takes precedence over the fictional narrative. It is also the documentary scenes, in particular those with demented hospital patients, that have reawakened claims from Seidl's critics that he is a "social pornographer" (see, e.g., Buß 2007), or, as one critic has put it, a salesman of "poverty porn" (*Elendspornographie*) to healthy, young, educated middle-class cinemagoers (Heine 2007). His apologists, for their part, have reiterated the point made by Schmid that he is "a moralist rather in the manner of a Michel Houellebecq" (Schmid 2003: 49).

Good Will

What is remarkable about *Import Export*, in the context of such polarized critical reactions, is that both of Seidl's protagonists are unexpectedly peaceable, chaste even. Paul censures his stepfather for cheating on his mother in Slovakia, claims that his goal in life is "harmony," rejects the cut-price sex offers of the Roma pimps in Luník IX, and refuses to participate in his father's brutal exploitation of the young Ukrainian prostitute in Uzhhorod. Olga chooses to migrate to Austria rather than join her girlfriend in Snizhne working in the internet sex trade. In Vienna, she rejects the advances of both a young male nurse and an old patient at the hospital. In their incorruptibility and passivity—they are invariably victims of physical and psychological abuse rather than perpetrators of it—they remind one of the migrant protagonist of Kafka's *Der Verschollene/Amerika*, Karl Roßmann, whose flight from Germany to America (as reported by the narrator in the Stoker episode) is precipitated by a sexual misdemeanor forced on him by a maid. There is, moreover, a striking similarity between the unwholesome sexual encounters in *Import Export* and those in Kafka's novel:

> Then she lay down beside him, and asked to hear some secret or other, but he was unable to tell her any, then she was angry with him or pretended to be angry, he wasn't sure which, and shook him, then she listened to the beating of his heart and offered him her breast for him to listen to, but Karl couldn't bring himself to do that, she pressed her naked belly against his, reached her hand down, it felt so disgusting that Karl's head and neck leapt out of the pillows, down between his legs, pushed her belly against his a few times, he felt as though she were a part of him, and perhaps for that reason he felt seized by a shocking helplessness. (Kafka 2007: 22)[26]

In his responses to the punishment of forced migration, Karl's stoicism borders on resignation: "'Oh well,' said Karl, 'it won't be that bad,' after what he had heard, he no longer believed that things might take a good turn" (ibid.: 113).[27]

It is significant that in the case of both Paul and Olga this resignation does not translate into the defeatism that has consumed Roßmann's companion Robinson, who self-deprecatingly acknowledges that "if you're treated like a dog the whole time, you end up thinking that's what you are" (ibid.: 154).[28] However, Roßmann's conclusion when faced with the allegations thrown at him by the tyrannical head waiter of the Hotel Occidental—"It's impossible to mount a defence of oneself without a certain amount of good will" (ibid.: 126)[29]—certainly has a powerful resonance for Seidl's film. As in *Good News*, the migrants may well retain an "upright stance" (*aufrechter Gang*), but this does not, evidently, guarantee fair and just treatment. Whether, like Karl Roßmann and the protagonists of Fassbinder's *Angst essen Seele auf*, Olga and Paul fail to defend themselves adequately, is not a question that *Import Export* attempts to answer. In this it is true to its director's repeated claim that he is not offering any political solutions to the problems he shows: "The spectator must be encouraged to form his own opinion. It's not my job to say what is good and what is bad. Images are moral and have meaning per se" (Seidl, in Schmid 2003: 55).[30]

The audience's response to the most shocking scenes, and to the central characters themselves, is rendered more complex by the recognition that so much of the film's *mise-en-scène* is non-fictional: the demented patients, the Slovakian Roma, and—to a certain extent—Ekateryna Rak and Paul Hofmann are revealing themselves to the camera. Whilst Hofmann was known to Seidl from an earlier project (he and his working-class family had been interviewed for *Zur Lage*), Seidl chose to do a casting call in the Ukraine for the part of Olga. This elicited several hundred responses and Rak herself was chosen as someone who did not speak German and had never been to Austria.[31] In drawing on the life experience of his actors, and allowing himself to be inspired by locations—very much in the manner of Werner Herzog or American documentarist Errol Morris[32]—Seidl remains close to the "shared anthropology" program of *cinéma-vérité*. Whilst he does not engage in post-shoot debriefings or other democratic gestures of the kind made famous by Rouch and Morin in *Chronique d'un été*, his films remain, for all their stylistic formality, improvisational and spontaneous in their dialogue and dramaturgy.

According to Grissemann, *Good News* was "a film of indiscreet gazes: Ulrich Seidl's cinema wants to reveal the unseen" (Grissemann 2007: 88).[33] It is the fine balance of implacable visual stylization and "freedom of staging" (*inszenatorische Freiheit*) that distinguishes Seidl's docu-fictional anthropology (ibid.: 19). In the case of the three films discussed here, Seidl's systematic anthropology is certainly indiscreet in its relentless framing of "acts of self-portrayal" (*Selbstdarstellungsakte*), but also compassionate in the democracy of its gaze (ibid.: 110). Moreover, there are moments in *Import Export*—for example, when Olga unexpectedly fixes the camera with an intense long-held gaze amidst the "limbo of the geriatric ward" (*Vorhölle der Geriatrie*; ibid.: 225)—when one is reminded of Karl Roßmann's simple conclusion, "I've had enough" (Kafka 2007:137).[34] However, whilst Karl only makes this remark to himself, Olga's gaze is fixed firmly on the audience.

Notes

This chapter first appeared in *German as a Foreign Language* 1, 2008. We are grateful to the editors for permission to present a revised version of it here.

1. In an interview in 2002, following the release of *Hundstage*, the affinity with Bernhard was put to Seidl: "You once said: 'If I feel close to anyone in Austria, then it is Thomas Bernhard.' What is it that makes you feel close to him?" To which Seidl responded: "The way he describes things Austrian, above all his humor. Thomas Bernhard is a very humorous writer, despite the fact he describes such alarming things, and I see that to some extent in my films as well" (*In seiner Beschreibung des Österreichischen, seiner Authentizität, vor allem in seinem Humor. Thomas Bernhard hat sehr viel Humor, obwohl er beängstigende Dinge beschreibt, und das sehe ich bei meinen Filmen auch ein wenig so*). "'Das sind Sittenbilder unserer Zeit.' Ulrich Seidl über seinen Film HUNDSTAGE". Retrieved 15 February 2008 from: http://www.artechock.de/film/text/interview/s/seidl_2002.htm.

2. *Seidl bricht in seinen Filmen ungeniert Scham- und Geschmackskonventionen, um die faszinierende Farce, für die er das Leben hält, darzustellen.... Tatsächlich aber erstattet Seidl den Menschen und Ereignissen, die er zeigt, durch seine rücksichtslose Bildsprache ihren Platz*

im Leben zurück: als wolle er das Unterdrückte, das Verdrängte unserer Gesellschaft und die Wut, die Irritation seiner Protagonisten für die Wirklichkeit retten.... Eine "emotionale Nähe zu Minderheiten, die abseits der bürgerlichen Normalität stehen" habe er stets gehabt, gesteht Seidl, weil er sich "auch selbst immer als Außenseiter gefühlt" habe. Er führt sein Interesse an Sozialverlierern und Exzentrikern auf die eigene katholische Erziehung zurück, in der er sich nie zurecht gefunden habe. Bloß "engagierte" Arbeiten lehnt er für sich selbst kategorisch ab. Er halte, meint er, dem Zuschauer vielmehr "einen Spiegel vor." Das Unbehagen, das verlässlich ausgelöst werde, wenn man sich darin wieder erkenne, führe eben zum simplen Vorwurf der "Entstellung" des Wirklichen.

3. The title of this section is also taken from the commentary of Marker's film.

4. In Marker's English language version the voice belongs to Alexandra Stewart who is also pictured "staring back" in the book of the same name (Marker 2007: 78).

5. Text transcribed from *Sans Soleil*.

6. Cooper is here referring to *Sans Soleil*.

7. Werner Herzog, who described *Good News* as "one of the best documentary films of all times", also noted that in his opinion the subtitle was "a clumsy choice, more misleading than anything else" (*ungeschickt gewählt, eher irreführend*). In his brief laudation (which appears on the inside cover of the Edition Der Standard DVD) he describes the film in terms that are close to Seidl's own: "Rarely has a film shown the terrible regularity of the everyday and the madness of normality with such rigour and such stylistic resolve" (*Mit solcher Konsequenz, mit solchem Stilwillen hat noch selten jemand im Film die furchtbare Regelmäßigkeit des Alltags, den Wahnsinn der Normalität gezeigt*). Herzog's text, provided at Seidl's request, was originally published in *Der Standard*, 13 March 1991.

8. *Es ist der Moment des Innehaltens, des Stillstehens im Film, ohne dass er angehalten wird. Die Personen posieren wie für einen Fotografen, und ihr Blick in die Kamera trifft sich mit dem Blick des Zuschauers. Das ist für mich ein magischer Moment, der mich berührt oder verstört. Dabei ist der Raum wichtig. Ich gebe den Menschen viel Raum, darum wirken sie oft sehr klein darin. Hier werden meine Bilder zu Altären.* This interview and accompanying article are an excellent source of information on Seidl and his films up to and including *Hundstage*.

9. This juxtaposition of economic and painterly poses can be seen to extend the investigations carried out into the politics and legislation of the body by such experimental artists as the Austrian filmmaker and performance artist VALIE EXPORT, who explored the disciplining of the female body within the rigid lines of the Viennese cityscape. Her most famous film, *Unsichtbare Gegner/Invisible Adversaries* (1977), is also—at least on a metaphorical level—a film of migration, although in this instance the immigrants are extraterrestrials.

10. Brecht uses the camera to similar effect at the beginning of *Kuhle Wampe oder Wem gehört die Welt?/Kuhle Wampe or Who Owns the World?* (1932). After a brief shot of the Brandenburg Gate there is a cross-fade to a working-class quarter with smoke-filled tenement blocks. From the courtyards to these blocks the camera points upwards to show how little natural light the inhabitants can afford.

11. *Die zuweilen rätselhaft anmutende Kultur der Migranten liegt gleich hinter Wiens Häuserfronten. Ein direkter Weg führt ohne Schnitt in die Fremde. Von grauen Straßen aus bewegt sich der Blick der Kamera durch Treppenhäuser und Vorräume in die verborgenen Zentren islamischer Kultur in Wien.*

12. *In GOOD NEWS etwa schaue ich den Kolporteuren nicht nur zu, sondern ich fühle mit ihnen und in ihre Existenz hinein.*

13. *Ich denke, meine Filme sind sehr artifiziell, weil sie durch meine Bildsprache stark geprägt sind. Ich nehme die Dinge, die passieren, also die Wirklichkeit, auf und bringe sie in einen Rahmen. Gleichzeitig versuche ich als Regisseur auch, die Dinge in Bewegung zu halten.... Es interessiert mich nicht, nur die Realität abzubilden, obwohl ich großen Wert auf Wirklichkeitsnähe und Authentizität lege.* Seidl acknowledges the affinity with the photography of Diane Arbus, which has been noted by numerous commentators (Grissemann 2007: 24).

14. On Rouch's "shared anthropology", see Stoller (1992: 99–103).

15. *Der Osten hat mich immer interessiert. Ich finde dort viel Interessantes und Gutes und Tolles. Ich fühle mich dort wohl und kann in den Chor derer, die die "Rückständigkeit" des Ostens verteufeln, nicht einstimmen.... Indem ich den westlichen Wohlstand der anderen Seite mit seinen Einbauküchen und Tiefkühltruhen in Frage stelle, ergreife ich ja für den Osten Partei.*

16. *Es ist symptomatisch, dass Seidl die Beziehungen zwischen dem postkommunistischen Osten und dem kapitalistischen Westen—ein Thema, dass er Jahre später in IMPORT EXPORT wieder aufnehmen wird—anhand zweier Dörfer untersucht, die in mancherlei Hinsicht fast ununterscheidbar, gewissermaßen zwei Seiten einer Medaille sind und einander in jedem Sinn nahe stehen.*

17. *Angefangen vom Verlust der Heimat, über den Verlust der Jugend, den Verlust der Liebe, den Verlust des Ehepartners, den Verlust der Sexualität, den Verlust des Geldes bis hin zum Verlust des Lebens.*

18. *Paula ging nicht zum Sepp hinüber. Sie zieht es vor, auch weiterhin ihr Essen von der Genossenschaftsküche zu beziehen. Sepp hingegen ist noch immer auf der Suche nach einer geeigneten Frau. Mit Verlust ist zu rechnen* was released in 2007 as part of the Standard edition of Austrian documentaries. It has English subtitles.

19. *Ich wusste nicht wie sehr ich dabei die Grenze vom Dokumentarfilm zum Spielfilm überschreiten würde.*

20. *[E]in besessener Stilist, ja geradezu ein Geometer am Visuellen, der seine Bilder ausmisst.*

21. *[K]eine äußere Grenze vorkommt. Äußere Grenzen fallen ja, aber innere Grenzen bleiben. Und die zeige ich.*

22. In an interview with Christoph Huber, Seidl remarked "What I show in the movie is pretty much what happened to me: I was offered girls, to buy, to take away if I wanted" (Seidl, in Huber 2008: 27).

23. Huber's review is of interest in the context of migration because it contrasts the film with Fatih Akin's *Auf der anderen Seite* (released in Britain as *The Edge of Heaven*, 2007), which Huber dismisses as a "German-Turkish mix-and-match of buzzwords ... heavy-handedly constructed connections ... and sensationally stupid symbolism" (Huber 2007: 47).

24. *Im Porträt seines männlichen Hauptdarstellers spielt Seidl von Anfang an mit den Signalen rechtsradikaler Kultur. Aber die Fährte führt ins Leere; Paul ist kein Rechtsextremer, weder Ausländerhasser noch Neonazi.*

25. In Petzold's case, his film is inspired by documentarist Harun Farocki's *Nicht ohne Risiko/ Nothing Ventured* (2004).

26. The original text of Kafka's *Der Verschollene* reads: *Dann legte sie sich zu ihm und wollte irgendwelche Geheimnisse von ihm erfahren, aber er konnte ihr keine sagen, und sie ärgerte sich im Scherz oder Ernst, schüttelte ihn, horchte sein Herz ab, bot ihre Brust zum gleichen Abhorchen hin, wozu sie Karl aber nicht bringen konnte, drückte ihren nackten Bauch an seinen Leib, suchte mit der Hand, so widerlich, daß Karl Kopf und Hals aus den Kissen heraus schüttelte, zwischen seinen Beinen, stieß dann den Bauch einigemale gegen ihn, ihm war, als sei sie ein Teil seiner Selbst und vielleicht aus diesem Grunde hatte ihn eine entsetzliche Hilfsbedürftigkeit ergriffen* (Kafka 2002: 42–43).

27. *"Na", sagte Karl, "es wird nicht so schlimm werden", nach allem was er gehört hatte, glaubte er an keinen guten Ausgang mehr* (Kafka 2002: 220).

28. *[W]enn man immerfort als Hund behandelt wird denkt man schließlich man ists wirklich* (Kafka 2002: 298).

29. *Es ist unmöglich sich zu verteidigen, wenn nicht guter Wille da ist* (Kafka 2002: 245).

30. *Man muss den Zuschauer fordern, sich selbst eine Meinung zu bilden. Es ist nicht meine Aufgabe zu sagen, was Gut und was Böse ist. Das Bild an sich ist moralisch, seine Aussage.*

31. It subsequently also transpired that she also had no intention of migrating there.

32. Herzog himself has noted the parallel between Seidl and Morris (Herzog, in Grissemann 2007: 121). It is not surprising that both have received his fervent support.

33. *[E]in Film des indiskreten Blicks: Ulrich Seidl will im Kino Uneinsehbares enthüllen.*

34. *Jetzt ist aber genug* (Kafka 2002: 266).

References

Barnouw, E. 1993. *Documentary: A History of the Non-Fiction Film*. Oxford: Oxford University Press.

Buß, C. 2007. "Parcours der Demütigungen," *Der Spiegel Online*. Retrieved 15 February 2008 from: http://www.spiegel.de/kultur/kino/0,1518,512151,00.html.

Cooper, S. 2006. *Ethics and French Documentary*. Leeds: Maney.

Danquart, D., S. Fröhlich, L.H. Gass, E. Hohenberger, W. Ružička, W. Schweizer, and C. Wulff. 1996. "How Provocative Can You Get? A Round Table Discussion on the films of Austrian director Ulrich Seidl," *Dox: Documentary Film Quarterly* 10: 34–37.

Eaton, M. 1979. *Anthropology—Reality—Cinema: The Films of Jean Rouch*. London: BFI.

Feld, S. 2003. "Editor's Introduction," in J. Rouch, *Ciné-Ethnography*. Minneapolis: University of Minnesota Press, 1–25.

Grissemann, S. 2007. *Sündenfall: Die Grenzüberschreitungen des Filmemachers Ulrich Seidl*. Vienna: Sonderzahl.

Heine, M. 2007. "Ulrich Seidl und die Pornographie des Elends," *Die Welt Online*. Retrieved 15 February 2008 from: http://www.welt.de/kultur/article1279225/Ulrich_Seidl_und_die_Pornografie_des_Elends.html.

Huber, C. 2007. "Import Export: Ulrich Seidl, Austria," *Cinema Scope* 31: 46–47.

———. 2008. "Ulrich Seidl's Song for Europe," *Cinema Scope* 33: 24–28.

Hughes, H. 1999. "Documenting the *Wende*: The Films of Andreas Voigt," in S. Allan and J. Sandford (eds), *DEFA: East German Cinema 1946–1992*. Oxford: Berghahn, 283–301.

Kafka, F. 2002. *Der Verschollene*. Frankfurt am Main: Fischer.

———. 2007. *Amerika (The Man Who Disappeared)*, trans. M. Hofmann. London: Penguin.

Marker, C. 2007. *Staring Back*. Cambridge, MA: MIT Press.

Rouch, J. 2003. *Ciné-Ethnography*, trans. S. Feld. Minneapolis: University of Minnesota Press.

Schmid, B. 2003. "Forscher am Lebendigen: Porträt von Ulrich Seidl," *Filmbulletin* 2: 46–55.

Stoller, P. 1992. *The Cinematic Griot: The Ethnography of Jean Rouch*. Chicago: University of Chicago Press.

Part IV

Re-visions, Shifting Centers, Crossing Borders

Chapter 16

Crossing Borders in Austrian Cinema at the Turn of the Century: Flicker, Allahyari, Albert

Nikhil Sathe

Questions of Austrian history and national identity are very much questions of borders: of openings and closings, of inclusion and exclusion, of creation and contestation. In particular, the shifts of post-1989 Europe and Austria's redefinitions after joining the European Union have positioned borders as a key topic in Austrian political discourse. Similarly, in numerous works since the mid 1990s Austrian filmmakers have contributed to this discourse by making the border perhaps Austrian cinema's principle site.[1] A frequent setting in art, borders function as a space that by definition creates, yet questions, conceptions of self and other, and that readily signifies personal transitions, since the border seems to demand its crossing. Engaging with these traditions and the current sociohistorical context, Austrian cinema has represented borders, both literal and figurative, in its interrogations of national identity and the country's response to increased migration.

The following discussion will examine these cinematic interrogations through a reading of the deployment of borders in three films. The first section reviews the sociohistorical context relevant to Austrian borders after 1989 and then establishes a conceptual footing from the interdisciplinary field of border theory. The second section then contains detailed readings of Florian Flicker's *Suzie Washington* (1998), Houchang Allahyari's *Geboren in Absurdistan/Born in Absurdistan* (1999), and finally Barbara Albert's *Nordrand* (1999). The concluding section examines how subsequent films both continue and expand the thematization of borders emerging in the previous three films. From this study it will become clear that the films' portrayal of borders, which illustrates their power, yet foregrounds their destabilization, enables a critique of Austria's migration policies and of the notions of exclusion and authenticity inherent to ethnicities and identities imagined as bounded and homogeneous. The border, as depicted in numerous films, appears as a restrictive barrier heralded as a defense against external threats, but it proves to be a porous membrane that is continually crossed and negotiated. Isolating these border transgressions will illuminate how the films undermine monolithic constructions of Austrian identity, which are often marshaled in response to the many continental shifts affecting Austria's self-image.

The momentous changes unleashed in 1989 were key events prompting a reassessment of Austria's borders. Although popular imagination has canonized it as the fall of the Berlin Wall, the Iron Curtain's first opening was indeed on the border between Austria and Hungary. While this did not change Austria's physical borders, it inaugurated redefinitions for Austria, which, while clearly linked to the West, had long imagined itself as a bridge between East and West. Given the collapse of the East–West divide, Austria's joining of the EU in 1995 must be seen as part of the country's post-1989 realignment, which, despite increased economic ties to the East, strengthened its alliance with the West at a political level. EU membership altered Austria's border dynamics, opening them to the West while tightening controls on those to the East and thus reinforcing the so-called *Festung Europa* (Fortress Europe), effectively replacing the Iron Curtain with what Eastern Europeans call a "Golden Curtain" (Liebhart and Pribersky 2001: 116). This was intensified with the Schengen agreement, which erased border controls between Western EU nations and made those with the Eastern countries stricter, even as they were admitted to the EU in 2004. Since December 2007, when Austria's eastern neighbors became part of the Schengen zone, Austria's borders are no longer the edge of Fortress Europe, but are now unrestricted with their defenses left to their neighbors, which has renewed some Austrirans' unease about the borders (Perterer 2007; Uwer 2007).

Concerns about Austria's border security arose well before the country joined the EU. As in much of post-1989 Europe, Austria saw increased numbers of foreigners attempting to cross its borders. In addition to asylum seekers and migrants from Eastern Europe, and from population movements resulting from globalization, a large number of refugees and migrants from the former Yugoslavia entered Austria. The xenophobic, radical Right across Europe took advantage of these developments and had its biggest successes in the shape of the Austrian Freedom Party (FPÖ) under its then leader, Jörg Haider. Haider's FPÖ exploited anti-foreigner sentiment for electoral gains and even held an unsuccessful national referendum in 1993 aimed at limiting foreigners' rights. The FPÖ created the specter of *Überfremdung*, "fraudulent asylum seekers," and Eastern European crime, all hyped up by the sensationalist media. Although an opposition party, the FPÖ succeeded in shaping political discourse as the ruling parties adopted elements of the party's platform to attract potential FPÖ voters, which lead to the passage of some of Europe's most restrictive laws concerning immigration and asylum. After substantial gains in the 2000 election, the FPÖ formed a coalition with the conservative People's Party (ÖVP). The FPÖ's entry into the federal government—the first radical right-wing party to attain such a position in Europe—ignited domestic protest and international uproar, culminating in the EU's imposition of diplomatic sanctions against Austria. The fallout of that election, party infighting, and Haider's departure to form a separate party, all contributed to the FPÖ's decline, but it still maintains, under Viennese politician H. C. Strache, platforms aimed at limiting immigration and the rights of foreigners.

This historical context is reflected in the films discussed below. They not only represent the actual border and its policing, but also address the conceptual significance of borders, and thus contend with issues that have figured prominently in the interdisciplinary theorizing of borders since the 1980s (Langer1999: 25). The impetus of this discussion, defined as "border theory," was the context of the US–Mexican border.[2] Border theory treats the border as a space of separation, but also of contact, and it imagines borderlands as places where cultures meet in dialogue and negotiation. As Jesús Benito and Ana María Manzanas note, "the border becomes fully meaningful not only when we consider it as a physical line, but when we de-center it and liberate it from the notion of space to encompass notions of sex, class, gender, ethnicity, identity and community" (Benito and Manzanas 2002: 3).[3] This conceptualization allows border theory to expand its inquiries beyond the US–Mexico context and to broader conceptions of spaces in contact. Austria's borders, in particular the southeastern borders depicted in many films, open new perspectives for border theory. Like the US–Mexican border, Austria's borders are sites of cross-border interaction and cultural antagonism and tension, yet they highlight a new geopolitical context as an EU border, functioning as an internal yet semi-external, national yet supranational border that should both prevent and promote the traffic of goods, people, labor, and ideas.

The films discussed below portray the border primarily from an Austrian perspective, from which the border is imagined as encapsulating and defining the whole. These functions have been the subject of border theory's most penetrating critique. Against the assumption that the border establishes and secures the solidity of a national or ethnic group, for which "[o]nly a closed border can presumably secure a fixed, stable and finished identity" (Benito and Manzanas 2002: 7), border theory has highlighted the border's arbitrariness and the liminality of borderlands. This enables a critique of visions of totality and authenticity inherent in conceptions of national and ethnic identity. Notions of the border as a sign denoting integrity and completeness are thus deconstructed, revealing the border to be an instrument of this fantasy. Instead of an alleged homogeneity defined by boundaries, border theory privileges the hybridity of the unstable, indeterminate borderlands. The images of transgressed borders that prevail in numerous Austrian films offer a similar critique of identity, as they both question the conflation of entrenched borders with national unity and security in response to increased migration, and also valorize the flux of borderlands.

Numerous critics, however, have questioned the celebration of borderlands for its uncritical overuse. David Johnson and Scott Michaelson, for instance, take border theory to task for too often assuming that borderlands are "a place of politically exciting hybridity, intellectual creativity and moral possibility ... *the* privileged locus of hope for a better world" (Johnson and Michaelsen 1997: 2–3). For them, the border becomes too quickly reduced to a locus for uncritical models of multiculturalism. Deborah Castillo notes how the often romanticized theorization of the border has often failed to account for the concrete realities and hardships of borders (Castillo 1999: 186).[4] While the films below vary in the degree to which they valorize the borderland, they portray the border as a space of violence and restriction, foregrounding the border as a physical imposition with real consequences for those it excludes.

Both the border's political implications and the privileging of hybridity and borderlessness factor into speculations on the aesthetics of border texts. While these considerations have limited utility for a discussion of cinema because they stem from literary analysis, they offer productive insights for understanding how films deploy and subvert border representations. Dieter Lamping's argument, for example, that border literature is inherently political because it calls into question both the erection of specific boundaries and also their ideological conceptualization, clearly applies to the films discussed below (Lamping 2001: 10–18). Highlighting the multilingualism of borderlands, Benito and Manzanas contend that border literature's project "clashes with the notion of writing as a discrete, coherently structured, monolingual edifice" and that it instead seeks to probe literature's "unfinished quality and the areas of exchange and negotiation it establishes with other languages and writings" (Benito and Manzanas 2002: 15). With its inherent capacity for visually and aurally recording everyday reality, cinema is well suited to represent the convergence of languages and peoples. Since language is only one element of the cinematic medium, textual interplay with other languages and literatures can only have limited application. But Benito and Manzanas's conception of the "grotesque" (ibid.: 17)—of a tendency toward inconclusiveness, stylistic freedom, and play that seeks to undo the border's logic of rigid division—can find cinematic equivalents in the episodic narratives, allusions, and other stylistic choices in the films discussed below. Even at their most conventional, these films attempt to unsettle the dichotomies created by the border.

Suzie Washington

Suzie Washington (1998) by director Florian Flicker illustrates the multiplicity of languages in the border film. The protagonist, an illegal alien, delivers most of her dialogue in English, itself a lingua franca for the film's characters. The film opens as Nana Iaschwili, a teacher from an unnamed former Soviet republic, lands in Vienna on her way to Los Angeles. But when her forged visa is discovered, she must remain in the transit area until her flight back. Unwilling to return, she escapes and makes her way into Germany and presumably then on to Los Angeles. Charting the protagonist's trek across Austria, the film implicitly indicts Austrian migration policies and their mechanisms of control, in particular through the ironic portrayal, both direct and intertextual, of the infrastructure of the dominant tourism industry.

Borders literally bookend this film, which starts with Nana's arrival at passport control and ends at an unpatrolled mountain stretch of the pre-Schengen border with Germany. The protagonist's initial interrogation introduces the questioning of Austrian policies regarding asylum and transit. After reviewing Nana's phony visa, the immigration officer tells Nana that she must return to her country and abruptly assures her that she faces no danger in returning, to which Nana, whose husband has disappeared in her country's civil war, can only utter skepticism. Later, Nana protests that she is a tourist, not a criminal, when the officer details her confinement to the transit zone, where any violation results in arrest and deportation. A social worker visiting Nana the following day expresses token sympathy, yet insists on the law's right to restrict her. Through the actions of these officials, the film portrays the border's function as one of selective exclusion and defense, which criminalizes any transgression by those deemed unwanted. The film leaves Nana's motivations unclear, but suggests both flight from dire straits and also a desire for change. The migrant's dilemma is reinforced through a short episode with an Iranian figure, who, like Nana, is forced to return. Attempting to resist, the Iranian takes a border guard hostage, only to be subdued by police. This migrant's desperation provides Nana with an opportunity to end hers: in the ensuing commotion, which the film intensifies by switching to a handheld camera for this scene, Nana exits the transit area and escapes.

Instead of concentrating on the migrants' motivations or treatment by border authorities, however, the film subtly engages its criticism by exposing the contradiction between Austria's restrictive policies and its tourism industry. Throughout the film the protagonist's movement is channeled along the touristic infrastructure: buses, boats, and even ski-lifts. This begins as Nana sneaks into a line of tourists boarding a chartered bus at the airport. Unlike the border police, the guides offer her a hearty welcome, a glossy itinerary, *Mozartkugeln* chocolates, and the strains of waltzes. These luxuries, however, are only transitory, as Nana leaves the bus at the first stop to escape from the tour guide's pleasant but persistent demands to see her ticket. She then progresses on foot, finding refuge in a lakeside resort crowded with summer vacationers. Here too, her security remains temporary: to complete registration, the innkeeper asks for her passport, which Nana cannot produce because she claims to be Suzie Washington, the name of an American tourist she met on the bus. By having the protagonist continue her flight by assuming touristic roles, the film not only reveals how mechanisms of control extend well beyond the border, but also underscores the irony that an industry welcoming guests from some locations flourishes alongside restrictive policies preventing entry to people from others. Through Nana/Suzie, the arbitrariness of determining who is and is not welcome becomes apparent.

Just as Nana becomes Suzie to evade the law and cross the border, the film uses intertextual parallels to play with its own identity for its border critique. Alysson Fiddler is correct that the film visits the "archetypal tourist scenery of Austria" (Fiddler 2006: 277), but it more accurately revisits films set or made in Austria, in particular those connected to tourism, in order to undermine both the narrative configurations associated with them and also their illusory gestures toward integration and acceptance. For instance, when Nana arrives at a Salzkammergut hotel, she befriends the German vacationer Herbert, a figurative descendant of the filmic tourists in the Wörthersee and Wolfgangsee *Heimatfilm*s of the 1960s.[5] Like those tourists, Herbert clearly desires the woman whom he meets at the lake, but Nana dismisses his advances and seems shocked by his apparent rejection after she confesses that she is an illegal alien. A further return to the *Heimat* genre can be found in the film's last act: After crooked smugglers help Nana reach the mountains near the German border, she stops for the night at a hut, and she gradually begins a relationship with its owner. This reenacts a scenario found in many *Heimatfilm*s, where the union between the host and the outsider guest often resolves narrative conflicts.[6] This lonely proprietor desires Nana and, as she later discovers, is even aware that she is a wanted fugitive and that she has stolen the passport of a French tourist, whom she resembles. The union that one would expect of a conventional *Heimatfilm*, does not, however, come to fruition, and Nana hopes to proceed westward with the stolen passport. The proprietor remains integral to the film's resolution: he not only helps Nana cross the mountain border safely into Germany, but also gives her money and the stolen passport that will enable her flight onward. Frustrating the *Heimatfilm* expectations of the outsider's harmonious integration, the film rewrites the cinematic encoding of the Austrian landscape, which both casts Austria as a space where outsiders do not feel welcome, and also highlights the protagonist's will to reach her goal.[7]

Whereas the film undoes *Heimatfilm* conventions, its final return to film history restages the conclusion of *The Sound of Music* (1965). The viewer is alerted to this allusion when the smuggler, who takes Nana into the mountains, arrives in a bus used for *Sound of Music* tours. Like the Trapp family before her, Nana, now by ski-lift, traverses the mountain peaks for her final escape into freedom. To be sure, the final alpine escape has different dynamics in each film: the Trapps are fleeing the Nazis, who would likely separate and incarcerate them, keeping them inside the state borders, but Nana is fleeing arrest by a state apparatus that will remove her from its borders. The restaging of the iconic closure of *The Sound of Music*, however, does allow *Suzie Washington* to reiterate its central critique and to cast the migrant's struggle in a more universal perspective: borders and their repressive control, even though the protagonists evade them, ultimately serve to imprison individuals and hinder their chances of arriving at their destinations.

Geboren in Absurdistan

The border continues to function as an agent of separation in *Geboren in Absurdistan* (1999) by director Houchang Allahyari. As the title indicates, bureaucratic absurdities provide the impetus for this comedy's representation of the hurdles facing migrants in Austria, and the film was inspired by reports of foreigners being deported on trivial grounds to a homeland that for many had become foreign.[8] This situation appears in the film, but its narrative focus is on the bureaucrat responsible for the deportations, Stefan Strohmeyer. This character, an official in the Interior Ministry, and his wife, Marion, think that their newborn son has been switched with the son of Emre and Emine Dönmez, the Turkish family in the next bed in the maternity ward. After learning first about the switch and then that the Dönmezs have been deported for a technical error, the Strohmeyers go to Turkey to find the Dönmezs and their son. Portraying the physical border as a space of brutal exclusion and political misappropriation enables the film to question constructions of ethnicity inherent to discourses concerning foreigners.

The opening immediately visualizes the concept of mistaken identities and takes the viewer to the national border to foreground Austria's conflicted policies towards migrants. With extreme close-ups of hands performing classical music, the first frames suggest a concert hall, but subsequent medium shots reveal that the musicians are actually outside. These images are juxtaposed with others of people surrounded by police, and a shot of a girl humming indicates her proximity to the musicians. The first pan follows several men in handcuffs rushed along by armed officers and then pulls back to an establishing shot of a highway checkpoint on the Austrian border, where the musicians are welcoming the Interior Minister, who has come to celebrate the checkpoint's renovation. The film thus first tricks the viewer about its initial setting, a concert hall, and then suggests a surreal element, classical musicians playing outside a border checkpoint, but then reveals its realistic portrayal of this moment – the celebration to open the new border facility. By deliberately playing with viewer's ability to interpret the location and meaning of the setting and by foregrounding the contrast between the classical music, a marker of humanistic and Austrian traditions, and the rough treatment of foreigners sets up the film's critique of Austria's border policies. This visual contrast is restated in the Minister's response to a journalist, who inquires whether Austria's new border facility constitutes Fortress Europe; he grudgingly replies that Austrian officials will protect genuine asylum seekers, but in the same breath warns against phony refugees seeking employment. Although the Minister promises a humane policy, the border is clearly designed to repel, and his attempt at political instrumentalization is confirmed when he adds that what is truly at stake is "the securing of our borders" (*die Sicherung unserer Grenzen*).

The question of border security is dramatized on a personal level through Stefan, who learns that the secure border around his family has been infringed. The film prefigures this by visually introducing the Dönmezs as intruders. In their first appearance at the hospital, they and their many visitors are transferred because of a lack of space to Marion's private room. Stefan protests and even threatens that he could have them deported. Later, when Emre and Emine try to obtain a birth certificate, they are told by different clerks that they are in the wrong place. This culminates in a deportation notice, which they receive after missing a deadline due to an address change. Hoping to contest this, they wind up in Stefan's office, who apologizes for his behavior and promises to help, but forgets to collect their paperwork. He tries to catch them, but stops when his racist superior berates him, which hastens their deportation. This becomes a problem when Stefan learns about the mix-up at the hospital. To enable the narrative's comedic structure, the film lets the viewer, but not the protagonists know about the switch, which sets up inside jokes for the viewer, in which the characters are unaware of the significance of their words. For instance, Marion's father gushes about family resemblances in his grandchild, and a neighbor describes the Dönmez child as a "purebred Viennese" (*Waschechter Wiener*) because he was born in Vienna, a claim one Turkish character skeptically derides as insufficient. These moments turn on an unsettling of conceptions of ethnicity and national identity, portraying them as projections and constructs rather than fixed essences.[9]

By sending the Strohmeyers to Turkey the film raises questions about *Heimat* and foreignness. One might expect this segment of the film to turn the tables on the Strohmeyers and portray their struggle as foreigners. This, however, only happens in the arrival scene, and the subsequent narrative focus remains on the identity of the children. With Emine and Emre, though, the film highlights how they have become foreigners in Turkey, their home country, after living ten years in Austria: Emre reveals how he owes the corrupt mayor money and will be at his mercy for years, and Emine notes that she is doubly displaced, since this is her husband's village. When the Dönmezs appear on screen in Turkey, they are nearly always working for someone else. Their portrayal is constructed to counteract the notion of *Heimat* that exists in Austrian legal discourse regarding foreigners: the law proscribes that they be returned to their *Heimat*, which for the Dönmezs has now become Austria.

The film returns to the Austrian border as the Strohmeyers must become smugglers so that both families can take a paternity test in Austria. Although this sequence is played for comedic effect, particularly through the casting of then cabaret star Josef Hader as the trucker hired to smuggle the Dönmezs, the border maintains the hard realities of the film's opening. For the border crossing scene, the film again plays with shifting identities, both for comedic effect and to foreground the arbitrary brutality of the border's impact. When Stefan and Marion cross in their car, the border guards recognize him and insist that he observe their work. Stefan agrees and uses the scanner himself when he sees that the next truck is driven by Hader's character, who is clearly dumbfounded to see the person who hired him to smuggle is now checking his vehicle for contraband. This allows Emre to cross safely, but all are then caught when Emine is discovered. As guards swarm around Emine and the baby in the trunk of Stefan's car, the insider Austrians become outsiders at the gates of Fortress Europe.

The film omits any consideration of the legal consequences and proceeds to a swift, utopian denouement. The Dönmezs' immigration problem is solved through political maneuvering and a dose of *Freunderlwirtschaft* ("pulling strings"). Marion's father strikes a deal with a journalist to publicize the incident, which lands both families on a talkshow, which, as the subsequent cut reveals, the Interior Minister is watching. He sees this situation as a campaign opportunity: he can show compassion, yet deflect criticism of leniency, because the case has become a media tragedy. Promising on air to help, he becomes the film's deus ex machina, which conforms to the conventions of a comedy of mistaken identities, yet undercuts the film's critique: perhaps acknowledging Austrian political realities, the film's resolution is driven by political instrumentalization, not the more humane treatment of migrants that the film implicitly advocates.

Similarly, the conclusion of the uncertainty regarding the children foregrounds and undermines its utopian dimension. After the minister's call, the film cuts to the head nurse watching the show, and she tells her underling that there never was a switch and then intimates, with her address to the camera—"that's exactly how it was planned" (*so war das geplant*)—that she instigated the confusion to teach a lesson to Stefan, whom she earlier dubbed a racist when he was upset about sharing a hospital room with the Dönmezs. The subsequent scene makes clear that the lesson was the acceptance of others, as the film then shows the families deciding to forgo the paternity test and presumably rear their children together. If the characters are willing to accept this idealized multicultural community and to suspend any claims to ethnic authenticity or parental identity, the radical potential inherent to it has already been undone for the viewer by the nurse's earlier revelation that each family does indeed have their own child. Her revelations invite the viewer to reaffirm the validity of this authenticity, making the utopian moment a further mistaken identity. The final scenes reinforce this dimension, as the film, as in the opening scene, alternates between realistic and surreal perspectives. As the characters walk away from the doctor's office, the *Blue Danube Waltz* plays on the soundtrack, and then musicians performing the music step into the frame and follow the characters. Unlike the musicians at the opening, however, these are clearly non-diegetic, recalling the surreal qualities of musicals. The setting then abruptly cuts to a bucolic Turkish landscape in which the characters now walk toward the camera, accompanied by Turkish music. The juxtaposition of these scenes encapsulates the film's inherent tensions: it hopes for a world without borders and the limits they impose, but can only imagine it as a fantasy.

From Albert's *Nordrand* to Kalt's *Crash Test Dummies* (2005)

A more tentative utopian union awaits the cast of Barbara Albert's film *Nordrand* (1999). This ensemble film has former schoolmates, Jasmin and Tamara, meet after a number of years in an abortion clinic and later befriend the Romanian Valentin and the Bosnian Senad. Albert has noted that her original conception of the film would have been an overtly political commentary on Austria, but later chose a more nuanced portrayal that emphasizes interaction between the film's multiethnic characters (Albert 1999). Events contemporary to the setting in 1995, however— such as the war in Bosnia, increased migration and sharper controls on immigration— all shape the film's stories. As the title suggests, borders are central to the film: "Nordrand" (northern edge) refers both to the film's setting in Vienna's northern districts, which are marked by strict class barriers, yet also to Austria's position with regard to southeastern Europe, from where many of its characters migrate. Depicting the national border and its legal ramifications for Vienna, the film employs borders, real and figurative, as the underlying aesthetic motor propelling its narratives and thematic concerns.

The aesthetic structure of *Nordrand* privileges the notion of transcending borders: it introduces separate narratives that become entwined as the different characters cross into each others' lives, which is underscored through editing that highlights spatial links and divisions. The sky, where physical borders cannot exist, creates this link when Jasmin and Tamara leave the abortion clinic where they first meet. They are surprised by the first snowfall, and the camera captures their reactions as they gaze up and then cuts to other protagonists, who, elsewhere in Vienna, look up with a similar sense of wonder and premonition. Their upward glances amid falling snowflakes forge a visual bond foreshadowing their emotional links. If the sky, associated with boundlessness, intimates the coming unions, the urban spaces of Vienna that prevail in transitional sequences suggest barriers that these figures have yet to overcome. Tracking shots of street scenes, often accompanied by pop music, segue into sequences with another character. For instance, as Jasmin returns from a hollow sexual encounter with her lover Wolfgang, the camera shifts from a shot of her inside the car to what she sees on the passing streets. In these images, Tamara can be seen leaving a subway station, which spatially links her to Jasmin, a connection that is further reinforced through the melancholic soundtrack, which alludes to their broken relationships and their impending pregnancies.[10] These street images can create further associations through the characters' memories, which transcend temporal and spatial boundaries. An example can be found in the sequence that begins with the interior of Valentin's van driving past snowmen, then cuts to propaganda film footage of enthusiastic supporters greeting Nicolae Ceauşescu's motorcade, and then cuts to a tracking shot from Valentin's car presenting blurred images of Austrian campaign signs. The images from Romania function like a restricting anchor that binds Valentin's past to his present and future. The inclusion of the election ads alongside Valentin's struggle in this uncertain historical landscape obliquely points to the parallel negotiations in the Austrian political landscape.

Metaphorically, the crossing of a border is pivotal to the individual narratives. Albert has noted that she conceived her stories around the difficult passage into adulthood, in which characters face the painful transition from youthful freedom to responsibilities and consequences (Albert 1999). The border's conceptual significance is apparent, as the protagonists face threshold decisions, which are underlined through a *mise-en-scène* whose spatial relationships emphasize boundaries. The Austrian character Jasmin, for example, is frequently shown along edges and barriers, such as walls, window, and even the banks of the Danube. When she tells her employer that she is pregnant and he is the father, for example, she has her back to a glass wall that reveals her busy coworkers yet also separates her from them, which underlines her condition and the breach of conventional workplace relations. One major transition, when she leaves her dysfunctional family, is visualized through a crossing of boundaries: after Jasmin locks her room to protect herself and sister from their father's sexual abuse, he retrieves the key and locks her in, but she then evades this restriction by escaping through the window. The conclusion of Jasmin's narrative and her transition is also visualized through her crossing literal and figurative borders. Again pregnant but now by Senad, Jasmin considers another abortion, but Tamara suggests she could help her with a child. Jasmin is then shown on a railway bridge where she approaches a group of ogling men, and after passing unscathed by their lewd remarks, she begins running with a joyful expression on her face. By portraying her mastering this brief, yet significant emotional challenge while crossing a physical barrier, this scene implies Jasmin's rejection of self-destructive, promiscuous relationships and her future acceptance of adult responsibilities.[11]

Tamara, a Serbian who has grown up in Vienna, is presented as living between two worlds, and her home is literally on the edge of the city limits. After she has her abortion, she is eventually abandoned by her jealous lover, Roman, who is completing his military service in a unit that patrols an isolated stretch of Austria's southeastern border. But she suffers her greatest loss when she learns that her brother, who has been living with her parents in Sarajevo, is killed in the Yugoslav civil war. This moment becomes integral to Tamara's friendship with Jasmin, which is made clear by the blocking of the *mise-en-scène* which stages their closeness through figuratively falling boundaries: Tamara relays the news while facing the camera with Jasmin behind her, and Jasmin slowly and hesitantly approaches, finally embracing her gingerly, suggesting that she is breaking an invisible barrier between them. Tamara's transition coincides with a true border crossing when she leaves for Sarajevo to visit her family. In the collage of transit images at the conclusion, the editing shifts between Tamara and the images she sees from her train, among them children running after a kite. This repeats her childhood memory shown earlier and suggests a final farewell to childhood as she moves toward her family's uncertainties and her promise to help Jasmin.

The Romanian character Valentin illustrates how the film envisions Vienna as a borderland. He resides in Austria illegally, which becomes clear when he is shown sneaking from a police raid, but only intends Vienna to be a transit stop on his way to America, where he can find work, presumably to support his pregnant girlfriend in Romania. In Vienna, his status only allows him illegal work. Frustrated by the delay in his visa application with a questionable dealer, Valentin returns to their office, to find that the swindlers have long since deserted with his money and hopes. Concretizing his confinement, the film portrays this realization by shooting Valentin outside behind a chained gate peering through windows. When Valentin later has a brief relationship with Tamara, he continues to tell her that he is soon leaving for America, even on their final night together, but the final images of him on a bus reveal that he is returning to Romania, where his child has just been born. His return and crossing of eastern borders suggests, as with the other figures, his postponement of his American dream and his move towards adult responsibilities.

The Bosnian Senad is the character whose threshold situation is literally a border crossing. He first appears illegally crossing the stretch of the Austrian border that Roman is guarding. He leaves Bosnia to resume his studies, but with his awkward silences about the war, his wedding ring, and the family of snowmen he later builds in a melancholic scene, the film hints at his traumatic past. Once in Vienna, Senad is able to find work as a laborer and shelter in a refugee center, but even here, far from the border, its policing and power remain omnipresent, as he, like Valentin, is shown escaping a raid on illegal workers. The film's critique of borders and the division that they enforce is reiterated through the depiction of Senad's relationship with Jasmin. When Jasmin, naive of the tensions between their respective identities, introduces Senad to Tamara, they refuse to speak. Jasmin's intervention, however, neutralizes their aversion, which the film visually underscores by having her sit down between them during a dispute, making Tamara's house on the border a utopian space immune from the sentiments fueling the bloodshed a few hours away.

The New Year's Eve sequence offers another visualization of this union, as the film's principals all waltz in front of the iconic St Stephan's cathedral. The handheld camera follows their revelries amid the chaotic masses and fireworks, imaging a community where multiple identities manage to coexist. The film then stresses the fragility of this union, though, by having the characters become separated during the commotion. This sequence acquires its resonance with regard to the border through a cut to a simultaneous scene, in which Roman lights a single firecracker at his border post while listening to the Vienna celebration on the radio. By contrasting Roman's meager celebration alongside the previous euphoric scenes, the film stages a pointed critique of notions of the border as the guarantor and sign of a secure and stable identity. St Stephan's Square is the premier central Austrian space and is laden with cultural significance as the national center (Zheng 2001: 65), but in Albert's film it appears as a cacophonous mix of languages and peoples where anyone, regardless of nationality, can participate in the rituals of national identity by waltzing at this site. In contrast, the border, which has already been pictured as porous, now seems empty and its policing insignificant, if not irrelevant. This juxtaposition thus offers an implicit critique of then contemporary demands both to tighten border restrictions and protect an imagined Austrian whole from the influx of foreigners. Just as the film's characters make transitions into complex uncertainties, *Nordrand* dispenses with fixed notions of borders to portray an indeterminate borderland where numerous cultures already exist in dialogue and flux. The actual physical border, though it has real power, appears flimsy, ill-equipped to fulfill its imaginary function of creating and containing a homogeneity.

This contemporaneous presence of borders that seem inherently permeable despite border policing and its powerful consequences is a hallmark of films released after those discussed above, and which continue to employ the border as a central site and thematic focus. In Ruth Mader's *Struggle* (2003), for example, the Polish protagonist Eva comes to Austria as a migrant worker hired to pick strawberries, but sneaks away at a rest stop before the bus returns to Poland. As in the previous films, the supposedly secure border becomes permeable, and *Struggle* exposes the economy's complicity in this process as it bends or dissolves capital and labor regulations under neoliberal globalization. Once in Austria, Eva evades raids on illegal workers at the black market, where she is hired for menial jobs, which are minutely detailed through a resolutely static, documentary-like lens. This detached style makes her relationship with a divorcee at the conclusion ambiguous, signifying stability or simply another demeaning stage that she, a migrant like Nana Iaschwilli, endures to reach her goal of providing for her daughter.

Like *Absurdistan*, Andreas Gruber's satire *Welcome Home* (2004) centers on a character's deportation, but here the process is depicted in detail. After Isaac, who conceals his true homeland, crosses the border, he is caught by two Austrian policemen, who then accompany him during his deportation to Ghana. The Ghanaian officials confiscate the two Austrian officers' passports on a visa violation, keeping them until Isaac's case can be resolved, which allows the film to subject the Austrians to the experience of being illegal aliens. Through this experience, the racist Austrian officer changes his ways and even allows Isaac to escape when they return to Austria. The film intensifies this transition by casting the lead officer with Georg Friedrich, a mainstay in Austrian cinema who generally plays unsavory, aggressive characters. Although ultimately penetrable, the border *Welcome Home* remains a space of violent repulsion, which is heightened through factual allusions: the story was inspired by an actual event where Austrians were detained in Africa, but the violence during the airplane deportation sequence invokes parallels with the case of Marcus Omufuma, a Nigerian who died in custody as a result of his treatment during deportation from Austria in 1999.

The shabby Viennese settings and episodic structure of Jörg Kalt's *Crash Test Dummies* (2005) recalls *Nordrand*. When Romanians Nicolae and Ana arrive in Vienna to pick up a stolen car, they learn that it has not yet been stolen, which necessitates that they stay in Vienna longer than their visa allows. After a squabble, they separate, and the film stages encounters with Austrian characters to articulate an image of Eastern Europeans torn between the desire for change and for stability. Nicolae, who longs to see Western capitals, has a brief affair with a capricious travel agent. Ana, who is worried about her child in Bucharest, finds a companion in an awkward surveillance clerk. These ties prove temporary, as Ana and Nicolae meet again and drive the car across the Hungarian border at the very moment that EU expansion takes effect. Whereas this film does present interrogations on the border and diverse checks on people's legal status, the border here, unlike in the previous films, loses its association with violent restriction. In the film's portrayal, for example, the body searches Ana and Nicolae endure seem more a hassle than excessive control, and on one occasion the film even uses them for comedic effect. Similarly, the protagonists' final crossing towards Romania is infused with a greater sense of potential and exhibits little of the uncertainty and loss concluding *Nordrand*.

The erosion of borders across parts of post-1989 Europe, fueled by the end of the Cold War and the expansion of the EU, has been coterminous with their reaffirmation in other places through the establishment of the EU's limits, violent nationalisms, tightened restrictions against migrants and refugees, and the mantra of security against "clashing" civilizations. The deconstruction of borders that is undertaken in the works discussed above exhibit this contradiction, which allows the films to highlight the border's illusions and fallacies, while not underestimating its power. As this chapter has shown, by placing the mobilization of the border in the context of

Austrian insecurities within a Europe that is itself undergoing a reconfiguration, the films engage in a critique of repressive Austrian policies and rhetoric against migrants and foreigners, and also reject constructions of Austrian identity defined by what it is not in favor of a more plural, inclusive notion. The films in this study reflect a context that has since ceased to exist, as Austria's physical borders have lost their defensive function following the Schengen expansion of December 2007. Released shortly before that shift, another Austrian film that explores both sides of the former border between east and West, Ulrich Seidl's *Import Export* (2007), perhaps anticipates future trends in the cinematic portrayal of borders. Seidl's film, in which an Austrian goes to the Ukraine, and a Ukrainian to Austria, portrays cross-border traffic, but consciously avoids depicting the border: as Seidl has noted, "I didn't want there to be any physical borders in the film, since in any case they are coming down. Contrary to borders within society, which remain".[12] Even if national borders diminish in significance, borders as sites of contact and separation will surely retain their utility for depicting tension and transition.

Notes

1. The border to the east has also appeared in German films, such as *Halbe Treppe/Grill Point* (2002), *Lichter/Distant Lights* (2003), and *Grenzverkehr /Border Traffic* (2005). See Halle (2007) and Kopp (2007) for readings of these films.
2. Cf. Sadowski-Smith (1999) for a discussion of how the US–Mexican border has been theorized in conjunction with the Iron Curtain, in particular the Berlin Wall.
3. Cf. Johnson and Michaelsen 1997: 1–2.
4. See also Benito and Manzanas (2002: 11–13) for further critique of the optimistic assumptions of border theory; and Morley (2000: 232–34) for a related critique of the romanticized view of nomads, mobility, and hybridity.
5. E.g., *Du bist die Rose vom Wörthersee/Rose of the Mountain* (1952), *Im weissen Rößl/The White Horse Inn* (1960), or *Happyend am Wörthersee/Happy End at the Wörthersee* (1964).
6. E.g., *Der Hofrat Geiger/Counsellor Geiger* (1947), *Ja, ja, die Liebe in Tirol/Yes, Yes, Love in the Tyrol* (1955), *Mariandl* (1961), or *Happyend am Wolfgangsee/Happy End in St Gilgen* (1966).
7. The proprietor is indeed most affected by the failed integration, which is suggested through the camera perspective when Nana leaves. Unlike the majority of the film, the camera does not remain fixed on Nana, but on the proprietor watching her walk away, foregrounding his loss.
8. See the interview on the website of the film's distributors: H. Allahyari and T.-D. Allahyari. 1999. "Absurdistan ist überall." Retrieved 20 October 2007 from: http://www.filmladen.at/gia_intv.htm.
9. This concern with the destabilizing of a fixed notion of ethnicity makes the inclusion of a scene at Marion's workplace now seem less extraneous to the film's plot. Just as Stefan's job is to control who may be admitted to Austria, Marion's profession, an entomologist, demands that she scientifically categorize difference.
10. The song, first heard diegetically on the car radio and then non-diegetically on the soundtrack, is the Kelly Family's "Angel," in which the singer muses, "Sometimes I wish I were an angel, sometimes I wish I weren't here."
11. This is further suggested by the song on the soundtrack, "Seven Seconds" by Neneh Cherry and Youssou N'dour, which describes the responsibilities and uncertainties that emerge when a child is born.

12. Seidl's remarks are taken from an interview contained in the online press kit that accompanied the release of the film. Retrieved 19 December 2007 from: http://importexport.ulrichseidel. com/Import-Export-Press-Folder.pdf.

References

Albert, B. 1999. "Ortsgespräche—Jenseits von Wien-Klischees" [interview], *Neue Zürcher Zeitung*, 20 December, p. 34.

Benito, J. and A.M. Manzanas. 2002. "Border(lands) and Border Writing: Introductory Essay," in J. Benito and A.M. Manzanas (eds), *Literature and Ethnicity in the Cultural Borderlands*. New York: Rodopi, 1–21.

Castillo, D. 1999. "Border Theory and the Canon," in D. Madsen (ed.), *Post-Colonial Literatures: Expanding the Canon*. London: Pluto Press, 180–205.

Fiddler, A. 2006. "Shifting Boundaries: Responses to Multiculturalism at the Turn of the Twenty-First Century," in K. Kohl and R. Roberson (eds), *A History of Austrian Literature 1918–2000*. Rochester, NY: Camden House, 265–90.

Halle, R. 2007. "Views from the German–Polish Border: The Exploration of International Space in *Halbe Treppe* and *Lichter*," *German Quarterly* 80(1): 77–96.

Johnson, D. and S. Michaelsen. 1997. "Border Secrets: An Introduction," in D. Johnson and S. Michaelsen (eds), *Border Theory: The Limits of Cultural Politics*. Minneapolis: University of Minnesota Press, 1–42.

Kopp, K. 2007. "Reconfiguring the Border of Fortress Europe in Hans-Christian Schmid's *Lichter*," *Germanic Review* 82(1): 31–53.

Lamping, D. 2001. *Über Grenzen: eine literarische Topographie*. Göttingen: Vandenhoeck and Ruprecht.

Langer, J. 1999. "Towards a Conceptualization of Border: The Central European Experience," in H. Eskelinen, I. Liikanen and J. Oksa (eds), *Curtains of Iron and Gold: Reconstructing Borders and Scales of Interaction*. Brookfield: Ashgate, 25–42.

Liebhart, K. and A. Pribersky. 2001. "'Wir sind Europa!' Österreich und seine Nachbarn am Goldenen Vorhang," in F.K. Hofer, J. Melchoir and H. Sickinger (eds), *Anlassfall Österreich: Die Europäische Union auf dem Weg zu einer Weltgemeinschaft*. Baden Baden: Nomos, 115–28.

Morley, D. 2000. *Home Territories: Media, Mobility, and Identity*. New York: Routledge.

Perterer, M. 2007. "Die Grenzen auch in den Köpfen abbauen," *Salzburger Nachrichten*, 20 December, p. 1.

Sadowski-Smith, C. 1999. "US Border Theory, Globalization, and Ethnonationalisms in Post-Wall Eastern Europe," *Diaspora* 8(1): 3–22.

Uwer, H. 2007. "Offene Grenze, Angst vor Kriminalität," *Salzburger Nachrichten*, 20 December, p. 6.

Zheng, A. 2001. "Contested Identities and Public Spaces in Recent Austrian Film," *Modern Austrian Literature* 34(1/2): 53–67.

Chapter 17

"The Resentment of One's Fellow Citizens Intensified into a Strong Sense of Community": Psychology and Misanthropy in Frosch's *Total Therapy*, Flicker's *Hold-Up*, and Haneke's *Caché*

Andreas Böhn

> For it was not only the resentment of one's fellow citizens that had become
> intensified there into a strong sense of community; even the lack of faith
> in oneself and one's own fate took on the character of a deep self-certainty.
> —Robert Musil, *The Man without Qualities*

Robert Musil's characterization of *Kakania*, the Austro-Hungarian Empire as it existed until 1918, in his novel *The Man without Qualities*, reflects a basic trait of Austrian culture which can also be recognized in recent Austrian cinema. A remarkable psychological depth and complexity is contrasted by a tendency towards an undermining mistrust of others and oneself, as well as of a rather pessimistic view on the human race in general and neighbors in particular. The peak of Austrian culture in the first decades of the twentieth century abounds with psychological vivisections, be it in narrative or theatrical representations (Schnitzler), in literary and social criticism (Kraus), or in the humanities (Freud). The New Austrian Film of the last two decades has taken up this tradition, often in constructing *huis clos* situations, where people are bound together despite their aversion to each other, and are not only shown as objects of psychological observation, but are depicted as using their skills in observing the other and analyzing their psychical mechanisms in order to manipulate or dominate them. This structure, identified and analyzed in the following films, may not be the ultimate characteristic of the New Austrian Film, if any such thing can be said to exist (Rebhandl 1999: 25), but it is at least one significant trait which can be related to a strong cultural tradition and is more specific than Lim's claim that "the salient quality of Austrian film's new wave is its willingness to confront the abject and emphasize the negative" (Lim 2006).

My first example is *Der Überfall/Hold-Up* (2000), directed by Florian Flicker, which features the anxiety of three people trapped in a little shop. The *huis clos* character of the setting is also stressed by the absurdity of the situation, and the grotesque change of power in the roles of dominator and dominated which subsequently takes place. *Die totale Therapie/Total Therapy* (1996) by director Christian Frosch, which deals with a far larger space and greater number of people, is a tragicomic thriller in which manipulative psychological treatment results in murder and chaos among the visitors to a retreat. To conclude, I will look at Michael Haneke's *Caché/Hidden* (2005), where the basic plot hinges on the idea that the perception by an "other" (here through videotaping) creates a sense of being trapped, generating hostility against those in close proximity (family and friends), and an increasing and destructive mistrust of oneself. Haneke's film seems to sum up my point of analysis vis-à-vis the aforementioned cultural trait(s) and *huis clos* situations.

According to Robert von Dassanowsky, New Austrian Film is characterized by three genres which deal with specific manipulations of popular film: "the cinematic treatment of the folk play; the social-critical drama, which had been transformed by the experience of Nazism, and now tended toward allegorical or psychological explorations; and the cabaret-inspired comedy film" (Dassanowsky 2005: 239–40). Some examples of the latter can even be seen as a combination of all three genres. The cabaret-inspired comedy film, or simply *Kabarettfilm*, appears in the early 1990s as a new genre which inherits the tradition of the Austrian *Volksstück*, traditional popular plays (Standún 2006: 67), at least with respect to the depiction of society and individual characters:

> The Austrian society shown within these Austrian popular plays is portrayed as being vicious and hypocritical, a baroque facade with a dirty backyard. Kindness is combined with falseness, and even humor becomes nasty. The main idea that motivates the new Austrian popular play is the aesthetics of the ugly, which is achieved by an attempt to portray Austrian life in all its squalor and harshness. (ibid.: 68)

Regina Standún also discerns three types of Austrian cabaret films and characterizes them as follows:

> stand-up comedy scripts that originate in stand-up comedians' programs (e.g. *Indien/ India* (Harather 1993)) ... Films that employ stand-up comedians, but whose original scripts were written either by the auteur-director or by a literary writer (e.g. *Komm, süßer Tod/Come, Sweet Death* (Murnberger 2000)) ... The documentary or semi-documentary (e.g. *Hundstage/Dog Days* (Seidl, 2000)) that can be classified as popular film, even though the cast does not consist of comedians. In such films the line between aesthetic staging and documentary is blurred ... All three categories of cabaret films

have one common thread: showing the harsh side of life in Austria, which strangely enough makes the audience laugh, albeit a laughter that sticks in the throat. (ibid.: 69)

To briefly illustrate the depiction of "normal" lives and what sort of humor this notion of popular film contains, I point to Ulrich Seidl's *Hundstage*, which observes what has been called the "everyday fascism" of an Austrian suburb. Richard Falcon highlights a scene of humiliation in the film which does not result in revenge, but another humiliation which takes place between the former humiliators, involving a grotesque employment of the Austrian national anthem: "Any director who devises a scene in which a pornographer with a lit candle up his arse is forced at gunpoint to sing the Austrian national anthem ("A nation blessed by its sense of beauty, Highly praised Austria") clearly has views on the subject [the actual situation of Austria at the turn of the century] that deserve to be heard" (Falcon 2002: 53). Taking this example into account, we can state that Standún's concept of cabaret film covers a rather wide range of the "comic" as well as the "popular." These films are popular in the sense of attracting a rather widespread audience, but also in depicting the life of "ordinary" people, mostly from the lower classes. This circularity of presenting an audience that which already forms part of everyday life can also be noticed at the level of characters and plot, because "these films, without exception, depict what might be best described as one of society's losers, who is trapped by his environment and remains so at the end of the film" (Standún 2006: 69–70). There is also no escape for the protagonists from their social milieu, just as the spectators cannot escape the norm of their lives upon entering the theatre of illusion.

People being trapped and their reaction to this threatening situation are common to the plots I will examine here. Of course, not all Austrian cabaret films are based on such a situation, but one of the first (and one of the most famous), Paul Harather's *Indien/India* (1993), begins with the encounter of the two protagonists who must work together as restaurant inspectors in the Austrian countryside, which means that they spend a great deal of their time travelling together in one car. The actors portraying this "odd-couple" are the comedians Alfred Dorfer and Josef Hader, who also wrote the script. So potent is their cabaret-style performance, that we are aware during the very first minutes of their appearance in the film that their relationship will be adversarial. The camera gives a static view of them through the windshield of the car. Neither speaks. As the film progresses, they take turns in delivering long monologues, and the spectator is able to relate to the lack of interest each has for the other's thoughts. Both seem to be trapped in a situation they cannot escape, and the restricted space inside the car is the perfect setting for this uncomfortable non-relationship. Antonin Svoboda bases his more recent *Immer nie am Meer/Forever Never Anywhere* (2007) totally on this sort of claustrophobic constellation. There, three men are trapped together in a Mercedes Benz for days following an accident. Instead of helping them escape, the boy who discovers them treats them like new pets in a cage.

Florian Flicker's *Der Überfall/Hold-Up* (2000) is related to the cabaret film through actors Josef Hader, one of the leading exponents of the genre, and Roland

Düringer, who had previously collaborated on the script of Harald Sicheritz's *Muttertag/Mother's Day* (1993)—an early example "of the successful transfer of cabaret theater to feature film" which "was one of the bona fide box-office successes of 1993–94 and demonstrated that contemporary social comedy about the average Austrian had the attention of the nation" (Dassanowsky 2005: 251)—and the highly popular *Hinterholz 8* (1998). In *Der Überfall*, Düringer plays Andreas Berger, an underdog with no job and no money, who lives separated from his wife and son in the apartment of his sister, whose husband, a policeman, constantly reminds him that he is living off the generosity of his relatives. Because he has no money to buy a present for his son, he decides to rob a bank, but just as he enters his target, he discovers someone has already done the job. He hides in a small tailor's shop and takes its owner, Böckl (Joachim Bissmeier), and his client, Kopper (Hader), hostage. Much of the action consists of these three men fighting, more verbally than physically. Utilizing the very restricted space, the camera follows the protagonists claustrophobically but avoids the cliché of emotionalizing close-ups. While it is apparent that these men are from the lower ranks of society, they each believe themselves better than the next and look down on one another. To deal with their trap, the trio regroup in various coalitions. The two hostages are originally united against the robber, but then Kopper attempts to befriend Berger, and in the end Böckl and Berger work together against Kopper, who is shot by the police because he is mistaken for another bank robber. Berger escapes with the stolen money and is happy that he can now buy his son a present; the bank clerk claims a far higher sum than was actually taken; and Böckl, who witnessed the robbery, does not correct the "error," so we can assume that he will share the profits with the clerk. The police have solved the case by shooting the (false) robber Kopper, though the money has disappeared. For everyone other than the dead victim, the conclusion provides a very happy ending.

Although the film vacillates between dark comedy and tragedy, it is rather funny, although laughter seems often quite inappropriate. The characters are presented in an exaggerated, but not totally unrealistic way. They show patterns of behavior and of speech that are characteristic of their social milieu. Nevertheless, they are more than clichéd types, and therefore we do not easily laugh at them, even if they act in a grotesque and awkward way. The source of the comedy stems primarily from the absurdity of the situation and the chain of events. Each step of the protagonist entails another disaster whereby his plans are continuously thwarted and damage is inflicted on him. He wants to rob a bank, but is outdone by someone else; he tries to hide in the tailor's shop and in his desperate state decides to rob the shop owner, although the available cash is hardly worth the effort; he feels compelled to take the shop owner and his client hostage, which deprives him of the possibility of immediate escape; he notices that he has trapped himself, gets angry and abuses his hostages, which he regrets. The conclusion of the film plays fortune and fate in a most cynical way, as Berger ultimately achieves his (criminal) goal despite his unskillful attempts, the robbery victims (shop owner and bank clerk) profit from being robbed, and the innocent bystander Kopper, who tried to be polite and helpful, is taken for the criminal and shot dead.

The often uncomfortable combination of tragic and comic elements which sabotage the spectator's expectation of a traditional thriller can also be found in *Die totale Therapie/Total Therapy* (1996), the feature debut of Christian Frosch, which is set in a country retreat where a therapist's murder sets the tone for chaos among the visitors. In a Hitchcockian manner, the audience is made aware that a client has obviously been freed from her problems and can bury her guru and her old life together. It is a "wry look at New Age religion and pop psychology, [and] the film metaphorically attacks political populism and cultism in Austria" (Dassanowsky 2005: 252).

The secluded situation of the retreat corresponds at the level of space to the construction of the plot. People from different social backgrounds come together more or less voluntarily because they suffer from psychological problems, troubled relationships, or simply want to improve their professional performance. The spatial isolation is paradoxically confronted with the therapeutic maxim of freeing oneself from all boundaries and restrictions, to open up the deeper emotional levels, to express oneself overtly. This methodology holds out the promise of improvement for clients if they follow these dictums to the letter. But in truth, this again signifies isolation as the sadistic cult leader and head therapist Dr Romero (Blixa Bargeld) attempts to break his clients' free will and force dependence on them. When he attempts to rape Gabi (Ursula Ofner), a woman who has proven to be the most reluctant of his patients, she stabs him to death, and ironically proves the success of his method. She feels transformed and freed of her mental constraints. Even her allergies disappear as she subsequently proceeds to kill all the therapists and clients at the center.

During the scene of the first killing, we see Dr Romero behind a closed window crying for help, but with the exception of the viewer, nobody hears or sees him, although the people we see in the foreground would only have to turn their eyes in his direction. A similar situation occurs at the end of the film, when Gabi's sister Hedwig (Sophie Rois) arrives by car. The camera shot from inside the car captures one of the participants signaling danger, but Hedwig does not notice and keeps on driving. Both scenes can be read as allegories of a secluded threat or horror in society, something which we should know about (possibly to save our and other's lives) but which nevertheless remains hidden from us, whether we block the threat consciously or unconsciously, or simply ignore the world around us. Hedwig is killed when she picks up her sister. The seclusion from the outside world frees up the secluded inside—a "total therapy"—which liberates one through the death of all others. Before this climactic ending, a great deal of violent aggression has been released among the "trapped" participants, which also manifests itself in the killing of therapists and clients. The isolation and abusive psychological training has strengthened the will and ability of the clients to fight each other.

While the director allows the audience to know what characters in the film do not, the film offers the spectator little conventional tension. A camera that remains predominantly in a neutral position only gives the spectator a detached view, which in its distancing underscores the sociopolitical allegory that plays here beyond the fantasy of horror and its expected emotional manipulation, but in order for the spectator to question what it is that they actually desire from this type of film. Only once does Frosch manipulate the spectator to "take sides" in traditional thriller/ horror film convention by murdering a character who is the most selfish and arrogant of all the participants. But in doing so, the spectator is made aware of this manipulation and it gives little satisfaction. Rather, the fact that the spectator has become numb to the slaughter and would easily fall to such "total therapy" becomes clear. The dispersed focalization of the film as it deals with a group of people rather than a few protagonists that a traditional camera would frame for moral or ethical spectatorial "leadership," contributes strongly to the overall experimental form of the presentation.

Michael Haneke's *Caché/Hidden* (2005) confronts us with a much more sophisticated and complex meditation on seclusion and its spectatorial possibilities. I will survey the wide critical reception of the film and concentrate on only one circumstance in the context of the other two examples; that is, *Caché's* metaperspective on isolation and observation. It is an intensification of a tendency which can already be observed earlier in Haneke's work, as Justin Vicari notes: "We are always aware in Haneke that we are helplessly watching—like his camera that only watches, never underscoring, never intervening" (Vicari 2006: n.p.). The spectator is forced into the position of being an uninvolved and detached viewer, although what they see is in fact very touching and calls for emotional participation, which might result in the feeling that we do not really want to see what the camera lets us see, that we feel uncomfortable in our position as observers of social experiments arranged before our eyes. Vicari follows this cinematic ideology through Haneke's films before *Caché*, pointing out the aspect of a counter-emotional satisfaction process with no alternative and a determined ending which the action on the screen has for the viewer:

> As a result, his films can be grueling. The systematic psychological and physical destruction of the family in *Funny Games* (1997) takes place seemingly in real time, uninterruptedly. Neither the authorities nor the filmmaker will step in to restore even a temporary sense of order or breathing room. Similarly, Erika Kohut's devastating self-destructiveness in *The Piano Teacher* is a mechanism that, once put into motion, cannot be stopped. One thinks of those little wind-up toys that hurtle spasmodically forward and will tumble off the edge of the table unless someone catches them. ("I'm just winding you up," a film director tells an actor and actress to prepare them for a scene, in one of the many sequences about filmmaking in *Code Unknown*.) But this saving agency rarely occurs. When it does occur, startlingly, in *Funny Games*—one of the killers suddenly rewinds the film to make the action turn out differently—it is not in the service of rescue, but rather of greater destruction. The only certainty in Haneke's films is that the world we know will come to a violent end, right before our eyes. The only questions are, how quickly and by what means. (ibid.)

In *Caché*, the camera view, that of a video monitor, is introduced in the situation itself. The first shot of the film shows us a narrow street in a French town which leads to an ordinary house where, we are invited to assume, the drama will evolve. This static establishing shot—that is what we take it for so far—lasts a bit too long and shows too little in terms of typical film convention. The spectator begins to detach from trust in the film at its very start: one begins looking for hidden clues and rethinking obvious details, like the street sign reading rue des Iris, which might refer not only to a certain flower but also to the iris of the eye and therefore the very act of viewing.

Ara Osterweil stresses the point that in reflecting on our act of watching we become involved in the relationship between viewer and viewed which is central to the film. The spectator has become complicit in the film's concept of spying and "official" monitoring in the post-private world.

> When Georges, the privileged white subject, is made the object rather than master of surveillance technology, he becomes stigmatized by the very technology designed to protect affluent people like him from criminal and racial otherness. Once he is under observation, not only is Georges incapable of deflecting the surveillance, but he is incapable of convincing his family and his colleagues (and the audience) of his innocence. (Osterweil 2006: 38)

The thriller-like plot involving a family under threat is common to *Caché* as well as to *Funny Games*, and in both cases the self-referential and reflexive use of the remote control causes a distancing from the genre structures these films display at first sight. Wheatley describes these genre rules, borrowed from Hollywood cinema, which contribute to the emotional involvement of the spectators but then are contrasted by the anti-illusionist use of the rewind or fast-forward in the movie:

> *Funny Games*, like *Hidden* [*Caché*], combines a familiar narrative scenario—the family under threat from an outside source—with classical suspense strategies in order to situate the film within the thriller genre. The earlier work, based on the question of whether, when and how the family might escape, uses the internal rewind as its trump card, hitting the spectator with it at the exact moment when they are most caught up in the film's fantasy of retribution and escape, thus violently shattering the cinematic illusion. In *Hidden*, centered on the epistemological conundrum of who is persecuting whom and why, the fast-forward functions as a warning to the spectator not to get too involved in what they see on screen, to be distrustful or at least skeptical. For it is introducing a film in which simulation and dissimulation form the twin pillars not just of the narrative but of the structure. (Wheatley 2006: 32)

We could also say the question of reliability arises not only at the level of the plot but also with respect to the film itself. The camera perspective of many shots that should be taken by a surveillance camera cannot be integrated into the constitutive assumption of the story that there is someone inside the story taking all these shots. Wheatley interprets this fact as a signaling of this assumption's fictionality: "One problem that poses itself is that the vast majority of the taped scenes are shot from seemingly 'impossible' angles.... So what's going on? As one of Haneke's anti-heroes tells us at the end of *Funny Games*, 'The fiction is real'. Or rather, the real is fiction" (ibid.: 33).

What at first sight may look like a classical transgression of the reality created inside the fictional work—a breaking of the illusion based on the coherence of a fictitious world and its presentation, or a Brechtian *Verfremdung*, as Tarja Laine (2004) suggests with respect to *Funny Games*—can also be taken as a repetition of the production of uncertainty and uneasiness, something which occurs at the plot level, then on the level of the reception of the movie, as Paul Arthur suggests:

> Haneke specializes in what Alexander Horwath labels 'boundary transgression' narratives, in which upscale professionals—cushioned from harsh realities by racial and class privilege, as well as by an illusion of control derived from televised news programming—become suddenly vulnerable to hostile outsiders or, alternatively, to subversive acts from within the family circle, frequently committed by children.... We feel insecure, stressed, threatened by elusive forces whose connection to us as individuals is obscure. Yet we can't quite shake rumbles of complicity, of having acceded to something for which we will ultimately be held accountable and from which our unprecedented standard of living cannot protect us. It is this heart of darkness that beats beneath the icy surface of Haneke's films. (Arthur 2005: 25)

By "we" Arthur is referring not only to the protagonists but also to the film's spectators, and we are forced into the role of voyeurs by someone we cannot locate inside the depicted world and by means we cannot clearly grasp with the intellectual and emotional tools of our trusted filmic conventions.

We as an audience are trapped in a role we do not like, and we feel obliged to accept a rather pessimistic view of human relations. Whereas in our first two examples isolation made the gaze of the other uncanny, in *Caché* it is the gaze itself that produces isolation. Dassanowsky states that:

> the new socially critical film has quickly become the genre typically associated with current Austrian cinema. But this type of filmmaking is not as new as it appears to be. It represents a resurfaced continuity of Austrian film and themes regarding national identity, national representation, and sociopolitical/gender-role-related dissension that were present at the very start of the national cinema. (Dassanowsky 2005: 283)

Whereas *Der Überfall/ Hold-Up* and *Die totale Therapie/Total Therapy* can be taken as still belonging to this sociocritical genre, prolonging a tradition of intertwined psychology and misanthropy, *Caché* goes one innovative and disturbing step further by intensifying this genre and its traditions to a point where it turns into its own transgression and reflection.

References

Arthur, P. 2005. "Endgame," *Film Comment* 41(6): 24–28.

Dassanowsky, R. von. 2005. *Austrian Cinema: A History*. Jefferson, NC: McFarland.

Falcon, R. 2002. "Cruel Intentions," *Sight and Sound* 12(9): 52–53.

Laine, T. 2004. "'What Are You Looking At and Why?' Michael Haneke's *Funny Games* (1997) with his Audience," in "A Slap in the Face: The Films and Philosophy of Michael Haneke," *Kinoeye: New Perspectives on European Film*, special issue, 4(1): n.p.

Lim, D. 2006. "Greetings from the Land of Feel-bad Cinema," *New York Times*, 26 November, p. 14.

Musil, R. 1995. *The Man without Qualities, Vol. 1*, trans. S. Wilkins. London: Knopf.

Osterweil, A. 2006. "Caché," *Film Quarterly* 59(4): 35–39.

Standún, R. 2006. "On the Road to Nowhere? Contemporary Austrian Popular Film," *New Cinemas: Journal of Contemporary Film* 4(1): 67–76.

Vicari, J. 2006. "Films of Michael Haneke: The Utopia of Fear," *Jump Cut* 48: n.p. Retrieved 14 May 2009 from: http://www.ejumpcut.org/archive/jc48.2006/Haneke/text.html.

Wheatley, C. 2006. "Secrets, Lies and Videotape," *Sight and Sound* 16(2): 32–36.

Chapter 18

Trapped Bodies, Roaming Fantasies: Mobilizing Constructions of Place and Identity in Florian Flicker's *Suzie Washington*

Gundolf Graml

When Nana Iaschwili, a teacher of French from the former Soviet republic of Georgia, arrives at the airport in Vienna, Austria, she only expects a brief layover before boarding her connecting flight to Los Angeles, where she wants to visit her uncle. However, the ticket agent discovers that Nana's passport and visa to the United States have been forged. Nana is arrested, interrogated, and then scheduled for deportation within forty-eight hours. Her request to remain in Austria or to be handed over to a neighboring country is rejected. By chance, Nana is able to escape from the airport and boards the bus of an American tourist group bound for the Austrian lake district. Pursued by the police, Nana begins an at times bizarre journey through Austria's tourist landscape. On her trip she encounters lonesome male tourists looking for a holiday fling, as well as smugglers and criminals preying on illegal migrants. Eventually, Nana will find her way across the Austrian–German border into an uncertain future.

Reviews of Florian Flicker's *Suzie Washington* (1998) highlight an interesting tension between, on the one hand, the film's depiction of the protagonist as a helpless victim of the collaboration between the tourism industry and state bureaucracy, and, on the other, as a resourceful and resilient agent. One critic emphasizes the first point when he writes that Nana's rejection at the airport rips the veil off "the postcard scenery of the Austrian countryside" (Rooney 1998). German film critic Thorsten Krüger addresses the second point when he applauds the film as "a road movie" (Krüger 1998), as does Nicole Hess (1999).[1] Both reviews use the term "road movie" to highlight the protagonist's seemingly unperturbed determination to reach her goal despite the many obstacles she faces.

I will elaborate on this tension between Nana as victim and as smart "survivor" in a strange tourism wonderland. First, I will discuss the film's critique of Austria's image and tourism industry in the context of the country's increasingly xenophobic immigration policy of the early 1990s. Specifically, I will argue that Nana's arrest at the airport and her subsequent journey through Austria reveal the racism underlying apparently objective differentiations between tourists and (im)migrants. Second, I will problematize the categorization of *Suzie Washington* as a road movie. I will show that Flicker's film is less concerned with the heroine's arrival at a particular destination, and more with the mobilizing of narratives of identities and places among a (presumably Western) audience.

How to Recognize a Tourist

Throughout the film, *Suzie Washington* highlights the collaboration between the tourist industry and police on both a local and a global level. Nana will encounter airline representatives, tour guides, and hotel owners who function as "double agents." It begins with the friendly ticket agent at Vienna airport, who does not just facilitate the flow of tourists by pointing travelers to their connecting flights, but who, by verifying passports, also serves the Austrian state, the supranational policing structure of the European Union, as well as the United States' immigration authorities. Later in the film, the Austrian guide on the American tour bus and a hotel owner also combine the welcoming of their guests with the demand to see their passports.

This double function also applies to spaces and places. While the airport symbolizes, at least in the Western imagination, almost unlimited mobility and freedom, it becomes an insurmountable barrier for people who do not meet the criteria of "traveler" or "tourist." *Suzie Washington* highlights the double function of the airport by cinematographic means. At first, Nana's arrival at the airport is filmed with a somewhat blurry handheld camera, which mimics the cinematography of holiday videos produced by tourists. Nana's interrogation by the airport police and, especially, her subsequent stay in the transit zone are captured by a much steadier camera, which follows Nana through a series of long shots as she aimlessly wanders among the duty-free shops and souvenir kiosks. Several horizontal long shots from outside the glass walls of the transit area underscore Nana's status as an object of a controlling gaze. Moreover, a high-angle shot of Nana provides the viewer with the perspective of a ceiling-mounted surveillance camera. As a consequence of this change in cinematography, the airport is transformed from a space representing freedom and mobility into a holding pen for undesirable foreigners.

The airport is the most obvious example of the double function of tourism, but other spaces and places are shown in similar ways. Whether Nana sits in a bus, takes a boat across a lake, hitchhikes on the autobahn, or takes a ski lift up into the mountains, instead of facilitating her travel, these spaces frequently force her to reveal her identity or to choose from a set of predetermined identity narratives. More than just an indication of the commodification of Austria's landscapes in the era of globalization (Zheng 2001: 60), the depiction of tourism and transit spaces as hindering the mobility of illegal migrants resonates with the heated debates about Austria's immigration politics of the early 1990s.

The fall of the Iron Curtain in 1989 and Austria's status as a prospective member of the EU produced irrational fears that Austria would soon be overrun by foreigners (Reisigl and Wodak 2001: 147). As soon as former communist countries in Eastern Europe relaxed their travel restrictions, the Austrian government felt compelled to reiterate "that it was not a country of immigration" (ibid.: 149). Moreover, in 1992 and 1993, the right-wing Freedom Party (FPÖ) under its chairman Jörg Haider pushed the more mainstream Christian Conservatives (ÖVP) and the Social Democrats (SPÖ) to pass a series of laws that severely restricted access to Austria for potential immigrants and political refugees.[2]

Nana's arrest in the airport's transit zone illustrates the significant change in attitude that Austria began to exhibit towards foreigners, especially when compared to Austrians' willingness to support refugees from Eastern bloc countries at crucial points during the era after the Second World War. The "various degrees of enthusiasm" (ibid.: 149) with which Austrians received those fleeing the Stalinist anti-revolutionary actions in Hungary, Czechoslovakia, and Poland was, to a certain degree, based on the fact that the vast majority of these refugees would move on to settle in other countries.[3] However, in these historical cases, Austria at least functioned as a transit zone, with revolving doors at both ends, so to speak. In the early 1990s, the doors had become harder for foreigners to open, except for one group: "Incidentally, the only foreigners entitled to *Gemütlichkeit* these days, it seems, are those who do not come from Eastern and Southern Europe and Third-World countries, and who come—as tourists—to spend money" (ibid.: 147–48).

The supposedly self-evident difference between tourists and illegal migrants or asylum seekers is what is under scrutiny in *Suzie Washington*. In often satirical ways, the film highlights the fact that these identity positions are constructed socially and culturally. Whether a person appears to be a tourist or a migrant is contingent not so much on this person's behavior but more on—often unacknowledged—Western traditions of seeing, identifying, and categorizing this behavior as indicative of a particular race, ethnicity, or gender. As Nira Yuval-Davis describes it, an ethnic "collectivity constructs itself and 'its interest'" through a series of "political processes" (Yuval-Davis 1997: 44) that often rely on ideas of "manhood and womanhood" (ibid.: 23). In several scenes, Flicker's film demonstrates how the interest of an ethnically "pure" Austria or the interest of Western male characters determine whether Nana is perceived as a threatening illegal migrant or an exotic foreign tourist.[4]

At the film's beginning, Nana's Georgian passport and her accented English frame her as an "ethnic other" in ways that attract the attention of the Austrian police. Yet, shortly thereafter, this apparently objective categorization is revealed as arbitrary and based on racist and gendered "interests" of the dominant Austrian/Western collective: When another illegal migrant resists deportation and causes an armed showdown with the airport police, Nana uses the confusion and slips out of the transit area. She dons the blue coat of a cleaning woman and pushes the cart with cleaning utensils down the corridors of the airport. The fact that none of the policemen she encounters pays any attention to her suggests that the threatening visibility of the foreign "other" can turn into invisibility when this other serves the economic interest of the Austrian/Western collective. As art historian Martin A. Berger writes, "[i]mages do not persuade us to internalize racial values embedded within them.... Instead of selling us on racial systems we do not already own, the visual field powerfully confirms previously internalized beliefs" (Berger 2005: 1). In other words, when the presence of the ethnic or racial "other" does not disturb the ethnic self-image of the dominant collective, it is not even included in the picture.

The film continues to mock Austrian/Western essentialist assumptions after Nana boards an American tour bus. The Austrian guide never questions the teacher's claim that she is an American tourist. In a stereotypical manner, he seems to accept Nana's accent and her appearance as typical for the ethnic configuration of the United States as a racial and ethnic "melting pot." His polite and welcoming attitude towards Nana might be prompted by his imagination of the American nation as a politically and culturally powerful collective with which Austria desires to have good relations. Later, the innkeeper of the small hotel where Nana finds a room displays a similar attitude: she treats the American "guest" very politely and, in the face of a persistent language barrier, postpones registration and payment until the next day.

Finally, *Suzie Washington* highlights how much the perspective of male erotic desire shapes the perception of ethnicity, nationality, and class. On her way to the above-mentioned hotel, Nana—who now travels under the pseudonym Suzie Washington—meets the German tourist Herbert Korn. The quiet and somewhat clumsy middle-aged loner is attracted immediately to the American tourist and invites her to dinner. He even buys a swimsuit for her, hoping that she will join him for a midnight swim in the lake. Herbert is pleasantly surprised to learn that Nana/ Suzie travels without a companion, obviously hoping for a holiday fling to spice up his vacation. Thus, although Herbert is not of the aggressive type, his demeanor nonetheless reflects a Western male perspective that perceives the body of the female "other" as a potential "destination," as an "imagined territory" open for exploration (Rojek and Urry 1997: 17).

These scenes illustrate that *Suzie Washington* criticizes tourism not just for its foregrounding of what Rooney calls "the postcard scenery of the Austrian countryside" (Rooney 1998). Rather, tourism is shown to be a set of discourses that shapes decisively the very objects and people it then represents. I contend that tourism should be included among what Stuart Hall calls the "'machineries' and regimes of representation in a culture ... [which] play a *constitutive* and not merely a reflexive, after-the-event, role" (Hall 1996: 443). While Nana's money and her claim that she is "not a criminal [but a] tourist" does not convince the female police officer during her interrogation at Vienna airport, Nana's performances as Suzie Washington become believable when they meet the tacit (male) desires and fantasies of the dominant collective, or when her performances match the visual traditions through which West European subjects identify racial and ethnic differences. In so doing, *Suzie Washington* reveals that Austria's defense of its immigration policies as simply separating the legal travelers from the illegal ones based on objective criteria relies on wishful thinking.

The Limits of Performance

It is safe to assume that Nana's/Suzie's temporarily successful performance as a tourist, and her flexibility in coping with constantly changing circumstances, among other things, prompted critics and audiences to view *Suzie Washington* as a road movie. In the context of my discussion of Nana's/Suzie's struggle with essentialist identity categories, David Laderman's definition of the European derivation of the road movie seems to fit well with Flicker's film. While American road movies often show their heroes engaged in criminal activities on their way "outside of society," Laderman argues that European road movies focus more on the "psychological, emotional, and spiritual states" of their protagonists and have them move "into national cultures, tracing the meaning of citizenship as a journey" (Laderman 2002: 248).

As viewers, we get an idea of Nana's/Suzie's psychological state of mind, her desires, and her worries through several postcards to her uncle in Los Angeles, which she narrates in voiceover at various moments in the film. Nana/Suzie "writes" the first postcard while she is locked up in the airport's transit zone: "Dear Uncle, I'm on my way. Not in time, but closer than ever before. I'm sorry to say my flight to Los Angeles will be delayed. But please don't worry. I'm fine. It's been years of waiting, so a few more days won't matter. See you soon. Maybe tomorrow. Love." Later, after she boards the tour bus, Nana/Suzie writes another postcard further explaining her delay: "Dear Uncle, Everything changed. I decided to take a little trip to the countryside. There was so much excitement over the last few days. I need some time to relax. So, I will travel around a little bit, take a deep breath and—you know."

At first, these postcard narratives seem to demonstrate that tourism is not just an oppressive subsection of the economy that collaborates with law enforcement, but, rather, an opportunity for emancipation insofar as it opens up new spaces. Numerous recent theoretical approaches in fact view tourism as a "set of cultural practices" that harbors the potential for spatial change through performative acts: "In the spaces of tourism and leisure, social and spatial identities collide and elide, creating moments of 'uncertainty.' The uncertainties expose the margins of categories, such as tourists and nontourists, and make present the struggles that arise as tourists and nontourists try to either reinforce or break down … tenuous social and spatial borders" (Del Casino and Hanna 2003: xxi). Along the same lines, David Crouch regards tourism as an example of a "spatial practice" whose aim is "not to return or imagine a past, but to creatively enliven, to repeat only the possibility of a new, unique moment" (Crouch 1999: 4).

Nana's performance as the American tourist Suzie Washington result in several creative and unique moments that help her to evade the police and fool tourism officials. By providing her own voiceover "captions" to images of these landscapes, Nana/Suzie creates an interactive relationship between the places observed and the narrative place of the observer, a practice that helps her to maintain an idea of agency: "I decided to take a little trip to the countryside," she writes, transforming the chance escape from the airport into a voluntary decision and the rather hostile spatial surroundings into an almost welcoming place.

Viewed from a slightly different angle, the postcard narratives also underscore the film's categorization as a road movie. While it is somewhat doubtful from the very beginning as to whether the heroine does have an uncle in Los Angeles, the postcards make it clear that this uncle is an invention. What drives Nana's/Suzie's journey is not the uncle, but rather the aura of Los Angeles. For the teacher from Georgia, a country traumatized by decades of Stalinist rule and then ravaged by civil war, Los Angeles means Hollywood, which in turn constitutes the final destination—either concretely or metaphorically—of innumerable road movies and filmic fantasies in general. In other words, in her postcards, Nana/Suzie readjusts her desires and fantasies of freedom according to her current situation. The distance between her and Los Angeles symbolizes the distance to freedom. By alluding to cinema's commercial side, *Suzie Washington* almost reflexively questions its genre and, by extension, postmodern interpretations of mass media as empowering and emancipating.

A closer look at a crucial scene will illustrate this criticism further. Both readings of the postcard narratives—as spatial performances and as a narrative construction of her desire for happiness—converge in a climactic scene that shows Nana/Suzie in her hotel room, lying on the bed and emptying the contents of the minibar. While she zaps through the TV channels, she formulates yet another postcard to her fictitious uncle:

> Dear Uncle, The weather is fine. And people here are rich and friendly. I found a nice hotel with hot water, drinks for free, and thirty-two TV channels. This is not America, but my first holiday since honeymoon, I guess, and a good place to hang around. So I will do my best. Los Angeles is far away, and so am I. Please don't forget me.

In this scene, Nana/Suzie seems to be able to forge a space for herself by performing as a tourist, by imitating a series of "cultural codes" that symbolize "proper forms of conduct" when engaging in a tourist trip (Edensor 2002: 95): she goes into the hotel room, takes a shower, lies down on her bed, watches TV, and consumes snacks and drinks from the minibar. The postcard narrative supplements this founding of a new space by providing a storyline that enables Nana/Suzie to "inscribe" herself into the social spaces of tourism. In this sense, the postcards illustrate Michel de Certeau's observation that "a story even has distributive power and performative force (it does what it says) when an ensemble of circumstances is brought together. Then it founds spaces" (de Certeau 1984: 123, emphasis removed).

By referring to the thirty-two TV channels, Nana/Suzie links this founding of spaces with mass-media influenced imagination. Her casual way of using the remote control and her almost childlike joy at the abundance of channels seems to resonate with cultural theorist Arjun Appadurai's claim that consuming globalized mass media also "provokes resistance, irony, selectivity, and in general, agency" (Appadurai 2000: 7). According to Appadurai, the consumption of globalized mass media must be understood as working in the space of "imagination," which he defines as "a space of contestation in which individuals and groups seek to annex the global into their own practices of the modern" (ibid.: 4). Appadurai emphasizes that though consumption is not a liberatory practice it is a pleasurable one, and, as he concludes, "where there is pleasure there is agency" (ibid.: 7).

The curiosity and also confidence with which Nana/Suzie zaps through the channels seem to prove that she is able to exert some form of control over the commodified world by successfully imagining herself on an extended vacation, reminiscent of her honeymoon. Indeed, for a moment it seems possible to view the film as a road movie whose heroine overcomes bureaucratic obstacles by relying on being street smart, imaginative, and exercising agency.

Yet, Nana's/Suzie's previously mentioned dinner with German tourist Herbert Korn exemplifies how the protagonist's spatial performances and imagination are insufficient to overcome the deeply ingrained essentialisms that shape narratives of national and cultural identity. At some point between the main course and dessert, Nana/Suzie decides to reveal that she is not an American tourist but, rather, an illegal migrant without a passport. Herbert, whose *Palatschinken* (sweet pancakes) have just arrived, reacts to the news by looking down at his plate and ripping apart the egg-and-flour omelets with the following words: "This is an Austrian specialty. The emperor liked it so much, he brought it with him from Hungary. He even refined it, shredded it. Now it's called 'Emperor's Delight' (*Kaiserschmarrn*). A specialty, too."

Herbert's description of how a Hungarian dish became an Austrian specialty seems to acknowledge that identities are socially and culturally constructed categories. However, by detailing further the dessert's Austrianization through an imperial act of simultaneous refining and shredding, Herbert illustrates what Homi Bhabha calls "the violence involved in establishing the nation's writ" (Bhabha 1990: 310). In other words, not by imaginatively appropriating and redefining spaces, but only by subjecting herself to a rather violent national and cultural reorientation, might Nana/Suzie be able to overcome the cultural and national boundaries that hinder her journey.

This reaffirmation of institutionalized power over definitions of individual identity is followed by several scenes that foreground Nana's/Suzie's inability to keep up with her performance as an American tourist. She wakes up the next morning only to discover her photo next to a large "Wanted!" headline in Austria's Yellow Press. After hitching a ride with a Viennese family to the nearest autobahn rest area, she negotiates with a trucker to take her to Hamburg. Unbeknownst to her, the trucker is part of a human-trafficking ring. Thus, after she spends the night in his truck cabin, he abandons her at a gas station, whose owner turns out to be yet another accomplice of the traffickers. The smugglers transport her and a couple of other illegal migrants to a ski lift which will carry them further up into the mountains.

While Nana's/Suzie's performances as an American tourist in the film's first part mocked the arbitrariness and artificiality of the tourism industry, the second part offers a view of the exploitative and criminal flipside of tourism enterprises. The transportation infrastructure with its freight trucks, gas stations, and roads in general, as well as the tourism infrastructure with ski lifts and tour buses in particular, now appear as engaged in both the legal and the illegal and exploitative movement of people by default.

Suzie Washington highlights this connection in the form of the van in which the human traffickers carry Nana/Suzie and the other illegal bordercrossers to the ski lift. In a brief shot of the van's door we glimpse a company logo identifying the vehicle as a tour bus for a "*Sound of Music* Tour." Florian Flicker calls the 1965 Hollywood production the "grandmother" of his own film and posits the use of this logo in connection with illegal bordercrossing as a symbol of hope: "In the same region, where *The Sound of Music* was shot 30 years ago, people are today still looking for an escape path into the 'new world'" (Flicker 1999: 102). While it is certainly legitimate to describe the historic event of the Trapp family's emigration from Nazi-occupied Austria as an escape to the New World, the 1965 Hollywood rendition of this event, as well as the several *Sound of Music* tours that have emerged in and around Salzburg are, if anything, escapist narratives rather than escape routes (see Vansant 1999; Graml 2005).

The misuse of the *Sound of Music* tour bus in an enterprise that further exploits people in an already desperate situation can only be viewed as an ironic comment on the powerful "mediascapes" (Appadurai 2000: 33) that have formed themselves around the *Sound of Music* narrative. The scene discredits mass-mediated fantasies and, by extension, also ultimately reveals Nana's/Suzie's goal to reach Los Angeles to be a flawed desire: as the van symbolizes, instead of delivering on the promise of liberation, globalized media fantasies and the corporate conglomerates behind them only take their consumers hostage.

The film finally discards the idea of imagination as potentially liberating in one of the last sequences. After the ski lift has transported Nana/Suzie to the alpine Austrian–German borderland, she loses her way and, in the impending darkness, seeks refuge in a mountain hut where hikers can buy dinner and stay overnight. The inn keeper seems to doubt Nana's/Suzie's narrative of the lost American tourist, but he does not ask further questions and provides the protagonist with a meal and lodging in exchange for her help in the kitchen. Affection begins to develop between the two characters, and there seems to be a possibility that the hut in the border zone becomes an actual place of refuge for Nana/Suzie.

Yet, the film anticipates the not-so-idyllic turn of events when it shows Nana/Suzie cleaning the hut's dormitory. Under the bunk beds she finds a pair of broken sunglasses with pink-colored lenses. Several times she holds the glasses before her eyes and each time the camera cuts to a point-of-view-shot of the mountains in pink. During the last point-of-view-shot, the jeep of the border patrol drives into the frame in order to inform the inn keeper about illegal migrants in the area. Thus, at the very moment when the repeated act of looking through the sunglasses seems to indicate an improvement in Nana's/Suzie's situation, the film disrupts the imagination of a better world by bringing the forces of law and order onto the *mise-en-scène.*

Conclusion

This pivotal scene constitutes the final evidence that Florian Flicker's *Suzie Washington* is concerned less with the potential spatial and visual movement of its protagonist, but, rather, with mobilizing the ideas of identity construction among its audience. Nana's/Suzie's playing with the pink-colored sunglasses and the border police's disturbance of the idyllic moment function as the film's ultimate signal to the audience to let go of the desire for a traditional happy ending in which Nana/Suzie might find long-term refuge in the Austrian–German borderland. It is also a signal cautioning viewers not to put too much hope in postmodern conceptualizations of new and hybrid identities based on metaphors of the "traveler," "migrant," or "tourist" finding their place in vaguely defined "borderlands." When Nana/Suzie eventually crosses the border into Germany with a new passport stolen from one of the hut's patrons, she attests to the fact that "few of us can live without a passport or an identity card of some sort" (Kaplan 1996: 9).

The protagonist's sometimes funny and often bizarre encounters with the Austrian tourist landscape, as well as with tourists, tourism officials, and locals, open up a "contact zone" both between the protagonist and the people she meets, as well as between Austrian (or Western) audiences and their traditional images and narratives of identity construction. Mary Louise Pratt, whose concept of the "contact zone" I borrow, uses it in her investigation of colonialist travelogues in order to "invoke the spatial and temporal copresence of subjects previously separated by geographic and historical disjunctures" (Pratt 1992: 6–7). The concept applies to *Suzie Washington* insofar as the tourist performances of a female traveler/migrant from the border zone of Europe and Asia question the hegemonic and allegedly natural self-image of Western audiences. The disturbingly comic effects created by Nana's/Suzie's experience are only possible because Western viewers are so familiar with tourism's conventional symbolic order. When an airport turns into a prison cell and a ski lift is used—in the summer no less—by illegal border crossers, it confuses a conventional sense of spatial order and sparks critical awareness.

Thus, by introducing a female heroine from beyond the conventional borders of Europe, *Suzie Washington* enacts a filmic "provincializing [of] Europe." Dipesh Chakrabarty coins this term in order to describe the task of "renew[ing] European thought," which is "at once both indispensable and inadequate" for an understanding of modernity "from and for the margins" (Chakrabarty 2000: 16). As I have shown in my above discussion of imagination and spatial performances, Nana Iaschwili is clearly influenced by Western narratives and fantasies of identity and happiness. However, it becomes apparent that her life experience as a woman hailing from a country suffering from a destructive civil war also changes the meaning of these narratives and desires. Nana/Suzie questions apparently progressive and liberatory constellations such as the EU and she mobilizes alternative imaginary and performative spaces. In so doing, she produces what Foucault calls a "heterotopia," a set of "other spaces" that contrast, contradict, and sometimes complement the imagined space of a supranational and equalizing European Union that, in public discourses, has become an iconic emblem for the supposed post-national era (Foucault 1986: 25). Instead of focusing on the margins of hegemonic space—the fringes of the ever-widening EU—Flicker's film temporarily marginalizes the "heart of Europe," to cite the label used to describe Austria in the tourist brochure handed out on the tour bus.

This transforms *Suzie Washington* into a road movie that is different from other contemporary films that focus on the question of a European identity. For instance, Wim Wenders's *Lisbon Story* (1994) features a male German protagonist who welcomes the prospect of peace provided by the supranational EU, but bemoans the cultural homogenization produced by it. Thus, when he travels to Lisbon in order to meet a friend, he begins to imagine this southwestern margin of the EU through the lens of "imperialist nostalgia," transforming it into a place that is culturally, socially, and economically behind the European center, but, precisely because of that, provides a refuge for the exhausted male citizen of the metropolis (Rosaldo 1993: 68). As Eva Mazierska and Laura Rascaroli point out, "although nominally ... Wenders reached the margins of Europe, metaphorically [he] did not travel very far" (Mazierska and Rascaroli 2006: 209).

Suzie Washington, by contrast, emphasizes the frictions of intercultural contact and highlights the existence of legal, political, cultural, ethnic, and gendered boundaries. However, while modeling a marginal perspective onto the "center," Nana/Suzie must not be misread as a kind of subaltern voice from the colonies critiquing the metropolis. As a teacher of French and as a fluent English speaker Nana/Suzie is versatile in different cultures and languages and she is perhaps described best as being suspended between different spaces and different historical narratives.

This might also explain the film's somewhat ambiguous ending: Nana/Suzie eventually manages to leave Austria for Germany with a stolen French passport. Her assumption of yet another nationally defined identity does not, however, constitute an unambiguous embrace of the national as the only viable identity category. Rather, it seems that for the fugitive from war-ravaged Georgia, a stable national identity is still highly desirable. While a Western perspective might see the nation as something "already overcome," Nana/Suzie might perceive it as "not-yet-achieved." Perhaps this is what she addresses in the last sentence of her last postcard: "Once upon a time there was, and there was not. A bientôt, Jacqueline Duron."

Notes

1. See the subtitle of Hess's review: "a *Heimatfilm* as road movie" (see Hess 1999).
2. The FPÖ started discussing a "people's petition" called "Austria First" in December of 1992 and launched it in January of 1993. Already in December of 1992, the Austrian parliament passed the Alien Act, in which the conditions under which foreigners could receive an entry visa were detailed. Before that, in June of 1992, parliament passed the Asylum Act that aimed to prevent the "suspected 'abuse' of the provisions for political asylum" (Reisigl and Wodak 2001: 147).
3. In 1956, approximately 160,000 Hungarians fled to Austria after the violent suppression of the anti-Stalinist uprising. In 1968, 100,000 Czechs arrived after Soviet tanks crushed the Prague Spring, and about 50,000 Poles came to Austria after the implementation of martial law in 1982 (Reisigl and Wodak 2001: 148–49).
4. While the notion of an "ethnic Austrianness" might sound strange at first, Reisigl and Wodak demonstrate convincingly that the language of the FPÖ's "Austria First" petition implies a definition of Austrianness based on biological and quasi-ethnic traits that can only be inherited by birth and not by other means (Reisigl and Wodak 2001: 155).

References

Appadurai, A. 2000. *Modernity at Large: Cultural Dimensions of Globalization.* Minneapolis: University of Minnesota Press.

Berger, M.A. 2005. *Sight Unseen: Whiteness and American Visual Culture.* Berkeley: University of California Press.

Bhabha, H.K. 1990. "DissemiNation: Time, Narrative, and the Margins of the Modern Nation,' in H.K. Bhabha (ed.), *Nation and Narration.* New York: Routledge, 291–322.

de Certeau, M. 1984. *The Practice of Everyday Life.* Berkeley: University of California Press.

Chakrabarty, D. 2000. *Provincializing Europe: Postcolonial Thought and Historical Difference.* Princeton, NJ: Princeton University Press.

Crouch, D. 1999. "Introduction: Encounters in Leisure/Tourism," in D. Crouch (ed.), *Leisure/Tourism Geographies: Practices and Geographical Knowledge.* New York: Routledge, 1–16.

Del Casino, V.J. and S.P. Hanna. 2003. "Introduction," in S.P. Hanna and V.J. Del Casino (eds), *Mapping Tourism.* Minneapolis: University of Minnesota Press, i–xxi.

Edensor, T, 2002. *National Identity, Popular Culture and Everyday Life.* New York: Berg.

Flicker, F. 1999. *Suzie Washington: Drehbuch und Notizen zum Film.* Weitra: Bibliothek der Provinz.

Foucault, M. 1986. "Of Other Spaces," *Diacritics* 16: 22–27.

Graml, G. 2005. "'The Hills Are Alive...': *Sound of Music* Tourism and the Performative Construction of Places," *Women in German Yearbook* 21: 192–214.

Hall, S. 1996. "New Ethnicities," in D. Morley and K.-H. Chen (eds), *Stuart Hall: Critical Dialogues in Cultural Studies.* New York: Routledge, 441–49.

Hess, N. 1999. "Suzie Washington: ein Heimatfilm als Roadmovie," *Neue Zürcher Zeitung,* 29 January, n.p.

Kaplan, C. 1996. *Questions of Travel: Postmodern Discourses of Displacement.* Durham, NC: Duke University Press.

Krüger, T. 1998. "Suzie Washington," *Artechock.* Retrieved 14 January 2008 from: http://artechock.de/film/text/kritik/s/suwash.htm.

Laderman, D. 2002. *Driving Visions: Exploring the Road Movie.* Austin: University of Texas Press.

Mazierska, E. and L. Rascaroli. 2006. *Crossing Europe: Postmodern Travel and the European Road Movie.* New York: Wallflower Press.

Pratt, M.L. 1992. *Imperial Eyes: Travel Writing and Transculturation.* New York: Routledge.

Reisigl, M., and R. Wodak. 2001. *Discourse and Discrimination: Rhetorics of Racism and Antisemitism.* London: Routledge.

Rojek, C. and J. Urry. 1997. "Transformations of Travel and Theory," in C. Rojek and J. Urry (eds), *Touring Cultures: Transformations of Travel and Theory.* New York: Routledge, 1–22.

Rooney, D. 1998. "Suzie Washington" [review], *Variety,* 5 October. Retrieved 14 January 2008 from: http://www.variety.com/index.asp?layout=print_review&reviewid=VE1117913463&categoryid=31.

Rosaldo, R. 1993. *Culture and Truth: The Remaking of Social Analysis.* Boston, MA: Beacon Press.

Vansant, J. 1999. "Robert Wise's *The Sound of Music* and the 'Denazification' of Austrian in American Cinema," in D.F. Good and R. Wodak (eds), *From World War to Waldheim.* Oxford: Berghahn Books, 165–86.

Yuval-Davis, N. 1997. *Gender and Nation.* London: Sage.

Zheng, A. 2001. "Contested Identities and Public Spaces in Recent Austrian Film," *Modern Austrian Literature* 34(1/2): 54–67.

Chapter 19

A Cinephilic Avant-garde: The Films of Peter Tscherkassky, Martin Arnold, and Gustav Deutsch

Erika Balsom

It is said that film is a dying medium. Proclamations of the "death of cinema" abound, awash in hyperbole but nonetheless containing persistent glimmers of truth. Perhaps the cinema has been dying since its birth: critics have long decried the medium's death at the hands of sound, television, or video, but it has always persevered, countering its predicted eclipse with a continued relevance. Now, in this age of medium convergence, it is the material substrate of celluloid that is in danger of becoming obsolescent. Even if the cinema as an institution persists, there is no assurance that it will always consist of a photochemical image on a filmstrip, as digital methods of storage and projection become increasingly the norm. Serge Daney has written, "Defunct as an industry, cinema will once more become an artisanal art, poor or affluent, and will talk of everything that remains in frame once the compressing rollers of mediated communication have gone by" (Daney 1988: 251).

Daney's assertion that the end of cinema-as-industry might carve a space for cinema-as-poetry suggests that the popular obsolescence of celluloid might not be thought of as a death at all, but rather as an occasion allowing work on film that would not exist as such by default, but rather would be *about film itself*: what it has been, what it has meant, and what it can do. Exciting and diverse strains of recent experimental cinema have actively engaged with such questions, spanning from Bill Morrison's melancholic meditation on the pathos of film decay in *Decasia* (2002) to David Gatten's insistence on the indexical receptivity of analogue film in his series *What the Water Said* (1997–2007). Such practices renew interrogation of the medium-specific qualities of film, but do so in a much different way than the modernist programs of reduction that characterized the ontological inquiries of

1970s structural film. The principal difference lies in the ways in which recent practices engage in what one might term a critical cinephilia: a love for cinema at the moment of its loss, or at the very least at the moment of its profound transformation. Critical cinephilia infuses considerations of ontology with a studied sense of film history, insisting on the perpetual becoming of the medium over time rather than attempting to isolate its stable or essential being. As such, the contemporary moment allows for work to be made that is about cinema in transition, a sort of "love at last sight" for what the cinema once was but will be no more.

Martin Arnold, Gustav Deutsch, and Peter Tscherkassky stand at the forefront of Austrian experimental cinema, and, indeed, are some of the best-known figures of the international avant-garde. Despite individual differences, their work stands together as one of the strongest manifestations of critical cinephilia. Infusing the paradigms of 1970s structural film with new vitality through the use of found footage and painstaking contact and optical printing, these films make a crucial intervention in the history of experimental cinema by reflexively examining the possibilities of analogue film underneath the specter of the digital. This is not to reduce these films to a mere reaction formation, nor to suggest that they are steeped in nostalgia for an unrecoverable object. Instead, Arnold, Deutsch, and Tscherkassky testify to the continued relevance of cinema while engaging with its history. They do not set themselves apart from a tradition considered to have reached its telos, taking the cinema as an object of distanced reflection, but rather immanently interrogate the past, present, and future of the medium, effectively creating film theory through practice.[1] This chapter will attempt to map the differences and similarities of their respective projects, from Tscherkassky's investigations into cinematic scale and the spectrality of technology, to Arnold's emphasis on the single frame articulation and the fetishization of detail, and Deutsch's great metahistorical undertaking.

Akira M. Lippit has suggested that Arnold's work stems principally from two traditions, the national heritage of the Austrian avant-garde (VALIE EXPORT, Kurt Kren, Peter Kubelka), and the genre of found-footage filmmaking (Bruce Conner, Craig Baldwin, Matthias Müller) (Lippit 1997: 9). One could certainly extend this appraisal to both Deutsch and Tscherkassky. However, if one wishes to fully conceptualize the interventions made by this triad in both of these traditions, an additional point of reference is necessary. Peter Tscherkassky has written that a single event changed the course of his life: a five-day set of lectures given in 1978 at the Austrian Film Museum by P. Adams Sitney, preeminent critic of the American avant-garde. With screenings that lasted up to six hours, followed by two-hour lectures, it was here that Tscherkassky was introduced to the work of such filmmakers as Stan Brakhage and Michael Snow, while Sitney's book on the American avant-garde, *Visionary Film* (Sitney 2002), became "a kind of bible" to him (Tscherkassky 2005: 104). Beyond partaking in mere anecdotal interest, this event marks a crucial meeting between Tscherkassky and what Sitney himself had termed "structural film": a tendency of sixties and seventies experimental film that interrogated the basic principles of cinematic specificity through reductionist measures that might be considered to be the filmic analogue of Clement Greenberg's prescriptions for the distillation of painting down to its essential principle of flatness.[2] Perhaps most exemplary of this modernist tendency is Michael Snow's *Wavelength* (1967), which consists of a 45-minute zoom across a New York City loft. Sitney describes structural film as a radical emptying of reference in favor of an axiomatics of form: it is "a cinema of structure wherein the *shape* of the whole film is predetermined and simplified, and it is that shape that is the primal impression of the film" (Sitney 2000: 327).

Certainly, structural film is not exterior to the Austrian tradition nor to the genre of found footage, but nor is it totally collapsible within them.[3] The relevance of structural film to Arnold, Deutsch, and Tscherkassky lies principally in its articulation of the problem of medium specificity and its relationship to history. As Rosalind Krauss suggests, structural film practice allowed for the formulation of an idea of the medium "film" that was unitary and essential, "producing the unity of this diversified support" through an expulsion of considerations of historical change or self-difference (Krauss 1999: 25). The understanding of medium specificity evinced by structural film engaged in a reification of the ontology of the film image by attempting to synecdochially communicate the essence of film by distilling it to a purified, singular element, such as the zoom. On the contrary, Krauss emphasizes the necessity of understanding media as self-differing, as "aggregative, a matter of interlocking supports and layered conventions" (ibid.: 44) that are never simply reducible to a physical substrate or single technical principle. The concept of medium specificity within, as Krauss would have it, a post-medium age, means conceiving of a medium as profoundly historical, imbued with restrictions and conventions that go beyond the purely material. Additionally, by historicizing ontological inquiry, Krauss' definition of a medium as lacking self-identity provides a way to interrogate the changing status of film as it is rocked by the wave of obsolescence: "it is precisely the onset of higher orders of technology … which allows us, by rendering older techniques outmoded, to grasp the inner complexity of the mediums those techniques support" (ibid.: 53).

In order to grasp the intervention of Arnold, Deutsch, and Tscherkassky, it is necessary to interrogate their work in the context of a relationship to structural film and to changing discourses of medium specificity. The legacy of filmmakers like Kubelka and Snow looms large in their work, but is distinctly reformulated by infusing the singular purity of structural-film paradigms with the productive contaminations of found footage, generic conventions, and narrative—in a word, by asking the question of history. As Arnold has written: "In the 1960s, some film-makers attempted to get to … the 'ultimate elements' of the medium. This was a very ahistorical and normative view, which cannot be taken seriously anymore" (Arnold, in MacDonald 1994: 7). Film is no longer considered to have a secret essence that must be uncovered through violent reduction; instead, the medium is conceived as generating a sense of conventions, limitations, and possibilities—all profoundly historical—out of which the artist can work. As such, the paring down of the 1970s has been replaced by a love of the cinema in its multifarious manifestations, including an engagement with that entity most often considered the monstrous "other" of the avant-garde, Hollywood. The cinephilia of this avant-garde does not reside in a mystified love,[4] but in a critical interrogation into the medium's internal differences at an exciting moment of profound transformation.

Peter Tscherkassky

> The two techniques [analogue film and digital video] *have absolutely nothing in common*, except that they both make visible moving images.... I insist on the *radically different* possibilities that open onto an artistic, reflexive usage of material in these two media.
> —Peter Tscherkassky (2002: 84)

Between 1997 and 2001, Peter Tscherkassky launched a major investigation into the specificities of cinematic scale with his CinemaScope trilogy. Consisting of *L'Arrivée* (1997/98), *Outer Space* (1999), and *Dream Work* (2001), the trilogy eschews the small-gauge formats most often adopted by experimental filmmakers in favor of 35mm CinemaScope, an anamorphic widescreen process featuring an aspect ratio of 1:2.35, invented in 1953 to counter the looming threat of the nascent technology of television. CinemaScope recast the pleasure of cinema as one of giganticism, of reveling beneath an on-screen expanse that refused apprehension at a single glance. In a world where films are consumed less and less in the traditional architectural situation of the movie theatre and increasingly on portable screens of various dimensions, Tscherkassky's turn to CinemaScope constitutes a polemic against medium convergence. In Godard's *Le mépris/Contempt* (1963), Fritz Lang famously remarks that CinemaScope is only suitable for filming snakes and coffins due to its emphasis on horizontality. Certainly, this is a compositional principle afforded by the format that has been exploited throughout film history: one might think of such clear examples as Sergio Leone's *Il buono, il brutto, il cattivo/The Good, the Bad, and the Ugly* (1966), which indeed constitutes the source material for Tscherkassky's fourth CinemaScope film, *Instructions for a Light and Sound Machine* (2005). However, one equally finds tendencies in CinemaScope cinematography of fragmenting the image into multiple planes or using its vastness to orchestrate an intricate visual spectacle, evident in Nicholas Ray's *Rebel Without a Cause* (1955) and Max Ophüls's *Lola Montès* (1955), respectively. It is more to this tradition of CinemaScope that Tscherkassky belongs, fracturing the frame into numerous sections and exploiting the spectacularity of the gigantic image to its fullest.

To this connection with the visual splendor of classical Hollywood, Tscherkassky adds the emphasis on hand processing dear to the avant-garde. His films are made in a photographic dark room, using the painstaking process of contact printing with a laser light pen. Tscherkassky transfers sections of his found footage onto raw film stock one frame at a time, at a rate of about 45 to 70 minutes for one meter of film. This process is repeated to accumulate layers of images: each frame of *Outer Space* is composed of up to five shots, while *Dream Work* uses as many as seven. This fragmentation and superimposition troubles the representational work of the image, emphasizing instead its graphic dimension. There is a sense that the title of

Tscherkassky's *Instructions for a Light and Sound Machine* should be taken very seriously indeed: his films interrogate what the cinematic apparatus might be like if it were truly concerned with the sensations of light and sound rather than realistic representation or narrative plausibility. However, this is not to suggest that he is an empty formalist. Rather, the strength of his work lies in his ability to make use of the specific content of his found footage while simultaneously fragmenting it into abstract principles of light, motion, and sound. The title of his 1985 film *Manufraktur* emphasizes this intertwining of the processes of production and deconstruction, creation and ruin. In his manuf(r)acturing of films using found footage, cinema's past comes into a productive collision with its future, as the choice of found footage provides Tscherkassky with a set of generative conditions for the work he will create.

This engagement with film history is particularly evident in *L'Arrivée*. The film is Tscherkassky's second homage to the Lumières, following his 1984 film, *Motion Picture*, which was made by projecting a single frame of *La Sortie des ourvriers de l'usine Lumière à Lyon* (1895) onto blank strips of film pinned together on a darkroom wall so as to form a sort of screen. These strips were then printed and assembled into a running film, resulting in a completely non-objective composition of light and shadow. *L'Arrivée* harkens back *L'Arrivée d'un train à la Ciotat* (1895), but is composed entirely of footage from a 1968 Terrence Young film, *Mayerling*, set in Vienna and starring Catherine Deneuve. As the film begins, the white light of the projector floods an empty screen. There is a reversal of centre and margin as sprocket holes (resembling train tracks) move toward the centre of the frame while snatches of the image lurk at its edge. Gradually, two identical images of a train arriving at a station emerge from either side to fill the frame, mirrored across an axis of symmetry at its centre. As the trains approach each other, a collision ensues, manifesting itself as graphic chaos. The legible image gives way to abstraction, when suddenly we glimpse a woman's face. Deneuve's train arrives and she descends onto the platform to receive the kiss of a man who waits for her as the film concludes. The analogy between the cinema and the locomotive has been well-rehearsed (Kirby 1997), as both are nineteenth-century technologies marked by speed, movement, and the ability to reveal a theretofore unseen world. Here, Tscherkassky plays with this equation to narrate the history of cinema through the representation of the train: "Reduced to two minutes *L'Arrivée* gives a brief, but exact summary of what cinematography (after its arrival with Lumières' train) has made into an enduring presence of our visual environment: violence, emotions. Or, as an anonymous American housewife (cited by T.W. Adorno) used to describe Hollywood's version of life: 'Getting into trouble and out of it again'" (Tscherkassky n.d.). In a film noteworthy for its materialist examination of celluloid, what is striking is the resolute emphasis on narrative. The film posits the Lumière train as a forgotten arrival, as emblematic of a cinema concerned with documenting the pure event, a cinema that has since been narrativized into the happy endings of romance movies. This concern with historical change makes Tscherkassky's engagement with early cinema distinctly different to that of other experimental filmmakers such as Ken Jacobs (*Tom, Tom, the Piper's Son*, 1969) or Ernie Gehr (*Eureka*, 1984), who have used early cinema in order to circumvent a narrative tradition and return to what Tom Gunning has termed the "cinema of attractions" (Gunning 1986).[5] Unlike Jacobs and Gehr, Tscherkassky does not return to early cinema to recover a lost purity of film specificity. Instead, he takes a detour through a 1968 narrative film to engage in a questioning of this narrativization rather than to refuse it wholesale.

Outer Space and *Dream Work* continue this interrogation into the relationships between representation and abstraction, narrativization and sensation. Using the source material of *The Entity*, a 1981 Sidney Furie horror picture starring Barbara Hershey as a woman menaced by an unseen force, Tscherkassky takes his exploration of contact printing far beyond its use in *L'Arrivée* to displace the terror visited upon Hershey's character in the narrative of the source footage onto the filmstrip itself. Abiding by the principles of displacement and condensation, identified by Freud in *The Interpretation of Dreams* as central to oneiric narratives, Tscherkassky turns narrative violence into formal violence: the jagged lines on the original film's magnetic soundtrack intrude upon the image, the bright projector light shines through, images merge and separate, printed negative and positive, and at one particularly revealing moment of *Dream Work* we see hands cutting a film strip. The perceptual intensity and attention to materiality of the films recalls the strobe light assault of 1970s flicker films such as Paul Sharits's *T.O.U.C.H.I.N.G.* (1969), but Tscherkassky goes beyond formalist interrogations into the basic cinematic articulation of the single frame. *Outer Space* and *Dream Work* attempt to achieve the same mimetic affects of fear and surprise that are associated with the horror film, and, indeed, import important conventions of the genre to engage, albeit in a very different way, with some of its central preoccupations. As Alice Lovejoy has written, "With multiple exposures, inversions, and abstraction, *Outer Space* and *Dream Work* play off issues of visual truth—the question of whether or not images carry an indexical relationship to something that was really there, especially in the wake of trauma, and the ways in which aesthetic disorder mirrors psychic disorder" (Lovejoy 2002: 31). The image is brutally destabilized, acted upon by an external force, just like Hershey's character. This thematic of spectrality carries over from the source material to the film's form at the cost of representational clarity, but it also functions at a meta-level to comment on a cinema threatened by obsolescence, descending into chaotic ruin.

Martin Arnold

> To put it in general terms: in the symptom, the repressed declares itself.
> Hollywood cinema is … a cinema of exclusion, denial, and repression.
> I inscribed a symptom into it, which brings some of the aspects of repression
> onto the surface, or, to say it in more modest words, which gives
> an idea of how, behind the intact world being represented, another
> not-at-all intact world is lurking. Maybe this is my revenge on film history.
> —Martin Arnold, in MacDonald (2004: 11)

Although in recent years Martin Arnold has turned his attention towards working with large-scale digital installations,[6] his three best-known works—*Pièce touchée*

(1989), *Passage à l'acte* (1993), and *Alone. Life Wastes Andy Hardy* (1998)—are optically printed 16mm films that explore both the basic cinematic articulation of the single frame and the latent libidinal energies of the family as depicted by classical Hollywood cinema. Like Tscherkassky's process of manuf(r)acture, Arnold's use of found footage causes "Hollywood's waste [to return] ... as fuel" (Lippit 1997: 9). Seemingly possessed by a sort of repetition compulsion, these films shudder, glitch, twitch, and convulse their way through familiar domestic situations, making the recognizable strange. Arnold's practice consists primarily in reprinting Hollywood found footage frame by frame to rupture continuity and create a perpetual oscillation between forward and backward movement. Proposing the existence of an optical unconscious, Walter Benjamin asserted: "it is another nature which speaks to the camera as opposed to the eye. 'Other' above all in the sense that a space informed by human consciousness gives way to a space informed by the unconscious" (Benjamin 2003: 266). Arnold accentuates this capability of the apparatus by according attention to minute, overlooked gestures, not endowing them with new significance so much as revealing that which lies dormant, prompting the repressions of the classical form to manifest themselves as external symptoms. Scott MacDonald has suggested that Arnold's practice is like a "revenge on film history" (MacDonald 1994: 2) for having forgotten the lessons of the pioneers, resurrecting early filmmaking approaches— related to an analytics of motion and magic—that were left behind after D.W. Griffith. This however, seems to neglect the very basic fact that Arnold is interested precisely in the narrative cinema of classical Hollywood that MacDonald would see him bypassing. Like Tscherkassky, Arnold's engagement with early cinema is not a return to prelapsarian innocence. As his response to MacDonald (reproduced as the epigraph to this section) suggests, he is not attempting to circumvent the narrative tradition entirely, but to demonstrate that the "attraction" (in Gunning's sense) is not opposed to narrative but lurks within it. Similarly, Tscherkassky has written of watching *The Entity* repeatedly, scrutinizing it, "searching for some detail that might be hidden in the original film" (Tscherkassky 2005: 154).

Pièce touchée was photographed on a homemade optical printer from an 18-second shot culled from *The Human Jungle*, a relatively unremarkable 1954 film noir, directed by Joseph M. Newman, about a good cop fighting vice and moral depravity in the big city. Requiring a year and a half of work and the rephotographing of 148,000 single images according to the dictates of a 200 page score, the film begins with a still image of a woman sitting in an armchair that begins to subtly quiver as Arnold prints a few frames forward, a few frames back. The frozen image is disrupted by the barely perceptible twitching of the woman's finger, as she uncannily seems to stir to life. She does not appear to move of her own volition, but seems propelled by an unseen force; the time of the apparatus has overtaken that of the onscreen world. As the film progresses, her entire body is possessed by this animation, but any forward movement is immediately doubled by a pulling back into reverse motion, contributing to an impression of time as flux. The film plays not only with cinema's status as the progeny of investigations into the analytics of motion, such as those undertaken by Eadweard Muybridge and Etienne-Jules Marey, but also with its alignment with the irreversible temporality of the second law of thermodynamics, that of entropy.[7] Defying the inexorable forward progression of time's arrow, *Pièce touchée* contests the reification of cinematic time as a linear unspooling of narrative advancement and progress. A man enters the room from a door at rear and the scenario is recognizable at once: a husband coming home from work, who will greet his waiting wife with a chaste kiss. Arnold refuses the relentless forward movement of the projected image by exploiting cinema's capacity to figure the reversibility of time, playing on the spectator's expectation so that the husband's entrance appears as a battle to the death with the door, while his attempt to kiss his wife is ever frustrated. In this sense, like *L'Arrivée*, the film interrogates the contrivance of the "happy ending" of the heterosexual couple's kiss. Indeed, each film of this trilogy prominently features a heterosexual kiss, be it between husband and wife, father and daughter, mother and son, boyfriend and girlfriend. The centrality of this trope to classical Hollywood is undoubtable; in Arnold's hands it is denaturalized, opening onto a questioning of narrative conventions and the configurations of gender that underlie them.

Unlike *Pièce touchée*, *Passage à l'acte* makes use of synchronized sound, pulverized into bursts by the violence of Arnold's printing. The sounds of a door closing or the pointing of a father's finger resound like machine gun fire, while, like the soundtrack of *T.O.U.C.H.I.N.G.*, the stuttering motion causes repeated dialogue to blend and metamorphosize into other words—is it "sister" or "sit down," "crying" or "trying"? Made from a thirty-three-second clip of *To Kill a Mockingbird* (1962), starring Gregory Peck and directed by Robert Mulligan, the film is perhaps the most overtly assaultive of the trilogy. Arnold transforms an uneventful family breakfast into a relentless visual and aural onslaught that reveals the narrative's latent tensions through so many violent eruptions. These agitations work on the body of the spectator, frustrating any desire for continuity by insisting on the perpetuity of disruption. In the vocabulary of psychoanalysis, *passage à l'acte*, often translated into English as "acting out," is defined as: "an exit from the symbolic network, a dissolution of the social bond. Although the passage to the act does not, according to Lacan, necessarily imply an underlying psychosis, it does entail a dissolution of the subject; for a moment, the subject becomes a pure object" (Evans 1996: 137). The title of the film thus suggests the manner in which the film undoes the stable subject of classical Hollywood, giving way to the chaos that lurks beneath. Arnold's film releases the repressed tension of the source footage in the form of direct affect that punctures the fabric of normalcy. The jittery repetitions speak of an attempt to manage the underlying chaos, the "not-at-all intact world" that always persists beneath the thin veneer of convention.

Laura Mulvey discusses Arnold's films in terms of their reinterpretation of the structural-film paradigm under the sign of historicity, blending the interrogation of the photogram pursued by Peter Kubelka with an accentuation of "the vulnerability of old cinema and its iconic figures." She writes, "As Arnold combines stretched time with the manipulation of human gesture, he combines reference to the strip of celluloid with the presence of the cinema machine, the uncanny of the inorganic and the automaton" (Mulvey 2006: 172). Mulvey's invocation of the uncanny, of that undecidability between life and non-life, raises the question of cinema's dialectic of animation and mortification, Eros and Thanatos. The cinema has been described by André Bazin as "change mummified" (Bazin 1967: 15): the preservatory technology par excellence, it brings its spectators animated images only at the cost of a certain mortification, by freezing the world's movement into isolated photograms. The precious continuity of dominant cinema is achieved only by eliding this process of embalming, by denying the absence that subtends the overwhelming presence of the moving image. Arnold's films remind the viewer of the discontinuity of individual frames that underlies all cinema and the ways in which conventional spectatorial pleasure is inextricably yoked to the desire for movement and continuity. However, by highlighting the ghostly specter of death and discontinuity that haunts all cinema, Arnold is by no means engaged in a destruction of visual pleasure. Rather, his films heighten an awareness of the terms of our pleasure, even accentuating it: they are accessible, enjoyable, even funny.

Alone. Life Wastes Andy Hardy, for example, is the most explicit of the three films to exploit the repressed sexuality that undergirds classical Hollywood to humorous ends. Featuring Judy Garland and Mickey Rooney and using footage taken from MGM's *Babes in Arms* (1939) and *Andy Hardy Meets Debutante* (1940), the film stages the basic oedipal narrative for all of its comic cadence. Arnold opens with Andy Hardy (Mickey Rooney) kissing his mother (Fay Harden) in a scene that would normally be an innocent and inconsequential goodbye. Here, though, optical printing transforms the encounter to maximize its oedipal resonances and imbue it with an incestuous indecency. Later in the film, when Andy is leaving the house, he tells his mother, "You know where I'm going," prompting crosscutting with Judy Garland's stuttering voice, which rings out on the soundtrack as the siren of the mother's alarm at her son's detachment. At work is a renarrativization of the source material that transposes its concern from an unthinking recapitulation of dominant ideological positions on the nuclear family and heterosexual union to a scathing critique. Despite being less formally aggressive than *Passage à l'acte*, *Alone. Life Wastes Andy Hardy* is perhaps more radical than the earlier film in its interrogation of gender. As Michael Zryd has noted, Arnold shifts the focus of the oedipal triad from the son's anxiety to the mother's desire: the film "is intent on discovering more sublime expressions of emotion in a subtle choreography of unconscious kinetics. Thus, while it looks like Andy is simply 'humping his Mom, ha ha,' the scene also gives expression to the Mother's desire as Holden's heavy-lidded eyes and sighs suggest a sensuality caught in pensive regret at her treatment in the hands of Rooney's callow youth" (Zryd 2002). In a similar vein, the film can be seen to interrogate the glittering spectacle of the female star, Judy Garland. Arnold allows portions of Garland's song to pass uninterrupted ("On a night that was meant for love"), setting them up as strategically calculated releases in the midst of a glitchy withholding of the pleasures of continuity. Garland acts as the object of desire not only within the diegesis, but also for the spectator, a position that is problematized by Arnold's refusal to deliver the image of the star in a glittering, unmediated presence. Instead, he looks back to the materiality of the medium—emphasizing the filmic dimension of the individual photogram that is elided to produce the presence of the cinematic—to remind the spectator of the illusionism of continuity and the constructedness of cinematic pleasure.

Gustav Deutsch

> This project does not attempt to be a theoretical work, but tries, on the basis of extensive work with the subject, to track down some of the building blocks of perception and some of the effects of moving images. The product is neither a scientific analysis nor documentation but rather an artistic experiment. The gaze back to the beginnings of the medium is meant to be focused in the present by its use of contemporary means...and at the same time to face the direction of the future.
> —Gustav Deutsch[8]

Although less well known than Tscherkassky and Arnold, Gustav Deutsch's ongoing *Film ist.* series, made with the assistance of five international film archives, merits particular consideration for its engagement in a critical cinephilia to undertake the great ontological inquiry of what exactly film might be. Deutsch began the project in 1996, completing chapters one through six in 1998, with the following six released between 1999 and 2002. The first six chapters use footage from scientific and educational films to interrogate formal properties of the medium, as well as its basis in nineteenth-century experiments in the analysis of motion; as such, the chapter titles include "Movement and Time," "Light and Darkness," "An Instrument," "Material," "A Blink of an Eye," and "A Mirror." The second half eschews this epistemological function of the medium to treat its ancestry in magic and the fairground through chapters entitled "Comic," "Magic," "Conquest," "Writing and Language," "Emotions and Passion," and "Memory and Document." While the notion of ontology is traditionally held to interrogate the essential, stable qualities of an object, Deutsch chooses to problematize such determinism by placing a period at the end of the film's title, making it into a reflexive statement that is tautological, self-enclosed. This allows for the questioning of what "film is" to generate many answers that can shift over time while all remain valid. As Tom Gunning has noted, echoing Krauss, *Film ist.* advocates a notion of medium specificity as contaminated by multiple, even contradictory concerns that are historically contingent. He sees each chapter of the film as articulating "a perception, a facet, of film's continuous metamorphosis... Thus the succession of film's affinities becomes multiple and transitory. No single term can occupy this space for long.... While there may be an end to film history, the theory of film will also be an ongoing story, always 'to be continued'" (Gunning n.d.). Indeed, the *Film ist.* project continued, with an installment titled "A Girl and A Gun"—after Godard's famous formulation—released in 2009. This chapter is feature length and uses footage drawn from the birth of cinema to the end of the 1930s to explore the ways in which the medium has figured relations between the sexes. As the variety of chapters demonstrates, for Deutsch, the ontology of film cannot be reduced to a merely formal property of the medium, as was the case for structural film. Instead, he has expanded his thinking about medium specificity to include the multifarious ways we think about cinema, contributing to the creation of a theory of film through practice.

In this respect, Deutsch's project recalls the notion of metahistory set forth by Hollis Frampton (2009). While often categorized as a structural filmmaker because of axiomatic films such as *Zorns Lemma* (1970), Frampton actually provides a way of looking beyond structural film towards the creative engagement with film history that has since become such an important part of avant-garde practice. He writes, "The metahistorian of cinema ... is occupied with inventing a tradition, that is, a coherent wieldy set of discrete monuments, meant to inseminate resonant consistency into the growing body of his art. Such works may not exist, and then it is his duty to make them" (ibid.: 113). Where the historian would be responsible for every frame of celluloid ever produced, Frampton's metahistorian, by contrast, invents a tradition very much his or her own. There is no teleological progression of an aesthetic program, nor a technological determinism, but rather a tradition fabricated according to the useful fictions of the metahistorian which are, above all, artistically generative. There is no pretence of delivering the objective historical truth or an essentialized ontology of film; instead, metahistory retains the status of a self-conscious poesis that annihilates chronology and causality in favor of a "set of rational fictions" invented by the filmmaker (ibid.: 108). For Deutsch, this means fabricating certain organizational constraints for his found footage, generating more and more ideas about what film "is," thus contributing to a notion of medium specificity that is both plural and additive rather than singular and reductive. The tautology of the film's title leads to the assertion that "film is what it is," a notion that suggests a certain mutability. This is to say, film is both a musical instrument as well as a surgical instrument that can penetrate the human body ("An Instrument"), the dream of a universal language ("Writing and Language") as well as a conveyer of cultural difference ("Conquest"), a guarantor of documentary truth ("Memory and Document") as well as a charlatan trickster ("Magic").

It is certain that cinema occupies an incredibly different position in contemporary culture than it did in its heyday, when it could lay claim to being a dominant mass medium. Cinema's hegemony has been usurped by the digital, with films seen more often on television sets, computers screens, and iPods than they are in a movie theatre. It is precisely this passage into obscurity that prompts ontological inquiries such as *Film ist.* Deutsch recognizes film in all its mortality and frailty, something made painfully evident in the "Material" chapter, which examines decaying footage, frame by frame. At the end of the nineteenth century, the advent of cinema was aligned with the shock of the new: a different way of seeing and knowing the world. Now, when the digital paradigm refigures the medium as imbued with history and nostalgia, it becomes more important than ever to undertake investigations into its specificity. Thus, instead of confirming the "death of cinema" so often discussed and so often exaggerated, Deutsch reaffirms the unique capabilities of cinema by re-examining its multiple uses throughout its life. Cinema has died many deaths before, but the present moment is the first time that the material substrate of the medium has been threatened, while the challenges to the traditional exhibition situation of the movie theatre begun with the birth of television and the dissemination of the VCR have been further exacerbated by high-bandwidth internet access. It is certain that the institution will survive, but perhaps in a digitized form stripped of its traditional exhibition situation, begging the questions: What was cinema compared to what it is? When does cinema cease to be cinema and mutate into a new cultural form? The films discussed here may be seen as hypotheses that respond to such questions. Deutsch, along with Arnold and Tscherkassky, mark this juncture in film history with the strong assertion that projected celluloid in a movie theatre possesses its own medium specificity that may not be usurped by the new media, despite its increasing dominance.

Notes

1. This relation to the cinema is to be contrasted with, for example, that of gallery artists such as Douglas Gordon or Pierre Huyghe who deliberately set themselves outside of the film context. While also partaking in what I have termed "critical cinephilia," a work such as Gordon's *24 Hour Psycho* (1993) is less engaged in an interrogation of cinema as such than it is in mobilizing the history of cinema in order to pose questions of spectatorship and temporality that are specific to the institutional and formal constraints of gallery installation.
2. The reductive program of Greenbergian modernism may be viewed as a response to the onslaught of mass culture, asserting artistic autonomy through a hermetic sealing off of the artwork from its social context: "Content is to be dissolved so completely into form that the work of art or literature cannot be reduced in whole or in part to anything not itself" (Greenberg 1961: 6).
3. One finds, for example, the work of Peter Kubelka—particularly *Arnulf Rainer* (1960) and *Unsere Afrikareise* (1966)—as central to Sitney's account of structural film, while structural filmmakers Ken Jacobs and Ernie Gehr engaged extensively in found-footage work.
4. For a canonical account of such a pathologization of cinephilia, see Metz (1982: 11–16).
5. For an in-depth discussion of the relationship between structural film and early cinema, see Testa (1992).
6. On Arnold's 2002 installation at the Kunsthalle Wien, *Deanimated: The Invisible Ghost*, see Cahill (2007).
7. On the relation between cinematic temporality and thermodynamics, see Doane (2002: esp. 108–39).
8. This epigraph is taken from "Introduction: *Film ist.* Attempt and Approach," a booklet which accompanies the DVD of *Film ist.* (Vienna: Arge Index, 2004, p.3).

References

Bazin, A. 1967. *What Is Cinema? Vol. 1*, trans. H. Gray. Berkeley: University of California Press.

Benjamin, W. 2003. "The Work of Art in the Age of its Technological Reproducibility (Third Version)," *Selected Writings, Vol. 4, 1938–1940*, trans. and H. Zohn and E. Jephcott, eds. H. Eiland and M.W. Jennings. Cambridge, MA: Belknap Press, 251–83.

Cahill, J.L. 2007. "...and Afterwards? Martin Arnold's Phantom Cinema," *Spectator* 27: 19–25.

Daney, S. 1988. *Le Salaire du zappeur*. Paris: Editions Ramsay.

Doane, M.A. 2002. *The Emergence of Cinematic Time: Contingency, Modernity, Archive*. Cambridge, MA: Harvard University Press.

Evans, D. 1996. *An Introductory Dictionary of Lacanian Psychoanalysis*. New York: Routledge.

Frampton, H. 2009. "For a Metahistory of Film: Commonplace Notes and Hypotheses," in *On the Camera Arts and Consecutive Matters: The Writings of Hollis Frampton*, ed. Bruce Jenkins. Cambridge, MA: MIT Press, 131–39.

Greenberg, C. 1961. *Art and Culture*. Boston: Beacon Press.

Gunning, T. 1986. "The Cinema of Attractions: Early Cinema, its Spectator, and the Avant-garde," *Wide Angle* 3–5: 63–70.

———. n.d. *"Film ist.*: A Primer for a Visual World." Retrieved 9 March 2009 from: http://www.sixpackfilm.com/archive/texte/01_filmvideo/filmist_gunningE.html.

Kirby, L. 1997. *Parallel Tracks: The Railroad Silent and Cinema*. Durham, NC: Duke University Press.

Krauss, R. 1999. *"A Voyage on the North Sea": Art in the Age of the Post-medium Condition*. New York: Thames and Hudson.

Lippit, A.M. 1997. "Martin Arnold's Memory Machine," *Afterimage* 24(6): 8–10.

Lovejoy, A. 2002. "Space Invaders," *Film Comment* 38(3): 30–31.

MacDonald, S. 1994. "Sp... Sp... Spaces of Inscription: An Interview with Martin Arnold," *Film Quarterly* 48(1): 2–11.

Metz, C. 1982. *The Imaginary Signifier: Psychoanalysis and the Cinema*, trans. C. Britton, A. Williams, B. Brewster, and A. Guzzetti. Bloomington: Indiana University Press.

Mulvey, L. 2006. *Death 24 x a Second: Stillness and the Moving Image*. London: Reaktion.

Sitney, P.A. 2002. *Visionary Film: The American Avant-garde, 1943–2000, Third Edition*. Oxford and New York: Oxford University Press.

——— 2000. "Structural Film," in P.A. Sitney (ed.), *Film Culture Reader*. New York: Cooper Square Press, 326–48.

Tscherkassky, P. 2002. "Comment et pourquoi? Quelques remarques sur la réalisation technique de la trilogie CinemaScope," *Trafic* 44: 83–87.

———. 2005. "Epilogue, Prologue: Autobiographical Notes Along the Lines of a Filmography," trans. A. Dereig, E. Heller and V. Heller, in A. Horwath and M. Loebenstein (eds), *Peter Tscherkassky*. Vienna: Synema Publikationen, 101–60.

———. n.d. "L'Arrivée," Retrieved 9 March 2009 from: www.tscherkassky.at.

Testa, B. 1992. *Back and Forth: Early Cinema and the Avant-garde*. Toronto: Art Gallery of Ontario.

Zryd, M. 2002. "Alone: Life Wastes Andy Hardy," *Senses of Cinema*, October. Retrieved 9 March 2009 from: http://www.sensesofcinema.com/contents/cteq/04/32/alone_life_wastes_andy_hardy.html.

Part V

Stefan Ruzowitzky and
Neo-classic Trends

Chapter 20

Screening Nazism and Reclaiming the Horror Genre: Stefan Ruzowitzky's *Anatomy* Films

Alexandra Ludewig

In recent years the filmmakers Stefan Ruzowitzky, Robert Schwentke, and Oliver Hirschbiegel have revived the horror genre in German language cinema, and used it to challenge accepted images of Hitler and the excesses of the Nazi era. This reconceptualization and reclamation is particularly intriguing after a lengthy hiatus in Germany and Austria. To date, however, the available literature is yet to fully recognize the true value of the contemporary German variety of the horror genre as a field of research,[1] a genre in which varying portrayals of evil offer the potential to provide information about associated and shared community values, perceptions, and fears.

German-speaking filmmakers are regarded as cofounders and masters of the horror genre, having directed many silent films considered to be expressionist classics. These include *Das Kabinett des Doktor Caligari/The Cabinet of Dr Caligari* (1920), directed by Robert Wiene and based on the script by the Austrians Carl Mayer and Hans Janowitz; Arthur Robison's silent film *Nächte des Grauens/Nights of Terror* (1916); F.W. Murnau's feature-length *Nosferatu, eine Symphonie des Grauens/Nosferatu: A Symphony of Terror* (1922); and Robert Wiene's classic expressionist *Orlacs Hände/The Hands of Orlac* (1924). By the mid 1920s the genre in German-language film was already in decline and the situation worsened after 1945, with Nazi history rendering on-screen horror inappropriate, an unnecessary reminder of the "bad German." This perception was reinforced by Siegfried Kracauer's study *From Caligari to Hitler* (Kracauer 2004 [1947]) in which he depicted the genre as particularly problematic for Germans, by tracing a linear development from horror to Nazism. In postwar cinema, horror and gore were trademarks of imports from Hollywood, while German television productions in related genres such as crime and detective stories were dominated by conservative and moderate public servants solving much less ghastly crimes.[2] In general, critics expressed a disdain for genre films, and for most of the second half of the twentieth century—especially regarding the horror genre—considered them to be B-grade movies made purely for entertainment (White 1971: 1).

It has taken over sixty years for German-speaking directors to bring the horror genre back to cinemas, although there was a resurrection of sorts on television in the 1950s and 1960s with the Edgar Wallace horror films.[3] The most prominent proponents of the current revival are Austrian Stefan Ruzowitzky and Austrian resident Oliver Hirschbiegel, who have created films which reconnect to the pre-1938 cinematic tradition as well as the Nazi period. *Das Experiment/The Experiment* (2001) by Oliver Hirschbiegel, and *Anatomie/Anatomy* (2000) and its sequel *Anatomie 2/Anatomy 2* (2003) by Stefan Ruzowitzky, make use of contemporary settings in an attempt to highlight timeless human traits at play. Their films have also fused these historical references with elements of popular genre and utilize present-day society as a backdrop in order to appeal to a younger viewing public in particular. In doing so they have created—arguably—a new school of film, as they reveal a novel perspective on Nazi crimes, not only because of their setting in twenty-first-century society, but also due to their choice of genre. In Hirschbiegel's and Ruzowitzky's films, Nazi and fascist traits are packaged in a genre which most German and Austrian filmmakers have shied away from—as much as they have from films that could be misunderstood as portraying fascism as human. However, Ruzowitzky and Hirschbiegel break with both of these unwritten laws by creating horror movies in the "best" Hollywood tradition, while provocatively suggesting at the end of their films that such evil potentially exists in all of us. As such, both *Anatomy* films, as well as *The Experiment,* can be interpreted as allegories of Nazism, while making viewers wary of humans in general and, in particular, of professions and institutions generally revered as pillars of civilization: the medical fraternity and universities.

Ruzowitzky's second successful feature film, *Anatomy* is a horror-fantasy about the medical profession. The protagonist Paula Henning is a promising medical student with a strong background in the field: her grandfather is a celebrated surgeon and her father runs a medical clinic for people on low incomes. Winning second prize in a competition lands Paula a place at the prestigious Heidelberg University, employer of the brilliant anatomist Professor Grombek. While on the train en route to the historic university town, Paula saves the life of a young man with a heart problem, only to see him again shortly afterwards, this time as a candidate for dissection in her anatomy class. Paula's curiosity is piqued by this unlikely coincidence, which leads her to discover the sinister dealings of a group of doctors who secretly pursue medical research at all costs. They call themselves "Anti-Hippocratics," deliberately rejecting the Hippocratic oath, and performing experiments involving dissection or plastination on unwilling, still-living victims. Members of the Anti-Hippocratics kill Paula's room-mate and attempt to do the same to her when she pursues them. With the help of Caspar, a fellow student—who turns out to be writing a Ph.D. on the history of secret medical societies—Paula succeeds in exposing their evil activities.

Set in Germany, the film certainly evokes connotations of the horrors of the Holocaust, especially as the viewer is visually reminded of the similarities between the cruel operations being depicted and Nazi medical experiments. This parallel is supported by the symbolism surrounding the film's antagonist, Hein, who is reminiscent of Gevatter Hein ("godfather death"), a mythical figure of doom, as well as a caricature of a Nazi poster boy: all neatly-parted blond hair, vital, and ready for combat. The violence acted out by the hypermasculine medico Hein marries murder and sexual pleasure, and the visual language of his black lab coat mirrors the aggression of neo-Nazi groups in Germany during the 1990s as much as the Nazis' treatment of Jews in the 1930s and 1940s. This parallel is highlighted by the first victim whom Paula encounters, symbolically named David. Ruzowitzky's message is, however, not too overt: he has created a hybrid film combining elements of popular entertainment and academically informed social critique in a manner that does not foreground a didactic message.[4]

Extremely popular in German-speaking countries, *Anatomy* was also successfully marketed abroad (particularly in the US, UK, and Australia) by its American distributor, Columbia Pictures. It was followed by a sequel in 2003, an unusual occurrence in German-language cinema, with the German subsidiary company Deutsche Columbia TriStar Filmproduktion endeavoring to cash in further on the success of its first production in Europe. As a result, with regard to visual aesthetics as well as to marketing, *Anatomy* and *Anatomy 2* have a very American feel about them, with their MTV-inspired stylistic elements including fast-paced cuts, swirling camera movements and the techno-inspired musical score. The films also derive a lot of their popular appeal from intertextual horror-genre citations from American "teen-horror" and slasher-film conventions. These references are especially apparent in the sequel, which, despite being set in Berlin, does not foreground national iconography and tells a much more generic story. In *Anatomy 2* there are no longer any of the direct references to Mengele or Nazism which provided the national framework in the first film.

In *Anatomy 2*, once again the labyrinth of a university clinic devoid of daylight serves as a metaphor for the dark side in all of us: the suppressed urges, the forces that are usually part of the unconscious and repressed sphere of our being. This underground world is presented as a microcosm reigned over by the neurosurgeon Professor Dr Müller-LaRousse, a prime example of the authoritarian type (Horkheimer and Flowerman 1950: ix).[5] He manipulates his colleagues and interns—and initially also the film's male protagonist, Jo Hauser—in order to conduct unethical research into muscle transplants and synthetic tissue. This dystopian leader is an integral part of a society which is itself based on manipulation, as the professor's medical advances are designed to broaden his powerbase rather than to help relieve suffering. His aim is to achieve external control of people by taking over their nervous systems; a mad scientist's contemporary Frankensteinian vision based on the latest techniques derived from biomechanics and chemistry. Though nominally a member of a humanitarian institution, he is instrumental in selling out to market interests—chiefly insurance companies and pharmaceutical multinationals—at the expense of ethics. The fundamental ideal of helping people in need is suspended in instances where the patient in need is unable to produce a valid healthcare card or the appropriate payment in exchange. Medical care—if provided at all—is based on a business model rather than on the Hippocratic oath. Chief physician Müller-LaRousse's neuroscience laboratory becomes the site where scientists are prey to their own delusions, wanting to improve on nature by experimenting on themselves with drugs and implants in the pursuit of creating the prototypical alpha male. The film's horror is largely derived from the cold detachment evident in the doctors' interaction with other human beings. The procedural mechanics acted out by the men in white are contrasted with the human carnage they cause, but do not mourn.

The film's commentary on history is as poignant as that on the possible future of mankind. The frailty of civil society and its tendency to descend into chaos are integral aspects of any microcosm. Evidence of the latter had already led the philosophers of the Frankfurt School in the late 1940s and 1950s to ask how it could be "that in a culture of law, order, and reason, there should have survived the irrational remnants of ancient racial and religious hatreds [leading to] the willingness of great masses of people to tolerate the mass extermination of their fellow citizens" (ibid.: v). As in Hannah Arendt's interpretation of Nazism (Arendt 1963), it is the banality of evil that is emphasized in the form of an everyday person who becomes part of the group of aggressors. As Jo Hauser's case confirms, it is thoughtlessness and the framework of a totalitarian system that breeds abuse of power; not innate evil traits, but rather cold pragmatism at the expense of (com)passion or personal will and thoughtfulness. In both *Anatomy* films, surgeons dissecting bodies or performing procedures on the living are seen mindlessly chatting about the mundane. Ruzowitzky thus juxtaposes the visual horror—enhanced by close-ups of body and scalpel—with a matter-of-fact dialogue. Nevertheless, most of the doctors remain likable, corresponding with Arendt's rejection of the idea that SS-men were by and large psychopathic sadists (ibid.: 286–87). To demonize them and portray them as monsters is precisely to miss the most disturbing fact about the average Nazi perpetrator; namely, that in an overwhelming majority of cases they were dutiful, law-abiding citizens who, in their role as civil servants, carried out orders that they did not question or dare to disobey. This very point was proved by Stanley Milgram, who conducted a series of experiments on obedience to authority at Yale University in 1961 and 1962. Historically, Milgram's experiments followed the capture of Adolf Eichmann in 1960, and coincided with Eichmann's trial in Jerusalem in 1961 at the time when the term "Holocaust" was starting to be used and associated with the massacre of European Jews during the Second World War. Milgram devised the scenario of his experiments in such a way as to answer the question of whether it was possible that people like Eichmann (as well as American soldiers in Vietnam executing women and children in the 1960s and 1970s) were just following orders (Milgram 1974: 5–6). Milgram found that "almost two-thirds" of his subjects, ordinary local residents who were given the role of teachers, were willing to give apparently harmful electric shocks to their students when commanded to do so by a scientific authority (ibid.: 5).[6] Both Arendt and Milgram consequently proved the tendency of "normal" humans to fall victim to totalitarianism.

Ruzowitzky follows suit, by initially showing Jo Hauser, the film's protagonist, to be a well-integrated, law-abiding member of German society—before outlining how easy it is for him (as it is for others) to transgress. Just like his fellow colleagues, Jo is no monster emerging from outside the normal spectrum of humanity. Rather, his shortcomings and mistakes are shown to be natural behavior instead of abnormality or psychopathology. Thus Ruzowitzky stresses that the evil mindset is banal and commonplace in an environment which allows it free rein, thereby commenting less on Nazism and fascism than on the universal law that power breeds abuse.

Capitalism—as exercised by pharmaceutical companies—is exposed as being in collusion with the uncanny, and apparently benefits from violence and even murder. While the medical fraternity serves as an example of human interaction which starts out with the most admirable of intents but becomes corrupted by power, the *Anatomy* films point to this failing as symptomatic. Closely related to the logic of crude capitalism is the abandonment of care; this male-dominated society can only be humanized by a female. As such, patriarchy and pure science without a social focus are depicted as dystopias in both *Anatomy* films. In contrast to the microcosm of the clinic, which mirrors misguided forms of institutionalization and defeats the very ideals of civilization, the female protagonist (played in both cases by Franka Potente, in the first film an integral part of the story, though in *Anatomy 2* a mere dea ex machina) is scripted as an example of an alternative: an ethical and intelligent force which can reinstate social order and humanistic values.

Ruzowitzky produced these horror movies in Germany utilizing an American genre formula, rather than referring visually and aesthetically back to the expressionist tradition of early Austrian and German cinema. Even *Anatomy*'s visual aesthetics, despite capitalizing on the tourist appeal of its city locations, highlight the undeniable Americanization of Austrian and German culture in general, and also respond to commercial expectations on behalf of his production company, which clearly had a secondary overseas market in mind. However, Ruzowitzky's films must also be understood as part of a film history in which tentative steps are once again being taken onto horror terrain. His two *Anatomy* films have been welcomed as a successful step towards the dark genre and a movement out of the shadow of post-Nazi self-censorship. The latter was achieved by the films' obvious connections to the Nazi substrate of Austria and Germany, packaged in such a way as to fascinate the audience, due to the gory yet stylish and suspenseful narrative and framing, as well as to historical references in the form of spine-chilling remnants of fascist ideology. Like Hirschbiegel in *The Experiment* and Schwentke in *Tattoo* (2002),[7] Ruzowitzky successfully fuses elements of the horror genre with twentieth-century European history in his *Anatomy* films, while commenting on contemporary matters with regard to the very Austrian failure to deal appropriately with its Nazi heritage (despite both films being set in contemporary Germany). In contrast to West

Germany, where a willingness to deal with its dark past has manifested itself in public and academic discourse, many Austrians have preferred to see themselves as the first victims of Nazism.[8] As such, the idea of horror in *Anatomy* (just as in *The Experiment*) is political, in that it is related to the resurfacing of what has been repressed: in the form of a group of medical doctors employing fascist-inspired practices. Biological selection and the relentless pursuit of a science aiding the creation or survival of the *Übermensch* ("super human") indicate that the Third Reich remains a potent legacy, with the actions of the Anti-Hippocratics providing the basis for a critique of contemporary society, in which Ruzowitzky sees similar ideologies and practices still alive—against all expectations and despite official denials.

Even after the exposure of the Anti-Hippocratics' conduct in the present day, Paula finds distinguished professors such as Grombek applauding the secret society's objectives in—as he says in the movie—not restricting "itself to narrow-minded traditions." If this were not the case, it is suggested that Heidelberg University's leading role in the medical field, potential Nobel prizes, government funds for research, commissions from the pharmaceutical industry, and finances to educate "the elite," would be in doubt. Science in a global context is competitive and it is less national than international pressures that come to bear. Although Grombek admits that during the Nazi-era people like Josef Mengele "went awry," he claims that their scientific achievements, specifically in the field of anatomy, have not been given proper recognition. "He admits that they 'play God' while experimenting on terminal patients, but states that the patients do not usually even notice what is going on" (Dolan 2000). As if this claim alone justifies their dealings, he continues to support the actions of professional societies that dare to compete in the global arena and describes them as "unremarkable" in this modern age of cloning and genetic modifications. With this statement by Grombek, Ruzowitzky invites comparisons of the achievements of Nazi-era scientific research with those of present day science.

The conduct of some researchers as reported in the media, as well as discussions about euthanasia and Gunther von Hagens' exhibition *Körperwelten*, or "Body Worlds," are but a few representative contemporary examples which make the chilling action in *Anatomy* less fantastic than real. While employed as a lecturer at Heidelberg University's Institute for Anatomy and Pathology, von Hagens invented "plastination" in 1978 as a teaching aid and to further research. Since then his technique has become widely accepted in medical circles and is carried out in many institutions throughout the world, including, apparently, those depicted in *Anatomy* and *Anatomy 2*. Von Hagens, who initially marketed his specimens for public spectacle under a professorial title that Heidelberg University (also the setting of *Anatomy*) has since revoked, made international headlines with his "Body Worlds" art project, with its deliberate fusion of horror and research. His anatomical exhibitions show real human bodies and organs that have been preserved through his invention, the process of "plastination". Since the late 1990s, von Hagens has made his bodies and body parts available to the public in increasingly daring exhibitions which have attracted audiences exceeding 15 million worldwide, making

"Body Worlds" the most successful traveling exhibition ever created. The first of these exhibitions opened in Austria in 1997, attracting some 6 million viewers and stirring subsequent public debate with his progressively more provocative presentations.[9] Von Hagens has been engulfed in controversy, particularly in his native Germany, where the historical burden of Nazi Germany has alarmed audiences more than anywhere else. While he has quite intentionally provoked many discussions in Austria and Germany, von Hagens has always proudly claimed that each of the plastinated entire-body exhibits was a voluntary donation. Indeed, in recent years many people have explicitly donated their bodies to him in their wills. Nevertheless, there has been considerable controversy surrounding some of the corpses used for the exhibits featuring plastinated hearts and other internal organs, as some of those organs were bought from prisons or mental institutions in countries such as China and Russia. Although this is strictly speaking not illegal, many feel that it is unethical to use people's bodies for artistic purposes without their permission.

The parallels to Ruzowitzky's film are unmistakable. Von Hagens, like Professor Grombek, claims that:

> plastinated organs and body slices are a novel teaching aid for cross-sectional anatomy which is gradually gaining importance and can be easily correlated with radiological imaging. Series of transparent body slices are helpful for manifold scientific research activities. In addition, they are a suitable diagnostic means in pathology, as they allow rapid macroscopic and diagnostic screening of entire organs or operation preparations; they still allow for selective analyses of pathological tissue regions with conventional microscopic methods. (von Hagens 2004)

Human subjects are transformed into specimens and objectified, while the ideals expressed in the Hippocratic oath are devalued further and further. Advances in science and the cut-throat competition for the Nobel Prize at times become more important than service to humanity; indeed, the scientists' inhumanity is startling and reminiscent of scientific activities carried out under Nazism. Thus, *Anatomy* "explores the fictional premise that underneath the democratic surface of contemporary Germany, and within its technocratic elites, traces of the country's fascist past still linger" (Hantke 2000). The film not only highlights a malaise which applies to other Western societies, it also points out the reason for the thrall with the past, one which people have not been able to come to terms with. This is explored through the examination of Paula's family.

Paula is shattered when Professor Grombek reveals that her own grandfather was once the head of the secret society, as well as the inventor of the drug Promidal that is used in the plastination process. Now an ailing, though still strong-willed man, Paula's grandfather has been her mentor all her life. Even from the confines of his bed in the very hospital in which he used to practice and teach, he has been able to influence Paula's career. Symbolically and parallel to Grombek's revelation, Paula's grandfather dies and ceases to be her idol, although he also passes away before she has an opportunity to confront him. With this new insight into her family, Paula is forced to renegotiate her relationship with her father. She has disassociated herself from him up to this point in her life, as she has been unable to understand his career choices. He seems to have rejected pure scientific research, fame, money, and ambition—as Paula eventually comes to understand—as a way of protesting against tendencies in the medical world that he perceives to be inhumane. He made the decision early in his profession to go back to the fundamentals of the Hippocratic oath (by caring for the needy, the most vulnerable and least advantaged) as a deliberate and provocative departure from his own father's practices and principles. While his motivations may have been noble, Paula's father has failed to communicate them to Paula. This behavior is depicted as paradigmatic for members of the 1968 generation, who often rejected the world of their fathers outright without engaging in a personal or differentiated way with the past and their personal involvement in it. The film thus suggests that "[t]he grandchildren's generation is susceptible to the proto- or crypto-fascist stance of the Anti-Hippocratics because the previous generation has failed to break this silence" (Hantke 2004: 128). However, the film's critique of German society goes further by implying that fascist ideology has survived into the present because of the failure of the 1968 generation.

Paula initially falls victim to the same black and white logic that sees only good or bad, when she quickly exposes Hein as the culprit, while being unaware that the matter is infinitely more complex. This is evident in the concluding scene of *Anatomy*, which focuses on two of Paula's fellow students talking about their immediate plans following the end of the summer programme in Heidelberg. One mentions rumors that a branch of the secret society is still operating in Berlin, while the female student reveals that she has decided to take over her father's practice. She explains that government supervision is not quite as strict in the case of private practices such as her father's, thus providing some freedom for scientific experimentation. When their conversation is interrupted by the morgue attendant asking how things are going, they respond tellingly that everything is the same as always; it seems that the technocratic elites controlling institutions—however large or small—will continue to provide a safe haven for fascist ideology.

Thus the Austrian-born Ruzowitzky—just like the long-term resident of Vienna, Oliver Hirschbiegel in *The Experiment*—exposes institutional as well as human shortcomings which aid the continuation of fascist practices in Western societies in general, while drawing on Austrian and German history—and present day society— as an example. The *Anatomy* films and *The Experiment* present a challenge to conventional ways of reading films about Nazism and fascism, because they situate their protagonists within educational facilities: a university's medical faculty in the *Anatomy* films, and a university's make-believe prison in *The Experiment*; the former an institution that should advance civil society, the latter intended to safeguard it. The directors seem to revel in presenting contemporary implosions of civil society and the regression of members of an educated middle class to barbarians in a matter of days. As with Hannah Arendt's interpretation of Nazism, it is the corruptive force and seduction of elites that is emphasized, with the ordinary person becoming part of the group of aggressors. *The Experiment*, like *Anatomy* and *Anatomy 2*, explores that which "within the individual organism responds to certain stimuli in our culture with attitudes and acts of destructive aggression" (Horkheimer and Flowerman 1950: v). In trying to address this issue, the films by Hirschbiegel and Ruzowitzky prepare the ground for a broader understanding of evil.

This shift in the representation of evil in Ruzowitzky's *Anatomy* films highlights the successful workings of the confluence of a new depiction of evil and Nazism. With regard to other German-language films, such as Robert Schwentke's *Tattoo*, Ruzowitzky's foray into the horror genre can be contextualized more broadly within a trend that heralds a change in the understanding of evil on a sociohistorical, sociocultural, and sociopolitical level. This highlights the complex nature of humankind, memory, and history in our comprehension of good and evil, and sheds light on the representation of evil in contemporary German-speaking culture in relation to broader developments, as well as on the instrumentalization of value judgments in media-saturated societies. Indeed, despite the cinematic shortcomings of the largely generic *Anatomy* films, the novelty value in Ruzowitzky's case is—in my opinion—that he has shown a way to move beyond national modes of explanation in his exploration of evil. In his rediscovery of the horror genre for German-language film he has stressed that evil is a timeless, primordial tendency which is more or less prevalent depending on a complex mix of conditions. He has thus broadened our perspective and challenged our values and taboos in commonly-held representations of evil and of Nazism alike. Moreover, Ruzowitzky deals with Nazism not as a discrete period of history but rather as an ever-present tendency in any civil society. Considering the obsession of many Austrians with their own victimhood and support for right-wing political parties such as Austria's Freedom Party (FPÖ) since the late 1980s, Ruzowitzky provides his social commentary not in the aesthetics of realism but instead in the form of a parable. This foregrounds the universality of evil: the fact that each and every one of us is capable of despicable acts of cruelty. Both *Anatomy* films can thus be read as a reminder of the process of "how a present contemplating a future generally invents the past it deserves" (Bosworth 1999: 117).

The hypergraphics and hyperreality of contemporary cinema in this instance explicitly represent the horrors that usually remain off-screen events in films about the Holocaust. While many critics of Hollywood's attempts at Holocaust movies have rejected "visual images that saturate and ultimately wipe away the reality of the horror" (Leventhal 1995), Hirschbiegel's, Schwentke's, and Ruzowitzky's images are very graphic. However, their contemporary (if not futuristic) rather than historical settings ensure that it is not the Holocaust that is solved, explained, or commercialized, but its remaining traces in any modern society. Their ultimate message, therefore, is that the Nazi past cannot be dealt with as a historical issue, but that it is part of every contemporary society.

The films deliberately focus on evil as a constant in the world, thus reminding the audience that crimes associated with the Nazis are, in reality, crimes associated with humankind. They cannot be relegated to the past, but must instead be seen as a fixity of the human condition. However cruel the protagonists or antagonists are depicted in the films, they can neither communicate the unspeakable horrors of the past, nor silence the unease about the potential for humanity to do it all over again. These contemporary horror films thus consciously accentuate evil using graphic imagery, while providing an explanation of the Holocaust that is removed from the cultural and historical context. This is achieved by rendering timeless the evil acts that are being committed, through the use of ancient motives and contemporary settings. The viewer is thus given another point of reference from which to understand the events as human traits.

> Hitler is and remains an anthropological possibility that will occur again and again. That is, so to speak, his legacy. However, this has scarcely been noted up to now. For 200 years after the Enlightenment we had an image of humankind that was based on the assumption: Man is good, Evil can be eliminated through education and improvement of social conditions. Hitler has destroyed this positive image of humankind. We know, or ought to know, that Evil exists.... According to Freud: Under the thin veneer of civilization there is a pack of murderers in every person. An insight which we have to gain once again when we look at the twentieth century. (Joachim Fest, in Amend 2004: 57)

Both *Anatomy* films, as well as *The Experiment* and *Tattoo,* can therefore be interpreted not only as allegories of Nazism, but also as commentary on a universal truth about mankind's natural inclination toward totalitarianism. While making viewers wary of humans in general, the films also raise concerns about society's trust in those of its institutions that promote law and order. It is generally believed that anarchy is prevented by the rules and values which are promoted and upheld by the pillars of society: the Church, the family, schools, and universities. However, such horror films seem to imply that it is these very institutions which can aid abuse, by serving as a cover for sinister activities. Nevertheless, these films also show the viewer a way out, by presenting role models who display the courage to stand up for what they believe in. The ultimate truth presented by the films is that people are always responsible for their actions, no matter what situation they find themselves in: whether they are "working for an institution that tells them to do certain things, or in an army ... It is always you, as an individual, that is responsible for your actions" (Hirschbiegel, in Cavagna 2004). This in turn serves as a commentary on Nazism. The potential to do good is vested in all of us, as too is the potential to do evil. Existential questions relating to self-control and responsibility therefore loom large.

In summary, Ruzowitzky's *Anatomy* films, as well as *The Experiment* and *Tattoo,* have been novel in their treatment of Naziism and evil. As recently as 1996, Goldhagen claimed that the Holocaust would not have happened without the help of "ordinary" Germans. Hirschbiegel's, Schwentke's, and Ruzowitzky's films have addressed and corrected this misconception and any related emphasis on "national character."[10] These directors have worked creatively with their heritage, having moved beyond the attribution of nationalistic traits in their exploration of evil. In their rediscovery of the horror genre for German-language film they have stressed that evil is not solely a "German master"— as in Célan's comment "Death is a Master from Germany" (*der Tod ist ein Meister aus Deutschland;* Célan 2002: 21–26)—but a human predisposition, thus broadening our perspective and challenging values and taboos in their representations of evil and of Nazism alike. In contrast to Freeland's definition of "uncanny horror: a disturbing and relentless vision of evil 'out there' in the world" (Freeland 2000: 244), Ruzowitzky's two films—not least due to their respective codas, which point to the possibility of yet another sequel—produce a feeling of the uncanny in the viewer; a disturbing and relentless vision that evil is "in them" and in the world due to all of us, individually and collectively, thus serving as a reminder of the fundamental law: *Homo homini lupus*, "man is a wolf to [his fellow] man."

Notes

1. There has been little, if any, research into the rediscovery of the horror genre in either Germany or Austria in recent years, making an investigation of this reorientation as well as the novel presentations of Nazism in horror film, necessary. For example, the horror genre post-1945 does not rate a mention in *The German Cinema Book* (edited by Tim Bergfelder, Erica Carter and Deniz Göktürk, 2002) in which attempts are made to include otherwise forgotten genre films such as the *Heimat*, western and crime film traditions.

2. "While courageous German police inspectors solved all kinds of crimes, sheer horror was left mostly to Hollywood and to specialists operating away from the mainstream, such as Jörg Buttgereit" (*Während tapfere deutsche Kommissare alle möglichen Verbrechen aufdeckten, blieb das nackte Grauen meist Hollywood und abseits des Mainstream agierenden Spezialisten wie Jörg Buttgereit überlassen*) (Bühler 2000).

3. While horror films adapted from Edgar Wallace's novels were considered *Straßenfeger* ("blockbuster", literally: street sweeper) as the streets were empty when they were screened on television in the 1950s and 60s, Ruzowitzky's *Anatomie* films are the first commercially successful big-budget horror films produced in German-speaking countries since the Third Reich (cf. Halle 2006).

4. Only the informed viewer will detect the deliberate references to Nazi doctor Josef Mengele and his medical experiments in Auschwitz-Birkenau.

5. "In contrast to the bigot of the older style," Horkheimer adds, "he seems to combine the ideas and skills which are typical of a highly industrialized society with irrational or anti-rational beliefs" (Horkheimer and Flowerman 1950: ix).

6. Milgram's work, as well as the infamous Stanford prison experiment, was the source of inspiration for Hirschbiegel's film *The Experiment.*

7. The memories of Nazism and fascism are evoked here by way of the body-art collection. Nazi concentration camps were playgrounds not only for scientists (as implied in *Anatomy*) but also for other hunters and collectors, who saw inmates' corpses as a resource awaiting exploitation. Just as it is depicted in Schwentke's *Tattoo*, skin (particularly decorated pieces of skin) was sought after by the Nazis for further use. While human skin was used for lampshades that were given to members of the SS, tattooed skin was popular for book covers, as well as for other decorative displays.

8. This myth was primarily made possible and acceptable by Document 1 of the Moscow Declaration (1943) which stipulated: "The Government of the United Kingdom, the Soviet Union and the United States of America are agreed that Austria, the first free country to fall victim to Hitlerite aggression, shall be liberated from German domination" (quoted in Keyserlingk 1988: 207).

9. He invited strippers to the exhibition openings and exhibited his works in Hamburg's Erotic Art Museum, fusing sex and death. He also participated in the annual Berlin rave party "Love

Parade" on a float using skeletons, seeking every opportunity to enlist media support for his business ventures (see Röbel and Wassermann 2004: 36–50).

10. Although Goldhagen refers to ordinary Germans living during the 1930s and 1940s, he nevertheless makes reference to a "German national project" as if to remind his readers that if there had been no Germans there would have been no Holocaust (see Goldhagen 1996: 11).

References

Amend, C. 2004. "Was für ein Land?" *Die Zeit*, 7 October, 57–58.

Arendt, H. 1963. *Eichmann in Jerusalem: A Report On the Banality of Evil.* New York: Viking.

Bergfelder, T., E. Carter and D. Göktürk. 2002. *The German Cinema Book.* London: BFI. Publishing.

Bosworth, R.J.B. 1999. "Film Memories of Fascism," in R.J.B. Bosworth and P. Dogliani (eds), *Italian Fascism: History, Memory and Representation.* London: MacMillan, 102–23.

Bühler, P. 2000. "Gelackte Kommilitonen: Wenn sich Jünglinge auf Seziertischen wiederfinden: *Anatomie* von Stefan Ruzowitzky," *Berliner Zeitung*, 3 February, p. 23.

Cavagna, C. 2004. "Star Moritz Bleibtreu and Director Oliver Hirschbiegel talk about their new film, *Das Experiment.*" Retrieved 12 June 2007 from: http://www. aboutfilm.com/features/dasexperiment/ interview.htm.

Célan, P. 2002 [1949]. *Todesfuge*, 2nd edn. Aachen: Rimbaud.

Dolan, S.P. 2000. "Anatomy aka Anatomie." Retrieved 12 June 2007 from: http://www. cinema-nocturna.com/d_anatomy _review.htm.

Freeland, C.A. 2000. *The Naked and the Undead: Evil and the Appeal of Horror.* Boulder, CO: Westview.

Goldhagen, D. 1996. *Hitler's Willing Executioners: Ordinary Germans and the Holocaust.* New York: Knopf.

Hagens, G. von. 2004. "Körperwelten." Retrieved 5 October 2004 from: http://www. koerperwelten.de/de/pages/ gunther_von_hagens.asp.

Halle, R. 2006. "Chainsaws and Neo-Nazis: Contemporary German Horror Film Production," *German as a Foreign Language* 3: 40–61.

Hantke, S. 2000. "Germany's Secret History: Stefan Ruzowitzky's *Anatomie* (*Anatomy*)." Retrieved 3 August 2004 from: http://www.kinoeye.org/printer. php?path=01/01/hantke01.php.

———. 2004. "Horror Film and the Historical Uncanny: The New Germany in Stefan Ruzowitzky's *Anatomie*," *College Literature* 31(2): 117–42.

Horkheimer M., and S.H. Flowerman. 1950. "Foreword," in T.W. Adorno et al. (eds), *The Authoritarian Personality.* New York: Harper and Row, i–xxxiii.

Keyserlingk, R.H. 1988. *Austria in World War II.* Montreal: Kingston.

Kracauer, S. 2004[1947]. *From Caligari to Hitler: A Psychological History of the German Film*, rev. edn, ed. L. Quaresima. Princeton, NJ: Princeton University Press.

Leventhal, R.S. 1995. "Romancing the Holocaust, or Hollywood and Horror: Steven Spielberg's *Schindler's List*." Retrieved 12 June 2007 from: http://www.iath. virginia.edu/holocaust/ schinlist.html.

Milgram, S. 1974. *Obedience to Authority: An Experimental View*. New York: Harper and Row.

Röbel, S., and A. Wassermann. 2004. "Händler des Todes: Gunther von Hagens' Ausstellung 'Körperwelten' fasziniert Millionen von Menschen. Doch die vermeintlich künstlerische Präsentation der Toten entpuppt sich als skrupelloses Geschäft: Viele Leichen werden billig gekauft, darunter sind offensichtlich auch die hingerichteter Chinesen," *Der Spiegel,* No.4, 36–50.

White, D.L. 1971."The Poetics of Horror: More Than Meets the Eye", *Cinema Journal* 10(2): 1–18.

Chapter 21

Beyond Borders and across Genre Boundaries: Critical *Heimat* in Stefan Ruzowitzky's *The Inheritors*

Rachel Palfreyman

Stefan Ruzowitzky's film *Die Siebtelbauern/The Inheritors* (1998) might appear not only explicitly, but even exclusively, focused on the German-language cinematic tradition. A critical *Heimatfilm* in the tradition of Volker Schlöndorff's *Der plötzliche Reichtum der armen Leute von Kombach/The Sudden Wealth of the Poor People of Kombach* (1971) and Peter Fleischmann's *Jagdszenen aus Niederbayern/Hunting Scenes from Lower Bavaria* (1969) does not instantly suggest broad international ambition, for the *Heimat* genre is not an especially well-traveled one. Indeed, the international success of Edgar Reitz notwithstanding, it is generally seen as a quintessentially German/Austrian genre, the product of particular German/Austrian aesthetic and historical constellations. But although Ruzowitzky's *The Inheritors* is a clear attempt to engage with the critical *Heimat* tradition, it enriches the genre with a diverse mix of other influences. We shall see in the following that his bold fusion draws on the radical fairy tale tradition of the 1920s and 1930s, the lush tragic idyll of Terrence Malick's *Days of Heaven* (1978),[1] as well as the bleak analysis of Volker Schlöndorff's *The Sudden Wealth of the Poor People of Kombach*. The result is a political film which, while engaging seriously with the *Heimat* tradition, is not tied to the specifics of German and Austrian culture. In this discussion I first consider Schlöndorff's German critical *Heimatfilm*, then the American drama *Days of Heaven*, before concentrating on Ruzowitzky.

The *Heimat* of 1930s films and books conveys a conservative sense of belonging, a spiritual and literal connection to land and a community that depends on the exclusion of unsuitable groups and individuals.[2] In the 1950s, conservative *Heimatfilm* papered over the cracks of the fractured nation and soothed a traumatized and displaced population with tales of potential outsiders being included in traditional, wholesome communities, and broken families patched up again into patriarchal wholeness.[3] However, this is very far from being the whole story of the *Heimat* mode. In this discussion I will focus on a subversive turn in the *Heimat* mode—particularly Volker Schlöndorff's *The Sudden Wealth of the Poor People of Kombach*, a generic cornerstone for Ruzowitzky's *The Inheritors*—though the deployment of the critical *Heimat* mode operates in combination with other aesthetic modes and cinematic influences.

The Sudden Wealth of the Poor People of Kombach is one of a little flurry of critical *Heimat* films that came out from the late 1960s to the early 1970s. Artists like Volker Schlöndorff, Rainer Werner Fassbinder, Reinhard Hauff, Peter Fleischmann, and Martin Sperr were influenced by the critical Italian westerns of Sergio Leone (Rentschler 1984: 111–12), and driven in part by a desire to overturn the 1950s *Heimatfilms* hated either for their anodyne, uncritical ahistoricity or for their nationalistic Cold War rhetoric. Nevertheless, filmmakers felt that the *Heimat* genre might be "salvageable" in their efforts to connect both with audiences and with a usable German cinematic identity (ibid.: 112). The films they produced ranged from bitter and violent rejections of provincial life, where the oppressed are themselves despised as colluding perpetrators ("anti-*Heimat*"), to more differentiated realist work which explored a critical and more honest view of peasant life while retaining a basic sympathy for the plight of the rural poor and dispossessed ("critical *Heimat*").[4]

Kombach is based on historical source material concerning the robbery of a tax coach by desperately poor peasants. The conspiracy is uncovered and the peasants are executed. The film is shot in black and white in a conscious rejection of the color of 1950s films. Explicit and repeated reference to the source material and other historical references in a voiceover put a clear aesthetic distance between this work and the 1950s evocation of *Heimat*. The grim naturalist aesthetic reveals the *Heimat* as a place not of nurturing family and spiritual connections but of poverty and deprivation. Family values are inverted: Heinrich Geiz and his common-law wife have an illegitimate child and in scenes with direct reference to Georg Büchner's play *Woyzeck*, they argue about the fate of this wretched unbaptized creature. Geiz angrily forces his wife onto the kitchen table to rape her. She only manages to prevent him by warning, "you'll give me another one" (*du machst mir noch eins*); thus the *Heimat* ideal of family joy is violently inverted. This and other references to *Woyzeck* place Schlöndorff's film within the tradition of German critical drama, one of the most important aesthetic legacies taken up by young filmmakers in the late 1960s.[5]

Schlöndorff and co-writer Margarethe von Trotta's peasants do not enjoy any kind of privileged bond with nature; their *Heimat* is no Technicolor idyll, but a grim forest which dominates them like some evil realm in a fairy tale: "nothing indicates an emotional affinity to the space they inhabit" (ibid.: 115). While earlier *Heimat* films show characters striding over the moors or hills and present majestic vistas conquered by authentic sons of the *Heimat*,[6] Schlöndorff's protagonists get lost in the fog, slosh about pathetically in the mud, and make several unsuccessful attempts to complete the ambush—once, farcically, because they have failed to agree in advance who will give the signal to attack.

Inevitably, the conspirators are undone by the sudden wealth they acquire when they finally manage a successful ambush. As soon as they spend the money, money that people of their standing cannot possibly have, they are revealed as the conspirators, and their poverty-stricken neighbors queue up to shop them to the state investigator Danz for a financial reward. Their only hope of successfully profiting from their crime would have been to flee, and throughout the film the characters as well as the narrator talk of emigration to America, described implausibly as a land of coffee, wine, and meat. However, they are stuck in Kombach precisely because of their *Heimat* ties and all attempts to leave lack conviction, to the extent that Ludwig Acker, who appears to have escaped, returns without explanation and gives himself up. Even Danz seems slightly taken aback at the success of the ideological hold of Church, State, and Law over him. The one person who escapes (because of his marginalized position he is disregarded as a conspirator) is the Jewish initiator of the plan, David Briel. The generic tradition of rewarding authentic *Heimat* folk is ironically reversed—it is a Jew, a paradigmatic rootless "other" of the *Heimat*, who survives to benefit from the robbery.

The role of the Church as an instrument of ideological oppression is made brutally clear as the conspirators are compelled to take communion prior to their execution. Heinrich Geiz refuses to bow to the Church to the end, an inspiring if futile gesture of defiance; though a scene where his accomplices try to force him to accept absolution is as depressing a demonstration of false consciousness as German cinema can muster.

Taking historical source material and using an off-screen narrator reflects Schlöndorff's attempt to challenge the irritatingly partial representation of historical change in 1950s films and at the same time to use the genre's potential for exploring the unwritten history of the voiceless poor (Boa and Palfreyman 2000: 89–102). But critical naturalism laced with historical documentary is not the only aesthetic mode the film alludes to. There are moments where austere naturalism breaks down in favor of joyous song and dance, and when the ambush finally succeeds there is an uncharacteristic extreme long shot showing the conspirators skipping off into the sunset. The opening credits show a naive drawing of the village and von Trotta's narration slides from the informative manner of an educational film to sounding like a children's storyteller. There are allusions to fairy tales in the wedding scene too. Briel refers skeptically to the tale "The Magic Table, the Golden Donkey and the Club in the Sack" (*Tischlein deck dich*) where a feast is provided by magic, while the goose-girl comments apparently without irony that life is not so hopeless as she has been told many tales where girls tending geese eventually became queens.[7] By juxtaposing Briel's skepticism and the goose-girl's naive faith, Schlöndorff and von Trotta present the tales as part of a system of ideological control that keeps the poor content.[8]

As Briel walks away to America—not into the distance, but into the foreground, towards the spectator, as it were—he recites the names of American cities and states, some of which did not yet exist in 1822, a date which is repeated in titles and narration so as to leave the viewer in no doubt about the historical setting. Such moments clearly undermine the appeal to historical authenticity, as does the music, which has a distinctly contemporary sound. Such flashes of highly ironized fairy-tale utopianism, whether tales of America or "The Magic Table", help to establish the transhistorical relevance of the film's anti-authoritarianism. Traces of utopianism, sometimes naive, sometimes ironic and knowing, gesture towards an unsettling generic mix far more powerful than a mere inversion of 1950s offerings.

Terrence Malick's *Days of Heaven*, noted (and awarded an Oscar) for its intensely warm cinematography, might seem a far cry from *The Sudden Wealth of the Poor People of Kombach*. Cinematographers Nestor Almendros and Haskell Wexler famously filmed much of the film at the so-called "magic hour," between sunset and dusk, so that the sun would never be visible in the sky, with a resultant soft, deep quality to the available light.[9] This technique delivers an extraordinary lyrical quality to the story of itinerant laborers in the 1910s who seize what seems to be a miraculous opportunity to improve their lives. Bill and Abby travel with Bill's sister, Linda. Though a couple, they pretend to be brother and sister. While working on a large and prosperous farm in Texas, Bill learns that the farmer is terminally ill. When the farmer falls for Abby, Bill encourages her to marry him in the hope of improving all their lives and eventually inheriting his wealth. However, what is embarked upon as a sham marriage is complicated by Abby's growing affection for the farmer and the farmer's apparent new lease of life following his marriage. Tensions lead to conflict and after Bill kills the farmer he is himself hunted down and killed.

What *Days of Heaven* shares with *The Sudden Wealth of the Poor People of Kombach* and *The Inheritors* is the prospect of the poor attaining sudden wealth. Schlöndorff's conspirators are ultimately engaged in a pointless exercise, for money alone, illegally acquired, will not release them from a system of ideological control that they have no hope of conquering. Bill and Abby are not trapped by quite the same system of ideologies. Indeed, in Schlöndorff's analysis their very rootlessness might give them a faint hope of coming out on top, as David Briel might, if he makes it to America and manages to build a life there. Malick instead emphasizes their isolation, shown in numerous shots, especially of Bill and Linda alone in the landscape as well as in Linda's lonely attempts to find friends. He does not attempt a forensic social analysis of the kind undertaken in Schlöndorff's film, despite the gesture towards social critique (Morrison and Schur 2003: 55). These differences aside, though, their attempt at getting rich through a sham marriage and subsequent inheritance, in a plot reminiscent of Henry James's *Wings of a Dove*, is quite as doomed as the tax robbery; in seeking the settled existence of marriage and then widowhood, their ambitions eventually implode in unwanted violence, futile flight, and precarious drifting for Abby and Linda.

Days of Heaven's lyrical embrace of the magic hour and astonishing landscape cinematography might suggest the idyll which the Kombach conspirators believe awaits them in the United States. Certainly the characters' relationship with landscape in this film is quite different from the grimy, bitter struggle of Schlöndorff's film. Although one could argue that Bill, Abby, and Linda are ultimately undone by a longing for a stable home and more secure lives, they are neither blighted nor blessed by ties to a *Heimat* in the same way as the poor of Kombach. There is no close examination here of the collusion of such institutions as the Church, the State and the law. Nevertheless, the glowing idyll of magic-lit wheat fields does not gloss over the tough conditions and exploitation endured by itinerant workers, and in common with *The Sudden Wealth of the Poor People of Kombach*, Malick's film is precisely dated with a newspaper from 1916, scenes of troop movements, as well as numerous examples of technology.

In *Days of Heaven*, the historically critical and the lyrically romantic variously collide and cohere. Scenes of characters alone in an overwhelming landscape and the elliptical emotions of the love triangle suggest an intense preoccupation with the individual; yet this preoccupation is balanced, or perhaps challenged, by scenes showing crowds of laborers, exploring communities at work and play. Teetering on the edge of a folksy sentimentality, Malick's workers and dancers are represented with an edge of irony in a complex fusion of the romantic, the naturalist, and pastiche (ibid.: 46–55). Indeed, in its efforts to explore the interrelation of the personal and the historical, the narrative itself is "at once impacted and tightly condensed with narrative economy, like a fable, and digressive and broadly sketched, like a ballad" (ibid.: 43). One might add that Old Testament influences on the narrative, such as the plague of locusts and the story of Abram and Sarai (who also pretend to be brother and sister), add an epic quality to the storytelling. Malick's tense and intense synthesis between apparently disparate elements and styles serves as a model for Ruzowitzky's reading of Schlöndorff, for his attempt to engage with both utopian and dystopian elements of the complex generic field of *Heimat*.

Like Schlöndorff's critical revision of the *Heimat* genre, which owes much to Büchner and Brecht as well as Sergio Leone, Malick locates his film within a complex cultural and literary field. The elliptical vernacular narration of the "wise child" Linda echoes Twain's Huckleberry Finn and alludes to a broad tradition of child or adolescent narrators encompassing J.D. Salinger and Henry James's *What Maisie Knew* (Latto 2003: 93–96). Indeed, the veritable "catalogue" of American literature from Whitman to Steinbeck that informs Malick's work is discussed by a number of critics (e.g., Morrison and Schur 2003: 29–31, 43–51; Mottram 2003: 13–14). There are obvious visual allusions to paintings like Andrew Wyeth's *Christina's World* and Edward Hopper's *House on the Railroad*, and the photographs in the opening credits include works by photographers such as Lewis Hine, William Notman, Chansonetta Emmons, and Frances Benjamin Johnston (Morrison and Schur 2003: 69–72). Myriad influences are worked through in a complex tension between the disillusionment of modernity and an almost nostalgic romantic irony (ibid.: 51).

Stefan Ruzowitzky's *The Inheritors* is a direct answer to *The Sudden Wealth of the Poor People of Kombach*, one which draws on the tensions between lyricism and social critique evident in Malick's film. Again a mix of aesthetic modes tells the story of a reversal of fortune among a group of rural poor; this time a legal mechanism poses a challenge to the powerful. In Ruzowitzky's film the peasants are bequeathed land legally by Hillinger, their landowning master in a mischievous but apparently incontestable will. Hillinger's will expresses the hope that his ten peasants will kill each other over the land, and although this is not quite what happens, the challenge to the established order does lead to a brutally violent crisis. *The Inheritors* tells the story of the conflict between the new property owners and the Establishment, which fears widespread insurrection among the wider peasantry. Seven peasants decide to call the bluff of their late employer and seek to make a success of the farm as a collective enterprise. The established landowners, led by the wealthy Danninger, conspire to bring the new farmers down, initially by placing an absurdly high value on the farm in the hope that the seven peasants who want to make a go of it will never be able to pay off the three who prefer to accept cash in lieu of the land. When this does not work, violence and arson are deployed against the fledgling collective. A further complication for one of the new farmers, the foundling Lukas, is that the former landowner Hillinger was murdered in an act of revenge by Rosalind, who Lukas discovers is his mother. Her pregnancy was the result of rape by Hillinger, and when she dares to report the crime she is imprisoned on a trumped-up charge. Thus her long-awaited vengeance initiates the utopian-tinged adventure.

Along with key thematic and narrative elements common to all three films—the prospect of wealth for the very poor, the more or less open endings, the interludes of music and dancing offering more or less ironic moments of idyll—*The Inheritors* has parallels with *Days of Heaven* in crucial scenes and narrative motifs. Both films have scenes showing characters working in a foundry, in both there are catastrophic fires on the respective farms, which lead to events of violence that result in Bill (*Days of Heaven*) and Lukas (*The Inheritors*) being killed. Scenes of the protagonist being chased through woodland occur in both films,[10] and a further parallel is the visit of traveling entertainers, who arrive by plane in *Days of Heaven*, and circus performers accompanying their elephant in *The Inheritors*. In both films there are scenes where the newly rich characters explore the house that they now appear to have a share in. In Malick's film, Bill (Richard Gere) is seen on his own exploring the farmer's house. Beyond Bill's obvious astonishment at the comfort and space, an implied criticism of injustice, there is no additional comment. In *The Inheritors*, a parallel scene occurs when three of the new farmers have a pillow-fight in the previously out-of-bounds "master" bedroom, delighting in the unfamiliar luxury. However, this sequence is intercut with Emmy learning from Old Nane, one of the other heirs, that Hillinger raped her there twice a week. On the ceiling of the room is a quotation from Proverbs warning against wickedness. Emmy declares that none of them will use the room. Like Schlöndorff, Ruzowitzky explores the nature of the exploitation that the peasants suffer, the collusion of property, patriarchy, and religion.

The Inheritors has in common with *Kombach* that life in the *Heimat* consists of unending servitude. Women peasants are raped by landowning farmers who exploit their laborers in a quasi-feudal manner, determining every detail of their peasants' lives. Such bonds of exploitation are neither so carefully picked apart nor in any case so tightly defined on Malick's Texas farm, where the very rootlessness of the laborers precludes this particular misery and opens the way to others. But in *The Inheritors*, as in *Kombach*, America is the utopian "other" of the *Heimat*, a refuge for outlaws, where land can supposedly be obtained with ease. When Lukas kills his former overseer during an attack on the farm, his comrades persuade him to head for America. Yet his attempt to leave is not much more convincing than that of Ludwig Acker in *Kombach*. At first he evades capture in the romantic forest where he was born, but when he learns there that the prisoner Rosalind is his mother, he ignores all rational advice and breaks into the gaol to see her. Even then his courage and chutzpah might see him escape, but he is finally caught when Danninger correctly guesses that at a time of crisis he will return to the farm, and sets a trap for him there. As in *Kombach*, only the *heimatlos*—Severin, the outsider, and Emmy, denounced as a whore with an illegitimate son, characters lacking *Heimat* bonds—have a realistic chance of making it to America, where the odd family grouping might resemble the inscrutable family connections of Bill, Abby and Linda. *Heimat* ties, whether the irresistible pull of land for a new farmer, or the family tie of a hitherto unknown mother, prove to be a peasant's downfall here as in the Kombach tale.

In a further gesture to the critical *Heimat* tradition, *The Inheritors* is full of uncompromising violence: Emmy suffers multiple rapes, the mute stable boy is beaten, the story begins with a vengeful murder, and it ends with the murders of Lukas and Danninger. A bleak critical *Heimat* narrative like *Kombach*, it emphasizes the exploitation of the rural poor, where the *Heimat* oppresses rather than nurtures them. Here, too, the defiant hero Lukas is ultimately defeated. However, *The Inheritors* is a critical *Heimat* narrative which combines the traces of futile utopianism in *Kombach* and the lyricism of *Days of Heaven* and makes them key generic pillars of the story. Fairy tales, which smother the peasants of Kombach in a comforting blanket of false consciousness, are amplified and accentuated in *The Inheritors*, to the point where the revolutionary potential of fairy tale, fused with critical *Heimat* in the manner of Malick's syncretic narration, becomes dominant in the film. Thus *The Inheritors* mixes critical *Heimat* with the utopian tradition of the literary fairy tale, despite apparent contradictions between the two aesthetic modes.

As a fairy tale narrative, *The Inheritors* draws on radical appropriations of the genre which are as much a part of its history as those which promote conservative, bourgeois values and a patriarchal understanding of gender.[11] Leaving aside the progressive aspects of the Romantic fairy tale,[12] there is also a vibrant twentieth-century tradition of politically radical fairy tales. In the Weimar period especially, writers such as Hermynia Zur Mühlen, Lisa Tetzner, and Béla Balázs wrote proletarianized fairy tales, some of which were published in anthologies by left-wing and radical publishing houses.[13] Their tales sought to show how class exploitation functioned and how it could be defeated by bold characters capable of insight, solidarity, and action against the powerful classes.

As well as proletarian fairy tales aimed at children, there is a philosophical tradition in which writers such as Walter Benjamin, Siegfried Kracauer, and Ernst Bloch explore the radical utopian potential of the fairy tale. Benjamin comments in his essay on storyteller (Benjamin 1977) on the importance of the folk tale in narration as a "quasi-magical mode of connecting the people with their own nature and history" (Zipes 1992: 95), particularly emphasizing the folk tale's exhortation to meet the challenge of powerful forces in the world with "cunning" (*List*) and "high spirits" (*Übermut*) (Benjamin 1977: 458). For Kracauer, magical fairy tales actually rehearse the defeat of supposedly "natural" mythologies by the truth (Giles 2003: 214).

Bloch, too, sees in fairy tales a rational, enlightened strategy in which cunning and courageous characters master the situations they face even with the odds stacked against them (Bloch 1965: 198–99). Fairy tale narratives and aesthetics lend themselves to a politically radical, critical reading of oppression in the rural *Heimat*. For Zipes, Bloch's utopian call for *Heimat* is fundamental to the way fairy tales operate in tension between the *heimlich* and the *unheimlich*, or uncanny: "the uncanny setting and motifs of the fairy tale ... open us up to the recurrence of primal experiences ... The pattern in most fairy tales involves the reconstitution of home on a new plane" (Zipes 1983: 175–76).

The liberating fairy tale does not end with a perfect resolution but its end is a beginning—the tale reflects an ongoing struggle, the emancipatory "happy end" is in fact the start of a development (ibid.: 182). Emancipatory tales have, in Zipes's view, an upsetting effect: they scrutinize social relations and force audiences to reflect on their own situation and social role (ibid.: 182). Thus a synthesis of the critical *Heimat* film and the emancipatory fairy tale, channeled by Malick's fusion of social critique, biblical epic, and individual tragedy, is a peculiarly appropriate and effective generic encounter in *The Inheritors*, a challenge to the spectator that goes beyond the forensic social analysis of *Kombach*.

The fairy tale heart of *The Inheritors* is evident from the very opening of the film. In common with *Kombach*, there is an off-screen narrator, though in this case, as in *Days of Heaven*, the narrator is one of the characters, Severin, the outsider. His elliptical storytelling is much closer to Linda's narration in *Days of Heaven* than to Margarethe von Trotta's dispassionate and explanatory narration, and immediately locates the film as a folk tale with violent twists.[14]

In addition, while *Kombach* uses titles and narrative to give precise (if knowingly disrupted) historical chronologies, *The Inheritors* is difficult to pin down to a specific historical moment. Some sources suggest that the film is set in the early 1930s,[15] some in the 1920s,[16] though Dor Film and the Austrian distributor of the film remain less specific, "a village in the Mühlviertel [Upper Austria] between the wars."[17] Robert von Dassanowsky gives an allegorical reading of the film based on the 1930s political context he identifies: the dead farmer could be seen as the missing monarch, the landowning farmers represent the "Austrofascist aspect of the Ständestaat," and the departure of Emmy, Severin and Florian "evokes the Austrian exiles from 1934–8" (Dassanowsky 2003: 140, 142). However, the packaging of the UK release refers to the period as "turn of the century," in the grand tradition of errors on such packaging. This error, though, is more forgivable than most. For, *pace* von Dassanowsky, how exactly are we supposed to date this film? There is not a single motor vehicle present in the entire film. Many of the clothes worn are traditional or working clothes. Agriculture is organized on quasi-feudal lines with the *Bauer*, the landowner, ruling supreme over *Knecht* and *Magd*, his peasants. There is electric lighting at least and there are telegraph wires, though the narrative at first lures the viewer into supposing it is set earlier.[18] The non-diegetic music is Satie—in particular his darkly childlike *Gnossienne*, written at the end of the nineteenth century—but this seems to see the film wriggling into a more modernist key. In the story itself, there is a Caruso recording of "La donna è mobile" from *Rigoletto*, though Caruso made a number of recordings of this aria (in 1903, 1904, 1908, and 1917). Ultimately Emmy's dress with its hemline skimming the knee and the chic hat which tempts two of the newly anointed farmers are the most convincing suggestion of a 1930s setting, or at the earliest 1920s. But the difficulty in dating the story seems to be as important and interesting as the date itself.

For *The Inheritors* flirts deliberately with the timeless effect created in fairy tales with their slippery chronology and vague monarchies and empires. There are a number of occasions in the film where a precise date would have been almost easier to include than to omit, which suggests that there is a deliberate effort to cloud chronologies rather than illuminate them. Legal documents—Hillinger's will, the statement identifying Rosalind, Rosalind's own statement, extracts of Rosalind's police file—for example, are all referred to conspicuously without a date. Ruzowitzky himself commented, "precisely because I studied history, I know that it is impossible to reconstruct anything completely accurately. I think that a consciously personal and consciously contemporary perspective is more honest and ultimately more authentic" (Ruzowitzky n.d.).

In his review, Rùppert Koppold captures such ambiguities when he refers to the film taking place "somewhere in the Austrian Mühlviertel and at some time when there were still no tractors in the fields, and hierarchies seemed still to be set in stone" (Koppold n.d.). The "once upon a time" setting of the narrative, the ambiguities of time and place, are fundamental to the effectiveness of the film as a critical *Heimat* tale. A film that looks to a classic of German political cinema might well incorporate political allegories related to the 1930s. But the presentation of the film's setting is not tied to a specific chronology and its political and aesthetic modes suggest a broad and allusive critique.

The storytelling of *The Inheritors* is also expressed by simple, strong rhythms and repetitions which add to the sense that we are watching a cool, ironic fairy tale. The repetition in Old Nane's telling of Rosalind's story is a striking example: "it was wrong, a great wrong … a great wrong" (*ein Unrecht war das, ein großes Unrecht … ein großes Unrecht*). The film is also full of the characters one might expect in a revisionist fairy tale of the Weimar period: the old wise woman, the poor, mute stable boy, the villainous farmer, the simple foundling hero, and the clever, resourceful young woman, reversing the "comatose princess" stereotype. In addition, Ruzowitzky uses intense colors, which reflect and radiate light, the kinds of colors a children's illustrator might use. According to Ruzowitzky such colors are everywhere in the countryside despite misconceptions that tasteful restraint dominates the palette of vernacular architecture (Ruzowitzky n.d.). Indeed, the careful effort to work with particular lighting and color effects to create narrative and aesthetic tensions is something which *The Inheritors* has in common with, and perhaps even learns from, *Days of Heaven*.[19]

The peasants in *The Inheritors* have a slim glimpse of the utopia of *Heimat*. The mere attainment of what they desire will not perforce bring with it their inevitable destruction as is the case with the crime in Kombach, nor are they subject to the conflict that accompanies Abby's marriage to the farmer. Instead of being necessarily outlawed they legally own the land, a classic fairy tale "miracle". The problem of identification with the land is thus very different from *Kombach* and *Days of Heaven*. The Kombach conspirators are alienated by their very position in the Heimat; Bill and Abby attain access to land only at the expense of their relationship. Ruzowitzky's peasant farmers are suddenly included in the *Heimat* system in a way they never thought possible. As *The Inheritors* ends, the spectator is left angry but not despairing. Severin, Emmy, and her son Florian might make it to America, though what awaits them there is clearly no heaven on earth. Old Nane and the stable boy remain and might make a success of the farm even after the arson attack. The mute boy has started to speak, though he has also been beaten up. Danninger has been killed, presumably by the otherwise cautious Severin, so at least Lukas has been avenged. Severin has thus in one sense acknowledged his rather repressed love for Lukas. And Lukas, who literally and metaphorically sowed the seed of rebellion, will never be forgotten, though (as Severin comments) even he cannot have sired all the children named Lukas who were born that year. This is precisely the end that is actually an open beginning, so beloved of the emancipatory fairy tale. The management and ownership of the farm are shared by an old woman and a boy. Taken together with Emmy, Severin, and Florian's departure from the *Heimat* to find a new life, this suggests a new struggle, new possibilities.

The key to the utopian gesture in *The Inheritors* is the revolutionary motif that is pointedly missing from *Kombach*, which explicitly declines to show even the faintest glimmer of solidarity amongst the oppressed poor. Such solidarity is not even conspicuous by its absence in *Days of Heaven*. But in *The Inheritors* other peasants volunteer their labor in the evenings to help pay off the three heirs who choose the cash alternative to land inheritance. When an attempt is made to bury Lukas quietly and without ceremony to prevent radical ideas fomenting among the peasantry, the peasants nevertheless attend, and even go on strike. to mark his life, not even feeding the animals that day. The church bell is rung for Lukas, and the shocked priest who tries to stop it is confronted with a peasant casually flicking a knife.

A further source for utopian celebration points clearly forward to the present day. The peasants of Kombach are crushed at least in part by the cage of morality constructed around them by the Church in dubious alliance with the State. Marriage and legitimacy are luxuries they cannot afford. In *The Inheritors*, the Church, which would have benefited financially were it not for the farmer's will, is against the inversion of what it regards as the natural order of things. The priest preaches against the peasant farm, declaring it immoral: the seven farmers are living in sin, in more ways than one. Their response is simple: they simply stop going to Mass. Only Old Nane is still afraid of Hell and carries on attending; the younger men and women are no longer bound by these particular ideological chains. Tellingly, while even the defiant Heinrich Geiz is undone by his wish to marry the mother of his baby, Lukas the simple foundling knows no sexual prohibition. Bill and Abby, who try to use marriage to their benefit in order to inherit legally, also find that a desire for moral legitimacy is no basis for people of their class to thrive.

These films are political texts for their respective generations. Schlöndorff and von Trotta present a fairly orthodox Marxist analysis of the mechanisms of ideology transmission. Church, State, school, the military, and the law are all shown to be colluding in the oppression of the peasants who are incapable of any form of class solidarity. The Church imposes moral systems backed by the fear of Hell that bolster the power of the State. Education amounts to teaching children the desirability of the status quo: children chant a poem that asserts that the peasant woman is ennobled by her labor, an assertion belied by the sight of actual women plowing the field. Schlöndorff grapples explicitly with a German aesthetic and historical legacy: historical source material from Hessen, *Woyzeck*, and the critical *Volksstück* (folk play) are all part of his effort to reckon with a counter-cultural German creative tradition. The film follows the preoccupation of the 1968 generation and is concerned with an examination of how institutions transmit ideology to maintain the status quo and keep the poor and dispossessed ignorant of their true power.

Ruzowitzky, on the other hand, specifically shows the Church as a defeated power, or at least a force on the wane. Education is not criticized, but a way out: when Lukas is prevented from attending school, this is presented as an unjust limitation. Positioned between the romantic irony of *Days of Heaven* and the Marxist critical *Heimat*, Ruzowitzky mixes the rural Austrian *Heimat* narrative with the revolutionary fairy tale and gestures towards a critical idyll, with the result that his film has a broader international appeal. Ultimately, Ruzowitzky's political concerns are not solely Austrian. Though his film is otherwise closely related to Schlöndorff's critical Heimat film which grapples with the legacy of German cinema and German political history, here *The Inheritors* contrasts sharply in that it is highly accessible to an anglophone audience: no particular knowledge of Austrian history or culture is necessary to understand it.[20]

Unlike *Days of Heaven*, *The Inheritors* offers both a critique of social organization and a model for a new society, however idealized, which chimes with the issues of our age, an era of globalization, refugees, citizenship rights, global agricultural issues, fair trade, and the question of who owns the land. Though the film does not suggest abolishing the concept of property as an orthodox Marxist treatment might, the collective nature of the farming experiment alludes to a revolution in property ownership as well as a social revolution in terms of the alternative lifestyles of communal living. Emmy's enterprising search for profit from the farm strikes a very modern chord: she understands that happy cows will give more milk, so lines them up not according to the alphabet, but according to their preference. The farm work is done almost entirely by women as Lukas and Severin need to bring in a wage from the foundry in the nearest town. This is a thoroughly modern, or even postmodern, farm: fully diversified, dependent on outside wages, offering accommodation to travelers and with a commitment to animal welfare. The fact that the film is hard to date makes these parallels all the more obvious.

Perhaps one of the specific political discussions in *The Inheritors* is an invitation to consider that there is something quasi-feudal about our late-capitalist, globalized world. After all, the clerical feudalism of the film's setting is clearly hanging on well past its sell-by date. Some critics of corporate culture, especially in the United States, are using the term neo-feudalism; it is suggested that ordinary people globally are becoming new serfs, that there is something faintly medieval about the current concentration of power and wealth in the hands of a few giant corporations that resemble a bloated aristocracy in that they have done nothing to deserve or create their wealth.[21] This may or may not be a respectable term in academic political science but it is at the least a powerful metaphor amongst many critics of globalization and it is one of the contexts in which we can read *The Inheritors*, just as *Kombach* invites us to consider how populations can be controlled and duped by the institutions of ideological control.

As Ruzowitzky reckons with one of the crucial and enduring genres of German-language cinema, he infuses his story with the rebellious and utopian spirit of the radical fairy tale, taking Schlöndorff's bleak analysis, Malick's melancholic, mysterious idyll, and suggesting a new answer to the question of how to make an accessible and differentiated political film. Quite in the spirit of Malick's aesthetic syncretism, Ruzowitzky deploys a number of aesthetic modes and narrative strategies, which operate in tension with each other. The critical *Heimat* genre given the form of an ironized idyll, a politically radical fairy tale with a dash of the western proves highly appropriate for the telling of a political fable for the era of globalization. He harnesses the power of an entertaining, artful and charming mode of storytelling, one that is "rooted in the people" (*im Volk wurzel[t]*), as Benjamin (1977: 457) puts it, to create a political film that engages as well as challenges. But by putting critical *Heimat* and revolutionary fairy tale together, he also restores the co-operation of two aesthetic modes that belong together: the "happy ending" of the revisionist fairy tale is Bloch's utopian *Heimat*, and the critical *Heimat* text has much to gain from revealing the utopian potential of the uncanny. In searching for an internationally readable mix of aesthetic modes, Ruzowitzky suggests that it is the rootless and the enterprising that might survive, or even, possibly, thrive. With the vital element of solidarity, we can see what might in a fairy tale world have come of the anger and tenacity of Heinrich Geiz: *The Inheritors* celebrates and, crucially, rewards courage (*Mut*), dialectically divided in Benjamin's text into cunning (*Untermut*) and high spirits (*Übermut*).

Notes

An earlier version of this chapter was published as "Once Upon a Time in the Critical Heimat Film: *Der plötzliche Reichtum der armen Leute von Kombach* and *Die Siebtelbauern*," in R. Rechtien and K. von Oppen (eds), "Local/Global Narratives," *German Monitor* 68 (special issue), 2007.

1. I am grateful to Michael Woodward for pointing out *Days of Heaven* as a significant intertext.
2. In Luis Trenker's *Der verlorene Sohn/The Prodigal Son* (1934), for example, the *Heimat* hero and his true sweetheart are set against rich American tourists who attempt to purchase

authentic artefacts of the *Heimat* and lure the hero to a soulless and cosmopolitan New York, before a triumphant return to where he truly belongs.

3. See, e.g., Hans Deppe's *Das Schwarzwaldmädel/Black Forest Girl* (1950), Harald Reinl's *Die Fischerin vom Bodensee/The Fisherwoman of Lake Constance* (1956), and Paul May's *Heimat, deine Lieder/Heimat, Your Songs* (1959), to name but three.

4. A key example of the anti-*Heimat* tendency is the rarely screened *Hunting Scenes from Lower Bavaria*, in which a young woman, who claims to be pregnant, is stabbed in the abdomen by the reviled outsider who is the putative father. Hated as a homosexual even before this crime, he is in turn hunted down by the villagers.

5. Fassbinder dedicated his film *Katzelmacher* (1969) to Marieluise Fleisser. *Katzelmacher* is an example of the anti-*Heimat* tradition in that it subverts the notion of the nourishing relationships of the *Heimat* idyll and replaces the jolly provincial or rural setting of the 1950s with a suburbia of energy-sapping tedium, incessant bickering, and petty exploitation.

6. This tendency is clear in Luis Trenker's films—e.g., *The Prodigal Son* and *Flucht in die Dolomiten/Flight into the Dolomiten* (1955)—but a tendency to include long shots and extreme long shots of characters in their rural element is very common in 1950s *Heimat* films: e.g., Alfons Stummer's *Der Förster vom Silberwald/The Gamekeeper of the Silver Forest* (1954), and Otto Meyer's *Dort oben, wo die Alpen glüh'n/Up Where the Alps Glow* (1956).

7. The Brothers Grimm's "The Goose-girl" is perhaps alluded to. A princess is usurped by her servant and forced to tend geese before she is eventually restored to her royal station.

8. The textual tapestry that makes up this call for obedience and contentment also includes the Bible and a number of literary texts by writers such as Christian Fürchtegott Gellert and Jeremias Gotthelf which tended to idealize the peasant's lot. See Daniel Schacht (1991: 72–86) on this point. On David Briel's insight into such ideologies, see Dieter Bahlinger et al. (1989: 120).

9. Almendros received the Oscar; Wexler a credit for additional photography.

10. Hunting scenes in woodland are an important motif of the critical *Heimat* genre: e.g., in the climax of *Hunting Scenes from Lower Bavaria*, which like *The Inheritors* and *Days of Heaven* turns the tables in that a human protagonist, not an animal, is hunted down.

11. For a summary of critical readings of the fairy tale tradition, see Zipes (1983: 170–71; 1994: 29–48).

12. "No matter what has become of the fairy tale, its main impulse was at first revolutionary and progressive, not escapist, as has too often been suggested" (Zipes 1992: 36).

13. For an account of the development of these tales, see Jack Zipes's introduction to his edited collection of Weimar fairy tales (Zipes 1989).

14. Malick said that he wanted Linda's narration to deliver an "innocent fairytale ambience" comparable to *What Maisie Knew* (Malick, in Combs 1978: 84).

15. See "Die Siebtelbauern", http://www.votivkino.at/textlang/321press.htm, retrieved 28 October 2008. Robert von Dassanowsky describes the film as located in "the impoverishment, political instability, and national identity trauma of the Austrian First Republic" (Dassanowsky 2003: 135).

16. Publicity for a screening in Jena suggests that the film is set in 1920s Upper Austria: http://www.jenaonline.de/events/filmev/die_siebtelbauern.htm, retrieved 28 October 2008.

17. Source: http://www.filmladen.at/vkat/v5395sie.htm, retrieved 28 October 2008. See also the Dor Film website, http://www.dor-film.com/page.php?modul=Article&op=read&nid=48& rub=3, retrieved 3 December 2008.

18. The confusion in establishing the period recalls Kafka's *Das Schloß/The Castle*, in which telephone and electric light sit uneasily within the otherwise vaguely feudal setting.

19. While color is frequently part of the aesthetic complaint against 1950s *Heimat* films, it is not the filmstock alone that causes the rather nauseating excess or (sometimes) insipid lack of precision in the color, but the way that the filmstock interacts with narrative, lighting and *mise-en-scène* to create such effects. In the same way, the effect of the color in *The Inheritors* depends

on its interaction with lighting and narration to evoke a beautifully illustrated and cherished edition of folk tales.

20. *The Inheritors* has been marketed on VHS and DVD with subtitles, a sharp contrast with *Kombach* and other critical and anti-*Heimat* films, which are difficult to obtain even without subtitles.
21. See, e.g. Chomsky (2004: 118–121); also Klein (2000) and Willers (2003).

References

Bahlinger, D., et al. 1989. *Der Deutsche Heimatfilm: Bildwelten und Weltbilder: Bilder, Texte, Analysen zu 70 Jahren deutscher Filmgeschichte.* Tübingen: Tübinger Verein für Volkskunde.

Benjamin, W. 1977. "Der Erzähler: Betrachtungen zum Werk Nikolai Lesskows" [1936/37], in *Gesammelte Schriften, II*, eds R. Tiedemann and H. Schweppenhäuser. Frankfurt am Main: Suhrkamp, 438–65.

Bloch, E. 1965. "Das Märchen geht selber in der Zeit," in *Literarische Aufsätze.* Frankfurt am Main: Suhrkamp, 196–99.

Boa, E. and R. Palfreyman. 2000. *Heimat – A German Dream: Regional Loyalties and National Identity in German Culture 1890–1990.* Oxford: Oxford University Press.

Chomsky, N. 2004. *Hegemony or Survival: America's Quest for Global Dominance.* London: Penguin.

Combs, R. 1978. "Days of Heaven," *Sight and Sound* 47(2): 84.

Dassanowsky, R. von. 2003. "Going Home Again? Ruzowitzky's *Die Siebtelbauern* and the New Austrian Heimatfilm," *Germanic Review* 78(2): 133–47.

Giles, S. 2003. "Limits of the Visible: Kracauer's Photographic Dystopia," in S. Giles and M. Oergel (eds), *Counter-Cultures in Germany and Central Europe: From Sturm und Drang to Baader-Meinhof.* Oxford: Peter Lang, 213–39.

Klein, N. 2000. *No Logo.* London: Flamingo.

Koppold, R. n.d. "Die Siebtelbauern: Landleben mit Enrico Caruso", *Stuttgarter Zeitung Online.* Retrieved 28 October 2008 from: http://www.stuttgarter-zeitung.de/stz/page/358300_0_2147_-filmkritik-stuttgart-zeitung-die-siebtelbauern.html.

Latto, A. 2003. "Innocents Abroad: The Young Female Voice in *Badlands* and *Days of Heaven*," in H. Patterson (ed.), *The Cinema of Terrence Malick: Poetic Visions of America.* London: Wallflower, 86–99.

Morrison, J. and T. Schur. 2003. *The Films of Terrence Malick.* Westport: Praeger.

Mottram, R. 2003. "All Things Shining: The Struggle for Wholeness, Redemption and Transcendence in the Films of Terrence Malick," in H. Patterson (ed.), *The Cinema of Terrence Malick: Poetic Visions of America.* London: Wallflower, 13–23.

Rentschler, E. 1984. *West German Film in the Course of Time.* New York: Redgrave.

Ruzowitzky, S. n.d. "Aus dem Presseheft: Die Siebtelbauern. Interviewstatements von Stefan Ruzowitzky." Retrieved 28 October 2008 from: http://www.votivkino.at/textlang/321press.htm.

Schacht, D. 1991. *Fluchtpunkt Provinz: Der neue Heimatfilm zwischen 1968 und 1972.* Münster: MAkS Publikationen.

Willers, B. 2003. "Privatization and Neo-Feudalism." Retrieved 9 December 2008 from: http://www.populist.com/03.12.willers.html.

Zipes, J. 1983. *Fairy Tales and the Art of Subversion: The Classical Genre for Children and the Process of Civilization.* London: Heinemann.

———. 1989. "Introduction," in J. Zipes (ed.), *Fairy Tales and Fables from Weimar Days.* Hanover: University Press of New England, 3–28.

———. 1992. *Breaking the Magic Spell: Radical Theories of Folk and Fairy Tales.* New York: Routledge.

———. 1994. *Fairy Tale as Myth/Myth as Fairy Tale.* Lexington: University Press of Kentucky.

Chapter 22

A Genuine Dilemma: Ruzowitzky's *The Counterfeiters* as Moral Experiment

Raymond L. Burt

When Hollywood's Academy of Motion Picture Arts and Sciences awarded Stefan Ruzowitzky's film *Die Fälscher/The Counterfeiters* (2007) with the Oscar for Best Foreign Language Film, one sensed a bit of déjà vu. Here is a film based on historical events in which a small group of Jews in a concentration camp find themselves protected to some measure from the Nazi death machine. They owe their survival to the efforts of a morally ambiguous and unlikely hero, who uses the power of money and his personal skill to protect these few inmates from the surrounding inhumanity and destruction. To some extent the film calls to mind Steven Spielberg's Oscar-winning film *Schindler's List* (1993). The fact that both films begin with tango music confirms the suspicion that there is more at play here than coincidence. *Schindler's List* is a tribute to the moral courage of those facing the Holocaust and an "artistic" remembrance of human suffering and loss. While no doubt influenced by Spielberg's monumental and monumentally successful film, Ruzowitzky's work explores moral stances and, ultimately, seeks universality and not historical memory.

As both the director and screenwriter of most of his films, Stefan Ruzowitzky has had considerable artistic control. It is therefore tempting to see him as a rising film auteur, with *Die Siebtelbauern/The Inheritors* (1998) and *The Counterfeiters* as evidence. Like Stanley Kubrick, Ruzowitzky moves from genre to genre, trying his hand at a wide range of cinematic styles: a coming-of-age film, a horror film, a *Heimatfilm*, a light adventure film, and in this case, a Holocaust film. He has also completed a children's film and has indicated that he is planning a science-fiction film (Suchsland 2007). Nevertheless, the designation "auteur," with its avant-garde, arthouse significance, does not quite fit a director who does not distance himself from industry expectations and openly admires Hollywood. Ruzowitzky's German-made horror film *Anatomie/Anatomy* (2000) was directly aimed at popular tastes and box-office success, as was its sequel, *Anatomie 2/Anatomy 2* (2003). *All the Queen's Men* (2001), scripted in English with a British and American cast, attempted perhaps too much in its misguided attempt to combine the transvestite humor of Billy Wilder's *Some Like It Hot* (1959) with the war sabotage exploitation film, *Kelly's Heroes* (1970), and garnered neither critical acclaim nor box-office success. It is, however, the only one of Ruzowitzky's films in which he does not have a screenplay credit. On the other hand, his very personal and enigmatic recontextualization of the *Heimatfilm* genre, *The Inheritors*, is rendered with masterful cinematic flair and has been read as a powerful historical allegory (Dassanowsky 2003). *The Counterfeiters* blends both aspects of the filmmaker, and its critical and popular reception has established Ruzowitzky at the forefront of the Austrian and Central European film industry.

Following *The Inheritors*, a film rooted firmly in a traditional Austrian cinematic genre if not in its anti-idyllic critical interpretation, Ruzowitzky moved away from Austria, both as a filming location and cinematic subject. In explaining his filming in Germany, he also criticizes current Austrian film support: "In Austria the budgets are too small for much of what I make. Besides, I am a 'German by training,' as I grew up here [in Germany]. I 'tick' somewhat differently than the classical misanthropic Austrian" (Ruzowitzky, in Suchsland 2007).[1] Like Michael Haneke, who was born in Germany but raised in Austria, Ruzowitzky explains the production of his films outside Austria as being due to lack of government support. Interestingly, *The Counterfeiters* may ultimately help change this situation. The former Austrian chancellor, Alfred Gusenbauer, in an initial burst of national pride after Ruzowitzky's work became the first Austrian film to win the Best Foreign Language Film Oscar, declared: "We must support European film production to a greater degree than is currently the case through an enhanced national and European subsidy."[2] It is, of course, ironic that despite distancing himself from his country's film scene, Ruzowitzky, with this film, has achieved a lasting place in its film history. His obvious pride in the importance of Austrian talent in golden-age Hollywood did not preclude a volley of criticism against Austria's long avoidance of dealing with the Nazi period: "There have been some great Austrian filmmakers working here [Hollywood], thinking of Billy Wilder, Fred Zinnemann, Otto Preminger. Most of them had to leave my country because of the Nazis, so it sort of makes sense that the first Austrian movie to win an Oscar is about the Nazis' crimes" (Ruzowitsky 2008).

The Counterfeiters begins at the end of the Second World War, as a French newspaper declaring *La Guerre est finie!* reveals. We see a lone figure sitting on a pebbly beach, dressed in a ragged suit and hat, staring without expression at the sea. He silently stands up and walks inland, passing a family of refugees, soldiers sleeping off an alcoholic stupor, a black marketeer hawking his wares, and a prostitute teasing her customer—a visual catalogue of the aftermath of any war. The man silently climbs the stone staircase from the shore up to the opulent casino. Salomon ("Sally") Sorowitsch (Karl Markovics), holding a suitcase filled with stacks of dollars, sheds his ragged suit for a tuxedo, checks into the luxury hotel and joins the gambling tables at the casino. His winnings draw admiration from the crowd and in particular from one woman (Dolores Chaplin) who joins him in his room that evening. During the course of their lovemaking, she spots the serial numbers tattooed on this arm. This raises a dramatic question: how can a concentration camp survivor have such riches?

At this point there is a flashback to 1936 and a night club in Berlin. The National Socialists have been in power for three years, and their might is growing. Sorowitsch is a kingpin, with people vying for his favor. A man who owes him money is begging for a reprieve. "It's not about the 150. It's a matter of principle. It's about my very existence, and for that I could be driven to take extreme measures."[3] This sets the expectation for the character's personal ethics and behavior—he is a survivalist at all costs. The sign of the times is evident for the Jews and Sorowitsch plans his escape, but it is deterred by a romantic encounter. The next morning the police break into his apartment and find Sorowitsch still in bed with the woman. With ironic admiration, Commissar Herzog (Devid Striesow) informs Sorowitsch that he has the honor of arresting him for counterfeiting. Following his time in prison, Sorowitsch is transferred to Mauthausen concentration camp (in Austrian territory) in 1939. Here he experiences the inhumanity of a labor camp, although he discovers how to gain special favors from the guards by drawing heroic portraits of them in the style of National Socialist Realism.

In 1944 Sorowitsch is transferred to the Sachsenhausen concentration camp, joining others in Operation Bernhard, an SS-sponsored project in which prisoners were used to counterfeit British and American currency. Upon arrival he meets other new transferees, including Adolf Burger (August Diehl). They are greeted by Herzog, now an SS officer in charge of the counterfeiting operation. The new arrivals are marched through the rows of huts to a special barracks sealed off from the rest of the camp. Here they join the special team of inmates involved in the massive counterfeiting operation. Sorowitsch is placed in a leadership role in the operation and begins counterfeiting British currency. The assembled team of inmates represents a microcosm of society, with members from all walks of life and social statuses, all equally engaged in helping the Nazi war effort in order to stay alive. The reactions to this moral dilemma vary greatly, but the central focus of the film is on the contrast between Sorowitsch's pragmatic struggle to survive and Burger's principled resistance in the face of certain death. The team is successful in counterfeiting the British pound and is told to turn its attention to the American dollar. Fueling the dramatic tension of the film, the special treatment of the counterfeiters is also contrasted with the horrific treatment of the prisoners in the surrounding concentration camp, indicated mostly by horrific sounds penetrating the operetta music piped into the barracks which is sealed off from the rest of the camp. The pressure to produce the dollar is intensified by Burger's sabotage. Sorowitsch refuses to betray Burger, even though his act threatens the lives of the team. Finally Sorowitsch secretly accomplishes counterfeiting the dollar, which saves Burger and four others from being executed by Herzog. With the imminent collapse of the Nazi war effort, Herzog bargains with Sorowitsch for false passports for himself and his family. The fleeing Nazis dismantle the counterfeiting machinery and abandon the inmates along with the emaciated Sachsenhausen camp survivors.

Next, the film returns to postwar Monte Carlo. Sorowitsch is back at the gaming tables, but has decided to rid himself of the money he produced and saved. He begins losing spectacularly in a cavalier manner until he is completely broke. He walks out to the beach and is followed by the woman who brings a bottle of champagne. In the final scene they are dancing a tango in the sand. She sympathizes about how much money he has lost, but in a comment that reveals his opportunism, Sorowitsch remarks, "We can always make us some more."

Film critics quickly recognized the moral predicament facing Ruzowitzky's finely drawn characters. Despite the significant literary and political discourse in West Germany regarding Nazism, the popular tendency (certainly in films before the New German Cinema of the 1970s and 1980s) was to avoid examination of these issues. Parents of the postwar generation did not want to discuss how they reacted to the Nazi regime. In Austria, the traditional stance was to embrace the view that Austria was a victim of Nazi aggression. In recent decades, however, a belated *Vergangenheitsbewältigung*, or "coming to terms with the past," has dominated a variety of cultural expressions and social dialogue in Austria. The question of individual responsibility and response is a difficult one when protest meant imprisonment or death. That this question is still a very complex one in reunified Germany, which has "placed Naziism into history," can be seen by the emotional debate caused in 1996 with the publication of Daniel Goldhagen's book about the the way in which "ordinary" Germans collaborated with the Nazi regime (Goldhagen 1996). Goldhagen argued that there has been a virulent anti-Semitism throughout German history. Raul Hilberg and other Holocaust scholars, however, rejected Goldberg's claim, and Hilberg's has himself examined the variety of Jewish and non-Jewish responses to Naziism (Hilberg 1993). Ruzowitzky's film appears to reflect this latter, more nuanced approach.

One reviewer has identified the central question of the *The Counterfeiters*, one it holds in common with *Schindler's List*: "What is the value of a single human life in the face of unspeakable evil? During World War II, one of Europe's greatest counterfeiters decides, for a while, that his own survival is more important, until inevitably he learns that surrendering one's soul and humanity may be worse than losing your life altogether" (Wiegand 2008). In *Schindler's List*, Steven Spielberg develops an epic morality play around this theme, as his version of Oscar Schindler grows from a self-centered, playboy entrepreneur into a humanitarian, bargaining with the vicious Nazi Commandant Goeth over the price of individual lives. The question is thrown back at Schindler (and the spectator) by Goeth with equal forcefulness: "No, the question is, what is a human life worth to you!" At the conclusion of the film, Schindler experiences his tragic epiphany: he might have saved even more lives. The film's message is intentionally and emphatically unmistakable: one person can make a difference in the confrontation with evil. The epilogue shows the actual survivors and their families filing by Schindler's grave in his honor. Similarly, but with more realistic character development and narrative dissonance, Ruzowitzky's central figure is the reverse of Spielberg's middle-class, Aryan, German opportunist. Salomon Sorowitsch may also be an amoral bon vivant, but he is Jewish and a criminal. Through the adversity of the concentration camp and the horrors of the Holocaust, he must face his true self and find his humanity without the power, pathos, and spectatorial identification that Spielberg's flawed classic movie hero evokes.

We first see Sorowitsch at his prime and in his element in 1936 as the "king of forgers," holding court in a nightclub during the death throes of the decadent Weimar Republic. In a manner uncharacteristic for this film and its strong "documentary style" visual movement, the camera whirls around the dapper Sorowitsch, much like the scantily clad dance-hall girls, the beleaguered creditor begging for more time, the opportunistic underling who proudly shows off his new Nazi Party pin, and the arrogant anti-Semite social climber who sneers knowingly at "Salomon" Sorowitsch.

That evening, as he is asked to forge a passport for a fellow Jew: "Don't you see what's going on around you? What the Nazis are doing to us?" Sorowitsch refuses to identify with the plight of the Jews. "Know why the Jews are always persecuted? Because they refuse to adapt! It's not that hard." At Mauthausen concentration camp, Sorowitsch comes to realize the genocidal intentions of the Nazi regime include him, regardless of his desire to assimilate or his proven talent to survive in the illegal world of a lawful society. A fellow prisoner tells him, "This is not a prison, they want to kill us." Sorowitsch, however, understands criminality and the impulses of assimilation—Jews becoming Austrians and Germans; Austrians and Germans becoming Nazis—and uses his talents to flatter the sensitive egos of his captors. Transferred to the Sachsenhausen concentration camp, he is initially regarded an outsider by other prisoners due to his status as a "career criminal," but he eventually gains their respect as he attempts to protect them.

Wiegand (2008), who praises the director's subversion of typical Hollywood constructions and his attempt at actually dealing with moral complexity as opposed to resorting to a simplistic reductionism, considers the closing scene in which Sorowitsch dances with the woman on the beach a disappointing flaw in the film. Indeed, if the core of the film is a message of moral development and growth, the ending would be highly incongruent. But Ruzowitzky has not created a morality play. The beach scenes which bracket the story of Sorowitsch in the concentration camps are a key to a more viable interpretation of the film.

It is clear that *The Counterfeiters* deals with a moral dilemma: How does the individual respond to the overwhelming evils of the Nazi system? The choices are known from historical accounts, debates, depictions, and speculations. Like Sophie Scholl and members of the White Rose, one can resist at the cost of one's own life with little chance of effective success. Like the prisoners in the Warsaw ghetto, one can fight back against overwhelming and hopeless odds. Like many artists and intellectuals, one can withdraw into "inner exile" and avoid open resistance. Like millions of citizens, one can passively obey the system and succumb to the authoritarian will, casting a blind eye to the atrocities. Like many officials and bureaucrats, one can adapt to the system and use it to promote one's career. Or one can simply give up in despair and hopelessness.

In contrast to *Schindler's List*, which provides the single, clear moral choice of a Hollywood film, *The Counterfeiters* can be seen as a moral experiment, or, as film critic Rainer Gansera has referred to it, a *Gewissensdrama*, a "drama of conscience" (Gansera 2007). It asks: How should one respond to pervasive and prevalent evil? In effect, Ruzowitzky has crafted a film that looks at people's responses. It begins with Sorowitsch's transfer to Sachsenhausen, where he becomes part of a constellation of characters, and the film expands its focus from the individual to the community, albeit one in isolation from the world. Karl Markovics has pointed to the intimate theatrical feel of the endeavor, "because at some point it is no longer about Nazis/Jews, but rather an extreme situation as people react to the dictates of their consciences."[4] Instead of an epic on the Holocaust or the Nazi era, we are given a small ensemble on an enclosed stage. There are no wide vista shots as the camera stays narrowly focused on events within the nightclub, Sorowitsch's apartment, and, most importantly, in the barracks of Operation Bernhard. This is primary to the opening scene of the Sachsenhausen sequence, which places Sorowitsch as a member of a team. Five prisoners are standing in a row in a large, dark warehouse, illuminated by the large open doors through which the SS officers approach them. I will return to this pivotal scene later, but it is important at this point to underscore that these men find themselves in a puzzling situation. We have witnessed the brutality to which they are accustomed by following Sorowitsch's story: the dehumanizing insults, the beatings, the indiscriminate executions, the hunger, the overcrowded and filthy living conditions. Now, however, they are greeted individually and by name, respectfully offered cigarettes and civilian clothing. A single and abrupt interruption of their special treatment is a sharp reminder of Nazi brutality and their true status: they find slips of paper pinned to the coats bearing the name of the original owners who no doubt have died at Auschwitz. Here, the first illustration of divergent moral responses emerges. Sorowitsch pauses and removes the tag without expression. Burger defiantly rejects the coat, which he folds and places on the floor.

Barracks 18 and 19 in the camp form a closed environment in the midst of the horror of the Nazi death machine. It becomes the hermetically sealed laboratory in which the director tests a constellation of moral stances. It becomes the world in microcosm. As seen from a point-of-view shot of the new transferees as they pass through rows of barracks with inmates staring at them out of the windows, barracks 18 and 19 are boarded shut and covered in barbed wire. The guards open the large entrance door, and the inner courtyard with its open roof resembles a stage. The first entrance into the interior of the barrack, which is made with a trailing camera shot, reveals a room filled with men in white lab coats, with typical propaganda slogans painted on the walls, which in this environment become ironic moral commands: "Do More than Duty Requires" or "To Each his Due." While the slogans remind us of the infamous *Arbeit Macht Frei*, "Work Makes One Free," on the gates of Auschwitz, within the confines of this experimental stage they are reflections of the moral dilemma: What does duty require? Resistance or Survival? What will each different response bring?

The stage is set with the players. Sorowitsch is the artist seeking to hide his true intentions in order to survive; Burger, who like the White Rose is guilty of publishing anti-Nazi tracts, is the idealist seeking to fight back with little regard for self-preservation; and Herzog, the police detective turned SS officer, opportunistically uses the system. The roster is completed with the compromised financier, Hahn; the innocent victim, Kolya; the sadistic guard, Holst; the complacent citizen, Atze; and the despairing Loszek.

What sets these barracks apart is that they are an anomaly, a sealed-off world in the midst of the concentration camp. Even the Sachsenhausen commandant does not know what is happening in them. The inmates are given normal clothes and provided with amenities and basic comforts which in comparison to life in a concentration camp seem miraculously luxurious. Having the Nazi's fetching them toothbrushes is both shocking and absurd, both to the arriving inmates and the audience. These "shocks" reoccur throughout the film and have two effects: on the one hand, they heighten the moral dilemma by reminding the counterfeiters of their fate if they do not continue to cooperate with the Nazis; on the other, it delivers in small and seemingly insignificant points the horror and inhumanity of the Holocaust to the spectator. One is reminded of the view that the Holocaust cannot be represented in art, and that only silence can convey the enormity of the event. These small amenities reveal through silent contrast an enormous inhumanity: Kolya's hand stroking the clean bed linen and smelling it with eyes closed, as if flooded with memories of a forgotten life; Zilinski smelling a bar of soap and reciting the lines of a commercial, which seems a sign of madness, until he turns to Sorowitsch and says, "I was a commercial photographer in Berlin." The most poignant shock comes with the shower scene. This scene is a direct reference to *Schindler's List*, in which the female workers are mistakenly diverted to Auschwitz. There, the women, who had earlier heard rumors of gassing in the showers, are forced into the shower room in terrified anticipation. As the doors slam shut, the panicking women (and consequently the film's spectators) await the gas, only for the women to be doused with water from the showerheads. The overall effect is of a cinematic thrill akin to a scene from a horror film: a cat jumping out of the dark instead of a monster. With the release of the women and their rescue by Schindler relieving this highly constructed and exploitational tension, Spielberg is quick to restore the monstrous reality of the Holocaust by having the women watch a faceless group of inmates herded toward the actual gas chambers. Ruzowitzky's approach is far more subtle and thus more effective. In the dressing room, Kolya sits staring blankly: "They are going to gas us." Given their special treatment and role, neither the characters nor the audience believe this to be the case. The terror which strikes the innocent Kolya, out of place as it may be, still conjures the terror which struck those trapped in the shower rooms when the poison gas was released. The horror of the Holocaust is depicted in a small scene that utilizes not imitation settings and effects, but palatable fear of a sympathetic character, and the memory of the Holocaust in the spectator. Kolya panics and Sorowitsch has to force him into the shower room. As he doubles over in fear and panic, naked on the floor, water suddenly pours from the showerheads. "Water! It's water!" Sorowitsch shouts in Russian. Water as the "miracle" of a hot shower; water as life. The visual power of this simple reworking of Spielberg's epic Auschwitz segment comes from communicating the unspeakable by not actually showing it.

The image of the moral experiment is enhanced by the placement of the camera. Its angles place the spectator in the perspective of the neutral observer of this "experiment" by avoiding point-of-view shots. Instead of shot and reaction shots, the tendency is to position the camera to view the protagonists from the side, so that the spectator becomes an "unsafe" voyeur as opposed to the omniscient viewer of classical cinema and the manipulative point-of-view of *Schindler's List*, which reassures the spectator of both distance and moral guidance. Cinematographer Benedict Neuenfels most striking work to this end is the use of the behind-the-shoulder shot. The camera is consistently placed behind and to the right or left of one of the characters. This provides a quasi point-of-view shot, but without the concomitant subjective perspective, and it is one of the most dominant and reoccurring shot choices in the film. The only concentrated use of point-of-view shots in the film occurs at the approach of barracks 18 and 19, as was mentioned earlier. At that point the audience is allowed a direct and personal view of the world in which they are entering. This point of view continues as the camera trails the group entering the barracks, but once inside, it pans back to the now familiar behind-the-shoulder perspective. This choice also skews a direct head-on view. The camera creates a slightly obstructed frame, which parallels the moral uncertainty of the situation. As each one of the participants confronts their situation, the audience is never given a fully unobstructed view. As observers of the experiment, we cannot have direct access to the experience, nor are we presented a "show" to satisfy traditional genre expectations.

Each character brings his own moral code to the mix, and these clash with one another. The former banker, Viktor Hahn (Tilo Prückner), imbued with the ethics of the upper classes and high capitalism and forced to serve as "quality control" for the counterfeited bills, continues to operate as if he were in his bank. Upon first meeting Sorowitsch, he becomes disdainful and haughty when he sees the green triangle identifying him as a professional criminal. The cage bars between them in the reaction shots indicate their shared status as prisoners, and yet Hahn refuses to see the reality of his situation. Sorowitsch asks, "So it insults your honor that you people have to work with a fellow jailbird?" Hahn replies, "If a man has nothing else, he has his honor." As a representative of the industrialist cadre that aided Hitler's rise to power, Hahn remains blind to the threat of the Nazi mindset and vainly clings to the moral code of his former social elitism. The absurdity of this stance is demonstrated when Hahn approaches the SS officers after the success of counterfeiting the British pound. He wants his identity and personal social code acknowledged by the authorities. "I want you to know that I am being coerced into performing dishonest acts," he says to the officers. Herzog and Holst stare at him and then burst into laughter, walking away in bemused disbelief.

Sorowitsch follows the system of the prison. Survival is paramount and one simply does what must be done to survive. Although he is often laconic, being mostly an observer and listener, when he speaks his statements reveal his own moral code as if they were commandments: "A man must have respect, but cannot not lose face." "Every prison is the same." "Never betray your jailmates." He lies, flatters, and steals to survive, but he risks his life to save others. This is not a sign of lessons learned in the moral experiment of the setting. It is a code he has brought to the camp.

The idealist Burger initially understands Sorowitsch through his own socialist lens. He joins Sorowitsch when he is sitting alone with his meal after Hahn's rejection. In a series of shot and reaction shots, Sorowitsch poses the question: "Fraternizing with a common criminal?" Burger responds that the real criminals are the financiers who made fascism possible and the camera pans to Hahn and his fellow diners. In obvious reference to Sorowitsch's selfless act of having previously given the starving Kolya his own rations, Burger frames "the criminal" in a communist context but Sorowitsch indicates the banality of ideology in a circumstance of human need:

> BURGER: If a proletarian steals bread to feed his children…
> SOROWITSCH: That's not exactly what I did.
> BURGER: You gave a comrade some bread to eat. That was solidarity.
> SOROWITSCH: It was soup.

This exchange opens the main debate in the "experiment." Burger recognizes Sorowitsch's moral leadership and tries to convince him to resist the Nazis, first by sabotage and later by forceful resistance. In an exchange in the bunk room, Burger explains how he survived Auschwitz for so many years as part of the clean-up brigade, collecting the possessions of those being sent to the gas chambers. Doing what is necessary to survive is something Sorowitsch comprehends:

> SOROWITSCH: You have to adapt or you will die.
> BURGER: I can't go on like this. We have it so good in here while outside…
> SOROWITSCH: I will not give the Nazis the pleasure of being ashamed that I'm still alive.

Burger concludes that the Nazis must be resisted, even if it costs the lives of the entire counterfeiting team. This puts him into direct conflict with Sorowitsch, and yet Sorowitsch's own moral code does not allow him to betray Burger to the Nazis. Though logical with regard to their respective codes, both positions would lead to the same result: no one will survive. The conflict intensifies until Sorowitsch and Burger come to blows. The rest of the inmates reject Burger's idea of an idealistic suicide, but they are prevented from betraying him by the power of Sorowitsch's leadership. In a scene parallel to an earlier one in which a Jewish prisoner beats up a fellow prisoner on behalf of the Nazis, the inmates attack Burger, beating him bloody. No moral guidance or lesson for the spectator here, as demonstrated after the withdrawal of the Nazis and the rescue by the rest of the Sachsenhausen survivors. Atze hypocritically tries to identify himself with Burger's attempt to sabotage the counterfeiting of the dollar: "Here is Burger. He is a hero."

What have we learned from this moral experiment? Which position is correct: heroic resistance or pragmatic survival? Was this question not the function of the experiment? Perhaps something else is at work here. A theme which is inherent in the film but obscured by the moral struggle deserves attention. The driving force behind Operation Bernhard is the power of money. When we are introduced to the operation, we learn that money will be used as a weapon of war, to undermine the British economy. The initial plan involved air-dropping millions of pound notes onto the British Isles like bombs. Its success is dependent on the expected individual greed and self-interest of the British "victims," since the circulation of so much extra currency would undermine the financial system. Later, Burger, whose communist perspective sees money as the sustaining force behind fascism, points out the changing goals of the operation. "The Nazis are bankrupt. We are financing the war." This observation intensifies the moral dilemma of the inmates. Their counterfeiting activity has a direct effect on sustaining the Nazi system. Symbolically, the focus on money also poses some additional questions. In Spielberg's morality play, money was the false path that Schindler had to overcome. As the moral hero, he had to recognize the true value of the world and traded money for lives. In the *Counterfeiters*, the central motif of money plays a more complex and cynical role. Money is the underlying force of organized society. As such, money has the power to transcend all human interaction, even the extreme animosity of Nazi racism. In order to obtain money, the Nazis are willing to be "humane" to the Jews. In an ironic twist, the stereotype promoted by the Nazis—that is, that Jews are obsessed by money—is here reversed. It is Herzog, the SS officer, who repeats his adoration of "the dollar!"

In this light, the film also points to the demystification of money. There is ultimately no distinction between the counterfeit bills and the real thing. The Swiss bank scene, in which the counterfeited pounds are verified as genuine, and the fact that the Bank of England confirms this, casts doubt on the actual difference between the "real" and the "counterfeit." If the bills are recognized as genuine then they are, in effect, the same as real currency. The simulation of money represented by the counterfeit bills reveals the fact that genuine currency is also a mode of simulation, a construct of society, and not "reality." In this regard, the film's German title, *Die Fälscher*, with its connotation of falsification, is more apt in that Sorowitsch's team is simultaneously falsifying money and revealing money to be false.

Additionally, the "moral experiment" is framed by the casino scenes, where the power of money reigns supreme. At the start of the film, Sorowitsch is seen winning, while at the end he rapidly loses all his money. Does this imply that following the war and his captivity Sorowitsch has changed his values? Has he indeed moved from avarice and self-interest to a moral understanding born of the terrors of the concentration camp? This is certainly the implication of the final camp scene, in which Sorowitsch carries his dead comrade beyond their compound, through the camp beyond, surrounded by the dead and dying. Before this scene is over, casino noises overtake the immediate diegetic sound. The tuxedoed Sorowitsch, in a close-up shot holding four aces in his hand, has been remembering the previous scene, the entire film, perhaps, as a flashback memory. He hesitates, then throws in the winning hand face-down. In rapid cuts and montage, we see Sorowitsch gambling away all his money. Is he ridding himself of "blood money" and rejecting his former values?

For Sorowitsch, counterfeiting was more than the pursuit of wealth. There is a development of this character over the course of the film, but it is not in moral terms. In prewar Berlin, Sorowitsch had not mastered his art. He was doing well, but ultimate success eluded him. "Whoever can do the dollar," he states, "can do everything." This is more than a wish to counterfeit money. Sorowitsch is presented as a talented gambler who can easily control the gaming tables. It is clear that he does not need to forge money. What then is his motivation? Sorowitsch's art has already taken him to a point where he can negate social differences. When questioned about the Jews, he insists that the problem with Jews is that they haven't learned to assimilate. His forgery skills enable him to change anyone's identity. He boasts: "Do you want Aryan papers? I can make you a direct descendant of Siegfried and the dragon." The acceptance of fake pound notes as "real," and falsified passports as an easy means of changing national and ethnic identities, reveals Sorowitsch's art as both transformative and transcendent. In the film, the dollar is identified as the pinnacle of this art: "I haven't perfected it yet, but someday." It is hard to ignore Herzog's enthusiastic, ecstatic exclamation to Sorowitsch, "The dollar!" He first utters it at his initial arrest of Sorowitsch upon finding an attempted counterfeit bill. He issues the challenge, "Have we bitten off more than we can chew?" The use of the inclusive plural is telling here, as the relationship between Herzog and Sorowitsch is presented as a partnership—a Faustian pact, with Herzog's Mephisto prodding and enabling Sorowitsch to attain his goal at the cost of his soul. This "pact with the devil" is highlighted at Sorowitsch's arrival at Sachsenhausen. The camera pans the four new arrivals, stopping at Sorowitsch. Avoiding directly gazing at Herzog, he dutifully recites his prisoner number, but is interrupted as Herzog identifies him as: "Salomon Sorowitsch, king of counterfeiters." The camera moves from a close up of Sorowitsch down to his hand accepting a cigarette from Herzog, and then follows Herzog's arm up to his face in one continuous shot. This connecting pan is immediately repeated with their handshake. The relationship is established. During the rest of the film, Herzog reminds Sorowitsch that they are on the same side. Both of them want to achieve the dollar. "Only we two," Herzog says, "you and I. The most perfect forgeries ever. First the pound and then the dollar." Herzog promises him survival in return. Sorowitsch acknowledges this connection to Herzog when he states: "Herzog is a crook. I can work with him." In Goethe's *Faust*, Mephistopheles misunderstands the nature of Faust's longings. Herzog, too, does not understand Sorowitsch's motivation. Herzog is captivated by the power of money, hiding a suitcase of dollars for his postwar escape. Groveling on the floor after a confrontation with Sorowitsch, he is a pitiful figure, not worthy of a bullet and Sorowitsch releases him. It is interesting that Burger recognized Sorowitsch's motivation: "What are you actually concerned about? About survival or to prove to everyone that you can create the dollar?!" Sorowitsch, like Faust, was seeking to reach his highest achievement, but Ruzowitzky doesn't let us revel in romantic German myth. There is a hint regarding the psychological genesis of Sorowitsch's obsession. In a rare glimpse into his tragic past, Sorowitsch confesses when asked about his family: "Taken away ... Killed ... I could have bought them freedom if I had had money." This is a haunted, tormented Faust.

Spielberg's *Schindler's List* is a monument to the victims of the Holocaust and a solemn tribute to moral courage. Ruzowitzky's film, by contrast, does not look at the specific historical situation. It is not a monument of remembrance but a question posed to the present. In their first meeting, Kolya asks Sorowitsch why he prefers to speak German instead of Russian, considering how he has suffered at the hands of the Nazis. While being transported to a concentration camp, Sorowitsch answers with a hint of irony: "I don't like speaking Russian. Reminds me of bad times." This film is not about the Holocaust as a historically unique incident. In an interview, Ruzowitzky mentions that we cannot know what life was like in a concentration camp, but we, today, do face the moral dilemma of the counterfeiters: living in luxury while people are starving in the world. What is our responsibility?[5]

Wars and inhumanity are universal and recurrent. The waves on the beach washing over the newspaper: *La Guerre est finie*, again. The cyclic nature of reality frames this unresolved moral experiment. Still, Ruzowitzky posits that there is a transformative possibility for those who recognize and transcend social definitions. For these "falsifiers" the dance continues on the shore of the endless sea. "We can always make us some more."

Notes

1. *In Österreich sind die Budgets zu klein für vieles, was ich mache. Zudem bin ich gelernter 'Deutscher,' ich bin hier aufgewachsen. Ich 'ticke' etwas anders, als der klassische misanthropische Österreicher.*
2. *Wir müssen durch eine verbesserte nationale und europäische Förderung die europäische Filmproduktion weitaus besser unterstützen, als dies bisher der Fall ist.* Gusenbauer's comments are taken from "Österreich feiert Oscar für Ruzowitzkys Die Fälscher," *Reuters Deutschland*, 25 February 2008. Retrieved 15 March 2009 from: http://de.reuters.com/article/worldNews/idDEKOE53699820080225.
3. All English translations from the film are from the subtitles of the DVD released for the US market (Sony Pictures, 2008).
4. *Das Kammerspielartige an diese Situation ...weil das irgendwann mal nicht darum geht, Nazis – Juden, sondern eine Extremsituation wie sich Menschen ihr Gewissen gegenüber verhalten.* Markovics's remarks are taken from the "Making of" special feature on the US DVD.
5. Ruzowitzky's remarks come from an interview among the special features of the US DVD version of *The Counterfeiters*.

References

Dassanowsky, R. von. 2003. "Going Home Again? Ruzowitzky's *Die Siebtelbauern* and the New Austrian Heimatfilm," *Germanic Review* 78(2): 133–47.

Gansera, R. 2007. "*Die Fälscher*: Überleben im KZ," *FILM: Das Kino-Magazin* 3. Retrieved 8 March 2009 from: http://www.epd-film.de/33184_48572.php.

Goldhagen, D.J. 1996. *Hitler's Willing Executioners: Ordinary Germans and the Holocaust*. New York: Knopf.

Hilberg, R. 1993. *Perpetrators, Victims, Bystanders: The Jewish Catastrophe, 1933–1945*. London: Lime Tree.

Ruzowitzky, S. 2008. "Acceptance Speech," *The Oscars*. Retrieved 1 November 2010 from: http://oscar.org. Path: Research & Presentation: Resources & Databases: Academy Awards Acceptance Speeches.

Suchsland, R. 2007. "Alles andere, als Geschitsunterricht ...," *Artechock*, March. Retrieved 15 March from: http://www.artechock.de/film/text/interview/r/ruzowizky_2007.htm.

Wiegand, D. 2008. "Moral ambiguity in *The Counterfeiters*," *SFGate: San Francisco Chronicle*, 19 February. Retrieved 8 March 2009 from: http://www.sfgate.com/cgi-bin/article.cgi?f=/c/a/2008/02/29/DD9VV8V9H.DTL.

Chapter 23

National Box-office Hits
or International "Arthouse"?
The New *Austrokomödie*

Regina Standún

On 31 December 2006, one of the official websites of the Austrian film industry released the following audience numbers:[1]

Hinterholz 8 (Harald Sicheritz, 1998)	617,558 (KF)
Poppitz (Harald Sicheritz, 2002)	441,017 (KF)
Müllers Büro (Niki List, 1986)	441,000 (KF)
Schlafes Bruder (Joseph Vilsmaier, 1995)	307,300
MA2412 – die Staatsdiener (Harald Sicheritz, 2003)	272,849 (KF)
Komm, süßer Tod (Wolfgang Murnberger, 2000)	230,261 (KF)
Indien (Paul Harather, 1993)	223,680 (KF)
Sei zärtlich, Pinguin (Peter Hajek, 1982)	210,000
Silentium! (Wolfgang Murnberger, 2004)	204,802 (KF)
We Feed the World (Erwin Wagenhofer, 2006)	201,567

Seven out of these ten box-office hits in Austrian cinemas are *Kabarettfilme* (KF), "cabaret films" or Austro-comedies, a genre that seems to have no counterpart in any other European country. It is astounding that Harald Sicheritz's *Hinterholz 8* (1998), for instance, attracted almost the same number of viewers in Austria as Hollywood blockbusters did. These figures reflect a trend in Austrian filmmaking that has become increasingly visible since the late 1980s and early 1990s, a trend which, in every aspect, is marked by the local, the parochial. Another indicator that this type of film has become substantially significant in Austrian cinema is the Austrian Edition Series of DVDs, a collection of fifty Austrian films, coproduced by the publisher Georg Hoanzl, Filmarchiv Austria, and the Austrian national newspaper *Der Standard*. Since the anthology was launched in 2006, 200,000 DVDs have been sold, a noteworthy success for Austrian filmmaking (Grissemann 2007: 132). This anthology contains, among rarities, classics, and new developments of Austrian film history, at least seven films which can be classified as Austro-comedies, or *Kabarettfilme*.

Firstly, I seek to trace this genre's relationship to the *Volksstück*, the popular folk play, often performed in dialect, and other predecessors in Austria, and debates about its artistic value. Secondly, this chapter analyzes common trends in relation to the ingredients of these films, how they work, and what models in international film guide the directors of these Austro-comedies. Thirdly, I will provide an insight into the commercial aspect, approaching the drive in contemporary Austrian mainstream film to remain domestic.

Optimistic critics claim to see hope for the present-day Austrian film industry in these films due to their obvious appeal to a wide range of viewers and the resulting potential for Austria as a film nation to gain new publicity and respect, even if only within Austria itself (see Jaschke 1999). However, the tension between commercial success and art has become omnipresent in the debate about the quality of these films. Directors of Austro-comedies are accused of creating pseudo art films by using unusual film techniques, but at the same time their films are accused of being superficial, and critics have pointed out the pretentiousness of this kind of filmmaking. Another aspect of these films that is often held against their makers is the origin of the scripts. Since many scripts for this genre were originally written as stand-up comedy routines, they appear to lack real storylines and plots; consequently, critics claim that these films consist of a series of jokes without any deeper meaning (Kralicek 2000: 65). This negative press has stigmatized the label *Kabarettfilm* to the extent that the term itself has become equal to a "denunciation" (Freund 2000: 10). Hence critics and people in the film industry have introduced a new terminology; for example, *Austrolustspiel* or *Austrokomödie*. These films have even been castigated as "incestuous products" because the actors and directors seem to reappear in varying constellations repeatedly, following the principle of success—what once worked will work again. Film critics have also referred to this genre as mainstream, and the debate about commercial success as opposed to artistic value has become prominent in debates over these films' worth.

In particular, the films of the *Kabarettfilm* genre are reminiscent of the *Volksstück*, or folk play. Questions about the value of art, about high art versus low art, art of the elite versus art of the masses, high culture versus popular culture, have been omnipresent in debates about the *Volksstück*. Pamela S. Saur (1993), for instance, analyses the classification of rural drama in Austria and in the USA, and comes to the conclusion that in Austria rural drama suffers from a tendency to play down its literary value, whereas in America the same type is considered high literature without restriction or doubt. In my own comparative study of rural *Volksstücke* in Austria and Ireland, I was able to show that in Ireland peasant plays have been considered national literature for over a hundred years.[2] In Austria, however, similar plays are not considered appropriate for the national stage, but instead are performed on provincial amateur stages. In the 1920s, writer and critic Karl Kraus complained about the administration of the Burgtheater (the leading German-language stage) in Vienna which underestimated Johann Nestroy's *Volksstücke* and performed them purely for superficial entertainment rather than for their social criticism. Herbert Herzmann (1997: 17) emphasizes that the German language utilizes a specific term—*Volksstück*—for which other languages merely use the neutral term "play" or *obra de teatro*. This, he suggests, is a sign that these plays are discriminated against by the main theater scene.[3] The same applies to the term *Kabarettfilm*; like *Volksstück*, it seems that the term is used to segregate the genre from more serious types of film.

Nevertheless, since Bertold Brecht, Marieluise Fleisser, and Ödön von Horváth, one of the main features of this allegedly lower form of theater—and likewise film— is a critical sociological and sometimes also psychological dissection of society. The plays and films achieve this by displaying the cruelty and the ugliness within society, ranging across the whole of Austria's social spectrum. The Austrian theater producer and critic Heinz Gerstinger (1971: 108) generalizes his evaluation of Austrian and German trends in theater by stating that in the Austrian *Volksstück*, criticism is not aimed at political targets but at society—unlike in German theater. Hence, the Austrian variant might be perceived as lighter than the "more serious" German one.

In these plays and in Austro-comedy films, Austrian society is portrayed as nasty and hypocritical, a baroque façade with a dirty backyard. Kindness is combined with falseness, and even humor becomes vicious. The main principle which motivates the Austro-comedy is the aesthetics of the ugly, originally created by Antonin Artaud's experimental avant-garde theater. In the Austro-comedy, this aesthetics is no longer avant-garde, but has instead become less radical and more mainstream. The aim is to criticize by merely showing the ugly without further commenting or explicitly evaluating the actual issue. And whenever the unpleasant side of Austrian society is not clearly visible, there remains an undercurrent of unease.

The function of such theater and film derives from Brecht's and Horváth's ideas about the *Volksstück* (Brecht 1990: 1169–70). They utilize preexisting theater traditions, and recognizable plot patterns, characters and language in order to subvert them. The audience's expectations are not fulfilled and, ideally, the shock should make the audience attempt to question the status quo of society. In this respect, these *Volksstücke*, which are indeed anti-*Volksstücke*, and these films— which, analogically, could be classified as anti-*Heimatfilm*—are of educational value. The intended target group is a mass audience, the *Volk*, the people. The Austrian *Volksstück*, rooted in nineteenth-century Viennese comedy and in the alpine passion play, peasant farce and local customs, seems to have succeeded in transgressing the limits of social class and education (Herzmann 1991: 174–75). Nevertheless, despite the efforts that were put into making the theater a place for the *Volk*, the people, it has remained a space for an intellectual minority in Austria.[4] Going to the theater continues to be a formal act, in particular in Austria, not least because it is an unwritten rule—and sometimes a written rule—that the audience must wear formal dress, even in smaller local theaters.

This is where cinema differs from theater: it is more accessible, and has taken over the egalitarian role of the theater. From the 1960s onwards, playwrights who produced *Volksstücke*, for instance Peter Turrini or Felix Mitterer, have often turned to the film, in part because of the more democratic concept of film. What they all have in common is the anti-*Heimat* aspect, an antidote to the sentimental *Heimatfilm* productions of the postwar period led by Franz Antel, whose *Heimatland/Homeland* (1955) became paradigmatic (Horwath 1999: 150). In the 1960s and 1970s, authors and directors, above all Rainer Werner Fassbinder in Bavaria, played with this idea of deconstructing the traditional *Heimatfilm* á la Franz Antel. However, these attempts were considered too "arty" for mass audiences (see Suchsland 2005). Perhaps they were perceived as being too depressing and lacking in humor. For instance, Fassbinder's *Satansbraten/Satan's Brew* (1976), allegedly a comedy, is a rather bleak and cynical attempt to introduce humor in its most subtle form.

Since the beginning of the 1990s, the Austro-comedy appears to have bridged the gap between arthouse and mainstream film in a way that has attracted a very wide audience in Austria. These films portray the Austrian population as a rather morbid species. They play upon clichés, sometimes overplaying them and hence ridiculing what and whom they depict. The targets of their criticism are their own fans; that is, the audience, all classes of the Austrian population of all provinces. And the magnet for the audience is not the plot but the stand-up comedians who have turned to acting. According to film director Wolfgang Murnberger, there have been two phases within this genre: stand-up comedy scripts which originate in stand-up comedians' routines—Paul Harather's *Indien/India* (1993) being a good example— and films that employ stand-up comedians, but whose original scripts were written either by the director or by a literary writer—such as Wolfgang Murnberger's *Komm, süßer Tod/Come Sweet Death* (2000).[5] These two strands have one common thread: they portray one or more stand-up comedians showing the harsh side of life in Austria, which strangely enough makes the audience laugh, although sometimes it might be laughter that sticks in the throat.

In Britain, stand-up comedians, such as Lee Evans, Ricky Gervais, and Mel Smith, have also featured in films and TV series, but they were not remarkably successful as actors in the sense that they have not reached a wide audience. The success of the *Kabarettfilm*, the Austro-comedy, is perceived as a specifically Austrian phenomenon. "The connection between stand-up comedy and film is an Austrian domain and is nowhere else in Europe as lucrative as here".[6] Austrian film production companies and directors have invented a type of film that seems to suit the Austrian audience in particular, a phenomenon that deserves closer examination. The Austrian soul is portrayed at a crossing point between tragedy and comedy. These films show a segment of reality and present it as a colorful human biotope with all its eccentric features. The rich and the beautiful are never seen; the main feature is the anti-hero and his milieu, a kind of anti-*Heimat*. Elements of the Austrian 1970s and 1980s series *Kottan ermittelt/Kottan Investigates* (1976–1983) are discernible, which in turn received inspiration from 1970s America; for instance, from films like Guercio's *Electra Glide in Blue* (1973). The influence of Dogme films of the 1990s is occasionally visible, and these films are also similar in tone to the work of the British director Mike Leigh and the productions of Finland's Aki and Mika Kaurismäki. Without exception, these films depict losers trapped by their environment and remaining stuck there at the end of the film. In some films, the protagonists might find consolation and encounter some sort of happy ending that is paradoxically bleak and always within their social milieu. They do not succeed in lifting themselves out of their surroundings. Sometimes the protagonist is unemployed, as in the case of the main character in Peter Payer's *Ravioli* (2002), although he later finds a job as a pool attendant. If he is lucky enough to have a job, it is always at the lower end of the social ladder or among the middle class: minor civil servants (Sicheritz's *MA 2412*, 2003), catering inspectors (*India*), private-ambulance drivers (*Come Sweet Death*), car sales assistants (Sicheritz's *Poppitz*, 2002), minor office clerks (*Hinterholz 8)* or teachers (Sicheritz's *Freispiel/Free Game, Replay*, 1995), and the like. And what they all have in common is that they are extremely unsuccessful and lacking in any career prospects. Usually, they are walked on by their colleagues or bosses and sometimes they get themselves into violent arguments. Their private lives are equally unsuccessful—they invariably suffer from broken marriages, if they have a relationship at all. The films confront the audience with the cinematic version of average Austrians living a morbid existence, full of disillusionment, and rarely experiencing a positive event that might make their lives better or even have a cathartic effect on their lives. Whatever these anti-heroes do, they only sink deeper into their own misery and exacerbate their situation.

In contrast to the *Heimatfilm*, the setting is the non-touristy side of Austria. If the films do show urban centers, we see backyards, filthy bars, and bare council houses, particularly vivid in *Come Sweet Death*. If the countryside makes up the backdrop of these pitiful anti-heroes' existence, the audience gets to know the endless and unattractive plains of the Marchfeld in Lower Austria, as for instance in the "road movie" *India*, or rough looking blocks of flats on the outskirts of a town, unpleasantly displayed in Sicheritz's *Muttertag/Mother's Day* (1994). Small towns or villages, in the traditional *Heimatfilm* romantic and idyllic enclaves, are, in this genre, claustrophobic spaces, where non-locals are not wanted or at least treated with suspicion—the audience might notice an affinity to Kehlmann's *Kurzer Prozeß/ Investigations are Proceeding* (1967) with Helmut Qualtinger in the lead role. For example, in Sicheritz's *Hinterholz 8*, the protagonist settles down in such a village, where instead of being welcomed the villagers betray him and make his life miserable. In Niki List's *Helden in Tirol/Heroes in Tyrol* (1998), the only Austro-comedy that uses a rural setting exclusively, the powerful image of the Alps serve as part of the satire. The film employs clichés of the stereotypical Austrian alpine *Heimatfilm*, such as traditional music, costumes, and setting in order to pervert them, and the end result is a rather bizarre black comedy.

In general, the films only show beautiful scenery when the directors approach unfulfilled desires or wishes, and then, according to Peter Payer, Super8mm film is used to capture wider frames, which in Western cultures triggers associations of happiness and creates a feel-good effect (Krobath 2005). Such scenes are in a strong contrast to the general tone of the films. The prominent themes of these films are the desire for happiness and love as well as the desire to be loved, but these desires seem out of reach for the hapless protagonists. The montage technique of contrast often underlines the protagonists' hopelessness even more. For example, in *Free Game, Replay,* unsuccessful teacher and musician Robert Brenneis, played by the stand-up comedian Alfred Dorfer, has a vision of his success on stage, but when he wakes up, he finds himself in his apartment all alone, and even worse, the radio broadcasts music by his successful competitor Roland Pokorny, played by the stand-up comedian Lukas Resitarits. In *India,* the two protagonists are reconciled after an argument and begin dancing to Indian sitar music in front of an almost unreal intensely red sunset, but suddenly Fellner writhes in pain and finds himself in a cold white hospital room diagnosed with terminal testicular cancer. This quick cut is unemotional and destructive. The anti-heroes' or anti-heroines' world appears even more ugly when compared with their fantasy worlds.

All this seems to align these popular films more with tragedy than comedy, and yet, paradoxically, they are known for their humor, for their entertainment value, for their jokes, and for their funny figures—similar to those of the old Viennese popular plays of the nineteenth century. It might seem that audiences are rather cruel if they consider such tragic lowlifes funny, in particular when directors and scriptwriters claim that they depict authentic milieux—be it the teacher's, the civil servant's or the sales assistant's. The focus is on everyday life, and according to these films, ordinary people lead a very tragic existence in Austria.

However, the scriptwriters and directors manage to neutralize the sting at the end. These anti-heroes go back to where they came from, but, surprisingly, the ending does not seem too bad in view of the misery that they have had to go through in the course of the film. Inspector Brenner in the Wolf Haas adaptations by Wolfgang Murnberger, for instance, successfully solves his murder cases, and even the *Hinterholz 8* protagonist, who goes through a house-owner's hell, is offered a science-fiction solution to their problems, to be beamed away from it all into space. A more spiritual solution ends *India*: after Kurt Fellner dies of cancer, leaving his friend Heinzi Bösel devastated, the latter encounters a cat who he thinks is his friend's reincarnation. Hope seems to override the immense grief. These examples show that the directors of Austro-comedies do not want to leave the audience with a tragedy, but with a positive outlook on life; obviously, the feeling of reconciliation rather than devastation should prevail.

In most of these films, alcohol and drugs play significant roles. The protagonists are all too aware of their invidious position. Hence, they drink or smoke or take drugs, not for fun or to make life more interesting, but out of boredom or a need to escape daily life. Under the influence of alcohol or drugs, the anti-heroes behave embarrassingly and make fools of themselves, leaving them to appear tragic or even ridiculous. This has a double effect for the audience. On the one hand, the audience feels sympathy because these anti-heroes are trapped within and mistreated by their society but, on the other hand, they make their situation worse by behaving like fools and so spectators laugh at them. In addition, a certain amount of blunt slapstick often emphasizes the levity of the film. Despite the actual tragedy in the protagonists' lives, the audiences are offered reasons to laugh. Judging by their commercial success in Austria, it would seem that these films create the right balance between the tragic and the comic, not the least through the directors' film techniques. They tend to employ simple, laconic filmic narration combined with montage techniques and unexpected cuts; they use surreal sequences mixed with a documentary style and handheld cameras. Sometimes, classic Hollywood visual clichés are exploited, such as the loser. In *Free Game, Replay*, for example, the teacher wanders through the rain, and a long camera close-up combined with kitschy background music makes the audience feel sympathy for this anti-hero, but it also makes the audience laugh due to the stereotyped presentation. On other occasions, "anti-Hollywood" techniques create an unusual, also funny, cinematic experience. For example, the static camera in *Come Sweet Death* captures a car accident without focusing on detail. A Hollywood camera would have followed the car movements revealing the power of the destruction; Murnberger's camera just records a car flying by the screen and, with a tinny sound, hitting the ground. Above all, the mere presence of well-known stand-up comedians as the identifiable comic personae is an important feature and implies in most cases that the film must—at least in part—be funny.

Dry humor blends with a detailed presentation of milieu. This humor is based on the ability to laugh about oneself and to be politically incorrect. In the first half of the twentieth century, Roda Roda, an Austrian humorist and comedian in his own right, made the point that there is no need for parody when the original is funny enough (see Greuner 1977), an idea that was also employed by the father of Austrian stand-up comedy and popular film, Helmut Qualtinger, whose routines often just consisted of "voices of the people" played by himself. In his one-hour TV film *Der Herr Karl/Mr Karl* (1961), he lets the supposedly average postwar Austrian male talk about his life. The film was a scandal, and the public rejected Qualtinger as a *Nestbeschmutzer*, "he who fouled his own nest," who deliberately tried to damage the reputation of Austria and its inhabitants. Nevertheless, he grew in popularity with his approach to film and comedy and, posthumously, he is celebrated as a genius, worshiped by the contemporary generation of stand-up comedians who have introduced and developed the Austro-comedy. Nowadays, this principle of showing ordinary people seems to be programmatic for modern mass entertainment, which has in turn also created a new genre: reality TV. Here, the audience watch real people and see them as they are, and as Roda Roda suggested, the originals are entertaining enough, and in general, they are not the rich, refined, and beautiful.

This concept is complemented by the language used in the Austro-comedy. Similar to Austrian *Volksstück*, a very strong use of dialect or accent marks all films of this genre. Dialect combined with a rather crude phraseology creates a form of speech that is considered "real," although it has been argued that it is an exaggerated form of reality and thus quite unrealistic (Hess-Lüttich 1992). In general, the language is characterized by a repetitive simplicity. No hermetic encoding requires the audience's skilled reading; no symbolism or metalanguage has to be deciphered. People speak in a rather blunt, direct, sometimes shockingly straightforward manner. The language corresponds to the "unpolished" pictures.

Cinema-going is an act of consumption, and in the case of these Austro-comedy blockbusters, the audience has absorbed parts of the language used by the protagonists. On the one hand, the language is taken from ordinary people, and on the other, ordinary Austrian people take phrases from the films and incorporate them into their own speech. "Thanks, very kind!" (*Danke, ganz lieb!*) is a phrase repeatedly used by main actor and stand-up comedian Alfred Dorfer in *India* and has become a popular phrase in Austrian speech. Lines from the same film, such as "ninety per cent of guest-house owners are one-hundred per cent idiots" (*Neunzig Prozent von de Wirtn san zu hundert Prozent Trottln!*), and "I am on a kiwifruit diet—anything but kiwifruit" (*I bin auf Kiwidiät—alles außer Kiwi*), have become commonplace catchphrases in Austria. Meanwhile, in *Ravioli*, even Descartes is doubted: "I think, therefore I am, if my neighbour exists too?" (*Ich denke, also bin ich! Wenn mein Nachbar auch existiert?*) Many of these and other phrases have no meaning—for instance, *da hopst er, der Lobster* (*MA 2412*), *Ruck-zuck* (*Hinterholz 8*), and *bist denn du deppert* (*Die Viertelliterklasse/The Quarter-Litre Class*, 2005)— but they are used instead to mark idiosyncrasies in an individual's speech. They are catchphrases that are not recognized because of their content, but mainly because of the rhythm and intonation. Whether it is the slow rhythm and broad melody of Alfred Dorfer's smug sing-song, Roland Düringer's noisy rattling voice, Monika Weinzettl's silly giggling sounds, or Günther Pal's incredibly powerful bass, all these aspects make up what has been called the "acoustic logo" of these films, a kind of "high concept sound design" (Robnik 2004: 82).

Directors of Austro-comedies employ recognizable stand-up comedians, and their speech has become a trademark of the films. They have appropriated the idea of showing the downside of life in a crude way and in a specifically local and rough language from the *Volksstück*, spicing this up with extremely black humor. This humor, which has become so attractive to Austrian audiences, is based on black comedy, on satire, and partly on the ability to laugh at oneself. The Bavarian Radio channel Bayern 3 Radio remarked when introducing "this new type of Austrian film" that it is "typical for Austrian filmmakers to mercilessly expose their own milieu and at the same time pretend that this all had nothing to do with them."[7] These films indeed deploy a morbid sort of humor that adds to the fun, which seems to work in Austria due to the basically masochistic structure of the Austrian psyche (Hager 2005: 108). Apart from the linguistic features and comic performances mentioned above, self-mockery is also a hallmark of the humor of Austro-comedies. In addition to the critical *Volksstücke*, Peter Handke's experimental monologues *Selbstbezichtigung/Self-Accusation* (1966) and *Publikumsbeschimpfung/Public Insult* (1966), in which he shows up his fellow Austrians by accusing them of being lazy, over-saturated, ignorant, mediocre, and crude middle-class people, could be seen as ground-breaking texts for the self-mockery (*Selbstironie*) in the presentation of life in Austro-comedies. This phenomenon possibly derives from the fact that officials in

Austria have always tried to make Austria appear as a victim nation, in particular after the Second World War; hence this self-accusation might counteract such distorted official versions of history, also represented in the postwar *Heimatfilm*. The new Austrian *Kabarettfilm* could be seen as an antidote to these films. Another explanation for the masochistic psyche revealed in these films might be found in twentieth-century Austrian Jewish literature and comedy, to which the Austro-comedy is partially indebted. In particular, between the 1930s and the 1960s, Karl Farkas, Gerhard Bronner, Fritz Grünbaum, Ernst Waldbrunn, and Hugo Wiener's stand-up comedy shows contained a great deal of self-mockery. However, this trend is not only visible in Austria; the best example beyond the Austrian borders would probably be Woody Allen's films, which ironically depict his own American Jewish roots. The directors and producers of the Austro-comedies of the past fifteen years might have gained inspiration from these predecessors, but they were the first to make this self-mockery successfully accessible to a mass audience, if only in Austria.

Austrian film directors and producers have created their own genre, the Austro-comedy, a genre that depends upon showing the unpleasant side of life in a realistic way. The authenticity of such films is revealed by the fact that they even cause public debate with regard to their alleged voyeurism, which is said to mock ordinary people. Another striking trend has recently emerged: while it used to be the modus operandi to turn comedy or theater scripts into screenplays, now screenplays are turned into theater or comedy. For instance, Florian Flicker and Susanne Freund's script for the Austro-comedy *Der Überfall/Hold-up* (2000) was rewritten for the stage and performed at Theater 89 in Berlin, not as a comedy but as a serious psychological drama; and within the comedy scene in Austria, parts of the reality TV series *Alltagsgeschichte/Everyday Stories* (1985–2002), which works on the same basis as the Austro-comedy—that is, it shows ordinary people—have been transformed into a stand-up comedy routine by Andrea Händler and Dolores Schmidinger, two of the handful of women in the male-dominated comedy scene. TV, theater, and cinema are interwoven and borders between media are transgressed.

Popular culture on stage, mainly in the shape of the *Volksstück*, has been an important form of mass entertainment in Austria since the Middle Ages. TV and cinema are the new facilitators of this kind of entertainment, which has resulted in the adaptation of many variants of this type of drama, recast in a modern framework by scriptwriters and film directors in Austria. Judging by the fact that these films have almost no commercial or critical success outside of Austria, they represent arguably a sort of humor that is understood only by an Austrian population, which recognizes the characters and their milieu as their own. In particular, the figure of the stand-up comedian as actor and his individualized dialogue have made these films an Austrian phenomenon. These Austrian blockbusters are hardly intended for export and remain national successes only (Robnik 2004: 81). One could argue that they constitute proof that comedy does not travel. The idea that comedy serves as an identity-forming cultural phenomenon could be of significance against the political backdrop of Austria joining the EU in 1995, a step that was and is observed with suspicion by the Austrian public. The emergence of this new genre at the same time as Austria became more integrated into a globalized world might be a form of artistic disassociation from the rest of Europe. Wendelin Schmidt-Dengler, the doyen of Austrian literary criticism, believes that he recognizes a trend towards "provincialization" (*Provinzialisierung*) and "parochialism" (*Österreichisierung*, literally "Austrianization") in post-1945 Austrian literature, and particularly in more recent writing (Schmidt-Dengler 2000: 9). He argues that this is dangerous because the writers he analyzes limit themselves to a specifically Austrian readership: "The more we concentrate on asserting our Austrian identity, the more we deal with specifically Austrian problems, and, if the literary style is not of exceptionally high value, we will always be regarded as some sort of side product" (ibid.: 10). The same could also be said of the Austro-comedy film.

However, every "national" comedy also consists of supranational elements, above all in their structure, which may be responsible for their occasional success abroad. Film, which uses many elements apart from the spoken word, would appear to be the ideal medium for overcoming language barriers and political borders. If this is true, then perhaps the reason for the lack of recognition of Austro-comedy films outside of Austria lies not in their choice of particular images or their language; rather, it comes down to the business of distribution. At a parliamentary symposium in Vienna on 3 July 2002, experts from the film industry, business, and politics came together to discuss "the future of the Austrian film in Europe—possibilities for enhancing Austria's profile as a film-producing country."[8] The report does not mention international marketing and distribution of Austrian films nor does it contain figures concerning film promotion abroad. According to Austria's Ministry for the Arts, subsidies for filmmakers are awarded individually, depending on the strength of the application, but the Ministry emphasizes that there exists a strong will to promote Austrian films abroad.[9] The state body responsible for promoting Austrian films abroad is the Austrian Film Commission, whose focus is on Austria's presence at film festivals. Yet the managers of production companies—such as Danny Krausz of Dor Film, who is a member of the executive board of the Association of Film Producers, and Helmut Grasser of Allegrofilm, who is president of the same association—claim that the Austrian Film Commission's efforts do not go beyond festival promotion.[10] All parties concerned—that is, the Ministry for the Arts, production companies, and directors—seem to identify the real problem faced by Austro-comedies as lying with the film distribution companies, which provide dubbing or subtitles. Film director Wolfgang Murnberger, for instance, is convinced that film distributors abroad consider Austrian "local comedies" to be too much of a risk to spend money on dubbing or subtitles.[11] However, these Austrian popular films are shown at international festivals, and so there are subtitled or dubbed versions already available. Peter Zawrel, president of the Vienna Film Fund (Filmfonds Wien), which is one of the three main organizations providing financial support to filmmakers, criticizes the structure of distribution in the Austrian film business: "In Austria, producers are more concerned with raising funds for new projects than selling their film products. Film marketing involves a lot of work, which is not always understood in Austria; in particular, because it is easier to finance new films" (Zawrel 2007: 136). It seems that in the case of the mainstream Austro-comedy, art and business do not coincide when it comes to matters of international marketing.

Notes

Parts of this article have been published as "On the Road to Nowhere? Contemporary Austrian Popular Film," *New Cinemas: Journal of Contemporary Film* 4(1), 2006.

1. Information from: www.filminstitut.at/downloads/11280709Endbericht_Lang_17_12_04_ Original.pdf, retrieved 11 September 2007.
2. *Ein Vergleich: Das österreichische und irische Volksstück des 20. Jahrhunderts als Ausdruck nationaler Selbstdarstellung auf der Bühne.* Dissertation. National University of Ireland Maynooth. 2008.
3. Herzmann does not mention, however, that other languages use derivatives of the basic term, for instance "peasant play," which also signify a certain form of discrimination.
4. This is still true despite efforts since David Josef Bach established the so-called Kunststellen in the 1920s, which was aimed at making theatre accessible to a working-class audience, or the left-wing propaganda of the late 1960s, for instance, by the literary magazine *Wespennest*, whose editors appealed to authors to create a literature for all classes.
5. Information from an e-mail interview with Wolfgang Murnberger (February 2004).
6. Quotation from: "Spaßkultiviert," *Profil*, 7 October, p.76.
7. Quotation from: http://www.br-online.de/kultur-szene/thema/oesterreich/oesterreich1.xml, retrieved 11 September 2007.
8. *Die Zukunft des österreichischen Films im europäischen Kontext—mögliche Maßnahmen um Österreich als Filmland attraktiv zu gestalten.*
9. Information from an e-mail interview with Johann Hörhan (February 2006).
10. Information from e-mail interviews with Danny Krausz (February 2006), and Helmut Grasser (February 2006).
11. Information from an e-mail interview with Wolfgang Murnberger (February 2004).

References

Brecht, B. 1990. *Gesammelte Werke: Schriften zum Theater 3, Vol. 17.* Frankfurt am Main: Suhrkamp.

Freund, R. 2000. "Haas im Interview," *Wiener Zeitung*, 22 December, p. 10.

Gerstinger, H. 1971. "Das Volksstück auf dem gegenwärtigen Theater," in Institut für Österreichkunde (ed.), *Das österreichische Volksstück.* Vienna: Ferdinand Hirt Verlag, 93–111.

Greuner, R. (ed.) 1977. *Zeitzünder im Eintopf: Antifaschistische Satire 1933–1945*, 2nd edn. Berlin: Buchverlag der Morgen.

Grissemann, S. 2007. "Reisende Apokalyptiker," *Profil*, 26 March, 132–36.

Hager, A. 2005. "Bist denn du deppert?" *Profil*, 7 March, 108–9.

Herzmann, H. 1991. "The Relevance of Tradition: The Volksstück of Felix Mitterer," *Modern Austrian Literature* 24(3/4): 173–82.

———. 1997. *Tradition und Subversion: Das Volksstück und das epische Theater.* Tübingen: Stauffenberg Verlag.

Hess-Lüttich, E.W.B. 1992. "Die Sprache der Sprachlosen: Sperrs Jagdszenen aus Niederbayern," in U. Hassel and H. Herzmann (eds), *Das zeitgenössische deutschsprachige Volksstück*. Tübingen: Stauffenburg Verlag, 151–66.

Horwath, A. 1999. "Filmbrief aus Wien. Normalform, Sollbruch: Österreich ist frei!" *Cinema: Das Private* 44: 150–62.

Jaschke, B. 1999. "Keine Schublade, bitte: Der Kabarettfilm," *Wiener Zeitung*, 12 March. Retrieved 27 March 2008 from: www.wienerzeitung.at/Desktopdefault.aspx?Ta bID=WZO&lexikon=Kino&letter=K&cob=7009.

Kralicek, W. 2000. "Ich will was probieren," *Der Falter*, 7 December, pp. 63–65.

Krobath, P. 2005. "Ist Optimismus nur eine Form von Informationsmangel?" Retrieved 6 July 2005 from: www.dorfer.at/austausch/ravioli/htm.

Robnik, D. (2004),"Ob Amt, Haus, Zeit, Bild: Es wird durchgearbeitet! Zur Ästhetik, Pragmatik und Ethik der Blockbusterkomödien mit Düringer und Dorfer" *Kolik*, Sonderheft I, 81–86.

Saur, P.S. 1993. "Classifying Rural Dramas: O'Neill's *Desire under the Elms* and Schönherr's *Erde*," *Modern Austrian Literature*, special issue, 26(3/4): 101–14.

Schmidt-Dengler, W. 2000. *Literatur in Österreich nach 1990*. Vienna: Basisgruppe Germanistik.

Suchsland, R. 2005. "Komödie und Weltgericht," *Münchner Merkur*, 30 May. Retrieved 2 April 2008 from: http://www.lyrikwelt.de/hintergrund/fassbinder-bericht-h. htm.

Zawrel, P. 2007. "Interview: Kein zivilisierter Umgang," *Profil*, 26 March, p. 136.

Part VI

Austria and Beyond as *Terra Incognita*: Glawogger, Sauper, Spielmann

Chapter 24

Austria Plays Itself and Sees *Da Him*: Notes on the Image of Austria in the Films of Michael Glawogger

Christoph Huber

"Shit," says the young man, "I am myself. When you look into the mirror, you see who you are." The young man is one of the car drivers who took along Michael Glawogger on his hitchhiking tour of Austria for his episode *Die Reise/The Journey* in *Zur Lage – Österreich in sechs Kapiteln/State of the Nation – Austria in Six Chapters* (2002), an omnibus effort inspired by the conservative victory in the Austrian elections of 2000. When the film opened in Austria, I wrote that Glawogger's contribution to the film was overshadowed by Ulrich Seidl's, and I still think that I was justified to some degree. Both directors in essence let people vent their prejudices and disappointments, which leads to a convincing chronicle, but not necessarily in-depth analysis, of the perceived right-wing backlash that shocked Austria's cultural scene. Seidl's gift for confrontational tabula-rasa, still-life tableaux, in which the ravings of his protagonists seem stripped down to their naked, near-psychotic core, while the baroque beauty of their spilled verbiage is all the more pronounced, leaves more of an impression. Yet having watched Glawogger's piece again on its own, I am moved by its floating quality and melancholy tone—shrouded in wet and foggy visuals of the Austrian landscape gliding by, the often similarly frightening and funny declarations of the various car-drivers who picked him up on his twenty-three-day ride throughout Austria acquire a poignant sadness, down to the last stop, an image of a hitchhiker's hand resignedly dropping out of the frame.[1] What seemed a lack back then can in hindsight be explained as a problem with the film as a whole, which never quite coheres. A case in point is the disastrous third contribution of Michael Sturminger, which attempts pretty much the same thing as Glawogger and Seidl, yet falls totally flat.[2]

LIVERPOOL JOHN MOORES UNIVERSITY
LEARNING SERVICES

What Sturminger's attempt lacks, but is on display on abundance in both Seidl's and Glawogger's segments, is personal handwriting and genuine curiosity—which, backhandedly, brings us around to the theme of this piece: how Austria is represented in the films of Michael Glawogger, or—per the name of a former popular newscast—their *Österreich-Bild*, literally their "image of Austria." As with most things in that sometimes maddeningly dialectical complex of Glawogger's filmography, it is something that cannot be pinned down easily to serve one point. Indeed, this is proven by "The Journey," which in retrospect seems a much less didactic (admittedly also less dryly stringent) foreboding of the digital-video method for which Abbas Kiarostami would be hailed only a few months later when his *Ten* (2002) premiered at Cannes.

What Glawogger draws from his encounters in the confined yet paradoxically, because of its privacy, "open" space of the inside of various cars, is, by his own admission, "the document of a confusion." Private and political concerns mingle: a man's ultra-conservative, extended rant about the "loss of values" in contemporary society, the rise of "homosexual men and other such perversions … the sickness in the heads of people, sickness of physical nature," turns out to be closely related to his personal disappointment as a "failed family-man" (his wife left him with the kids). In a similar vein, the first driver (in a statement that seems to encapsulate the entire film) embarks on a complaint with the disclaimer that he will probably be "damned as a defeatist"; actually he uses the wonderful, much richer dialect word *Motschkerer*, which cannot be adequately translated but incorporates the very Austrian notion of expressing one's defeatism preferably in long, pissed-off rants—and that is exactly what follows.

Racist and fascist remnants proliferate throughout *The Journey*. One driver chides the Eastern European nations, which after the First World War "could not wait to escape the people's prison" of the Austro-Hungarian Empire, yet now want to come back into the fold of the European Union, "because life in that people's prison wasn't so bad after all." But the most interesting figure is the young man I quoted at the start. Like many of Glawogger's interviewees, he is referring to the *bête noire* of the film: Jörg Haider, the populist right-wing politician and leader of the Freedom Party whose successful rise in Austrian politics—and, most controversially, into a government position in 2000—had much to do with his skillful fueling of precisely such prejudices. Haider, the young man opines, echoing a popular sentiment, may have gone to far on occasion, but is right on many things, especially "foreign infiltration"— there are way too many aliens in Austria. In a sadly familiar rationale the boy says that Hitler may have had the right ideas back then, "he just shouldn't have exterminated the Jews," but a "more understated method" would have been agreeable. It is after this that things start to get really interesting, and decidedly Glawoggerian. When the young boy talks about his frustrations, the lack of possibilities, which lead him to hang out at cemeteries (a recurring motif in Glawogger's "Austrian" films) to forget about the seemingly pre-planned life route for his kind—settling down, finding a job, and going to the discotheque every Saturday "to drink oneself into stupidity"—he finds a momentary escape in the image of "Da Him." In a nice coincidence, the Austrian dialect word "da" means the same as it does in hip-hop slang: "the."

"Da Him" is shorthand for Ville Hermanni Valo, singer of the then-popular Finnish doom rockers Him, and the young man's resemblance to Valo (whose name incidentally means "light") is lighting up his life: helping him to pick up girls, a constant source for inside jokes, and, on occasion, the chance to forget himself. "There was a time when I thought I didn't want to be myself any longer. Shit, I want to be that guy!" Of course, when looking in the mirror, the unavoidable realization of being just oneself after all is what follows. This accidentally captured moment may—though not quite accidentally, given how Glawogger's films undermine common notions of fact and fiction, document and staging—be a key scene in the entire Glawogger oeuvre. In the semi-utopian image of "Da Him" also lies a dialectical realization of the self. It is not the blunt antithesis of the "other" in which Glawogger's Austria sees itself, but something at the same time more elusive and somewhat closer. Gazing back through Glawogger's work there's a fascinating interplay of similarity and difference at work in the contrapuntal interplay of home and elsewhere. There is Paulus Manker as a hard-drinking poet who regains footing abroad only after having been unwittingly transported over the Austrian border into Czech territory in *Slumming* (2006). There is the most exemplary comparison of Austria and various "others", achieved by intercutting Austrian and opposing nations' (Cameroon, Chile, Italy) soccer fans' reactions, as well as the strikingly varied tone and degree of enthusiasm of the different commentaries on TV, in the World Cup documentary *Frankreich, wir kommen!/France, Here We Come!* (1999). There is the cross-pollination of Austrian ambition and international inspiration (and vice versa) in *Kino im Kopf/Movies in the Mind* (1996). And of course, interlaced and in between all this, and decidedly on a more meta level, there is another kind of cross-pollination in tracing auteurial themes and interests through Glawogger's "strictly Austrian" films, *Nacktschnecken/Slugs* (2004) and *Die Ameisenstraße/Ant Street* (1995), and his "global" documentaries, *Workingman's Death* (2005) and *Megacities* (1998). Also, the mind boggles at the added possibilities if Glawogger had shot his steel-factory segment of *Workingman's Death* in Austria's VOEST complex and not in Anchan, China, which he had considered for some time. That it was bureaucratic problems that ultimately got in the way is in itself a nicely Austrian touch, however. All this can be traced back to Glawogger's first feature-length effort, which—completing another circle rather beautifully—was also a collaboration with Ulrich Seidl, and in its more even-handed mixture of their approaches achieved a more successful superstructure: *Krieg in Wien/War in Vienna* (1989).

The "war" in Vienna which the title of the latter film announces is in many respects already a decidedly global affair, setting up a hall of mirrors, images crossing borders and producing a dazzling ambiguity of meanings, which seems central to the Glawogger project. A collage of news clips from all over the world interspersed with freshly shot material from home, *Krieg in Wien* startles with its wealth of associations. It kicks off with the familiar setting (familiar to Austrians, that is) of the studio from which the country's big news program is broadcast, and the promise from Horst F.

Mayer, then its anchorman, that the news programme's duty is "to inform in the most precise and fastest way" possible. But the found footage quickly segues into reports from places as diverse as Korea, Germany, and Africa, proving that in the age of ever-expanding media, information has become a very random thing. The defamiliarizing impact of this material on the Vienna footage invites one to ponder ever-more complex meanings and ideas, if one can keep up. "All cities are the same," announces a voiceover, as the camera first glides into town, but indeed the specific aspects of the city soon seem questionable, or at least often negligible, within the larger context.

While some of the shots carry Seidl's signature, the playful structure seems to anticipate the bombardment of ideas characteristic of Glawogger, especially in his other film about generating and generated images, *Movies in the Mind*. "A movie about News, Life, Love, and Death," announces the opening title, heralding themes that have to varying degrees become even more pronounced in the careers of both directors. It also anticipates the ironic-sounding tagline for *Slugs*, which promised "a moving film about the big themes of life: sex, love, parents, cars, and wild animals," whereas one of the many intertitles that follows will also double as the ironic title of Seidl's next film, his breakthrough documentary about newspaper vendors, *Good News* (1990). Other text inserts include "News for Happy People" and "War in the Home Country," the latter followed by images of people working out in a fitness center and street traffic.

So the announcement of "War in Vienna" may feel somewhat ironic for quite a while. Is it what the media flow brings to daily lives, as recurring international topics like the Iran–Iraq war or the catastrophic shipping accident near the Philippines suggest? Or is it the daily struggle itself, keeping afloat in the midst of media bombardment? Near the end, in one of the many humorous juxtapositions of the film, an announcement by Ronald Reagan on TV that "there's a time for hope and optimism" is followed by a statement of an interviewed Austrian worker that there's so little time just for the evening walk with his wife, "then I come home, grab a beer, and sit down in front of the box. That is the whole routine." But by that time the tables have already been turned in a most interesting fashion. Long past the movie's midway point a US news report about violent demonstrations by youth in Vienna literalizes the title, after all. The reason is the Waldheim affair, provoked by the very selective memory of Kurt Waldheim, former UN Secretary General and then Austria's president, about his knowledge of war crimes during the Nazi era, when he served as an SA officer. This led to his being subsequently put on the US "watch list," among other things, which in turn led to a campaign by Austria's singularly influential reactionary tabloid *Kronen Zeitung* that successfully roused nationalist non-interference sentiments. That very tabloid is also prominently displayed in *Good News*.

Pointing towards a very specific Austrian problem—and notions that, as *State of the Nation* amply proves thirteen years later, have never quite subsided—this crucial scene anchors the kaleidoscopic film, whose onslaught of material otherwise suggests a product of the proliferating visual media. It was only during the 1980s that the widespread introduction of cable TV brought about the fast growth of channels in Austria. In retrospect, the film has only gained in substantive richness, its quick-paced mosaic approach a harbinger of what was to come. This is not to mention the moment when Horst F. Mayer declares (about newscasting) that, "however, we cannot influence it the way we would like to," a statement that must have seemed east to believe at face value then, when "official" state-sponsored TV was still held in high regard as a quasi-autonomous and reliable source—particularly regarding news coverage, with Mayer then being "the face" of its integrity—when compared to the sensationalist tendencies of privately financed stations. These days, the difference often is hard to tell, something that the tumultuous *Krieg in Wien* anticipates with merciless clarity.

Starting with a protagonist obsessively counting his steps home over the still-black screen, Glawogger's first fiction feature, *Ant Street*, establishes a key theme of the director's work that appeared submerged in the previous film: that life is not quantifiable. Significantly, other characters include a watchmaker obsessed with time, a young kid who pierces and collects insects (Glawogger stresses the motif by occasionally resorting to the presentation of objects in pronouncedly display-case-like arrangements), and a narrator who spends much of their time building and pondering a model of the house in the titular street they all live in, always stressing that "one has to be prepared." That he "disappears" for himself by closing his eyes and for the audience in a *trompe-l'oeil* effect recently used again in Zach Braff's *Garden State* (2004), where the protagonist's clothing is identical to the wallpaper (both here, of course, with ant patterns), give a taste of Glawogger's slightly surrealist leanings. But *Ant Street* seems most important for being an Austrian comedy that actually bears a semblance to reality. By the mid 1990s, the comedy genre had already fallen firmly into the hands of stars coming from the stage. The Austrian *Kabarett*—which is not exactly cabaret, but a kind of stand-up comedy, often leaning towards "filmic" (and definitely film-inspired) one-man performances—had brought on an exaggerated tone, fueled by a lowbrow-gags-at-any-price concept, and lacked any semblance of relaity.

In its aggressively assertive music track and the repeated stretching for punch lines, *Ant Street* is slightly tainted by these tendencies, resulting in an occasional artificiality that—given the free-spirited nature of his later work—by now marks it as a decidedly minor, yet still amusing, Glawogger work. Especially in *Slugs*, Glawogger has made good on the genuinely tragicomic promise of this film, which then seemed like a miraculous breath of fresh air, and whose down-to-earth sense for cleverly stylized décor is still impressive. Impressive too is the slightly overcrowded plot structure that follows the death of the owner of the house in Ant Street, when everybody is pitched against everybody else, but especially against the house's heir, who wants to drive out the residents and make their inherited property more lucrative for himself. It even channels the Austrian TV series *Kottan ermittelt/ Kottan Investigates* during the course of its increasingly daffy seven-year run.[3] The series' magnificent first episode, "Hartlgasse 16A" (1976), was named after the tenement it mostly takes place in, with the anti-hero, police detective Kottan (in the beginning played with melancholy overtones by the incomparable Peter Vogel), investigating a murder amidst residents who are always prone to prove the proverbial perfidy that lurks in the cliché "golden Viennese heart." The arguments and mishaps in *Ant Street* also lead to some memorably morbid demises which are always commemorated with an intertitle "plaque" featuring the dead person's name, birth and death dates. The notoriously macabre Viennese sense of humor also manifests itself, for instance, in the presence of an elderly citizen with a hearing aid who sits in front of the television, smiling, eyes twitching, immersed in an undoubtedly uneventful live report from Vienna's great cemetery, the legendary Zentralfriedhof.

Even in a completely high-spirited work like *France, Here We Come!* the return to the cemetery seems unavoidable. Here, one of the soccer fans chosen as the main protagonists regularly visits the grave of his father, who—some 60 years ago, in the golden age of Austrian football—introduced himself to one of the nation's great soccer idols, Mathias Sindelar (1903–1939), the legendary "Man of Paper." The elderly fan dutifully recounts the fate of the Austrian team at the 1998 World Cup to the deceased—not a pleasant task under any circumstances, since the national team's disappointing performance led to a rather deserved demise after the group games. Of course, the true soccer fan—Glawogger being a prime example, as the buoyant tone of his film proves—will be crushed only temporarily by such a disaster. Indeed, the cemetery visitor ends his report by looking forward to the next World Cup, another chance.[4] A more grounded approach is guaranteed the film's co-writer, Austrian sport journalist Johann Skocek, whose philosophical comments, wearily spoken into a video camera in his French hotel room late at night, show some critical distance. In fact one of his first statements is, "This rubbish hasn't started yet, and already I'm completely tired." Skocek's funny and analytic meditations—a particular highlight is when he explains how (Austria's national trainer) Herbert Prohaska "would have to build a gothic cathedral, yet he's only a bricklayer . . . who can no longer find the building site"—are in stark contrast to the reactions of the other soccer-savvy main characters, including a probably alcoholic retiree, an accountant who has devotedly followed his team of choice for years, always dragging along his mother, and, most moving and most typical of Glawogger, a blind man, who nevertheless seems to imbibe every detail of the game.

Blindness is also something the referees are accused of, especially when their verdicts go against Austria and a multitude of angry voices are raised in pubs and homes. Similarly, *France, Here We Come!* is constantly piling up material, rising to the media-saturated occasion, its polyphonic structure paying off especially when confrontations on the field of play yield even richer confrontations of cultures. Cutting between continents, Glawogger juxtaposes the reactions of Austrian fans with those of Austria's opponents. And while some things, not least the ardor and excitement, are similar around the world, differences between the game commentators are telling: mostly desperate in Austria, but poetic in Cameroon ("the Austrian aristocrats ... cropped our wings"), ecstatically febrile in Chile ("we have to believe in this team ... this will be the longest three minutes of our lives"), first self-assured, then unusually unsettled in Italy (in this game, the last one, the Austrian players for once do better). Ironically, it is also the one match they lose, after managing to score (even only during injury time) disappointingly defensive stands. "The beautiful game was our death," Skocek muses afterwards.

Tellingly, the Austrian fans employ a defensive, self-deprecating strategy throughout, justifying the film's subtitle, a "drama in three acts." In the end they take comfort in their fate, since the last game gives "reason to be proud of our team," and the tem's fate is explained as not having had the luck which is always bestowed "only on the Germans" (who in the history of Austrian soccer have always served as the existentially, it seems, favored and much-maligned "big brother"). This pleasure in "noble" resignation, typical of the Austrian penchant for self-pity, is only the most pronounced critical aspect Glawogger cunningly captures; others often seem to have gone unnoticed due to the frenzied temper of the film. Choice bits include the traditionally patriarchal circumstances of soccer viewing (at home, the woman has to prepare everything while the men look and talk knowingly), and the sport as a springboard for nationalist sentiment (once again, the *Kronen Zeitung*—who else?— takes first prize, featuring the front-page caption "Ivo, now you're really an Austrian!" after legionnaire Ivica "Ivo" Vastic, recently naturalized for World Cup eligibility, scores the last-minute goal against Chile). In a masterstroke, the last bit of the crowded soundtrack perfectly captures the Austrian spirit of hope in the face of deeply savored despair: Creedence Clearwater Revival's "As Long as I Can See the Light."

No less brilliant is the intricate interplay of comedy and secretly accumulating sadness in *Slugs*. This film must be seen as Glawogger's true *Heimatfilm*, with the director's typical wit applied to one of Austria's most detested mainstays of commercial cinema in the 1960s and 1970s: the lowbrow sex comedy, which itself often took place within the earlier *Heimatfilm*'s regional settings. A kind of Styrian slacker movie (which does wonders with the special tone of the regional idiom), it does not overly empathize with the protagonist's illusions. The all-too-perfect dream of horny students balancing their budgets by shooting a sex movie which is determined to fail, since the only thing that really works is their camera. Just as the redevelopment plans in *Ant Street* ultimately result in a revealing disaster, the more benevolent, yet never sentimental or misguidedly faux-humanist, *Slugs* unearths deep truths in a deceptively light manner. Despite the acknowledgement of tragedy, it also stands alone as a triumphantly comic treatment of themes—not least among them sex itself—that have been a source of depression in the increasingly cliché-threatened bulk of contemporary Austrian cinema. And, as Glawogger's most recent, and again, in that miraculously unpretentious manner, truly complex effort proves, this singular stance is happily *Slumming* on.

Notes

The original version of this essay was published by the *Lisbon International Independent Film Festival*, 2006.

1. In German this makes for a sly, yet almost mournful pun, since hitchhiking is called "Auto-Stop."
2. The fourth episode, in which Barbara Albert strains for a more dialectic approach, seems to belong to another movie entirely.
3. *Kottan ermittelt/Kottan Investigates* was directed by Peter Patzak and written by Helmut Zenker, and ran from 1976 to 1983.
4. That Austria has not managed to even qualify since then is of course quite another issue.

Chapter 25

Configurations of the Authentic in Hubert Sauper's *Darwin's Nightmare*

Arno Russegger

What is a documentary? The images flickering across the screens of security staff in a subway station, or the recordings of a video camera mounted over an automatic teller machine? What about the countless home-video amateur filmmakers—do they come close to approaching the documentary ideal when they capture their children or cats, vacations or misadventures on film or video? Does a faithful cinematic treatment of reality—in accordance, one might say, with the commonplace concept we use to define it—require the submission to a purist concept of reproducing reality or does reality constantly open itself up to several possible approaches? Is it not the case that we expect a documentary also to deliver a story that captivates us, touches our humanity and presents a new, interesting view on life? Or is it sufficient simply to use a minimum of technical equipment, in order to bestow upon a message an expression of immediacy and authenticity?

Hardly, we will respond in answer to these many questions. But then what does the authentic element—the truth and the credibility of a documentary—stand for if it does not just happen but is instead obviously the result of a particular cinematic structure, or rather dramaturgy? Using concrete examples and some general considerations we will attempt to fathom this out, specifically with regard to Hubert Sauper's *Darwin's Nightmare* (2004), an extremely successful film seen both from an artistic and a box-office point of view, but one that was nevertheless the subject of intense discussion. With this, Sauper, who was born in the Tyrol in 1966 and subsequently raised in Carinthia, gained international recognition and numerous prizes, culminating in the award of a César in France and a nomination for an Oscar by the American Film Academy. *Darwin's Nightmare* is representative of the remarkable boom Austrian film has enjoyed in recent years, particularly in the genre of documentaries; it also demonstrates the extent to which the particular creative determination of directors is relevant today, within the context of an exceedingly diverse tradition of documentary.

Some Starting Points and Basic Principles

A review of the pertinent specialist literature shows that no clear position exists among the makers of documentaries themselves, no normative notion of what is permitted and what is not. However, it is precisely this uncertainty, which dictates the extent to which documentarians should hold themselves back, in order to report in a manner that is as distant as possible, or which indicates how deeply they can introduce themselves into their work as a kind of auteur. In this context, the German director Peter Nestler, speaking for many of his colleagues, believes that "no pure prototypes exist for the documentary that can be seen to be free of arranged scenes" (Nestler, in Schadt 2002: 17). Often, a vague delineation between non-fiction (for the documentary) and fiction (for the so-called feature film) is taken as the lowest common denominator; this implies that in the one case the people, events and locations within a film already exist in a pre-filmic reality, while in the other case they do not. At the same time, however, practically all filmmakers are convinced that a documentary that truly deserves the name is also a work of art; it is this that distinguishes it from mere reportage, or journalism. And as long as the poetic and rhetorical means of representation used in a documentary (such as background music, contrast montage, or re-enactments) are supported by a responsible, critically engaged attitude towards society, it also remains immune to the purely illusionist entertainment function, which, in the eyes of many recipients, is the hallmark of feature films. In view of the existence of multiple audiovisual hybrids, formats and new (electronic) media, it is no coincidence that it is frequently impossible for a modern audience to make a clear distinction about how a film was intended to be understood, or which genre it belongs to, given that "the documentary increasingly pursues the formal perfection of the feature film," while "the feature film opts for the less perfect aesthetics of the documentary more and more often" (Schadt 2002: 20).[1] Thus, nowadays, documentarians no longer risk the immediate accusation of being fraudsters and manipulators simply because they have a comprehensive cinematic repertoire at their disposal and pursue advanced creative strategies.

The origins of the documentary can be traced back to the very dawn of film itself. One simply has to think of *The Arrival of a Train* at the Parisian station La Ciotat, filmed by the Lumière brothers, who organized its first public viewing in a cafe in 1895. Since those early days, the documentary genre has evolved to include an impressive stylistic diversity according to cultural conditions and changeable political circumstances, ranging from the early 'actualities', then newsreels, right up to specialized documentary and news channels on cable and satellite TV (see Barsam 1992; Hattendorf 1995). In the process, the traditional opposites—real/false, true/contrived, and reputable/commercial—have become less useful as a means of assessing the documentary form; they have dissolved into a relational mesh of perspectives that co-exist as alternatives.

In order to continue to be able to satisfy the "basic need for orientation in a complex and disorganized world", Peter Krieg, manager of the High Tech Center in Babelsberg, points to the pivotal moment of credibility of a given medium; that is, the "key term" for our comprehension of authenticity:

> The language clearly reveals what the issue is really about: not proof, not ultimate reliability, but faith and trust. A faith in images as incorruptible, objective witnesses of reality is much older than photography.... The concept of a copy as the true duplicate of a given model is also older than photography. The category of similitude flows not only through the debates on art, but can also be traced in the legends and creation myths of arguably all cultures and suggests that the question of authenticity is not a question of technical perfection, but rather of cultural conventions in a certain period of time. (Krieg 1997: 85–86)

Because the perceived world is "produced exclusively in us and by us" in accordance with the systemic functionality of our sensory organs and our brain (though "conveyed and marked by social communication"), this means, as Krieg expounds further, that:

> Statements about reality, truth, authenticity, genuineness etc. ... are always subjective and ... are merely matched to social or cultural arrangements. As the possibility to compare with the 'real reality' is not given, adjustments of this kind are always conventions and not objective conclusions, that is to say conclusions that are independent of the observer. Every human being is the ultimately autonomous, legitimate—but also responsible—creator of his own world. (ibid.: 86–87.)

These are, in short, the most essential principles with regard to cognitive theory and constructivism that contemporary documentary makers should use as their starting point. They step before us with their works just like witnesses at a legal trial and then have to communicate with their critical audience in a way that allows the story they are telling to appear plausible. No more, no less, as we cannot make a statement about how things "really" relate to each other in an ontological sense—in other words, independently of their being perceived and communicated in the context of our interpersonal, sociocultural system of interaction.

Hence the category of the authentic is not an absolute parameter, but rests upon a certain arrangement:

> In the documentary context the cinematic image takes on a representative function: It refers to a defined view of reality beyond the cinematic, but it is not a copy true to scale, to say nothing of a 1:1 replica of this reality. A common understanding about the reference character of the cinematic image is a precondition for the reception of a documentary—in other words, an understanding that aspects of reality are being arranged, produced before our very eyes, in order to facilitate a discussion about this extract of reality. Every documentary—in this there is no difference to a feature film—is a complex and complicated esthetic construction. (Kreimeier 1997: 29)

In the end, the authentic elements emerge as a signal of quality that, as in the case of organic food, should permit conclusions to be drawn about natural origins and unadulterated cultivation and production (see Krieg 1997: 93). In both cases, the consumers hardly have an opportunity to verify the validity of the asserted claim and match it with reality. They have no choice other than to place their trust in a certain brand or delegate quality assurance to a certain institution, where once more they can only trust in conscientious execution of the assigned task. Taking this comparison to the extreme, documentaries are therefore no more than "organic products" in the audiovisual vegetable patch of media production that are electronically bred and modified with the aid of computer technology.

Background

Let us now return to Hubert Sauper. The first confidence-building measure he undertook—after several months of intensive research and preparation—was traveling to Tanzania in person and with only a modest amount of equipment in order to confront himself with the local circumstances and people during the course of filming. Sauper has attributed an almost allegorical significance to this sometimes dangerous journey, on which "it was easy to get into trouble," and which he stylized—in an allusion to Joseph Conrad—as a journey into the "heart of darkness".[2] Similar connotations and associative relations are also hinted at later in the finished film and lead to a kind of symbolic underpinning and to a mythological super-elevation of the whole story respectively. In due course we will return to this point.

Sandor Rieder, the director's friend, was his only constant companion, and nearly the entire raw footage for the film was produced by the two men alone, using only a small, lightweight camera, with the occasional aid of a sound engineer or additional assistant.[3] This was not Sauper's first experience of Africa, however, having shot the film *Kisangani Diary* in 1997 about the massive flood of refugees into the country after the civil war in Rwanda. It was on the occasion of shooting that film that the director hit upon the story of the Victoria perch. On an airfield in Mwanza, Tanzania, Sauper happened to witness the unloading of UN aid deliveries for Rwandan refugees, which included inferior provisions such as yellow peas, while at the same time fresh fish fillets destined for European consumers were being loaded onto another aircraft. Appalled by this cynical reality he started to investigate the issue, which—as he sees it—eventually led him to carrying out his "most ambitious personal and cinematic venture to date."[4]

Form and Content

Once upon a time in Africa, in the early 1960s, a small biological experiment was launched in the course of an OECD development program, which consisted in introducing three dozen Nile perch into Lake Victoria. The Nile perch was previously unknown in this area, and locals had never before seen an example of this large-bodied species of fish. But what started as a fairytale and should have initiated an amazing boom for the economy of the entire region, including neighboring countries, very soon degenerated into a nightmare involving the destruction of the lake's ecosystem—a nightmare now dreamed by fish-factory owners and prostitutes, World Bank representatives, street children, EU Commissioners, Russian pilots, Tanzanian authorities, arms dealers, security guards, violent criminals and victims alike. For the Nile perch, just like many of its human business partners, turned out to be a voracious predator, and since its introduction the fish has eradicated over 400 other species of fish and other life forms. This, in turn, has led to a continuous over-fertilization of Lake Victoria. At the same time, the creature, now called the Victoria perch, proved to be a popular export to half the world, targeted mainly at European and Japanese markets, yielding high profits for all those people involved in some way in its trade. That is why neither the state of Tanzania, the EU, the owners of the fish-processing plants, nor the carriers and operators of special aircraft fleets, are interested in changing the situation, which is becoming increasingly precarious overall—in particular for nature and the environment.

But how, exactly, does Hubert Sauper's film present this dark side of so-called globalization, exemplarily examined here in regard to social-Darwinian phenomena such as exploitation and enrichment, impoverishment, violence, disease and, last but not least, war-mongering and profiteering?

While the credits emerge against a black background, the sound—very faint at first—of radio noises and some added atmospherics become distinguishable by the attentive listener. Then a female voice can be heard, singing a song in a foreign language; we will get to know the young woman this voice belongs to better later on, as it is Eliza (Elizabeth Maganga Nsese), who suffered a cruel fate during the shooting of the film and will presumably be long remembered by most viewers—not least because of the striking, acoustically accentuated introduction she provides to *Darwin's Nightmare.* Then the shutter opens, and the shadow of an aircraft glides across an endless expanse of blue water—this being Lake Victoria, as a text insert explains. Quite apart from the beauty of the shot, due to its shape and floating lightness, the shadow calls to mind a fish in the water below and thus manages to incorporate the two central themes of the film (aircraft and fish) in an integral way using purely optical means. What is more, the scene refers to the fundamental character of film; that is, a kind of shadow play.

Digression

In a film it is not the objects themselves that we become aware of, but their reflection; and this is doubly so, with regard to, firstly, the photographic process, and, secondly, the act of projection within the cinema apparatus. Hubert Sauper possesses a keen sense of different types of self-referential structures; their materials drawn from reality, they can be built into his films without great effort, discreetly and casually, as visual ambivalences, contrasts or analogies. Paradoxically, these self-referential structures amplify the perception of the authentic because, despite the chaotic impression reality evokes at first glance, we nevertheless gain the impression that it still offers evidence that (an) order can be imposed. Besides, it is evident that the person at work here is acting in a highly reflexive manner and knows exactly what he is doing and how far he can go, despite the simplicity of means at his disposal; this, in turn, adds to the leap of faith one is prepared to undertake when viewing Sauper's film. The climax of his film-in-film dramaturgy is reached a little later on with recordings from a conference in Kenya, attended by high-ranking government officials from all the states bordering Lake Victoria. In an interview,[5] Sauper sheds some light upon the reasons for the unplanned presentation of an accusatory report about the catastrophic quality of the water in Lake Victoria by a French environmental group: he himself had made sure it would happen, so he could immediately document the reactions on film of those assembled, spouting pat phrases and quite clearly not minded to do anything that might harm their business.

Admittedly, in this approach Sauper avails himself of certain postmodern methods, such as we may know from Michael Moore for example, in order to manipulate reality itself. He does not do this, though, in order to satisfy his egocentricity. The sincerity with which he comments on his actions corresponds to the general diagnosis of the film, which is that in order to successfully construct a documentary project a trusting attitude is not only required of the cinema audience, but is also required during the actual shooting of the film from the people who come into direct contact with a documentarian in the course of their work. First of all, it is they who must have the feeling that the person focusing on them is open, sincere, and authentic in the pursuit of their interests. This, presumably, is the reason why Sauper remained unchallenged during the Kenya conference:. The attendees appear rather guilty and defensive, they stall; they were not expecting to have to defend themselves and attempt to answer the criticism leveled at them with something positive.

Continuation

After a hard cut we are no longer hovering above Lake Victoria, but are instead in the midst of the confusion at the control tower of Mwanza airport. Now we can finally identify the radio element of the soundscape from the start of the film, and we are confronted with an air traffic controller (Marcus Nyoni) who explains the light signals that have to be used to regulate the brisk air traffic when the radio is not working properly, while also being occupied with chasing pesky insects and beating them dead with a newspaper. Receiving what is obviously a wrong connection, he dismisses the caller with authoritative affectation. He is fine, he says, because he is employed. In a different scene, a former peasant woman, who moved into town and is now rummaging in maggot and worm-infested fish filth in the hope of picking out something useable, drying it and turning it into food for other people like her, will say exactly the same thing.

The air-traffic controller sometimes appears to be speaking as if to himself, so not always towards the camera and interviewer, Hubert Sauper, who never makes an appearance and always asks his questions in (awkward) English off-screen. In combination with different subtitles for otherwise unintelligible passages of conversation or dialogue, this kind of off-screen speaking belongs to the code of the authentic in the classical documentary genre. With this classical format, no subsequent dubbing of a film into another language occurred, whereas today it is increasingly the case that a translator's voice is simply laid over the original sound recording, to save the audience the trouble of reading a subtitled translation.

The air-traffic controller ostentatiously tries to demonstrate the power of the man he would like to be. In doing so, he introduces a further central theme of the film, namely the social-Darwinian behavior of many people, leading to a cycle of exploitation (with few winners and many losers) that can subsequently be observed on the most diverse social levels, right up to the priests, Tanzanian politicians, and EU emissaries. Despite the unfortunate circumstances, he does his best to remain composed; however, as there is obviously much that is beyond his control, he occasionally loses his nerve and reveals through involuntary gestures and facial expressions the extent to which he, too, is exposed to the prevalent system. It is precisely because of his fits of rage and aggression that he displays a singular helplessness he would presumably prefer to conceal. With reference to scenes such as these—and he might have drawn on any one of Hubert Sauper's interviews for this—Thomas Schadt speaks of a "double subjective factor," resulting from the fact that the director of the documentary has to "establish a relationship between his own subjectivity and that of his counterpart and then has to proportionate himself and his motive above that.... To be able to subordinate one's own subjectivity and to stand with the people (not alongside them), but not to pressurize, smother, or even 'violate' them" (Schadt 2002: 41) can be seen as one of the most important aspects of documentary dramaturgy. Otherwise the "real theme remains decoration" (ibid.: 41–41) in the service of one's own vanity, inevitably leading to a weakening of authenticity.

It is almost unbelievable what people from the most diverse backgrounds and professions have told Hubert Sauper, although he presumably held technical recording devices up to them and never denied his intention to work on a critical film. Their frankness is probably due to the fact that Sauper does not engage in discussions but allows the images and words to speak for themselves and reveals the conclusion of the whole film only after the separate scenes have been arranged and edited. As questionable as the role of one or the other person may appear in the end, nevertheless no one is paraded purely for effect, or villainized or condemned through the way they are depicted. In fact, for Sauper it is essential to show the inherent restraints that gleam through all the portraits and significantly impair each individual's decision-making ability. What is treated in a discursive manner in the conversations thus receives a quasi-objective, intersubjective, that is, common dimension that is visibly reflected in the people and their actions.

Sauper did not play upon the power he holds as a European, an intellectual, and a filmmaker and use it against the other contributors; if anything he moved around on their respective level and simply spent a lot of time in Tanzania. The footage that eventually made it into the edited version of *Darwin's Nightmare* represents only a fraction of the footage piled up high in Sauper's Parisian office. He made very deliberate gestures of personal respect and gratitude—such as the frequent gift of video recordings to the interviewees—even though it was clear that most of his conversational partners do not possess adequate equipment to watch them. Notwithstanding the apparent futility of this, it must nevertheless have contributed to the conveyance of a sense of confidence in a better future, one where Tanzanian people can also enjoy more opportunities for shaping their own lives, and it led to an affection that the film bears witness to time and again. Meanwhile, Sauper calls many of the contributors his friends—"I feel like they are an important part of my existence now," he has said—and tries to help them often and with a variety of actions.

The next scenes show the crew of an aircraft after landing. The (non-diegetic) background music of a Russian folk song hints at the nationality of the men. Almost daily they arrive in their ancient, huge Ilyushins, to collect hundreds of tons of fish for European markets. An insert fades in to inform us that the area around Lake Victoria is known as the "Cradle of Humankind," producing a mythical-allegorical substrate for the entire story as mentioned previously (in the sense of a journey into the "heart of darkness"), elevating the subsequent events to a general, almost paradigmatic level. For this purpose, after tracking shots lead the viewer through the slums of Mwanza and desolate villages on the shores of the lake, a few fishing boats come into view, one of which displays the name "Jesus". This specific tailoring to Christian mythology, which the dramaturgy of the film likes to employ, confers upon the Victoria perch and its unimpeded proliferation a vicious significance, because the alleged Tanzanian fish miracle appears as a travesty of the biblical multiplication of fish accomplished by Jesus to sate the hunger of the thousands who listened to the Sermon on the Mount. The promises made at that time have not seen fulfillment in the course of two millennia, at least not literally and not in Tanzania, where radio reports inform of an ongoing famine affecting 2 million people. Locals cannot afford to buy and eat the Victoria perch—or rather nothing more than the heads and skeletons that are dried on specially erected racks and prepared for consumption— and live in the midst of the ubiquitous filth, crawling with insects, larvae and grubs, in a constant battle against birds that, just like the vultures of the apocalypse, pitch into the remains of God's judgment day. The poor of Mwanza and other parts of the world are still poor, if not even poorer; and for them there is no redeemer, for the modern successors of Jesus, if they even get as far as Africa, are proving to be Pharisees and sanctimonious fundamentalists who, without hesitation, sacrifice practical advice, such as the use of condoms for protection against the rampant and pervasive HIV virus, to principles that are drenched in hypocritical morality. They cannot help those who even have to fight for the refuse left behind by the international trade in raw materials, neither economically nor in a spiritual sense. Instead the walls of the fish factory are adorned with calendars bearing sayings from the neoliberal Gospel that pronounce, among other things: "You are part of the big system!"

An attentive camera registers a multitude of further details. Seen as a whole, the film provides a cross-section of all segments of the population. It introduces both the manager of a factory, who eulogizes the creation of new jobs, and the employees of different companies, who appear completely anonymous in their hygienic overalls and pursue a monotonous activity at the assembly line. Also imprinted on our memory are: a one-legged boy with two crutches, who is unbelievably nimble and is placed in drastic contrast with fish cadavers being filleted in the factory; the pilots, who do not always visit the whores, but sometimes comfortably spend the evening in each other's company, looking at family photographs and telling each other little adventures from past travels. Most enduringly though, it is Raphael (Raphael Tukiko Wagara), who knows war from personal experience: he used to be a soldier and now guards the local fish research center for one dollar a night, a job he holds because his predecessor was slain whilst on duty. To prevent the same from happening to him, he carries bow and arrows with him, ready to shoot anyone who dares to scale the fence and enter the grounds of the institute. For in here, only the right of the stronger prevails, you simply have to be faster than anyone else; in here, Raphael may do whatever is necessary to repel the enemy. He speaks softly, a gentle smile playing around his lips whilst envisioning the most ghastly things, and he considers war to be basically a good thing that, in his opinion, many of his fellow countrymen would wish for, because then the army would employ them, an impossibility during times of peace. Raphael is a specialist for skewed stories such as this one. A little later he gives an account of a crocodile in Lake Victoria that appears suddenly, like the Loch Ness monster, to bear down upon its victims. In the next instant he speaks of his son, who is dreaming of becoming a pilot, something which would fill Raphael with pride, as then his boy too could carry out fish shipments.

Hubert Sauper captures the paradoxical status of this world in images that weave a subtle net of opposing references. He employs effective analogies and visual contrasts—for example, juxtaposing squashed flies and aircraft wrecks, planes that failed to lift off upon departure due to overloading and which now lie scattered over the ground. He contrasts songs on the wireless with others sung by contributors in front of the camera, at times ending in an abrupt fade out—this has an altering, disillusioning effect, for example when a group of little girls in uniform is singing. There are the colorful paintings by a black artist called Jonathan (Jonathan Nathanael), who sees himself as a "citizen of the world" since moving into town in the course of the general rural exodus; Jonathan's motifs come from the streets, where children who have to fend entirely for themselves spend day and night, beating each other up, getting drunk, and prostituting themselves. Some also sniff a gelatinous substance they manufacture out of the plastic packaging that the perch fillets are sealed into prior to shipment. On another occasion we learn from the factory manager that he considers the collaboration with the plastics company in question a success story spanning decades; he is probably completely unaware of the intoxicated children. Once more the film has a clear advantage as far as authenticity is concerned, if one makes a direct comparison with Jonathan's naive paintings.

In the hotel occupied by the pilots ("Sergey, Dima, Jura, Vladimir, Stanislaw") we meet Eliza, who sells her body for ten dollars a night, because she has no other means of making money. Nevertheless she intones a song of songs for her native Tanzania. She "knows many pilots" and is out and about with Dima (Dima Rogonov), who treats her roughly and toys with a young woman unable to fend him off. She appears to be fun-loving on the outside, but surely grew up under the same circumstances as the boys and girls that roam the streets, orphaned and homeless, the girls tending to stick with groups of smaller boys, who clearly do not emit such an immediate threat of sexual abuse as the older adolescents do. Eliza's mother has died, her father is very ill. Later, when she speaks of her innermost hopes and plans, it is already dark; it is touching, the special tone of voice and glances aside, when Eliza is ashamed of her situation and dreams of going to school and eventually taking up computer studies. Actually, most of the young people questioned would like to read something or, in the case of one boy, become a teacher himself—a clear sign that he views knowledge as common property, not to be kept to oneself but to be shared with others.

As if they had a pleasant evening out together, Eliza swaps ideas with Sauper, who listens and is interested in her words rather than he body. As usual, he does not only get his counterpart to answer questions. He appreciates the significance of the poetry of the moment—which may be why Nick Flynn was employed as special "field poet," who makes comments on the unfolding story, pointed and garnished with additional significance, in a series of inserts—and presents the contributors as complex personalities. The apparent proximity to these people is enough to release strong emotions in the viewer that are not based on a superficial identification; the biographies drawn are not suited to this purpose. Nevertheless, as viewers we gain such an intimate insight into Eliza's life that we feel as if struck by lightning at the subsequent news that she was brutally stabbed to death by an Australian punter. Eliza's colleagues watch the recording of her last interview; this scene, already familiar, is shown to us again on the monitor as a self-referring element of film-in-film aesthetics.

Darwin's Nightmare manages both to have thematic concern for itself and challenge its own effect, and to authenticate the uniqueness of its images as documents; for example, by demonstrating that it costs the women great effort to remain "cool" as viewers of the film extracts featuring Eliza. This results in a typical mixture of tactical composition and open improvisation by the director, making it possible to provoke the unexpected, only to freeze it on camera the next instant. In this way, the originality of life retains its uniqueness and its secret from which one can sometimes wrench brief true moments (see Schadt 2002: 108–09).

Hubert Sauper does not just show an affirmative relationship to film. He is aware of the manipulative power of the medium and explores it quite critically, which also strengthens his own credibility. To give a distinctive example, in another key scene a missionary appears; in the course of his open-air speech, recited in the aggressive style of an American television evangelist, he shows a Christian propaganda film of the kind that is still being produced and deployed by many faith communities and churches in the so called Third World for conversion purposes. Of course, Sauper chooses the episode in this film when through a miracle Jesus brings about a massive catch of fish for his apprentices, several of whom were also fishermen by profession. Their nets are eventually so full of fish that they can barely haul them aboard and the boats almost capsize—itself a fatal reminder of the overloaded Russian airplanes mentioned above. The population of Mwanza (and surrounding area) is being confronted with an ideologically sugarcoated cinematic version of their own fate as a kind of promise that cannot be beaten for cynicism in the context of the present globalized economy. Without having to invent anything, it is quite sufficient to record the events actually taking place and leave the audience to reflect on their symbolic importance. The resulting conclusions—in other words, the understanding of the "revealing" function that, according to Siegfried Kracauer automatically adheres to each film image alongside its "registering" function—can be drawn by the film's viewers. They will usually appreciate not having every last detail and its significance spelt out to them, but instead prefer to be allowed to think for themselves about (and beyond) what is made explicit.

Of course this is particularly true for the subject of arms dealing that Sauper picks up on additionally. The point here is that the weapons that are brought into the country by the haulage aircraft on their inbound journey are never shown. The first person to speak of arms dealing is Jonathan, who does so with reference to relevant reports in the Tanzanian news media. Previously, the government had played dumb and ordered an enquiry, but that proved inconclusive. When the pilots are asked about it, we hear that they had indeed loaded some large crates onto the aircraft when they started in Russia or Belgium, but that they did not know what was inside. They all provide evasive answers, suggesting that their freight must be aid supplies of some kind, but no one has seen them, just as we never see the guns, grenades and mines destined for Angola, Zaire, or the Congo in the film. Later on, a journalist speaks frankly about the arms deals brokered by Tanzania, because making direct deliveries to a nation at war is illegal. It would not have been difficult to present some fake crates containing the secret cargo. But Sauper does not need to avail himself of such tricks; with his indirect approach he proves that it is not necessarily a disadvantage not to be able to show everything that exists in reality.

The dramaturgy of *Darwin's Nightmare* is based on a deliberate restriction of information because it is actually about more than reporting. Around the symbolic vacuum, as it were, that spreads out in the bellies of the aircraft on the inbound flight, the space and time for different considerations is created, challenging the viewers to follow their own thoughts and to take a stand. The person who, following the example of the biblical Thomas, only wishes to believe what they have seen for themselves, or (as an alternative) what has been prepared by news technology in the media, is fighting a losing battle nowadays. The former is not representative and is entirely devoid of meaning, and the latter drowns in the sheer plentitude of frequently contradictory information and is marked by a general loss of authority, this being particularly the case with television (see Krieg 1997: 91). A documentary like

Darwin's Nightmare on the other hand is the expression of a discussion at a meta level, where the relevance of the experiences of a more or less large group of people is negotiated because film is not subject to the dictates of daily updated news and has at least a theoretical chance of surviving as a manifestation of historical positions.[6]

Closing Remarks

Hupert Sauper, like other postmodern film directors, disposes of an individual cinematic calligraphy; he is an auteur in the best sense of the word. His interpretations of what happens rest on the knowledge that there is no such thing as objective reality and there certainly can be no neutral reproduction of it. He disavows clichés on the status of reality, not just by creating a plot about the political and economic machinations of international high finance, but also by providing a story with emotional logic and motivation. *Darwin's Nightmare* distinguishes itself through a visual language that easily transcends the cinematic design of the single moment. Tanzania ultimately emerges as a microcosm that facilitates a concentrated, because exaggerated, recording and presentation of the general structures of contemporary society.

Of course, Sauper's film did not turn out to be "objective." What would that be anyway, given these issues? The director has sided with people who are at great risk of going to the dogs. He distinguishes himself as the conceptual core of a creative process in which he uses technical and aesthetic strategies to shape something new out of the perceptions, statements, actions, and abilities of the persons concerned. He is able to extract a very specific message from the raw material of reality and that is authenticated solely by Sauper himself and his crew and interview partners.[7] A film like *Darwin's Nightmare* opens up new visual and aural spaces that reach out beyond that which is presented and reflects our own existence like a mirror. In a paradigmatic manner we are shown that today the production of the authentic and credible does not happen once and for all, but at best in a relative sense—as in the case at hand with regard to our European, postcolonial history of awareness. Because of this, Sauper, several contributors to the film, and their families are frequently attacked, violently persecuted, arrested, and incarcerated, banished from Tanzania or threatened in other ways, so that in the summer of 2006 it even became necessary for the Austrian Ministry of Foreign Affairs to intervene at a diplomatic level.[8] So, be it Eliza, who did not live long enough to see the completion of the film, or Raphael, who smears his arrows with poison like a fighter from the archaic past, or the boys who quickly stuff their mouths with a few fistfuls of the rice they have just snatched in their daily struggle for survival—in word and picture they all represent a specific substance of truth that lies on this side of fictional storytelling and also touches upon the concrete conditions of Western society. The need for this kind of investigative enlightenment is clearly no longer or not sufficiently satisfied by the primary news and information media of television and daily newspapers, which is why the documentary form has become appreciated internationally. Every successful film,

Sauper once remarked, is an "internal journey, where one finds more than one seeks."[9] There is no better way than this to describe the aesthetic and ideological program of *Darwin's Nightmare*.

Notes

Translated by Karen Meehan and Arno Russegger.

1. The following subgenres are listed by Schadt: reportage, feature, docu-drama, docu-essay, docu-soap, docu-fake, reality TV and reality soap (Schadt 2002: 21).
2. Sauper's remarks are taken from the booklet that accompanies the DVD release of *Darwin's Nightmare* (Homevision, 2007).
3. Reider is identified as "stills photographer and assistant director" on the DVD edition of *Darwin's Nightmare*, while in the opening credits of the film he is listed under the heading of "artistic collaboration."
4. Quoted from "Conversation with Hubert Sauper," one of the special features on the DVD of *Darwin's Nightmare*.
5. This interview is one of the special features on the DVD of *Darwin's Nightmare*.
6. In fairness, however, it should be noted that documentaries such as *Darwin's Nightmare*, cofinanced by Arte and WDR, would not even exist without public television.
7. See Heiner Stadler: "If ... the distinction between 'fiction' and 'reality' were to collapse, more would be gained than lost.... We would only be measured by our own credibility, whatever means we use to tell our stories" (Stadler, in Schadt 2002: 17).
8. "In August 2006 the Tanzanian government claimed that *Darwin's Nightmare* had tarnished the image of Tanzania and caused a decline in the fish trade. The Tanzanian parliament passed a resolution according to which all contributors to the documentary were to be punished as public enemies" (quoted from "Darwin's Nightmare," http://www.wikipedia.de, retrieved 10 November 2006).
9. *Der Standard*, 1 February 2006, n.p.

References

Barsam, R.M. 1992. *Nonfiction Film: A Critical History*, rev. edn. Bloomington: Indiana UP.

Hattendorf, M. 1995. *Perspektiven des Dokumentarfilms*. Munich: Schaudig & Ledig.

Kreimeier, K. 1997. "Fingierter Dokumentarfilm und Strategien des Authentischen," in K. Hoffmann (ed.), *Trau-Schau-Wem: Digitalisierung und dokumentarische Form*. Konstanz: UVK Medien, 29–46.

Krieg, P. 1997. "Die Inszenierung des Authentischen," in K. Hoffmann (ed.), *Trau-Schau-Wem: Digitalisierung und dokumentarische Form*. Konstanz: UVK Medien, 85–95.

Schadt, T. 2002. *Das Gefühl des Augenblicks: Zur Dramaturgie des Dokumentarfilms*. Bergisch Gladbach: Bastei Lübbe.

Chapter 26

The Lady in the Lake: Austria's Images in Götz Spielmann's *Antares*

Sara F. Hall

In a deceptively straightforward moment of narrative transition in Götz Spielmann's *Antares* (2004), a married nurse (Petra Morzé) named Eva has just departed from a hotel-room tryst with her lover, Tomasz (Andreas Patton). In a tight shot, a blue and white train carriage picks up speed and rolls off to the right. As the locomotive moves away, multiple rows of concrete apartment and office buildings become visible in the distance to the left, and an advertising billboard comes into view center screen. On it hangs a photograph of a surrealistically large bikini-clad woman reclining in a crystal clear lake, her head tossed back in relaxed ecstasy. Her face, breasts and knee surface through the water, forming peaks and valleys paralleling the Alpine crags in the background. A glimmer of light reflects off her submerged abdomen. The red and white logo of the Austrian National Tourist Office hovers above the scene. Designed to resemble a luggage sticker, it bears the Tourist Office's official URL and its mass-marketing advertising slogan: *Alltag raus. Österreich rein* ("Out with the day-to-day. In with Austria"). Eva walks past the billboard without looking at it. The top of her head lines up with the tip of the billboard model's nose, a contrast in scale that threatens to render the protagonist visually insignificant. However, Eva's purposeful gait and the film's established investment in her story bind the viewer's attention as she moves out of the frame to the left.

The camera does not respond immediately; instead, in a stylistic gesture typical of the film as a whole, it lingers on the train platform for an extra beat, leaving the viewer to contemplate this lady in the lake a moment longer. When the scene eventually cuts to Eva on the asphalt path that traverses her apartment complex, the camera pans quickly left, stopping on a young, dissatisfied, bleach-blond woman sitting smoking a cigarette. This woman is Sonja (Susanne Wuest), seen earlier working as a checkout girl at the grocery store where Eva does her shopping, and whose own story will be narrated in the film's second strand. The two women nod respectfully to one another, but do not speak. Coming after the shot of the tourism billboard and its legible slogan, this scene could well bear the caption *Alltag wieder rein* ("In with the day-to-day"). This seemingly banal transitional sequence thus evokes the aesthetic and thematic challenge *Antares* poses as a whole: how can the everyday experiences of Austrians, and Austrian women in particular, be reconciled with a national fantasy that tries to eradicate the quotidian by using images of women and nature to distract attention from modern life's rootedness in an often unspectacular manmade environment?

This provocative advertisement is shown twice more as part of a sequence that moves the narrative back in time. Forty minutes into the film, the viewer sees the Alpine photograph at a juncture that must necessarily be before Eva would have walked past it—which is to say, as the poster is being assembled and hung by Marco, Sonja's boyfriend. Standing on a ladder with his hand hovering just above the left breast of the bikini-clad model, Marco answers a call from Sonja, who has ended her shift at the grocery store. In the preceding scene, she has revealed to a co-worker that she lied to Marco about being pregnant so that he will marry her, a story he has taken for true. Now seen doing his job, Marco promises Sonja he will call her back. The scene then cuts between a shot of her sitting in the spot where, as the first narrative chapter has shown, Eva will pass her the following day, and shots of Marco and his co-worker, Robert, putting the final touches on the Austrian tourist poster and then hanging more ads selling cars, jam, and lingerie in unpopulated urban and semi-suburban settings. A conversation between the two men about the hypothetical possibility of sleeping with a woman like the lingerie model whose image they are assembling reveals that Sonja is justified in her insecurities and her suspicions that Marco is not committed to a monogamous relationship.

A multitude of visual, aural and diegetic repetitions—such as Eva buying her groceries from Sonja, and Marco's hanging the Austrian tourism billboard that Eva will walk past on the train platform—connect the three forty-minute segments of *Antares*. Spatial markers—such as the three establishing shots of concrete apartment buildings, the brief appearances of characters in the same places at the same time, and the sounds of voices and music that originate from one scene in one segment and are subsequently heard in another—tell the viewer that despite what their appearances and lifestyles might otherwise tell you, Eva, Sonja, and Nicole (Marco's lover, whose experiences are the core of the third segment of the film)[1] share a common world, one which both literally and metaphorically centers on their deteriorating postwar apartment complex. Temporal markers—such as the shift from day to night, images of clocks, references to the time of day, and the representation and reorientation of memorable events and encounters between characters—offer a vague sense of the shared passage of one weekend in that shared world.

While Spielmann does employ parallel editing to show simultaneous events within each individual narrative strand, the three overarching stories are very deliberately not intercut. Instead, they unfold in succession, bookended within a framing narrative involving a car accident that results in one character's death and another's injury. Rather than using intercutting, which today's viewers have come to expect from popular narrative films as the standard means for providing an immediate grasp of multiple events, achieving spectator effects such as suspense or a sense of causality and implying thematic relations between disparate experiences and actions, Spielmann leaves it to the viewers to recognize moments of coincidence and simultaneity and to draw their own conclusions about whether they are meaningful. In fact, many of the connections between the characters' lives (and the consequences of the connectedness) can only be recognized after the events are iterated a second or third time; some can only be recognized upon a systematic dissection of the film.

Structurally and thematically, the film harkens back to G.W. Pabst's film *Joyless Street* (1925), whose legacy in the development of the conventional film narrative and the international consumption of cinematic images of modern Austria it deconstructs and reworks in ways relevant to the twenty-first century (Hall 2008). Pabst, an Austro-Hungarian-born Berlin director, used the support of the pan-European producers backing his independent production company Sofar-Film to adapt Hugo Bettauer's novel documenting the misery of the post-First World War inflationary period in Vienna for the big screen. As an antecedent of *Antares*, *Joyless Street* tracks the impact of various men's economic engagements on the day-to-day lives of women from different class backgrounds, three of whom are cast as the sympathetic protagonists (Elsie, Maria, and Greta). Pabst and his editor Michael Sorkin constructed a narrative pattern that puts the lives of these three women into motion within a common set of spaces along the "joyless street" of the title, in particular in an apartment building, as well as a hotel, brothel, dress shop, and butcher's shop linked across a single courtyard. Similar to Spielmann's later film, Pabst's masterpiece employs in its set design a multitude of mirrors, windows, walls and curtains that offer moments of revelation while also creating metaphorical blind spots and literal barriers between socially symbolic spaces. Both films refer to an increasingly steady economic and cultural exchange with not only the United States, but also regions of new economic opportunity: South America for Pabst's film; Eastern Europe and Asia for Spielmann's. For his part, Pabst emphasizes Vienna's dependence on foreign economies in the sub-plots involving an Argentinean real estate investor whose schemes leave the male lead bankrupted and a young American Salvation Army worker who rescues the recently impoverished bourgeois heroine from a potential life of degradation. And not only were Pabst's own funders international (French and Russian), but so too was his cast, which included established and emergent talent from Russia, Sweden, and Denmark. Spielmann, meanwhile, includes in his cast of characters not just Marco, an immigrant from the former Yugoslavia, but also bit characters who represent the global labor force supporting Vienna's bourgeois households, commercial enterprises, and tourist economy: cleaning ladies, chambermaids, bell hops, and prostitutes.

At two distinct historical moments, *Joyless Street* and *Antares* demonstrate that the human beings living and working on the margins of Austrian culture and the Austrian economy are crucial players in a social and political system that ultimately serves the interests of white, usually male, Western Europeans. Whereas Pabst engages with issues of economic marginalization at a moment of crisis and disintegration in the former capital of the Habsburg Empire, Spielmann interrogates the emotional and social consequences of Austria's re-established contact with regions that were once part of that Empire, but which had been closed off to Vienna during the Cold War.[2] And whereas Pabst reminds the viewer of the continuing dominance of patriarchal power, Spielmann shows both men and women at a loss in a world where gender and power relations have been destabilized, but where no productive public or private discourse adequately addresses what should come next. The lingering images of the inscrutable, but visibly strained, young characters in both films—Mariandl, the sister of Grete in *Joyless Street*; and Iris, Eva's daughter, and Mario, Nicole's son in *Antares*—remind the viewer to think, even after the films come to their carefully crafted endings, about the future world that extends beyond the frame.

One of the reasons *Joyless Street* is considered a landmark in film history is because of the impressive assembly of its tripartite structure. Although a long history of censors' interventions and a distribution path that manifested multiple international release versions have complicated all assessments of that structure, it is undeniable that Pabst and Sorkin made strides in developing their own variations on the editing techniques that were starting to dominate cinematic storytelling under the influence of the growing U.S. studio system after the 1910s. Repeatedly praised and elucidated, and alternately criticized and misread, for both conforming and not conforming to the emergent "rules" of continuity editing, *Joyless Street* remains notable for standing outside of, while in dialogue with, the developing Hollywood mainstream. Much the same can be said for *Antares*, which was made in an era in which many "indie" films were (and still are) produced by Hollywood studio executives and in which the international festival circuit serves the needs and interests of big-ticket distribution networks. Given that the turn of the twenty-first century has set notions of the foreign and independent film in flux, it seems to be no accident that Spielmann shows Eva's daughter, Iris, dancing to music with English lyrics and Nicole's son, Mario, wearing a Mickey Mouse pajama top while drinking his morning cocoa from a mug displaying the Disney character, Aladdin. It is telling that in the year when Spielmann made his film, Disney controlled Miramax (in a twelve-year relationship that ended in 2005), whose name has come to serve as shorthand for semi-independent, arthouse film production in a global market dominated by Hollywood studios.[3] What is more, to many the name Disney has long represented the fantasy factory responsible for unrealistic images of Europe promulgated through both movies and tourist spectacles. Austrian youth like Iris and Mario are part of the most lucrative consumer base for the contemporary global entertainment culture industry Disney represents, yet the producers of mainstream culture show little interest in representing, let alone exploring, Austria's particular history or culture in all its depth and unique complexity. The world of pop music and Disney cartoons thus often alienates bourgeois defenders of a finer Austrian culture, like Iris's father, Alfred, a classical music aficionado who thinks that what she listens to is not really "music," bemoans the lack of quality programming on television, and derides the German film titles he reads aloud from the newspaper. These and other intertextual, intermedial references in *Antares* prompt the viewer to consider how Spielmann's own film fits into the contemporary global media landscape.

On a formal level, the director's choice not to intercut the stories of Eva, Sonja and Nicole certainly marks *Antares* as an art film with a correspondingly challenging plot structure. Spielmann's macro-scale parallel editing pattern gives a stronger sense of "real time" unfolding than the conventional Hollywood narrative does. His film's unique realist effect is achieved at once by overlapping the most quotidian of moments and by employing restrained camera movements and flat lighting that do not glamorize or romanticize the characters' experiences. In particular, the scenes of graphic sex and physical violence remind the viewer that while movie-watching is an inherently voyeuristic enterprise, the classic escapist view onto a hermetically sealed diegetic fantasy world (to which traditional parallel editing usually contributes) is very different to what someone would see if he or she looked in on private events from a realistically close proximity. His film seems as shockingly and uniquely realist today as Pabst's earliest new objectivity films, including *Joyless Street*, did during the mid to late 1920s and early 1930s.

Both the structure and title of *Antares* point to a vastly broader context in which the personal, quotidian events portrayed might be considered: that of the whole planet. As mentioned above, Spielmann's narration occasionally moves back in time, in a retrograde fashion, a pattern that bears astronomical and cosmological associations with what is known as the retrograde motion of heavenly bodies. Each character can be compared with a planet, which, while it appears from earth to move consistently in one direction (in the case of the northern hemisphere from east to west) across and along with the other visible objects in the sky over the course of one night, will, when observed over the course of several nights, sometimes be seen to reverse its direction. Without going into an elaborate explanation of the reason for this optical effect (related to the direction of each planet's rotation, including the Earth and each planet's position relative to the sun), it suffices to say that the apparent retrograde motion of a planet requires that the on-lookers reorient their views of that planet according to its new stellar context. This astronomical allusion, along with others, including the large photograph of Earth from outer space that Sonja has wallpapered on her bedroom wall, reminds the viewer to consider how the narrative events might indeed look very different when considered from a radically distanced point of view.

Spielmann's film title further encourages such considerations. Antares is a supergiant star in the constellation Scorpion; about three-hundred times larger and three-thousand times brighter than our sun, as seen from Earth, it is often mistaken for Mars, with which it sometimes shares a red color and a proximate location in the night sky. This star is also notable for its relationship to a smaller companion star that is barely detectable in Antares's bright glare. The larger star's future is an uncertain one, as it is gradually disintegrating under the fierce wind that encircles it and its massive size means it is likely to explode into a supernova, although it is impossible to predict when. According to astrologers, because of these qualities, Antares has the power to move people to act in creative and powerful ways to change the status quo and to challenge authorities when they no longer serve the individual's best interest or support positive evolution, freedom, or fulfillment. In the winter months of 2004, when *Antares* was made and appears to take place, the planet Mercury ended its retrograde movement (a time period in which astrologists encourage people to reconsider, re-evaluate and reformulate matters of concern) over the star Antares, which is believed to have provided the right conditions for living honestly and facing and speaking the naked truth with little regard for established convention.[4] At the most basic level, one can deduce from its title that the film was conceived to present a small set of people sharing various qualities with the star Antares, individuals who manifest that destiny each in their own way. Such an interpretation then raises the question of whether they are all struggling within and/or reacting against the same set of established conventions, conventions that might be understood as particular to Austria in the globalized twenty-first century.

The billboard described above offers an entry into this line of inquiry. Spielmann includes it in a location shot, thus drawing into his film an actual advertising campaign launched by the Austrian National Tourist Office in the years around the making and release of *Antares*. The campaign's logo was the luggage sticker, which in the larger campaign bore a variety of slogans ranging from the English phrases "Discover the joy of Austria" and "Austria. Holiday break away," to the German *Lebensquelle Österreich* ("Lifesource Austria") and the tag line displayed in the film, *Alltag raus, Österreich rein*. A DVD entitled *Lebensquelle Österreich*, produced by Faudon Movies for the Austrian National Tourist Office and distributed by Austrian cultural and diplomatic units abroad, typifies the campaign's visual and linguistic rhetoric.[5] Its cover features a couple reclining romantically on a fog-shrouded lakeside pier. They are dressed in eveningwear, but have loosed themselves from the constraints of whatever cultural activity engaged them prior to the shot: his black bowtie lies unfurled over his shoulder, the hem of her red dress has been pushed high up her thigh, and she wears no shoes. Her eyes are closed as she basks in the dawn light. He casts a dark and deep gaze across the lake, a gaze the viewer can follow by opening the plastic DVD case where the picture of the lake continues. The video clips on the DVD consist of brightly colored, rhythmically edited scenes of people young and old, many of them couples, enjoying what is offered as the best of Austrian culture: fresh food, crisp wine, beautiful music, and historically significant architecture. These images are intercut with spectacular scenes of nature, most of which revolve around crystal clear waters and blindingly white snow, cutting to fanciful depictions of people performing traditional dance rituals and wearing folkloric costumes from a range of periods and regions. While the men are all seen in full attire, ranging from Loden jackets and trousers to ski wear and modern business suits, almost all the women are shown in bathing suits and revealing dresses, or even receiving a massage topless or stripping down to a corset (to the pleasure and applause of male companions) after a rainstorm has interrupted an outdoor meal set on the veranda of a majestic chateau.

Including a billboard from this marketing campaign in the narrative framework of *Antares* allows Spielmann to remind viewers, in a rather tongue-in-cheek manner, that the touristic Austria is not the Austria of his characters. For example, as sexualized as its visual rhetoric is, the DVD made by the National Tourist Office does not show graphic close-ups of both male and female genitalia. No one is cheating on his or her partner. Men do not beat their ex-wives or harass Polish prostitutes. Immigrants from Eastern Europe and Asia are not insulted, exploited, and relegated to jobs that others might consider beneath them. No one tries to kill him or herself on an overdose of pills and liquor. No dubious real estate agents lie to well-intentioned customers about the properties they represent. And there is not a single run-down, suburban mass housing complex in sight. Correspondingly, with the exception of the woman on the billboard poster, no one in *Antares* luxuriates in a bucolic landscape. The only allusion to clear Alpine waters is the brand name Waldquelle imprinted on the plastic crates next to the bottle-recycling conveyer belt in the dank backroom of the grocery store where Sonja works. The only green meadows, contented cows, and plump goats are those printed on the milk cartons she stocks in the dairy section. People drink wine, perhaps local, but they are not savoring it in stunning historical or natural settings. Classical music is presented as a pretense of good Austrian cultural values (recall how Eva's husband Alfred complains that their cleaning lady, presumably an immigrant from the former Yugoslavia, has wreaked havoc on the organization of his DVD collection, particularly his Schubert), often as the background sound in a series of stilted encounters in a family that represses much more than it expresses.

In addition, the production design of *Antares* is boxy and geometrically precise, using vertical and horizontal lines to emphasize the uniformity and inherent limitation of the spaces inhabited by the characters (which in the case of their homes occupy the same location on the same floor plan, but in different buildings of the shared complex).[6] Cinematographer Martin Gschlacht's camera is still for the most part, except for some jarring quick pans to catch characters' reactions and more drastic movements during scenes of agitation and excitement; it emphasizes the edges and corners of rooms and encourages the viewer to understand the individual shots as components in an architectural arrangement that emphasizes mass uniformity and standardization. Even when the camera does curve around corners, pan quickly across spaces, or track motion in an automobile, there are none of the sweeping, graceful traveling shots (let alone helicopter shots) that befit the spectacular Alpine landscapes usually associated with Austria and highlighted in videos like the one distributed by the Tourist Office.

The touristic billboard in *Antares* seems to represent the direct antithesis of Spielmann's cinematic aesthetic, yet does something more complicated than provide a simple rhetorical contrast: it demonstrates that the Austria of *Antares* exists in a productive dialectic with the Alpine fantasy. The billboard tells the viewer that the only way to more deeply understand the characters' experiences is to recognize that they are shaped by the same cultural assumptions and ideologies that underpin the visual representation of "the lady in the lake." Central to this line of reasoning is the recognition that this figure's position is ambivalent. On the one hand, her body is offered in a heteronormative gesture to a desiring male gaze for commercialized consumption as part of a feminized landscape: the same gaze operative when Marco and his co-worker discuss the finer features of the lingerie model whose sexual availability they muse over. On the other hand, she enjoys isolated rapture, gazing away from the viewer, seemingly oblivious to the needs or desires of any onlookers, male or female, something Eva will learn to do once she is finally alone in the hotel room she has shared with Thomasz. Spielmann has remobilized this marketing campaign as part of his own effort to interrogate the ways gender norms, sexuality, body politics, bourgeois family values, ethnocentrism, visuality, and the circulation of mass-reproduced images structure both everyday Austrian life and the creation and circulation of an exportable image of the Austrian nation.

In this context, it is significant that the first two storylines joined by the billboard thematize the manipulation of photographs in negotiations over the female characters' self-esteem, the place of sexuality in their relationships, and the fraught quality of encounters between Austrian residents of Vienna and those who have emigrated from regions to the east. The film opens with a scene of Thomasz, Eva's lover, riding in the back of a taxi on a dark evening. His face is obscured by the play of light and shadows until he deferentially asks the taxi driver to turn on the light, to which the driver responds with the highly respectful, *Ja gern, netter Herr* ("But gladly, kind sir"). What then happens disrupts with ever-increasing intensity the polite Viennese veneer of the situation. Thomasz pulls a small stack of photographs out of his pocket, which the camera presents in close-up point-of-view shots. They are highly personal images of a woman (who we will soon learn is Eva) reclining on a bed, her face and then her breasts and genitals on display in close-up. Suddenly, while Thomasz quietly examines the pictures, a run-away car, horn blaring, careens around the corner and collides with the taxi. The film has begun in medias res and the framed narrative strands will provide the backstory revealing exactly how Tomasz and his manifest memories of Eva got into the accident in the taxi.

The pictures are shown to be the result of a series of sexual encounters in an upmarket hotel room in the continuation of an affair presumably begun outside of Vienna. After Thomasz has tracked Eva down by calling her apartment and finding out from her daughter that she works at the Rudolf Hospital in the heart of historic Vienna, the two engage in what appears to be physically satisfying, but rather impersonal sexual relations. Their interactions are focused not only on reaching climax, but also on maximizing the sexual tension of unspoken negotiations over who will kiss whom and how (Eva does not let Thomasz kiss her on the mouth and subsequently performs fellatio on him), over who will be on top (Eva climbs on top of Thomasz on the hotel room floor, but they move to the bed and adopt the missionary position), and finally over visual access to Eva's body and her image, for when Eva returns from dressing off-screen in the bathroom and sits on the bed to say her goodbyes, Thomasz (covered up to his waist by a neatly arranged sheet and blanket) snaps a photograph of her face before she comprehends what he is doing. The expression on Eva's face is soulful and the image highly personal. Paradoxically, despite the intervention of the photographic apparatus, the camera will offer Thomasz his most intimate views of his lover, who otherwise does all she can to avoid meaningful eye contact or substantive conversation with him.

As if in response to this visual and verbal withholding, on their second meeting in the hotel room Thomasz asks if he can blindfold her. This time she lets him kiss her, but as was the case in the first the sex scene, although the act of intercourse is shot with both bodies in the frame, the two are shown in isolation afterwards. Eva takes the blindfold off her eyes and the two awkwardly discuss her spending the night with Thomasz and their going out for dinner. During their foray into the city streets, Eva and Thomasz run into Eva's daughter strolling with a friend; mother and daughter exchange deep glances but deny knowing one another. The visibility of Eva's intimacy with this man who is not her husband tests their trust and loyalty in unspeakable ways. Later that night, in their third sexual encounter, perhaps in an attempt to even the visual power score, Eva tries to turn the tables on Thomasz by using a series of telling glances to encourage a room service waiter (Stefan Stojetz), who has come in to serve a bottle of wine, to watch through a half-closed door as Thomasz performs oral sex on her in the shower. Eva makes eye contact with the young man the whole time, although her lover does not know he is there. Earlier Thomasz had broken the line of vision between them, so Eva substitutes for that connection a direct visual exchange with someone who seems to be a willing voyeur.

When Eva tells Thomasz afterwards that she has done this, he looks slightly perturbed and asks for the camera, with which he then takes a rather aggressive photograph of her with his finger in her mouth, an image that was shown in the opening sequence in the taxi. The two make love again, this time with Eva on top. Very much the more active partner, Eva tells Thomasz that she loves him right before he reaches climax; however, this verbal proclamation only casts more doubt on the depth of Eva's emotions. Taking control of the visual interactions, and diminishing Thomasz's position in their relations, seems to have given Eva the power to find pleasure (and the pleasure of finding power) in her emotions, her senses, and her words. She wields them just as Thomasz wields the camera. Eva professes in rather rough language that she has never had had such good sex and encourages him to do what he wants with her—an expression of intimacy and sexual desire on her part, but at the same time a display of her willingness or need to relinquish control momentarily. Thomasz responds by interjecting the distancing photographic apparatus between the two again, instructing her to touch herself while he takes close-up photographs from between her legs. She tells him shyly that she cannot, but does so anyway, in another ambivalent moment of concession. It is not clear whether her movements and quiet gasps are an expression of embarrassment or pleasure, or both. Thomasz later awakens to find Eva taking close-ups of his un-erect penis with his camera.

His next move in this mounting game of power and vision is to pay a female Asian hotel employee (Jay Lees), whom he speaks to in English in a demonstration of her immigrant status, 100 Euros to join them in the room and watch them having sex, unbeknownst to Eva. The woman takes the money and watches as Thomasz enters Eva, who is once again blindfolded, from behind. Thomasz removes the blindfold, and at first Eva appears pained. But she then smiles sympathetically and pleasantly at the other woman, whose expression softens in return in a shot-counter-shot exchange. Either both women are turned on, or they are both smiling because they know that the understanding achieved between them undermines Thomasz's attempt at gaining control of their bodies and eyes, or they offer one another moral support in what could otherwise be an uncomfortable situation. The beauty of the expression achieved by each actress lies in the fact that any and all of these meanings are present and possible. After a quick cut to the next shot, Eva is shown fully dressed. She says a cool goodbye to Thomasz, leaving him looking somewhat lost, sitting in his bathrobe on the bed. The door closes and the scene cuts to the shot of the train and billboard that links Eva to Sonja as cohabitants of a milieu that radiates from their apartment complex outward through all of Vienna, Austria, Central Europe and the globe.

Like Eva's illicit relationship with Thomasz, Sonja's domestic arrangement with Marco is negotiated through photographic images. As recounted above, Sonja competes for Marco's affections not only with actual women in her environment, but with all the imaginary women that the commercial media imply might come into her boyfriend's life. As part of her belief that having a child could provide insurance against infidelity, Sonja fetishistically collects pictures of babies, tearing them out of women's magazines at the supermarket and storing them along with photos of her and Marco in keepsake boxes in the room the two are setting up for their non-existent offspring. When she discovers that Marco has been using evening walks with her dog Fipsi as a pretense for a regular rendezvous with Nicole, Sonja destroys the photos and discards them over her balcony ledge. She then tries to kill herself. After effectively stealing the reassuring and romanticized images of babies from her fellow female magazine consumers, Sonja recognizes that these false images cannot conjure the life she fantasizes about, a realization that makes her give up on herself entirely. Unlike the very adult, bourgeois Eva, she has no opportunity for a personal or sexual awakening. With her thin, nubile body and her cutesy pink and fuzzy clothing, Sonja is cast in the part of the perpetual adolescent. She does not participate actively in the struggle over the power of the gaze and access to the apparatus of mechanical reproduction and influence over its products. Her moment of recognition, unlike Eva's, does not arise out of an exchange of glances evoking mutual respect, shared sexual frisson, and camaraderie with another female global citizen, but instead comes when she is forced to recognize another working-class Austrian woman as competition in a territory dispute over a man, and in particular an immigrant who offers something the resident alternative embodied by Austrian men like Alex and Alfred do not. Lying in her hospital bed at the end of the film, Sonja tells Marco that she has tried to kill herself because she lost the baby, which was, as the viewer knows, a phantasmagoria to begin with. When the film ends, there is no sense of what lies ahead for her. In stark contrast, Eva returns at the close of the film to the hotel room after Thomasz has checked out; there she dwells on memories of her pleasure, even finding a photo of herself that Thomasz has left behind and masturbating to climax. She calls her husband and tells him that no, she does not want a divorce; she simply has taken a lover.

Spielmann's film thus aligns but refuses to tie entirely together two different stories of how women consume and are affected by photographic images that are both distinct from but related to the image of the lady in the lake on the Austrian National Tourist Office billboard. Eva is able to take possession of the images and the desire and objectification they represent because these images are produced in a very personal context and are only passed between her and her lover. At the close of the film, when Thomasz ends up in the hospital where Eva works as a result of the accident, he leaves an envelope for her with one of her colleagues, which we are left to surmise contains the remaining photos he still had in his possession in the taxi. We have learned that Alex was killed in the accident, which makes it all the more significant that Thomasz was not. Although still alive and well, or perhaps, because he finds himself still alive and well, Thomasz removes himself from his positon behind the camera lens. In the context of Eva's story, the Austrian billboard thus stands for the possibility of female independence, self-exploration, solitary pleasure, and self-fashioning. In the context of Sonja's story, however, it serves as a reminder of the media's continued interference in women's relationship to their own desire, for it projects a feminine ideal that remains unattainable to someone like her. If the glimmer reflecting off the abdomen of the lady in the lake stands for the hope that Sonja has placed in her imaginary baby (a hope that Eva and Nicole may or may not have placed in their own children), then the billboard also represents the dangers of an idealized femininity that revolves around an oversimplified and romanticized ideal of motherhood as the result of sexual relations.

The critical gesture represented by the billboard is a complicated one. In making an art film about the lives of these three women, Spielmann himself feminizes an exportable image of Austria. Like the lady in the lake, his female protagonists can be reduced to archetypes and allegories. Yet with its framing device and discreet parallel—sometimes retrograde—storylines set in the unspectacular built environment of the apartment complex, *Antares* offers a range of alternative views on the dynamic relationship between gender, sexuality, body politics, media history, and the national imaginary. Spielmann denaturalizes the mythology of beautiful women and Alpine scenery as the focal points of a consumer-friendly vision of Austria. His film thus functions as a contribution to an Austrian counter-cinema, which in this case means a cinema counter both to the dominant Hollywood paradigm and to the image of Austria being mass-marketed by the tourism industry. Interestingly, *Antares* was presented to the Academy of Motion Picture Arts and Sciences as Austria's 2004 pick for the Best Foreign Language Film, but was not chosen as one of the Oscar finalists that year. Its dismissal in a category that tends to reinforce the mainstream film industry's faith in the ambassadorial function of morally elevated and deeply moving products of discreet national cultures provides a strong testament indeed to the incisive critical potential of Spielmann's cool tone, provocative imagery, and ambivalent narrative outcomes.

Notes

1. This segment focuses on Nicole's attempts to break out of an abusive relationship with Alex (Andreas Kiendl), the father of her son.
2. On postmodern Austrian filmmaking trends in this geopolitical context, see Dassanowsky (2008).
3. Interestingly, although Spielmann and his production team could not have known it at the time, in 2006 Disney would also purchase Pixar, the animation company that made *Monsters Inc.* Mario is shown bringing a stuffed animal representing a *Monsters Inc.* character home from an excursion with his father. This unforeseeable coincidence attests to the depth of the American corporatization of artisanal filmmaking Spielmann appears to be engaging with.
4. See: http://www.lunarplanner.com/LunarMonths2004/lunarmonth.04.12.12.html and http://members.aol.com/terriastro/mercury.htm. Retrieved 15 October 2008.
5. I received this DVD, also titled "Discover the Joy of Austria," at an event at the University of Illinois at Chicago to which the Austrian Consul General of Chicago contributed educational materials of interest to Germanic Studies students.
6. Katharina Wöppermann won an award for her production design on *Antares* at the Hof International Film Festival, 2004.

References

Dassanowsky, R. von. 2008. "A Wave over Boundaries: New Austrian Film," *Film International* 6(1): 31–44.

Hall, S. 2008. "Inflation and Devaluation: Gender, Space, and Economics in G.W. Pabst's *The Joyless Street* (1925)," in N. Isenberg (ed.), *Weimar Cinema: An Essential Guide to Classic Films of the Era*. New York: Columbia University Press, 135–54.

Chapter 27

"Children of Optimism": An Interview with Götz Spielmann on *Revanche* and New Austrian Film

Catherine Wheatley

Götz Spielmann's *Revanche* (2008) begins with a static shot of a rural idyll, inverted in the cool, torpid waters of a lake. The peaceful pastoral, bathed in crepuscular sunlight and cast in a warm, autumnal palate, is quite suddenly splintered by the abrupt splash of an object hitting the water, fragmenting the landscape, casting centrifugal ripples over its reflection. As the shot lingers, these ripples expand and dissipate, one by one, until gradually calm is restored; it is as if nothing had ever happened.

It's an apt opening for a film which incorporates elements of New Austrian Film's "feel-bad" aesthetic, only to subvert them by producing a film which, overall, could hardly be described as pessimistic or hard to take. Indeed, perhaps the most outrageous aspect of Spielmann's film is its optimism: as the film draws to a close it is the possibility of grace, redemption, and reconciliation which endures long after the closing credits have scrolled over the screen.

Immediately after these opening images, a pair of matched cuts shows a woman and a man standing at windows: she in her kitschy countryside kitchen, he at the window of a grim, neon-lit flat. These characters are Susanne, a contented wife and would-be mother, and Alex, a petty thug in the heady throes of an illicit affair with prostitute Tamara, in whose bedroom we first meet him. Before Alex even speaks, we watch him indulge in an explicit and tender bout of sex with Tamara, which the two follow with a casual meal of pizza, eaten naked on her grimy sheets. In keeping with much of New Austrian Film's aesthetic, the cold, hard, hallucinogenic urbanity of Alex and Tamara's existence is juxtaposed with Susanne's soft-lit rural routine. Cinematographer Martin Gschlacht frames the two locations with a series of cool, precise, static takes and sequence shots, calling to mind the ascetic form of Michael Haneke's films, while Spielmann's prevalence for found settings, naturalistic lighting and sound effects, and Bressonian types reflects Ulrich Seidl's working methods. Further convergences with the two blue-eyed boys of the nation's contemporary film industry emerge within these opening scenes. The director takes pains to establish a pervasive atmosphere of dread through the use of generic convention: like *Dog Days* (2001) and *Funny Games* (1997), *Revanche* draws on thriller conventions, casting its scenes in a sinister light, as the camera lurks on certain objects—a gun, an axe, a knife slicing through an apple—and populating its narrative with a cast of ominous characters, such as Alex and Tamara's faux-friendly boss Konecny, a smiling pimp whose benevolent demeanor is undercut by his unsmiling eyes.

If the arthouse film disguised as genre flick has become something of a cliché in recent European cinema, however—one that comes with its own set of stereotypes and audience expectations—Spielmann scores an understated coup by cleaving from type, and refusing to supply the brutal, punitive, and nihilistic images which have come to be associated with such works. When, for example, Konecny arrives unexpectedly at Tamara's apartment and forces the young woman onto her knees to perform fellatio on him, it is both a relief and a frustration of sorts that instead of confronting us with an excruciating scene of sexual abuse, such as might appear in Seidl's *Import Export* (2007), Spielmann let's his audience off the hook, as Konecny hauls Tamara to her feet, chiding her for believing he would subject her to such indignity. There's perhaps an analogy to be drawn here with the director himself: "relax" he might tell us, "it won't be as bad as you think." Like the gun that Alex wields, *Revanche*'s chamber is not loaded. It is a motto which could underpin the film as whole, which time and again sets us up for a nasty surprise, only to pull back at the last minute, leaving us with a far more gentle experience than we might have expected. Granted, there is one nasty shock in store for viewers, the death of Tamara some fifty minutes into the film, but its tone is tragic rather than aggressive, a terrible accident which takes place almost entirely off-screen. Not for Götz Spielmann the sudden shock of *Benny's Video* (1992), the endless ordeal of the drawn-out suicide scene in *The Seventh Continent* (1989), nor the abrasive, aural violence of *Dog Days*. Tamara's death is not a reflexive assault on the audience but a narrative trope, the consequences of which will reverberate throughout the ensuing character study.

As such, *Revanche* might be better placed alongside films by young filmmakers such as Valeska Grisebach, Jessica Hausner, and Ruth Mader than with the more abrasive works of Seidl and Haneke. These are films that, as I have argued in chapters 9 and 12 in this book, are more interested perhaps in depicting emotional states than scoring political points. Indeed, one might speculate that Spielmann is typical of a new trend among Austrian filmmakers for "enjoy[ing] telling their stories," as producer Gabriele Kranzelbinder (Otti, 2009) puts it. The director himself claims: "I don't believe in art that has the aim of getting a political message across ... my characters aren't symbols for something else. They don't stand for something else, they stand for themselves" (Otti 2009). And it is precisely this aspect of the film that Roger Ebert picks up upon in his characteristically succinct summation of *Revanche*'s impact: "These actors create characters who are above all people, not performances. That's why the film is peculiarly effective; it's about their lives, not their dilemmas.... How often, after seeing a thriller, do you continue to think about the lives of its characters? If you open up most of them, it's like looking inside a wristwatch. Opening this one is like heart surgery" (Ebert 2009).

It is interesting in this regard that religion enters Spielmann's purview in a manner hitherto unseen in recent Austrian cinema. For while Haneke's *The White Ribbon* (2009) sees him level his scathing gaze at Christianity for the first time, and Seidl has frequently cast caustic glances at Catholicism—dedicating his documentary *Jesus, You Know* (2003) to a more fulsome consideration of the subject—and while other European directors such as Jessica Hausner (*Lourdes*, 2009), and Bruno Dumont (*Hadewijch*, 2009) have produced extended studies of faith and its significance, for Spielmann, in *Revanche*, the Christian faith is given as a positive force as well as an analogy for the human condition. Both Susanne and Alex's elderly uncle find solace in their beliefs; but beyond this, biblical imagery resonates throughout the film, in the proliferation of apples offered, refused, and accepted, the recurring image of a crucifix (most obviously in the woods but also around the necks of the film's two female leads), and most poignantly perhaps in the recurring question of guilt, grief, responsibility, and forgiveness,

The film's title, a neologism of sorts, denotes both revenge and rebirth, or a second chance. And it is this second meaning which ultimately comes to describe the tone of Spielmann's film. What initially appears to be a more-or-less straightforward revenge thriller transforms over the course of its narrative into a meditation on compassion and human kindness. The dreadful act which we anticipate never occurs; and in fact Alex's sexual encounter with Susanne, the wife of the man who killed Tamara, emerges not as an act of revenge but of grace. By impregnating Susanne with the long-hoped-for child her husband Robert could not give her, Alex in fact offers the couple a miraculous gift. Rather than evening the score by taking another life, Alex redresses the balance by giving another life. The film's denouement is not without its ambiguities of course; while the loose ends are superficially tied up, the possibility remains that that Alex's cuckolding of Robert may itself be a form of revenge. But *Revanche* nonetheless resolves itself not as a "cinema of disturbance," but one of conciliation. Its neat conclusion closes one chapter, and opens up the possibility of a new one—a fresh start.

This seems an appropriate note to sound for a film that maintains links with its cinematic forebears—not only the aggressive cinema of Haneke and Seidl, but also the explicitly political works of Christian Berger and Wolfgang Glück, and further back, beyond that, to the *Heimatfilm* and the melodramas of the 1950s—but which also marks a break with these models, incorporating formal and thematic aspects from them but rearranging them to form new patterns and tropes. Perhaps *Revanche* is indicative of a new direction for Austrian cinema, in which the nation's cinematic eye is no longer focused on its troubled history or disaffected present, but on its future: a future which, in Spielmann's film at least, contains hope. As the director himself puts it, "My movies are children of optimism."

An Interview with Götz Spielmann

This interview was conducted on the 29 October 2008, following *Revanche*'s British premiere at the London Film Festival, which took place on the previous evening.

CATHERINE WHEATLEY: There are a lot of correspondences between *Revanche* and your previous film *Antares*. You've been quoted as saying that *Revanche* is a kind of sequel to the earlier film.

GÖTZ SPIELMANN: *Revanche* is a sequel to *Antares*? There are hopefully some thematic similarities, because hopefully all my movies have something in common. But I don't think about what that could be—it should just happen.

C.W.: Guilt and redemption seem to be strong themes within both films.

G.S.: Maybe, yes.

C.W.: The locations in both films are also very striking. There's a strong urban–rural divide in *Revanche*. How do you go about finding the locations—do you have them in mind when you start writing?

G.S.: It's a question of style, you know. As regards the locations, the general idea is very clear in my mind when I start to prepare a movie, but I keep my mind open to be influenced by reality again, because finding the locations, finding the actors, and so on is in a way the last draft of the script. Reality gives me answers to my ideas and I listen to those answers and change a little bit or find new ideas. It gets richer in that case. For example the cross, in the woods, that was not in the script. And when we were looking for locations from time to time I saw similar crosses standing in places, and then because I try to stay open-minded then I got the idea that there should be a cross like that standing in the picture. So we put it there— it wasn't originally there. I loved the energy of original locations but in truth it's not always that natural, we sometimes have to adapt the locations. But always with sensitivity to the original locations—so there could be such a cross standing in that place.

C.W.: It worked very well with the natural light. And obviously the sound effects are very natural too. Was it a deliberate decision to keep these elements as true to life as possible?

G.S.: Yes. On the one hand we wanted it as naturalistic as possible and then on the other hand also in a very clear form. I would say that the sound of the movie itself is like music. We worked on the sound design, or my sound designer did, like a musician would, for weeks and weeks. That's one thing. The second thing is that I have used film music in former times—although there was no music in *Antares*— but more and more I find a more puristic energy in filmmaking, and music is very often just used to tell the audience something that the picture, the story, cannot tell; to bring about emotions that the audience should have. Well, I dislike it as a method, because I feel the will and the effort to manipulate my emotions with music, and to my mind music is much too important to do this with.

C.W.: The accordion music was very moving. Did Hannes already know how to play?

G.S.: Yes. I wrote the part for him knowing that he plays the accordion so I used the things I knew about him to invent the character.

C.W.: His character has a purity about that the other characters seemed to be trying to come to.

G.S.: I like that interpretation.

C.W.: And did you write with the other cast members in mind too?

G.S.: Well, Johannes hasn't acted in films before—he's acted in some television things but no films. Hannes was the only the actor I specifically wrote the character, the character of the old man for. And when I was writing the script Ursula came into my mind for the policeman's wife. But the others were cast after the writing was finished. I didn't want a famous actor; that is, an actor's reputation, the name, the celebrity, isn't important to me at all. I mean, if one actor has a good reputation and he's right for the part, then he's welcome. But if not, it doesn't matter. What I look for is actors who come as close as possible to the emotional character of the parts. Or who bring a new aspect to the part that I hadn't foreseen and which is interesting for the story.

C.W.: Did any of them surprise you?

G.S.: All of them surprised me, because they were all even better than I expected. Without any exception, they all played their roles very truthfully. But maybe the character of Susanna, played by Ursula, talked more than she did in the first version of the script. I think Ursula changed the character, and I liked that she talked so much.

C.W.: It's interesting that she talks so much, because for the rest of the characters within the film the dialogue is really quite minimal. Johannes performance in particular is very physical. Coming from theatre, which is a very verbal medium, is this something you're very aware of when making films?

G.S.: Theatre and film are very different things, which have the same centre. At the centre you have a hidden energy behind the story. And out from that centre you go different ways to emerge and to show what has to be shown. They are very different paths. But yes, there's something very virile about Johannes's performance, and about him as an actor.

C.W.: Was the film completely scripted? Was there any improvisation?

G.S.: It was completely scripted. But there was a phase of rehearsal which was about two weeks before shooting. During this period we worked with improvisation a little bit, and some interesting things came up which I then incorporated into the script. So the improvisation period can change the film's dynamics, can make them richer. But by the time we start shooting it is all on the page. To give you an example, when Alex comes to the house for the first time and Susanna offers to fetch a new bottle of wine, but then suddenly panics that he will think she's been drinking alone – that was new material that came from the improvisations.

C.W.: Both this film and *Antares* feature some very powerful sex scenes—are they harder to write, since there has to be something very spontaneous about them?

G.S.: Well, *Antares* was completely different of course, because those scenes were much more demanding for the actors and they needed much more preparation, much more thinking about, and a lot more rehearsal to get them right, whereas the sex scenes in *Revanche* were not as taxing. Not to me at least, maybe for the actors. Of course, actors get nervous before, but I think I know how I can help them now. It wasn't as special in the case of *Revanche*.

C.W.: There's been a tendency to group a lot of European films that have emerged over the last few years together under the banner of "New Extremism." Is that something you feel comfortable with?

G.S.: I feel some affinities with some of the directors who are placed in this category. I feel some affinity, in formal terms, rather than in terms of story, with Michael Haneke, for example. I like the way he films. His simplicity—the precise mentality. But I don't see that many similarities between my films and those of Catherine Breillat, or Ulrich Seidl, for example.

C.W.: Your fellow Austrian Valeska Grisebach has said that her films are not about politics, but people. Would you say that's something that applies to your work too?

G.S.: Yes, very much. I don't believe in art that has the aim of getting a political message across. I think that the power and energy of art goes deeper than politics. It doesn't interest me very much. Not active, and not passive. I mean I'm interested in politics, but not political art. I hope my films allow the viewer more space to understand the film in their own terms. And maybe that space has to do with energy and our own energy and that energy can also be needed to change to society. I think we need space and energy to change society—not messages.

C.W.: There are a lot of young Austrian directors, and I'm thinking of Grisebach but also maybe Jessica Hausner, who seem to be deliberately forging a break from the political cinema of the past—the work of Peter Patzak and Wolfgang Glück. Is this something you're consciously trying to do?

G.S.: Not at all. It would be a very poor artist's position, just wanting to be different. You don't need to be different to someone else, you need to be similar to yourself. That's the beginning. Being different would be a childish beginning for an artist. I'm not against generations; I'm going my own way.

C.W.: Are there any directors who have influenced you?

G.S.: I couldn't say. I'm influenced by such a lot of things. Everything I read, everything I see, every experience in the past and the present; everything influences me. And for sure there are a lot of directors and a lot of movies that influence me, but I couldn't tell you which ones.

C.W.: *Revanche* is being marketed as a thriller. But to me it seemed to use elements of the genre—for example, when we see Johannes chopping wood—but it does something very unexpected with them.

G.S.: I'm not interested in genres; I just try to make my own movies. As I say, there are a lot of movies in my life, and a lot of thrillers, and I suppose those have influenced me. But I'm just interested in cinema. A genre gives me some material to play with, and I don't hesitate to take it; but I'm not out to make a genre film, or an anti-genre film. There's a nice journalist in the United States, who wrote a good review of the film, and she said that maybe *Revanche* is the first artistic thriller. I liked that. But genres don't influence me consciously.

C.W.: Could you tell me something about the pacing of the film? It feels quite slow, particularly by comparison with *Antares*.

G.S.: Well, yes and no. The first part of *Antares* had quite a similar pace to *Revanche*. And in *Antares* the general pace of the movie was leading the stories more and more to a kind of intensity. The last sequence was done just with a hand-held camera. So it got more and more nervous and then at the end it was very quiet again. And then *Revanche* was the opposite—starting quite fast and then getting slower and slower. They were two very different general rhythms. But there are parts of *Antares* which are as slow, I think, as parts of *Revanche*. And one thing I used the first time and I liked very much is the steadicam—I'd never used steadicam before, and I used it a lot in *Revanche*. And that again gave me new possibilities of pace.

C.W.: Is time very important within the film?

G.S.: Time is important. With every movie time is very important. I always want to create movies in which one can be aware of time when watching them, and in which time is full of intensity. I don't want to make movies where you forget the time, like simple entertainments. I think time can and should be felt.

C.W.: Let's talk about the ending of the film. Austria has recently been described as the world capital of feel-bad cinema. And yet, although you've said that the ending of *Revanche* isn't a happy ending, it certainly leaves room for optimism.

G.S.: I have to give a larger answer to this question, because I personally don't believe that art can be pessimistic. Not true art. Art (at least I have this impression) is something that is strong, and has energy, and has quality. But not that is pessimistic. Never. And never, never, never, not for one second, would I want to think that I make pessimistic movies. My movies are, I would say, children of optimism. And that doesn't mean to say that they are sentimental, or kitschy, or blind to reality. But in my opinion they have a strength and energy that's bigger, and more profound, than the problems, the conflicts, the injustices, that we're talking about. So I dislike pessimistic art. Just as strongly as I dislike kitsch. Pessimism doesn't go deep enough. Because if you look deep enough, you might find something beautiful. But pessimism doesn't do that. And kitsch and sentimentality... Well, they just fear to look deeper. That's my position. So *Antares*, for example, shows a lot of pessimistic things, but it's not a pessimistic movie. The movie itself—its energy, the form—that's not pessimistic.

C.W.: I think as a director you demonstrate a kindness to your characters that many directors don't.

G.S.: Exactly, because my characters aren't symbols for something else. They don't stand for something else, they stand for themselves. That maybe makes the difference.

C.W.: So when you're writing a screenplay, do you start with the characters and then develop the story, or does it work the other round?

G.S.: The storyline is the last thing that comes. I start with feelings, with vague ideas or with pictures, or perhaps with the characters, it's a mixture... And then from time to time the larger picture comes in and a real idea emerges out of these fragments. With *Revanche*, it was the idea of a journey, and of a big change in the life of the main character. The idea that the journey ends in quietness.

C.W.: Both *Revanche* and *Antares* were nominated for the Austrian Oscar contention. Have you found that's made a difference to your ability to get funding for your films?

G.S.: No, it makes no difference. There are a lot of good and interesting directors in Austria and there is not that much money so it is never that easy. But it is not easy anywhere in the world as far as I know. That's just how it is, and that's what you have to deal with.

C.W.: It seems to be an exciting time for Austrian cinema all the same.

G.S.: It's strange that so few movies are made and so many of them get distributed overseas and get well known. I think that the average level of Austrian filmmaking is very high, maybe—I'm not sure—because competition for funding is so fierce. I mean in France, 120 movies are made in a year, so there are bound to be some bad ones. And obviously you'll see the best, but you don't see the average level. Yes, I think Austrian cinema is in quite good shape at the moment. I don't know where it comes from. Maybe when you're in a very small country with a very small market you have to be better, to concentrate more, you've got your back against the wall at the beginning more than people in other countries might do. A second reason is maybe that the film community in Austria is very vibrant.

There are a lot of directors who will criticize my work, with whom I can discuss my movies. I think that also helps a lot—that there's a kind of community and not only isolated, egomaniacal, directors.

C.W.: This is the first time you've worked with your own production company—how was it?

G.S.: Wonderful!

C.W.: And why did you decide to do it?

G.S.: Because I couldn't find a producer I really felt comfortable with. And when you take everything into account its easier to be my own producer. But I didn't do it completely alone, I worked with another company. I'll definitely do it again in future—there's no way back. For my own movies at least—if a producer has an idea and would like to work with me, well, I'd consider it. But for my own movies—the movies I invent, I write, I direct, I'll produce them myself, together with another company, a coproduction. It's somehow more economic, and I don't mean the money, I mean the energy. You don't lose your energy in dead ends.

C.W.: Would you consider working abroad, as Haneke has done for example?

G.S.: Of course. I'm open to everything. It's not my dream, I mean I don't live for the possibility of making a Hollywood movie—if that was the case I would have gone to Hollywood when I was twenty! But I'd consider all the possibilities. And of course, it would be very different to having my own production company—but I can deal with that, I'm really very open. I don't need special circumstances to be able to make a movie, I can always find a way in different circumstances and different possibilities.

C.W.: Are your films very personal to you then, or do you feel quite detached from them?

G.S.: Yes and no. Hopefully they're personal. Because I think only personal movies can communicate deeply with the audience. At least, I'm just interested in personal movies as a spectator, because then someone really wants to tell me something, to reach out to me, not just use me to show tricks to. But on the other hand, they're not autobiographical stories or anything like that. Making movies is not talking about myself, but telling stories. I'm a storyteller, that's who I am.

References

Ebert, R. 2009. "*Revanche*," *Chicago Sun Times*, 5 August. Retrieved 21 December 2009 from: http://rogerebert.suntimes.com/apps/pbcs.dll/article?AID=/20090805/REVIEWS/908069995.

Otti, A. 2009. "*Revanche* Could Help Shed Austria's 'Feel-bad Cinema' Image." Retrieved 21 December 2009 from: http://topnews.us/content/23654-revanche-could-help-shed-austrias-feel-bad-cinema-image.

Select Filmography

24 Realities per Second – A Documentary on Michael Haneke (Austria 2004) Director/
writer: Nina Kusturica and Eva Testor; Production companies: Mobilefilm/
ORF.

38 – Auch das war Wien/Vienna Before the Fall (Austria/Federal Republic of Gemany
1986) Director: Wolfgang Glück; Writers: Wolfgang Glück, Lida Winiewicz,
Friedrich Torberg (source novel); Cinematography: Gérard Vandenberg;
Production companies: Satel-Film/Almaro Film/Bayrischer Rundfunk/ORF.

71 Fragmente einer Chronologie des Zufalls/71 Fragments of a Chronology of Chance
(Austria/Germany 1994) Director/writer: Michael Haneke; Cinematography:
Christian Berger; Production company: Wega Films.

Ägypten/Egypt (Austria 1996) Director/writer: Kathrin Resetarits; Cinematography:
Gundula Daxecker, Christine A. Maier, Kathrin Resetarits; Production
company: Filmakademie Wien.

All the Queen's Men (Germany/Austria/USA 2001) Director: Stefan Ruzowitzky;
Writers: David Schneider, Digby Wolfe, Joseph Manduke, June Roberts;
Cinematography: Peter Kappel, Wedigo von Schultzendorff; Production
companies: BA Filmproduktion/Dor Film/Phoenix Film/Atlantic Streamline.

Alone. Life Wastes Andy Hardy (Austria 1998) Director/writer/cinematography: Martin
Arnold; Production company: Martin Arnold/Sixpack Film.

Alpensaga/Alpine Saga (Austria 1976–1980) Director: Dieter Berner; Writers:
Peter Turrini, Wilhelm Pevny; Cinematography: Xavier Schwarzenberger;
Production company: Studio-Film Wien/ORF.

Anatomie/Anatomy (Germany 2000) Director/writer: Stefan Ruzowitzky;
Cinematography: Peter von Haller; Production companies: Claussen & Wöbke
Filmproduktion/Deutsche Columbia TriStar.

Anatomie 2/Anatomy 2 (Germany 2003) Director/writer: Stefan Ruzowitzky;
Cinematography: Andreas Berger; Production companies: Claussen & Wöbke
Filmproduktion/Deutsche Columbia TriStar.

Antares (Austria 2004) Director/writer: Götz Spielmann; Cinematography: Martin
Gschlacht; Production Companies: Lotus Film/TeamFilm Produktion/ORF.

Auswege/Sign of Escape (Austria 2003) Director: Nina Kusturica; Writer: Barbara Albert; Cinematography: Tim Tom; Production company: Filmakademie Wien.

Benny's Video (Austria /Switzerland 1992) Director/writer: Michael Haneke; Cinematography: Christian Berger; Production companies: Bernard Lang/ Wega Film.

Blue Moon (Austria 2002) Director/writer: Andrea Maria Dusl; Cinematography: Wolfgang Thaler; Production company: Lotus Film.

Böse Zellen/Free Radicals (Austria/Germany/Switzerland 2003) Director/writer: Barbara Albert; Cinematography: Martin Gschlacht; Production companies: Coop99/Fama Film/Zero Südwest.

Brüder, lasst uns lustig sein/Brothers, Let Us Be Merry (Austria 2006) Director/writer/ cinematography/production: Ulrich Seidl.

Caché/Hidden (France/Austria/Germany/Italy 2005) Director/writer: Michael Haneke; Cinematography: Christian Berger; Production companies: Les Films du Losange/Wega Film/Bavaria Film/BIM Distribuzione/ France 3 Cinéma/arte/ Uphill Pictures.

Code inconnu: Récit incomplet de divers voyages/Code Unknown (France/Germany/ Romania 2000) Director/writer: Michael Haneke; Cinematography: Jürgen Jürges; Production companies: Bavaria Film/Canal+/Filmex/France 2 Cinéma/ Les Films Alain Sarde/MK2 Productions/Romanian Culture Ministry/ZDF/ arte France Cinéma.

Contact High: The Good, the Bad, The Bag (Austria/Germany/Poland/Luxembourg 2009) Director: Michael Glawogger; Writers: Michael Glawogger, Michael Ostrowski; Cinematography: Attia Boa, Wolfgang Thaler; Production companies: Boje Buck Produktion/Iris Productions/Lotus Film/Ozumi Films.

Copy Shop (Austria 2001) Director/writer: Virgil Widrich; Cinematography: Martin Putz; Production companies: Virgil Widrich Filmproduktion.

Crash Test Dummies (Austria/Germany 2005) Director/writer: Jörg Kalt; Cinematography: Eva Testor; Production companies: Icon Film/Amour Fou Filmproduktion.

Darwin's Nightmare (Austria/Belgium/France/Canada/Finland/Sweden 2004) Director/ writer/cinematography: Hubert Sauper; Production companies: Mille et Une Productions/Coop99/Saga Film/WDR/arte.

Das Experiment/The Experiment (Germany 2001) Director: Oliver Hirschbiegel; Writers: Mario Giordano (source novel "Black Box"), Christoph Darnstädt, Don Bohlinger; Cinematography: Rainer Klausmann; Production Companies: Fanes Film, Senator Film, Seven Pictures, Typhoon.

Das Vaterspiel/Kill Daddy Good Night (Austria/Germany/France/Ireland 2009) Director: Michael Glawogger; Writer: Michael Glawogger, Josef Haslinger (source novel); Cinematography: Attila Boa; Production companies: Degeto Film/Lotus Film/Newgrange Pictures/Polaris Films/Schenk Productions/ Tatfilm/WDR/arte/ORF.

Das weiße Band/The White Ribbon (Austria/Germany/France 2009) Director/writer Michael Haneke; Cinematography: Christian Berger; Production companies: Wega Film/Les Films du Losange/X-Filme Creative Pool.

Der Ball/The Ball (Austria 1982) Director/writer: Ulrich Seidl; Cinematography: Paul Choung; Production company: Wiener Filmakademie.

Der Bockerer (Austria/Federal Republic of Germany 1981) Directed by Franz Antel; Writers: Kurt Nachmann, Ulrich Becher and Peter Preses (source play), H. C. Artmann; Cinematography: Ernst W. Kalinke; Production company: Neue Delta/TIT Filmproduktion/Wien-Film.

Der Bockerer II – Österreich ist frei/The Bockerer II – Austria Is Free (Austria 1996) Directed by Franz Antel; Writers: Franz Antel, Martin Becher, Beatrice Ferolli, Wilhelm Pribil, Carl Szokoll; Cinematography: Helmut Pirnat; Production companies: EPO-Film/Terra Film.

Der Bockerer III – Die Brücke von Andau/The Bridge at Andau (Austria 2000) Directed by Franz Antel; Writers: Franz Antel, Kurt Huemer; Cinematography: Hans Selikovsky; Production Company: EPO-Film.

Der Bockerer IV – Der Prager Frühling/Prague Spring (Austria 2003) Directors: Franz Antel and Kurt Ockermüller; Writers: Franz Antel, Kurt Huemer, Fedor Mosnak; Cinematography: Martin Stingl; Production company: EPO-Film/ ORF.

Der Knochenmann/The Bone Man (Austria 2009) Director: Wolfgang Murnberger; Writers: Wolfgang Murnberger, Josef Hader, Wolf Haas (source novel and screenplay); Cinematography: Peter von Haller; Production company: Dor Film.

Der Schüler Gerber/The Student Gerber (Austria/Federal Republic of Germany 1980) Director: Wolfgang Glück; Writers: Wolfgang Glück, Werner Schneyder, Freidrich Torberg (source novel); Cinematography: Xaver Schwarzenberger; Production companies: Arabella Film/Almaro Film/Satel-Film/Bayrischer Rundfunk.

Der siebente Kontinent/The Seventh Continent (Austria 1989) Director: Michael Haneke; Writers: Michael Haneke, Johanna Teicht; Cinematography: Anton Peschke; Production Company: Wega Film.

Der Überfall/Hold-Up (Austria/Germany/Canada 2000) Director: Florian Flicker; Writers: Florian Flicker, Susanne Freund; Cinematography: Helmut Pirnat; Production company: Allegro Film.

Die Ameisenstraße/Ant Street (Austria 1995) Director: Michael Glawogger; Writers: Michael Glawogger, Barbara Zuber, Peter Berecz; Cinematography: Jirí Stibr; Production company: Dor Film.

Die Fälscher/The Counterfeiters (Austria/Germany 2007) Director: Stefan Ruzowitzky; Writers: Stefan Ruzowitzky, Adolf Burger (source novel); Cinematography: Benedict Neuenfels; Production company: Magnolia Filmproduktion/ Babelsberg Film/Beta Film/Josef Aichholzer Film/ZDF.

Die papierene Brücke/Paper Bridge (Austria 1987) Director/writer: Ruth Beckermann; Cinematography: Nurith Aviv, Claire Bailly du Bois; Production company: Ruth Beckermann-Filmproduktion.

Die Praxis der Liebe/The Practice of Love (Federal Republic of Germany/Austria 1985) Director/writer: VALIE EXPORT; Cinematography: Jörg Schmidt-Reitwein; Production companies: VALIE EXPORT Filmproduktion/Königsmark & Wullenweber Filmproduktion/ORF/ZDF.

Die Siebtelbauern/The Inheritors (Austria/Germany 1998) Writer/Director:
     Stefan Ruzowitzky; Cinematography: Peter von Haller; Production
     Companies: Bayerischer Rundfunk (BR), Dor Film Produktionsgesellschaft,
     Österreichischer Rundfunk (ORF).
Die totale Therapie/Total Therapy (Austria 1996) Director/writer Christian Frosch;
     Cinematography: Johannes Hammel; Production company: Prisma Film.
Die Viertelliterklasse/The Quarter-Litre Class (Austria 2005) Directors: Roland Düringer
     and Florian Kehrer; Writer: Roland Düringer (source play and screenplay);
     Cinematography: Thomas Kürzl; Production companies: Dor Film/Nanook
     Film.
Dream Work (Austria 2001) Director/writer/cinematography: Peter Tscherkassky;
     Production Company: Peter Tscherkassky/Sixpack Film.
Ein Augenblick Freiheit/For a Moment, Freedom (Austria/France/Turkey 2009)
     Director/writer: Arash T. Riahi; Cinematography: Michael Riebl; Production
     company: Wega Film/Pi Film/Les Films du Losange.
Ein flüchtiger Zug nach dem Orient/A Fleeting Passage to the Orient (Austria 1999)
     Director/writer: Ruth Beckermann; Cinematography: Nurith Aviv; Production
     company: Josef Aichholzer Filmproduktion.
Eine blaßblaue Frauenschrift/A Woman's Pale Blue Handwriting (Austria/Italy 1984)
     Director: Axel Corti; Writers: Axel Corti, Kurt Rittig, Franz Werfel (source
     novel); Cinematography: Edward Kłosiński; Production companies: ORF/RAI.
Fallen/Falling (Austria/Germany 2006) Director/writer: Barbara Albert;
     Cinematography: Bernhard Keller; Production companies: Coop99/ZDF/ORF.
Film ist/Film is (Austria 1998-continuing) Director/writer/cinematography: Gustav
     Deutsch; Production company: LOOP.
Flora (Austria 1995) Director/writer: Jessica Hausner; Cinematography: Robert
     Winkler; Production company: Filmakademie Wien.
Frankreich, wir kommen!/France, Here we come! (Austria 1999) Director: Michael
     Glawogger; Writers: Michael Glawogger, Johann Skocek; Cinematography:
     Wolfgang Thaler; Production company: Lotus Film.
Freispiel/Free Game, Replay (Austria 1995) Director: Harald Sicheritz; Writers: Alfred
     Dorfer, Harald Sicheritz; Cinematography: Helmut Pirnat; Production
     company: Fernsehfilmproduktion Dr. Heinz Schneiderbauer.
Fremde/Strangers (Austria 1999) Director/writer: Kathrin Resetarits; Cinematography:
     Martin Gschlacht, Marcus Kanter, Robert Winkler; Production company:
     Filmakademie Wien.
Funny Games (Austria 1997) Director/writer: Michael Haneke; Cinematography: Jürgen
     Jürges; Production company: Wega Film.
Funny Games (USA/France/UK/Austria/Germany 2008) Director/writer: Michael
     Haneke; Cinematography: Darius Khondji; Production companies: Celluloid
     Dreams/Halcyon Pictures/Tartan Films/X-Filme International/Lucky Red/
     Kinematograf.
Geboren in Absurdistan/Born in Absurdistan (Austria 1999) Directors: Houchang
     Allahyari, Tom Dariusch Allahyari; Writers: Houchang Allahyari, Tom
     Dariusch Allahyari, Agnes Pluch; Cinematography: Helmut Pirnat; Production
     company: EPO-Film.

Gebürtig (Austria/Germany/Poland 2001) Directors: Lukas Stepanik, Robert
   Schindel; Writers: Lukas Stepanik, Robert Schindel, Georg Stefan Troller;
   Cinematography: Edward Klosinski; Production companies: Cult Film/
   Extrafilm/DaZu Film/Akson Studio/Tor Film Studio.

Geschichten aus dem Wiener Wald/Tales from the Vienna Woods (Federal
   Republic of Germany/Austria 1979) Director: Maximilian Schell; Writers:
   Christopher Hampton, Maximilian Schell, Ödön von Horvath (source play);
   Cinematography: Klaus König; Production companies: Arabella-Film/Franz
   Seitz Filmproduktion/BR/MFG Film/Solaris Film.

Gfrasta (Austria 1993) Director: Ruth Mader; Writers: Barbara Albert, Martin
   Leidenfrost, Ruth Mader; Cinematography: Christoph Hochenbichler;
   Production company: Filmakademie Wien.

*Good News oder: Von Kolporteuren, toten Hunden und anderen Wienern/Good
   News* (Austria 1990) Director/writer: Ulrich Seidl; Cinematography: Hans
   Selikovsky; Production company: Selikovsky Film.

Grbavica (Austria/Bosnia and Herzegovina/Croatia/Germany 2006) Director/writer:
   Jasmila Zbanic; Cinematography: Christine A. Maier; Production companies:
   Coop99/Deblokada/Noirfilm/Jadran Film/ZDF/arte.

Hannah (Austria 1996) Director: Reinhard Schwabenitzky; Writers: Susanne M. Ayoub,
   Reinhard Schwabenitzky, Jonathan Carroll; Cinematography: Fabian Eder,
   Johannes Kirchlechner; Production companies: Star Film/EPO Film.

Heidenlöcher (Austria/Federal Republic of Germany 1985) Director/writer:Wolfram
   Paulus; Cinematography: Wolfgang Simon; Production companies:
   Bayerischer Rundfunk/Marwo Film/Voissfilm/ORF.

Helden in Tirol/Heroes in the Tyrol (Austria/Switzerland 1998) Director/writer: Niki
   List; Cinematography: Martin Stingl; Production company: Cult Film.

Hinterholz 8 (Austria 1998) Director: Harald Sicheritz; Writers: Roland Düringer
   (source play and screenplay), Harald Sicheritz; Cinematography: Walter
   Kindler; Production Company: Dor Film.

Homemad(e) (Austria 2001) Director/writer: Ruth Beckermann; Cinematography:
   Nurith Aviv, Ruth Beckermann, Peter Roehsler; Production company: Ruth
   Beckermann-Filmproduktion.

Hotel (Austria/Germany 2004) Director/writer: Jessica Hausner; Cinematography:
   Martin Gschlacht; Production companies: Essential Filmproduktion/Coop99/
   WDR/ZDF/arte/ORF.

Hundstage/Dog Days (Austria 2001) Director: Ulrich Seidl; Writers: Ulrich Seidl,
   Veronika Franz; Cinematography: Wolfgang Thaler; Production company:
   Allegro Film.

Ich bin Ich/I Am Me (Austria 2006) Director/writer: Kathrin Resetarits;
   Cinematography: Sandra Merseburger; Production company: Nikolaus
   Geyrhalter Filmproduktion.

Im Spiegel Maya Deren/In The Mirror of Maya Deren (Austria/Czech Republic/
   Switzerland/Germany 2001) Director/writer: Martina Kudlácek;
   Cinematography: Wolfgang Lehner; Production companies: Dschoint
   Ventschr Filmproduktion/Navigator Film/ TAG-TRAUM Filmproduktion/
   arte.

Immer nie am Meer/Forever Never Anywhere (Austria 2007) Director: Antonin
Svoboda; Writers: Christoph Grissemann, Jörg Kalt, Dirk Stermann, Heinz
Strunk, Antonin Svoboda; Cinematography: Martin Gschlacht; Production
company: Coop99.

Import Export (Austria 2007) Director: Ulrich Seidl; Writers: Ulrich Seidl, Veronika
Franz; Cinematography: Edward Lachmann, Walter Thaler; Production
companies: Ulrich Seidl Filmproduktion/Société Parisienne de Production/
ZDF/ORF.

Indien/India (Austria 1993) Director: Paul Harather; Writers: Paul Harather,
Josef Hader, Alfred Dorfer; Josef Hader and Alfred Dorfer (source play);
Cinematography: Hans Selikovsky; Production company: Dor Film.

Instructions for a Light and Sound Machine (Austria 2005) Director/writer/
cinematography: Peter Tscherkassky; Production Company: Peter
Tscherkassky/Sixpack Film.

Jesus, Du weißt/Jesus, You Know (Austria 2003) Director: Ulrich Seidl; Writers: Ulrich
Seidl, Veronika Franz; Cinematography: Wolfgang Thaler, Jerzy Palacz;
Production company: MMKmedia/arte.

Kaisermühlen Blues/The Kaisermuehlen Blues (Austria 1992–2000) Directors:
Reinhard Schwabenitzky (1992–1995), Harald Sicheritz (1996–1997), Erhard
Riedlsperger (1998–2000); Writer: Ernst Hinterberger; Cinematography:
Gérard Vandenberg, Constantin Kesting, Mathias Grunsky, Walter Kindler,
Karl Hohenberger, Judith Stehlik; Production companies: MR-TV Film/ORF.

Kassbach – Ein Porträt/Kassbach – A Portrait (Austria 1979) Director: Peter Patzak;
Writers: Peter Patzak, Helmut Zenker (screenplay and source novel);
Cinematography: Dietrich Lohmann, Attila Szabo; Production companies:
Patzak Filmproduktion/Satel Film.

Kino im Kopf/Movies in the Mind (Austria 1996) Director/writer/cinematography:
Michael Glawogger; Production company: Dor Film.

Kisangani Diary (France/Austria 1998) Director/writer: Hubert Sauper;
Cinematography: Hubert Sauper, Zsuzsanna Várkonyi; Production companies:
Nikolaus Geyrhalter Filmproduktion/Flor Films Paris.

Komm, süßer Tod/Come Sweet Death (Austria 2000) Director: Wolfgang Murnberger;
Writers: Wolf Haas (source novel and screenplay), Josef Hader, Wolfgang
Munberger; Cinematography: Peter von Haller; Production Company: Dor
Film.

Kottan ermittelt/Kottan Investigates (Austria 1976–1983) Director: Peter Patzak;
Writer: Helmut Zenker; Cinematography: Dietrich Lohmann (1978–1993),
Heinz Hölscher (1976–1981), Jirí Stibr (1978–1980); Production Company:
ORF.

Krieg in Wien/War in Vienna (Austria 1989) Directors: Michael Glawogger and
Ulrich Seidl; Writers: Michael Glawogger, Ulrich Seidl, Ortun Bauer;
Cinematography: Ortun Bauer, Hans Selikovsky, Wolfgang Thaler; Production
company: Filmakademie Wien.

L'Arrivée (Austria 1997–1998) Director/writer/cinematography: Peter Tscherkassky;
Production company: Peter Tscherkassky/Sixpack Film.

La Pianiste/Die Klavierspielerin/The Piano Teacher (Germany/France/Austria/Poland 2001) Director: Michael Haneke; Writers: Michael Haneke, Elfriede Jelinek (source novel); Cinematography: Christian Berger; Production companies: Bayerischer Rundfunk/Canal+/Centre National de la Cinématographie (CNC)/Les Films Alain Sarde/MK2 Productions/P.P. Film Polski/Wega Film/ arte France Cinéma/ORF.

Lemminge (Teil 1 & 2)/Lemmings (Austria, Federal Republic of Germany 1979) Director/writer: Michael Haneke; Cinematography: Walter Kindler, Jerzy Lipman; Production companies: Schönbrunn Film/Sender Freies Berlin (SFB)/ ORF.

Le temps du loup/Time of the Wolf (France/Germany/Austria 2003) Writer/director: Michael Haneke; Cinematography: Jürgen Jürges; Production Companies: Bavaria Film, Canal+, Centre National de la Cinématographie (CNC), Eurimages, France 3 Cinéma, Les Films du Losange, Wega Film, arte France Cinéma.

Life in Loops (A Megacities RMX) (Austria 2006) Director: Timo Novotny; Writers: Timo Novotny, Michael Glawogger; Cinematography: Wolfgang Thaler; Production company: Orbrock Filmproduktion.

Lourdes (Austria/France/Germany 2009) Director/writer: Jessica Hausner; Cinematography: Martin Gschlacht; Production company: Coop99.

Lovely Rita (Austria/Germany 2002) Director/writer: Jessica Hausner; Cinematography: Martin Gschlacht; Production companies: Coop99/Prisma Film/Essential Filmproduction.

MA 2412 – Die Staatsdiener/MA 2412 (Austria 2003) Director: Harald Sicheritz; Writers: Alfred Dorfer, Roland Düringer, Harald Sicheritz; Cinematography: Thomas Kürzl; Production company: MR Filmproduktion.

Manufraktur (Austria 1985) Director/writer/cinematography: Peter Tscherkassky; Production companies: Peter Tscherkassky/Sixpack Film.

Megacities (Austria 1998) Director/writer Michael Glawogger; Cinematography: Wolfgang Thaler; Production companies: Lotus Film/Fama Film.

Mein Stern/Be My Star (Austria/Germany 2001) Director/writer: Valeska Grisebach; Cinematography: Bernhard Keller; Production companies: Filmakademie Wien/Hochschule für Film und Fernsehen Konrad Wolf/ZDF/3Sat.

Menschenfrauen/Human Women (Austria/Federal Republic of Germany 1980) Director: VALIE EXPORT; Writer: Peter Weibel; Cinematography: Wolfgang Dickmann, Karl Kases; Production companies: VALIE EXPORT Filmproduktion/ZDF.

Mit Verlust ist zu rechnen/Loss is to be Expected (Austria 1992) Director: Ulrich Seidl; Writers: Ulrich Seidl, Michael Glawogger; Cinematography: Peter Zeitlinger, Michael Glawogger; Production company: Lotus Film.

Models (Austria 1998) Director/writer: Ulrich Seidl; Cinematography: Ortun Bauer, Hans Selikovsky, Jerzy Palacz; Production company: MR Film.

Motion Picture (Austria 1984) Director/writer/cinematography: Peter Tscherkassky; Production companies: Peter Tscherkassky/Sixpack Film.

Muttertag/Mother's Day (Austria 1993) Director: Harald Sicheritz; Writers: Peter Berecz, Alfred Dorfer, Roland Düringer, Harald Sicheritz; Cinematography:

Helmut Pirnat; Production company: Fernsehfilmproduktion Dr. Heinz
Schneiderbauer.

Müllers Büro/Mueller's Office (Austria 1986) Directors: Niki List, Hans Selikovsky;
Writer: Niki List; Cinematography: Hans Selikovsky; Production company:
Wega Film.

Nach Jerusalem/Toward Jerusalem (Austria/Israel 1990) Director/writer: Ruth
Beckermann; Cinematography: Nurith Aviv; Production company: Ruth
Beckermann-Filmproduktion.

Nacktschnecken/Slugs (Austria 2004) Director: Michael Glawogger; Writers: Michael
Glawogger, Michael Ostrowski; Cinematography: Wolfgang Thaler;
Production company: Dor Film.

Nordrand/Northern Skirts (Austria/Germany/Switzerland 1999) Director/writer:
Barbara Albert; Cinematography: Christine A. Maier; Production companies:
Fama Film/Lotus Film/Zero Film.

Outer Space (Austria 1999) Director/writer/cinematography: Peter Tscherkassky;
Production companies: Peter Tscherkassky/Sixpack Film.

Passage à l'acte (Austria 1993) Director/writer/cinematography: Martin Arnold;
Production Company: Martin Arnold.

Pièce touchée (Austria 1989) Director/writer/cinematography: Martin Arnold;
Production companies: Martin Arnold/Sixpack Film.

Poppitz (Austria 2002) Director: Harald Sicheritz; Writers: Roland Düringer, Harald
Sicheritz; Cinematography: Helmut Pirnat; Production company: Dor Film.

Postadresse: 2046 Schlöglmühl (Austria 1990) Director/writer: Egon Humer;
Cinematography: Peter Freiss; Production company: Prisma Film.

Radetzkymarsch/Radetzky March (Austria/Germany/France 1995) Directors: Axel
Corti, Gernot Roll; Writers: Axel Corti, Georges Conchon, Louis Gardel, Jean
Lagarche, Erik Orsenna, Joseph Roth (source novel); Cinematography: Gernot
Roll; Production companies: Satel Film/ORF.

Raffl (Austria 1984) Director: Christian Berger; Writers: Christian Berger, Markus
Heltschl; Cinematography: Christian Berger; Production company: TTV
Filmproduktion.

Ravioli (Austria 2002) Director: Peter Payer; Writers: Alfred Dorfer, Markus Pauser,
Gregor Stampfl; Cinematography: Thomas Prodinger; Production companies:
Arge Heimat/ORF.

Revanche (Austria 2008) Director/writer: Götz Spielmann; Cinematography: Martin
Gschlacht; Production companies: Spielmannfilm/Prisma Film.

Richtung Zukunft durch die Nacht/Direction Future Through the Night (Austria 2002)
Director/writer: Jörg Kalt; Cinematography: Eva Testor; Production company:
Filmakademie Wien.

Schlafes Bruder/Brother of Sleep (Germany/Austria 1995) Director: Joseph Vilsmaier;
Writer: Robert Schneider (source novel and screenplay); Cinematography:
Joseph Vilsmaier; Production companies: BA Filmproduktion/Dor
Film/Iduna Film/Kuchenreuther Filmproduktion/Perathon Film- und
Fernhsehproduktion.

Sehnsucht/Longing (Germany 2006) Director/writer: Valeska Grisebach; Cinematography: Bernhard Keller; Production companies: 3Sat/ Home Run Pictures/Peter Rommel Productions/ ZDF.

Sei zärtlich, Pinguin/Be Gentle, Penguin (Federal Republic of Germany/Austria 1982) Director: Peter Hajek; Writers: Peter Hajek, Fritz Müller-Scherz, Barbara Ossenkopp, Peter Weibel; Cinematography: Walter Kindler, Jaques Steyn; Production company: Dieter Geissler Filmproduktion/Günther Köpf Filmproduktion/Popular Film/Regina Ziegler Filmproduktion.

Silentium! (Austria 2004) Director: Wolfgang Murnberger; Writers: Wolfgang Murnberger, Josef Hader, Wolf Haas (source novel and screenplay); Cinematography: Peter von Haller; Production company: Dor Film.

Slumming (Austria/Switzerland/Germany 2006) Director: Michael Glawogger; Writers: Barbara Albert, Michael Glawogger; Cinematography: Martin Gschlacht; Production companies: Coop99/Lotus Film/Dschoint Ventschr Filmproduktion.

Somewhere Else (Austria 1996–1997) Director/writer: Barbara Albert; Cinematography: Chrisitne A. Maier; Production company: Filmakademie Wien.

Sonnenflecken/Sunspots (Austria 1998) Director/writer: Barbara Albert; Cinematography: Christine A. Maier; Production company: Filmakademie Wien.

Spiele Leben/You Bet Your Life (Austria/Switzerland 2005) Director: Antonin Svoboda; Writers: Antonin Svoboda, Martin Ambrosch; Cinematography: Martin Gschlacht; Production companies: Coop99/Triluna Film.

Struggle (Austria 2003) Director: Ruth Mader; Writers: Barbara Albert, Martin Leidenfrost, Ruth Mader; Cinematography: Bernhard Keller; Production companies: Amour Fou Filmproduktion/Struggle Films.

Suzie Washington (Austria 1998) Director: Florian Flicker; Writers: Florian Flicker, Michael Sturminger; Cinematography: Robert Neumüller; Production company: Allegro Film.

Syntagma (Austria 1983) Director/writer: VALIE EXPORT; Cinematography: Fritz Köberl; Production company: VALIE EXPORT Filmproduktion.

Ternitz, Tennesee (Austria 2000) Director: Mirjam Unger; Writer: Manfred Rebhandl; Cinematography: Jürgen Jürges; Production company: Thalia Film.

Tierische Liebe/Animal Love (Austria 1995) Director/writer: Ulrich Seidl; Cinematography: Peter Zeitlinger, Hans Selikovsky, Michael Glawogger; Production company: Lotus Film.

Überfall, Der /Hold-Up (Austria 2000) Director: Florian Flicker; Writers: Florian Flicker and Susanne Freund; Cinematography: Helmut Pirnat; Production Company: Allegro Film.

Über Wasser – Menschen und gelbe Kanister/About Water – People and Yellow Cans (Austria/Luxembourg 2007) Director: Udo Maurer; Writers: Udo Maurer, Michael Glawogger, Ursula Sova; Cinematography: Udo Maurer, Attila Boa; Production companies: Lotus Film/Samsa Film.

Unser täglich Brot/Our Daily Bread (Germany/Austria 2005) Director: Nikolaus Geyrhalter; Writers Nikolaus Geyrhalter, Wolfgang Widerhofer;

Cinematography: Nikolaus Geyrhalter; Production companies: Nikolaus Geyrhalter Filmproduktion/ZDF/3Sat/ORF.

Unsichtbare Gegner/Invisible Adversaries (Austria 1977) Director: VALIE EXPORT; Writers: VALIE EXPORT, Peter Weibel; Cinematography: Wolfgang Simon; Production company: VALIE EXPORT Filmproduktion.

Vollgas/Step on It (Germany/Austria 2001) Director: Sabine Derflinger; Writers: Sabine Derflinger, Maria Scheibelhofer; Cinematography: Gerald Helf, Wolfgang Lederer, Natascha Neulinger, Bernhard Pötscher; Production companies: Prisma Film/ZDF/arte.

We Feed the World (Austria 2005/2006) Director/writer/cinematography: Erwin Wagenhofer; Production company: Allegro Film.

Welcome Home (Austria 2004) Director: Andreas Gruber; Writers: Andreas Gruber, Martin Rauhaus; Cinematography: Hermann Dunzendorfer; Production company: Wega Film.

Wien Retour/Vienna Revisited (Austria 1983) Directors: Ruth Beckermann, Josef Aichholzer; Cinematography: Bernd Neuburger, Tamas Ujlaki; Production company: Ruth Beckermann-Filmproduktion.

Wiens verlorene Töchter/Vienna's Lost Daughters (Austria 2007) Director: Mirjam Unger; Writers: Sonja Ammann, Lisa Juen, Mirjam Unger; Cinematography: Eva Testor; Production company: Mobilefilm.

Wohin und Zurück/Somewhere and Back (Austria/Federal Republic of Germany/ Switzerland 1980–1986) Director: Axel Corti; Writers: Georg Stefan Troller, Axel Corti; Cinematography: Gernot Roll, Otto Kirchhoff; Production companies: Thalia Film/ZDF/ORF.

Workingman's Death (Austria/Germany 2005) Director/writer: Michael Glawogger; Cinematography: Wolfgang Thaler; Production companies: Lotus Film/arte/ Medien- und Filmgesellschaft Baden-Württemberg/Quinte Film/ORF.

Zorros Bar Mizwah/Zorro's Bar Mitzvah (Austria 2006) Director/writer: Ruth Beckermann; Cinematography: Leena Koppe; Production company: Ruth Beckermann-Filmproduktion.

Zur Lage – Österreich in sechs Kapiteln/State of the Nation – Austria in Six Chapters (Austria 2002) Directors: Barbara Albert, Michael Glawogger, Ulrich Seidl, Michael Sturminger; Writers: Barbara Albert, Michael Glawogger, Ulrich Seidl, Michael Sturminger; Cinematography: Michael Glawogger, Ulrich Seidl, Eva Testor; Production company: Lotus Film.

Notes on Contributors

Erika Balsom is an Andrew W. Mellon postdoctoral fellow in the Department of Film Studies at the University of California, Berkeley. She received her Ph.D. in the department of Modern Culture and Media at Brown University where she completed a dissertation entitled "Exhibiting Cinema: The Moving Image in Art After 1990." Her writings have appears in publications such as *Screen*, *The Canadian Journal of Film Studies*, and the edited collection *Outsider Films on India 1950–1990* (2010).

Andreas Böhn is Professor of German and Media Studies at KIT/University of Karlsruhe. His research interests include intermediality, metareference, the comic, and the relation of culture and technology. His most recent publication is a coedited volume, *Gender and Laughter: Comic Affirmation and Subversion in Traditional and Modern Media* (2009).

Martin Brady teaches film in the German and Film Studies Departments, King's College London. He wrote his Ph.D. on documentary and fiction in the early films of Jean-Marie Straub and Daniéle Huillet. He has published on German and French film (Straub and Huillet, Haneke, Bresson, experimental film, literary adaptation, East German documentary film, Kafka and film, Adorno and film, Brechtian cinema, *Der Untergang/Downfall*), music (Schönberg), literature (Celan), and Jewish exile architects. He is the translator of Victor Klemperer's *LTI* and Alexander Kluge's *Cinema Stories* (with Helen Hughes). He has recently coauthored a volume on the collaborative films of Peter Handke and Wim Wenders and is currently working on foraging and gleaning in the work of Stifter, Handke, and Beuys.

Raymond Burt is Professor of German and the chair of the Department of Foreign Languages and Literatures at the University of North Carolina, Wilmington. His research interests include *fin de siècle* Vienna, and, most notably, the life and work of the infamous ethnologist and sexologist, Friedrich Salomo Krauss, whose papers he discovered in Los Angeles. In addition to publishing his biography, he has coedited a major portion of Krauss's papers in the volume *Volkserzählungen der Südslaven: Märchen und Sagen, Schwänke, Schnurren und erbauliche Geschichten* (2002). Additionally he publishes articles on contemporary Austrian literature and culture and is examining the influence of the film medium on Austrian literary narratology.

Robert von Dassanowsky is Professor of German and Film and director of the Film Studies Program at the University of Colorado, Colorado Springs. He is cofounder of the International Alexander Lernet-Holenia Society, editor of *The Gale Encyclopedia of Multicultural America*, 2nd Ed., and editorial advisor to the *International Dictionary of Films and Filmmakers*. His examinations of Austrian film and literature have appeared in *Germanic Review, Austrian Studies, Senses of Cinema, Central Europe, Austrian History Yearbook, and Modern Austrian Literature* (guest editor of a special issue on Michael Haneke, 2010). His most recent books are *Austrian Cinema: A History* (2005) and the coedited *Hugo von Hofmannsthal's Der Schwierige: A Classic Revisited* (2011). He is currently working on a collection examining Tarantino's *Inglourious Basterds* (2011) and is active as an independent film producer.

Mattias Frey is Lecturer in Film Studies at the University of Kent. His writings have appeared in *Cinema Journal, Screen, Quarterly Review of Film and Video, Literature/Film Quarterly, Framework, Film International, Senses of Cinema,* and numerous anthologies and reference works. His book on recent German film, entitled *Goodbye, Hitler: Postwall German Cinema and History*, will be published with Berghahn Books.

Gundolf Graml is Assistant Professor of German and Director of German at Agnes Scott College, Decatur. His research interests are twentieth and twenty-first-century Austrian and German film and cultural studies in general. He has published articles on *Sound of Music* tourism and on the representation of blackness and whiteness in films by Luis Trenker. He is currently completing a book on the role of tourism in Austrian identity construction after 1945.

Christina Guenther is Associate Professor of German at Bowling Green State University. Her teaching and research focus on German and Austrian culture, Jewish identity, and the Holocaust. Most recently, she has published articles on the work of Ruth Beckermann, Anna Mitgutsch, Barbara Honigmann, and Robert Schindel. She recently coedited the volume *Trajectories of Memory: Intergenerational Representations of History and the Arts* (2008).

Sara F. Hall is Associate Professor of Germanic Studies and the Chair of the Minor in Moving Image Arts at the University of Illinois at Chicago. She received her Ph.D. from the University of California, Berkeley, and is the author of a forthcoming book on the application of film technology to law enforcement in the Weimar Republic. Her studies of German and Austrian silent film and questions of gender and ethnic identity have appeared in such journals as *German Quarterly, Modernism/Modernity, German Studies Review,* and *Journal of European Studies,* and in a number of edited collections.

Christoph Huber is film and music critic for the Austrian daily *Die Presse*, European editor of *Cinema Scope* magazine, and writes the program notes for the Austrian Film Museum. He has contributed to several books and numerous publications on cinema.

Helen Hughes is Head of Film at the University of Surrey. She wrote her Ph.D. on aspects of bureaucracy in Austrian prose fiction and has published articles and chapters on linguistics (Thomas Bernhard), experimental film (VALIE EXPORT), historical film and literature (Adalbert Stifter and Robert Bresson), German cinema (Heinrich Boll's contribution to *Deutschland im Herbst/Germany in Autumn*, Kafka and film, *Der Untergang/Downfall*), and East German documentary film (Andreas Voigt, Barbara and Winfried Junge). She is the cotranslator of Alexander Kluge's *Cinema Stories*. She is currently working on Austrian and environmental documentary film.

Eva Kuttenberg is Associate Professor of German at Pennsylvania State University, Erie. Her research focuses on twentieth and twenty-first-century Austrian literature and film. Her publications range from visual culture in Vienna in the 1920s to Austria's topography of memory. She has also published on Thomas Bernhard, Melitta Breznik, Lilian Faschinger, Margarethe von Trotta, and Arthur Schnitzler.

Margarete Lamb-Faffelberger is Professor of German and Director of the Max Kade Center for German Studies in the Department of Foreign Languages and Literatures at Lafayette College, Pennsylvania. She is general editor of the Austrian Culture Series of Peter Lang Publishing, New York, and co-editor of the *Women in German Yearbook*. She specializes in contemporary Austrian literature and film and has published several edited and coedited books, including *Elfriede Jelinek: Writing Woman, Nation, and Identity* (2007), *Visions and Visionaries in Contemporary Austrian Literature and Film* (2004), *Post-War Austrian Theater: Text and Performance* (2002). The volume *Festschrift in Honor of VALIE EXPORT* appeared in October 2010.

Dagmar C.G. Lorenz is Professor of Germanic Studies and Director of Jewish Studies at the University of Illinois at Chicago. Her research focuses on nineteenth and twentieth-century German and Austrian literature and culture, German Jewish writing, and Holocaust literature and film. She was editor of *German Quarterly* from 1997 to 2003, and has held offices in professional associations such as AATG, GSA, MALCA, and MLA. Her publications include *Keepers of the Motherland: German Texts by Jewish Women Writers* (1997), *Verfolgung bis zum Massenmord. Diskurse zum Holocaust in deutscher Sprache* (1992), as well as edited and coedited volumes: *From Fin-de-Siecle to Theresienstadt: The Works and Life of the Writer Elsa Porges-Bernstein* (2007), *A Companion to the Works of Elias Canetti* (2004), *A Companion to the Works of Arthur Schnitzler* (2003), *Contemporary Jewish Writing in Austria* (1999), *Transforming the Center, Eroding the Margins: Essays on Ethnic and Cultural*

Boundaries in German Speaking Countries (1998), and *Insiders and Outsider: Jewish and Gentile Culture in Germany and Austria* (1994).

Alexandra Ludewig is Associate Professor and Convener of German Studies at the University of Western Australia. She studied in Germany, South Africa, and Australia, and completed a Ph.D. at the University of Queensland on Jewish German migration. After this she returned to LMU, Munich, where she completed a thesis on Thomas Bernhard and a study of *Heimatfilm*. Throughout her career, she has managed to span the distance between continents and disciplines, writing and teaching in both German and English. German and European cinema have captured her interest in recent years and she recently published her *Habilitationsschrift* entitled *One-hundred Years of German Heimatfilm*.

Imke Meyer is Professor and co-chair of the Bryn Mawr–Haverford Bi-College Department of German. At Bryn Mawr, she teaches courses on German and Austrian literature and film. She has published widely on writers and filmmakers such as Ludwig Tieck, Hugo von Hofmannsthal, Arthur Schnitzler, Franz Kafka, Ingeborg Bachmann, Elfriede Jelinek, Michael Haneke and Barbara Albert. Her new book, *Männlichkeit und Melodram: Arthur Schnitzlers erzählende Schriften*, appeared in 2010.

Joseph Moser is Assistant Professor of German at Washington and Jefferson College. He has served as book reviews editor for *Modern Austrian Literature* for the past three years. His dissertation, "Thomas Bernhard's Dialogue with the Public Sphere," was completed at the University of Pennsylvania in 2004. His recent publications have focused on Thomas Bernhard, Franz Antel's *Bockerer* films, and Austrian Jewish culture in Czernowitz.

Verena Mund is Film Studies Coordinator at the University of Minnesota. She has previously worked for the film/video department at the Walker Art Center in Minneapolis, the International Short Film Festival Oberhausen, Germany, as well as for Feminale: International Women's Film Festival Cologne. She has taught at several universities and art schools and is coeditor of *Girls, Gangs, Guns: Zwischen Exploitation-Kino und Underground* (2000) and *Working Girls: Zur Ökonomie von Liebe und Arbeit* (2007).

Rachel Palfreyman is Lecturer in German Studies at the University of Nottingham. She is the author of *Edgar Reitz's Heimat: Histories, Traditions, Fictions* (2000), and coauthor of *Heimat – A German Dream: Regional Loyalties and National Identity in German Culture 1890–1990* (2000). She has published on German cinema from Weimar to the present, and is currently working on the animator Lotte Reiniger.

Arno Russegger completed his studies in German Philology and Anglo-American Philology with a thesis on Robert Musil's theory of images. At present he is Associate

Professor at the Institute of Germanic Studies, University of Klagenfurt. His teaching and research activities focus mainly on Austrian literature since 1900, the relationship between film and literature, film analysis, literature for children and adolescents, and the literary business community.

Nikhil Sathe is Associate Professor of German and Language Program Coordinator at Ohio University. His research interests are focused on Austrian Studies, language pedagogy, and literature and culture from the twentieth century to the present. His publications include articles on Norbert Gstrein's text *Einer*, films by Ruth Mader and Barabara Gräftner, Uwe Timm's memoir *Am Beispiel meines Bruders*, as well as a number of pedagogically oriented articles.

Oliver C. Speck is Assistant Professor of Film Studies at the School of World Studies, Virginia Commonwealth University. His scholarly writing focuses on narrative strategies and the representation of memory and history in European cinema. His new book, *Funny Frames: The Filmic Concepts of Michael Haneke* (2010), explores how political thinking manifests itself in the oeuvre of the Austrian director.

Regina Standún was with the Department of German at the National University of Ireland, Maynooth, from 2000 to 2008. Her doctoral dissertation was a comparative study of rural Austrian *Volksstück* and Irish peasant plays of the twentieth century. She has published several articles on modern Austrian film and literature, and teaching German as a foreign language. She currently works at the Technical High School in Innsbruck, Austria.

Felix W. Tweraser is Associate Professor of German at Utah State University. He works on the literary and cultural legacy of turn-of-the-century Vienna, film theory and criticism, and the instrumentalization of arts and letters during the Cold War. Recent articles include: "Leo Golowski as Minor Key in Schnitzler's *Der Weg ins Freie*: Musical Theory, Political Behaviour and Ethical Action" (2009), and "Elisabeth Reichart's *Komm über den See*: Upper Austria and the Excavation of its Past" (2008). He is the author of the book *Political Dimensions of Arthur Schnitzler's Late Fiction* (1998), and is currently working on a monograph which traces the contributions of Austrian émigrés to the US film industry and Hollywood's golden age.

Justin Vicari's book, *Male Bisexuality in Current Cinema: Images of Growth, Rebellion and Survival*, is forthcoming from McFarland in 2011. He has translated François Emmanuel's *Invitation to a Voyage* (Dalkey Archive Press) and Octave Mirbeau's *Twenty-One Days of a Neurasthenic* (Dalkey Archive Press), and is the author of a forthcoming collection of poems, *The Professional Weepers* (Pavement Saw). His film writing has appeared in such journals as *Jump Cut*, *Postmodern Culture*, *Senses of Cinema*, and in the Czech journal *Filmovy Casopis FPS*. He lives in Pittsburgh.

Mary Wauchope received her Ph.D. from the University of California, Berkeley, and is currently Director of German Studies at the Department of European Studies, San Diego State University. She has published a book and articles on Germanic linguistics and European cinema, in particular postwar German and Austrian film.

Catherine Wheatley is Lecturer in Film and Media Studies at the University of East London. She is the author of *Michael Haneke's Cinema: The Ethic of The Image* (2009), the first full-length English-language study of the acclaimed director's work, as well as the forthcoming BFI Film Classics guide to Haneke's *Caché/Hidden*. In addition, she is a regular contributor to *Sight and Sound* magazine.

Gabriele Wurmitzer is a Ph.D. candidate in German Studies at Duke University. Her doctoral research focuses on postwar Austrian literature, performance art, and film. For the academic year 2009–2010 she received a James B. Duke International Fellowship to conduct research for her dissertation in Vienna and Berlin and to participate in the graduate colloquium "InterArt" at the Free University, Berlin. Her research interests include twentieth-century Austrian literature; postwar avant-garde experimental literature, art, and film; and semiotics and performance studies.

Index